"A nuanced look into the hearts and minds of three very different women who deserve to be better known."

—Amanda Foreman, author of *A World on Fire*

"With an encyclopedic knowledge of the historical record and a novelist's alertness to detail, Catherine Kerrison brings Thomas Jefferson's three daughters (one of them the child of Sally Hemings) achingly to life. This is a brilliant and beautiful book, as fascinating for what it tells us about the virtues and grave moral failures of our 'philosopher president' as for what it reveals about the lives of the women who lived in his shadow."

—Stephen O'Connor, author of
Thomas Jefferson Dreams of Sally Hemings

"Fascinating and infuriating, Catherine Kerrison's well-researched book shows the contradictions and compromises built into the foundation of our nation. Details abound about Jefferson's free, white daughters while his enslaved daughter lives in the shadows. Even after she leaves Monticello, Harriet Hemings's very survival depends on being separated from her family and hidden from history. But in some ways that is an answer to our questions about her life: Harriet Hemings could not be herself and be free."

—Laila Ibrahim, author of *Yellow Crocus*

"Catherine Kerrison's imaginative and exhaustively researched book recreates the worlds of Jefferson's daughters in Virginia and beyond. Martha and Maria were white and privileged; Harriet was enslaved and unacknowledged. With a keen eye for detail, Kerrison tells the stories of all three and shows how gender and race profoundly—and sometimes in surprising ways—shaped their lives."

—Cynthia A. Kierner, author of
Martha Jefferson Randolph, Daughter of Monticello

"Written with clarity, empathy, and grace, *Jefferson's Daughters* presents the triumphs and tragedies of three brave women coping with life in the shadow of a paternal self-absorbed genius. Kerrison's achievement is a page-turner that explores and explains hidden complexities of our shared national story."

—Jon Kukla, author of *Mr. Jefferson's Women* and
Patrick Henry: Champion of Liberty

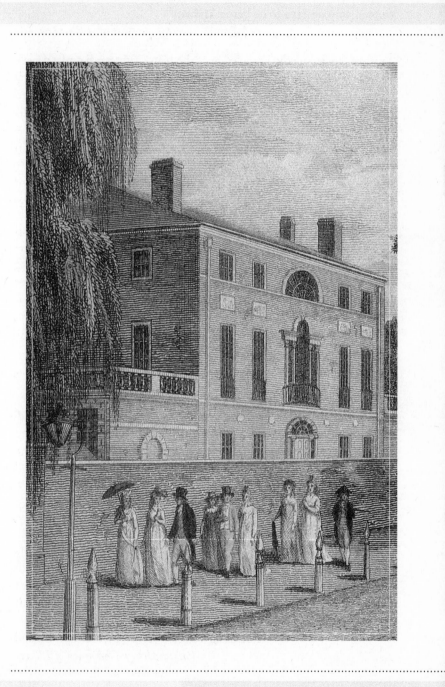

Jefferson's Daughters

....

THREE SISTERS, WHITE and BLACK, in a YOUNG AMERICA

....

Catherine Kerrison

BALLANTINE BOOKS · NEW YORK

Published in the United States by Ballantine Books, an imprint of
Random House, a division of Penguin Random House LLC, New York.

BALLANTINE and the HOUSE colophon are registered
trademarks of Penguin Random House LLC.

Originally published in hardcover in the United States by Ballantine Books,
an imprint of Random House, a division of Penguin Random House LLC, in 2018.

Image credits begin on page 403.

Grateful acknowledgment is made to the following for permission
to reprint previously published material:
UNIVERSITY OF GEORGIA PRESS: "Harriet Hemings: Daughter of the
President's Slave" by Catherine Kerrison from *Virginia Women: Their Lives and Times,
Vol. 1*, edited by Cynthia Kierner and Sandra Treadway, copyright © 2015 by the
University of Georgia Press. Reprinted by permission.
UNIVERSITY OF PENNSYLVANIA PRESS: "The French Education of Martha
Jefferson Randolph" by Catherine Kerrison, *Early American Studies*, v. 11, no. 2
(Spring 2013): 349–394; copyright © 2013 by the McNeil Center for
Early American Studies.
All rights reserved. Reprinted by permission.

LIBRARY OF CONGRESS CATALOGING-IN-PUBLICATION DATA
NAMES: Kerrison, Catherine, author.
TITLE: Jefferson's daughters : three sisters, white and black,
in a young America / Catherine Kerrison.
DESCRIPTION: First edition. | New York : Ballantine Books, [2018] |
Includes bibliographical references and index.
IDENTIFIERS: LCCN 2017043540 | ISBN 9781101886267 (paperback :
alk. paper) | ISBN 9781101886250 (ebook)
SUBJECTS: LCSH: Randolph, Martha Jefferson, 1772–1836. | Eppes, Maria,
1778–1804. | Hemings, Harriet, 1801– | Jefferson, Thomas, 1743–1826—Family. |
Women—United States—History—18th century. | Women—United States—
History—19th century.
CLASSIFICATION: LCC E332.25 .K47 2018 | DDC 973.4/60922—dc23
LC record available at https://lccn.loc.gov/2017043540

Printed in the United States of America on acid-free paper
randomhousebooks.com
4689753
Book design by Barbara M. Bachman

For James P. Whittenburg,
who encouraged my study of the past,
and
For Everett, Luke, and Madeleine—
my hope for a more just future.

. . . .

Contents

. . . .

Introduction   ix
Author's Note   xiii
Partial Hemings Family Tree   xiv
Map   xvi

CHAPTER 1   *First Monticello*   3

CHAPTER 2   *To Paris*   23

CHAPTER 3   *School Life*   47

CHAPTER 4   *Families Reunited*   73

CHAPTER 5   *Transitions*   98

CHAPTER 6   *Becoming American Again*   126

CHAPTER 7   *A Virginia Wife*   161

CHAPTER 8   *Harriet's Monticello*   189

CHAPTER 9   *An Enlightened Household*   215

CHAPTER 10   *Departure*   242

CHAPTER 11   *Passing*   275

CHAPTER 12   *Legacies*   309

               Acknowledgments   335
               Bibliography   339
               Notes   351
               Image Credits   403
               Index   405

Introduction

. . . . .

SUMMER 1789

$\mathcal{I}$T WAS A DECEPTIVELY QUIET Sunday in Paris. The very air of these summer months seemed laden with menace, as news of peasant revolts in the countryside filtered into the city and apprehensive Parisians watched the king position his troops to defend it. Political tumult had convulsed the city that summer as well, as the king, nobles, and bishops had stridently resisted the urgings of commoners to join them in their newly formed National Assembly. But finally, in a clear nod to the people's will, Louis XVI conceded and a crisis appeared to have been averted. As the carriage of Thomas Jefferson, American minister to the French court, rattled through the streets that day, he was confident that with its "victory . . . complete," the assembly was "in complete and undisputed possession of the sovereignty."

Unbeknownst to Jefferson, however, that very day infuriated aristocrats had forced the king to backpedal. As "news of this change began to be known at Paris about 1. or 2. o'clock," Jefferson later recalled, the city began to stir again. Passing through the elegant Place Louis XV (now the Place de la Concorde), Jefferson saw, with a start, three hundred mounted German and Swiss mercenaries amassed along one side. Along the other, an angry crowd had gathered and "posted themselves on and behind large piles of stones, large and small, collected in that Place for a bridge which was to be built adjacent to it." Jefferson found himself in the thick of it. No sooner had he passed through than their fury erupted, as the people pelted the cavalry with the rocks. On the front lines, the Germans drove their horses toward the crowd but were resolutely beaten back. Leaving one of their number dead, they abandoned the square. It was, Jefferson recognized in retrospect, "the signal for universal insurrection." Two days later, on July 14, another Paris crowd would storm the Bastille to arm themselves for the fight.

JEFFERSON HAD BEEN IN PARIS since 1784. After his wife's premature death, Congress had asked him to represent the United States at the peace table with Great Britain, and he grasped at the appointment as a drowning man would a rope. Escaping the painful memories etched into the very landscape of his home at Monticello, Jefferson crossed the ocean to France with his twelve-year-old daughter, Martha. Three years later, Martha's younger sister, Maria, joined them, accompanied by her slave, Sally Hemings.

By that fateful summer of 1789, Paris had changed them all. Famous for his role in drafting the American Declaration of Independence, Jefferson was sought after by French revolutionary moderates who persuaded him to host meetings as they hammered out their ideas to reform their government. But Paris was also the place where he had adopted the aristocratic wigs and elegant silk suits made fashionable by the French, and where he had fallen in love with their art, architecture, furniture, and books. Like her father, Martha took an eager interest in the political ferment. Sporting a revolutionary cockade, she was the envy of her friends when General Lafayette, riding through the streets of Paris, recognized her with a chivalrous doff of his hat. Even little Maria was changed. Initially left behind in Virginia, she had not wanted to go to Paris when Jefferson wrote to have her join him. But once arrived, the nine-year-old became so acclimated to the beauties of Paris that she broke down in tears on their return to Virginia as she surveyed the burnt-out ruins of Norfolk, their port of arrival. Sally Hemings had learned how to care for Jefferson's silk suits and linens, as well as the fashionable clothing of his daughters. She also learned French. By this pivotal moment in French (and Jefferson family) history, then, she had learned marketable skills and had seen the possibility of a way of life that was different from the slavery she had known in Virginia.

In the fall of 1789, however, she would agree to join Jefferson and his daughters as they boarded the *Clermont*, bound for Virginia. But what kind of nation awaited them? As the newly elected president, George Washington, assembled his government, he faced the challenge of transforming the political system inscribed on paper in the Constitution into a working and workable government. Chief among the questions to be resolved was who, exactly, was included in the ringing phrase "We the People" with which that document opened. In this age of revolutions, the idea of independence did not only refer to a national government, free of monarchical ties. It also meant individual self-determination. But who was eligible to claim that right? More particularly, what changes might the American Revolution begin to effect, especially for women, free blacks, and slaves?

As the Jefferson party sailed home, they would have pondered these questions in very different ways. But Paris remained imprinted upon them all forever, shaping the courses of their lives and the choices they would make.

Author's Note

....

EIGHTEENTH-CENTURY NAMING, spelling, and punctuation conventions can pose a challenge to twenty-first-century readers. Thomas Jefferson's daughters, named Martha and Mary at birth, were called different names during their lifetimes: Martha was called Patsy as a girl and Martha in adulthood, and Mary was called Polly as a child and, later, Maria, although she continued to sign her letters "Mary." For the reader's convenience, however, I will use their adult names, Martha and Maria, throughout the text.

Eighteenth-century spellings were not yet standardized; to remain faithful to the original, I have retained the writer's spelling. Where needed for clarity, I have silently corrected quotations for twenty-first-century punctuation, and I have supplied the full spelling when the writer used an abbreviation.

For ease of reading in some quotations, I have sometimes inserted my own words in square brackets.

Partial Hemings Family Tree

· · · · ·

= UNMARRIED UNION

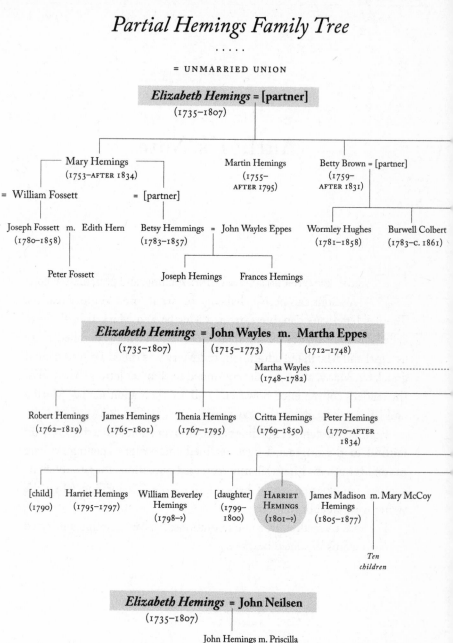

Elizabeth Hemings = [partner]
(1735–1807)

Mary Hemings
(1753–AFTER 1834)

= William Fossett

= [partner]

Martin Hemings
(1755–
AFTER 1795)

Betty Brown = [partner]
(1759–
AFTER 1831)

Joseph Fossett   m.   Edith Hern
(1780–1858)

Betsy Hemmings = John Wayles Eppes
(1783–1857)

Wormley Hughes
(1781–1858)

Burwell Colbert
(1783–c. 1861)

Peter Fossett

Joseph Hemings   Frances Hemings

Elizabeth Hemings = **John Wayles**   m.   **Martha Eppes**
(1735–1807)   (1715–1773)   (1712–1748)

Martha Wayles -
(1748–1782)

Robert Hemings
(1762–1819)

James Hemings
(1765–1801)

Thenia Hemings
(1767–1795)

Critta Hemings
(1769–1850)

Peter Hemings
(1770–AFTER
1834)

[child]
(1790)

Harriet Hemings
(1795–1797)

William Beverley
Hemings
(1798–?)

[daughter]
(1799–
1800)

HARRIET
HEMINGS
(1801–?)

James Madison
Hemings
(1805–1877)

m. Mary McCoy

Ten
children

Elizabeth Hemings = **John Neilsen**
(1735–1807)

John Hemings m. Priscilla
(1776–1833)

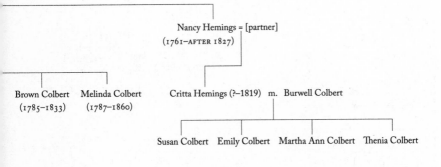

Nancy Hemings = [partner]
(1761–AFTER 1827)

Brown Colbert   Melinda Colbert   Critta Hemings (?–1819) m. Burwell Colbert
(1785–1833)   (1787–1860)

Susan Colbert   Emily Colbert   Martha Ann Colbert   Thenia Colbert

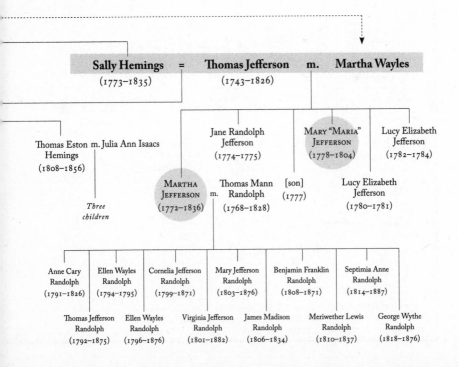

Sally Hemings = **Thomas Jefferson** m. **Martha Wayles**
(1773–1835)   (1743–1826)

Thomas Eston m. Julia Ann Isaacs   Jane Randolph   MARY "MARIA"   Lucy Elizabeth
Hemings   Jefferson   JEFFERSON   Jefferson
(1808–1856)   (1774–1775)   (1778–1804)   (1782–1784)

                    Three   MARTHA   Thomas Mann   [son]   Lucy Elizabeth
                    children   JEFFERSON m. Randolph   (1777)   Jefferson
                                    (1772–1836)   (1768–1828)   (1780–1781)

Anne Cary   Ellen Wayles   Cornelia Jefferson   Mary Jefferson   Benjamin Franklin   Septimia Anne
Randolph   Randolph   Randolph   Randolph   Randolph   Randolph
(1791–1826)   (1794–1795)   (1799–1871)   (1803–1876)   (1808–1871)   (1814–1887)

     Thomas Jefferson   Ellen Wayles   Virginia Jefferson   James Madison   Meriwether Lewis   George Wythe
     Randolph   Randolph   Randolph   Randolph   Randolph   Randolph
     (1792–1875)   (1796–1876)   (1801–1882)   (1806–1834)   (1810–1837)   (1818–1876)

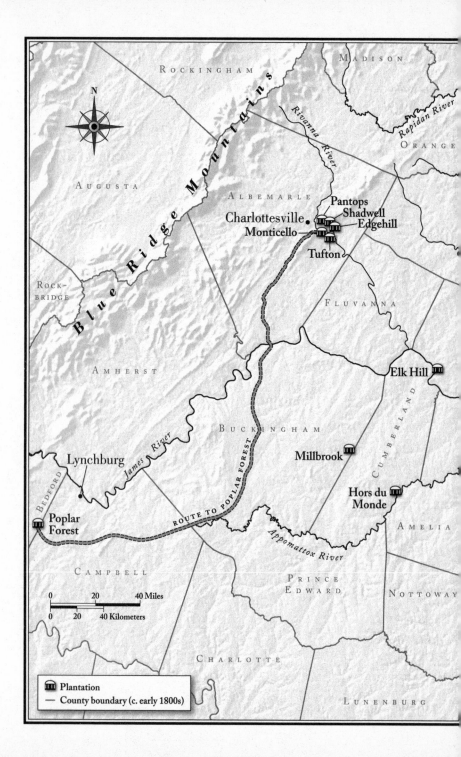

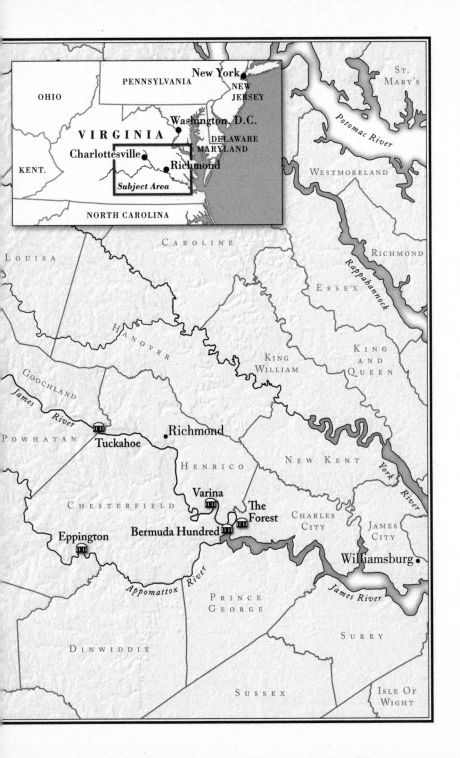

JEFFERSON'S
DAUGHTERS

First
Monticello

. . . .

1770

. . . .

A FAVORITE TALE, RETOLD COUNTLESS TIMES at the Jefferson
family hearth, was the story of Martha Wayles Jefferson's
arrival at Monticello as a new bride. A beautiful young widow, Martha
married Thomas Jefferson at her father's estate in Charles City County,
just up the James River from Williamsburg, on New Year's Day in 1772.
The beaming couple were well matched. At six feet two inches tall, Jefferson carried his lanky frame erect, towering over his bride. Although
petite, Martha carried her slim figure with the elegance of a queen. She
had auburn hair and hazel eyes that sparkled with wit and vivacity. Her
groom was likewise fair, although his red hair was lighter and his eyes
blue. Although no one ever described Jefferson as handsome, one of his
earliest biographers said his face shone with "intelligence, with benevolence, and with the cheerful vivacity of a happy, hopeful spirit." A young
lawyer and planter, Jefferson was just beginning his political career, having won his seat in the Virginia legislature barely three years earlier.
With his prospects and the good-humored temperament they each
possessed, they were confident their future boded fair.

Immediately after the wedding festivities, Martha and her new husband left for the home Jefferson had only just begun building in Albe-

marle County, almost a hundred miles west. Although it had begun to snow as they set out, it was not heavy, so they were taken aback as the storm got progressively worse as they traveled westward. Forced to abandon both their carriage and the main road, they unhitched the horses and rode them for the last eight miles of their journey, trudging along the mountain track Jefferson knew so well, despite the two feet of snow that covered it.

The south pavilion (left) was the first structure Jefferson finished at Monticello and served as his bedroom, office, and dining room. It was also his honeymoon cottage and the site of the birth of his first child, Martha. The south wing connected it to the main house by an L-shaped "dependency," featuring a walking terrace above and essential services, such as the kitchen, laundry, and dairy, below. The south wing also contained the room in which Sally Hemings would live and raise her four children.

Their destination that January night was a tiny one-room building, today an appendage connected to Monticello by a long terrace, but then Jefferson's home, furnished only with a bed and books. "They arrived late in the night, the fires all out and the servants retired to their own houses for the night," their daughter Martha wrote, remembering the story her parents loved to tell during her childhood. Still, the groom was not entirely unprepared. They broke out a bottle of wine he had stowed away behind his books and lit up the night with their songs and laughter. It was the beginning of ten years of "unchequered happiness," as Jefferson would lovingly recall. On that night, with a beloved wife in

his arms, he could lay out his hopes for the future for his family, plantation home, and successful political career.

THOMAS JEFFERSON HAD CHOSEN the location of his home carefully; he
had been born at Shadwell, within sight of the mountain he would call
Monticello. In his youth, he would walk its summit and sit there for
hours, reading and plotting the future with his boyhood friend Dabney
Carr. He and Carr made a pact to be buried at the very oak tree under
which they had spent countless hours together. Peter Jefferson, Thomas's westward-looking surveyor father, and Jane Randolph Jefferson, his
elegant mother, shaped his vision of what he would build there. Their
influence was unmistakable in the finished house, in which specimens
of the New World from the Lewis and Clark westering expedition
mixed with the art, plate, and silver of the Old.

Peter Jefferson was an up-and-comer in colonial Virginia. At his
father's death in 1731, Peter had inherited lands in Goochland County,
just west of where Richmond would be founded six years later. But he
hankered after additional lands farther west. For the price of a bowl of
arrack punch in a Williamsburg tavern, a family story goes, he bought
four hundred acres on the Rivanna River, adjacent to land he already
owned, thanks to a good friend. He named the new tract Shadwell,
honoring his wife's home parish in England. His later career as a surveyor positioned him to see and claim the most desirable land first as
Virginia settlers pushed west. By the time he died in 1757, he had
amassed seventy-five hundred acres, more than sixty slaves, and a substantial inventory of horses, cattle, and hogs. Even so, his son was
prouder still of his father's other accomplishments. For Thomas, Peter's
chief legacies were the map he had drawn (which was published in
1757) after a grueling surveying expedition, the "first map of Virginia
which had ever been made, that of Captain [John] Smith being merely
conjectural," Jefferson noted dismissively in his memoirs; and that his
father was one of the founders of Albemarle County, "the third or
fourth settler, about the year 1737." For Thomas Jefferson, nothing in
the Old World could compare to the natural beauty of the Blue Ridge
Mountains and the promise that lay beyond them to the west.

Jefferson's mother, Jane Randolph, came from a family that was wealthy and socially prominent in both England and Virginia. Jane's father had been born in Virginia but moved back to England in the course of a seafaring career. He later returned to Virginia in 1725, with a wife and two children, when little Jane was just five. Armed with wealth and plenty of family connections, Isham Randolph entered into the highly lucrative slave trade. It may bring us up short today to hear that his great-great-granddaughter characterized him as a man "whose name associated itself in his day with all that was good and wise," but Randolph's success as a slave trader, tobacco planter, and military man would have commended him to his contemporaries. Jane Randolph was proud of a lineage that she traced far back to England and Scotland. No hardscrabble backcountry farmers, then, the Randolphs built a lavish Virginia estate, known for its hospitality. There Jane learned how to supervise the labor of a plantation household, from setting a table to slaughtering hogs. She was also taught to dance a minuet, to embroider, and to preside over her husband's dinner table. From her, Thomas gained his appreciation of fine food and wine, beautifully bound books, and elegant furniture.

Peter Jefferson's genius in situating his house surely inspired his son's choice thirty years later, when he selected his site for Monticello eight miles due west. "To the south," a great-granddaughter reported of Shadwell, "are seen the picturesque valley and banks of the Rivanna, with an extensive peaceful-looking horizon view, lying like a sleeping beauty, in the east; while long rolling hills, occasionally rising into mountain ranges . . . stretch westward." The whole panorama, she sighed, presented "landscapes whose exquisite enchantment must ever charm the beholder." While one cannot see the Rivanna River from Monticello, the view from the plateau carved from the top of Jefferson's mountain likewise charms. To the east, the rolling valleys seem to stretch endlessly toward the Chesapeake Bay; a French visitor in 1796 believed that "the Atlantic might be seen were it not for the greatness of the distance." To the west, the Blue Ridge Mountains bear the color, in infinite variations, of their name. Summer fog sometimes scatters small clouds about the mountain, so that, viewed from the valley below, the house seems set apart from the rest of the earth.

Slaves, many of them hired from neighbors, began the backbreaking work of leveling the top of the mountain in the spring of 1768. By the following year, the hilltop site of Thomas Jefferson's future home was ready for the cellar to be dug. Because the land lacked a water source, a well had to be dug through sixty-five feet of rock. By 1770, the south pavilion, just twenty by twenty feet, in which Jefferson would honeymoon with his bride, had been completed. The following year, the dining room in the north wing had been built.

Scholars differ about some of the chronological details of the building of the house, since Jefferson did not keep a diary tracking its rise. But there is no doubt that it was to a construction site, rather than to a home, that Jefferson brought his new bride. He had hoped for "more elbow room" by the summer, he wrote to a friend in February 1771, eleven months before his wedding. The completion of the dining room by the end of that year may have relieved the Jeffersons from taking their meals in the tiny pavilion. But it would be two years before the first stories of the north wing and central block were completed and the south wing begun, another two years before the upper story of the central block was begun, and not until 1778 were the attics begun and completed. Yet even this litany of progress refers only to the outer shell of the house; finishing touches on the interior, the work of expert joiners, would not be completed until 1783. It is unlikely that these rooms bore even a simple plastered finish much before then.

Thus Martha Jefferson would live out her married life in a noisy, dusty construction zone—except for the times she left Monticello. Indeed, it was only a matter of days after her first arrival that she and her husband left their new home for Elk Hill, the house she had shared with her first husband, Bathurst Skelton. After just two short years of marriage that produced a son, John, Bathurst died suddenly, leaving his twenty-year-old widow in possession of their house at Elk Hill. In the course of her married life with Jefferson, she would live a peripatetic existence: now with one sister or another in their homes, while her husband served as a representative of his county in the colonial assembly in Williamsburg or later as a Virginia delegate to the Continental Congress in Philadelphia; at Elk Hill; in Williamsburg and Richmond as the governor's wife; or on the run, fleeing the British incursions deep into Virginia during the Revolution. To the extent that it is possible to track from the records, Monticello was her home for only a little over half of her married life.

But that nomadic existence was still in her future. By the end of June 1772, the couple had returned to settle in at Monticello. A scant nine months after her wedding, Martha Jefferson gave birth to their first child on September 27. Her formal name was Martha, after Martha's mother, Martha Eppes Wayles. But throughout her childhood, her parents would adopt the popular nickname of that era and affectionately call her Patsy. Her birth was a harbinger of hope for a new beginning for the young mother, whose only child from her first marriage, John, had died in 1771 at four years of age.

The infant Martha gave her mother some cause for worry at first, however. She was a sickly, underweight baby, and her life may well have been saved by the "good breast of milk" provided by a newly acquired slave, Ursula Granger. Martha had known Ursula, a slave of a friend, and at Martha's request (she was "very desirous to get a favorite house woman of the name of Ursula," Jefferson wrote), Jefferson bought her and her two sons at an estate auction in January 1773. Shortly thereafter, he bought Ursula's husband, George Granger. The Grangers would take trusted positions in the Jeffersons' service: Ursula as supervisor of the kitchen and smoke- and washhouses, and George as the only paid black overseer on any of Jefferson's plantations. Well nourished, little Martha soon grew strong, but Ursula's own baby, Archy, born in 1773, died the next year.

THAT AN ENSLAVED WOMAN, purchased to bring her invaluable housekeeping talents to the work in progress that was Monticello, was then put to work as a wet nurse to her owner's child was just one of the innumerable ironies of the workings of a slave society. The same system that declared Ursula unfree also relied on her, literally, to nourish and sustain itself. As it had developed in colonial Virginia, slavery became predicated upon a finely striated system of law and custom designed to make clear the separation between free and unfree. It had not always been that way. The arrival of the first Africans in Virginia in 1619 had not, in itself, signaled the beginning of a fully formed slave system. True, the English in Virginia had the example of the Spanish and Portuguese sugar plantations in the Caribbean and South America; and the Dutch would later establish a thriving transatlantic slave trade system that kept those plantations supplied with labor. But not all blacks in early Virginia were enslaved. Some were kept as servants, in temporary bondage. Others bought their freedom and moved to the Eastern Shore, where many purchased land, married, raised families, and hired or bought laborers of their own.

To meet their insatiable appetite for labor, white Virginians would make the transition gradually from white English servants to black slaves over the course of the seventeenth century. Time and again in these early years, the newly formed assembly in the provincial capital of Jamestown legislated what it meant to have white skin or black, to be free or enslaved. The representatives, called burgesses, debated such questions as: Are all men, black and white, permitted to carry guns? (No, only whites, 1639.) Are African women counted as tithable (that is, taxable) in the same way as all men, white and black, sixteen years of age and older? (Yes, 1643.) To clarify, are *free* African women taxable, as well as enslaved? (Yes, but white women remain exempt, 1668.) Is the child of an enslaved woman and an Englishman free? (No, the child takes the condition of the mother, 1662.) So then, the child of a free white woman and a free black man is free? (No, not quite; such children will be held in service until their thirtieth birthday. In addition, the mother must pay a fine of £15 sterling or herself be sold into servitude for five years, 1691.) May blacks and whites marry? (No, 1691 and 1705. To prevent such "abominable mixture and spurious issue," the white person will be jailed for six months and pay a fine of £10 sterling. And clergymen who conduct such ceremonies will be fined ten thousand pounds of tobacco—half of which goes to the informer.)

Laws can be revealing, and as in the case of Virginia's racial codes, they cannot always disguise self-interested intentions. So, for example, as the burgesses wrestled with what constituted murder in the colony, they concluded, in their 1669 "act on the casual killing of slaves," that neither a master nor his agent could be convicted of murder if a slave died from overzealous punishment. It defied common sense, they agreed, to think that any master possessed "that prepensed malice" that would "induce any man to destroy his own estate." In deciding that even free African women were subject to the tax on laborers (arguably the best measure of wealth in a colony where the cash crop was labor-intensive tobacco), the burgesses were explicit that "negro women . . . though permitted to enjoy their freedome yet ought not in all respects to be admitted to a full fruition of the exemptions and impunities of the English." Black women, the burgesses warned, should never think themselves equal to white Englishwomen. But most significantly, what these examples demonstrate is that slavery was more than a labor system. In their increasing reliance on African labor, Virginian slaveholders had to contrive a rigid legal system to govern social, as well as economic, relations between blacks and whites.

Although Virginia's evolving racial code made plain the slaveholders' vision of colonial society, it also revealed the behavior of non-elite whites, servants, and slaves. Laws against miscegenation would not have been necessary if blacks and whites in Virginia had not been having sex. Laws controlling tithable labor would not have been necessary if free African women had not tried to assert the same status as white Englishwomen, who were considered too delicate for hard agricultural work. For all the order the burgesses intended their laws to impose, it was clear from the growing numbers of what they called "mulattoes" that the legal system was failing in its attempt to keep the races apart.

Of course, many of the lawbreakers were the slaveholding legislators themselves. In 1662 they had reversed centuries of English common law by mandating that children take the condition of their mothers. Not unintentionally, that legislation also benefited masters in two very tangible ways. First, it gave them free access to the bodies of their enslaved women, who had no legal standing to prosecute sexual assault; second, masters quite literally profited from the additions to their slave force that resulted from these assaults. Most insidiously, over time that law would take on the veneer of natural and divine law, as slaveholding whites justified their view of slaves as inferior beings by pointing to their birth into slavery. One's birth rank, they pontificated, revealed God's will and judgment. And by rendering any white person immune to prosecution for harming or even accidentally killing a fugitive slave, the slaveholding burgesses enlisted the acquiescence even of nonslaveholders in a system that made them feel superior to a permanent underclass over whom they effectively had the power of life and death.

By Martha and Thomas Jefferson's day, this system of racial hierarchy, designed to enforce white supremacy, was firmly in place. With the exception of a handful of radical Quakers, few thought to dispute it;

certainly Martha Jefferson, the daughter of a man who dealt in the slave trade, would not have. Unable to pay his passage to America, her father, John Wayles, an English immigrant, had contracted himself to work for a prominent Virginia planter and member of the colonial governor's council. That business relationship proved especially lucrative, as it threw him into the path of other leading men of the colony. Wayles worked his way toward independence by doing the kind of work others were not especially eager to do. Trained in the law and representing English business firms, Wayles dunned their American debtors for payment. In addition, he became enmeshed in the slave trade as a broker. The daughter of such a scrappy go-getter, willing to do whatever it took to rise in the world, was hardly likely to question a system that was the means of her father's success and her own comfort.

So when Martha heard about the estate sale that put Ursula Granger on the auction block, she thought nothing of acquiring a slave who could help bring order to a household under construction. Ursula was even worth the cost of buying her two sons as well. But although Ursula relieved Martha of one anxiety in the spring of 1773 by nourishing the newborn Martha, another arose to take its place. As Thomas headed east to Williamsburg to take his seat as an elected representative of Albemarle County, Martha packed up her baby and traveled with him, veering off the road just a few miles short of Williamsburg to her father's home of The Forest, where Wayles lay seriously ill. Her nursing efforts notwithstanding, her father died May 28.

With his death came the revelation of his entangled finances. Just before he died, Wayles had become involved in a massive investment in the slave trade that had gone very wrong: Disease and death had reduced a shipment of 400 slaves from Africa to Virginia to 280. The entire transaction had rested on the extension of credit, and Wayles had counted on a booming tobacco market to pay for the deal. Instead the market crashed and he died before he had paid a penny for his shipment. Unraveling the whole mess fell to his executors: Thomas Jefferson and his two brothers-in-law. Wayles had taken care to divide his assets equitably. To Martha he left eleven thousand acres of land—much of which he had amassed by taking advantage of foreclosures under the auspices of his elite connections—and about 130 slaves. Martha also inherited her share of his debts. Or, to put it more precisely, because of the law of coverture that rendered a married woman legally invisible, her husband inherited the land, the slaves, and the debt.

Thomas quickly sold six thousand acres of the inheritance to pay his share of the debt, then for the first time sat down to record all his holdings in his Farm Book. This little book, now housed at the Massachusetts Historical Society, is available in published facsimile to anyone who would care to read Jefferson's notes on managing his plantations. Here slaves are sorted, births and deaths recorded, dispensation of clothing and blankets organized, harvests tallied, and future ventures planned. Here, in his exactingly neat hand, he listed first "A Roll of the proper Slaves of Thomas Jefferson, Jan. 14, 1774," followed by "Slaves conveyed by my mother," and finally, the longest, "A Roll of the slaves of John Wayles which were allotted to T.J. in right of his wife." Then he merged all three into a fourth list entitled "Location of Slaves," obliterating their various origins and asserting his ownership of them all (187 souls) by allocating them to his various plantations. He could not know at the time that the Wayles debt would not be so easily expunged. At that moment in mid-January, as he sat totting up his inheritance, he must have felt like a rich man.

The process of sorting out which slaves would go where would take some time; decisions made on paper that January day would be revised as needed. And, as she had with Ursula, Martha let her husband know her preferences. Elizabeth Hemings and her family were at the top of her list.

Martha Jefferson had known Elizabeth Hemings all her life. When Martha's mother, Martha Eppes, married John Wayles in 1746, she brought Elizabeth Hemings, a young slave then about eleven, with her to her new husband's estate of The Forest. But before her wedding, Martha Eppes protected her property with a marriage settlement. The law permitted a single woman, as feme sole, to enter into contracts without a male signatory. Martha Eppes's prenuptial agreement specified that her property would remain hers and not be sold away to pay her husband's debts if she was widowed; if she died first, it would be held in trust for her children. In other words, John Wayles might profit from the use of his wife's slaves during his lifetime, but he neither owned nor could sell them. Two years into her marriage, Martha Eppes

Wayles was dead, after giving birth to her only surviving child, Martha. During the next twelve years, Wayles remarried twice. But after burying his third wife, he apparently decided that he could endure no more such losses. Instead he turned to a slave to serve as his "substitute for a wife" (a phrase later used by one of Jefferson's neighbors to describe this not uncommon practice). He turned to Elizabeth Hemings.

Elizabeth Hemings was light-skinned (one of Jefferson's slaves at Monticello described her as a "bright mulatto woman") and, judging from later descriptions by her daughter and granddaughter, beautiful. At twenty-six, she was already the mother of four children (by unrecorded fathers, likely slaves). In the relationship that would last the rest of his life, John Wayles fathered six children with her, the last, Sally, in 1773, the year he died. Hence, Elizabeth Hemings had been part of Martha Jefferson's world from her earliest memory. Hemings may well have served as a nursemaid to the motherless infant, and as a maid to the young girl. A teenager when Elizabeth Hemings gave birth to her children with John Wayles, Martha would certainly have been aware of their relationship. White Virginia women learned to live with such open secrets. In his will, John Wayles rewarded his eldest daughter's loyalty with his own: He honored the wishes of his first wife and was careful to bequeath the Hemings family to Martha.

There are a number of reasons why Martha Jefferson could have wanted the Hemings family at Monticello. One should not sentimentalize any of them. She may have been fondly attached to a maid who had cared for her as she was growing up. She may have been relieved that her father did not take a fourth wife, since she apparently did not care for either of her stepmothers. She may have been following the lead of her father, who gave Elizabeth Hemings and her children special privileges. She may have wanted them as a legacy of her father. Whatever the reason, Martha got what she wanted, and the Hemingses came to Monticello in 1775.

MARTHA NEEDED HELP. HER life became an almost unrelenting cycle of pregnancy, childbirth, and recovery. Less than a year after her first daughter was born, Martha was pregnant with her second child. Jane Randolph Jefferson was born April 3, 1774. But 1775 brought grief for the young mother: Eighteen-month-old Jane died in September, and Martha may have suffered a miscarriage that year as well. As her husband was laboring in Philadelphia that fall, the ominous silence from Virginia worried him incessantly. "I have never received the scrip of a pen from any mortal in Virginia since I left it," Jefferson complained to his brother-in-law Francis Eppes in November 1775. "If any thing has happened, for god's sake, let me know it."

Martha almost certainly miscarried in the summer of 1776, when reports of her poor health made Jefferson frantic to return to Virginia from his assignment as delegate to the Second Continental Congress in Philadelphia. Martha had been staying with Elizabeth and Francis Eppes, her sister and brother-in-law, at The Forest, near Williamsburg; by July, she was recuperating at her beloved Elk Hill, and Francis could assure the anxious husband that Martha "is perfectly recover'd from her late indisposition and except being a little weak, is as well as she ever was." Jefferson finally arrived home in September; shortly thereafter, Martha was pregnant again. Her son was born on May 28, 1777. The despairing parents never even named him, so doubtful were they of his survival; he lived but seventeen days. Less than six months later, Martha was carrying the only other child besides Martha who would survive childhood; Mary—called Polly in her childhood, and then later Maria—was born on August 1, 1778. Lucy Elizabeth followed two years later, on November 3, 1780, but died in April the next year. Four months later, at almost thirty-three, Martha became pregnant for the last time. Lucy Elizabeth, named for her dead sister, was born in May 1782. Martha endured far worse than the 10–30 percent average mortality rates of the era.

This saga of birth and death exacted a predictable cost on Martha's health. Although she left no letters describing her ordeals, the account book in which she recorded the seasonal cycles of hog slaughtering and candle- and soap-making yields important clues about her energy and faltering stamina. She began her married life with vigor, recording the winter butchering of hogs and sheep, salting and smoking them to keep through Virginia summers. She brewed beer; she made soap. She kept track of when she "opened a barrel of flower" or broke into a loaf of sugar, and of which hams fed her own family and which the construction crew. But her final pregnancy took its toll; from that point on, Martha recorded no spending, slaughtering, or production.

Of course, Martha had not wielded the knife herself, nor did she stir the vats or churn the butter. Her slaves did that for her. Jefferson's account book records money doled out to his wife to tip slaves, to pay for the chickens and vegetables she bought from them, and for other miscellaneous household expenses. But it is unclear who at Monticello took care of paying the household bills during the nine months of silence in 1779, when Jefferson did not record giving his wife a penny for household accounts. The September 1781 entry, when Martha returned the unused £120 of the £165 her husband had given her, is the last record in his memorandum book of money changing hands. Another period of silence follows, signaling that she was no longer supervising the household a full year before her death.

Illness accounted for some of the lapses in Martha's account book; so, too, did war. During Jefferson's absences, she would frequently take refuge with her sister Elizabeth at The Forest, or at her own Elk Hill. When Jefferson was not in residence at Monticello, she could find little relief from anxiety or illness at the grand home he was building for them. She traveled from Albemarle to The Forest to stay with Elizabeth in June 1776, even though she was pregnant, had a three-year-old in tow, and for all she knew was heading straight into the brewing war the closer she drew to Williamsburg. When Jefferson was elected governor of Virginia in 1779, she and her daughters joined him in Williamsburg and then in Richmond, when the state capital was relocated there in April 1780. The move inland did not protect the legislators from British assaults, as had been hoped; Jefferson's political reputation would sustain a severe blow from his unpreparedness as governor to protect his state.

Twice Martha and her daughters fled, barely ahead of the British advance. In January 1781, Jefferson packed his family into a carriage headed west as he remained behind in Richmond, belatedly attempting to mount a defense against Benedict Arnold's attack. They left behind the slaves they had brought to the capital to serve them—George and Ursula and their children, and several Hemingses, including Elizabeth and her daughters Mary and Sally. So panic-stricken was the patriots' flight, Ursula's son Isaac recalled that "in ten minutes not a white man was to be seen in Richmond." Jefferson, too, joined the exodus. After destroying the abandoned ammunition and capturing the slaves, the invading British left to join forces with General Cornwallis, who was making his way east down the peninsula through Williamsburg and on to Yorktown. Resting his troops in the little town on the York River, Cornwallis looked in vain for the reinforcements that he expected to sail into the Chesapeake Bay from New York. Reunited with his family, Jefferson spent some time in safety at his father's old plantation at Fine Creek just west of Richmond before they all returned to the state capital. The war news got progressively bleaker, however, as the governor received reports that the British land forces were amassing at Yorktown while their navy maneuvered to seal off the entrance to the Chesapeake Bay to protect them.

In those dark days, as it appeared that the Revolution might be lost in his own state, Jefferson suffered another blow. On April 15, 1781, his infant, Lucy, died, a grievous loss to the couple. A week later, the British were on the move again. With no time to recover from Lucy's death, Martha and her daughters, now eight and two, fled to Elk Hill. But whatever respite they may have enjoyed in Martha's peaceful home was short-lived. By June they were back at Monticello, as Jefferson sought to move the government from the hazards of Richmond to the safety of Charlottesville, farther west. Determined to capture the man whose Declaration of Independence was a clarion call for rebellion, however, Cornwallis sent his most fearsome lieutenant, Colonel Banastre Tarleton, to Monticello, while he turned his own fury on Elk Hill. For the third time in less than six months, Martha was forced to flee with her two little girls, leaving her husband behind to an uncertain fate. This time, they traveled deep into southwest Virginia, finally arriving at Poplar Forest near Lynchburg, part of the estate they had inherited from John Wayles. Jefferson joined them en route, having eluded capture by a scant few hours.

Inexplicably, Monticello was spared depredation; Elk Hill, they would later learn, was not. Cornwallis's army destroyed the corn and tobacco; likewise "all my barns," Jefferson complained bitterly. They slaughtered any animals too young to be of service or used to feed his soldiers and stole about thirty slaves, according to Jefferson's count. His term as governor having expired, Jefferson and his family remained at Poplar Forest through the end of July. They returned to Monticello in early August. Before the month was out, Martha was pregnant again.

Yet as she looked back on those harrowing days of her childhood, it was not the trauma, the dislocation, and the horror of war that, as an adult, Martha would remember years later. She said nothing of the terror of sudden warnings and flight, of a grieving and exhausted mother, or of a distraught and overworked father. Perhaps that omission indicates how successful her parents were in protecting her from the worst effects of the war. It certainly suggests a remarkably strong mother, who, despite her failing health and the deaths of several of her children, conveyed confidence in her ability to keep the family safe—even in wartime. Each time they fled, they did so, at least initially, without Jefferson. When the Marquis de Chastellux, a French visitor to Monticello, described Martha Jefferson as a "mild and amiable wife," he was observing her in the spring of 1782, toward the end of her final pregnancy. If she seemed quiet and somewhat reserved, it is understandable in the context of her failing health. But his phrase, a universal compliment to the good wife in the eighteenth century, does not quite comport with the history of her married life, with what she had endured, or with the terrors from which she shielded her daughters.

The little girls' travels about Virginia, whether prompted by British troop movements or by their father's political obligations, may not have been, in and of themselves, traumatic. Indeed, extended visits among the eighteenth-century gentry were common. And in the Jeffersons' case, these visits—forced though they were—brought Martha and Maria a sense of safety and security, drew them more closely to their extended family, and encouraged them to view the Virginia landscape as dotted with the homes of friends and relatives ready to receive them. Martha Jefferson frequently turned to her half sister Elizabeth Wayles Eppes for help during her pregnancies and ill health. And, as we have seen, Elk Hill was a favorite haven, as was Poplar Forest, a plantation that fell to Jefferson from the Wayles inheritance. Martha frequently took her daughters to Elk Hill while Jefferson was away, as slave Isaac Jefferson recalled, and little Martha came to love it as her mother had.

Maybe it was also the place of Martha's happiest childhood memories from when her mother was still alive. Certainly it did not harbor the aura of death and grief associated with Monticello, where little Jane, her nameless brother, and her grandmother Jane Jefferson had died. And it was a refuge from the dust and commotion of Monticello's construction. At Elk Hill, Martha and her daughter could spend quiet hours together. Scholars have missed this point; typically they contrast what they regard as an emotional distance between mother and daughter with the extraordinarily close relationship that Martha would develop with her father over the course of her life. But they forget how much time mother and daughter spent together and how much Martha would have learned at her mother's knee.

In keeping with the conventions of her day, Martha Jefferson would have been her child's first teacher. The village of Charlottesville, which one traveler noticed could boast no more than a court house, a tavern, and a tiny cluster of houses when Martha was growing up, did not have a school. In any event, in this period, female education was hardly a priority. Privileged girls would be fortunate to learn to read and write, play a musical instrument, dance, embroider, and perhaps speak a little French. Martha Jefferson could play the harpsichord very skillfully and was, in the estimation of a Hessian officer held as a prisoner of war in Charlottesville, "in all respects, a very agreeable, Sensible & Accomplished Lady." Martha likely schooled her daughter to read and write (girls were taught a different hand than boys), began her music lessons, and trained her in the manners expected of a young Virginia lady. It is possible that it was at Elk Hill that the young Martha learned to ride, taught by the mother who had first arrived at Monticello on horseback, or plied the first stitches of the needlework exercises required of gently raised Virginia girls under the watchful eye of her mother.

Given both her age and the itinerant quality of her childhood, little Martha would not have had lessons in household management. Unlike her future daughters, then, Martha did not have any bitter complaints about household chores in her recollections of growing up. But the mother who possessed "considerable powers of conversation," according to her daughter, plus "all the habits of good society, and the art of welcoming her husband's friends to perfection," was the perfect guide for this girl who would grow up to be universally admired for her ability to charm all who met her.

Only two accounts of Martha's childhood in Virginia exist: one by a

French visitor, the Marquis de Chastellux, in the summer of 1782, and the other by Martha herself as an adult. Both remembered Jefferson, and not his wife, as the guiding force of Martha's education. Although newly met, Chastellux was quickly welcomed into the family circle. Long conversations about books, travel, and architecture endeared the two men to each other. Jefferson discovered Chastellux's "worth and abilities [that] impressed me with an affection for him which under the then prospect of never seeing him again was perhaps imprudent." For his part, the Marquis was captivated by the architecture of Jefferson's home, the nimbleness of his mind, the depth of his learning, and the quality of his conversation. So it is no surprise that he deduced that Jefferson took charge of educating his children, whether Jefferson told him so or not.

Martha remembered that "during my Mother's life he bestowed much time & attention on our education, our cousins the Carrs and myself." These memories do not quite match those of Jefferson himself, however. In 1818, he admitted to a friend that "a plan of female education has never been a subject of systematic contemplation with me," and that his own daughters' education only "occasionally required" his attention. Jefferson had sketched out in broad strokes his recommendations for girls' reading: select novels only (most being inclined to result in "a bloated imagination [and] sickly judgment"), select poetry (for the same reason) to promote "style and taste," and French, dancing, drawing, and music. It was an utterly conventional program, essentially unchanged by thirty eventful years of revolution and republic-building. Of lessons in budgeting household accounts, Jefferson knew, "I need say nothing," since he assumed all parents would teach their daughters not to spend the hard-won earnings of their future husbands. In other words, Jefferson described precisely the program of female education his wife had been well equipped to administer to her daughter forty years earlier.

But it is also clear, as we shall see, that when Martha Jefferson entered her convent school in France at almost twelve, she began her studies with classical, not juvenile, literature. This suggests some prior preparation, although we know nothing from Jefferson's hand or her own about what that may have been. Martha may have provided a clue, however, when she mentioned her cousins the Carrs. Martha Jefferson

Carr, Jefferson's sister and the widow of his boyhood friend Dabney, was probably living at Monticello by the troubled spring of 1781. The arrival of Martha Jefferson Carr's brood—three sons and three daughters—may well have been the impetus for Jefferson's serious thought about children's education generally, and about his daughters' in particular. Jefferson became a second father to his six nieces and nephews, particularly to Carr's eldest son, Peter. Jefferson was busy with public life when the boy first came under his tutelage at age eleven, but back at Monticello he was able to devote more time to Peter. After his disastrous second term as governor, in which he had been unable to repel invading British forces, a determined Jefferson swore to have "taken my final leave of every thing of that nature [politics], have re- tired to my farm, my family and books from which I think nothing will ever more separate me." Thus freed, he turned his attention to the eight children under his roof.

This brief period of respite from public life at Monticello is why both the adult Martha and Chastellux could report with confidence that Jefferson had taken charge of the children's education that spring of 1782. By March, Peter Carr was already reading Virgil, probably in Latin, and Jefferson planned to start schooling him in French. Ten- year-old Sam Carr was halfway through a beginner's Latin primer, and at nine the youngest son, Dabney, was almost ready to begin his studies in Latin. Around this time, too, Jefferson probably began to frame a program of reading for his precociously bright nine-year-old daughter.

Martha may well have sat alongside Peter in an improvised school- room at Monticello; the sons and daughters of Robert Carter, one of the wealthiest planters in the Northern Neck of Virginia, shared the same tutor and classroom, in spite of the considerable range in their ages. But proximity did not necessarily mean access to the same cur- riculum; male and female education in the colonial period had very different aims. There is no evidence, for instance, that young Martha learned Latin alongside her cousins.

This period of domestic peace was shattered, however, not by yet another British attack but by a momentous family tragedy. For all the dangers the Revolution posed for her family, it was not the attacks on Richmond, the frantic departures, the destruction at Elk Hill, or the attempt of the British to capture her father that daughter Martha recorded in her memoir years later. Her war story, which she recounted in detail, was that of her mother's death and her father's grief.

IN MAY 1782, JEFFERSON's wife had given birth to their last child, Lucy Elizabeth. Martha was dangerously ill and sinking, and this time it was clear that she would not recover. Her husband devoted himself to her care. "For the last four months that she lingered he was never out of calling," daughter Martha remembered. "As a nurse no female ever had more tenderness or anxiety; he nursed my poor Mother in turn with aunt Carr and her own sisters setting up with her and administering her medicines and drink." When forced to attend to work, he did so "in a small room which opened immediately at the head of her bed."

At nine, little Martha may have been barred from the room by her concerned aunts. Almost one hundred years after these events, her granddaughter told a story that had been passed down to her. "Mrs. Jefferson had been too ill to see the child for some time, when one day the latter was called in to see her mother dressed and sitting up in a chair, as something that would please her." Instead "for the first time the truth flashed on her as she saw death stamped on the invalid's pale face; and so overcome was she by the shock that she was obliged to leave the room."

Therefore, more than her mother's death, Martha remembered better her father's response, observed, perhaps, from outside the sickroom door. Jefferson's wife died on September 6. "A moment before the closing scene he was led from the room almost in a state of insensibility," she wrote, his response a perfect image of her own earlier one, "by his sister Mrs Carr who with great difficulty got him into his library where he fainted and remained so long insensible that they feared he never would revive." When, in fact, his wife was gone, the distraught husband gave way altogether. "The scene that followed I did not witness but the violence of his emotion, of his grief when almost by stealth I entered his room, right to this day I dare not trust my self to describe," Martha wrote almost fifty years later.

In that instant, Martha became her father's emotional caretaker, a role she would fill for the rest of his life. "He kept to his room three weeks and I was never a moment from his side," she recalled; there he "walked almost incessantly night and day." Martha's sisters remained at Monticello for weeks afterward, no doubt helping to care for the three children whose father was incapacitated by grief. "When at last he left his room he rode out and from that time he was incessantly on horseback rambling about the mountain," Martha remembered; "in these melancholy rambles I was his constant companion, a solitary witness to many a violent burst of grief."

The cataclysm of Martha Jefferson's death accomplished what the British armies had not been able to do: It brought an end to Martha's childhood, caused the family's departure from Monticello, and fractured Martha Wayles Jefferson's two families, Jefferson and Hemings. Within two months, Jefferson would grasp at the congressional appointment to represent the United States in final peace negotiations with Great Britain. When at last he would leave Virginia, he would deposit his two youngest daughters with Elizabeth Eppes, the younger sister of their mother and the aunt most like her, and make the decision to take with him to Paris eleven-year-old Martha. He would also part Elizabeth Hemings from two of her children: nineteen-year-old James would accompany him to Paris, while nine-year-old Sally, he decided, was old enough to accompany Maria and Lucy to the Eppes plantation until his return. These directives, made at the will of the master of Monticello, would have enormous repercussions in all their lives. Nothing would be the same again.

To Paris

. . . .

1782

. . . .

*I*T WAS NOT THE FIRST time Congress had tapped Jefferson to represent his country in France. In June 1781, Congress had appointed him minister plenipotentiary, to round out a diplomatic commission consisting of Benjamin Franklin, John Jay, and Henry Laurens. Since France had joined the war as an ally of the United States after the American victory at Saratoga in October 1777, the United States had maintained a diplomatic presence at the court of Louis XVI to sustain the alliance. As minister plenipotentiary, Jefferson would rank just lower than Ambassador Franklin but could exert full power and authority in the commerce treaties he was to negotiate. The summons had found him in the midst of deep political troubles: the Virginia House of Delegates had decided to launch an investigation of the former governor's conduct during the British invasion. Determined to remain in Virginia to fight for his reputation, Jefferson refused the appointment, resolving to leave public life forever to enjoy the domestic comfort of Monticello. The news of Martha Jefferson's death almost a year later, however, prompted James Madison to resubmit Jefferson's name for the appointment. "All the reasons which led to the original appointment still existed," Madison argued, and as an intimate friend of Jefferson's, he rightly guessed that "the death of Mrs. J. had probably changed the sentiments of Mr. J. with regard to public life." Congress readily agreed; it passed the motion unanimously.

The commission, dated November 12, reached Jefferson two weeks later at Ampthill, the Chesterfield County plantation of his friend Colonel Archibald Cary. "Your [letter] finds me at this place attending my family under inoculation," Jefferson replied to Madison on the twenty-sixth. The return of Jefferson's captured slaves, who had been exposed to smallpox during their captivity at Yorktown, posed a significant risk to his daughters' health. Inoculated himself in Philadelphia in 1766, he knew the process well. Just as faithfully as he had tended to his dying wife, he now served Martha and Maria as their "chief nurse," as Martha called him. It is likely that he had left the infant Lucy, too tiny to be subjected to the infection, with her aunt Eppes. By this time, Francis and Elizabeth Eppes had moved from The Forest west and south to the banks of the Appomattox River, where Francis had built a home he called Eppington. After visiting them there for the first time—or so it seems, since he hired a guide to show him the way—Jefferson then went to Ampthill and spent November in seclusion with his daughters.

The inoculation procedure probably followed the method developed by the famous English doctor Robert Sutton in the mid-eighteenth century. Earlier versions of inoculation involved taking a sample from the sores of an already infected person and inserting it into a deep incision on the patient. There were considerable risks in this method, of course, either death or the permanent scarring George Washington suffered. But Sutton took the inoculum from a previously inoculated person and avoided deep incisions. As a result, he and his doctor sons enjoyed phenomenal success in defeating a fearsome disease: little scarring and only a 1 percent fatality rate among the thousands they treated. The Suttons also insisted upon outdoor exercise for their patients. Familiar with the Suttons' methods, Jefferson took his daughters away from Monticello. While contagious, his patients needed to live in the quarantine that Ampthill provided.

However solicitous of his daughters and grief-stricken by his wife's death Jefferson was, he could not contain his eagerness to start for France. His daughters' recovery from fever, aches, and pains could hardly be rushed, so the preparations that could only be done from

Monticello would just have to wait. But, he assured Madison, he would lose no time in preparing once he got home. "From the calculations I am at present enabled to make," he estimated, "I suppose I cannot be in Philadelphia before the 20th. of December, and that possibly it may be the last of that month." There, he knew, he would need several days to prepare for his mission, "as I could not propose to jump into the midst of a negotiation without a single article of previous information." His mind raced his pen as he planned ahead. Could he be ready in time to take advantage of a French naval officer's offer to carry him and the Marquis de Chastellux to France? He fired off a letter to Chastellux the same day. Maybe luck would favor him with a delay in the ship's departure, he hoped, so that he could catch Chastellux before he left Philadelphia for home. He anticipated the pleasures of their voyage, the chess games and the continued conversations begun that spring at Monticello with his new friend. "My only object now is so to hasten over those obstacles which would retard my departure as to be ready to join you in your voiage," he wrote with anxious urgency.

On December 2, he tipped the slaves who had served them at no small risk to themselves—we have no idea if they had been inoculated or not—and left Ampthill for home. Within two weeks, Maria had joined her sister Lucy at Eppington; so, too, very likely, had her nine-year-old maid, Sally Hemings. With his affairs in order, Jefferson left Monticello with Martha and twenty-year-old Robert Hemings, another of Elizabeth Hemings's children, arriving in Philadelphia on the twenty-seventh. It was not Robert's first trip to the city; he had accompanied Jefferson in 1775 and been safely inoculated there.

They boarded at the home of Mary House and her daughter, Eliza Trist, probably at the recommendation of James Madison, who also rented there. They stayed for a month, delayed by threats of capture by the vigilant British, who, smarting from their unsuccessful attempts in Virginia to capture the author of the Declaration of Independence, still had not issued him safe passage on the seas. Jefferson and Martha then made their way to Baltimore, hoping that the French ship that had been outfitted for him was ready for departure. Three weeks later, they returned to Philadelphia, having been warned that British attacks on French shipping continued to render a winter crossing hazardous for the American minister. Finally, in early April 1783, after this series of creeping delays and false starts, sufficient progress had been made in the peace negotiations being held in Paris to reinforce the American commitment to their French ally that Congress informed him that his services were no longer needed.

Formally released by Congress, Jefferson collected Martha and headed for home. It was a leisurely trip. They stopped when the phaeton needed to be repaired, or the washing done, or a horse shod, or people visited, or business conducted. In Richmond, Jefferson met up with James Hemings, Robert's eighteen-year-old brother, and gave him ferry money to go to Elk Hill. Did Martha look wistfully after him, wishing that she too could see her mother's beloved home again, or was she consoled by the prospect of their next stop, seeing her Randolph cousins at their plantation home of Tuckahoe? Jefferson and Martha finally arrived home at Monticello on May 15.

Within weeks of their arrival, they knew that the stay would be temporary. In June Jefferson was elected to Congress, a position to which he would report that fall. Although the distance separating family members obviously would be considerably shorter than if he had gone abroad, the arrangements would be the same: Martha would head north with him, while Maria and Lucy would return to Eppington. Exactly where Jefferson himself would be was another question. Fearing a mutiny by Pennsylvania soldiers to force payment for their service, Congress had bolted from Philadelphia to Princeton. But by the time Jefferson arrived there, he found that Congress had adjourned to the safety of Annapolis, where it would receive the Treaty of Paris in January 1784 that would formally end the American Revolution.

The best place for Martha was clear, however: Philadelphia. At eleven years old, Martha Jefferson was poised to begin her education as a young lady; as the largest city in the United States and its cultural center, Philadelphia was the perfect place to begin to acquire the polish required of young women of her class. As her father put it, "Her time in Philadelphia will be chiefly occupied in acquiring a little taste and execution in such of the fine arts as she could not prosecute to equal advantage in a more retired station," like the tiny village of Charlottesville. True, he also wanted her to know something of "the graver sciences" in the event that she was responsible for educating her children because she had married a "blockhead"—a possibility that Jefferson had calculated "at about fourteen to one." But he intended to supervise her science education himself when she was once again under his roof. In the meantime, two popular novels, *Gil Blas* and *Don Quixote,* would suffice. As one historian observed, while Jefferson insisted on what he called the "natural equality" of women, he meant women's duty to serve men, as nature intended. Thus, enhancing Martha's ability to sing, dance, draw, and converse—that is, to be pleasing to men—would be the prime object of her time in Philadelphia.

There was, then, the question of where Martha would live and be schooled. During their fruitless stay in the city the winter before, her father had displayed some sensitivity in thinking ahead to arrangements for her once they arrived in France. He had written to John Jay, already settled in Paris as one of the American peace negotiators, to inquire about housing that would be suitable for a motherless girl. Now preparing for his return to Philadelphia for the extended stay of the congressional term, he asked Madison to intercede for him with Mrs. House and her daughter, Eliza Trist, with whom they had boarded the previous winter. At first he hoped Martha could lodge with her again. If it turned out that Congress sat elsewhere, however, he still wanted Martha to stay in the city. But where? He knew Eliza was planning on leaving Philadelphia eventually to join her husband in New Orleans, but Martha required a more permanent place to stay. Trusting the warm friendship that had developed the year before among them all, Jefferson decided, "I will ask the favor of Mrs. Trist to think for me on that subject, and to advise me as to the person with whom she may be trusted. Some boarding school of course," he ventured, "tho' I am not without objections to her passing more than the day in such a one." Dislocated yet again from her home, his daughter would fare better, he believed, in the embrace of a congenial household than among strangers in a boarding school.

Eliza Trist agreed. On November 19, Martha moved to the home of Mary Hopkinson, the mother of Jefferson's much-admired friend Francis Hopkinson. In accordance with Jefferson's wishes, Martha followed a traditional curriculum for elite eighteenth-century girls that continued in the track of her mother's tutelage, her school days punctuated by music, dancing, French, more music, reading, and writing. Her father had hired a range of exclusive tutors: a dancing master from

Paris, a Swiss artist, an English musician, and on the recommendation of French diplomat François de Barbé-Marbois, a Frenchman to instruct her in the language. By the time he repaired to Annapolis, Jefferson was confident that Martha's education was in good hands. The thought consoled him greatly. "The conviction that you would be more improved in the situation I have placed you than if still with me, has solaced me on my parting with you, which my love for you has rendered a difficult thing," he admitted to her.

But Martha Jefferson would have received much more training than her schedule suggests. Mary Hopkinson was a formidable woman. Widowed at thirty-three and responsible for the care of her seven children (Francis, the eldest, was fourteen at the time), Mary won the admiration of Benjamin Franklin for her ability to educate her children and launch them into the world "without much diminishing their portions," that is, their inheritance. Her children were devoted to her and taught their children to be so as well. When her youngest daughter, Anne, married and moved to Baltimore in 1775, she remained bound to her mother by letters and regular visits. Although growing rapidly, Baltimore could not yet match the cultural milieu of Philadelphia, but the letters and literary extracts composed by Anne's daughters make clear that Anne conveyed her mother's passion for reading, reflecting, and writing to her own children. Letters flew from Baltimore to their dear "GrandMama" in Philadelphia, reinforcing a female network in which the younger generation learned from the strong models before them. Mary Hopkinson also embraced her daughter's friends. One of Anne's correspondents was warmed by the memory of "the many happy hours I have spent in your agreeable society and the Worthy Circle of friends who were accustim'd to meet at your dear Momma's." Martha's own passion for reading and writing was certainly nurtured in Mary Hopkinson's home.

Even so, Martha's mentor apparently held religious views decidedly at odds with Jefferson's. A devout Anglican (one of her daughters married the rector of the prestigious Christ Church, whose spire made it the tallest building in colonial America), Mary Hopkinson no doubt brought Martha to services frequently. Although Anglicans stressed reason as well as revelation in their theology, Hopkinson evidently harbored some notions that natural phenomena could predict future catastrophe and passed them on to Martha. Jefferson would have none of it. "Disregard those foolish predictions that the world is to be at an end soon," he told his daughter bluntly. "The almighty has never made known to any body at what time he created it, nor will he tell any body when he means to put an end to it, if ever he means to do it." Hopkinson's alarming forecasts may explain why Martha never warmed up to the woman her father urged she "consider . . . as your mother." She never wrote to Mary Hopkinson after her departure from Philadelphia, although she did form a lifelong friendship with the good-natured Eliza Trist.

Mary's son Francis, a fellow signer of the Declaration of Independence with Jefferson in 1776, also took an active interest in Martha's progress and happiness. Son of Thomas Hopkinson, first president of the American Philosophical Society and trustee of the College of Philadelphia (later, the University of Pennsylvania), Francis's interests ranged widely in politics, music, and the literary arts. He loved music, wrote satirical essays, songs, and poetry, and built a distinguished career that included serving as a lawyer and jurist. His home, which still stands on Spruce Street, was a center of political and social conviviality. The lively young Martha would have found the cheerful society of her father's like-minded friend and his children more appealing than that of the well-meaning older woman whose doomsday warning was so frightening. That winter, Francis hosted a New Year's Eve gathering that Martha attended; she "danced out the old Year in Company with Mr. Rittenhouse's Daughters and my Children. A Forte Piano served for a *Fidle* and I for a Fidler," Francis added playfully. "I was much indisposed the whole Evening, but their mirth alleviated my Pains." His son Joseph, three years older than Martha, may well have been one of her dance partners that evening.

As a father of a daughter about Martha's age, Francis Hopkinson could understand Jefferson's anxiety about her education; but in his sprightly way, he also knew how to temper it. "I have the Pleasure to inform you that your Girl comes on finely in her Education; but Mr. Simitiere"—the drawing instructor—"declares he will leave her at the End of the Month," Hopkinson reported. Insisting that "he is no *School-Master*," Simitiere had sniffed disdainfully that he was "not obliged to go thro' the Drudgery of teaching those who have no Capac-

In addition to his larger family home in Bordentown, New Jersey, Francis Hopkinson maintained a Philadelphia town home on Spruce Street between Third and Fourth streets. Here Martha Jefferson spent many happy hours during her stay in that city, visiting with Hopkinson's children.

ity." Hopkinson dismissed the artist's imperiousness, softening the sting of his words. "You will not be disappointed at this," he soothed Jefferson, "as you know the Man." Martha enjoyed her visits with the Hopkinson family; four days after the New Year's Eve revels, she was back at their home again for another visit.

In the meantime in Annapolis, Jefferson was preoccupied with trying to collect the nine required state signatures mandated by the Articles of Confederation to ratify the peace treaty Congress had received from Britain in September 1783. Only seven states had sent delegates to Annapolis, and a delegate's impending departure threatened to reduce that number to six. A six-month deadline imposed by Great Britain caused an additional degree of urgency. Jefferson did not get his quorum until March, the month of the deadline. Legislatively paralyzed until then, the congressional session was marked by contentious squabbling; hardly a surprise, Jefferson thought, for lawyers "whose trade it is to question everything, yield nothing and talk by the hour." But substantive conversations on the organization of the western lands to be gained in the treaty did begin, laying the groundwork for new states to be admitted on equal terms with the original thirteen. And Congress agreed with Jefferson's practical suggestion to decimalize a dollar-based currency.

It is difficult to say how Martha felt through the better part of this six-month absence from her father; none of her letters from this period remain. Certainly Francis Hopkinson's five children, and the two daughters of David Rittenhouse (an eminent astronomer and inventor), were good and animated company, and Martha was probably eager to accept Rittenhouse's offer to meet the dreaded Mr. Simitiere for her drawing classes at his home, rather than her own. His daughters, born between 1767 and 1772, were just a bit older than she was, and part of the group that provided so much merriment for Francis Hopkinson that he forgot his indisposition. Drawing lessons with the temperamental Simitiere, whose pocketbook obliged him to continue teaching whether he liked it or not, would be more pleasant for Martha taken in the company of friends, as the kindly Rittenhouse realized.

Martha Jefferson's time with the Hopkinsons gave her a richer education than most young girls in the early republic would have enjoyed. A poet and songwriter—in fact, the first white native-born American to write a secular song in colonial America—who delighted in entertaining children, Francis Hopkinson would have done more than relieve her loneliness with his cheer. In his household, she would also have heard serious conversations about science and politics, such as those he shared with his famous friends Benjamin Franklin and David Rittenhouse. Two years after he left Philadelphia, Jefferson would sigh for the Wednesday evening conversations he used to enjoy with Rittenhouse and Franklin. "They would be more valued by me," he recalled, "than the whole week at Paris." In their homes, Martha enjoyed the company of young people and the society of the most important Enlightenment figures in Philadelphia. If Mary Hopkinson did not teach her how the Church could coexist with reason and science, her son and his friends certainly could.

Martha's sojourn in Philadelphia came to an abrupt end in May

1784. Although the Congress meeting in Annapolis agreed on little, they did agree on the appointment of Jefferson as minister plenipotentiary to France. John Jay was returning to the United States, and the southern contingent—warily eyeing Franklin and John Adams, northerners both—wanted their interests represented in the ongoing trade agreements with the various European states. After preparing a final report to the Speaker of the Virginia House of Delegates, Jefferson resigned his seat in Congress and returned to Philadelphia.

Preparations for their departure were frantic. On May 7, the day of his appointment, Jefferson sat down to dash off a flurry of letters. There was no time for a quick trip to Eppington for goodbyes to Maria and Lucy. Instead he had to settle for a series of what his letter journal called "valedictory" letters (none of which survive): to his sister Martha Jefferson Carr and brother-in-law Henry Skipwith, invitations to make themselves at home at Monticello during the "hot season" when he was away; and farewells to Elizabeth Eppes, with an enclosure for little Maria, and to his other sister-in-law, Anne Skipwith. He wrote urgently to his friend William Short in Virginia. Could Short drop everything to join him as his secretary in Paris, as he had earlier hinted might be a possibility? And would he also track down James Hemings and either bring or send him to Philadelphia immediately? Two days later, he prepared a power of attorney for his trusted friend and brother-in-law Francis Eppes, and for Nicholas Lewis, a friend and neighbor in Charlottesville, to conduct business in his name during his absence.

By the twenty-eighth of May, James Hemings had arrived in Philadelphia (Short would travel later), and together he, Jefferson, and Martha left the city bound for Boston. It would take them three weeks, occupied by the usual maintenance requirements of eighteenth-century travel and a week's stay in New York City. Jefferson used the time to acquaint himself with northern commercial interests, which, as an ambassador for the entire country, he must also represent. For that purpose, he added a week's tour of New England when they discovered that they could not depart for France until early July. He lodged Martha with John Lowell, a judge and antislavery activist who offered his services to any Massachusetts slave suing for freedom. She never spoke of her time among Lowell's family, so we do not know what the young Virginia girl thought of their antislavery activities. Of course, she had spent time in Philadelphia with Francis Hopkinson, who later helped to write the constitution of the newly revived Pennsylvania Abolition Society and served as its secretary, so Boston may not have marked her first encounter with antislavery ideas. Still, New England would have revealed a different kind of society to all three Virginians: father, daughter, and slave.

At long last, Jefferson and Martha walked up the gangplank to the ship that would take them across the ocean, nearly two years after Martha Jefferson's death. The *Ceres* was beautiful: new but already proven seaworthy by a previous crossing. They would have it practically to themselves, sharing it with only six other passengers, "all of whom papa knew," Martha reported later. It was a perfect passage: short—nineteen days—sunny, and calm. "If I could be sure it would be as agreeable as the first," she later said, she would happily make another.

We can imagine the three voyagers standing at the ship's rail, watching as land disappeared from view. It is not likely that Jefferson mourned the sight, although he no doubt regretted his inability to see his younger daughters before he left. But they were in the best of hands, so he would not worry. Instead he may have stood at the bow, looking forward now after his years of sorrow. "The vaunted scene of Europe," for which Jefferson had longed and which had been promised for the better part of two years, would finally be his. The trip would have been monumental for nineteen-year-old James Hemings as well. Unlike Jefferson, Hemings had made a point of visiting Monticello to say his goodbyes when he heard that Jefferson wanted him for a sojourn that was likely to last two years. The land disappearing over the horizon proclaimed liberty for all men but enslaved him; it was not his country in the same way as it was his master's. Did he look backward, toward Virginia and his family, or forward? And as he watched the ship cut through the waves, did he ponder the marvel of his eastward destination, the reverse of the voyages his ancestors had made from England or Wales, or packed in the bowels of a slaver from Africa?

When Martha wrote about the trip a year later, she spoke with the voice of experience, as a young girl who had mastered the challenges of living among strangers, first in Philadelphia, then in Boston, and finally in Paris. Her memory of an idyllic passage was selective, entirely editing out the last two days of the voyage, when she had fallen ill. What she was feeling as she left her sisters and aunts behind, we cannot know. It was a key moment, however, as the paths of the Jefferson sisters diverged markedly. Left behind to be raised by her aunt, Maria would find what Martha did not, a second mother. Trained in the mode of upper-class Virginia girls, Maria, like her peers, would seek marriage and motherhood, with little interest in exploring the wider world beyond her home. For her elder sister, Philadelphia had served as a kind of bridge from rural Albemarle to the splendors of Paris; her travels to New York City and Boston would have amplified her broadening view of the world, including, possibly, her views on slavery. Paris would not be her first time living among strangers, but it would require a transition from the New World to the Old. As she stood at the ship's railing, she must have wondered what awaited her there, and how she would adapt.

THEY ARRIVED IN PARIS on August 6. They had left Triel, twenty-five miles to the northwest of the city, that morning, changing horses four times. En route, they stopped to see the Machine de Marly, whose fourteen huge wheels, groaning and creaking with effort, another admiring visitor had noted, "threw every day more than 27,000 hogsheads of water up a height of 600 feet into the aqueduct." Traveling along the aqueduct, the water propelled from this engineering marvel supplied the beautiful fountains at Versailles, about four miles away. At last, they crossed the bridge at Neuilly, a wide stone structure Jefferson thought "the handsomest in the world," which had been completed just ten years earlier. A scant two and a half miles away, the great city rose before them. Perhaps the day was fair, like many August days in Paris, and the walls of the city gleamed white in the summer sun.

After their progress from the coast, through countryside that Martha had thought "a perfect garden," they arrived in the teeming, boisterous, reeking city of Paris. Nothing could have prepared them for what they saw. A city whose population was variously estimated at between five hundred thousand and a million inhabitants, Paris was—even conservatively—at least a dozen times bigger than Philadelphia. Its maze of more than eight hundred streets defied the efforts of visitors, foreign and provincial alike, to find their way to the city center. Most streets were narrow and crowded, filled with stalls where Parisians hawked their wares or brought their work, their socializing, and their arguments. Hazards abounded: dangling shop signs, projecting additions to overcrowded homes, overhanging flower boxes. There were no sidewalks. People, animals, wagons, and carriages all jostled for position, colliding with one another and tipping over the makeshift stalls, adding to traffic and din. There is not a sliver of daylight in a 1787 depiction of a typical Paris street: A country rustic, clutching a whip, drives his plodding workhorse past several women who press their backs to the house behind them to give way; a dog daringly darts under the horse's hooves; a delivery man with an enormous mirror strapped to his back leans heavily on his walking stick as a young boy, clutching a loaf of bread, ducks beneath his arm. A well-dressed bourgeois attempts to clear the way for his deliveryman, but a further complication is emerging: A carriage approaches from around the corner, the driver looking dismayed as he surveys the congestion from the height of his seat. Not until 1783 were city streets required to have a minimum width of thirty feet.

Less obvious from pictures of eighteenth-century Paris were its smells. Rivers could be the source of odors sweet and foul, from the abundant flower markets that lined the banks and the sewers that dumped into the Seine. Mornings brought the pleasant aroma of fresh-baked bread and coffee; later in the day, if the breeze was blowing just so, one could detect the distinctive smell of hops from the breweries south of the city, as well as the sickening stench from the tanneries. Even the most fashionable areas of the city were not immune to rank odors: Some days, the terraces of the pleasure garden attached to the Tuileries Palace could be overwhelmed by the stink of human excrement.

Initially, Martha was spared this view of the seamier side of Paris, since she and her father approached their destination from the northwest. The city had been undergoing a building boom since the 1760s, expanding in all directions but particularly to the west. There, neighborhoods such as the Faubourg Saint-Germain on the Left Bank drew aristocratic families, both French and foreign, seeking lodging. The elegance of the neighborhood is on display in an eighteenth-century engraving of the rue de Grenelle: Newer buildings of neoclassical design are interspersed with older but tasteful townhouses, in a tableau of graceful order. If the anonymous artist exaggerated the width of the street (and he did), he nonetheless made his point: beauty, serenity, and cleanliness could be had in Paris, if you could afford them. By the time the Jeffersons arrived in 1784, half of the city's aristocratic families lived in the Faubourg Saint-Germain, and it is still one of Paris's most exclusive neighborhoods, housing embassies, diplomats, and the well-heeled.

Building had proceeded apace on the Right Bank as well. As they entered the city outskirts, Jefferson's driver guided their phaeton down the main thoroughfare, the Champs-Élysées. On their left, a whole

A depiction of the rue de Grenelle in 1789, this engraving is an idealized view showing the street to be much wider than it actually was. La Fontaine des Quatre-Saisons, the colonnaded building seen here on the left side of the street with four small fountains at street level (two of which are barely visible here), was just two blocks from Panthemont. Both buildings still stand along a street that has not altered dramatically since Jefferson's day.

new quarter was being built in what had been, until recently, the royal orchards. Once owned by a younger brother of Louis XVI, the orchards were sold off by lots in the 1770s, spurring entrepreneurial construction projects of individual luxury homes for the nobility and the creation of new streets off the boulevard for further development. These lovely houses, enclosed by carefully kept gardens, made an immediate impression on Jefferson. Close enough for a commute to the city, but with their delightful rural aspect, they would be precisely what he would choose when it was time to look for his Paris home.

Proceeding down the Champs-Élysées, the carriage carrying Jefferson and Martha reached the great Place Louis XV. Twenty years in the making, the square had only been completed seven years before. At its center stood an enormous statue of Louis XV, which the joyous city of Paris had voted to erect in order to commemorate the king's reputedly miraculous recovery from illness in 1748. Jefferson admired the statue from a distance but as they drew closer thought the immense proportions made it "appear a monster." But the square, gracefully connecting the gardens flanking the Champs-Élysées on the west with the gardens of the Tuileries on the east, formed a beautiful prospect along the Right Bank of the Seine and a spectacular entrance to the city.

Their carriage turned left onto the rue Saint Honoré, toward another fashionable district, the Faubourg Saint-Honoré. Nobility who did not reside in Saint-Germain could be found here. The family of Adrienne de Noailles, who had married the Marquis de Lafayette, the famous French hero of the American Revolution, lived on this street, as did the Comte and Comtesse d'Houdetot (*salonnières* who were avid admirers of Benjamin Franklin). Then as now, exclusive shops lined the street; Jefferson would log in his memorandum book the many livres he spent there. But the rue Saint Honoré was narrower than the Champs-Élysées and lacked sidewalks; here the Jeffersons would have encountered the traffic and congestion for which Paris was notorious. They arrived at their lodgings, the Hôtel d'Orléans, on the rue de Richelieu, where they stayed for a few days before realizing their mistake and moving to the more spacious (and expensive) lodgings of the other Hôtel d'Orléans, on the Left Bank.

They spent the first three weeks getting acclimated. Even their first drive through the rue Saint-Honoré, the center of haute couture, had made them realize that their provincial Virginia clothing marked them as country rustics. Jefferson addressed this immediately. The very day they arrived, he spent 167 livres on clothes for Martha and 120 livres for a single pair of sleeve lace ruffles for himself—this in a society in which a female servant was doing well if she earned 12 livres a month. He also bought a couple of yards of cambric and lots of edging—perhaps to be made up for ruffles for Martha. Four days later, he bought himself a sword and belt to add to his presentation before moving to their more luxurious hotel on the Left Bank. More clothes for Martha, and more lace ruffles, shirts, knee and shoe buckles, and a cane for him soon followed.

A year later, Martha laughed at the memory of those first few days. "I wish you could have been with us when we arrived," she wrote to Eliza Trist. "I am sure you would have laughed, for we were obliged to

Painted two years after Jefferson's arrival in Paris, this portrait reveals his adoption of the elegant French style he discovered in his first days in France. He wears a rich blue coat, silk waistcoat, a crimped double-pleated jabot, and powdered wig. Completed in London in 1786 while Jefferson was visiting John Adams, this is the earliest known portrait of Jefferson. He gave it to Adams to mark their deep friendship.

send immediately for the stay maker, the mantumaker [dressmaker], the milliner and even a shoe maker, before I could go out." But even though Abigail Adams had reported that in Paris, "there is not a porter nor a washer woman but what has their hair powderd and drest every day," Martha saw the friseur but once. Regardless of what was à la mode in Paris, Martha Jefferson was *not* going to subject herself to the torture of French hairdressing. "I soon got rid of him," she told Trist mischievously, "for I think it always too soon to suffer." She must have learned a few styling techniques in that one session, however, since she crowed in triumph that she "turned down my hair [myself] in spite of all they could say."

JEFFERSON'S OFFICIAL DIPLOMATIC DUTIES notwithstanding, a most pressing personal matter was the selection of a proper school for Martha. His friend the Marquis de Chastellux, who had visited Monticello shortly before Jefferson's wife died and returned to Paris that same year, came to the rescue. He suggested the Abbaye Royale de Panthemont, one of the most fashionable schools in the city—and, by a mile, the most expensive. A noble reference was required for admission, and Chastellux secured that as well. He had been so impressed by Jefferson on his Virginia visit that he had included Jefferson in an account he published in Paris in 1786 of his travels in America. Such a well-placed advocate may explain why the Comtesse de Brionne, the niece of the Abbess of Panthemont, agreed to serve as Martha's sponsor for admission on such a brief acquaintance, if indeed she even met Martha at all.

On August 26, just three weeks after their arrival, Martha and Jefferson left their lodgings at the Hôtel d'Orléans on the rue des Petits-Augustins for the one-mile trip to the abbey. They entered the grounds through an extensive garden and pulled up to the entrance of the school. An enormous building—the garden façade was two-thirds the length of a modern-day football field—the Abbaye Royale de Panthemont was designed to impress. The product of fifty years of planning, renovation, and rebuilding (ongoing, even while Martha was there—she never could escape the din of construction), Panthemont was as elegant a presence in the Faubourg Saint-Germain as any of its other aristocratic neighbors. Indeed, a walk along the rue de Grenelle today remains one of the best ways to see the Paris that Martha and her father knew. Martha's school building still stands; occupied by the Ministry of Defense for many years, national austerity cuts prompted its sale in 2014 to a private developer.

The full splendor of Panthemont is best appreciated from the main entrance—the double white doors shown here—rather than the plainer street façade. The garden would have been in full flower on that August day when Jefferson brought his daughter to her new school and home. Directly above the double doors through which Martha entered was the Abbess's office, graced with a little balcony and bathed in the sunlight that streamed through the floor-to-ceiling windows.

Martha and Jefferson alighted from their carriage in front of the imposing entrance. Tall sets of double glass doors adorned the façade on both the first and second floors. Capped by transom and fanlight windows, they drew Martha's eye continuously upward to the elaborately carved pediment that heralded the entrance to the school. Graceful arches bonneted the rows of windows on the upper floors; a cupola elegantly capped the third floor. Nothing in Philadelphia, New York, or Boston had prepared her for the grandeur of her new school. Looking up, she suddenly felt very small.

They made their way into the spacious vestibule, with its high ceilings and elaborately carved moldings, and were ushered up the flight of stairs, to the office and reception rooms of the Abbess, the Mother Superior of the convent and head of the school. Martha nervously scrutinized the magnificent surroundings as she climbed the grand staircase, her dread mounting as the moment of separation from her father drew closer with each step. Reaching the second-floor landing, she could see a long hallway that led to the rooms that would be her home. The abundant sunlight coming in through the windows that faced the inner courtyard may have cheered her. She was not allowed to linger, however, and following their guide, Martha was taken to meet the Abbess, whose impressive office boasted the same high ceilings and carved woodwork that she had seen downstairs. No record of this first meeting exists. Maybe Martha tried out her elementary French from her lessons at home, or maybe she was utterly tongue-tied from grief over her impending separation from her father. Next they were led to an office where Jefferson paid his daughter's tuition to Sister de Vis, Amariton, or d'Elbée, the nuns in charge of the convent's accounts. Undoubtedly Martha was also introduced to Sister Tonbenheim, the headmistress, who supervised all the students.

Jefferson bid his daughter farewell, assured her he would come to visit often, and left her to the care of the nuns. Writing to Eliza Trist a year later, Martha still could not bring herself to describe her utter desolation as she watched him go. "I leave you to judge my situation" was all she would say. At just eleven, she was abandoned to navigate the waters of this new world alone.

THE CONVENT SCHOOL PRESENTED innumerable mysteries to a girl from Virginia, from the female government that controlled such a prominent institution to the strange clothing of the nuns. Martha entered her new school with all the anti–Roman Catholic sensibilities then held by Protestant Americans, who abhorred what they saw as the slavish obedience required of Catholics to a foreign ruler in Rome and who were deeply suspicious of the mysteries of their liturgy. Even after the passage of England's 1689 Act of Toleration, colonial American Catholics remained marginalized, and Martha had not entirely escaped this cultural disdain. Years after her return from Paris, she would describe the Catholic doctrine of transubstantiation as "the most monstrous article of their creed . . . absurd and disgusting." Although no doubt reassured by the recommendation of the Marquis de Chastellux and by her father's decision to place her at Panthemont, she must have wondered how a Catholic convent school would prepare her for her adult life in America.

In fact, in the Age of the Enlightenment, convent schooling was the target of criticism and ridicule even by Frenchmen. Enlightenment philosophes such as Voltaire and Jean-Jacques Rousseau believed that nature endowed men with rational capacities, which, when cultivated through learning, enabled them to contribute to the advancement of society and its happiness. They rejected the ancient Christian idea that men were tainted by original sin; rather, they believed that men were inclined toward goodness. Thus they rejected institutionalized religion and the monarchy as oppressive fetters on man's innate freedom to reason toward and to choose what is right. The strong arm of the Church, imposing its restraints on the self-interested inclinations of men, was irrelevant—even harmful—in this new view of society. In time, the belief in this natural tendency of men toward improvement, and their resulting capacity for self-government, would become a central argument in the overthrow of the monarchy in America.

Devoted to reforming children's education according to this new worldview, Enlightenment thinkers were therefore highly critical of French nuns and the curricula they offered their students. The philosophes portrayed the convents as cloistered islands, devoted to the perpetuation of an outmoded and superstitious way of understanding the world. They were also suspicious of the nuns' credentials: When Enlightenment philosophes referred to the rational capacity of *man*, they did not mean a universal understanding of humanity. Although they acknowledged that women were capable of some learning, they generally agreed that women were inferior, emotional creatures. Ultimately incapable of controlling their passions, therefore, women required the governance of men. A favorite method of discrediting convent education was to portray the convents as dens of female iniquity ("the sewer into which society's waste is thrown," Diderot had called them) in racy novels that spun tales of lewd and unscrupulous nuns corrupting their innocent charges.

Revered in European and American culture as the harbingers of modernity, the philosophes launched attacks that left enduring impressions. It is only in recent decades that their portrayal of ignorance and venality in French convents has been debunked. As historians have documented two centuries of tensions between the French government and female religious orders, a very different picture has emerged of the nuns' strength, pragmatism, and steely resolve in their struggle for survival. Beginning in 1610, the government tried to herd these religious communities of women into cloisters, quite literally to isolate and contain them. But the nuns fought back by creating teaching orders that brought them into daily contact with French families and enabled them to support themselves. So successful were they that by the time Martha Jefferson was in school there, Parisian parents could choose from no fewer than forty-three convent schools for their daughters.

French convents and convent schools came to serve important functions for their exclusive clientele: They were places to educate daughters to the conventional religious beliefs expected of aristocratic women. They frequently served as places of refuge for widows, unmarried women, and royalty. And, particularly in the case of the more prominent convents, they provided a way to shore up family alliances and add prestige to the family. The Mother Superior of the nuns, or the Abbess, was typically drawn from an aristocratic family, and her connections enabled the economic survival of the community when the government mandate to cloister prevented the women from going outside the convent walls to earn their support. Thus, far from being ignorant, passive, and out of the mainstream, French nuns knew exactly how to use their social, political, and economic connections to offset the deprivations imposed by their government.

Not all students were aristocratic however, and the schools these nuns founded were a study in contrasts, as varied as the economic classes they served. Martha Jefferson's Panthemont stood at the pinnacle of all of them. For one hundred livres per year, the annual wage of a male servant, a young girl might attend the charity school of Sainte-Famille; for a thousand, she could attend Panthemont. Charity schools attended to the basics of reading and writing for students who could barely be spared from home; at Panthemont, lessons ranged from classical history to music and dance, to train the daughters of nobility for their entry into the glittering world at court. A thin soup served in a pewter plate would feed the charity school student; an additional fee of

two hundred livres admitted Panthemont's pensionnaires to the sump-
tuous fare of the Abbess's table. Combined with Martha's basic tuition,
Jefferson's tab for the additional fees of board, specialty masters, and the
privilege of dining with the Abbess totaled three thousand livres per
year (very roughly comparable to twenty-three thousand dollars today).

These differences mattered little to the philosophes, of course, who
derided all convent schooling; indeed, many of the calls for the reform
of female education in the eighteenth century were attacks on the education provided by French nuns. This was due in part to the secular
leanings of the philosophes, and to the proliferation of their views by
people who admired them. The dismal state of female education in
Paris could also be explained by the short amount of time girls actually
spent in formal learning: One study of seven Paris convent schools
found that 60 percent of the students attended for less than two years.
By 1800, only 27 percent of French brides could sign their names in the
marriage registers, as opposed to 40 percent of English ones. But there
was a deeper, more fundamental problem with female education in
1780s Paris. Although some had begun to argue that women also possessed intellectual ability and the capacity for rational thought, pragmatic parents had to groom their daughters for a marriage market that
still abhorred the *femme savante,* a disparaging term for the woman
who made herself ridiculous by proudly displaying her learning.

Elite French convent schools walked this tightrope carefully. Marie-
Catherine de Béthisy de Mézières, the Abbess of Panthemont between
1743 and 1790, was eminently suited to the challenge. She was a well-
born woman, although not of nobility. Her mother was the daughter of
an English brigadier general and courtier of King James II. A Catholic,
James II was deposed by a rebellious parliament and replaced by James's
sister Mary and her husband, William of Orange. Fleeing with her
family to France, where they continued to plot the restoration of James's
monarchy, Marie-Catherine's mother landed on her feet with her marriage to Monsieur de Béthisy de Mézières, a French general who was
known more for his ugly visage than for his military talents. More important, he possessed a shrewd head for business, and his speculations
in far-off Mississippi had succeeded where many others' had failed. His
money and her political savvy equipped this unusual pair to raise their

four daughters to occupy exalted positions in French society: Two married nobility and two headed religious communities.

Marie-Catherine saved Panthemont, rescuing the convent from falling into ruin. Founded in 1217, the Cistercian order had been relocated to Paris in 1672 from its original site on a mountainside outside Beauvais (the word *pentemont* loosely translates as mountain slope), after a flood all but destroyed their convent. They had settled for a building on the rue de Grenelle, then on the western reaches of the city. Barely a third of a mile farther west, Louis XIV was building the Hôtel des Invalides, a beautiful structure to house his wounded soldiers. (Les Invalides still stands and is the site of Napoléon Bonaparte's tomb.) Of course, by the time Martha Jefferson met this indomitable woman, the area around the school had profited from the building boom and was already quite fashionable. But when Madame de Béthisy de Mézières became abbess in 1743, her convent was steps away from the westernmost city walls and was rapidly deteriorating.

She boldly recruited Pierre Contant d'Ivry, a member of the Royal Academy of Architecture, who held the title of "architect to the king" and whose career included the design of the Palais Royal and La Madeleine. Undeterred by significant cost overruns and even d'Ivry's attempts to scale back her ambitious plans, she unapologetically importuned wealthy patrons for funding. One of them, the Cardinal of Luynes, was clearly taken aback by her methods. "I must admit," he told her, barely able to contain himself, "that I was quite surprised to read that you were counting on a donation, on the part of the Commission of 60,000 livres, and that you were so confident about receiving this aid that you consequently were planning arrangements with your creditors." She successfully recruited postulants to her order of nuns and wealthy young students to her school, and even attracted women of quality seeking respectable refuge, such as Rose de Beauharnais, the future Joséphine, wife of Napoléon Bonaparte. Madame l'Abbess, as Martha called her, presented a model of female energy, capability, and authority that the girl would have found extraordinary, especially as she cast back to the memory of life in Virginia, in which most women (with the exception of widows) lived under the daily government of men.

Still a month from her twelfth birthday, Martha Jefferson from Albemarle County, Virginia, stepped into a very different world that August day in 1784. With its all-female environment, its days devoted to studies and conversation with her peers and worldly boarders, and the formidable leadership of the Abbess, Panthemont was unlike anything she had ever experienced at Monticello, where her father was master over all. These were uncharted waters, indeed.

CHAPTER

3

School Life

. . . .

1784

. . . .

ARTHA'S FIRST PRIORITY WAS TO learn French. Of the fifty to sixty other boarders, only one spoke English—and she was two years old. The Abbess spoke English, of course, but neither she nor the two-year-old would be part of Martha's daily rounds of lessons, meals, and play. As she settled in, she tried to draw upon the French lessons she had taken in Philadelphia. They had failed her, she had to admit to herself—a testament to the limits of ornamental female education in Revolutionary America, even in Philadelphia. She remembered with chagrin how her father had been overcharged for baggage transfer on their arrival at Havre de Grace because he "spoke very little French and me not a word." On the lookout for such innocents abroad, French handlers charged Jefferson "as much to have the bagadge brought from the shore to the house, which was about a half a square apart, as the bringing it from Philadelphia to Boston." In this place where none of her classmates understood her, she would have to start again. She was a quick study, however, and determined, "so that speaking as much as I could with them I learnt the language very soon."

Within a year of her arrival, she was cheerfully describing her new life. "I am very happy in the convent and it is with reason," she reported firmly to an American friend; "there wants nothing but the presence of my friends of America to render my situation worthy to be envied by the happiest." So adept at French had she become by the following year, she began to worry because she was having "really great difficulty" writing in English.

Martha may have begun feeling utterly bereft of friends and footing, but that situation seems to have been remedied fairly quickly. The Abbess allowed her father to visit her every evening for the first few weeks until she got her bearings. Indeed, with no other option in the daily routine of the convent, Martha quickly surpassed him in her mastery of French. She donned the same crimson uniform worn by all the other pensionnaires, no longer noticeable as a newcomer. The students' uniforms were based on the court dress Louis XIV mandated for women one hundred years earlier. In the only surviving letter she wrote to her American friends about her stay in Paris, she described it as "made like a frock laced behind with the tail like a robe de cour hooked on muslin cuffs and tuckers." The *robe de cour,* or stiff-body dress, had a straight bodice, shaped by stays, which narrowed at the waist and laced up the back. A separate train (Martha's "tail") fell either from the shoulders or the waist. The formal dresses worn at court had detachable lace sleeves, but for everyday wear, the students at Panthemont wore the more practical and washable muslin sleeves and neckerchiefs.

Martha was pleased with her accommodations. There were, she said, "four rooms exceedingly large for the pensionars to sleep in, and there is a fifth and sixth one for them to stay in in the day and the other in which they take their lessens." Other French girls' schools were improvised arrangements, superimposed upon already existing monastic buildings that had been designed for cloistered nuns. Panthemont, on the other hand, was spacious and convenient, thoughtfully planned for the various usages of students, nuns, and boarding women, as a result of the Abbess's determined renovations. It is no wonder that Martha soon came to regard her life there as worthy of envy. And if she had harbored any Protestant fears about the tyranny of Catholic religious orders, they were dispelled by the "cheerful and agreeable" nuns who took care of her. In fact, as she told Nabby Adams, the daughter of John and Abigail Adams, it seemed to Martha that the nuns actually took pleasure in making the students happy.

As she gradually became accustomed to this new world, and even happy in it, Martha's contentment increased further with the addition of new English-speaking students. "There comes in some new pension-ars evry day," she reported to Eliza Trist in Philadelphia. Several were daughters of English diplomats, who, notwithstanding the politics of the recently concluded American Revolution, befriended the only American girl in the school. Their surviving letters to Martha (we have none of hers) allow us an insider view of school life and girlhood friend-ships at Panthemont, and of the vivacious personality that endeared Martha Jefferson to everyone who met her. As an adult, Martha would be universally admired for her lively wit, high intelligence, graceful manners, and animated storytelling. One might be tempted to attribute those qualities to the grooming of her French education, but it seems she already possessed them even before she left Virginia. Begging her to write all about her Paris adventures, her cousin Judith Randolph fully expected "great entertainment from your Epistles," for she knew that eleven-year-old Martha could already be counted on to provide it. Martha's irrepressible temperament forbade her from indulging in iso-lated despair in her new situation. Instead she threw herself into speak-ing frequently with the other girls and drawing them, magnetlike, to her.

It is endearing to see the list of her schoolmates that Martha kept, carefully marked with an X alongside the names of those she consid-ered her closest friends. Julia Annesley was the thirteen-year-old daughter of Irish peer Arthur Annesley, 1st Earl of Mountnorris, who was serving in the English delegation to the French court. When Julia arrived at Panthemont, she was delighted that Martha accepted her overtures of friendship, especially the exchange of notes, although they saw each other daily. Julia pounced on the opportunity immediately, beginning confidentially, "I will first give you my opinion of the class." But she grew impatient when Martha did not reply right away. "I am very angry with my dear Jeffy for not having yet answered my letter, and am resolved to be revenged by not speaking to you for 100 years to come, if I do not hear from you this very day," Julia wrote playfully, after waiting a week for a response. She peppered Martha with many of the questions typical of first acquaintance: "Pray where are your friends? Do you often go out?" and "How many brothers have you? And when does your sister come? I wish you slept in our room, ask the first time there is a vacancy to come." The letters the two exchanged while at school would bear their most important secrets, so confidentiality was crucial. "I am very glad no one here understands English," Julia confided; nonetheless, she begged Martha to "take care not to lose the letters I write to you" and promised, in turn, that "I will take equal care of yours." Martha would preserve her notes and a lock of Julia's hair all her life.

Julia was just one of a number of Martha's classmates who had singled her out as a friend worth having. Caroline and Elizabeth Tufton also became part of Martha's circle. They were the nieces of John Frederick Sackville, the Duke of Dorset, who was serving in Paris as the English ambassador to France. The two sisters struck up an intimate friendship with Martha. So close had they become, when they were discussing how to maintain their friendship across the ocean, Martha dispensed with the rules governing formal correspondence. They would write simple informal letters, she told Elizabeth, rather than a journal kept over time, as many young girls did. Later, when Jefferson named one of his smaller outlying farms Tufton, it was surely in deference to a request from Martha, as a memento of her friends.

Bettie Hawkins was a particularly close friend with whom Martha also exchanged locks of hair and shared deep confidences. Their friendship endured even after Bettie, three years older than Martha, left Panthemont to return to England in 1787. In spite of the distance between them, the girls gave each other commissions to fill: Martha sent a black cloak to Bettie, and in return Bettie sent the latest plays, books—particularly novels—and tea. Acutely missing her little circle at Panthemont as she prepared for her marriage in England, Bettie charged Martha to keep her fully informed: "I shall be indulged with every incident that has lately occur'd within your Holy Walls," she wrote in 1789. "Give me a description of all the new pensioners that *enter*," she asked in another letter, so that she could keep abreast of all the news.

But perhaps no one was more effusive in her love for her "dear Jeff" than Marie de Botidoux. Over the course of twenty years after they had all left Panthemont, Marie wrote more than one hundred pages of journals and letters for her friend, although she only ever received one letter in return. Nevertheless, she gives us one of the most spirited glimpses of the youthful Martha, who she remembered as "always wild, your petticoat dragging on one side and with coffee stains on the other, descending the stairs four by four." Marie also adored Martha's father with a "veneration and an enthusiasm I cannot express" and remembered fondly her visits to his Paris home, the Hôtel de Langeac, where he patiently let them "derange his library." "I still love you with all my heart and miss you every day," she wrote, six months after Martha left Paris.

In her loneliness, Marie had even gone for a stroll in a little lane near the house, in an attempt to relive the old times they had spent walking there. When she finally received a letter from her old friend two decades later, her pain at having been neglected for so long was palpable. Dismissing the adult Martha's feeble excuse that she was "held back for twenty years by *foolish 'amour propre,'*" Marie replied with disbelief, "How could you have that with me, who wrote you without pretension and who wrote *very badly*?" Frankness and impulsively sloppy handwriting were, for Marie, the two clearest literary signs of intimacy between friends. True friends forgave candor, errors, and ink splotches. Yet Marie was still willing to reopen the door to her heart. "At a certain age one . . . sees that the few pleasures of this life are in an intimate society where one can say what one thinks and feels. You have come to that age dear Jeff," she wrote pointedly.

Marie may have been one of the first to befriend the young Virginia girl as she began her classes and mapped her way in this very different world. Not everything was new, at least. Some of the subjects were similar to those she had studied in Philadelphia, since ideas about the necessary ornamental education required for upper-class girls transcended barriers of language, political boundaries, and even oceans. Martha continued her lessons in drawing, dancing, and music. Included in the three thousand livres Jefferson paid for her tuition, room, and board (including firewood, candles in the classes, and her instruments) were the extra fees for the respective masters, among them Claude Balbastre, the renowned church organist, who alone charged an additional 144 livres per month. Her studies expanded, however, to include classical history, French, Italian, geography, and arithmetic. She struggled through a sixteenth-century translation of Titus Livius's *History of the Roman People* in an ancient version of Italian, produced landscapes for her drawing master, mastered her history "pretty well," and worked hard at the challenging piano music her father sent her in order to be ready to perform when he called upon her. But the needlework Jefferson thought essential to prepare for the isolated life of a Virginia plant-

Martha Jefferson's devoted friend during their school days, Marie de Botidoux remained so for many years after Martha returned to the United States. Her youthful exuberance, seen here in her barely repressed smile, was undimmed by Martha's long years of silence or by the loss of half Marie's fortune and her stint in a revolutionary prison. In an 1801 letter to Martha, Botidoux professed her delight at Jefferson's election to the presidency and mentioned her own undying passion for republican politics.

er's wife was not available in an elite school that catered to royalty. "The only kind of needlework I could learn here," Martha informed her father in 1787, "would be embroidery, indeed netting also. But I could not do much of those in America, because of the impossibility of having proper silks." But perhaps, she concluded doubtfully, eager to please him, "they will not be totally useless."

This much can be gleaned from the very limited number of letters that have survived of Martha's Paris years: six letters to her father, written between March and May of 1787 as he was touring Europe, and the one she wrote to Eliza Trist in Philadelphia a year after her arrival. (Jefferson had told her not to write to him when, in the spring of 1786, he went to England to assist with the negotiations for commercial treaties; the trip was so short, he was sure he would be on his way back by the time her letter arrived.) But when we look to a broader variety of sources, we can piece together additional particulars of her reading to get a better sense of what Martha was learning and how her thinking was being shaped by the nuns' curriculum. For example, Monticello now houses a collection of family books that include a number of volumes she owned while at Panthemont. We know that she studied natural history: Martha Jefferson's copy of *Nature Displayed. Being Discourses on Such Particulars of Natural History as Were Thought Proper to Excite the Curiosity, and Form the Minds of Youth* bears a London imprint from 1750, suggesting that she may have relied on this English translation as she worked to perfect her French. Her French grammar book, inscribed "Mademoiselle Jefferson/L'Abbaye Royale de Pantemont/Paris," was indispensable in her transition to life in Paris. It must have also been a treasured keepsake; Martha kept it and later gave it to her daughter.

Her education immersed her in French literature: fables, novels, romances, poetry, and plays. Like most French children—even today—Martha Jefferson owned and memorized Jean de La Fontaine's famous fables. She read Alain Lesage's picaresque novel *Gil Blas* and his *Diable Boiteux* (*Devil on Crutches*), as well as *Don Quixote* in French. And she relished romances. Her enjoyment of novels was well known among her friends: "Are you still reading novels?" classmate Bettie Hawkins had asked her from England as she prepared to recommend another. She was introduced to the French theater in her reading by the much-respected Madame de Genlis; and she studied both French poetry and

Italian, such as the work of the Renaissance poet Francesco Petrarca. Reading these works at Panthemont normalized literature that was largely discouraged for American girls, for whom romances and novels were viewed as harmful to the female character. Americans also generally frowned on the worldliness of the theater; although Virginians had a longer history of performances of plays dating back to the 1730s, Boston did not build its first theater until 1793.

From Fontaine's fables, Martha learned the value of work over play ("The Grasshopper and the Ant"), the dangers of flattery ("The Fox and the Crow"), and the rarity of true friendship ("The Saying of Socrates"). The novels of Alain Lesage taught her about the different levels of French society and illustrated that humanity's foibles were not confined to the lower classes. Indeed, Lesage's popular novels turned the hierarchical world of the ancien régime upside down: nobles were disreputable, lustful, and treacherous, but honest commoners (like Gil Blas) succeeded by dint of hard work and perseverance.

To perfect the art of natural letter-writing, she was taught to imitate the much-vaunted style of Madame de Sévigné, whose letters exhibited the delightful spontaneity that was a standard for female writing in the eighteenth century. Panthemont students learned their Sévigné well: A letter written by Marie de Botidoux just weeks after Martha left Paris began with the teasing opener "I am going to say to you, like Mde de Sévigné, that I am giving you one hundred tries [to guess] of what news I am going to inform you."

Because Martha left us so little about her life in a convent school, it is helpful to compare the clues we do have about the curriculum at Panthemont with other girls' schools in Paris, such as the highly regarded Abbaye-aux-Bois. One of its students, Hélène Massalska, remembered a typical day there as a ten-year-old: rising at seven-thirty A.M.; catechism class at eight; breakfast at nine and Mass at nine-thirty; lecture at ten; music at eleven; drawing at eleven-thirty; geography and history at noon; lunch and recreation at one P.M.; writing and arithmetic at three; dance at four; afternoon tea and recreation at five; harp or harpsichord at six; supper at seven and in bed by nine-thirty. The convent school at Liège, in Belgium—attended from 1789 to 1794 by the Marylander Catherine Carroll, who was the daughter of Charles Carroll, the only Catholic signer of the Declaration of Independence—

likewise outlined the same basic curriculum, with a few additions that Martha Jefferson would have recognized for older students: "reading and writing; the principles of English, French, and Italian; sacred and profane history; arithmetic . . . the art of writing letters at all stages of life . . . geography; use of the globes; of the sphere, &c. the principles of natural history to the extent that they are suitable for young ladies; embroidery and all needlework; drawing and the painting of flowers." At Liège, as at Panthemont and most girls' schools, Latin was excluded. These comparable elite schools thus help us fill out the picture of the kind of education that Martha Jefferson received at Panthemont: an acquaintance with broad varieties of knowledge, but nothing too deep to be deemed taxing for these delicately bred students.

Following the lead of the Enlightenment philosophes, historians in the late nineteenth and early twentieth centuries dismissed this curriculum as providing not much more than the veneer of polished manners designed to distinguish the aristocratic society of the ancien régime from their social inferiors. But these critics ignored the seriousness with which some nuns and students took female education. Manon Phlipon, a student at the Congregation of Notre-Dame in Paris, fondly recalled her teacher, Sister Sainte-Sophie: "This good woman soon attached herself to me because of my taste for study; after having given a lesson to the entire class, she took me aside and made me recite grammar, pursue geography, extract bits of history." Sister Sainte-Sophie's assessment of her pupil was unerring: Phlipon, later famous as Madame Roland, would become an integral part of the radical Girondist group that challenged Robespierre during the French Revolution. Indeed, some have thought that she was the mastermind behind the work of her husband, Jean-Marie Roland de La Platière, the prominent minister of the interior in 1792.

At Panthemont, Martha Jefferson liked her instructors and pronounced them "all very good"—except for her drawing teacher, but then again she had struggled with that subject in Philadelphia as well. She labored, too, over an older Italian translation of Titus Livius. "Titus Livius puts me out of my wits," she cried on one occasion, and "it serves to little good in the execution of a thing almost impossible" on another. But her letters to her father, reporting both progress and struggles, show the challenges of her classes and her dogged application to her studies. So, too, does the knowing remark of a classmate, who advised Martha that she should not try so hard to impress the Abbé, their instructor, saying, "Remember, *Priests* can't marry." Certainly Martha studied hard to produce the results that would please her father and instructors. But unlike her classmates who saw their schooling as ornamental preparations for the marriage market, Martha took the content of her studies seriously. Years after the Jeffersons had left Paris, Madame de Staël, a salon host and the most famous female author in Europe, told Jefferson that "I remember her as more brilliant than all the grande dames of this old world."

For both serious scholars and more casual ones, the lessons taught at the convent schools were crucial to the formation of elite female identity, and perhaps none was more important than the art of letter-writing. The challenge for parents and teachers, who knew that their young charges would live lives of leisure, was to prepare them to fill their idle time profitably while still preserving the privileges of rank. The solution, as one historian explains, was writing, which was a "useful pursuit without, however, working" and "became central to the education of young ladies as it took its place in the new morality of leisured femininity." Stiffly corseted in their *robes de cour,* young ladies were taught how to sit perfectly straight at their writing table (never leaning on their left hand, as men did), holding their pen just so and transcribing the words of elegant writers such as Sévigné, who would eventually serve as models for their own words. This is precisely what Martha learned at Panthemont. In fact, so standardized was this type of instruction in French schools that the distinctive lowercase *d* of Martha's handwriting is almost indistinguishable from that of Marie Marguerite Émilie Lavoisier, the younger sister of the famous French nobleman and chemist, whose careful pen had traced out letters in her copybook thirty years earlier.

Their teachers may have conveyed these lessons as a mark of rank and status, but young girls gained much more from their letter-writing. Between 1767 and 1780, for example, young Manon Phlipon maintained a voluminous correspondence with her friend Sophie Cannet, whom she met at their Paris convent school in 1765. Their friendship had begun when Manon was just eleven; it flourished through a correspondence maintained through their teens, ending when Manon married at twenty-six and became Madame Roland. In her letters, she shared her deepest thoughts, as well as those "little nothings to which friendship gives so much importance," which she would not divulge even to her beloved mother. Today we recognize this as a process of self-differentiation, child from parent, much encouraged in the twenty-first century. But a strong sense of self was never the goal of female education for eighteenth-century French girls. Even so, it is clear that while writing to her friend, Manon grew into herself, as over time her letters conveyed fewer news reports and more reflections of an increasingly self-aware young woman who was becoming an independent and confident thinker.

Although Manon and Sophie began their correspondence to maintain their girlhood friendship across the miles that separated them when they each returned home, Manon also gives us a clue about what these letters meant to the girls who exchanged them. "The need to write to each other made itself felt almost at the moment when we began to care about each other," she recalled in a letter to Sophie; "the need to satisfy it put the imagination in play, forced ideas to hatch and feelings to be expressed." For the students at Panthemont, this need to connect emerged while they were still at the school as we saw with Julia Annesley's notes; and like Manon and Sophie did, Bettie Hawkins, Marie de Botidoux, and the Tufton sisters would use letters to bridge the thousands of miles with Martha after they had parted.

Marie's playful imitation of Madame de Sévigné's letters is therefore only one small example of how girls took this lesson to heart. Friendships were serious business, and so were even the most sprightly of notes. At Panthemont, the students themselves established their own groups; the letters that Martha kept for the rest of her life from her faithful correspondents show who was in her circle. Even after her return to England, Bettie Hawkins wanted to know how those groups were reshuffling in her absence. "Tell me who are friends now at the class, who Bellecour, Botidox, D'Harcourt & your ladyship associate with? & who are my rivals?"

Introducing new friends into the old set raised concerns for those who had left and a rethinking of their improvised rules. From London in 1789, Bettie Hawkins wrote to Martha about one of her new friends. "Tell me all about her & of your new regulations," she asked, trying to divine, from across the channel, who had been admitted to their little circle and how candid her letters could be. Letters could also mend ruptures or mourn lost friendships. Unable to mediate at a distance, Bettie told Martha that she was "very sorry D'Harcourt & you never settled matters. A *racommodement* [rapprochement] would have been desirable for both parties." (In fact, whatever the problem was between Martha and Gabrielle D'Harcourt, the two girls did settle it—at least well enough to resume the exchange of notes at school that marked particular friendships. "I am grateful to La Charière for having tried to bring us back together," Gabrielle wrote to Martha in 1789, although she was still uncertain how to approach Martha, "because I saw that you greeted me coldly.")

These strongly felt alliances, and the letters that document them, show how these educated young women—American, English, and French—grew into their understandings of their identity, status, and rank. That a girl from England should address the American as "your ladyship" is telling; Martha learned to imitate the regal bearing of her aristocratic friends and to uphold strict protocols in her letter-writing. Bettie Hawkins once saucily chided her, "Your lady ship stands much on *Punctilio* & has a great deal of the 'old maid' in her composition." The provincial American may have been a bit more naïve and restrained than her more worldly European friends. Nonetheless, she entered fully into their schoolgirl cliques, ensuring by language and the rules they created (regulations that, tellingly, were never specified in their letters) that their correspondence would remain safe from prying eyes.

Perhaps the best example of the significance of confidences among friends can be found in Martha Jefferson's encounter with Roman Catholicism at Panthemont. With its majestic architecture and music, mysterious rituals, and opportunities for women, Catholicism was profoundly transformational for Martha, and it was with her friends—rather than her father—that she first shared her spiritual journey. She had been struck by the beauty of Catholic churches from the very first. On their arrival in France, as Martha and her father completed their journey from the coast to Paris, their carriage followed the roads that hugged the Seine. His planter's eye noticed the richness of the soil, but she was taken with the beautiful architecture of the churches, which "had as many steps to go to the top as there are days in the year," the statues, and the stunning stained-glass windows that were so foreign to American Protestants. Upon installing her at Panthemont, Jefferson had to calm the anxious fears of relatives and friends, who fretted that Catholicism would claim such an impressionable young girl. He himself seems not to have been worried. As his friend Jean Armand Tronchin, minister of the republic of Geneva to France, recalled Jefferson having told him, "The abbess in charge is a woman of the world who understands the direction of young Protestant girls. There are often English girls. The daughter of Mr Jefferson is a pupil there, and I know it is understood that one does not talk to them about religion, or rather controversial topics are not discussed. They certainly emerge quite as good Protestants as when they entered." The Abbess's well-known reputation in this area may explain Jefferson's confident reassurance to his sister at home in Virginia that "there are in it as many protestants as Catholics, and not a word is ever spoken to them on the subject of religion." His frequent visits (at least once a week when he was in town) would allow him to keep a close eye on his daughter's interests, and the large number of English students also at the school might have convinced him of the truth of the Abbess's assertions. As events would show, however, Jefferson miscalculated.

THE JEFFERSONS HAD NOT been in Paris two months when they invited Abigail Adams and her daughter Nabby to a profession ceremony at Panthemont's chapel for two young women entering the convent. The setting itself was magnificent, having been restored during the Abbess's ambitious renovations. The chapel's arched ceilings stretched several stories high, culminating in a dome constructed of an exquisite stone, its hues gradually transfiguring from light tan to a rosy pink with the changing light of the sun during the course of the day. The chapel's pre-revolutionary incarnation may have had stained-glass windows; it certainly would have had flickering candles, fragrant incense, and a crucifix bearing the image of the slain Christ. Empty niches today suggest the presence of impressive statues of the sort that had caught Martha's eye when she first arrived in France, before they were removed by the revolution. As she entered this lovely space, she was treated to a feast for the senses before the profession ritual had even begun.

The betrothal ceremony they witnessed possessed all the drama of a theatrical spectacle: Nabby left a detailed description that captured all

its solemnity, majesty, and pathos. It began with a procession from behind the iron grates where the nuns were usually cloistered, into the
chancel. The Abbess parted the curtain and led her nuns and students,
each bearing a lighted candle. Attended by two richly dressed English
classmates of Martha's, also holding candles, the two candidates for the
convent followed, attired in simple cloaks and with their hair shaved, a
dramatic symbol of their rejection of worldly vanities. Then began the
rituals of endlessly kneeling and rising that so bewildered the Protestant Nabby that she found them "impossible to describe." A sermon
impressed upon everyone assembled, but especially the two candidates,
the solemnity of the vows the young women were about to take. The
priest detailed all the worldly pleasures they would forego and warned
them of the privations of life within the convent. Their resolution un-
wavering, the young women received a kiss from each of the nuns, who
then withdrew from the altar. Then "there was brought in, by eight
pensioners, a pall of black, crossed with white, which was held over
them." For half an hour, while the priest prayed and the nuns chanted,
the candidates lay prostrate on their faces, dead to the world under the
funeral cloth. "This was an affecting sight," Nabby admitted in spite of
herself; "I could not refrain from tears."

Rising—symbolizing the new life into which they were being
born—the pair presented themselves to the Abbess. She dressed them
in the nun's habit, "fine, white woolen dresses and white veils," and
crowned their heads with flowers. When the priest then exhorted the
other students to consider following their example, Nabby noticed one
of the two English attendants "looked sharp" at the other, "whose countenance expressed that she . . . had no such intention." If the nuns had
hoped that their participation in the profession ritual would inspire
them to do so, they were sorely mistaken. Nabby agreed wholeheart-
edly. "Quite right she," she judged firmly.

At nineteen, Nabby Adams observed these proceedings with a
somewhat jaundiced eye, her attitude toward Catholicism likely in con-
cert with her mother's, who once shamefacedly admitted her anti-
Catholicism to Jefferson. But Nabby had also been touched to see the
smile that lit up the face of one young nun as she received the habit she
would wear for the rest of her life, and the unruffled serenity of the
other. And, in spite of herself, she had been moved to the point of tears.

Panthemont's magnificent organ (1846) draws the eye to the soaring dome above. The engraved names of the four evangelists (Luke and John are seen here) survived the depredations of the church by the French revolutionaries, even if their images did not. Converted to a Protestant church in 1844, today's Temple de Pentemont retains the magnificent carvings, proportion, and beauty that so entranced the twelve-year-old girl from Virginia.

How much more affecting might the scene have been for a less worldly twelve-year-old, who now lived within this community?

    Martha was smitten. Nominally, at least, she was an Anglican, but her childhood religious observances had probably been limited to prayers taught by her mother and some Scripture readings at home. The first church building in Charlottesville was not completed until 1825; until then, the various sects took turns using the county courthouse, the largest assembly space in the town. So for Martha, both the profession ceremony and its setting were a striking departure from anything she would have seen in Virginia. How could it have failed to stir her imagination?

Her curiosity piqued, Martha turned to her classmates, asking questions at first, later sharing with them her deep interest in Catholicism, and finally confiding her resolution to abjure her Protestantism. In several letters shortly after her departure from Panthemont, Bettie Hawkins asked repeatedly about a mysterious matter that had clearly been the subject of their conversations at school but that required complete discretion in their correspondence. "When do you make abjuration?" she asked abruptly on one occasion, wondering "how you intend telling your father?" In another letter, she fretted about Martha's long silence, worrying it might have been occasioned "by some tragical event concerning your abjuration." Bettie was sorry she could not be there to support her; "I regret much having quitted Panthemont before your *revolt* . . . my fidelity & respect at least you might have depended upon."

In May 1788, Bettie had been appalled to see a report in *The Morning Post,* an English newspaper attentively read in Paris by English and American diplomats, that the nuns "seduce[d] Miss Jefferson, daughter of the American minister, to change her religion." The "daughter of Lord Valentia," Julia Annesley, had also been subject to that "infection," the paper noted, and had withdrawn from the school. Bettie raced to her writing table early the next morning to transmit "the earliest intelligence of it, that you might prepare your answer to any questions your Father (who will certainly see it) might ask you on the occasion." Aware that father and daughter would receive the paper in the same post, Bettie strained to alert Martha, knowing that "you have never talked to him on *that* subject I imagine, as I think you never mentioned it to *me* in any of your letters." The tumult in Martha's soul—not to mention the danger of political embarrassment to her father, the American minister to France—was too precious for her to trust it to paper, even with all the precautions they had taken.

A revolt (that may never have happened) or the newspaper account (that did) may well explain the nineteenth-century family legend that is still told today: After Martha sent her father a letter informing him of her desire to enter the convent, the story goes, he unceremoniously arrived at the Abbess's doorstep and politely but firmly removed Martha from her school. (In fact, it would not be until April 1789 that Jefferson withdrew her, a full year after the newspaper notice, so it is unclear if or when Martha ever wrote such a letter.) If the point of the family story is to depict Martha's attraction to Catholicism as a mere romantic girlish infatuation, easily dismissed, it was serious enough to have attracted the attention of the papal nuncio in Paris, Antonio Dugnani, as Martha approached her fifteenth birthday. Reporting information he had heard, probably from Jefferson himself, Dugnani told the Bishop of Baltimore that Martha "seems to have great tendencies toward the Catholic religion." Her interest was deep enough to require her father to distract her, in hopes that she would forego making any decision before she turned eighteen. And his concern was warranted, as her closest friends knew, even better than he did. Marie de Botidoux, who had also been taken into Martha's confidence, astutely observed that to protect her newfound faith, Martha would have lived the rest of her life as a nun, staying in France forever.

All Martha Jefferson saw and learned at Panthemont seems to have inspired far more than a heady, youthful infatuation with ceremony, as her friends and eventually her father recognized. Bettie Hawkins's letters do not specifically talk about reception into the Roman Church, but taken together with Dugnani's letters (and his continued interest in Martha into the 1790s), Jefferson's concern, and the newspaper report, that is the most likely interpretation of the revolt Martha was planning. And it was prompted by her encounter with Catholic theology, not just youthful impressionability. Almost four decades later, she could still vividly recall the earnestness of her Catholic faith, imprinted upon her layer by layer, by the daily regimen of chapel attendance, prayer at meals, catechism classes, clergy teachers, her French and English Catholic friends, and the example of the nuns—their assurances to Jefferson notwithstanding. "At your age," she wrote to a daughter, then eighteen and thinking about converting to Catholicism, "I believed most religiously that it was the only road to heaven, and looked forward with fear and terror to the possibility of never again having it in my power

This Day was published,
In One Volume Octavo, Price 6s. 6d. in boards,
THE ANALOGY of RELIGION, Natural
and Revealed, to the Constitution and Course of
Nature.
To which are added,
TWO BRIEF DISSERTATIONS.
1. On Personal Identity.
2. On the Nature of Virtue, together with a Charge
delivered to the Clergy of the Diocese of Durham, at
the Primary Visitation in the year 1751.
BY JOSEPH BUTLER, LL.D.
Late Lord Bishop of Durham.
A New Edition, corrected, with a Preface, giving some
Account of the Character and Writings of the Au-
thor.
By SAMUEL, Lord Bishop of GLOUCESTER.
Printed for J. F. and C. Rivington, and G. and T.
Wilkie, in St. Paul's Church yard; and S. Hayes, Ox-
ford-street.
Of whom may be had,
In One Volume Octavo, price 6s. bound,
Fifteen Sermons, preached at the Rolls Chapel; to
which are added, Six Sermons on Public Occasions.

For RHEUMATISMS, SPRAINS, BRUISES, &c.
DR. STEERS's OPODELDOC.
SOLD in London only by the Proprietors, H.
STEERS (Son of the late Dr. STEERS the In-
ventor), at his Medical Warehouse, No. 10, Old Bond-
street, on the left hand from Piccadilly, three doors be-
yond Stafford-street; and F. NEWBERY, at the only
Warehouse for Dr. James's Powder, No. 45, the East
End of St. Paul's, five doors from the Trunk-maker's,
the Corner of Cheapside, in bottles of one size ONLY,
price 2s. each, duty included, or six for 10s. 6d.
CAUTION
All purchasers are requested to give particular directions to their servants, when they are sent for Dr.
STEERS's Opodeldoc, to procure it from either of the
above places, and to observe, that the name of F. NEW-
BERY is engraved in the stamp, as none can be genuine

PITT is right in urging the Company to liquidate
the sum; as it certainly is much better to collect
what is justly due to the Public, than to adopt the
oppressive maxim of the leaders of Opposition,
viz. that of borrowing, and loading the people
with additional taxes.
Opposition may almost as confidently hope for
the repeal of *Magna Charta*, as for that of the
Commutation Bill. Nothing but a general infa-
nity in the House of Commons could induce its
Members to overthrow a measure so replete
with wisdom, and so productive of useful effects.
It may not be improper to inform those parents
who are partial to foreign education, and impatient to send their children to Convents, under the
idea of œconomy, that they risque having their
principles corrupted, and their minds poisoned
by superstition and bigotry; as the first object of
the Nuns and Priests is to convert the children,
confided to their care, and particularly in the
English houses on the Continent, as they are generally the most bigotted. The Nuns at the
ABBEY of PANTLEMON at Paris, having seduced MISS JEFFERSON, the daughter of the
American Minister, to change her religion, it is
said have received a severe reprimand; nor have
they been less attentive to the *salvation* of British
souls, as a daughter of LORD VALENTIA's has
been taken from thence on that account, but unfortunately not early enough to escape the infection.
Few men in public situations have met with

Founded in 1772 by the Reverend Henry Bate, The Morning Post *published sensational news tidbits such as that revealing Martha Jefferson's
scandalous interest in Catholicism. Anticipating today's tabloids, paragraph men—as they were called—picked up their information from cof-
feehouse gossip and composed and submitted their paragraph news items,
little concerned about their accuracy.*

[in America] to profess myself a member of that church which I believed the true, and original." Many of her new beliefs countered those
of her father. Unlike Jefferson, who took a razor to cut out every miracle
narrative from his Bible, Martha thoroughly believed in them. Martha's
exposure to Catholicism raised serious philosophical questions with
which she had to contend. The stakes were high. How was a young girl
to judge? What if she made a mistake?

There were very real, pragmatic reasons for a young woman to consider Catholicism. With the Reformation, the convent as an alternative
to marriage had been closed to Protestant women. As Martha saw in
Paris, however, the Church provided opportunities for women to teach
as a profession, supported fully without having to marry: Many nuns at

Panthemont were former students. For aristocratic women, such as the school's abbess, Marie-Catherine de Béthisy de Mézières, the Church also provided opportunities to govern, not unlike running a business, and even to flex some muscle in the world beyond the convent walls. The Abbess had persuaded the Dauphin of France to lay the ceremonial cornerstone of her new chapel, and in fact was so respected—even by the revolutionaries who overthrew the old order—that she was permitted to spend the rest of her life in her quarters at Panthemont, although they had abolished her school in the summer of 1790. Indeed, nuns in revolutionary France showed the same determined resistance to government efforts to define them as their spiritual ancestors had displayed the century before. In spite of the abolition of teaching convents in August 1792, most nuns continued their adherence to the old Church. This is not to argue that the Abbess exemplified a kind of proto-feminist model that Martha Jefferson found appealing. But it is to say instead that in the old regime, with its intricate systems of hierarchy (which Martha, coming from the slave society of Virginia, would have well understood), Catholic women could offset the disadvantages of their sex in religious communities: Women of all ranks could elude the governing hand of a husband; aristocratic women could run institutions such as schools, hospitals, orphanages, and asylums, presiding over their huge government-subsidized budgets; and even women of lower orders could find fulfilling work and satisfying friendships. In such a setting, Martha Jefferson saw how the right education could firmly uphold and even improve one's status.

BUT A WOMAN DID not necessarily have to be a religious to exert influence in French society. In addition to the nuns at Panthemont, other women also taught Martha the pleasures of status and learning. The daughter of the American ambassador had occasion to meet many luminaries of French high society and of its salon culture. Jefferson had immediately renewed his friendship with the Marquis de Chastellux, who had visited him at Monticello in 1782 and who (with his wife, after his marriage in 1787) was a frequent visitor to Jefferson's Paris household. As we have seen, the Marquis had a hand in helping Jefferson find a school for Martha. As well, the Marquis de Lafayette ebulliently laid his home—barely a ten-minute walk from Panthemont—"entirely at your disposal." He also volunteered the help of his wife, Adrienne, since her "knowledge of the country may be of use to Miss Jefferson." Martha enjoyed excursions with her, including one to Versailles, and dined at their home. Just blocks away from Panthemont, Madame de Tessé, Adrienne de La Fayette's aunt, presided over a salon in which she pressed a little too enthusiastically for a new constitution for France, according to the New Yorker Gouverneur Morris; indeed, she grew impatient with the rather conservative Morris (a member of the Constitutional Convention), whose views were entirely too cautious for her. With their shared interest in gardening and political sympathies, she became a great friend of Jefferson's, corresponding with him until her death in 1814.

Probably the most brilliant salons in Paris were presided over by Mesdames Houdetot, Helvétius, and Necker, where literature, politics, philosophy, and the sciences were the primary topics of conversation. As a young woman, Houdetot had been Jean-Jacques Rousseau's lover and was forever memorialized as the "Julie" of his *Confessions*. In her fifties when Jefferson met her, she lived with the Marquis de Saint-Lambert, the poet and philosopher who would later translate into French Jefferson's famous Act for Establishing Religious Freedom, which became law in Virginia in 1786. Jefferson seems to have been better acquainted with the latter two women. Helvétius, the widow of a noted philosopher, was the beloved of Benjamin Franklin, who introduced Jefferson into her charmed circle before Franklin returned to America. Suzanne Necker was the wife of the banker and chief financier of King Louis XVI. The naturalist Buffon, whose theories about America Jefferson refuted in his *Notes on the State of Virginia*, was a regular attendee at her salon, as was the famed philosophe Denis Diderot. Madame Necker was the mother and teacher of the more famous Germaine de Staël, who was already published by 1786 and who presided over what Morris called "quite the first salon in Paris." Jefferson admired the entire family.

We have nothing in Martha's hand to say that she knew these women, but between visits to her father's home (and full-time residence after April 1789) and outings typical of Parisians—balls (no more than three per week, her father decreed), the opera, the Palais Royal, and

Versailles—it is hard to believe that she would not have met them in one or more of these places. Gouverneur Morris made a note of many dinners at the Jefferson household "en famille," attended by a variety of people, as did Nabby Adams. Young as she was, Nabby still accompanied her parents to dine with Madame Helvétius; Jefferson's close association with her makes it entirely likely that Martha would have known her as well. Madame Houdetot helped Martha shop for gifts to bring home to Virginia before her departure. The affectionate relationship between the Jeffersons and the Lafayettes would have given Martha and Madame de Tessé time together and common ground on which to connect.

Family stories of Martha's social life in Paris include an account of a conversation with Georgiana, the Duchess of Devonshire. The duchess was renowned on both sides of the channel for her trendsetting fashions as well as her active political campaigning back home in Britain. Attending a dinner given by the Duchess, Martha's height drew the attention of this celebrity. "It gives me pleasure, Miss Jefferson, to see any one as tall as myself," Georgiana told her, smiling. Martha also socialized with the duchess on more intimate and informal terms. On one occasion, her friends Caroline and Elizabeth Tufton invited Martha to join them at their home to hear music with the Duchess. "You need not dress as there really will be nobody else," Caroline assured Martha. On another, Caroline wrote, "the Dutchess of Devonshire will be here at eight o' Clock, so pray come as soon as you can, as we shall be happy to see you, as much before as you like, *on ne* peut pas vous voir trop souvent [we cannot see you too often]."

Family stories also preserved memories of Martha's love of dancing and balls. At one ball, Martha danced with a member of the aristocratic Polignac family (her partner's mother was Marie Antoinette's great confidante) eight times. Because etiquette forbade two dances in a row with the same person, she must have had at least sixteen dances that evening. At another ball, the Duc de Fronsac observed that she danced well that night. "And beaucoup [a lot]," was her happy rejoinder, to which the duke reiterated, "Et bien [And well]." At these balls, Martha frequently saw the celebrated *salonnière* Madame de Staël, who she remembered as always "surrounded by a circle of gentlemen under the spell of the wonderful charm of her conversation." Handed down by a granddaughter, these stories may well have been burnished over the years; nonetheless, they underscore Martha's delighted participation in a lively social scene populated by exemplary women who reveled in the life of the mind and were celebrated for it.

Martha Jefferson kept company with less exalted women as well. Neither an aristocrat nor a *salonnière*, Madame de Corny was a particular favorite of the Jeffersons. Her husband had served as a commissary for the French army in America and was a minor political official in Paris. Madame de Corny devised especially amusing outings for Martha, such as escorting her to the opera and taking her out of the convent to view the Longchamp parade, an annual procession of the wealthy, in which both people and horses were arrayed in their finest livery. Jefferson's lodgings at the Hôtel de Langeac provided the perfect vantage point from which to enjoy this annual spectacle. Kitty (Catherine) Church, Alexander Hamilton's niece, stayed with Corny, so Martha came to know her as well.

Jefferson's home had quickly become a center for Paris-based Americans, many of whom Martha also met. At her father's request, she would bring her music to entertain his guests with her latest accomplishments, although he once had to remind her to dress the part of an accomplished young woman. "Make it a rule hereafter to come dressed otherwise than in your uniform," he admonished her, when she had not dressed to the occasion when venturing out of the school. Martha probably also knew Anne Willing Bingham, a stylish Philadelphia woman who frequented the salons and the gardens of the Palais Royal and debated gender and politics with Jefferson. Martha would have been less conflicted about Bingham than the staid New Englander Nabby Adams, who was alternately wowed by her beauty and intelligence and distressed by her enthusiastic adoption of French fashion—especially rouge.

The venues of these encounters varied, but one place where Parisians of all ranks met was the Palais Royal, which had just been converted from a private residence into a kind of walking mall. Newly opened when the Jeffersons arrived (their first lodgings on the rue de Richelieu were only a block away), the Palais Royal featured shops, cafés, and entertainments in the three galleries, which together with the original palace enclosed an enormous garden. There, Parisians dressed in their best finery gathered by day to promenade the graceful allées, sip coffee and chocolate, shop, and visit. Sundays featured concerts so crowded the air was thick with the perfume of men's hair powder and the nose-gays women carried as a refuge from the noisome city smells. Even today, the Palais Royal is breathtaking on first sight; leaving the noise of Parisian street traffic behind, one walks through an enclosed gallery until it opens to reveal a tree-lined garden oasis of beauty and elegance. Jefferson loved it; he thought it "one of the principal ornaments to the city." Martha did, too. She, Caroline and Elizabeth Tufton, and their uncle the Duke of Dorset had made quite a day of it on one occasion, staying until nearly dusk (when all respectable women needed to leave to preserve their reputations). Perhaps one of the charms of the Palais Royal (and indeed of Paris itself) for American women was the apparent freedom enjoyed there by French women. Nabby Adams had noticed that "in company here, every one consults his own pleasure; the ladies walk about, view the pictures if there are any, chat with any one who pleases them."

But these freedoms also harbored perils, particularly for young women unaccustomed to them. Panthemont and other convent schools like it appealed to parents precisely because they were designed to shelter their daughters. With its strategic mix of the worldliness of the boarders and strict protocols for its students, Panthemont both prepared and protected its young charges. These older women boarders, called *dames des chambres,* also lived at Panthemont, although in a different wing from the students. This was a common practice in France, allowing a safe haven for women whether unmarried, widowed, or seeking refuge from a bad marriage. Although required to attend chapel, they were otherwise free to receive visitors and leave the convent at will, subject only to a nightly curfew.

So just as profane and respectable rubbed shoulders at the Palais Royal, so too did the women and pensionnaires at Panthemont. A former student from the Parisian convent school of Port-Royal (like Panthemont, a "four star" girls' school) remembered many evenings in which she spent two hours at a time in the rooms of the worldly boarding women, who taught her how to talk about politics with manners, wit, and style. Dining at the Abbess's table provided Martha with lessons in deportment, voice modulation, and the art of pleasing conversa-

Vue du Nouveau Palais Royal.

This 1788 view shows the recently refurbished Palais Royal, playground and meeting place for Parisians of all ranks. Note the promenades formed by the trees planted in al-lées. Shops and restaurants occupied the galleries surrounding the enclosure and the subterranean area, capped by the structure in the center.

tion; it may have also provided her a glimpse of French marital mores, courtesy of the *dames des chambres*. Martha's report (pointedly ignored by her father) of a man who killed himself because he thought his wife did not love him—concluding with her arch observation that "if every husband in Paris was to do as much, there would be nothing but wid-ows left"—certainly echoes gossip overheard at school. The Abbess may well have tried to suppress such talk among the boarders when her students joined them, but it would not have surprised her. She was very much a woman of the world; many parents counted on her to engineer suitable connections for their daughters among the privileged and powerful families represented at the school.

Other news filtered through Panthemont's permeable walls as well. It is not surprising that the daughters of nobility, royal officials, and diplomats should be particularly interested in political news, especially in the changeable climate of 1780s France. Three princesses, distin-guished by the blue ribbons they wore over their shoulders, attended the school, and a dozen of the 129 families represented at Panthemont in that decade were English. While her father was touring southern France in the spring of 1787, Martha reported that she was hearing a swirl of rumors about the political activities of the Assembly of Notables, a group of high-powered nobles and clergy called together by the king to advise him. She refused to divulge any of the rumors, however, "for fear of taking a trip to the Bastille for my pains, which I am by no means disposed to do at this moment." On another occasion, a copy of one of the king's speeches to this assembly was circulating in the school. So too were speculations about who was to occupy the cell at the Bastille being prepared by a minister of the king's household. Some thought it might be Madame de Polignac, the Dauphin's governess and the mother of one of Martha's dance partners, who—it was whispered— might have been pocketing some of the royal allowance.

After Martha's departure from France, her friend Marie de Botidoux gleefully recounted heated arguments in which she delighted to take the republican view (arguing for the sovereignty of the people), was unrepentant in the face of a political conservative's efforts to exorcise her "demon of democracy," and begged to know what Jefferson thought of the National Assembly's latest decrees, for "you know he is my oracle." Botidoux's lively letters also dispensed the latest gossip of pairings, alliances, and intrigues at court. Even lodged at Panthemont, Botidoux was able to keep up with the dizzying pace of the French Revolution: the doings of the newly renamed National Constituent Assembly that represented the common people, their fight for a constitution, and the rise and fall of various notables of Paris society.

The Abbess had strict rules to protect her charges against the hazards of this world. Pensionnaires were allowed to leave the convent on outings, but, Martha found to her chagrin, only if the Abbess had written permission from the parents. Even when out with their parents, students had a curfew that was apparently enforced to the minute. "Know exactly at what hour they will shut your doors in the evening," Jefferson warned his daughter, apparently stung from past experience, as she prepared to go to the opera, "and as you come down to the carriage see exactly what oclock it is by the Convent clock that we may not be deceived as to the time."

The Abbess also maintained strict protocols of rank, by station and age. The daughter of the Duc d'Orléans took her meals apart from the other pensionnaires, in company only with a girl whose family was also associated with the royal household. Students wore different-colored uniforms depending on their ages but were housed in common sleeping quarters. Martha's good friend Julia Annesley complained petulantly, "I think *we* are kept rather too strict for such great girls, and that there ought to be some difference made between ours and an infantine age. But," she admitted ruefully, in a clear acknowledgment of the Abbess's iron-clad law, "it is of no use to complain, as it will not mend the matter." Entrusted with the most prominent daughters of the land, the Abbess was immovable on matters respecting their status and virtue, knowing their futures depended upon it.

Nevertheless, within a year of living under the Abbess's rule, Martha was "charmed" with her new life. She had learned to speak French like a native and, in her bearing and posture, was indistinguishable from the nobility. When her sponsor, not recognizing Martha on the playground one day, was informed who she was, she replied, *"Ah! Mais vraiment elle a l'air très-distingué."* ("Oh, but truly, she has a very distinguished air.") In these critical years of her life, Martha Jefferson developed a sense of herself that was shaped by mutually reinforcing elements: the curriculum, Catholicism, and female friendships, both within and without the convent school. She learned about the benefits of status and education for women and saw the ways in which even the Roman Church not only countenanced but took full advantage of female ability. In their salons and their letters, French women had achieved the social and intellectual leadership that positioned them to take on the pressing issues that erupted in their own revolution. As the daughter of the American ambassador, it had been Martha's enormous good fortune to live in the city at the very height of female influence and to move in those circles.

It was the best of times for the bright, vivacious young girl, who soaked it all in.

Families Reunited

. . . .

1787

. . . .

*S*o FRENCH HAD MARTHA BECOME by the time her sister appeared in France in 1787, three years after her own arrival, that Maria literally did not know her. But, truth to tell, neither of them would have recognized Maria, either, Thomas Jefferson admitted to Elizabeth Eppes, "had we met with her unexpectedly" on a Paris street. As it was, it fell to Jefferson's French servant, Adrien Petit, to reintroduce Maria to her father and sister. To Maria's great dismay, Jefferson had sent Petit to London, where her Atlantic voyage ended. She was staying with Abigail and John Adams, who had been living there since their move from Paris upon his appointment as the first American ambassador to the court of George III.

It was a fair July day when Maria Jefferson alighted from her carriage in the courtyard of the Hôtel de Langeac, her father's home in Paris. The warmth of the day (a balmy seventy-five degrees that afternoon) most likely persuaded her to leave off wearing her brand-new beaver hat trimmed with feathers, the latest fashion in London's danker summer weather. Instead she may have been wearing fingerless mitts made up of soft linen diaper cloth, a gift from Abigail Adams, to keep her hands and arms protected from the sun while she traveled. She was undoubtedly wearing one of her new fine Irish linen frocks that Abigail had also provided, perhaps overlaid with a blue sash at the waist, for her first presentation to her father in almost four years.

No one preserved the memory of those first moments of reunion on paper, perhaps because they were painfully awkward. The French-speaking Petit was in no position to smooth things over between Maria and the father who had sent him in his stead. Maria may have banished her tears at being forced to part with Abigail Adams, but she would not have met her father as happily as she might have had Jefferson gone to London himself and Abigail facilitated the introductions. "As she had left all her Friends in Virginia to come over the ocean to see you," Adams told Jefferson, reporting Maria's crisp assessment of Petit's errand, "she did think you would have taken the pains to have come here for her." How many times, during the trip across the channel and along the same roads traversed by her father and sister three years earlier, did she steal a sideways glance at Petit and add silently what she had pointedly asked Mrs. Adams: Why did her father have to send a man she could not understand? Abigail had tried to make excuses for Jefferson, but Maria remained unmoved. "I express her own words," Adams warned him.

Why Jefferson did not go to London himself is a puzzle. He pleaded the press of business that awaited him on his return to Paris after a three-month tour of southern France and Italy. Or perhaps the Virginia plantation owner did not want to face his two discerning New England friends as he retrieved his daughter and her beautiful young enslaved maid. Or perhaps he felt himself bound to Paris, waiting as anxiously for news of the arrival of a friend there as Maria was waiting for his in London. Maria Hadfield Cosway, the exquisite golden-haired, diminutive artist wife of miniaturist Richard Cosway, was due back in Paris that summer and Jefferson did not want to miss her.

Introduced in August 1786 by the American artist John Trumbull, Jefferson had been immediately smitten. He admitted to dispatching "lying messengers . . . to every corner of the city" to cancel his many engagements so that he could spend the day in her company. For weeks, they stole time when they could—although usually in the company of others—touring the beauties of Paris and its environs. It was while on a walk with her in September that, in an ill-calculated attempt to impress the young woman with his agility, he tried to hop a fence. Instead he fell and dislocated his wrist; never properly set, it plagued him for the rest of his life. Mrs. Cosway's departure from Paris in early October occasioned his famous "Head and Heart" letter to her, an internal debate over which should have precedence and much analyzed by scholars since. (It was a tie: Morality, goodness, and happiness could only flow from the Heart, he believed; but the Head forbade a relationship with a married woman.) In the dozens of flirtatious letters that followed, the two looked forward to her return to Paris the following summer. Whatever the reason, Jefferson had sent Petit to London.

Now, in the summer sunshine, Maria stood before her father, resplendent in his Paris fashions, a stranger yet her family. In his absence, Elizabeth Eppes had tried to teach Maria and Lucy to love him. But as far as Maria was concerned, her family, from whom she had been torn against her will, was back in Chesterfield County. In those eyes that held nothing back—"What she thinks in her Heart You may read in her Eyes," Abigail Adams saw—Jefferson may well have been able to read her reproach. By his own admission, he did not see the five-year-old he had left at Eppington in this extraordinarily pretty young girl, now just days away from her ninth birthday. But as his vision focused, did he begin to see traces of his wife's features in those of his daughter, who had grown up so much in his absence? Or vague shadows of Lucy, a toddler of fifteen months the last time he had seen her? With what combination of joy and sorrow, eagerness and hesitancy, did he greet his lovely but heartsick child?

We do not know if Martha was with her father at that moment, or at school, daily awaiting the news of Maria's arrival. Abigail Adams had thought it would be a good idea for Jefferson to bring Martha to London with him when he came to claim Maria, the better to "reconcile her little Sister to the thoughts of taking a journey. It would be proper," she explained, "that some person should be accustomed to her." Well acclimated indeed, delighting in her life at Panthemont, Martha no doubt greeted her sister with affection and the confidence of experience. But apprehension may also have colored their meeting. Jefferson had been preparing Martha for Maria's arrival for some time. "When she arrives," he instructed his elder daughter, "she will become a precious charge on your hands. The difference of your age, and your common loss of a mother, will put that office on you." Not yet fifteen, Martha was still a schoolgirl herself and hardly eager to take on the responsibility of motherhood to a sister she had not seen in four years. She responded dutifully that a family reunion would "render my happiness complete" but then dropped the subject.

Now face-to-face, the sisters were a study in contrasts. No portrait was ever taken of Maria in her lifetime, and the identification of a miniature of a young redheaded woman as Martha Jefferson at seventeen has now been questioned. But verbal portraits do remain and are strikingly consistent for both. Throughout her life, Maria's beauty was repeatedly remarked upon and admired. Abigail Adams thought her a "beautifull girl," as did Nathaniel Cutting, a Boston ship captain who met her when she was eleven. A "lovely Girl," he called her, whose "engaging smile ever animates her Countenance"; Maria Jefferson was "a distinguish'd ornament to her sex," Cutting gushed. In her twenties, she was described by a family friend as "beautiful," with "winning manners." Her memory was still vivid to Monticello slave Isaac Jefferson more than forty years after her death. "She was low like her mother"—by this he meant petite—"and longways the handsomest, pretty lady jist like her mother," he recalled. Her eyes, "fine blue," another family friend remembered, "had an expression that cannot I think be described." Her face, he said, "was divine. Her complexion was exquisite; her features all good, and so arranged as to produce an expression such as I never beheld in any other countenance: sweetness, intelligence, tenderness, beauty were exquisitely blended."

As much as Maria seems to have taken after her mother, Martha favored her father. A Virginia friend described her as "large, loosely made, and awkward"—probably owing to her unusual height. It may also explain why she could so easily bound down the stairs of the convent, taking them four at a time. Like her father, she had red hair and blue eyes. She was, as her good friend Margaret Bayard Smith tactfully observed, "a delicate likeness of her father." Her children would later describe her "dignified and highly agreeable appearance" but concede that she "bore too many of her father's lineaments to be termed beautiful." Her lack of beauty was probably more apparent when she was contrasted with her sister, but without exception those who described her were drawn to a face "beaming with intelligence, benevolence and sen-

sibility," with features that were "flexible, playful and agreeable." Even
meeting the twelve-year-old, just two months after the Jeffersons' arrival
in Paris, Nabby Adams had been struck by the "delicacy and sensibility"
that she "read in every feature." Her lively interest and "frank, communicative disposition," which "melts into cordiality," was the way a granddaughter thoughtfully described Martha in her mature years.

Now, seeing her younger sister again, did Martha, too, mark out
Maria's resemblance to their dead mother, the memory of whom would
have been much more vivid for Martha than for Maria? She may have
been apprehensive about the responsibility she was to bear for her. She
may also have recognized a rival for the already limited time and attention of her father. So often had she been disappointed in not hearing
from him that she once wrote to him purposefully to "break so painful
a silence by giving you an example that I hope you will follow." Instead
Martha's hopes were met with his rejoinders that "I have not been able
to write to you so often as expected, because I am generally on the road;
and when I stop any where, I am occupied in seeing what is to be seen."
Too busy with sightseeing to write to his daughter back in Paris (she
received only four letters throughout his thirteen-week tour of Europe
in the spring of 1787), he nonetheless admonished her that "this need
not slacken your writing to me, because you have leisure." Whatever
Martha felt as she met Maria again, the benevolence for which she was
known throughout her life won out as she saw the homesickness in
Maria's eyes. She moved back to the Hôtel de Langeac during Maria's
first week in France and, "leading her from time to time to the convent,"
gently introduced Maria to her new life there.

How DIFFERENT PARIS WAS from Eppington, the plantation home of
her beloved aunt and uncle Eppes. Francis Eppes was a wealthy man,
but the frame home he had built in Chesterfield County, twelve miles
west of Petersburg, could not compare with Monticello, much less
Paris. It stood about a mile from the Appomattox River on a ridge
overlooking the valley. Winterpock Creek ran through his property and
for decades had given its name to the Eppes estate. By 1782, when
Eppes returned after the war to resume work on the house he had begun
a dozen years earlier, he had renamed it Eppington.

Today, approached by a winding rural lane, the vista of the house pleases as it comes into view. Visitors admire the lovely wide lawns and the double rows of Lombardy poplars that frame the house. But it was to a considerably smaller home that Maria Jefferson had moved in the fall of 1783: just two large rooms on the ground floor and two bedrooms upstairs. The front door opened into a narrow passage, barely three feet across, that ran along the length of one room, from which stairs rose to the second floor. Maria stepped from one construction zone to another, as Eppes had just begun his expansion plans, which continued through the 1790s.

Still, to cross the threshold into this home was to enter a joyous if somewhat noisy household, whose warm hospitality welcomed visitors and made them loath to leave. At its center was Elizabeth Wayles Eppes, a half sister of Jefferson's wife. The two sisters were obviously close: Martha had spent many an anxious month during the war at The Forest in refuge, and she had traveled there to help her sister nurse their father in his final illness. Elizabeth Eppes had been at her sister's death-bed. It was to her that Jefferson had poured out his anguished heart in a rare display of trust from a man who typically kept his feelings tightly tethered. "This miserable kind of existence is too burthensome to be borne," he cried to his sympathetic sister-in-law three weeks after Martha's death. If it were not for the three little daughters who depended on him, he would "not wish its continuance for a moment."

Jefferson took comfort in his relationship with Elizabeth Eppes, whom he considered "mightily like her sister" and whose warmth radiated beyond the members of her extended family to all who came to her door. When traveler Benjamin Latrobe visited in 1796, he planned no more than a quick stop to pay his respects to Francis Eppes, the leading man of the neighborhood. Instead he was waylaid by their conviviality. "Here all is good humor, kindness, and mirth," he wrote in his journal. "We breakfasted with him and his charming family, and forgot ourselves so far as to stay almost till noon." Jefferson regretted that during her visit to Virginia in 1786, the Philadelphian Eliza Trist had not visited Elizabeth Eppes, whom, he declared, "you would have found among the most amiable women on earth. I doubt whether you would ever have got away from her."

Eppes's cordial empathy, her likeness to her sister, and their long

Although larger than most Virginia houses, Eppington was considerably smaller than Monticello, particularly during Maria Jefferson's childhood stay, before either wing had been added to the house. Unlike Monticello, its architecture was entirely conventional. But Eppington, more than Monticello or Paris, shaped Maria's life; here she found the warmth and stability to which she happily returned again and again.

friendship no doubt explain why Jefferson felt unlimited confidence, as he told her husband, in leaving his two younger daughters with her during his anticipated two-year absence. It may be something of an overstatement to say, as has one historian, that four-year-old Maria Jefferson was scarred by a "terror of abandonment" after her mother's death, but certainly the motherly Elizabeth Eppes was the perfect person to embrace and raise her and her baby sister, Lucy. Jefferson's sister Martha Jefferson Carr, who spent five or six weeks at Eppington in the summer of 1786, "very much admired that amiable Ladies management of the little Girls. She pays the upmost attention to them and harmony seems to rein among them." To ease Maria's homesickness, Eppes had even proposed taking her home to Monticello for a month's holiday. Eppes coordinated her plans with Martha Carr to meet there in September 1786, although in the end their plans were foiled when one of Eppes's own children took sick.

Recognizing a kindred spirit, Maria responded fully to Eppes's mothering. "Dear little Polly (who shares an equal proportion of her tenderness) appears more attached to her than her own" children, Carr reported to her brother. Nonetheless it was an adjustment, and Maria missed her father and sister. "Polly," as her family called her during this period, "often mentions you . . . and begs you to make haste home, for she longs to see you," Francis Eppes told Jefferson in December 1783, three months after he had left her at Eppington. As he bid his daughters goodbye, Jefferson may have pried himself away with promises of dolls he could buy for her in Philadelphia. Almost immediately after his arrival in that city, he asked Eppes to tell his "dear Poll" that he had not been able to find a ship "to send with the babies" he had promised her. By the following spring, Maria was growing impatient for her doll. At her dictation, Elizabeth Eppes obligingly wrote, "I was mighty glad of my sash's," which her father had sent to adorn her dresses. But with a child's tenacious grip on a parental pledge, Maria still wanted to know "what day you are going to come and see me, and if you will bring Sister Patsy, and my baby with you."

But sashes and dolls were poor substitutes for an absentee father, so Maria entered fully into the life of the Eppes household and its growing family. Francis and Elizabeth Eppes had eight children, born between their marriage in 1769 and 1788, six of whom survived infancy. Maria's cousin Jack was ten when she arrived at Eppington. There were at least two daughters as well, Martha Bolling (like Maria, born in 1778) and Lucy Elizabeth (likely the daughter whose November birth Francis Eppes announced in a letter to Jefferson). The arrival of two young cousins and a new daughter certainly took a great deal of Elizabeth Eppes's attention, but according to Jefferson's sister, she clearly met the challenge.

Elizabeth Eppes attended as well to the girls' education. Although she served as secretary for Maria Jefferson's first letter to her father, ever after Jefferson received letters written in the large, awkward hand of a child. At six years old, Maria could read "prittyly," Martha Jefferson Carr reported. "Mrs Eppes is Extreemly anxious for her Improvement & pays the greatest attention to her," she added later. At almost eight years old, Maria was "a Sweet Girl, reads & Sews prettily & dances gracefully." Her education included all the necessary lessons for Virginia girls of her class, but Elizabeth Eppes wanted more for her charges. It was probably at her urging that Francis Eppes wrote to Jefferson in the summer of 1786, inquiring about proper tutors (over forty years of age) who could school the girls in "French English erethmatick and musick."

So successful was Eppes in her efforts that by the time Maria arrived in London she had acquired a love for reading. "Books are her delight," Abigail Adams wrote to Jefferson, "and she reads to me by the hour with great distinctness." But even more, Maria had learned to think about what she was reading, for Adams added that she "comments on what she reads with much propriety." Maria also learned to appreciate music. As she listened to her sister play a haunting composition of Francis Hopkinson's in their Paris home, her father noticed that she had dissolved in tears. Concerned, he asked if she was sick. "No," she replied, "but the tune was so mournful."

Elizabeth Eppes taught Maria Jefferson how to behave in company, as well as among family. An inventory taken of her home in 1810 allows us to imagine the large rooms on the first floor and their care to put guests at ease. Ten beds (three curtained), a cradle for the ever-present infant (her own or Jefferson's), and four extra mattresses ensured a place to sleep; seventeen counterpanes (bedspreads, perhaps worked by Elizabeth Eppes and her slaves), four pairs of blankets, and fourteen pairs of sheets ensured comfort and warmth. Her several dining tables and sixty-six chairs enabled large parties, but she also had several additional small tables and forty-six more chairs to accommodate any overflow. Towels, napkins, tankards, silver, ladles, serving vessels, china, brandy snifters, decanters, and card tables spoke to the hospitable entertaining that had rendered Benjamin Latrobe blissfully ignorant of the time.

Very young girls did not participate in adult dinners, card games, or parties. Nonetheless, they needed to learn how to make themselves agreeable in company and how to perform their "courtesies" (bows for boys and curtsies for girls) for introductions and meetings. Elizabeth Eppes sent a very polished young girl to Europe. Abigail Adams was impressed with the "quickest sensibility and the maturest understanding, that I have ever met with for her years" that she found in Maria Jefferson. No matter where she went in her young life, Maria endeared herself to adults, from her Virginia relations to the sea captain she encountered during her Atlantic crossing to fellow travelers in a French stagecoach to the wives of government officials.

But life in eighteenth-century Virginia was not an idyll, even in this hospitable household. Tragedy struck shortly into Maria's stay, precipitating further wrenching change for her. Whooping cough carried off her younger sister, two-year-old Lucy, and the Eppes's youngest, also named Lucy Elizabeth, in October 1784. Francis Eppes had sent a worriedly foreboding letter to Jefferson in September, unable to reassure him of his daughters' health. "They as well as our own are laid up with the hooping cough. Your little Lucy and our youngest [Lucy, born in November 1783] and [five-year-old] Bolling are I think very ill." One month later Elizabeth Eppes, stricken with grief, forced herself to deliver the news to Jefferson. "It is almost impossible to paint the anguish of my heart on this melancholy occasion," she wrote through her tears. "A most unfortunate Hooping cough has deprived you, and us of two sweet Lucys, within a week. Ours was the first that fell a sacrifice. She was thrown into violent convulsions linger'd out a week and then expired. Your dear angel was confined a week to her bed, her sufferings were great though nothing like a fit. She retain'd her sense perfectly, calld me a few moments before she died, and asked distinctly for water." Older, Maria was able to fight the wracking coughs without even taking to her bed. "Dear Polly," Eppes added, "is now quite recovered." But the heartbroken mother was beside herself with grief and worry. "My heart shudders for my poor Bolling, who is reduced to a skeleton, and the cough still very obstinate. Life is scarcely supportable under such severe afflictions," she concluded, echoing Jefferson's own cry of grief after his wife's death.

Jefferson received the news not from the Eppes's letters, which took almost seven months to reach him, but from Dr. James Currie, who had been called to attend the sick children. Hand-delivered by the Marquis de Lafayette on January 26, 1785, Currie's letter attributed Lucy's death to "the Complicated evils of teething, Worms and Hooping Cough." A bacterial infection easily transmitted through sneezing and coughing, the cough had been "carried there by the Virus of their friends without their knowing it was in their train." Currie was called "too late to do any thing but procrastinate the settled fate of the poor Innocent." Even today the antibiotics used to treat the disease have limited if any effectiveness if the victim has been ill for three weeks or more. The strain that struck the Eppes household must have been particularly virulent; just one child in a hundred who suffers from it is seized with convulsions, although infants, like Lucy Eppes, are particularly susceptible. Only with difficulty was Currie able to save Bolling, who was Maria's age. Lucy Jefferson's heartbroken relatives pressed her father with her praises; not quite two, she "prattles Every thing she hears"; at two and a half, she was a "Child Of the most Auspicious hopes" and had inherited from her parents "among other early Shining qualities an ear nicely and critically musical."

Jefferson was stunned. "It is in vain to endeavor to describe the situation of my mind," he told Francis Eppes days after receiving Currie's letter. "It would pour balm neither into your wounds nor mine; I will therefore pass on from the subject." He and Martha canceled social engagements for months and withdrew into a grief almost as incapacitating as when his wife had died giving birth to this child who now lay in a Virginia grave. Watching them relive this grief anew, Nabby Adams was deeply touched. "Mr Jefferson is a man of great sensibility and parental affection. His wife died when this child was born," she noted insightfully, "and he was almost in a confirmed state of melancholy, confined himself from the world and even from his friends for a long time, and this news has greately affected him and his daughter."

Not two weeks before receiving Currie's letter, Jefferson had toyed with his "wish to have Polly brought," but believing that he would soon be returning to Virginia, he discarded the idea. By May, however, Jefferson learned that his stay in France was to be extended. Benjamin Franklin was going home, and Jefferson would take his place as the American ambassador. On the eleventh of May, his mind made up, he wrote to Francis Eppes. That letter is lost, but the terse notes in the summary journal he kept of his correspondence remain. "I must have Polly. As would not have her at sea but between 1st Apr and Sep, this will allow time for a decision—is there any woman in Virginia who could be hired to come." What did the Eppeses think, he wanted to know? Hearing nothing, Jefferson wrote again on August 30. Thoughts of his last daughter in Virginia "hang on my mind night and day," he said. "I must now repeat my wish to have Polly sent to me next summer." Again he was precise about how this should be accomplished: in the summer months to avoid storms, in a ship that had been tested on the Atlantic but had not plied those waters for more than four or five years, and with a suitable companion: "some good lady . . . or a careful gentleman." Even "a careful negro woman, as Isabel, for instance," he wrote, suggesting his slave Isabel Hern, "if she has had the small pox, would suffice under the patronage of a gentleman." This time he did not ask the Eppeses what they thought of his plan.

Jefferson did not hear from Eppington until June 1786, when Francis Eppes's reply, dated April 11, came to hand. Eppes bemoaned "some strange fatality attending our correspondence," insisting he had received only the May 1785 letter, which had not acknowledged the letters Eppes had written the previous fall and winter. But then, emphatically, he came to the point. "In my two last, I gave my opinion very fully with respect to Polly's trip to France," he declared, and since they did not arrive, he repeated, "I think it impossible she shou'd ever reach France, even if you insisted on its being attempted." He had mentioned the idea frequently to Maria, but "the situation it throws her into satisfies me that the scheme is inpracticable." Martha Jefferson Carr agreed. Although she was not at Eppington, she had heard of Maria's aversion to the plan. Maria may have overheard the adults discuss ways around her intransigence, for Carr reported that she was "very much afraid they will fool her and carry her there."

Jefferson's request threw the Eppes household into uproar. Yet another letter from Jefferson—this one warning about the possibility of capture on the high seas by warring Barbary powers—unleashed a barrage of protest from Virginia. Martha Carr attempted to intervene with her brother by presenting the distraught child's case. Jefferson's letter precipitated a torrent of tears from Maria, "tho after much ado she is so far pacified as to wipe her eyes and set down to write to you." The adults tried to make France sound more appealing by describing all the amusements and luxuries to be found there, but to no avail. Certain that her father's wishes would prevail, however, Maria eyed her relatives' suggestions warily. Her shrewd watchfulness would make it all but impossible for the adults to trick her into submission, Carr warned her brother. So convinced was Maria that Elizabeth Eppes was her only ally, that even after a two-week visit, Carr could not persuade Maria to accompany her on a visit to a nearby relative's home. Refusing to leave Elizabeth Eppes's side, the little girl "cannot be carried off without compultion," Carr concluded helplessly.

Francis Eppes agreed. "Nothing but force will bring it about," he told Jefferson. Eppes rashly suggested that Jefferson could cross the ocean to meet her in Philadelphia, where Eppes himself would carry her. But since even this offer had "no affect except distressing her," he resolved to do nothing until he heard further from Jefferson. Buying Maria another year, Eppes would later blame his procrastination on the late receipt of Jefferson's letters and the difficulty of inoculating slave Isabel Hern for the trip. Even twelve-year-old Jack rushed to Maria's aid, assuring his uncle Thomas that "not withstanding your great desire to have Cousin Polly with you, it cannot be effected without forcing her, for she seems very much averse to it."

For her part, Elizabeth Eppes could not believe what she was hearing. Utterly "unhinged" by her brother-in-law's suggestion, she could not bring herself to add to the packet of protesting letters. "She says she has once written to you very fully on the subject," Martha Jefferson Carr wrote to her brother, "and concludes that her letter has not reached you or that the multiplicity of business you are engaged in has prevented your acknowledging the receipt of it." Disbelieving that a fond father would insist upon his young daughter crossing the ocean, Eppes told herself and all within earshot, he must not have received her letter. Surely he would not have continued to insist, after having the dangers laid out for him. How could he?

Maria composed herself so far as to primly assure her father that "I long to see you, and hope that you and sister Patsy are well." But then she came to the point. "I am very sorry that you have sent for me. I don't want to go to France, I had rather stay with Aunt Eppes." She had a better idea: "that you and she will come very soon to see us." And, still waiting, she continued to hope that her father "will send me a doll." Jefferson had attempted to woo her across the Atlantic with firm attestations of his love and tantalizing promises of "as many dolls and playthings as you want for yourself, or to send to your cousins." But so intractable was Maria's resistance, Eliza Trist heard about it all the way up in Alexandria and presumed it would thwart Jefferson's plans. A regular visitor to Eppington, James Currie also warned Jefferson from Richmond that Maria would not leave Elizabeth Eppes.

Maria lived her last year at Eppington in an agony of dread. Francis Eppes had at last capitulated, and suspecting the change in tactics, Maria had made no secret of her increasing trepidation of the journey. As late as March 1787, she continued to insist that "I can not go to France." Elizabeth Eppes told Jefferson that she too prayed daily for a last-minute reprieve, "countermanding your orders with regard to dear Polly." But the mail failed to deliver, so Elizabeth Eppes knew that when the day arrived, Maria "must at last be dragged like a calf to the slaughter." She attempted to ease the pain by planning the very sort of decoy Maria feared. Taking her to Osborne's Wharf, on the James River near Richmond, "the children will spend a day or two on board the ship with her, which," Eppes hoped, "would reconcile her to it." She knew Martha Jefferson Carr, stranded at home without transportation, would be distressed because she could not be there for Maria's leave-taking, but that could not be helped; Eppes could not spare a carriage to collect her.

The pangs of grief and anxiety that emanate from their unhappy letters to Jefferson contrast markedly with the one he wrote to Francis Eppes the same month, cheerily expressing his pleasure in sending him some of the fabulous French wines he had been sampling during his travels. Jefferson's sister Mary Bolling described utter dejection at Eppington, Martha Carr felt for Maria's "sufferings at parting with . . . Mrs. Eppes from whom she has experienced the tenderness and fondness of a parent," and Elizabeth Eppes's wretchedness still echoes two centuries later in her plea: "For God's sake give us the earliest intelligence of her arrival." As Maria napped in her cabin, lulled to sleep by the lapping waves of the James, her relatives crept away, leaving her to awaken under sail and heading out to the Atlantic. The only familiar face on board was that of her slave.

The captain of the *Robert,* Andrew Ramsay, was so unnerved by her "vexation and the affliction she underwent" when Maria awoke, he was afraid that she would make herself ill. To his relief, "she soon got over it and got so fond of me that she seldom parts with me without tears." By dint of her "sweet disposition and good nature," Maria secured his attention and, judging by what Abigail Adams observed on her arrival, a fair degree of free rein on the ship. After five weeks at sea in the company of men, Maria was "as rough as a little sailor," Adams reported to Jefferson, and her clothes, "only proper for the sea," were no longer wearable.

After a storm-free passage, in accommodations that her relations thought exceedingly comfortable, Maria Jefferson arrived in London, where the process of decoy and detachment began once again. "She was so much attached to the Captain and he to her, that it was with no small regret that I separated her from him," Abigail Adams told Jefferson in her letter announcing Maria's safe arrival. Adams tried every-thing to distract her. She told Maria that she had never seen her elder sister cry once. But, Maria replied smartly, Martha "was older and ought to do better," and "besides she had her pappa with her." Adams showed Maria her father's portrait. She did not recognize him. How could she when she didn't know him? Maria asked Adams bluntly. A proposed trip to Sadler's Wells, a popular amusement park, likewise failed to cheer. Maria would gladly trade "all the fun in the World" for "one mo-ment" with Captain Ramsay. At the end of that long first day, a relieved Abigail Adams reported that the exhausted child, resolving to "try to be good and not cry," had finally dried her tears and gone to bed.

Ever wary of adults' plans for her, Maria hovered over Adams's desk the next morning, asking if she wrote every day to her father. But by the time Jefferson's servant Adrien Petit arrived from Paris to collect her, Abigail had so won Maria's affection that the little girl confided that it would be as hard to leave her as it had been to leave her aunt Eppes. Almost twenty years afterward, Abigail Adams could vividly remember how Maria had "slung around my neck, and wet my bosom with her tears, saying, 'Oh, now I have learned to love you, why will they take me from you?'" But, resigned, the girl then climbed into the carriage that would take her to the coast for the last leg of her journey to France.

This pattern of detachment, tears, resignation, and passionate at-tachment, repeated several times in young Maria's life, certainly left a mark. "Polly had learned to get her way by alternately charming and raging," one historian concluded. Some of the people who knew her later in her life followed Abigail Adams's initial impulse to compare her unfavorably with her elder sister; she was never as brilliant, articulate, or outgoing as Martha. Others see her through the prism of Jefferson's expectations and his constant reminders to her of her shortcomings as a correspondent, student, and attentive and obliging daughter. Thomas Jefferson's biographer Dumas Malone, for example, regretted that Jef-ferson "did not succeed in molding his daughter in his own image." But none of these approaches takes Maria Jefferson on her terms.

Eighteenth-century children had no control over their lives, but the lack of stability in young Maria's was staggering. As a tiny child, she was always moving and being moved: first from Monticello to Rich-mond, when her father became governor; then the wartime flights to

Tuckahoe and back to Richmond; to Poplar Forest and then finally back to Monticello in safety, where her mother died just after her fourth birthday. Then followed the back and forth between Monticello and Eppington, until she was settled there when her father departed to take his seat in Congress, all but disappearing from her life for the next four years. (Recall, he had not been able to return to Virginia to say his goodbyes before he left for Europe.) If she was determined to hold on to the stable, loving family life she had with the Eppeses, that is not to be wondered at. Nor should we wonder that she used the only strategy available to an eight-year-old girl to effect her wishes: torrents of tears and grief that appeared to threaten her health.

Maria Jefferson was no pushover. She was the daughter of Martha Jefferson, who, as historian Virginia Scharff has crisply observed, "could

Painted in 1795, Abigail Adams appears here much as Maria Jefferson would have known her in Philadelphia. Adams was self-educated, but well traveled by this date, sharply observant, and an incisive thinker. The artist captures the no-nonsense confidence born of decades of active interest in political affairs, as well as the clear-eyed gaze that caused Maria to trust her.

ride a horse through a mountain blizzard, give orders to scores of people, run several households at once and preside over the slaughter of a herd of hogs." She was raised by an aunt who fought to keep her and was so thoroughly confident of the merit of her argument over the child's father's that she was convinced he could not yet have read it. Like them, Maria was a Wayles; she had their resolve and strength of character. When Petit arrived in London to claim Maria, presenting the fait accompli of paid reserved seats on the stagecoach, a defeated Abigail Adams had turned to Maria to persuade her to give up the fight. "If I must go I will," Maria replied with a maturity beyond her years, "but I cannot help crying so pray don't ask me to." She would do as she was told, but she was also sure of the legitimacy of her feelings, her right to them, and the need for adults to pay attention to them.

At Eppington, she had learned a different way of understanding and expressing herself than did Martha at Panthemont. She learned how to endear herself to family and to those who had authority over her. That she learned perfectly these lessons of gentrified Virginia girlhood is lost completely if the standard is her sister's five-year education program in Paris or Jefferson's loving but persistent demands that she read her Spanish and write letters on schedule. Even in the one letter he wrote to her from across the Atlantic, intended to woo her, he warned her not "to go out without your bonnet because it will make you very ugly and then we should not love you so much." The effusively warm Elizabeth Eppes never conditioned her love on Maria's performance or looks. Instead the Eppes household schooled Maria in another way of being, and that is who she was when she arrived in Paris.

Although affectionate, Maria Jefferson was also astute. She knew loving adults would trick her; she knew they didn't always take seriously their promises to a child. There is no indication that she ever received the promised "baby" from her father. Rather than meeting her in London and using the trip to introduce her to himself and to all the beauties and delights of France, he sent his servant. He also took lightly the pledges that she gave. "She fancies she is to pay you the visit she promised," the amused father told Abigail Adams two months after Maria's arrival in Paris. If Maria developed a thicker skin than Martha and would, later in her life, make decisions according to her own priorities rather than Jefferson's, it was because of the memory of her peripatetic childhood, punctuated by only brief periods of loving stability that came to sudden, unannounced ends.

HOWEVER MUCH MARIA JEFFERSON was outmaneuvered by her father, there is no question that her force of will had initially persuaded many adults that Jefferson's plan was impossible, and all who wrote to Jefferson assumed that ultimately he would back down. That is to say, although eventually overruled, Maria Jefferson's feelings still mattered to everyone in her family, even if to varying degrees. But Maria was not the only young girl wrenched from her family and sent across the sea. So too was Sally Hemings. She was fourteen years old when she was selected by Francis and Elizabeth Eppes to accompany Maria for an absence none of them could estimate. There are no records of tears, grief, resistance, or agonized leave-takings. Indeed, the record is so silent we do not even know how the choice was made. All we know is that Maria Jefferson awoke from her nap aboard the *Robert* to the only face she knew, that of Sally Hemings.

This same cloud of silence envelops much of Sally Hemings's life. The Pulitzer Prize–winning work of Annette Gordon-Reed has done much to dissipate it, yet a great deal still remains unknowable. That the Eppeses finally chose her to accompany their precious charge on a perilous trip when the older Isabel Hern, ill at Monticello, could not go permits several reasonable deductions. First, the choice of Sally Hemings suggests that she was on-site, that is, already living at Eppington. Ten-year-old Sally Hemings had probably been taken from her own mother at Monticello as companion-maid for little Maria when her father, heading north for his congressional term, settled her at Eppington in the fall of 1783. Five years older than Maria, Sally had been her playmate and maid, especially in their last year at Monticello before Martha Jefferson's death. Indeed, Hemings family tradition had it that Sally was present at Martha Jefferson's deathbed and received from her the ambiguous gift of a bell, the gift itself a reminder of their relationship as half sisters, the bell a reminder of their roles as mistress and slave.

Given Elizabeth Eppes's motherly considerations in trying to relieve Maria's grief and homesickness, it stands to reason that she would want to give her comfort during what she knew would be a traumatic experience. Living with her at Eppington, Sally Hemings was no stranger to the tempests of Maria's fears and grief. And we know from Abigail Adams's reports to Jefferson that the girls were very fond of each other. Elizabeth could have had several reasons why she wanted Sally Hemings to go, but not least of them would have been to supply the comfort of a traveling companion Maria had known her whole life and on whose affection and forbearance (as a slave, that was Sally Hemings's job) she could count. And if, as is reasonable to assume, Jefferson himself had permitted Sally Hemings to accompany Maria to Eppington for her solace and convenience, Elizabeth Eppes could be confident that he would also approve their decision to send her across the Atlantic for the same reason.

Abigail Adams, however, did not approve. When the girls arrived in London, one barely older than the other and both in clothes in dire need of replacement, Adams's dismay was evident. Surprised that "the old Nurse who you expected to have attended her" was instead replaced by a "girl about 15 or 16," she viewed Sally Hemings as "quite a child," and concurred with Captain Ramsay's opinion that she would be of so little use it would be better for her to return to Virginia. Ten days after their arrival, Adams was still insisting that "the girl she has with her, wants more care than the child, and is wholy incapable of looking properly after her." Adams's insistence on Sally Hemings's immaturity is curious, given the confidence of the Eppeses, who knew her much better and who clearly thought her responsible enough to send. It may be explained, in part, by Adams's overestimation of her age, or by her discomfiture with meeting a slave girl who may have borne a Wayles family resemblance, clearly apparent in the face of Maria Jefferson as well.

Whatever the cause of Abigail Adams's explicit disapproval, it did not bode well for the enslaved girl's reception into her household. Not once did Adams refer to Sally Hemings by name, although she wrote specifically about her three times. For two weeks, Hemings had to endure Adams's frostiness, so starkly different from the warmth with which she embraced Maria. At the end of an Atlantic voyage, Maria Jefferson had adults striving to please and comfort her; Captain Ramsay had even offered to personally escort her to Paris. Sally Hemings, an enslaved girl thousands of miles away from her family, knew no such attentions. It is doubtful that Elizabeth and Francis Eppes considered the impact of separation on Sally's family life; their calculations were all centered around Maria. Hemings certainly did not provoke Ramsay's anxiety for her "vexation and affliction" as had Maria; his report was utterly mute about her maid. (Maria's letter to Elizabeth Eppes, the only inkling we might have had about the girls' trip, is lost to us.) Abigail Adams discounted Sally Hemings entirely when she recommended that Jefferson bring Martha with him to London so that Maria would have someone "accustomed to her." Indeed, in Abigail Adams's view, Sally Hemings did not even merit the dignity of her name.

Sally Hemings's only comfort was her brother James, waiting at the end of the line in Paris. As she witnessed all the deliberations at Eppington about Polly's prospective trip, it is possible that Sally may have even looked forward to the prospect of visiting him. Certainly as a slave she had no leverage to influence the Eppeses' decision and had to go if sent. Yet at the same time, she would not have served Elizabeth Eppes's purposes if she had been as frightened and tearful as her younger charge. It required courage to cross the ocean, and the anticipation of her own family reunion could well have fortified her through challenges that none of the free white adults, who were ostensibly in control of her, thought to make easier for her.

James Hemings had accompanied the Jeffersons to Paris in the summer of 1784. Unless he stopped at Eppington when he received Jefferson's summons, he had not seen Sally for almost four years. She would have changed mightily from age ten, recognizable to him only because of the company with whom she arrived. Like Maria, she would have been wearing the new clothes Abigail Adams had made up for her, although her workaday calico would not compare with Maria's dresses, made from the finest linen that money could buy. For Sally's part, James, eight years older than she, was already an adult when they last saw each other, and the difference in aspect may not have been all that dramatic. But she may have detected something different in his manner and bearing, a new confidence and sense of self born of his three years in France. As Martha did for Maria, so too could James Hemings orient his younger sister to the sights, sounds, wonders, and dregs of daily life in Paris.

James had been training as a chef in French cuisine for about eighteen months, first serving an apprenticeship with Jefferson's caterer before advancing to French pastry-making under the direction of the chef of Prince Louis-Joseph de Bourbon, a member of the royal family. When his sister arrived in 1787, James was only six months short of his promotion to chef de cuisine, when he would become responsible for running Jefferson's kitchen. He was a paid employee in a society that recognized the existence of slavery in its colonial territories but was not invested in protecting it at home. Jefferson had made a point of evading the French legal requirement of registering slaves upon entry into the country, willing to risk a substantial fine in order to minimize the visibility of James Hemings's enslavement. Nor did he register Sally Hemings. And on Paris streets in a revolutionary age, James Hemings would have learned that a trip to a French court in pursuit of freedom would support his case, rather than his master's. In short, in three years James Hemings had learned a valuable craft but, more important, had seen that a different way of life was possible than existed in Virginia and that it could be his.

This was the world to which he introduced his younger sister. Of course, Sally Hemings would not be trained as a chef. Indeed, precisely what Sally Hemings's role would be was a question, as Abigail Adams foresaw. There is no indication that she was packed off with Maria, a week after their arrival, to Panthemont, although many students brought maids with them. Rather, Jefferson was first concerned to have Sally Hemings inoculated against smallpox, a requirement he had specified to Francis Eppes for Maria's travel companion. That fall, within a few months of her arrival, he paid dearly—240 livres (about one thousand dollars today)—to Dr. Sutton, whose procedures he had followed so carefully with his own daughters immediately after his wife's death. There followed several weeks of isolation, pain, fever, and undoubtedly fear and loneliness, as Sally Hemings was forced to endure this process alone, albeit under the best medical care money could buy. Yet, as the historian Gordon-Reed has pointed out, it also "may have been the first time she had ever been attended to by white people." With no work required of her, Sally Hemings had time to think about what she would like her life to be.

Following her lonely quarantine, Sally returned to Jefferson's home. In the new year of 1788, she, like her brother, received wages, although irregularly: twenty-four livres in January, then nothing until the following November, when Jefferson began several monthly payments of twelve livres. That monthly salary was, as Gordon-Reed pointed out, "well above that of the average female live-in servant in Paris" and matched the allowance that Martha was receiving. There is no record to suggest what Sally was doing to earn this pay, but there are many possibilities. She could have been assisting her brother the chef; sewing, mending, and doing some washing; perhaps engaging in some light housework. Jefferson's Paris household staff was unusual in that, before Sally Hemings's arrival, it was all-male. With no designated housekeeper, Sally Hemings may have taken on that responsibility. She was probably responsible for caring for his clothing and linens, as well as those of Jefferson's daughters when they visited him. In any event, for Jefferson, who believed that domesticity was the work nature fitted women to do, these tasks would have been completely reasonable for a female servant.

How and when their relationship changed during Hemings's two years in Paris have been the subject of much controversy, as has the question of the paternity of Sally Hemings's children. For generations, historians followed the lead of Jefferson's grandchildren, whose defense of him seemed sufficient to quash the first rumors of the relationship that surfaced in a Richmond newspaper in 1802. Not until 1974 did a white historian take seriously the words of Sally Hemings's son Madison, who had recounted his family history a century earlier in 1873. After laying out her theory in her book *Thomas Jefferson: An Intimate History,* Fawn Brodie was excoriated by a cadre of Jefferson experts, who did not shrink from personal attacks on Brodie herself. But a new trend in early American history of asking about the experiences of ordinary people of the past facilitated deeper questions about slavery and opened up additional avenues of research.

The path-breaking work of Annette Gordon-Reed and Monticello historian Lucia Stanton shed even more light on the Hemings-Jefferson controversy and opened up the history of the slave communities at Monticello. In 1998, DNA testing documented a connection between Sally Hemings's youngest child, Eston, and the Jefferson male line and conclusively refuted the assertions of Jefferson's grandchildren that their Carr cousins had fathered Hemings's children. While not direct proof of Thomas Jefferson's paternity, the science appeared to offer the best hard evidence to counter the stout denials of those who styled themselves Jefferson's "defenders." After a year's reexamination of all the evidence—historical and scientific—the Thomas Jefferson Memorial Foundation published a report on its website in January 2000, concluding that the preponderance of the evidence pointed toward a relationship between Jefferson and Hemings that resulted in four surviving children.

That relationship began in Paris. It is impossible to know precisely how or when. But it is possible to deduce why. Sally Hemings was a lovely young woman of sixteen or seventeen, who contrasted greatly with the educated and vocal aristocratic French women whose free expression of political ideas so distressed Jefferson. Domesticity was Sally Hemings's venue; care of Jefferson's rooms was her job. Nor was the age difference a problem. Jefferson and his elder daughter had teasingly encouraged James Madison's courtship of Kitty Floyd, a woman almost twenty years his junior, while in Philadelphia; and when Martha's future father-in-law took a second wife, no one batted an eye at the thirty-one years that separated them. Sally Hemings reminded Jefferson of the home he missed and likely of his wife, who was, after all, her half sister. Of course, at home, slave women were frequent targets of their owners' desire; and although Jefferson hated confrontation, preferring persuasion rather than force, his actions were entirely in line with the presumptions of all masters in a slave society. Such a woman answered all that Jefferson needed, without the complications of a broken deathbed pledge, an unwanted stepmother for his daughters, and a second set of heirs.

The calculations of this relationship were considerably more complicated for Sally Hemings. "She was just beginning to understand the French language well," her son Madison related in 1873, "and in France she was free, while if she returned to Virginia she would be re-enslaved." Undoubtedly she and James had talked about staying. He was equipped with a skill, and unwilling to sound like the country people so often hired for menial labor in the city, he had hired a tutor who would school him in aristocratic French. James Hemings was planning for his future clientele, and they were not in Virginia. Sally too had a marketable skill as a femme de chambre. And they both knew French law would be on their side if they pressed for their freedom. But if she stayed, she would never see the rest of her family again. She would never again see the breathtaking views from Monticello or experience the softness of a Virginia spring. The beauties of Albemarle County tugged at the heartstrings of Monticello's slaves as well as its master's.

As Jefferson's thoughts turned toward returning home, he made it clear to Sally Hemings that he wanted her to accompany him. But, according to Madison, she refused. Thus began Jefferson's persistent campaign of persuasion. "To induce her to do so he promised her extraordinary privileges," Madison continued, "and made a solemn pledge that her children should be freed at the age of twenty-one years." From their subsequent history, we can guess what some of these privileges were. Neither Sally Hemings nor her children would be forced to work "in the ground," the common phrase for agricultural work. Unlike Jefferson's other slaves, her children would not go to work until they were fourteen years old. They would spend their childhood at her side. Their clothing would be better than that of most slaves. Neither she nor her children would be compelled to serve Jefferson's daughters, her contemporaries.

The most extraordinary privilege that Sally Hemings won in her own treaty, as Madison called it, was freedom for her children. It was a remarkable promise, given and accepted, although she knew that no court in the United States would force Jefferson to keep it. Her son's words suggest that Sally Hemings was already pregnant with Jefferson's child as she deliberated. "During that time," Madison Hemings related, "my mother became Mr. Jefferson's concubine, and when he was called back home she was enceinte by him." Strictly speaking, the word *concubine* refers to the legal status occupied by a woman who lives with a man without marrying him. But marriage between a master and slave was a legal impossibility in every state; nor was Sally Hemings Jefferson's mistress, since he was not married. But Madison's use of the word to describe his mother's relationship with Jefferson is tinged with his own pain and humiliation at his mother's perpetually inferior status. She would never acquire the honor and respect that came with being a wife.

Madison's use of the French-derived word *enceinte* is also curious and equally suggestive. In its most common usage, it means pregnant. However, it has a longer history dating back to the medieval period, when it referred to the outer wall of a castle. Surrounded by moats, the castle's outer fortification could be breached only by a drawbridge, lowered from inside. That is, it served as a defensive military boundary. In an account of his mother's Paris negotiations with his father, Madison used not one but two martial terms: *treaty* and *enceinte*. Returning to slavery in Virginia, Sally Hemings may not have had the leverage to refuse Jefferson when he wanted access to her body. But her body certainly formed the line of fortification for her children. Through her body, the hereditary tie to slavery mandated in Virginia law in 1662 would be broken. In her line, she would be the last slave.

So when Jefferson finally received the long-awaited word from Congress granting him permission to come home, she had a life-altering decision to make. Whether their relationship would continue depended upon Sally Hemings. Perhaps she weighed her options in long conversations with her brother. Or perhaps she was already quite sure about where she wanted to live her life. In the end, Madison tells us, "in consequence of his promise, on which she implicitly relied, she returned with him to Virginia."

Transitions

. . . .

1789

. . . .

ONLY TWO DAYS AFTER JEFFERSON crossed the Place Louis XV and witnessed an angry Paris mob beat back Swiss and German mercenaries, another Paris crowd stormed the Bastille on July 14, 1789. It was the explosion that the king, the new National Assembly, and even diplomats like Jefferson had, with cautious optimism, hoped could be averted. In his role as American ambassador, Jefferson had enjoyed a front-row seat to the unfolding drama as France lurched, step by step, toward revolution. He had attended the first meeting of the Estates General at Versailles in May. A representative body composed of three estates—clergy, nobility, and commoners—the Estates General never acquired the status of a political institution over its almost five-hundred-year history; rather it was called only occasionally by French monarchs. It was in his desperation to deal with the worsening state of his nation's finances—in large part a result of its expensive participation in the American Revolution—that Louis XVI called the Estates General into being that spring. The question of taxes was almost immediately overshadowed, however, by that of representation, that is, the distribution of power. Would each estate have one vote, thus giving the advantage to the king when the first two estates outvoted the common people, the Third Estate, two to one? Or, would each individual representative have a vote, giving the advantage to the greater numbers of the Third Estate?

Jefferson followed the debates closely, attending the meetings at Versailles almost daily in May and June. There he witnessed the growing impasse between clergy and nobles on one side and the Third Estate on the other. Impatient, the Third Estate claimed the authority to conduct the nation's business and broke away in mid-June to form the National Assembly. They invited clergy and nobles to join them, but as equals. In doing so, they destroyed the notion that government should be based on a hierarchy of people, just as the American Revolution had so recently done. The king's concession, ordering the first two estates to accept the invitation of the third, had brokered the fragile peace Jefferson was enjoying that Sunday morning until furious nobles forced Louis to reconsider.

Jefferson decided to remove his daughters from the volatile city, although not because of the violence he knew would reverberate out from the streets of Paris into the provinces. Almost a year earlier, he had written to Congress asking for leave to return home, "with a view," as he diplomatically put it, "to place my daughters in the society & care of their friends." But he was a worried father. At seventeen, Martha had arrived at a marriageable age, and he had decided it was time to separate her from the temptations of French high society before she could be swept off her feet by a glittering aristocratic suitor. He had been thinking about this since the previous summer but had wanted the girls to stay in Paris long enough for Maria to perfect her French. By the explosive summer of 1789, however, "the necessity of my going is so imperious," he anxiously told James Madison, "that I shall be in a most distressing dilemma" if the family could not leave before the winter, when travel would become even more hazardous.

One wonders why the necessity had become "imperious." Martha certainly did not want to go. She had arrived in Paris a girl, but had grown into a cosmopolitan young woman. A year after their arrival in France, she was speaking French as easily as English, Jefferson admitted, while his secretaries "Humphries, Short, and myself are scarcely better at it than when we landed." Language was only the first mark of her cultural immersion. Martha was becoming French in other ways: in her religion (as we have seen), dress, appreciation of fashion, manners, and perhaps her views on love and marriage as well. And even in the few letters that survive from this period, it is plain that she was gaining confidence in her own voice. In Paris, she had formed and was unafraid to make clear her abhorrence of slavery (months before Sally Hemings arrived) and an interest in politics. These were developments that could easily alarm a republican from Virginia who infinitely preferred a society in which women were "too wise to wrinkle their heads" with the subject, as Jefferson diplomatically put it, to that which was "filled with political debates into which both sexes enter with equal eagerness."

Martha had not always cared about such things. As a child in Philadelphia, she had been so inattentive to her dress, for example, that Eliza Trist had quietly suggested that Jefferson may want to mention it in his next letter to her. Nor did Martha's admission to the convent school effect an immediate change, as indicated by Marie de Botidoux's recollection of her coffee-stained aprons and Jefferson's reproach that when she went abroad from the convent for visits, she was to change out of her uniform. Yet in her latter days at Panthemont she was receiving commissions from Bettie Hawkins in London to buy her a cloak, advise her about the latest fashion in hats "chez vous," and consult with others to "enquire what *skins* are the most in fashion for *Pelises*—a pale pink satin trimm'd with either white or red Foxes skin?" Martha's newly acquired taste pleased; Bettie thought "the cloak you have sent me, is the most beautiful thing of the kind I ever recollect to have seen." Jefferson's accounts also reveal her heightened interest in fashion, which began just before her withdrawal from the school in late April 1789 and increased steadily thereafter. Jefferson recorded expenditures for luxury summer fabrics, gloves, silks, shoes, stays, and a hat—and that was just in the month of May!

These purchases document preparations for Martha Jefferson's more formal entry into French society, at a time in her life when courtship and marriage loomed large on her horizon and marital calculations were of the utmost importance. The notes and letters she received from her school friends (which, significantly, she kept for the rest of her life) allow us to overhear their conversations, even when we cannot listen to Martha's side of them. As we have seen, these young women straddled the precarious divide between respectability and infamy, no small challenge in a school designed to maintain their childish innocence, even as they were expected to know how to fend off assaults on it. They shared stories, passed judgment, and spent hours considering the workings of the marriage market.

An English classmate named Rachel Dashwood was the subject of much discussion. Her "bold" conduct led Bettie Hawkins to fear for her "light character," although she hoped that separation from the bad influence of her "*infamous* cousin" might result in both "better principles" and "a little more virtue." Martha's opinion was more charitable on the subject of Miss Dashwood, but she, too, indulged in gossip about her. "The story you told me today of her and the Eaton boys really shocked me," Bettie gasped in response. Martha liked to tease Marie de Botidoux about her beau, apparently in front of their other friends. "I wrote some nonsense to Botidoux last week about Boident," Elizabeth Tufton told Martha. "I hope I have not affronted her. If I have it is all your fault, so you must prepare to be well scolded Tuesday."

Martha had her own romances and suffered teasing in turn. Her friend Julia Annesley noticed her early first crush: the Irish-born Abbé Edgeworth de Firmont. "Do you know I have an idea the Abbe has rather—a—a—a—penchant for you—" Julia began, before finishing slyly, "Oh Lord I beg your pardon, it is owing to your learning your lessons so well." A week later, ostensibly offended that Martha had not yet answered her note, Julia pretended to pout. "I wish out of mere spite that the Abbe may scold you tomorrow. I do not care—I think that is the greatest mortification you could possibly experience, therefore I wish it you—I am sure you look very pretty now you read this—Lord!" she laughed, mindful of her friend's fair skin, easily prone to blushing. "What a—pretty—color you have."

Well beyond the stage of first crushes by her last summer in Paris, Martha was sixteen, old enough among her aristocratic acquaintances to be seriously considered in marriage. In August 1789, Elizabeth Tufton thought she had detected a secret crush. "You cannot think how I laughed yesterday on somebody's asking me whether I was in love with Tom," she wrote from London, "upon which I answered that I was not but that I knew an American young lady who admired him above all things in the world."

Even though she had returned to England, Bettie Hawkins also thought she caught a whiff of romance. "I thank you for the Italian verses, which by the bye you never sent me—let me add en passant [in passing] that *absences* generally proceed from les affaires du Coeur cela ne fait ciel [affairs of the heart and not just out of the blue]," she wrote. Surely only Martha's preoccupation with a romance could explain her failure to keep up her correspondence with Bettie. "I ask no questions as one is shy," Bettie teased before turning to persuasion to extract more information. "*I have heard* of making those kinds of *confidences*." Precisely which romance kept Martha so distracted is difficult to say; there appears to have been several possibilities.

In addition to the mysterious Tom, there was an American, a Mr. St. John, who confessed to Marie de Botidoux that Martha was his first passion. St. John had been a student at Messieurs Loiseau and Lemoine's Institution Pour le Jeune Noblesse (school for the young nobleman) on the rue de Berri. From his perch across the street from the Hôtel de Langeac, St. John "spent the nights at his window, *contemplating your house*," Marie wrote to Martha years later. His account shocked Marie, who had never heard Martha mention him. But she remembered that Martha had received and then returned a ring from an unnamed young man. "Well, it is precisely me," St. John told Marie.

Several people appeared to have noticed that William Short, Jefferson's distant relative and secretary, had caught Martha's eye. He had many qualities to recommend him: He, too, was enamored of all things French, including making serious if not wholly effective attempts to learn the language; he was handsome and personable; and her father liked and trusted him. Indeed, when Jefferson left Paris, he left the management of his home, the Hôtel de Langeac, and his business affairs in Short's capable hands. Nabby Adams found him a sociable man who possessed pleasing manners, "without the least formality, or affectation of any kind," and he was a favorite of her mother's as well. Martha and Short had been thrown together during the summer of 1787, when Jefferson took his seven-week European tour. Short checked in on her frequently at the convent and delivered Jefferson's letters to her. Once the girls left Panthemont and returned to Jefferson's home for good, she would have seen even more of him.

The forty-four-year-old Duke of Dorset took an interest in these courtship proceedings as well; his niece Elizabeth Tufton once con-

Remaining behind in Paris after Jefferson's departure, William Short, whom Jefferson once called his "adoptive son," was entrusted with his diplomatic duties. Short served as the American chargé d'affaires in France until 1792, before going on to posts in the Netherlands and Spain. Disappointed in a long-standing love affair with a French noblewoman and in being passed over for the ambassadorship to Russia, Short returned to the United States for good in 1810.

veyed his message to Martha "that he hopes you like *Mr Short* as much as ever." But his words may have been the cutting sarcasm of a jilted rival. Martha had been much in the company of the duke and his nieces in the summer of 1789. A friend had noticed that "the duke seemed to care very much about you, which I am not surprised, my dear Jef—his choice can only honor him and make many, many people jealous." But when he offered Martha a diamond ring, she refused it, so he was forced to content himself with sending a simple ring instead as a token of his "fond remembrance."

Although she had spurned a duke, Martha's romance with Short did not go smoothly. It is impossible to know what happened to cause their rupture, but in the aftermath, each spoke peevishly about the other. Martha did not even want to hear his name mentioned, and Short did not wish her well. After Martha's departure from Paris, Elizabeth Tufton told her to look for a letter her sister had written that their uncle had "sent to the American charge d'affaires [Short], (I will not mention names for fear of offending you), who has promised to forward it." When Marie de Botidoux inquired of Short for news of Martha's return voyage to Virginia, he was still angry. "Mlle Jefferson was still at Harbor," Short informed her, her departure held up by "contrary winds." With no sign that the winds would let up, he feared that "the friends of Mlle Botidoux will have a very disagreeable journey." He added darkly, "There is one"—and by this he meant Martha—"who deserves it."

Marriage, of course, was serious business for women, who surrendered their names, legal identity, property, and bodies to their husbands with the pronouncement of their wedding vows. For all the levity of the young girls' letters, the calculations in choosing a husband were a vital part of their conversations. Perhaps remembering her own parents' loving marriage as she learned about matchmaking in aristocratic circles, Martha was incredulous to hear the manner in which some European men searched for wives. "I recollect you would not believe that now & then people advertise for a wife," Bettie Hawkins wrote from London, enclosing just such an ad from *The Morning Post* and hoping "you will believe your *own* eyes." In another letter, Bettie wrote of her forthcoming marriage in May 1788 to twenty-one-year-old Henry Francis Roper Curzon, recounting his credentials. "All I can tell you concerning him is that he is of an excelling family, his father is brother to Lord Leynham, whose title & estate Mr Curson in all probability will have," she wrote, a pragmatic nineteen-year-old, laying out her assessment of her own prospects for wealth, title, and security as his wife. "He would be a Baronet were he not a Catholick," she continued, "but this will luckily not prevent his being Lord Leynham, should the present heir *kick the bucket*." And happily she could also report that her intended "is remarkably sensible & handsome."

A year later their friend Julia Annesley married "a Mr Maxwell, oldest son of the Bishop of Meath." There was a cost, however, to that apparently favorable match. "One may conclude her sentiments on *an important point are changed*," the new Mrs. Curzon intimated tactfully, "or this marriage cou'd never have taken place." When Julia had left Panthemont she bemoaned the "fatal vessel" that had taken her away from France and from Abbé Edgeworth, Martha's beloved teacher and, it turned out, Julia's as well. "A charming man!" Julia wrote after her landfall in Dover. "What obligations am I not under to him! He has been the means of my salvation." Heavy-hearted, she feared for her newly acquired Catholicism in Anglican England. Her fears were justified; to marry the son of an Anglican bishop, she would have to abjure her new faith. Weighing her options, she decided to do so. Later that year, Bettie Curzon heard that Mr. Maxwell had become Lord Farnham, and his new bride "is now Lady Julia, which was her wish."

As a student at Panthemont, Julia Annesley had known she wanted a title and that she would marry to secure it. But for all her youthful teasing of her American friend's infatuation ("remember, *Priests* can't marry," she had teased), Julia learned that marital arrangements were about rank and wealth. In exchange for her future livelihood, Julia Annesley traded away a religion decidedly unfashionable in Britain. (Catholics could not vote in Britain until 1829.) As their own weddings approached, the lighthearted banter about the making and breaking of marriages grew serious. Two days before her wedding, Bettie Hawkins confessed to Martha that "I am really *un peu dérangée dans la tête* [a little deranged in my mind], the idea that I quit all my friends, my dearest and nearest relatives so soon, to follow a man who may soon forget the many promises he has made me. . . ." She trailed off. Her hard-nosed mother, clearly happy about the promising match, was unsympathetic; Bettie's fears revealed her "an idiot," she said. "Pity your distressed friend," Bettie wrote disconsolately.

Martha certainly entered into the spirit of courtship gossip and readily received her friends' marital updates, but she seems to have resisted the idea of marriage as mere negotiation of money and titles. When their classmate Miss Broadhead became engaged to "a Mr Dashwood, a most amiable young man, heir to a title & ten thousand a year," Bettie Curzon feared that Martha "may accuse him of the same fault for which you so *unmercifully* blame poor Sophie": mercenary motives for marriage. Martha wanted a love match, which Bettie believed that "you Jef—who I believe is capable of a sincere attachment" would be able to have. Like her aristocratic friends, Martha took her status and rank for granted as a natural consequence of her father's; she would no more sacrifice money for love than would her friends. But as an American, she rejected the titles so coveted by her aristocratic classmates. Still, after a five-year French sojourn, in her dress, self-assurance, and maturing ideas about courtship, love, and marriage, Martha Jefferson was no longer the ingénue her father had brought to Paris. By her final months there, Martha had grown out of her shyness, carrying herself with the self-assurance the more experienced Bettie knew was "necessary in the world, where every man judges you from the opinion you seem yourself to have of your abilities." And she had learned about the complex calculations she would have to make when it was time to select her own husband.

THE TRANSITION EFFECTED BY her years in France was much less dramatic for Maria than for her sister, in large part because of her age. Entering Panthemont at nine rather than twelve, and leaving the city shortly after her eleventh birthday, she was too young for the affairs of the heart that preoccupied the older students. The outline of her day and studies would have closely resembled that remembered by Hélène Massalska at the Abbaye-aux-Bois, another elite Parisian school. As they had been for Martha, French lessons would have been Maria's first priority; reading, penmanship, and arithmetic would follow. But they were not purely elementary; Maria had not arrived in Paris unschooled. Abigail Adams had exclaimed about Maria's "so mature an understanding, so womanly a behavior, and so much sensibility united" and noticed her love of books, all a credit to Elizabeth Eppes's training. "Her reading, her writing, her manners in general shew what everlasting obligations we are all under to you," Jefferson wrote gratefully to his sister-in-law, days after Maria's arrival. So it is not a surprise that Maria did well in her new school. After only a year, Jefferson told Elizabeth Eppes that Maria had begun to speak French "easily enough and to read as well as English. She will begin Spanish in a few days, and has lately begun the harpsichord and drawing."

Unlike Martha in her first weeks of isolation at Panthemont, Maria had an elder sister who gradually initiated her to her new surroundings. Martha's devoted friends, many of whom were English, also doted on Maria. Bettie Hawkins and Julia Annesley were there when she arrived in July 1787, as were several others whose close friendship with Martha was marked by the treasured exchange of a lock of hair. Maria's tendency "to attach herself to those who are kind to her" (as her father had observed) had served her well in the absence of her parents. "Her temper, her disposition, her sensibility are all formed to delight," Abigail Adams, too, had thought. And from her loving aunt Eppes to the strangers who vied to have her sit on their laps in the coach that bore her from the coast to Paris, people were naturally drawn to the endearing Maria Jefferson.

Within two weeks of her entrance into the school, she had secured the affection of Martha's friends and of the nuns as well. Even after her departure from Panthemont, Bettie Hawkins begged for letters from Maria, urging her not to worry about neatness. Eighteenth-century manners required that writers first draft their letter and then make a fair copy to send. But Bettie waived that rule for Maria. "It does not signify you know, if well or ill between friends. If it did, I should certainly write this over again, for in my life I never saw such a wretched scrawl," she admitted merrily. From London, Bettie sent storybooks and kisses to Maria and reassurances that she would "answer her charming letter." Elizabeth and Caroline Tufton never wrote to Martha without enclosing their love to her younger sister as well. Maria also made friends of her own, such as Kitty (Catherine) Church, the niece of Alexander Hamilton. So it was with some justification that Jefferson could report almost immediately to Elizabeth Eppes that Maria had become "a universal favorite with the young ladies and the mistresses" at Panthemont.

His view that Maria was "perfectly happy" at the school was probably more optimistic than accurate, however. As pampered and petted as Maria was by her friends, the regimen at Panthemont, presided over by the Abbess, was a far cry from the individual attention, loving care, and indulgence she had known at Eppington. Caroline Tufton must have noticed Maria's unhappiness at the convent school, for she guessed that after their return to Virginia, Maria was much happier there.

Indeed, Maria's thoughts in Europe appear to have been almost entirely preoccupied with Virginia. When in London, she would sometimes sit on Abigail Adams's lap, Adams told her sister, "and describe to me the parting with her aunt, who brought her up, the obligation she was under to her, and the love she had for her little cousins, till the tears would stream down her cheeks." She must have done the same thing with her father in her first week in Paris, for he assured Eppes "it is impossible for a child to prove a more sincere affection to an absent person than she does to you." A year later, her father could tell his sister-in-law that Maria still "looks to you as her best future guide and guardian," that is, like a mother. While they were in school, Jefferson's daughters spent Sundays with him, talking of nothing but their relatives at home in Virginia. But even if they spent every day of the week together, Jefferson believed, "the theme would still be the same."

There was another layer to Maria's unhappiness at Panthemont: her fear of displeasing her father. Although Maria notoriously hated letter-writing, she had composed a long letter—unfortunately lost to us now—to her aunt Eppes about her voyage, in time for Jefferson to enclose with his notification of her safe arrival. But a year removed from that traumatic experience, though her face "kindled with love" every time she heard her aunt's name, Maria could not bring herself to write another. It was not for lack of desire, as Jefferson knew. He would keep suggesting that she try again, he told Eppes, but he already knew it was hopeless. "I know she will undertake it at once as she has already done a dozen times. She gets all the apparatus, places herself very formally with pen in hand, and it is not till after all this and rummaging her head thoroughly that she calls out 'indeed Papa I do not know what to say, you must help me.'" Since Jefferson always refused, "her good resolutions have always proved abortive and her letters ended before they were begun."

Historian Dumas Malone called Maria Jefferson a "reluctant correspondent" because letter-writing seemed to present an insurmountable challenge to her. It was, he concluded, "hard for her to learn to be her father's daughter," a failure according to Malone, who measured her entirely according to Jefferson's standards. But Malone did not consider several other possibilities, not least of which was Maria's disposition to please. A family story, told by an Eppes descendant in the 1860s, gives another variation of the scene Jefferson had sketched: "He seated his little daughter at the desk with a pen, ink and paper, told her the date, and left her to write. When he returned after a reasonable time, only the date was written, and the paper, so white and fair at the beginning, was blistered with her tears." When Maria returned to Virginia, the story continued, and was asked by her aunt why she had never written, she replied, "Oh, Aunt Eppes, I did want to and I tried, but I just couldn't. . . . If I had written to you, I would have told you everything, and Papa was going to read it all." With her father looking over her shoulder, she could not unburden herself of her loneliness or homesickness, afraid he would read a rebuke of his decision to send for her. Because just starting the letter to her sympathetic aunt would open the floodgates, little Maria restrained herself altogether.

In any event, Maria Jefferson had learned an important lesson in Virginia, where she learned to write. Her first letters, trying to stave off her move to Paris, ended in disaster. Although she had spoken her mind quite firmly, she was overruled. She had also seen her aunt suffer a similar fate, as letters became events to dread rather than anticipate. Ultimately, she must have wondered, what did it signify if she wrote or not? If letters were only going to hurt, why write them? Nor did letters serve Maria Jefferson as the cement of friendship they did for her elder sister. She had known a second mother that Martha had not. As she had learned at Eppington and in London, it was so much more satisfying to unburden herself with a loved one, seated side by side, a sympathetic arm around her shoulders, than to write a letter.

So Maria probably did not object when Jefferson withdrew his daughters from Panthemont in April 1789 to reunite them in a family circle at the Hôtel de Langeac. Situated in a newly developed neighborhood, the house had a large garden that was the delight of both Jefferson and his daughters. He liked to experiment with American plants, and his purchase in June 1786 of a badminton set suggests that Martha played there with her friends from the convent. Away from the dirt and smells of the city, the convenient location permitted easy access down the Champs to the east to the capital's center and, to the west, to the Bois de Boulogne (a massive park, still a Parisian favorite, where Adams and Jefferson both liked to walk) and the western suburbs.

Martha Jefferson remembered the house as a "very elegant one even for Paris with an extensive garden court and out buildings in the handsomest style." The three-story house itself was in the shape of a trapezoid, following the irregular shape of the lot. One entered the property through a gated courtyard off the quieter rue de Berri. The entrance hall opened into a large domed room, adjacent to which were a large oval salon illuminated by a skylight, a smaller salon, and a dining room. A grand staircase ascended to the second floor, which had an "oval salon overlooking the garden and three suites, each complete, in the French manner, with a bedroom, study, and dressing room." Jefferson's rooms were on the top floor. With its lighting, elegance, and modern plumb-

The Hôtel de Langeac (Parisians referred to their town homes as hôtels*), on the corner of the rue de Berri and the Champs-Élysées, was in the westernmost part of the city, just inside the Grille de Chaillot, one of many customs gates built to collect duties from farmers and merchants entering the city from the countryside. In this east-facing view, down the Champs toward the city center, Jefferson's home is the lower building on the left. In spite of the beauty of the elegant government building on the right, it was a hated symbol of the crown's power to tax.*

ing (Jefferson paid fifty livres each year to have water piped into the house), the Hôtel de Langeac was the epitome of French design and comfort.

We do not know which rooms the girls used on their weekend visits or after their withdrawal from the convent. Indeed, the house would have been quite full with Jefferson and his daughters, Sally and James Hemings, Petit, and five other French servants all lodged there. Short also lived there when he was in town, as did the American artist John Trumbull and other visitors. As the home and office of the American minister, the Hôtel de Langeac was a semipublic building, open to all Americans who needed his help. But it was also the place to which Jefferson had brought his daughters during their last winter at the school. They had contracted typhus during one of the worst winters in Paris's history. He made light of their illness to Elizabeth Eppes in December 1788, "an indisposition," he called it, from which Martha had recovered but Maria had not. It was "not sufficient however to confine her to her bed," he wrote, not wanting to alarm her aunt.

To John Trumbull a month later, he was more direct. "My daughters have been sick two months, and still continue sick; the younger very seriously so." In fact, Jefferson feared for her life. Maria suffered all the classic symptoms of the disease. Contracted from fleas or body lice, typhus strikes when the bacteria they carry enters the bloodstream after the victim has broken the skin by scratching. A very high fever then follows, sometimes for as long as two weeks. Extreme cases, such as Maria's seemed to be, can also induce delirium and a subsequent stupor. By the end of January, however, Maria was on the mend and, Jefferson hoped, out of danger. He would send the girls back to their school once they were fully recovered.

Their permanent return to his home a few months later, in April 1789, was a happier occasion, even if it had been prompted by yet another worrisome event: Martha's desire to join the convent. Martha nonetheless continued to correspond with her English friends who had left Panthemont before her and those who remained behind. Marie de Botidoux was crushed when Martha's father remained intractable in his decision to withdraw his daughters. "At last, dear Jefferson, it has been decided that you will not come back here," she wrote to Martha, disconsolate. "I did not want to believe it but, unfortunately, there is no reason to doubt it. You have no idea how sad I am. I cried last night despite all my attempts to turn my mind away from such thoughts, and I am crying again at this very moment." To relieve the pain of their separation, however, Martha received visitors at her father's home, especially Marie, and went out in company with them.

Jefferson ensured that Martha's last few months in Paris were enjoyable. According to a granddaughter, she was "introduced into society at the brilliant court of Louis the Sixteenth" and importuned her father to let her go to more balls than the three-per-week limit (he said no). No longer needing to request the Abbess's permission, Martha enjoyed promenades in the parks and gardens near the Hôtel de Langeac. She continued to frequent the Palais Royal, including an outing in late June with the Duke of Dorset and his nieces. "A Gentleman told me he had seen you," one friend wrote, impressed by the duke's attentions to Martha, "& that you remain'd there till it was quite duskish."

Jefferson also showered Martha with gifts. In addition to her new clothes, he bought her a ring, increased her monthly allowance by a factor of five, and paid for a whip as she resumed riding. These purchases signaled Jefferson's tacit acknowledgment that Martha had arrived at courtship age; he well understood that marriageable young women "of course require to be clothed more expensively than at any earlier period." But shopping for these new items was also meant to provide sufficient distraction and entertainment so that her last few months in Paris would wipe out any desire for the cloistered life of a nun.

THE SUMMER OF 1789 brought an enormous transition in the life of Sally Hemings as well. It is difficult to reconstruct her life at the Hôtel de Langeac during this period. Certainly an attraction was growing, at least on Jefferson's part, since Hemings was pregnant by the time they left Paris in September. We do know she left the house for a five-week period in early 1789, unexplained in Jefferson's accounts except for the notation that he paid "Dupré 5. Wks board of Sally." Although we know that Dupré was Jefferson's launderer, we do not know the dates of Sally's absence from his household. Annette Gordon-Reed has suggested that Hemings's stay with Dupré overlapped with the earlier period of the Jefferson girls' illness, when Maria was at her lowest ebb. Perhaps Jefferson sent Sally Hemings away to prevent her from contracting the disease, easily spread through body lice, after seeing its harrowing effects on Maria.

With the girls' return in April, Sally Hemings's duties may have changed as well. The care of Martha Jefferson's new silk gowns may have fallen to her, as well as dressing her hair, mending, running errands, and generally attending to the girls' requirements of a lady's maid. But Jefferson's expenditures rose for Sally Hemings as well, as she more frequently accompanied them in public. The 168 livres that Jefferson spent in April on Hemings's clothes does not compare with the single purchase of 229 livres' worth of silk for Martha; nor does the 25-livre fee for making Sally's clothes compare with the bill for 303 livres that Jefferson paid Martha's tailor. Still, it was a significant amount of money to invest in a servant's clothing, considering that her wages of twelve livres per month already exceeded that of the best-paid female domestics in the city. Certainly Hemings needed to be well dressed as she accompanied Martha, since servants' dress reflected their employer's status. But whether this expenditure constitutes evidence of Jefferson's growing interest in her, we cannot be sure.

In the course of her duties as Martha's maid, Sally Hemings met her friends and made an impression on them. In her letters to Martha, Marie de Botidoux asked to be remembered to "Mlle Sallie." But if anyone was confused about Sally Hemings's place in the Jefferson household, with knowing French discretion, they refrained from asking. It was not unusual in French families for poorer relations to serve their wealthier connections in exchange for bed and board; nor were sexual predations of masters on their female servants unusual either. The young but worldly-wise Botidoux took the unusual household configuration in stride, diplomatically using the honorific "mademoiselle" (which normally was never used to address servants) to signal her acceptance of Martha's lead that Hemings was not an ordinary servant.

That was just one of many ways in which Hemings learned something about her position in French society: Whatever her status in Virginia, as far as Parisians were concerned she was not a slave in France. Sally Hemings saw a great deal of aristocratic Paris in her attendance on Martha Jefferson. She ate fine French cooking (her brother was a master chef, after all), she chatted with Martha's aristocratic friends, and she learned about French social mores from overhearing their talk. Thus, Paris had taught Sally Hemings a great deal about society, rank, presentation, dress, and language in addition to her skills as a femme de chambre by the time Jefferson decided to return to Virginia.

Added to the intelligence and maturity the Eppeses had already seen in Hemings, these lessons would certainly have bolstered her confidence in herself and in her ability to enter into negotiations with her master about returning home. These conversations did not go well for Jefferson, who fell ill with a migraine at the beginning of September, as he often did when faced with stressful situations. "She refused to return with him," Madison said of his mother, when Jefferson received word of his leave. Hating confrontation, he began the campaign to win her consent instead. In the end, she trusted her judgment of the man who made so many promises in exchange for hers, and went back to Virginia.

Departure preparations were not as extensive as they would have been had Jefferson been leaving Paris permanently. Having applied for a temporary leave to escort his daughters home to Virginia, he fully anticipated returning the following spring. Thus, the Hôtel de Langeac was not topsy-turvy with the crating of eighty-five boxes of furniture, paintings, sculptures, and plates that William Short, left behind to tend to Jefferson's affairs, would have to contend with later. Rather, Martha and Maria shopped for gifts for their Virginia relatives and arranged for the careful packing of their French fashions. Sally Hemings may have persuaded her brother to escort her on the shopping trip that secured a lotion pot from a pharmacy on the fashionable rue de Richelieu, hard by the Palais Royal. Almost two centuries later, the cracked remnants of that pot would be excavated from the soil of Mulberry Row, Sally Hemings's first home on her return to Virginia.

Martha's Paris goodbyes were limited. Julia Annesley and Bettie Hawkins had left long before, of course. But it seems that the Tufton sisters, Elizabeth and Caroline, were prevented from seeing Martha by a collusion of their elders. "We are in such confusion ever since nine oclock this morning when the Duke decided to go to England tomorrow," Elizabeth wrote in haste to Martha one August morning. "The idea of parting with you hurt us more than we can describe, but as we have a great deal to do, we think it better not to see you." Martha sent them parting gifts, including a ring for Caroline. "I shall value it for your sake and I will never part with it," Caroline wrote gratefully from London. Still, it did not make up for the hurt of not being able to say their goodbyes in person, "but Mr Jefferson likewise told the Duke it was better not so we must submit." Elizabeth's rationalization that a last visit would be a "very painful task" best avoided echoes the soothing platitudes of her uncle and her friend's father. Rather more likely, the two men preferred to avoid the awkwardness of a last meeting that would underscore the spurned suitor's disappointment. As he waited at Cowes to embark for America, Jefferson wrote several letters to Paris friends, such as that to Madame de Corny admitting that "adieus are painful; therefore I left Paris without sending one to you." But at least

Jefferson could look forward to renewed acquaintances in the spring; as far as they knew, his daughters were going home forever.

Jefferson's efforts to find direct passage from Havre, on the French coast, to Virginia were fruitless, so he, his daughters, and James and Sally Hemings were forced to make a channel crossing to pick up a ship leaving from England. Leaving Paris on September 26, the family group arrived in Havre two days later, where they lingered for ten days waiting for a break in the miserable weather. Nathaniel Cutting, a Massachusetts sea captain who had helped Jefferson make his travel arrangements, was waiting with them. The night of September 30 was particularly bad, he remembered. "I do not recollect to have heard the Wind blow so very violently before, since I have known this Country," the experienced seaman wrote in his diary. After a couple of false starts, the Jefferson party arrived in Cowes on the Isle of Wight at two A.M. on October 9. Weary with seasickness from their rough twenty-six-hour crossing, they fell gratefully into the warm, dry beds Captain Cutting had secured for them at the Fountain Inn. There the family spent another thirteen days waiting for their ship, shopping and sightseeing. At Jefferson's invitation, Cutting frequently took tea with the family as they whiled away the days before finally departing England on October 23.

They sailed aboard the *Clermont*, which Jefferson had secured exclusively for his own party and his baggage. Under the supervision of "as bold a sailor as a judicious one should be," as Jefferson described him, the ship made the crossing in twenty-nine days. What Jefferson had feared from a two-leg voyage came to pass: They suffered a second bout of seasickness, more severe than the first. But after several days they were all well enough to enjoy the rest of a pleasant voyage. As she had two years earlier, Maria made friends during her travels. "Maria, who is at my elbow desires me to tell you she has not forgot you," Jefferson later wrote to Cutting with a smile.

The smooth passage ended as dramatically as it had begun, however. Approaching the Virginia coast, Martha remembered, they were surrounded by "as thick a mist as to render it impossible to see the pilot" who would have guided them into port. After three days, the captain decided to make a run for it, even though he had not yet seen the capes that mark the entrance to the James River. "We had to beat up against a strong head wind which carried away our topsail and were very near being run down by a brig coming out of port who having the wind in her favour was almost upon us before we could get out of the way," Martha recalled later, the frightening memory of near catastrophe still vivid. The family safely disembarked, but their travails were not over. Less than two hours after its arrival, the *Clermont* caught fire and would have been scuttled had not the flames been discovered just in time to prevent it. An agonized Jefferson waited to see if any of his papers of state survived. By sheer accident, the captain, having seen the doors to the Jefferson family quarters open after they had left the ship, closed them, keeping the flames from penetrating their staterooms. The thickness of the trunks likewise protected their new French clothes from destruction.

The shock of the change of scene from Paris to Norfolk confirmed Martha's worst fears. Small and incommodious, Norfolk still bore the scars of the Revolution, during which, as a thriving commercial port, it had been burned by the British in 1776. The family party would not have even been able to find any lodgings "but for the politeness of the gentlemen at the hotel (Lindsay's) who were kind enough to give up their own rooms for our accommodation." As it was, James Hemings had to sleep in a hammock. The contrast with their first Paris hotels (either of them) could not have dismayed Martha more.

Clearly she had confided her fears about what she would find in America to her friends: Elizabeth Tufton hoped that Martha would find that "the *idea* you had formed of America was an unfavorable one, and that you will spend your time more agreeably than you imagined." Martha must have sketched a bleak picture of Charlottesville to Bettie Hawkins Curzon, since she also wanted a full accounting when Martha returned. "Pray tell me if you have Balls, Plays & all the amusements we enjoy in Europe?" the new Mrs. Curzon wanted to know, both curious and anxious. Assuming that in the backwoods of Virginia "you cannot get every article of dress with as much facility as we do," she also helpfully offered to procure for her anything Martha might want. Privy to many of her friend's secrets, Marie de Botidoux knew that Martha would have preferred even a nun's life in the convent in Paris to going back to life in Virginia. And although newly met as they waited in

Havre, Captain Cutting had noticed in Martha "some emotion of chagrin at the thought of being separated from the engaging circle" of her friends in Paris. Martha's heart sank as she surveyed the town before her. Norfolk presented such a dismal view that even Maria sobbed her distress at what she saw. *"Mais c'est bien different de Paris!"* she cried.

Maria was eventually comforted upon her arrival at Eppington, where she was reunited with her beloved aunt and uncle Eppes. There she met the twins, Matilda and Mary, who had been born in her absence. Maria's delight that Mary was named in her honor had been one of the bright spots of her Paris exile. Although they had made landfall on the twenty-third of November, it had taken the Jefferson party almost three weeks to reach Eppington. In the meantime, they had proceeded slowly through Virginia, stopping to visit friends and relatives. They had joyous reunions with Anne Skipwith, the half sister of his dead wife, and her husband, Henry, at their plantation of Hors du Monde, and with Jefferson's sisters Martha Carr at Spring Forest and Mary Bolling at Chestnut Grove. They stopped as well at the Randolphs' home at Tuckahoe, where Jefferson had spent so much of his childhood. There Martha regaled her cousin Judith with the stories of Paris that, five years earlier, Judith had predicted would be so entertaining. At some point on their trip home, she met again her cousin Thomas; they saw each other with different eyes now after their European education, hers in Paris, his in Edinburgh.

Two days before Christmas they arrived home at last. After a six-year absence, the master of Monticello returned to a joyous welcome. "The negroes discovered the approach of the carriage as soon as it reached Shadwell," Martha recalled at length, "and such a scene I never witnessed in my life. They collected in crowds around it, and almost drew it up the mountain by hand. The shouting, etc., had been sufficiently obstreperous before, but the moment it arrived at the top it reached the climax. When the door of the carriage was opened, they received him in their arms and bore him to the house, crowding around and kissing his hands and feet—some blubbering and crying—others laughing." Such a homecoming for Jefferson, seventeen-year-old Martha, and eleven-year-old Maria was indelibly impressed in their memories. The story was told and retold, Martha remembered, embellished by later generations of slaves who swore that "the horses were actually 'unhitched,' and the vehicle drawn by the strong black arms up to . . . the door at Monticello."

Somewhere in the scene that day—perhaps—was sixteen-year-old Sally Hemings, pregnant for the first time, with her master's child. It was a homecoming for her as well. She had been gone from Monticello as long as Jefferson had been. It was her childhood home, from which she had been called as a girl of nine or ten, a maid to a child. She returned a woman, committed to a lifetime relationship with Monticello's master. A new chapter was beginning for her and for the Hemings family: As Jefferson's "substitute for a wife" (in the phrase of one of his neighbors), Hemings was positioned to defeat the reach of slavery for her children and to ameliorate slavery's impact on her extended family.

But while the records reverberate with the exuberant celebration of the white family's return, they are utterly silent about Sally's. She may have arrived earlier with her brother James, if he had gone on ahead from Richmond. James was with Jefferson as late as December 10, when Jefferson gave him money to pay for their laundry, but there are no further notations in Jefferson's account book for the rest of the trip to track James's whereabouts. It is impossible to know.

The silence of the record is typical of white disregard for the significance of slaves' lives; it is striking how infrequently slaveholding families, particularly women, discussed the slaves on whom their daily lives depended. At the same time, the silence also underscores the deep significance of Sally Hemings in Thomas Jefferson's life as he returned to Monticello. As time would tell, Jefferson would arrange his life to accommodate the promises he made to her; he would refuse to acknowledge the accusations of his political enemies when they exposed his relationship with her; he never banished her from Monticello when it might have been easier for Martha and Maria if he did. His discretion protected his reputation as a Virginia gentleman, it is true; but it also provided some cover for Sally Hemings and her children. So effective was his silence, as Annette Gordon-Reed observed, it brought "down a curtain on his relations with Hemings and their children so heavy and thick that it took over a century and a half to effectively raise it."

OF COURSE, BOTH JAMES and Sally Hemings returned to slavery. Although France's revolution was just beginning, the American Revolution was over, concluded with the Treaty of Paris in 1783. But the changes it had effected for enslaved Americans were severely limited. Jefferson's own attempt to condemn slavery in the Declaration of Independence had been deleted by the Continental Congress. Even though Jefferson had—inaccurately—framed slavery as a grievous evil imposed on the colonies by a corrupt monarchy, its condemnation in an American founding document could have had far-reaching implications. Instead the Constitution, just barely ratified by the time Jefferson got back from France, engraved in the country's legal framework a variety of protections for slavery, not least of which was a provision that forbade Congress from ending the slave trade for twenty years.

Still, a combination of the Revolution's egalitarian rhetoric, economic considerations, and the press of evangelical Christianity had resulted in a more explicit reconsideration of slavery as a national institution after the war. By 1804, every state north of Delaware had either abolished slavery altogether or enacted a program of gradual emancipation. In the Upper South, particularly on the Delmarva Peninsula on the eastern shore of the Chesapeake, thousands of slaves would be manumitted, that is, formally freed. By 1810, free blacks formed almost a quarter of the black population in Maryland, three quarters in Delaware, and almost a third in the capital district.

The scope of those changes had not reached Albemarle County, however. And to the extent that the horrors of slavery were ameliorated somewhat for Sally Hemings and her brother, it was because of the choices Jefferson was free to make. His decisions may have been prompted by sentiment, to honor his wife's memory; they may have been selfish, to fool himself into thinking he was a benevolent slaveholder. They may have been entirely pragmatic, suiting his own purposes. Whatever his motives, they do not change the fact that like all southern slaveholders, Jefferson was the final law on his plantations. Jefferson would eventually free James Hemings, but grudgingly and not for seven long years. And he extracted a grievous price for doing so:

James would pay for his freedom at the cost of training his younger brother Peter, whose new skills ensured his captivity for the rest of his life.

Sally Hemings had been promised freedom for her children in her own remarkable "treaty" (as Madison called it) of Paris in exchange for her return to Virginia. But unlike the diplomatic treaty that ended the Revolution, Hemings's received no fanfare; it was made behind closed doors. It was both secret and unenforceable. Yet both treaties bore deep significance. Both were deeply rooted in past relationships: centuries of enmity between England and France that indeed would persist beyond 1783, and almost two centuries of slavery, legislation, and social practices that in their persistence were emblematic of the inconsistencies and limits of the Revolution. Both also looked forward, however: the first as it announced international recognition of the infant United States and its republican experiment, and the second in its promise that the ancient bonds of slavery would be broken for Hemings's descendants.

The transatlantic revolutions also prompted fresh questions about the role of women in society. This was not an entirely new subject; Enlightenment figures had been debating the nature and role of women since the seventeenth century. A variety of theories had crystallized into two main competing views. The first, promoted by the French philosopher René Descartes (1596–1650), asserted that men and women were equal; since both could think ("I think, therefore I am," Descartes famously wrote), both were set apart as equally human from the animals. The second, popular in Scottish Enlightenment circles, understood men and women as complementary beings, possessing characteristics unique to each sex's function in the world but incomplete without the other. Several French writers followed Descartes's thinking, most notably François Poulain de La Barre. Poulain's *On the Equality of the Sexes* (1673) pointedly took the common ability of men and women to reason as a starting point rather than as an analytical conclusion in his thought. Thus, rather than arguing as so many male thinkers did that women's inferior intellect justified male governance over them, he concluded that it was men's application of force, defying nature's dictates, that explained centuries of women's subordination.

Not until Mary Wollstonecraft, at the end of the eighteenth century, would a British writer follow Poulain's thinking. Instead the view of Scottish Enlightenment thinkers had overwhelmingly prevailed. David Hume believed that, over the centuries, the nurturing female had gradually exercised a civilizing influence over the more brutal male, resulting in progressively more rational civilizations. (The English philosopher John Locke, much read by prominent American revolutionaries, dismissed women entirely from his political tracts, however, believing that self-government could work only among independent men.) The eventual triumph of reason, Hume anticipated, would temper men's brutish nature, raise women's status, and produce a harmonious society. But even so, it could never forecast the equality of the sexes, since they were so fundamentally different.

Certainly Martha Jefferson's readings at Panthemont in history, moral philosophy, and literature assured her that she was of the class of thinking, rational beings. Indeed, her literacy alone marked her apart from most European women; only 27 percent of French women and 40 percent of English women could read by the end of the eighteenth century. But from her childhood, her education—however extraordinary it may have been by Virginia standards—had been circumscribed by gender conventions and by her father. Jefferson had made that quite clear in a letter he had written to her from Annapolis when she was eleven. "If you love me then, strive . . . to acquire those accomplishments which I have put in your power," he wrote, assuring her that her efforts "will go far towards ensuring you the warmest love of your affectionate father." Although the boundaries of music, dancing, drawing, writing, and French widened from Philadelphia to Panthemont, Martha Jefferson's opportunities—like those of all young girls—remained limited to those allowed and provided for by men.

But France had given Martha a different view and vision. She grew up in a kind of semi-independence from her father during her years in the convent, and her friendships with both English and French aristocratic women had refined her manners, polished her appearance, and bolstered her confidence. Like them, she was an eager spectator to the political theater playing out on French streets. She forever kept a red, white, and blue cockade, the kind sported by Lafayette's officers; and she told her story about witnessing Lafayette's procession into Paris so many times, it eventually found its way into print in the early twentieth century. Two days after the storming of the Bastille, the popular general had met the king on the outskirts of Paris and escorted him to the city center in an effort to calm the unrest. Sixty thousand people, armed with pistols, swords, and a variety of improvised weapons, formed a dubious welcoming party as they lined the streets through which the king, the assembly members, and Lafayette passed. Watching the excitement from the safety of her window perch, Martha Jefferson heard the roar of the crowd as Lafayette approached. Looking up, he spied Martha and bowed. "Her young friends declared they were filled with envy," a great-granddaughter reported at this mark of favor.

Should women remain on the sidelines in such times, however, content merely to accept the homage of men who lived in the thick of the action? Jefferson certainly thought so, but to his distaste he found this question increasingly debated in the salons he had previously enjoyed frequenting. Indeed, the salons, the acceptable sites of female intellectual engagement, had changed over the course of that crucial decade of the 1780s: Those that had earlier been devoted to literature, philosophy, and science had become increasingly politicized. From his regular attendance at her salon, for example, the American Revolutionary Gouverneur Morris recognized that Madame de Tessé's zeal for republicanism far outstripped his own. In that, she was hardly alone; Morris had observed in his diary that 1780s France was a "woman's country" in which wives were as keen to discuss politics as their husbands. Morris was entranced, but Jefferson grumbled sourly, "Society is spoilt by it."

French women of all ranks enthusiastically embraced political participation, as the events of the summer of 1789 signaled new possibilities for governing: a constitutional monarchy in which the people, previously subjects to a king, were recognized as citizens with equal rights, guaranteed by a national constitution. Madame de Staël's passionate interest in politics never wavered, even after she was forced into exile; in 1797 she published *On the Current Circumstances Which Can End the Revolution,* criticizing the excesses of the Jacobins and urging the creation of a representative government based on popular sovereignty. In 1791, Olympe de Gouges, the self-educated daughter of a butcher, published her "Declaration of the Rights of Woman and Female Citizen," an essay contesting the view of the world-renowned "Declaration of the Rights of Man," adopted by French revolutionaries in 1789, that women were inherently inferior to men. Women whose names are forever lost to us took their places in formation alongside the national guard, following the drumbeat as they marched Paris streets; they demanded (and won) entry into local electoral assemblies, occupied the National Assembly the night that thousands of other women marched on Versailles, and gathered on the Champ de Mars (familiar today to millions of visitors to the Eiffel Tower) to insist that the sovereign will of the people be considered as the assembly deliberated about what to do with the king when he was recaptured after his escape attempt. No wonder Marie de Botidoux had exulted in her republicanism. The heady excitement as the old gave way to the new was intoxicating, bringing forth the possibility that a new order might embrace the contributions of women. And who better to influence, inform, and lead than educated women of rank—such as those who had studied at Panthemont?

Across the ocean, the American Revolution had also politicized women. White women formed chapters of the Daughters of Liberty that ran spinning bees, published patriotic appeals, and supported boycotts to stiffen the resistance against Britain. During the war, they bought war bonds, donated food and clothing to the army, and stoically stood behind their soldiering husbands and sons. Men's public recognition of women's efforts, as one historian explained, "affirmed women's capacity to act as political agents." Still, in an age in which property qualifications excluded many white men as well as free black men from the vote, female suffrage was not a question that garnered much attention.

A single book changed all that. Mary Wollstonecraft's *A Vindication of the Rights of Woman*, published in 1792 and immediately devoured in England and America, generated a full-bore national conversation about the woman question. Wollstonecraft's appeals for equal educational and economic opportunities for women struck a chord among Americans of both sexes, for whom recent experience had made clear both women's capacities and the artificiality of societal limits on them. In the 1780s and 1790s, male college debating societies discussed questions like "Whether Women Ought to Have a Share in Civil Government." A 1793 graduate of the Young Ladies' Academy of Philadelphia was emboldened to excoriate "our high and mighty Lords," who, she charged, "have denied us the means of knowledge," so that "the Church, the Bar, and the Senate are shut against us." An article in a New York magazine judged women's exclusion from lawmaking as "both unjust and detrimental."

When Massachusetts writer Judith Sargent Murray exuberantly looked forward to a "new era in female history" in 1798, she echoed the enthusiasm of Martha Jefferson's French friend Marie de Botidoux, for whom the egalitarian rhetoric of revolution also seemed so rich with promise. Following the Revolution's human rights argument to its logical conclusion, New Jersey legislators had written a state constitution that allowed all propertied "inhabitants," male and female, to vote. Over the course of thirty years, several hundred single propertied women braved the raucous male milieu at the polling stations to cast their ballots until that right was retracted in 1807.

More Americans, however, agreed with the writer who found the prospect of a female politician "like a monkey in a China ware shop, where he can't do any good but may do a great deal of mischief." Women feared being labeled masculine or, worse, sexually aggressive if they took too great an interest in politics, falling afoul of those men for whom, to quote a minister of the era, a "dove-like temper is so necessary to Female beauty." And although many women took advantage of the liberality of New Jersey laws to vote, they voiced no public outcry when they were formally disenfranchised in 1807.

Martha Jefferson would not contribute a word to this international conversation about the rights of women. Perhaps she was persuaded by her father's assessment that a good wheat harvest in the fall would calm the bestirred Parisians, pulling them back from the extremes of their radicalism. Perhaps she agreed with him that women were better suited to soothing men rather than engaging in divisive partisan politics. Or perhaps, as she followed the slaves carrying her father into the house and the great door of Monticello was closed behind her, she heard its thump unequivocally bring her Paris life to a close. The end of a life of balls and plays, fashion and learning, outings and gossip. The end of sparklingly clever conversations about politics and literature with well-educated, self-assured aristocratic women. The end of Roman Catholic churches, with all their beauty, mystery, and grandeur. The end of the pleasures of urban life in one of the most captivating cities in the world.

There were other considerations now. Summoned by President George Washington to a new post almost as soon as they landed, her father was preparing for his imminent departure to New York to take his office as secretary of state. There apparently was no talk of his daughters going with him, but neither would he leave them at Monticello alone. Martha and Maria could be safely lodged with the Eppeses in their sleepy neighborhood on the banks of the sluggish Appomattox River. Elizabeth Eppes, he was confident, could supply those elements of female education so glaringly absent at Panthemont yet completely necessary in rural Virginia. She could teach them how to make a pudding, organize a household, and supervise slaves. It was the perfect solution for everyone but Martha, who no longer considered herself a child to be supervised. If she was not going to be buried alive at Eppington, she had to act fast.

Thus it was, on a winter's day in 1790, less than two months after her homecoming, she stood in the parlor of her father's home and pledged herself for life to Thomas Mann Randolph, her cousin with whom she had just become reacquainted. The new Mrs. Randolph was all of seventeen years old.

Becoming American
Again

. . . .

1790

. . . .

*I*T HAD BEEN A WHIRLWIND courtship. The cousins had barely known each other when they reconnected in 1789. They had met only twice before that we know of, during the war when eight-year-old Martha sought refuge from the British attack on Richmond with her mother and sister at the Randolph homestead of Tuckahoe, and again two years later in May 1783, as Martha and her father returned to Monticello from Philadelphia. Four years older than Martha, Tom Randolph saw his cousin with different eyes on her return from France, when she and her sister and father stopped in at Tuckahoe as they made their way back to Monticello.

An immediate and strong attraction drew Tom Randolph to follow Martha to Monticello in December. Like Martha, Tom was well educated, having returned from two years' study at the university in Edinburgh—the epicenter of the Scottish Enlightenment. He was tall, which would have suited Martha's own height, and darkly handsome; Tom's father, Jefferson's second cousin, would have passed on the family legend that the Randolphs descended from Pocahontas herself. Unlike most young men Martha met on her return to Virginia, Tom shone with the polish of his cosmopolitan European experience. Their court-

The only known portrait of Thomas Mann Randolph, Jr., shows a darkly handsome young man. Plainly dressed, Randolph is depicted more as the serious planter and man of business he strove to be than as a gentrified grandee recently returned from his European sojourn. As governor, he would propose a modest though unpopular antislavery bill, encouraging the emancipation of a "fair proportion" of young male and female slaves each year.

ship may well have featured rides in the Albemarle countryside; Martha was an expert rider from her childhood, and we know she continued to ride in Paris. Tom, too, sat well in the saddle. His reserve complemented her fun-loving temperament. One of Martha's favorite pastimes, perhaps more easily indulged in her native Albemarle County than in the aristocratic circles of Paris, was sliding on ice. Scottish immigrants who migrated to Virginia by the thousands in the mid-eighteenth century had popularized the sport when they introduced ice skates to colonial America. Her less adventurous suitor contented himself with watching her, although he must have seen skating often in Edinburgh. Tom Randolph did have a temper that exploded unaccountably from time to time, but both father and daughter may have chalked that up to youth; the bridegroom was only twenty-one, after all. He would soon grow out of it.

As Martha stood in her father's parlor that February day in 1790 to be joined to Thomas Mann Randolph forever, Jefferson beamed, pleased with her choice. Tom was the son of his former schoolmate Thomas Mann Randolph, Sr., a man Jefferson thought of as a brother. As the eldest son, Tom stood to inherit the Tuckahoe estate where Jefferson had spent so much of his childhood and of which they expected Martha would one day be mistress. Tom had pursued a variety of intellectual interests in Scotland but was particularly keen on science and politics—subjects that fascinated his future father-in-law as well and furnished hours of convivial fireside conversations during Tom's visits that winter. And there was comfort in taking a spouse from a family already well known to them: Martha and Tom were third cousins, hardly a problem among Virginia gentry who frequently married first cousins. Jefferson may have "scrupulously suppressed my wishes, that my daughter might indulge her own sentiments freely," as he wrote to a French friend, but once the couple told him of their plans, he probably pushed to get the business accomplished before he had to leave for New York by the end of the month to join President Washington's cabinet.

Still, one wonders if Martha had her doubts before the wedding. She later said that "her sufferings were greatly increased" when her father threw a dinner party on her wedding day. Understanding full well the legal suicide they committed as they took their vows, it was hardly unusual for eighteenth-century brides to express distress on the eve of their weddings, as Bettie Hawkins had done so plaintively with Martha. The choice of a husband was, as Abigail Adams's sister had once starkly put it, "*the* important Crisis upon which our Fate depends." Even so, most brides described nerves, jitters, or even anxieties, but not sufferings. For his part, Tom was sure very early on; by early December he knew that he loved her "and her only, with all of my faculties." Perhaps Martha was grief-stricken at the prospect of her father's imminent departure for New York or, as another historian has suggested, rebellious in the face of her father's new relationship with Sally Hemings. Either way, the strain of forced smiles during the great celebration could well have felt to her like suffering. Years later, she left a clue that she regretted the early timing of her marriage when she told a daughter's suitor that at seventeen "you are both too young to be entangled by an engagement which will decide the happiness, or wretchedness of your lives."

But as she pledged her life to Tom Randolph, the future held promise, if no guarantees, for both the new couple and the new nation to which they had returned. The Revolution had bound thirteen disparate states into a common cause proclaimed by the Declaration of Independence, but that union was a fragile one. In the years immediately after 1776, the infant United States had only two national institutions, the Continental Army and the Congress, both of which were relatively weak. General George Washington spent the war trying to hold his army together in spite of terms of enlistment that regularly expired, insufficient provisions for his men, mutinies, and runaway inflation that made it impossible to pay his soldiers. Under the Articles of Confederation, Congress functioned more as a league of friendship among sovereign states than as a central government. Each state had one vote, and delegates vociferously defended their own state's interests. Any amendment to the articles required a unanimous vote, effectively preventing any change. Hamstrung by such a weak system, Congress could only requisition, not require, the necessary money and supplies for the army. Washington's correspondence throughout the conflict is replete with his frustration at congressional inefficiency, but the delegates' fear of a strong central government frequently overrode the imperatives of war.

The joyous celebrations after the Treaty of Paris that formally ended the fighting in 1783, bringing international recognition of the new nation, did little to change this picture. Congress remained helpless to pay its war debts or to curb inflation. Instead state legislatures struggled on their own to combat the economic depression that followed the war. Some printed more currency to help their people pay their debts. When Massachusetts lawmakers refused to do so in the fall of 1786, however, farmers led by the former Continental Army captain Daniel Shays actually shouldered their arms again to close down the courts that were foreclosing on their farms, and to force measures that would relieve the widespread economic distress.

The violence of the Shays uprising made starkly clear the need for reform. In the summer of 1787, twelve states sent fifty-five delegates to Philadelphia to revise the Articles of Confederation. Instead the convention produced a wholly new constitution that created a strong central government and changed the terms of the states' relationship with one another. Unlike the old articles, the new Constitution empowered the federal government to tax, mint currency, regulate interstate commerce, resolve interstate disputes, and raise an army. Significantly, the Constitution resolved the question of sovereignty that had first propelled the colonies to war with Britain. The interim answer under the articles had been to invest sovereignty in the states, but the Framers in Philadelphia hammered out a new way of thinking about representative government. States would have equal weight in the Senate, but in the House, representation would reflect the people, proportionate to each state's population. But unlike the English and French systems, which balanced competing ranks of people (monarch, nobles, and commoners), the American system balanced powers: executive, legislative, and judicial. Most important, in the new federal system, sovereignty lay with the people rather than in any institution or claim to noble birth.

It was a bold experiment. As Jefferson headed to New York City in March 1790, the nation's financial center and the capital since 1785, he ruminated on the challenges of transforming a paper document into a functioning government. The Constitution had been in effect since June 1788, and George Washington had been inaugurated as the first president in April of the following year. Like all Americans, Jefferson had been kept in the dark about the convention's work in the summer of 1787, hearing about it from his friend James Madison only when he had been released from the delegates' pledge of secrecy. Madison had been highly instrumental in shaping the Framers' debates and the document they created. He fought hard for ratification in his home state of Virginia and, with Alexander Hamilton and John Jay, famously contributed to the Federalist Papers, a series of eighty-nine essays that persuaded New York to vote for ratification. Reading Madison's letter and the enclosed Constitution in France, Jefferson raised only two objections: the Constitution lacked a Bill of Rights and term limits for the chief executive. Both were answered in relatively short order, with the Bill of Rights ratified by the end of 1791, and Washington's retirement from office in 1796 after two terms.

The Framers were not the only ones to think deeply about what it meant to be an American; so, too, did the people. Old patterns of deference began to slip away in the new republic. Artisans and tradesmen marched together in parades, proud of the skills and hard work that had secured independence and now proved their own fitness to stand as an equal with any man at the ballot box. Cheering women lined parade routes and attended politically sponsored balls and barbecues. Educators began to think about the best ways to teach both boys and girls, now that they were no longer subjects to a monarch but future citizens. Noah Webster compiled a dictionary to standardize spelling, rejecting British conventions such as the *u* in *colour* to reflect the direct and plainspoken citizenry of the new republic. Print proliferated in these early years, knitting together newly literate readers in a common culture. There had only been twenty-three newspapers in British colonial America in 1764; by the end of the Revolution, that number had more than doubled to fifty-eight; by 1800 it had risen to 150. After the overthrow of King George III, magazines printed essays that questioned whether husbands in a republic should hold tyrannical sway over their wives; short stories about notable women gave readers models of exemplary female behavior. Novels spun plots that also challenged the old order, allowing women to imagine that the Revolution had opened a new world for them as well. In these ways, and many others, newly freed Americans sought to create a culture of their own to demonstrate and celebrate their break with the vestiges of the Old World.

Despite her intimate connection with the new secretary of state, the new Mrs. Randolph watched these developments from the sidelines of rural Virginia. She put a good face on her transformed life, announcing her marriage bravely to her Paris schoolmates. Less than a month after Martha's wedding, Elizabeth Tufton wrote from London that she was "most agreeably surprized in receiving a letter" that contained the announcement, adding, "*How* greatly my satisfaction was increased in finding you were so happy." Caroline Tufton and her uncle the duke congratulated her on "being settled so much to your own satisfaction."

The new bride may not have felt she had a choice. She did not want to disappoint friends who wanted the details of her new life and eagerly anticipated that "in the course of years our letters will make quite an history." When Bettie Hawkins moved back to London in the spring of 1788, she had been unable to write because "for this month past I have been in a continual bustle. We enter into all the amusements of the gay metropolis." She wrote gleefully of the number of her partners at a ball "that you cannot wonder at, as there were many people of taste there." From Paris, Marie de Botidoux continued to press Martha with gossip of courtships gone awry, her own beaux (sometimes four at a time), the latest scandal at Panthemont (one of the nuns fled and sold her story to a French newspaper), and the goings-on at the National Assembly, which she apparently attended. What adventures of interest could life in Virginia possibly produce that would satisfy her friends' dearest wish that her exploits continue?

The truth was that reentry had not been easy. So easily did French roll off her tongue, she had difficulty reverting back to English on her return. Martha's life could not have been more different from Paris, as she learned how to be a Virginian again. As she had made her way home, the view outside her carriage window was not Parisian architecture but a rolling landscape of fields, planted with tobacco or lying fallow, dotted with rude plantation homes, slave quarters, and the ubiquitous curing sheds. This agricultural world was marked by the rhythms of the seasons rather than the social calendar of the beau monde. She could see no apparent prospects for culture or amusements. The contrast between the world she left behind and the one to which her marriage had committed her could not have been greater. For the new Martha Randolph, the life of wife, mother, and plantation mistress— a goal to which all other white Virginia girls aspired—was, after Paris, a trial so arduous as to require heroism to be endured.

After a round of nuptial visits, Martha remained behind at Eppington, where her aunt Eppes gave her a crash course in the particulars of housekeeping that a planter's wife should know. Tom traveled to inspect Varina plantation, his father's wedding gift to them. Just south of Richmond and about eighty-five miles southeast of Monticello, the estate occupied 950 acres on the James River. But on that first visit, Varina presented a dismal prospect to Tom: It had only two two-room houses, sat on low-lying land, and in May was already broiling under the Virginia sun. Tom complained about the rashes and boils that so assailed him from the heat and humidity that he could only spend an hour outdoors each day. Worse, he knew, his father's gift was encumbered with a large mortgage. He rapidly concluded that he would need to pursue married life and work elsewhere. In the meantime, Martha was impatient to begin her life as mistress of her own plantation rather than continuing to impose on her aunt Eppes. But she was pleased that as Tom reevaluated his options, he began to consider Albemarle

County; she had privately confessed to her father that she was "much averse" to living so far away from Monticello at Varina.

Negotiations soon began with Tom's father for his acreage called Edgehill, just across the Rivanna River, barely two miles from Monticello. Recently widowed, however, the senior Randolph had decided to remarry and, as part of the nuptial agreement, planned to sell Edgehill to his new father-in-law. Jefferson quietly intervened in the negotiations, determined to establish his daughter close to him. But he was unable to prevent the rupture that occurred between father and son, when the elder Randolph abruptly changed his mind about the price he and Jefferson had agreed upon. Young Tom "took fire," as Martha anxiously observed, at his father's reversal. Tempers cooled, fortunately, and the elder Randolph eventually agreed to sell the fifteen-hundred-acre property to his son. But his father's remarriage posed another, greater threat to Tom's plans for his future: the inheritance of Tuckahoe. Fifty-year-old Randolph Senior's new bride was still in her teens and, as Martha and Tom feared, produced a son (whom, inexplicably, they *also* named Thomas Mann). Martha's hopes to become mistress of Tuckahoe were blasted. Jefferson's consolation letter makes clear that Martha had made her own premarital calculations, just as Bettie Hawkins had before her wedding, about the estate (if not a title) her future husband would be in line to inherit. Only four months into her marriage, she was already bitterly disappointed.

So painful was the disjuncture between her hopes and disappointments, she ducked it with silence. Begging for a letter in April 1790, Bettie warned her, "Take care my dear girl you do not justify my former apprehensions, remember how much you laughed at them & assured me our friendship was reciprocal & would be of long duration!" Elizabeth Tufton breathed a sigh of relief when she heard from Martha. "To own the truth I began almost to fear new connexions and friends had entirely obliterated in my dear Mrs. Randolph the remembrance *of one*." Marie de Botidoux, unaware even of Martha's marriage, scolded her roundly in May. "You are truly unbelievable for not having written anyone for six months. Lady Elizabeth [Tufton] tells me she believes your father has forbidden it. That's not possible because it doesn't make sense, what would he do that for?" she demanded. Marie hoped to bump into William Short in Paris so that she could find out if he had gotten over his infatuation with Martha. "I think so. You aren't worth getting attached to," she finished, pained by her friend's silence.

When Mrs. Randolph finally responded to her friends, she did so sparingly, reporting her satisfaction with her situation generally rather than supplying particulars. As she adjusted to the requirements of married life, she quickly realized that it would not be hers to command; rather it would be ordered by her husband's career and by her father's. On his return home from Edinburgh, Tom had hoped to continue his studies by reading in law to prepare for a political career. Marriage to Jefferson's daughter altered that plan, when he assumed the double responsibility of providing for a wife and managing his father-in-law's plantations in his frequent absences. But until Tom could wrestle Edgehill from his father, build a home, and establish a thriving plantation on that property, the couple would spend the first years of their married life largely migrating between Varina and Monticello.

After a discouraging summer at Varina, Martha and Tom returned to Monticello in September. Jefferson was visiting, his first respite from six months as secretary of state. Pregnant with her first child, Martha remained there when her father returned to work, this time to Philadelphia, the new temporary capital city. It was in Philadelphia that Jefferson received the news of the birth of his first grandchild, a girl, in January 1791. Martha was determined that her father should name the child, but not until his letter of March 24, when Jefferson responded to the new mother's repeated requests, was she called Anne Cary, after Tom's mother.

The following spring, Tom's father relented and sold Edgehill to his son. Staying at Monticello, Tom could much more conveniently begin to farm his new property. His family expanded that September, with the birth of his son, Thomas Jefferson, who they would call Jeff. But worryingly for the young father, financial difficulties also arose that year, with a disappointing wheat crop and the spoilage of his tobacco crop that had been pelted by rain as Tom moved it to market. His responsibilities mounted with his father's death in November 1793 and the birth of his third child, Ellen, in 1794. Hoping to sell Varina, Tom gradually began to establish roots in Albemarle County. In 1794, he became a justice of the peace, an office typically held by the county's leading men, and applied for and won a commission as captain of the local militia.

The rhythm of the Randolphs' lives changed with Jefferson's resignation from Washington's cabinet in December 1793, however, and his return to Monticello. Embroiled from the start of his term in a bitter political rivalry with Alexander Hamilton, Jefferson felt his advice ignored as the president sided with his treasury secretary on most policy decisions. Their battles had spilled over to the press with escalating acrimony. In the midst of it all, he had written to Martha of his desire to exchange the "labour, envy, and malice" of political life in Philadelphia for the "ease, domestic occupation, and domestic love" of his family. But as the attacks on him mounted, Jefferson decided to remain in hopes of forcing Hamilton to leave instead. By December, however, it was Jefferson who was packing for home.

Jefferson remained at Monticello for three years, in a semiretirement that he swore no political office would ever tempt him to abandon. He told a friend he had happily given himself up to "the enjoyment of my farm, my family and my books." His contentment was a startling contrast to the miseries that assailed Tom and Martha, beginning in 1794. Tom fell victim to mysterious illnesses that plagued him for the better part of three years, prompting trips to Boston and New York in search of treatment. His doctors were baffled. He sought relief in the healing springs of western Virginia. Several times Martha went with him, their children remaining behind at Monticello. Once, however, nursing eight-month-old Ellen, the young mother brought her along. They had gotten as far as Staunton, barely forty miles away, when Ellen died. Sending her little body back to Monticello for burial, the heartbroken parents pushed on in search of a cure for Tom.

The only respite for Martha during these difficult times were the birth of another daughter in 1796, whom she named Ellen after her dead baby, and a visit from one of her French classmates, Brunette Salimbeni, in the spring of 1797. Bruny, as Martha called her, spent two months with her at Varina. Together they took long walks and lingered over meals, recapturing the old candor and friendship from their days in Paris in countless hours of conversation. When in 1800, Bruny recalled her visit, she hoped that Martha was finally settled at Edgehill. "It was all you wished," Bruny still remembered vividly. On her return

to France, Bruny immediately contacted their old friend Marie de Botidoux; it was the first Botidoux had heard of Martha in eight years.
"Bruny has told me in some detail of your life," Botidoux wrote to Martha in October 1798. "I know that despite the loss of the fortune of
your father-in-law you are happy, that you have three charming children, an amiable and good husband who loves you very much and who
you love the same." Botidoux shook her head as she tried to reconcile
the image of the fond mother with her girlhood friend who loved to
take the stairs at Panthemont four at a time. "Have you become reasonable?" she asked. "I can't see you a mother of a family."

It was Jefferson's election to the vice presidency in 1796 that finally
committed the Randolphs to Albemarle County. Tom had not yet been
able to sell Varina, but he was needed to manage his father-in-law's
plantations during his four-year term serving under President John
Adams. They spent the summer of 1797 at Monticello and then for the
next two years rented a neighboring farm from which Tom could more
easily keep an eye on Jefferson's interests as well as his own at Edgehill.
After ten years of shuttling from one farm to another, Martha and Tom
finally moved into their new home at Edgehill in 1800. A modest two-
story frame house, Martha's home was sited for the view of Monticello,
prominently visible not two miles away through the intervening hills.
The biggest window facing that direction was in a second-floor
bedroom—the largest, and most likely Martha and Tom's during their
marriage.

Perhaps the most stark adjustment Martha had to make on her return to Virginia was learning to live in the slave society she had left as
a girl. In Paris, she had spoken of her hatred of slavery to her European
friends and to her father as well. "I wish with all my soul that the poor
negroes were all freed," she had written to him two months before Sally
Hemings's fateful arrival in Paris. "It grieves my heart when I think that
these our fellow creatures should be treated so terribly as they are by
many of our country men." She had clearly shared her hopes with Elizabeth Tufton that the American Revolution had forced change during
their absence, for Elizabeth optimistically predicted that on Martha's
return, "we shall see the newspapers as full of the progress of slavery
there when you arrive in America as they are now of that of liberty in
France."

Tom was no more enamored of slavery than was his wife. He had banned the whip on his own plantations and, unlike most white Virginians (including his father-in-law), acknowledged that slaves too were capable of moral character. "All men have a right to liberty," he believed; he thought it "impossible that the slave system should continue, without some check on their increase, and not in the end produce a great, long, and obstinate struggle." In fact, when Jefferson was pressing him to buy Edgehill, Tom had hesitated initially because of his "aversion to increase the number of my negroes" that would be required to farm over fifteen hundred acres. But, in fact, the young couple made the accommodation in fairly short order. By 1799, as the owner of thirty-eight men, women, and children, Tom Randolph was one of the largest slaveholders in the county. And as she and Tom struggled to get on their financial feet, Martha might have been hard-pressed to explain the necessity of such a thing to aristocratic French visitors who sought out the author of the Declaration of Independence. In Virginia, she knew, one could not make a living without controlling labor. But, despite her French education, perhaps she was not so very different from most white Virginia slaveholders in her privileged blindness to the evils of slavery. Not until she was in her fifties, as she reflected on the practice of selling family members away from each other, did she admit that slavery's "sorrows in all their bitterness I had never before conceived."

By the time they moved to Edgehill, Martha was an experienced mother; another daughter, Cornelia, had been born in 1799. Martha had probably long forgotten Bettie Hawkins's girlhood incredulity at a male acquaintance's assumption that motherhood was every girl's fantasy. "I wonder he could imagine a young girl would like to become in one day mother of half-dozen squalling brats—the man must be crazy," Bettie concluded. Rather, it is more likely that Martha remembered better Bettie's besotted introduction of her infant son in a letter she sent in July 1789, "my little darling, who is a remarkable handsome child, his eyes are large & of a very dark Blue, the rest of his face is as like his mother's as possible." At Edgehill, Martha tended to Tom's illnesses and her own—her stomach frequently rebelled at the plentiful amounts of radishes and milk in their diet—as she lived in a perpetual cycle of pregnancy, childbirth, and lactation. Within eight years, they had added four more children to their ever-expanding brood: Virginia

(b. 1801), Mary (b. 1803), James Madison (b. 1806), and Benjamin Franklin (b. 1808). After Ben's safe delivery, Martha confided to Dolley Madison that she "hoped tis her last." At thirty-six, Martha was already the mother of seven.

A long way from French fashion, urban life, and conversation, Martha gradually realized that she could re-create at least a version of it by giving her children the kind of rigorous and sophisticated instruction she had experienced at Panthemont. After ten years of marriage, she declared that she had grown tired of company, pronouncing instead that "the education of my children to which I have long devoted every moment that I could command" was her principal pleasure. Her children adored her and yearned to imitate her industry in reading and writing. Anne was days shy of her second birthday when she asked her mother to tell Jefferson that she was "yiting" (writing) a letter to him. He was not expected to be able to decipher the transcript, however; even her doting mother couldn't always understand her. The toddler loved to tell stories, earnestly supplying many details, Martha recounted merrily, "but in such broken language and with so many gestures as renders it highly diverting to hear her." Five-year-old Ellen also wrote to Jefferson, hoping he would bring some books back from Washington, urging him home quickly so she could show off her new bookcase and complaining condescendingly of the "children," who made so much noise, she could not write well. She treasured her first Shakespeare volume and writing desk, both gifts presented by her grandfather. Years later, Virginia recalled the dark winter evenings of her childhood, when the family gathered around the glow and warmth of the fireside, the slaves lit the candles, and "all was quiet immediately" when her mother and grandfather began to read. As the children grew old enough to follow suit, Virginia—the middle child of the seven—recalled, she saw Jefferson "raise his eye from his own book, and look round on the little circle of readers and smile, and make some remark to mamma about it."

Although the Randolphs no doubt welcomed many visitors to Edgehill, no account survives describing the family's daily routine there. However, Margaret Bayard Smith has left a detailed description of the precision with which her good friend Martha demarcated each day at Monticello. "After breakfast, I soon learned that it was the habit of the family each separately to pursue their occupations," she wrote the morning after her arrival in August 1809, when Martha was a matron of thirty-six. While Jefferson retired to his study, and Martha's husband, Tom, left for his farms, Martha organized the day's housekeeping chores with the house slaves and then gathered her children for a full day's instruction. Thus occupied, the family was not sighted again by visitors until the bell rang to assemble them for dinner, between four and five o'clock. Smith delighted in her long "agreeable and instructive conversation" with Jefferson that followed the meal, as he lingered at the table with the guests he had not made himself available to see until then. Frequently a group walk around the grounds closed the day.

Martha was determined to establish a household culture and raise her children with the Enlightenment lessons she had learned in Paris. With the proper education and nurturing, Enlightenment thinkers believed, even children could be trained in habits of self-discipline. In this attribute, Martha set a sterling example, not only in the order of her days but in her habits of industry that were remarked upon by all who observed her. Her father's overseer for twenty years, Edmund Bacon, commented that "Mrs. Randolph was just like her father . . . she was always busy. If she wasn't reading or writing, she was always doing something. . . . As her daughters grew up, she taught them to be industrious like herself."

Martha had also learned Enlightenment lessons of rational self-control. "Few such women ever lived," Bacon recalled admiringly. "I was with Mr. Jefferson twenty years and saw her frequently every week. I never saw her at all out of temper. I can truly say that I never saw two such persons in this respect as she and her father." And Martha was clearly successful in imparting this lesson to her many children. Her friend Margaret Bayard Smith was astonished at their impeccable behavior (eight had been born by the time of her visit in 1809) at the breakfast table at Monticello. "All Mrs. R's. children eat at the family table, but are in such excellent order, that you would not know, if you did not see them, that a child was present." As any parent knows, such behavior in children is not cultivated overnight; the admirable discipline Bayard Smith observed in action was the product of Martha's years of unflagging mothering at Edgehill.

So as her little children began to string together sentences with their broken language and endearing gestures, and her thoughts turned to their education, she drew on the French memories that remained so strong. They shaped her vision of motherhood to which she would devote the rest of her life, while the work of revolution and republic-building carried on without her. She would teach her children French, the value of reading and writing, and the all-important practice of self-discipline in their studies, whether in ancient history or the fortepiano. For her daughters, for example, she stipulated an hour's practice at the piano each day, "*honest* practicing," she emphasized smilingly, not easily fooled. It would not be painless, Martha knew, but as she remembered from her own parent's insistence when she resisted her Titus Livius, "the habit will in time be formed." She would practice what she preached: In spite of all the pain and disappointments of life, she refused to brood. As her father had for her, Martha prescribed exercise when her children were out of temper; a walk or a ride could reverse the downward slide in spirits like nothing else, she believed. Again, one hears the voice of experience in her advice to her children.

The new Mrs. Randolph had to work at maintaining that cheerful temper that had been so easy and magnetic in Paris. Rural Virginia presented a host of challenges to a worldly, well-educated young woman, and in her identification with her Parisian education and Jefferson's intellectual life, Martha Jefferson Randolph found a way to transcend them: She would launch a career as her children's teacher.

MARTHA ALREADY HAD OPPORTUNITY to practice her teaching skills even before her children were born, when Jefferson delegated to her the supervision of her sister's education. He had left Maria behind with the newlyweds while he settled into life in New York City as secretary of state. Maria remained with them through the spring of 1790 but must have been impatient at her delayed return to Eppington. The newly-weds had not been able to satisfy Maria's heartfelt wish to stay with her aunt Eppes; they lacked horses for the trip, and Tom was reluctant to ask his father to spare his own workhorses for so long a time. So Maria trailed Martha and Tom while they paid the requisite wedding visits to other relatives.

In the meantime, Martha directed Maria's continued studies, a challenge when they were so frequently on the road. Maria could work neither on her translation of *Don Quixote* ("the dictionary is too large to go in the pocket of the chariot," she protested) nor practice the fortepiano while she traveled. She may have been reading some American history, reciting some English grammar, and sewing under Martha's direction, but her schooling during these months remained a mystery to her father. "Your last letter told me what you were not doing," Jefferson wrote with exasperation. "I hope your next will tell me what you are doing." By the end of May, however, Maria was happily ensconced in Eppington, reading her *Don Quixote* daily, reciting her Spanish grammar under the tender tutelage of her aunt Eppes, and continuing her history. Elizabeth Eppes also provided the training in housewifery necessary for young girls; Maria had already been taught to make a pudding and, with her cousin Mary Bolling, had charge of a hen and her chickens. Jefferson was pleased. "You must make the most of your time while you are with so good an aunt who can learn you every thing," he wrote approvingly.

By September, however, when Jefferson returned to Monticello for a month's visit, both daughters were there to greet him. There they remained through the winter. In spite of being well along in her first pregnancy, Martha was a diligent teacher to her sister. Maria "improves visibly in her Spanish," Martha reported to her father, although "she was surprised that I should think of making her look for *all* the words and the parts of the verb." Maria's nonsense translations, as Martha called them, may have passed muster under her aunt's more indulgent tutoring, but Martha was more exacting. "Finding me inexorable she is at last reconciled to her dictionary with whom she had for some time past been on very bad terms," she told Jefferson. She also intended to make Maria toe the line with her music practice. Martha had had their harpsichord repaired and tuned, but Maria was little interested. She was dismayed at Maria's laziness. To the officious older sister, it seemed that the younger was making the most of her father's absence, neglecting anything that she thought would not be noticed.

It is difficult to reconcile Martha's picture of the recalcitrant pupil with the girl of whom Abigail Adams had observed, "Books are her delight." Someone—Elizabeth Eppes or maybe her son Jack—had taught her early to love books. In Cowes, where the family had broken their return journey to Virginia, Captain Cutting had been completely taken with the tableau he happened upon as he entered the breakfast parlor one morning and found Jefferson giving eleven-year-old Maria a Spanish lesson. "The lovely girl was all attention," he recorded in his diary; and as Adams had before him, Cutting observed a "degree of sagacity and observation beyond her years, in the very pertinent queries she put to her excellent Preceptor." In Maria's astute questions and the progress she was making in her Spanish, history, and geography lessons, Cutting saw the presage of the accomplished woman he was confident she would become.

So what caused this transformation of the reluctant pupil? Several things, we can venture. It was one thing to bask in the glow of her father's undivided attention, attending carefully to his Spanish lesson on the conquest of Mexico and plying him with intelligent questions as she sought to please him. But the father whom she had just gotten to know after a four-year separation had departed again. Leaving her behind. Again. His parting letter filled with life lessons—urging her to be good, warning her against the faults of anger and envy, and enjoining her to give rather than receive—was a poor substitute from a "vagrant" father (as he put it himself) for his daily presence. Over the years, Maria had blossomed in the Eppes household, as Jefferson well understood. "I am really jealous of you," Jefferson admitted to Elizabeth Eppes, "for I have always found that you disputed with me the first place in her affections."

But Eppes had never demanded academic excellence as the price of her approval; after all, just how critical was Spanish for a young lady in Albemarle County? Maybe effort was enough to satisfy her aunt, which is why Maria was so startled when her sister required accuracy as well. Martha may have been trying to live up to Jefferson's charge, rendered when she was still a young student at Panthemont, to be a mother to her sister when they met again in Paris. And as a young wife, Martha would have felt that responsibility even more keenly. But Maria may have bristled at the strict instruction of a sister not even six years older than herself. In any event, what does an ability to translate *Don Quixote* signify, when her father is gone, she already possesses the loving approval of the Eppes family, and she lives in rural Virginia, far from the academic discipline of Panthemont?

Unmoved by Martha's lessons, Maria was much more charmed with her first niece, born to her sister on January 23, 1791. "She is very pretty, has beautiful deep blue eyes," Maria told her father of three-week-old Anne, "and is a very fine child." But how helpful twelve-year-old Maria was to the new mother is questionable; she had not even known that Martha was on the verge of giving birth on January 22, when she wrote to the anxious grandfather-to-be that all was well. In fact, unbeknown to Maria, who spent the entire day in another part of the house, Martha had been in the throes of labor all that day. To relieve Martha as her time drew near, Maria and Jenny (Virginia) Randolph, Tom's younger sister, had been trading off weekly housekeeping duties, although how effectively is anyone's guess. In any event, when Jefferson's summer visit to Monticello came to an end that year and he took Maria with him to be schooled in Philadelphia, it is not likely that she was missed for her domestic skills.

They left Monticello on October 12, 1791, and broke their trip twice, first at Montpelier to pick up James Madison and then at Mount Vernon for a visit with the Washingtons. Arriving there on the sixteenth, the travelers discovered the president in a flurry of preparations to leave for Philadelphia, having just learned that Congress was meeting a week earlier than he had thought. "I had no more idea that Monday the 24th inst was the day appointed for the meetings of Congress, than I had of its being dooms-day," Washington had complained furiously to his treasury secretary, Alexander Hamilton. The next day, the three statesmen drove the twenty miles to Georgetown in a hard rain that did not let up in the ensuing five days it took them to reach Philadelphia. In the press of the men's urgency, Martha Washington took charge of Maria and brought her safely to Philadelphia in her own coach.

As they approached the city, Maria could spot the imposing spire of Christ Church—the tallest building in colonial America—from the hilltop as they drew near the Schuylkill River. They had taken the route used by travelers coming from the south, crossing the river at Grays Ferry, a floating bridge that had been built by the British during their occupation of the city in 1777 (today marked by Grays Ferry Avenue). It was an unimpressive sight in 1791, narrow and spindly. But Martha Washington likely diverted her young charge with the story of how, just two years earlier, Philadelphians had bedecked the bridge with the laurels, liberty caps, and flags—important symbols of the newly free republic—to welcome her husband as he made his way from Mount Vernon to New York City to take his oath of office as the nation's first president. As Washington passed under the arch fashioned at the entrance to the bridge, it was said, a laurel wreath fell precisely to his head, as Philadelphians borrowed an ancient custom from the Roman republic to honor their own military hero.

Contemporary maps show that Philadelphia occupied the two-mile stretch of land, east to west, between the Schuylkill and Delaware rivers, and extended about a mile, north to south. Laid out in an orderly grid by William Penn 110 years earlier, the city was to have been a "greene Country Towne, which," Penn resolved, remembering the great fire of London in 1666, would never burn. He designed a city bisected by two stately thoroughfares (the intersecting Broad and High streets were wider than any seventeenth-century road in London), with four large squares to serve the city's residents as parks, an even larger square in the city center to house its main public buildings, and tidy lots to accommodate homes and businesses. East-west streets were named after trees; north-south were numbered, beginning at the Delaware River and progressing west. It was a plan that allowed Philadelphia to grow and thrive.

By the time Maria arrived, the city had not yet overspread the land between the two rivers, but what had been a wooded area to the west was now cleared—the result of the British occupation during the war—and ready for expansion. With a population of forty-four thousand, Philadelphia was the second-largest English-speaking city in the world, far outstripping its nearest American competitor, New York, with its thirty-three thousand. It had become the temporary national capital in 1790, the result of a deal Jefferson had brokered with treasury secretary Alexander Hamilton and Virginia representative James Madison, trading congressional passage of Hamilton's debt plan for the permanent location of the capital city on the Potomac River. In exchange for their votes to seal the deal, Pennsylvania delegates had won Philadelphia as the temporary capital until Washington City would be ready for occupancy.

A booming commercial center throughout the colonial period, now vested with new importance, Philadelphia embarked on a program of building worthy of the nascent republic, in hopes that it could claim that honor permanently. Homes that had been ravaged by war now shone with new windows and coats of paint; public buildings used as hospitals and stables were thoroughly cleaned of stench. In 1787, the city flanked the State House (now known as Independence Hall) with a new county courthouse to the west and, in 1791, City Hall to the east. These new structures would conveniently house Congress and the Supreme Court, as Philadelphians readily improvised to make a capital city out of a commercial and cultural center. The new First Presbyterian Church on Market Street between Second and Third had yet to be built (1793), but it would be the first public building in the city to be faced with a classical temple façade and columns. Following suit two years later, the massive First Bank of the United States would proclaim both the stability and the republican ethos of the new nation.

Arriving in 1794, English artist William Birch recorded the building of the world's first republican capital since Ancient Rome in a series of remarkable paintings. They enable us to see the rows of neat red-brick buildings, trees, and brick-paved walkways that lined the city's streets. Pedestrians strolled unconcerned by the hum of activity in the streets, protected by the regularly spaced posts that kept wagons and horses from spilling over onto the sidewalks. By 1800, the city's development had crept as far west as Twelfth Street, although most of its population remained concentrated east of Seventh, where High Street's paving stopped—an improvement from 1776, when Seventh Street marked the outskirts of the city and Jefferson resided there for its quiet location. Birch's images show a prosperous though—in good republican fashion—not ostentatious city, a civilized and productive citizenry, and an already successful nation on the rise.

With the shift of the capital from New York to Philadelphia, Jefferson enlisted the aid of William Temple Franklin, Benjamin's grandson, to find a rental property that would accommodate both office and domestic space. None of Franklin's recommendations suited, however, even with the alterations Jefferson intended to make, adding a book room here or moving a wall there. In the end, budget constraints prevented Jefferson from renting the two adjoining houses that Franklin,

In one of many scenes of Philadelphia captured by William Birch, this shows the magnificent home built in 1789 for Anne Willing Bingham by her husband, William. In their richly furnished home, the Binghams hosted the political and social elite of the new nation on the model of the French salons they had admired in Paris. Both in the salons where men and women discussed politics, and in the neat, orderly streets of the capital where citizens could freely mingle, we see Americans' aspirations for what their republic could be.

understanding Jefferson's sensibilities, suggested would "constitute what the french call un Appartement complet," so he settled for just one of them instead.

Located on High Street (it was not renamed Market until 1853) between Eighth and Ninth, just two blocks west of the president's residence, Jefferson's new home was typical of Philadelphia row houses, with twenty-five feet fronting on the street and a back extension of forty-four feet. A narrow passage ran the length of the house on the ground floor, opening to the public rooms (parlor and dining room) and then extending back to the kitchen in the rear. A large drawing room overlooked the street on the second floor, which also had two additional chambers, one of which Jefferson used for sleeping. Wanting to have a quiet space at the rear of the house to work away from street noise, Jefferson also successfully negotiated for an extension of the second floor to add a book room. His landlord arranged a second rental, across the street, for office space. For all of these modifications for his comfort and convenience, however, nothing suggested that Jefferson was thinking of lodging his daughter with him as he planned his living arrangements in the new capital.

Maria stayed with him only briefly on her arrival, when the relieved father reported to her sister Martha that she was busy making new friends. Nelly Custis, Martha Washington's granddaughter, was a particular favorite. Jefferson noted that Maria remained "particularly attended to by Mrs. Washington," who continued her maternal kindness to the motherless girl in spite of her duties as First Lady.

A round of visits from leading ladies of the republic ensued; by mid-November, Jefferson told Martha, Maria had "been honored with the visits of Mrs. Adams, Mrs. Randolph, Mrs. Rittenhouse, Sergeant, Waters, Davies &c. so that she is quite familiar with Philadelphia." The reunion between Abigail Adams and Maria must have been particularly joyful, since Maria had never been able to make the visit she had promised during their tearful farewell in London four years earlier. Mrs. Randolph's husband, Edmund, was serving as Washington's attorney general. Hidden behind their married names were Hannah Rittenhouse and her stepdaughters, Elizabeth and Esther (Mrs. Sergeant and Waters, respectively), who had rescued eleven-year-old Martha from the venerable Mary Hopkinson during her stay in Philadelphia in 1783. These were the girls who had made bearable Martha's drawing lessons with the imperious Simitiere and with whom Martha had danced away a New Year's Eve to the merry tunes played by Francis Hopkinson. Now, eight years later, they descended upon Martha's beautiful young sister to embrace her as well. They squired Maria about the city so that Jefferson could reassure himself within two weeks of her arrival that she was comfortable in her new surroundings.

Whether the press of his affairs of state precluded Jefferson from giving her a tour of *his* Philadelphia, we shall never know. Only one of the letters Maria wrote to her sister from this period survives, and but a handful to her brother-in-law. But we can certainly imagine that Jefferson would have pointed out to her the house he had rented during the momentous summer of 1776; it was just a block away, after all, on the southwest corner of High and Seventh. It was now the home of James Wilson, a Pennsylvanian who had also served in the Continental Congress that year and signed the declaration Jefferson had drafted "right in that front room," father may have told daughter, pointing to the second floor. Jefferson may have taken her to the State House, where the Pennsylvania Assembly now met, to show her where he had helped declare a revolution. He may have taken her to the home of artist Charles Willson Peale, whose passion for natural science rivaled Jefferson's. Stuffed to capacity with his enormous collection of animal specimens, Peale's home proved insufficient to display them all; by 1794, he had established a museum in Philosophical Hall. One can only hope that Jefferson would not have delegated these outings to Adrien Petit, his French butler who had migrated to Philadelphia to supervise Jefferson's domestic staff there. Maria's reunion with Petit may have been tinged by the memory of their first unhappy meeting in London. Bringing his training in the art of French cookery, James Hemings, another alumnus of Paris, rounded out Jefferson's Philadelphia household.

Whatever her introduction to Philadelphia, on November 1—no more than a week at most after her arrival—Maria and Jefferson stepped out onto High Street, turned left at the corner onto Eighth Street, and, crossing the street to the east side, entered the lovely courtyard that fronted Mrs. Pine's boarding school. Mary Pine was the widow of Robert Edge Pine, an English portrait painter who had died three years earlier. In 1785, the artist had come to the attention of George Washington through his old friend George William Fairfax. Because Pine had been a staunch friend to the American cause, Fairfax told Washington, he had lost his business and friends in his own country and had migrated with his wife and six daughters to America. Moved by the story, Washington was persuaded and sat for what may have been the truest—although most forgotten—portrait of the general, worn out from the fatigues of war. The likeness did not suit the public's craving for a hero, but it did prompt its subject to invite Pine to Mount Vernon to paint his family members there. This mark of Washington's favor opened many doors to Pine. He maintained a studio in the Assembly

Room of the State House in the late 1780s and built the spacious home on Eighth Street to house his works. It was America's first art museum.

But when Pine died in November 1788, his widow struggled to stay afloat. She had apparently been operating a drawing academy in their home before her husband's death. In the spring of 1789, trading on the reputation of her late husband, she expanded her curricular offerings and advertised a new and improved school. By 1790, Mrs. Pine appeared to have given up the fight, for she put the magnificent home up for sale. Yet on this fall day in 1791, as Maria walked up the front path to be enrolled, Mrs. Pine had persevered and the school was still in operation. Word of mouth, from one elite government official to another, had been sufficient to garner the number of scholars necessary to keep her school open. Through his secretary, Tobias Lear, George Washington had made discreet inquiries about the program and fees for his step-granddaughter Nelly Custis; Deborah Bache, granddaughter of Benjamin Franklin, was a pupil there. Elizabeth and James Monroe also considered sending their daughter there if they did not return to Virginia.

Mary Pine's splendid home certainly did not hint at her financial distress. It sat on a lot fully four times the breadth of Jefferson's rental property and more than triple its depth. Unlike most Philadelphia row homes, which practically spilled out onto the street, Mrs. Pine's home enjoyed the luxury of a twenty-foot setback, protected from prying eyes and street noise by an enclosed courtyard. Jefferson had surely toured the school before he decided to board his daughter there. He would have approved of the six first-floor rooms, each heated with a fireplace, that Mrs. Pine's advertisement had proudly described; he had been incredulous when the workman hired to build a book room in his own lodgings failed to include a fireplace. ("It is possible that I may not have particularly spoken of the chimney," Jefferson complained to his landlord, but that was because he had taken a fireplace for granted.) Mrs. Pine's heated rooms served the students as a residence space, as they had for the Pine family when her husband was alive. Jefferson certainly would have appreciated the beauty and proportions of the second-floor ballroom, which Mrs. Pine had described as "being the whole front of the house in length and about thirty-three feet in breadth, with a very lofty ceiling, and lighted from above in an elegant stile." Jefferson had fallen in love with skylights in Paris. He had hoped to have one installed in his new second-floor book room, where he could enjoy both light and privacy, but the workmen had completely misunderstood his instructions. Instead, when he returned from his summer holiday in Virginia in 1792, he found to his disgust that the workers put the windows in the doors rather than in the ceiling, utterly thwarting his design. (He ended up using it as a storeroom.) But the large, light-filled room in Mrs. Pine's home must have made a wonderful schoolroom.

Jefferson gave Mary Pine a bank note for $33.33 that day to pay for Maria's tuition and board. If she remained that night, Maria's leave-taking of her father would not have been marked by the tears Martha had shed on her first day at Panthemont. Living just around the corner from her father's home and office, Maria could visit him every day. In fact, the proximity of Mrs. Pine's school to his home had influenced his choice. Another Philadelphia teacher, Ann Brodeau, ran a better school in Jefferson's opinion; but since it was much farther from his own rental, it would have precluded Maria's daily visits. Without her elder sister to smooth the transition, Maria was on her own to form new friendships and find her way in her new school. Jefferson may have been satisfied that she had "made young friends enough to keep herself in a bustle with them" two weeks after her enrollment, but Maria's report to Tom, after almost a month, that she had "been to Mrs Pines but I am not well acquainted with her or the young ladies there yet," seems more likely, given her habitual reticence.

Much as Jefferson scholars have tucked Martha away in Panthemont without comment, so too have they done with Maria in Philadelphia. A footnote here in the edited edition of Jefferson's family letters, or an editor's comment there in the print edition of Jefferson's voluminous memorandum books, and that is all the attention Maria gets. The sparse documentary record of Maria's tenure in Philadelphia helps to explain this. Yet in many respects, we should consider that Philadelphia was for Maria what Paris had been for Martha. As Martha had in her first month at Panthemont, Maria could see her father daily, without having to vie with a sister for his attention; she attended an elite female academy; she hobnobbed with a privileged group of girls and women and likely attended plays, assemblies, and other amusements around the city. Here she may have even felt the first stirrings of love.

Mary Pine's school for young women was small and exclusive: The 1790 census showed only ten females (including Mary Pine and her four daughters) in residence. However small her school, the English-born Mrs. Pine had a clear sense of educating her students for the elevated status they occupied. Young Deborah Bache, Franklin's grand-daughter, was delighted when Mrs. Pine seated her at the head of the table with Nelly Custis, the president's step-granddaughter, and Maria Morris, the daughter of the wealthy financier who underwrote so much of the war. Social patterns of deference had not disappeared just be-cause there had been a political revolution. This was particularly true for women, the struggling widow was well aware, as she tried to woo the custom of the nation's elite in the new capital. After her two years of ranked seating arrangements at meals at Panthemont with aristocratic English and French girls, Maria likely had a different sensibility about such things than did Deborah Bache's mother, who tartly told her daughter to inform Mrs. Pine that "there is no rank in this country but rank mutton."

In fact, Mrs. Pine offered her students exactly the curriculum Jef-ferson and other fathers of his standing thought proper for young women, both useful and ornamental. Under her tutelage, her students studied grammar, reading, writing, arithmetic, and geography, subjects reflecting the increasingly popular view through the eighteenth century of the rational capacities of girls and women. Still, in this transitional post-Revolutionary era, ornamental accomplishments were still con-sidered crucial to polish young women for their presentation on the marriage market, so Mrs. Pine also advertised needlework, French, drawing, music, and dancing under her particular "care and instruc-tion." With his firm belief in the importance of needlework to alleviate the tedium of plantation life, and his perpetual interest in his daughters' progress in drawing and music, Jefferson could rest assured that his re-quirements for Maria met an exact match in Mrs. Pine's offerings.

Robert Pine's art museum offered the perfect setting and inspiration for his widow's drawing lessons. The huge room on the second floor, so well lit by skylights, housed much of Pine's work. As a boy, Rembrandt

Peale had accompanied his artist father, Charles Willson Peale, to see the new museum. After paying the twenty-five cents admission fee, they climbed the stairs to the second floor. "Accustomed only to my father's small gallery of paintings," Peale recalled, "when I entered Mr. Pine's spacious salon, I was astonished at its magnitude and the richness of the paintings which covered its walls." When Pine emerged from his workroom, the young Rembrandt was surprised to see such "a very small and slender man as the author of the great works I had just left."

But Pine did not work alone. His wife was a portrait painter in her own right, and she was assisted by at least two of her four daughters. They often finished the portraits their father had begun on his southern tours. Pine painted the subjects' heads, and his daughters finished the pieces, adding bodies, clothing, and backgrounds, allowing their father to move on more rapidly to his next paying customer. Jefferson was not as easily impressed as the young Rembrandt had been (he bought a portrait of James Madison that he thought "indifferent"), but Mrs. Pine's expertise would have been entirely suitable for training a thirteen-year-old girl in that female accomplishment. And her young assistants would have been far less intimidating teachers for shyer students like Maria. If Maria ever kept any of her drawings, however, they have not survived.

Music was probably the most important of the decorative arts for young women to master. "Among genteel ranks, lord and master understood that idleness of his wife and daughters was a necessary feature of his prestige as a gentleman," music historian Arthur Loesser explained, but "it looked more ladylike to do something uselessly pretty than to do nothing." Maria had had something of a checkered musical career by the time she arrived in Philadelphia: On one hand, she had studied the harpsichord under the renowned Claude Balbastre in Paris; on the other, she had successfully ducked practice time despite her sister's attempts to sit her down at her instrument at Monticello. But Jefferson was determined, in spite of Maria's indifference. Now in Philadelphia, Maria was redirected to her music under Mrs. Pine's supervision. Jefferson had brought a spinet to Philadelphia for the purpose, and he hired John Christopher Moller, one of the most prominent organists in the city, as a music teacher.

Just as the company of the Rittenhouse girls had made Martha's drawing lessons more tolerable, Nelly Custis may have been enlisted to encourage Maria's musical proficiency. Jefferson knew that Martha Washington shared his views on the matter; Nelly's brother later recalled his sister's practice sessions: "The poor girl would play and cry, and cry and play, for long hours, under the immediate eye of her grandmother, a rigid disciplinarian in all things." "They often practiced together" was Jefferson's bland report to his son-in-law about the two girls. Perhaps his stratagem was successful; almost two months after her arrival, Maria was writing to Tom, asking in some desperation about some of her things that had yet to arrive in Philadelphia. "I am in great want of them," she wrote, "particularly my music."

Interestingly, Jefferson had not chosen for Maria one of the best-known girls' schools in the country: the Young Ladies' Academy of Philadelphia, founded in 1787. Located on Third Street, just a short walk from his home, the academy offered courses in rhetoric and bookkeeping in addition to all the subjects Mrs. Pine offered her students. Significantly, it did *not* offer classes in needlework. One of the academy's sponsors was Benjamin Rush, a signer of the Declaration of Independence and a lifelong friend of Jefferson's even after their politics took them down opposing paths. Rush had written a model curriculum for the academy, training young girls for their futures as wives of industrious American men. Rejecting European modes of female education, he emphasized the practical and dismissed the ornamental, which he believed unsuitable for citizens of the new republic.

If Rush's plan had been meant for boys, Jefferson would have heartily approved. But he would not have seen rhetoric as a subject necessary for girls. Of what use would it be to a girl to know how to frame and deliver an argument? Rhetoric certainly prepared academy students for the annual public examinations they would take to graduate, but both Jefferson and Maria herself would have found unpalatable such public displays of female intellect: Jefferson's patriarchal sensibilities had revolted in Paris as he listened to outspoken French women, and Maria would have cringed in agonies of shyness. The academy graduate Priscilla Mason's 1793 valedictory speech, condemning the exclusion of women from higher learning and the professions, likewise would have disgusted them. As the historian Margaret Nash has observed, with a fair degree of understatement, whatever Rush's intentions, the academy did not produce the most pliant of wives.

In Paris, Martha's association with worldly French women had augmented her classroom education and understanding of how the world worked beyond the prescriptions of books, but Maria's associations with the leading circles of the new republic would have strengthened, rather than challenged, conventional gender attitudes. Abigail Adams is a case in point. Although Adams took an avid interest in politics and by 1794 would describe herself as a pupil of Mary Wollstonecraft, the feminist English author of *A Vindication of the Rights of Woman* (1792), her views of women's involvement in politics by the 1790s had become somewhat more conventional. Yes, Adams had distributed copies of Thomas Paine's revolutionary *Common Sense* in the early months of 1776 and had insisted that her husband keep her informed of political developments, but she did not believe that women should participate in politics. She had not joined in the fund drives spearheaded by Philadelphia women in 1780 to raise money for the soldiers of the Continental Army and imitated by women around the country. Rather, she believed women's patriotism to be qualitatively different from men's: It was purer because it was disinterested, that is, women did not stand to gain from victory in the war, since they were excluded from the polity. Nor did she follow that observation with a plea for inclusion. Now meeting Maria again in the early 1790s in Philadelphia, she was becoming even more politically conservative as the horrors of the French Revolution unfolded.

As one of America's most cosmopolitan and forward-thinking women, then, even Abigail Adams would not compare with Georgiana, the Duchess of Devonshire, who by 1789 (when Martha met her in Paris) had already openly campaigned for the Whig party in England, or with Madame de Staël, who would be exiled by Napoleon for her outspoken political views. Like many American women, Adams fully supported Wollstonecraft's ideas that men and women were intellectual equals and that a woman should be a companion, rather than a helpless dependent, of her husband. But she drew back from Wollstonecraft's more radical claim that women enjoyed the same natural rights as men. Still, if American women rejected Wollstonecraft's more radical ideas, they nonetheless conducted avid conversations about her book. This was particularly true in Philadelphia, where one of the city's booksellers had printed fifteen hundred copies of it for sale. But Jefferson apparently never owned a copy of her *Vindication of the Rights of Woman;* nor did Martha or Maria ever discuss it in their letters.

It is not likely that Maria's circle of friends would have prompted feminist political musings, either. Deeply suspicious of the French Revolution, for example, Nelly Custis once declared she would not trust the revolutionary French government with the "life of a *cat.*" Nor did the return of the aristocratically minded Mrs. Pine to England in June 1792 and Maria's transfer to Valeria Fullerton's school that fall seem to encourage those considerations. Unlike Mrs. Pine, Fullerton was American, the young widow of a Revolutionary War veteran, Richard Fullerton. He had risen to some prominence in the city, organizing processions to commemorate Independence Day and eventually winning a seat in the state assembly and the Common Council. When he died unexpectedly at age thirty-five, his widow opened her school, and Jefferson enrolled Maria there in October 1792.

Maria boarded at Valeria Fullerton's school on Mulberry (now Arch) Street. She was very happy there, she assured her brother-in-law. "Mrs Fullerton . . . is so kind to us that we cannot be otherwise." She visited her father on Sundays, just a few blocks away. In Fullerton's congenial household, Maria acquired more independence from him as she developed her friendships. Sarah (Sally) Corbin Cropper, a year older than Maria, was a good friend. She was the daughter of General John Cropper of Maryland, a member of the Continental Congress whose reputation for patriotism was matched only by his hatred for Tories. Sally and Maria became close, continuing to correspond after Maria's departure from Philadelphia. Family lore told of a romance Sally had during her school days with a Thomas Sergeant, who later became a judge in Pennsylvania. But this would have been several years after Maria's tenure at Fullerton's school. Still, the story, passed down in a family history, hints at the same kinds of preoccupations with love, courtship, and marriage among the young girls at Mrs. Fullerton's school that Martha had known at Panthemont.

It may have been in Philadelphia that Maria felt the first stirrings of love for her cousin and childhood friend Jack Eppes. Jack had arrived in the city by the middle of May 1791, where he may have lived with

Jefferson, who was supervising his studies at the University of Pennsylvania. At the very least, Jack visited frequently; Jefferson's memorandum book regularly noted money given to Jack. Jack's day was rigorous: "2. to 4. hours a day at the College, completing his courses of sciences, and 4 hours at the law." In addition, Jefferson recommended "an hour or two to learn the stile of business and acquire a habit of writing," and reading "something in history and government." It was a two-year program that Jack completed in the spring of 1793, when he returned to Virginia to establish a law practice. By that time, the beautiful Maria was almost fifteen and may have thrown a wrench into Jefferson's plan to keep the young man "out of love" so that "he will be able to go strait forward, and to make good way." There are no family traditions or letters to suggest the flowering of a romance in Philadelphia that would culminate in marriage, but it is certainly possible that the cousins took another look at each other as Maria was leaving her childhood behind.

Of the curriculum at her new school and other details of Maria's life in Philadelphia, we know very little. Her distaste for writing hampers all efforts to recover her life in Philadelphia. If one week she wrote to her aunt at Eppington, her family at Monticello would have to wait until the next to hear from her. Jefferson likened her letters to the biblical Isaac's blessings, which were "but one at a time." When Maria did write, the process was tedious and the result meager. On one occasion, Maria spent three hours "scribbling and rubbing out" a letter to Tom Randolph; "we'll see how her labours end," the resigned father sighed. Her surviving letters to Tom typically comprised five sentences at most and frustratingly lacked detail. One letter to her sister took more than two weeks to complete; like all but one of Maria's other letters, Martha did not think it worth keeping.

Other sources offer a slightly clearer glimpse of Maria's life. Jefferson's memorandum book shows that he took full advantage of living in the bustling commercial center, regularly buying shoes, stockings, shawls, ribbons, and muslin for his daughter to equip her for a social life of visits and the occasional play or assembly. With the pocket money he gave her, Maria could make her own choices in the Philadelphia shops she passed every day. In January 1793, she accompanied her father to the yard of the Walnut Street prison—the largest open-air square in the city—to watch the ascension of a hot-air balloon. Jean Pierre Blanchard had already acquired an international reputation when he flew across the English Channel in 1785, so this event generated real excitement in Philadelphia. An enormous crowd had gathered to watch the launch, the first successful manned ascent in America. Blanchard's fifteen-mile trip to Gloucester County, New Jersey, demonstrated to Jefferson "the security of the thing," and he yearned for a balloon for himself to reduce his normal ten-day trip to Monticello to mere hours. Although Jefferson reported the flight to his daughter Martha, he deliberately saved the details for Maria to recount, since she was always at a loss for what to write about. Maria's letter to Tom disappoints, however. "I have been very much entertained by a balloon that went off" was all she had to say, noting only "the gentleman was in it himself."

By April 1793, Jefferson had taken a house outside the city, near Grays Ferry on the Schuylkill River. The bucolic setting took him out of both the urban and political environments that he found so odious, yet kept him close enough to keep an eye on enemies like Hamilton. An image painted that year shows an unimposing yellow two-story house; but it was beautifully situated on a rise above the river and under a cluster of trees, with a long sloping lawn that led from a sizable front porch to the water's edge. By the summer, Maria began spending more time with him there, two or three days a week. Father and daughter loved the riverfront property. Jefferson spent the summer outdoors. The tall plane trees that sheltered the house were a revelation to him. "Under them I breakfast, dine, write, read and receive my company," he told Martha. "I never before knew the full value of trees," he sighed contentedly. Maria enjoyed picnicking with her father on summer peaches and corn and sauntering along the riverbank. Across the river, she could see Bartram's Garden, modeled after the public pleasure gardens in London.

Maria invited friends out of the city to stay. Sally Cropper was probably visiting when Jefferson attempted to think of something to occupy "two young ladies at his house whose time hangs heavily on their hands." Since the drawing master was unable to come that day, Jefferson asked his friend David Rittenhouse if he could borrow Rittenhouse's camera obscura (a box device that refracts light, giving off an inverted image) so that the girls could create their own botanical sketches with nature herself as their teacher.

Jefferson rented this house near Grays Ferry during his last months as secretary of state. Father and daughter loved its beauty and remove from the city. Jefferson delighted in spending his days under the trees; Maria loved walking the lawns, where across the river she could see Bartram's Garden, today the oldest botanical garden on the continent.

Maria's social life may have been hampered by ill health during these years. Jefferson had complained that her first winter in Philadelphia, 1791–1792, was "long and severe." She was plagued with colds from the first, just as Jefferson and Martha had been during their first winter in Paris. Maria's health had never truly recovered from her illness in their last winter in Paris. Years later Martha wondered if Maria had suffered brain damage during her almost fatal bout with typhus, "having always retained a torpor which I thought was not natural to her." The following winter of 1792–1793 was little better. In the midst of packing up his city townhouse in March to move to Grays Ferry, Jefferson had also been preoccupied with Maria. In early April, he wrote with concern that Maria had been plagued for several weeks with mild fevers, nausea, and lack of appetite. He tried to minimize his worry. "Doctors always flatter, and parents always fear," he told his sister; but still he fretted, "It remains to see which is right." Even with the warmer weather, the best he could report was that she was "well . . . tho not in flourishing health." At least the yellow fever epidemic that struck the city so catastrophically in the fall of 1793 spared them both. Their pastoral location west of the crowded city enabled them to escape the epidemic's worst effects, which claimed four thousand lives in mere weeks. Still, by mid-August, both Maria and Jefferson were counting the weeks till they could go home to Albemarle.

They finally left the fever-stricken city on September 17, 1793, crossed the Schuylkill River at Grays Ferry, and headed for home. Maria's departure spelled the end of her formal education. Martha had been five months short of seventeen when her father withdrew her from Panthemont, although tutoring continued until their departure from Paris. But as she left Philadelphia behind, Maria had only just celebrated her fifteenth birthday. What had Philadelphia meant to her? It was clear that Jefferson was not thinking about Maria's education as seriously as he had her cousin Peter Carr's, or perhaps even Martha's. The school's proximity to his home, rather than its quality, had been his top consideration. In any event, Mrs. Pine's school was no Panthemont, and Mrs. Fullerton, a widow scraping to survive and struggling to hold her school together, was a far cry from the aristocratic Madame l'Abbess, who knew how to extract money from disinclined bishops. Maria does not appear to have been befriended by the kind of women that Martha had known in Paris. In the 1790s, Anne Willing Bingham hosted brilliant parties in her elegant Philadelphia home, trying to create a public space for female political participation in the new republic modeled on the Paris salons she had loved, but young Maria would not have attended any of them. Instead she seems to have lived the conventional, sheltered life typical of a young girl of her class, her education more a continuation of genteel grooming than a transformation.

This was precisely what her father intended. It explains why he packed up a spinet—a badge of his family's gentility—to ship to Philadelphia in 1791 and had paid to have it repaired and tuned at least twice. It explains why he joined forces with Martha Washington, insisting that Maria practice, and why Maria needed to locate the trunk that contained all her music. Maria had resisted, perhaps because she already saw that Martha's abilities exceeded her own in music as well as their other studies. Or maybe she was lazy, as her father and sister believed. Or she just may have considered such accomplishment superfluous. Endowed with a beautiful face, charming manners, and a desire to endear herself to the people she loved, she had in abundance the currency eighteenth-century girls needed to attract a husband and succeed in life. And if she had already decided that she would marry into the Eppes family, further ornamentation was hardly required for their approval. They already loved her mightily, she knew. But as they prepared to leave Philadelphia, Jefferson carefully crated Maria's instrument again and shipped it back to Monticello, even correcting the steward's entry on the packing list from "forte piano" to "the Spinet." Her formal grooming complete and her spinet safely ensconced on a ship to Richmond, Maria Jefferson headed south for home.

CHAPTER

7

A Virginia
Wife

. . . .

1795

. . . .

HERE IS NO INDICATION THAT Maria mourned separation from her school and friends, or even from city life, as Martha had after leaving Panthemont. Perhaps she looked forward to the tranquility of rural Virginia, where she would be closer to her much-loved Eppes relations. She may well have been quite ready to begin that next stage of her life, training for marriage, that her father directed her to do immediately upon their return: "Follow closely your music, reading, sewing, housekeeping."

But lessons in drawing, needlework, music, and Spanish had hardly taught Maria what she needed to know about courtship. And by the summer of 1795, as she turned seventeen, she needed to be ready. She was beautiful, educated, and the daughter of an evidently wealthy and well-respected political leader. In other words, she was a prize, and at least two men vied for her hand that year. "Mr. Giles is at Monticello on Business with Maria," Jefferson's sister Martha Jefferson Carr reported in August, "and Jack Eppes has spent the summer there it is said with the same motive."

A lawyer from Amelia County, forty miles southwest of Richmond, William Branch Giles was then serving in the House of Representatives. He was a vigorous supporter of Jefferson and had launched an inquiry into the ethics of Alexander Hamilton's conduct in running the Treasury, as part of Jefferson's effort to discredit him. Although the episode had actually vindicated Hamilton, Jefferson continued to sign his letters to Giles "affectionately, Th. J." This was but one episode in a career for which Giles would acquire a reputation for audacity and fearlessness in attacking the executive branch. Once, dining at Jefferson's home, he had launched a merciless attack on the artist John Trumbull, who a few days earlier had made him look ridiculous in front of a young woman he had been trying to impress. Jefferson's smiling encouragement of Giles's attack no doubt induced Giles to continue the bombardment from the predinner gathering to the end of the meal. Sixteen years older than Maria, and with a belligerent streak that she would have found overwhelming, Giles should not have been surprised when she turned him down.

Slave Isaac Jefferson saw it happen. One morning he "saw him talking to her in the garden, right back of the nail-factory shop," Isaac recounted. "She was lookin on de ground: all at once she wheeled round and come off. That was the time she turned him off." Watching the scene, Isaac was "never so sorry for a man in all his life: sorry because everybody thought that she was going to marry him." Given Jefferson's obvious favor and hospitality to Giles, he seemed to be the odds-on favorite in the neighborhood gossip network. But Maria, knowing her own mind and heart, turned on her heel and left him in the garden among Jefferson's experimental plantings. Knowing when he was beaten, "Mr. Giles give several dollars [tips] to the servants and when he went away dat time," Isaac finished, "he never come back no more."

Jack Eppes did not fare much better that summer. Jefferson had made a point of letting him know about his competition. "Mr. Giles joined us, the day after you left us," Jefferson informed Jack, and he stayed about ten days. Also alert to the rivals' strategic maneuvering, Martha Carr had nonetheless forecast that in spite of their cleverness, neither would succeed. She was right. Seven months later she wrote, "Maria Jefferson has discarded both Mr. Giles & Mr. Eppes."

A family story, written decades later by the wife of one of Maria's descendants, may help explain why she also refused Jack. One day, the story went, as the Philadelphia schoolgirls sat around in their sewing circle, a Miss Spotswood entertained Maria and her classmates with a cautionary tale of a Virginia acquaintance who had worn her heart on her sleeve. When she finally received the long-awaited marriage proposal, "she dropped like a ripe persimmon," but the suitor, by then tired of her, left. "I think we girls ought to band together," Miss Spotswood firmly concluded, "and pledge ourselves to have more womanly pride than that; in other words, never be a ripe persimmon." Remembering her pledge given solemnly that day, Maria refused Jack's first proposal, but "grew pale and thin" when he did not follow up with the second attempt she expected. The story finishes when Maria tearfully confesses her dilemma to Martha, who quickly put everything to rights.

The details of this tale may be questioned, but not its essential truth. The design of elite female education was to preserve girlish innocence rather than prepare young women for the realities of courtship and marriage. French, English, and American sentimental novels with titles such as *The History of a Young Lady of Distinction, The History of Charlotte Summers,* and *The Coquette* (all written by women) won an avid readership in the years following the Revolution. They offered not only entertainment but a more realistic view of the limited protection that their patriarchal society afforded young unmarried women. These stories of smooth-talking suitors who flattered and seduced innocent women supplemented the lack of such practical advice offered by the newer educational programs for girls. It is wiser and far safer to experience the perils of courtship vicariously through books than to fall victim to a suitor's flattery and false promises. But Maria was on her own that summer. Her father's preference seemed to be the argumentative Giles, who may have reminded Maria somewhat of the intemperate man Jefferson had allowed her sister to marry. In any event, he seemed oblivious to the anxiety his daughter felt as she weighed this most important decision. Instead he was focused on himself, exulting in the serenity of his pastoral life, "retired to my home, in the full enjoiment of my farm, my family, and my books, having bidden an eternal Adieu to public life which I always hated."

Nor could Maria rely on Martha's wise counsel. That summer, she had left Monticello, accompanying her husband on travels to the Virginia springs, seeking a remedy for the illness that had debilitated his body and his spirits. This was the trip on which Martha and Tom suffered the loss of their little Ellen and sent her body back to Monticello for burial. A worried wife and grieving mother, Martha was far too preoccupied to offer courtship advice. That the teenage girls of Maria's acquaintance in Philadelphia had talked about men, love, courtship, and marriage in the absence of their elders, pooling their collective (if limited) knowledge, is entirely likely. So, too, is the possibility that, left to her own devices and remembering their conversations, Maria drew from the font of that wisdom. Whatever her reasons, Jack Eppes returned to his law practice in Richmond empty-handed, forced to yield the field to his rival.

The next summer was an entirely different story. By this time, according to the log Jefferson kept of his correspondence, he and Jack Eppes had exchanged six letters, between September 9, 1795, and June 2, 1796 (all of which, unfortunately, are missing). Although they were all living in the dust clouds and noise of demolition as Jefferson launched the French-inspired renovations of his house, Maria's sister and her aunt Martha Jefferson Carr were in residence by the end of the summer of 1796. Perhaps one of the older women tactfully suggested that Jack should solicit the approval of Maria's father before continuing to express his feelings and hopes to Maria. In any event, visiting at Monticello that fall, Jack sat down and wrote the first (surviving) letter of his suit to Jefferson. "Could I hope, that should time and future attentions render me agreeable, my wishes may be crowned with your approbation," Jack wrote in his formal application to his sweetheart's father, "I should indeed be happy."

Jefferson did not write a reply, but rather most likely called the young man into his cabinet to talk. One guesses that a substantial consideration, for Jefferson at least, was where the young couple would live. As the eldest Eppes heir, Jack would inherit Eppington; indeed, as the heir he would be committed to take control of the property. Its distance from Monticello—at least two days' travel—would pose a considerable obstacle to Jefferson's happiness, however, if not to Maria's. By December, Jack had worked out the dilemma of living arrangements. "All obstacles to my happiness are removed," he notified Jefferson, assuring him that "in every arrangement as to future residence, I shall be guided by yourself and Maria."

Given the fact that Jack had wrapped up these negotiations by the end of 1796 and, it seems, that Maria had happily accepted him, it is a bit of a puzzle why Maria asked her sister the following spring to notify their father about her impending marriage. By May 1797, Jefferson was back in Philadelphia, having been elected vice president the previous fall. Martha's letter of May 20, 1797, is lost, but Jefferson's reply makes clear that in it Martha had presented the news of Maria's engagement. After having seen Martha so well settled, Jefferson replied, his only remaining anxiety was "to see Maria also so associated . . . She could not have been more so to my wishes, if I had had the whole earth free to have chosen a partner for her." To Maria he wrote, "I learn, my dear Maria with inexpressible pleasure that an union of sentiment is likely to bring on an union of destiny between yourself and a person for whom I have the highest esteem."

Given Jefferson's rather predictable response, Maria's reticence to tell her father about her choice is unclear. Perhaps he had urged her to wait a year or two to confirm her decision. Or maybe Maria feared that if she pressed for a wedding date it would appear to be a sign of disloyalty to her father. She easily could have been aware of the emotional tug-of-war between Jefferson and the Eppeses and so wisely delegated the task to the favored daughter who could handle it most diplomatically. In any event, in his letters to both daughters, Jefferson waxed eloquent about his vision of the family's future. "We shall all live together as long as it is agreeable to you," he planned with Maria. With Martha, he dreamed of a harmonious family gathered around the fireside, a vision distinctly at odds with the bitter political conflicts of which he was once again at the center, as vice president clashing with President Washington's successor, John Adams.

In September, the father of the bride-to-be wrote to Francis Eppes to begin the formal negotiations about wedding gifts and dowry. In the end, in keeping with his vision, Jefferson gave the newlyweds Pantops, a tract of eight hundred acres within sight of Monticello, and thirty-one slaves; Francis Eppes had already deeded his son acreage called Bermuda Hundred, south of Richmond along the James River (about a two-day journey from Monticello) and some slaves to be delivered that Christmas.

There are no details about their wedding celebrated on October 13, 1797, in the parlor of Monticello. We know Elizabeth Eppes was not there to see her beloved niece become her daughter. "To say how much poor Betsy [Eppes], and myself are disappoint'd at not being present," she wrote sadly, "requires a better pen than mine." It is not certain that Tom Randolph was present, either. He had not entirely recovered from his illness and in early November was making his way slowly home from Richmond, determined not to tax his waning energies. "Tell my Dear Martha that I shall hasten as much as I can without disabling myself," he wrote to Jefferson three weeks after Jack and Maria's wedding. He remembered too well what he called the horrors he had suffered two years earlier to take the risk; death would be a better alternative, he swore, than a relapse.

What is certain is that the marriage of Maria Jefferson and Jack Eppes was a happy union of lifelong friends. In Jack Eppes, Maria found the assurance of stability she had lacked all her life. He was an anchor from her earliest memory; he would never desert her. He had

A jovial, well-liked man, John "Jack" Wayles Eppes was successful in politics and as a planter. He served in the House of Representatives (1803–1811, 1813–1815), where he staunchly supported his father-in-law's policies; he also served in the Senate until ill health forced his resignation. After Maria's death, he left their home of Mont Blanco for Millbrook, his plantation in Buckingham County. He is buried there alongside his slave Betsy Hemmings, with whom he fathered several children.

stoutly pleaded her case to keep her in Virginia when her father had called her to Paris. He was part of the family that had embraced, loved, taught, nursed, and tearfully parted with her, and then happily welcomed her home again. She had long been part of the Eppes family, and with her marriage Maria cemented that relationship forever.

But Maria's marriage was successful not just because she loved her in-laws but because she adored her husband. John Wayles Eppes was a handsome man, according to slave Isaac Granger Jefferson, who had watched the courtship proceedings closely. Eppes wore his thick, curly dark hair long around his ears; he had a round prominent chin and dark eyes. His niece Ellen Randolph could not help but compare him to her father, Tom Randolph, who disliked Eppes intensely. "Mr Eppes was a gay, good-natured, laughing man," Ellen remembered, "inferior perhaps to my father in talent and cultivation, but of a much happier and more amiable temper." Jefferson enjoyed joking with Jack, whose warm, open, and engaging manners had been cultivated in the household infused with the warm cordiality of Elizabeth Eppes. It is no wonder that the affectionate Maria, who basked in the kindliness of others, would be drawn to such a man rather than to the cold reserve of her brother-in-law.

As Jefferson's biographer Dumas Malone ended his account of Maria's life, he concluded regretfully that "the author of the Declaration of Independence did not succeed in molding his second daughter in his own image, and may never have won first place in her heart." Her constant resistance to her father's wishes—whether about moving to France, writing letters, practicing her music, or visiting him—constituted ample evidence for Malone of Maria's failure to conform to Jefferson's wishes. Other scholars have followed suit, comparing the adult Maria to a "fretful child," because she balked at his pleas to visit him when he was in residence at Monticello. In particular, the newlyweds' choice about where they would live seemed to provide the best evidence of the weakness of Maria's attachment and loyalty to her father, especially as contrasted with Martha's. But if we shift our focus to Maria's aspirations for her marriage, our perspective on her feelings for her father looks distinctly different.

The newly married couple did not leave the mountain immediately upon their wedding. In the construction zone that was Monticello,

Maria had fallen twice that year. The first time was in January, when she fell through the floor to the cellar below, from which she emerged unscathed. The second time she was not so lucky. She injured herself falling through a door, so they remained at Monticello, as did Jefferson, until she was ready to travel. By mid-November, the couple had left, and as they approached Richmond, Jack could report that "Maria's foot improves with traveling—She walked last evening conveniently without her stick."

As was customary for newlywed couples, Maria and Jack made the visiting rounds. They went immediately home to Eppington, where they were kept busy seeing relatives and friends. After traveling to see extended family, they returned to Eppington, where they stayed through the spring, planning to join Jefferson at Monticello during his summer visit in 1798.

But like Martha and Tom, Jack and Maria needed to make a decision about which of their landholdings would be their primary home. There were several considerations. Jefferson, of course, had given them just over eight hundred acres at Pantops, a tract clearly visible to the north from Monticello, because, as he explained to Francis Eppes, "their inclinations concur with my wishes that they should live here." There was no house there yet, but no matter. "A plantation here will furnish him daily employment," Jefferson assured Jack's father, "which is necessary to happiness, to health and profit." In the meantime, Jefferson planned to be at home eight months of the year and wanted them to be there when he was in residence. The remaining four winter months, when Congress was in session (the schedule then was considerably shorter than it is today), he allowed expansively, "they can divide between their other friends." By living with him at Monticello, the couple could save money, "put off the expence of building till it shall be convenient," and Jack could easily make the daily commute to the Pantops plantation as it was being developed.

As she had been with his request to send an eight-year-old across the Atlantic, Elizabeth Eppes was incredulous at Jefferson's expectations; daughters should follow their husbands after they married, not the other way around. But she was more diplomatic this time. She refused to deal with such emotionally laden matters through correspondence, putting off the conversation until Jefferson could visit Eppington to talk with her in person. In the meantime, however, she did write that she was sure he was "too generous . . . not to let us have half their company." Of course, the appeal of Eppington, with its affable and loving relations, made it a magnet for Maria Jefferson Eppes, who easily made the adjustment from calling Elizabeth Eppes "Aunt Eppes" to "my dear mother" and then "Mama." Jefferson had not had to worry about sharing Martha with her in-laws, given the estrangement brought on by Tom's father's marriage to his very young bride; indeed, Tom's sisters had come to them, seeking refuge at Monticello. But it was a different situation when Maria married into the Eppes family. Now Jefferson faced competing claims on his daughter's time and was forced into negotiation with her in-laws. Certainly the absence of a dwelling on the land he had given them at Pantops made it easier for the young couple to justify looking elsewhere for a home. Indeed, there was no contest; back to Eppington they went.

Another consideration was the groom's financial independence. With a successful law practice and the endowment of lands from both his father and father-in-law, Jack had less need than his new brother-in-law, Tom Randolph, to live at Monticello. Tom had begun his married life in debt on heavily mortgaged land, and his indebtedness only increased through the years—the consequence, his daughter believed, of his generous nature in co-signing every note for friends and relatives, assured that he would never have to pay a penny but then finding himself tapped for the full amount. By 1809 his family had moved into Jefferson's home, almost entirely dependent upon Jefferson for their support. During Jack's marriage to Maria, however, his financial independence of Jefferson allowed them to make decisions based on their own goals.

But most important is the way in which Jack Eppes consulted with his wife so that they could make this monumental decision together. This becomes apparent in an exchange of letters in 1802, as Jefferson continued to press Maria and Jack to make their permanent home within sight of Monticello. He had begun his campaign the previous fall, when he laid out all the plans for Pantops, suggesting to Jack that the work "would give you so much to do in the upper country that I should think you and Maria had better make Monticello your head quarters for the next year as central to all your concerns." Forced to decline Jefferson's invitation to join him in the summer of 1802 at Monticello (Jack could not spare the horses for traveling when they were needed at his farm for that year's crop), Jack acknowledged it would be easier if they lived at Pantops. "If I could conveniently make the arrangement I would gladly leave this place and fix immediately at Pant-Ops, that Maria might always be with you when your public duties allowed of your being at Monticello," he diplomatically soothed his father-in-law. The couple had been splitting their time between their plantation of Mont Blanco, near Petersburg, and Bermuda Hundred, the land at the confluence of the James and Appomattox rivers given to them by Jack's father. But rather than squander his financial resources on several temporary homes, Eppes preferred to hold off on building until he and Maria decided on their permanent location. He did not have the money to do so yet, however, and had begun discussing with Maria the possibility of selling her dower land in Bedford County to finance the project.

Jefferson's reply is lost but can be deduced from Jack's next letter on the subject: He offered Jack a loan. Jack politely refused to tie up Jefferson's money when it was needed for Jefferson's own enormous renovation project at Monticello. Significantly, Jack would return only his thanks for the kind offer from his father-in-law but no more, since he was at Mont Blanco and Maria was at Eppington, taking the air. "As she is equally interested in the contents of your letter," Jack told Jefferson, "I shall postpone my answer until we have an opportunity of perusing it together."

In the meantime, Jack was laying an even firmer groundwork for his independence from Jefferson. Unlike Tom Randolph, who started to establish himself as a political figure in Albemarle County before he had officially moved there from Varina, Eppes quickly put down political roots near Eppington in his home county of Chesterfield. In 1801, he ran successfully for a seat in the Virginia Assembly as a representative from Chesterfield County. Asked to stand for reelection in 1802, his candidacy required that he maintain his residence there, so Jack could more easily reject Jefferson's offer without offending him. To live at Monticello was "out of my power," Jack wrote, employing the phrase much used in this period to foreclose any further discussion.

How remarkable for Maria—who had been shuttled across the Atlantic and back, and up to Philadelphia and back, without regard for her feelings on the subject—to have married a man who would not even consider entering into a financial discussion with her father without speaking with her first. Rendered a legal nonentity by her marriage through the law of coverture, Maria would have been legally hamstrung if Jack had entered into any contracts with Jefferson that she disliked. But she had married a man who considered her opinion on their home indispensable to his decision. Jefferson, who had told Maria—not three months after her wedding—that a wife's patient submission to her husband was crucial to marital harmony, would simply have to wait for her return home to Jack for his answer.

Jack's letter reveals the extent to which their marriage was a companionate one. True, Maria's travel plans depended on Jack's work schedule or his plowing needs; this was the nineteenth century, after all, when white men were expected to be the household head and enjoyed all the legal, social, political, and economic privileges necessary to ensure their primacy at home. Still, Maria's letters caressing her "best beloved husband" and Jack's respect for her vision of their lives together mark a significant change in marital expectations from Jefferson's time to their own. They made their decisions together and faced her father as a marital unit. This was not the dynamic of marital relations that characterized Martha and Tom's marriage, in which Jefferson clearly remained his daughter's emotional anchor. In one of many such instances, Martha had looked forward to Jefferson's homecoming from Philadelphia in 1798 with "raptures and palpitations not to be described," assuring him that "the first sensations of my life were affection and respect for you and none others in the course of it have weakened or surpassed that," including, presumably, her husband and children. With his illnesses, both physical and emotional, Tom required her care almost as much as her children did. "The agonies of Mr. Randolph's mind seemed to call forth every energy of mine," she wrote in 1801, when she was at the breaking point, caring for three children struck by whooping cough. Not only did she have to shoulder the burden of nursing three seriously ill children; her husband was as one of them.

This may be why Maria often found herself explaining to Jefferson that she could love him as much as her sister did, even as she also loved her husband. She frequently compared herself to her elder sister and in many ways had found herself lacking, but never in her love for their father. When she visited Martha at Varina early in 1796, Maria was impressed with how efficient a household manager Martha had become. "The more I see of her the more I am sensible how much more deserving she is of you than I am," Maria observed, "but, my dear papa, suffer me to tell you that the love, the gratitude she has for you could never surpass mine: it would not be possible." On another occasion, she ruminated that the deep affection she felt for her sister helped her understand Jefferson's love for Martha; still, Maria insisted, "in the most tender love to him I yield to no one." Jefferson replied immediately, assuring her in the most strenuous tone that there was no difference in his love for his daughters. But still Maria continually strove to assure him of her love. However inadequate her letters, she hoped they would nonetheless prove to him that love she could never quite express to him was part of her, "interwoven with her existence."

These letters have convinced Jefferson scholars that Maria was painfully conscious of her inferiority to Martha and of Jefferson's preference for her sister, and that she competed—unsuccessfully—with Martha for their father's love and attention. But these conclusions have always followed questions that placed Jefferson at the center of the inquiry: How did the sisters vie for his affection? Who pleased him the most? Whom did he love best? Or they follow Martha's daughter Ellen's obviously biased assessment of her aunt, endlessly repeated by succeeding generations of descendants, that Martha was "intellectually *very greatly* superior to her sister. A truth I never heard called in question," and so Maria "mourned over the fear that her father *must* prefer her sister's society, and *could* not take the same pleasure in hers."

But Maria was speaking a different language of love than Martha or even Jefferson may have understood. Close geographic proximity was a key idiom of Martha and Jefferson's shared language; so, too, was the expectation—like a silent vowel, never explicitly stated but clearly understood—that Jefferson would remain foremost in his daughters' hearts. But even as a little girl, Maria had insisted on the legitimacy of her feelings and desires. "If I must go I will, but I cannot help crying so pray don't ask me to," she had told Abigail Adams as she left London for Paris. And when she was grown, she would marry the man of her own choosing, and she would control where she wanted to go and when. Precisely because her way of loving Jefferson was different from her sister's—he was one of many, rather than foremost—she had to reassure him constantly that love was not diminished the more it was shared, and that her love for her husband did not lessen her love and devotion for her father. Indeed, one could argue that Maria exhibited an emotional maturity that has been entirely overlooked because scholars have let Jefferson and Martha's daughter and Dumas Malone set the standard. Today we would applaud the emotional and financial independence of an adult child who marries, moves out, and raises a family, rather than the one who brings a brood back home for grandparental support.

Taken from Edgehill, today a working cattle farm, this photo conveys the view from Martha Jefferson Randolph's home. Framed by branches, her father's house is shaded by the stand of trees at the crest of the mountain. It was always in her sight, as her home was in his.

But as long as Jefferson (and his complaints) remains our central focus, we lose sight of the strength of Maria's marriage and the wise choice she made for herself. And we miss entirely the ways that Maria Jefferson Eppes hit the jackpot in the marital lottery that eighteenth-century marriage could be for so many wives, her winnings much in excess of her sister's.

In the childbearing sector of that lottery, however, Maria Jefferson Eppes lost bitterly. She suffered a miscarriage the first summer after her wedding. Letters from July 1798 recount an unnamed illness that prevented her visit to Monticello. From the third of July, Jefferson had been impatiently awaiting her arrival, certain that "every sound we heard was that of the carriage which was once more to bring us together." It had taken ten days to hear that she had been unwell, but he still did not know the nature of her complaint. "A preceding letter of Jack's . . . must have miscarried," he guessed, unwittingly using the word that would have given Maria the most pain. Still, he urged her to "nurse yourself therefore with all possible care for your own sake, for mine, and . . . do not attempt to move sooner or quicker than your health admits." Impatient with the delays of the post, the anxious father sent an express rider to Eppington the next day to find out what ailed his daughter. Not until 1802 did Jack confirm what one suspects, naming "her miscarriage at Eppington" as the "unfortunate accident" that he had thought was at the root of her ill health for the previous two years. By the fall of 1798, however, Maria was much recovered, suffering only a cold because she had been "too thinly clad."

The couple tried again, and by the spring of 1799, Maria was pregnant. After Jack settled some overseer problems at Bermuda Hundred, they moved to Mont Blanco, south of Petersburg. "From Mont Blanco to Petersburg, opportunities are so rare that it is seldom in our power to write," Maria explained to Jefferson that summer. She had been unable to visit Monticello. Although Jack was as eager for a visit as she was, she assured him, his affairs in Chesterfield County required his attention. By the end of the year, when it was time for Maria's lying-in, they repaired to Eppington and the loving care of "her dear mother," Elizabeth Eppes. From there, on the first of January 1800, Jack joyfully wrote to Jefferson to announce the birth of his daughter the day before. The new father was jubilant now that he was able to make his father-in-law "a sharer in a species of happiness from which my Mary and myself have heretofore been debarred." Their daughter, "tho' very small has every appearance of good health," Jack reported happily, and Maria had made it safely through the birth, evading the fever that frequently felled new mothers. Childbed fever, also called then puerperal fever, could kill as infection invaded the uterus after delivery. Long before doctors understood the importance of cleanliness in avoiding infection, and the invention of antibiotics, expectant mothers prepared as much for their death as for the new life they would bring into the world. Jack was relieved that Maria showed no such symptoms.

Their joy was short-lived. Within two weeks, their little girl was dead and Maria was suffering greatly from abscesses on her breasts. It is possible that she had been instructed, as many eighteenth-century mothers were, to withhold milk for the infant's first few days. Today's mothers know that colostrum, the first secretions of the breast after childbirth, contain a rich combination of vitamins and anti-allergens that protect newborns. In the eighteenth century, however, colostrum was thought to be toxic, so mothers waited for what they considered a purer milk flow to be established before nursing. But the baby's death suggests that she had difficulty nursing, rendering Maria vulnerable to mastitis and infections. The milk ducts in her right breast became clogged, and, inflamed with infection and pus, sores broke through to her skin in several places. With the outbreaks, her fever rose worryingly. The Eppeses called in their trusted physician, Dr. Philip Turpin, to attend her. He prescribed bed rest and the daily administration of a few drops of medicines such as Elixir Vitae (literally, the elixir of life, probably a combination of alcohol and water), in addition to hefty doses of castor oil to reduce the inflammation. But the doctor's remedies made Maria worse, as the infection roared on essentially unchecked, utterly debilitating the patient.

Maria had been bedridden for a full month before word reached Martha and Tom at Edgehill about the loss of her child and her illness. A snowstorm that dropped over two feet of snow on Albemarle prevented them from setting out immediately. Martha was frantic, her heart broken by the loss of her cherished sister's fondest hopes for a child. She chafed at the two-week delay, wanting desperately to comfort her. She had been unable to be present for Maria's lying-in, detained at Monticello by a horrifying series of deaths of several slaves who had become seriously ill after taking medication (likely poisons) from a traveling quack doctor. Finally packing up their children, Martha and Tom undertook the dangerous three-day journey on the snowy roads and arrived at Eppington on February 18. Their arrival, Jack was relieved to see, "revived a little the drooping spirits of my poor Mary."

The Randolphs, on the other hand, were aghast at what they found. "We found Maria much worse than we expected," Tom told Jefferson, "still confined to her bed, greatly reduced in flesh and strength and suffering extremely from inflammation and suppuration of both breasts." A quick survey of the situation made clear to Tom that although Turpin was a doctor long known and much beloved by the Eppes family, his treatments were making her worse rather than better. Tom outdid himself with his tactful intervention. In spite of strong family opposition, even from Jack, Tom and Martha gently persuaded Maria to get out of bed and to stop taking the prescribed medicines, convincing her instead that her continued illness was the result of lying in bed in a stifling sickroom. They urged her to take gentle exercise and some fresh air. Tom even coordinated a visit to Maria by his own trusted physician and neighbor, Dr. William Bache, engineering it as a social call that Bache was making especially to see Tom, to avoid offending Turpin and the family.

In Philadelphia, where he was serving his last year as vice president, Jefferson heard with relief that within a week Maria had begun to respond to her new regimen. Jefferson was usually nonchalant about the childbirth process. He once told Maria that "some female friend of your Mama's (I forget whom) used to say it was no more than a knock of the elbow." But his alarm had increased with the length of Maria's persistent illness. "The continuance of her indisposition is far beyond any case of the same kind I have ever known before," he confessed to Jack. Her recovery was tediously slow, however. It would be almost another month before Jack could write that Maria was well enough to go from her room to an adjoining one, although she was not yet ready to go downstairs. But he remained consumed with worry. "The sores on her breast have proved most obstinate & will not I fear be easily healed without the aid of the knife to which she feels as is natural a great repugnance." Martha stayed at Eppington to continue to nurse her sister, while Jack left her side only once to make a quick trip to Richmond.

Finally, toward the end of April, nearly four months after the birth, Jack happily reported to Jefferson that Maria's health and spirits were entirely restored. He was much relieved. So well did she look, he said, it was not possible to tell that she had ever been ill. In fact, the relieved husband wrote, "she has not I am certain appeared more blooming for two years past." They took their leave from Eppington and settled back happily at Mont Blanco. Jack could even joke about the lame excuse Maria asked him to relay to her father about why she had not written. It was so bad, Jack laughed, he refused to waste his father-in-law's time by including it.

It was a happy ending to what had been a miserable winter for them all. Although Tom and Martha had finally moved into their new home at Edgehill, it had not been quite ready to receive them. They had been forced to live with smoky fireplaces, leaky windows, and mud tracked throughout the house from the dirt floor of the flooded cellar, in addition to the anxieties and dangers of their trip to Eppington. Jefferson had been wretchedly embroiled in fierce political battles while vice president. They all looked forward to their family reunion in May at Monticello. It was an indication of the severity of his anxiety about Maria that Jefferson traveled home by circuitous way of Richmond and Eppington, to collect his daughter himself for their summer visit.

The prospect of Jefferson's election to the presidency in 1800 meant a further postponement to his plans for a quiet life in retirement among his family at Monticello. When Washington retired from politics in 1796, whatever restraint his presidency had exerted on the developing and warring factions within his government evaporated. Part of the conflict was a result of a distinct flaw in the Constitution. Because its framers had not anticipated the party system that would emerge in the nineteenth century, the Constitution did not distinguish between president and vice president when the electors of the electoral college came together to vote. The winner became president; the runner-up became vice president. This is how John Adams, Washington's heir apparent, was saddled in 1796 with a vice president who opposed all his policies.

It had been a turbulent four years, as Vice President Jefferson emerged as the de facto leader of the opposition. His French sympathies induced him to oppose the administration's Quasi War with France, an undeclared naval war on French shipping that followed a period of worsening relations with France's frequently changing revolutionary governments. Provoked by French seizure of American ships and the demand by French diplomats of a bribe before they would arrange a meeting to discuss their differences, Congress finally suspended diplomatic relations with France in July 1798. Adams then sent to Congress the 1798 Alien and Sedition Acts, measures that sought to protect the United States at war by deporting threatening aliens and to protect his government by silencing its critics. Jefferson was so appalled that he, together with James Madison, secretly penned the Kentucky and Virginia Resolutions, which argued that states could and should "interpose" (Madison's carefully chosen word) their authority over congressional acts they deemed unconstitutional. Jefferson's Kentucky Resolution even argued that states could nullify unconstitutional federal law. Such a proposal itself would have been cause for Jefferson's arrest under the Sedition Act had his authorship been known.

In such harrowing circumstances, when it seemed that the very fate of the American experiment was hanging in the balance, Jefferson stood for election against his Federalist foe John Adams in the fall of 1800. Ironically, his fiercest opposition came not from Adams but from his supposed running mate, New York's Aaron Burr, with whom Jefferson was tied at the end of the electors' voting. Following the procedure set out in the Constitution, the election was then thrown to the House of Representatives, where it took six days and thirty-six ballots to finally elect Jefferson president. Jefferson and his supporters would later refer to the election as the Revolution of 1800, in which the government was taken from the hands of the monarchist Federalists and returned to the people.

As he awaited the outcome of that bitter election in the first weeks of 1801, Jefferson's thoughts were already turning to how his new position would affect his family in Virginia. He immediately seized upon the shorter distance to Charlottesville from Washington, D.C., where the capital had moved in 1800 from Philadelphia, as more convenient for both mail and visits. "The distance is so moderate that I should hope a journey to this place would be scarcely more inconvenient than one to Monticello," he told Maria brightly. His daughters were anxious about the outcome of the election, loyally wanting his happiness but also dreading continued separations. Maria assured him that if he won, she would be happy for all those who voted for him, although she would prefer to have him at home to herself. Martha agreed. Her letter at the end of January 1801 was the first one she had written to him in two months. Her silence seems to have sprung from her hurt that he had spent so little time with her on his earlier visits home. "Always in a crowd," she said resentfully, he was inaccessible to her, even when he was at Monticello. He might as well have remained away. Their lives during a Jefferson presidency, she suspected, would be more of the same.

In the meantime, Maria and Jack had apparently decided that Bermuda Hundred would be their homestead. "The carpenters are still at work in the house," Maria told her father, "but we have two rooms that are comfortable and I prefer it infinitely to living in a rented place." They were still awaiting the arrival of their furniture from Mont Blanco, but the mild winter had made the inconveniences of the move bearable. So too had the prospect of permanence and stability in a home of their own. By February, Jack could inform Jefferson that Maria was once again pregnant; his letter (now lost) probably also begged off travel to Monticello for Jefferson's spring visit on that account. Having suffered two grievous losses, the couple was unwilling to risk a third. Jefferson conceded that he could not "regret entirely the disappointment . . . because of the cause." Still, he pressed them to think about going to Monticello anyway, perhaps earlier in her pregnancy when it would be safer, he argued, before travel became too difficult for her. As an added enticement, he placed his house, its contents, and his slaves entirely at their disposal.

Jack declined the offer. For the time being, they were conveniently situated near his family, where Maria could count on the experienced help of her mother-in-law, only thirty-five miles away, if anything went wrong. That Jefferson would not be there for much of the time only made it easier to refuse. Maria wrote her excuses as well, adding, "the servants we shall carry up will be more than sufficient for ourselves and you would perhaps prefer yours being employed in some way or other." Whether or not she knew that Sally Hemings was also pregnant at this very moment, Maria tactfully gave advance notice that she neither wanted nor expected her former maid's service if, in fact, she was able to visit.

Maria waited out the early stages of her pregnancy at home until the most likely time for a miscarriage had passed. In June she left for Eppington, where she visited with Elizabeth and Francis while Jack, who had his hands full with coordinating the work of overseers and slaves at harvest time, attended to his farm. They eventually pressed on to Monticello in mid-July to await Jefferson's summer visit. When Jefferson arrived on August 2, the family reunion was complete. Martha did not think Maria looked well, as the sisters settled in to await the births of their children. Virginia Jefferson Randolph was born on August 22, 1801; her cousin Francis Wayles Eppes, named for his other grandfather, followed on September 20. Attended by a local midwife who enjoyed Jefferson's complete confidence, Francis's birth apparently went well. Nor did Maria endure nearly the postpartum sufferings with Francis that she had with her daughter.

There were other terrors that season, however. No sooner had Jefferson returned to Washington than his daughters' families faced an outbreak of whooping cough. "We have considerable apprehensions about the whooping cough which rages in every part of this neighbourhood," Jack told Jefferson from Monticello, and its spread, he feared, brought it so near, it would be impossible to escape. Maria's infant was not yet six weeks old when he caught it. "He has now struggled with it eleven days," Maria told her father, when she could finally bring herself to write about the ordeal. But, she hoped, "tho he coughs most violently so as to become perfectly black with it in the face he is so little affected by it otherwise that my hopes are great that he will go through with it."

The young mother must have been worried to distraction during those eleven long days. The whooping cough could not have failed to dredge up memories of loss and grief from her childhood at Eppington. Would it claim her son, as it had her sister Lucy? At Edgehill, Martha frantically nursed Ellen, Cornelia, and infant Virginia through fevers and coughs. Not until the crisis had passed could she bear to write about her own maternal agonies watching helplessly her two daughters in their delirium, one laughing and singing, the other gloomy and terrified. "My God what a moment for a parent," she cried.

By mid-November, Maria was satisfied that little Francis could make the journey safely home and began preparations to leave. Martha still thought him "in a very precarious state of being . . . the most delicate creature I ever beheld." But by early January, Jack could assure Jefferson that "Maria was entirely reestablished in her health, and her breast quite well. The little boy too was well and healthy." For the rest of her life, Maria dedicated herself to keeping him that way. She was anxious at his continued fussing but explained it as caused by teething. Both parents were relieved when the baby's distress disappeared even when no teeth were forthcoming but realized their past experiences had heightened their anxiety. "The perils he has passed through render him doubly dear to us," Jack explained to Jefferson when Francis was almost six months old, and they only gradually had learned to relinquish their apprehensions on his account. "The happiness we experience in his daily acquisition of strength, size and ideas," Jack reported gratefully, "is not at present dampt by the dread of losing him."

After a busy spring session in 1802—in which Congress had reorganized the federal judiciary, created a precedent for the admission of new states with the addition of Ohio to the Union, and at the president's behest authorized the establishment of a military academy at West Point—Jefferson looked forward to the summer recess. When he issued his annual summons for the family to join him at Monticello, however, an outbreak of measles in that neighborhood revived all of Maria's old fears. She had been very sick that June, unable to keep anything down and suffering constant mild fevers that she transmitted to Francis. Hearing of her illness, Elizabeth Eppes hastened to Bermuda Hundred to care for her. Eppes devotedly nursed Maria there until she was well enough to make the journey to Eppington, where her mother-in-law could more conveniently look after her. The measles outbreak in Albemarle filled Maria with a greater fear for Francis than had the whooping cough. There followed a flurry of letters between Washington, Edgehill, and Eppington. Were Martha's children clear of the infection? Jefferson asked. "We are entirely free from the measles here now," Martha replied from Edgehill with relief. What about the enslaved children on the mountain? Maria wondered. "There are no young children there but Bet's and Sally's [Hemings]," Jefferson replied, and he was sure the disease had already cleared them safely. "I think therefore you may be there in perfect security," he assured them from Washington.

Maria was not convinced, and neither, it seems, was Jack. "Mr. Eppes thinks we had best remain here My Dear Papa till we hear further from you about the measles. . . . Write as soon as you can conveniently after arriving at Monticello," she finished. Jack wrote to Jefferson as well, begging him to understand "how large a portion of our happiness depends on the safety of our child" and reminding him that they trusted him to let them know the soonest they could come without endangering Francis. Maria's hesitation was neither resistant nor undutiful; her letter makes clear her disappointment in their delayed arrival.

Francis's birth had been unremarkable to Jefferson; he had told a friend after the birth of Maria's first child that his elder daughter had made grandchildren "cease to be novelties—she has four children." But it was exactly the opposite for the young parents. Francis was the delight of Maria's life. She thrilled to his attempts to totter about the room, "with his hands extended to balance himself." He brought light to days darkened by illness and by Jack's absences during legislative sessions or the harvest. But the terror of losing her child was never far from her mind. On a cold February day in 1803, as Tom Randolph escorted Maria and her toddler back to Eppington from Edgehill, Jack told Jefferson, Maria came "very near losing our little Francis." For no apparent reason, "he became lifeless in an instant in the carriage and most probably would have expired but for the friendly aid of Mr. Randolph." Not willing to rely on the slow progress of the carriage, Tom clutched the child in his arms, and took off on foot to a house close by the road. There, Jack wrote, he "procured a warm bath by which Francis was gradually restored." Even when Francis had all the appearance of good health, Maria could not rest easy. "It is in the best health allways," Martha had noticed, "that he has been attacked with those dreadful fits," which she guessed was epilepsy, with its "noise in the throat the foaming at the mouth and drawing back of the head."

Looking more closely at these details of Maria's life weakens the interpretation of her as the petulant child who refused to be molded into her father's image. From the days of her childhood longing for the "baby" that her father had promised her from Philadelphia, Maria had wanted a family of her own. As an adult, her desire to create and preserve her own family with her husband was paramount, and Jack's letters to Jefferson show that he was as fully invested in that vision as his wife was. Finally, after two heartbreaking disappointments, they had their son. But he was sickly and delicate, as even others saw. Maria's reluctance to travel and expose Francis to disease was not the response of a peevish daughter or a neurotic mother but of a young couple united in their determination to preserve the fragile life of their child.

This charming little sketch of four-year-old Francis Eppes reflects the delicacy of his health, which so worried his parents. He lived a long life, however. After his move to Florida in 1828, he was a successful planter and an energetic civil servant in Tallahassee. Undoubtedly influenced by his grandfather's example, he was a founder of the West Florida Seminary, the precursor of Florida State University.

There are very few letters that allow us to see this marital bond in action, but those that survive attest to its strength. Jack and Maria Eppes planned their lives to allow the least amount of time apart, as Jack served first in the state legislature in 1801–1803 and then in the House of Representatives in 1803–1804. When Maria accompanied Martha to Washington in November 1802 to visit their father, leaving Jack behind in Virginia, she was immediately pulled into rituals of visiting and company. Yet shortly after her arrival at the White House, as she waited for her dress to be ironed, Maria stole a few minutes to write to her husband. Francis had borne the trip well, she said, although it had been rough. As she wrote, he was "now venturing across the room alone & begins to do it very boldly." Maria sighed, wishing that Jack "could behold his dear little figure." Although they were just four days into a weeks-long stay, Maria assured the "most beloved of my heart" that "nothing can equal the joy with which I shall return to you after so long a separation." This was a distinctly different pattern from the reluctant letter writer Jefferson described to Kitty Church (Maria's friend from Paris), who "resolved to answer" Kitty's letter "every day for a month" but didn't, and who would do anything to prove her love "except writing letters."

In the winter of 1803–1804, Jack's election to the House of Representatives forced another separation. Pregnant again, Maria joined her sister, who was expecting her sixth child, at Edgehill for the winter, since Tom also had stood for election and won. Both men made their way to Washington for the convening of the Eighth Congress in mid-October, while the sisters kept each other company through their pregnancies. Martha named Mary Jefferson Randolph, born on November 2, after Maria. All went well, and Jefferson hoped that Maria would find Martha's success in childbirth an example that would cheer. But Maria's spirits were low, Martha told her father wearily, in part because her sister's past experiences precluded "every thing like comfort or cheerfulness." Maria's pregnancies had never been easy, and even after Francis she had struggled with pain in her breasts. Without Jack's heartening presence to encourage her, Maria sank more easily into dejection during what she called "this tedious interval." Even seven-year-old Ellen noticed that her aunt Maria's "temper, naturally mild, became I think, saddened by ill-health." Martha thought the long winter's separation, while Jack served in Congress, was particularly difficult for Maria to bear. Although caring for a newborn herself in addition to five other children, Martha was striving to take as good care of Maria as Jack would have done if he were there. But she knew that she was a poor substitute for Maria's doting husband.

Jack's letters were not as frequent as Maria had hoped, as he dove into his new job with relish. A strong supporter of Jefferson's efforts to shrink government, Jack introduced a resolution that the House Ways and Means Committee look into methods to cut wasteful spending, and he energetically engaged the debates that followed. In January, as tempers frayed at Edgehill, Maria could not help but express her hurt at her husband's neglect. "I confess I think a little hard of not receiving a single line from you by the last post," she admitted, "yet though hurt I cannot let an opportunity pass without giving you the only proof in my power of the tenderness which I feel & with which I think of you." Perhaps it was Martha's exhaustion, supervising a household of young children, a baby at her breast, and the absence of both fathers that prompted her spiteful suggestion that she address Maria's reply to Jack, "by way of retaliation." Martha's handwriting would raise Jack's expectations for a humorous and newsy letter. But Maria could not agree. She would not subject her husband to "so much disappointment from a letter of mine." Neither, it seems, was there any room in her marriage for petty reprisals, even when her husband had disappointed her.

In late January, Jefferson wrote confidently that hereafter, the mail would be more regular with the institution of twice-weekly delivery from Milton, the Monticello neighborhood's post office; he also hoped that Congress might rise in March, rather than April, allowing him an early return home. That prospect, Maria told Jack in the last letter she would ever write to him, "would revive me more than any thing. I find it often hard to bear up against sickness, confinement and a separation from you," she confessed. Her health was gradually worsening. Unable to keep anything down, she was growing weak. But she took comfort that her trials could only last a week or two longer, when she would present him with "so sweet an addition to our felicity" that she was sure "would more than compensate for almost any suffering." She closed on a note of happy expectation to her "best beloved of my soul." "I live but in the anticipation of the happiness I shall feel when we meet again," she told him. Poignantly unaware that two months later they would be separated forever, she added, "it is not a little increased in knowing that it will not be followed by another separation." For the rest of his life, Jack kept these last letters.

She gave birth to a daughter, Maria Jefferson Eppes, just a week later, on February 15. On the twenty-sixth, Jefferson wrote his congratulations immediately after receiving a quick note from Martha about the birth. He had been hoping that Maria might deliver a little later, and Congress rise a little earlier, so that they could all be there for the event, but ultimately he rejoiced that all went well. Within days, however, things took a rapid change for the worse. Although informed the morning of March 3 of her illness, Jefferson was forced to remain in Washington until Congress had finished its business. But Jack Eppes bolted from Washington immediately, with Jefferson's anxious pleas pressed upon him to be kept informed by every post.

Everything seemed to go wrong for the frantic husband as he made his way to Edgehill. High winds made the ferry crossing over the Potomac River impossible, he got lost in the dark trying to find an alternate route, and more than once was forced "to get down and brake the Ice before my Horse could get forward." But he was somewhat cheered by what he found when he got there. "I found Maria on my arrival here free from fever and sitting up—She has no complaint at present but weakness—Her appetite is improving daily," he wrote Jefferson with relief. "I have no fear," he added optimistically, "but that in a short time she will be restored to health." She had lost her milk, so Martha was nursing little Maria along with her own infant, Mary.

Jack's updates to Jefferson chronicle the rise and fall of his hopes and fears as he watched his wife's life ebb away. Martha too had been hopeful at first, having moved into Maria's room to care for her around the clock. Her report to Jefferson on March 2 had lifted him from despair; indeed, he felt positively buoyant. He even sent Maria a jovial message to "be of good cheer and to be ready to mount on horseback with us" when he returned. But Jack's report on March 12 was more guarded. If Maria was getting better, he said carefully, "it cannot be discerned by me." Remembering Tom's prescription that had saved Maria's life when her first daughter was born, Jack resolved to "Prevail on her to leave her room immediately, to lay aside her phials, and depend on gentle exercise and fresh air for her recovery." From Washington, Jefferson suggested adding light food and cordials to the prescription. Raid the stores of Monticello for anything that would tempt her, Jefferson told Jack; "the house, its contents and appendages and servants are as freely subjected to you as to myself."

By the nineteenth, Jack was getting worried. "A rising of her breast" threatened to revive that habitual complaint, she was taking no food, and for the first time, he admitted, "I feel dreadfully apprehensive that the great debility under which she labours may terminate in some serious complaint." On the twenty-third, he allowed his hopes to rise again. Yes, Maria was "a mere walking shadow" of herself, but since weakness seemed to be her only complaint, Jack told Jefferson, "I have the pleasure of feeling that the recovery of her health although slow is absolutely certain." He planned to move her to Monticello in a few days to give her a change of air and scene. There, they could take her out on the lawn when the weather permitted. On the twenty-sixth, he could only tell Jefferson that "Maria is not worse," as they all looked forward to Jefferson's imminent departure from Washington.

By the time Jefferson finally arrived home on April 4, a much-debilitated Maria had been moved from Edgehill to Monticello. "I found my daughter Eppes at Monticello. Whither she had been brought on a litter by hand," a stunned Jefferson told his neighbor James Madison on the ninth. He found her "so weak as barely to be able to stand, her stomach so disordered as to reject almost everything she took into it, a constant small fever, & an imposthume [abscess] rising in her breast." He hoped that his arrival would act like a tonic and revive her spirits. But she remained in her weakened condition for days; like Jack before him, Jefferson could detect no discernible change a few days later.

By April 16, however, all reason to hope was gone. "We have no longer ground left whereon to build the fondest and most fantastic hopes of Mrs. Eppes' recovery," Tom Randolph wrote in despair to a friend. "How the President will get over this blow, I cannot pronounce," he continued, "I can tell you how he bears it now. He passed all last evening with her handkerchief in his hand." Overcome by grief and weeping, Tom confessed the need for his own handkerchief as well.

Maria died the following day. Jefferson opened his family Bible, and next to her name wrote simply, "died Apr. 17, 1804 between 8. and 9. A.M." He sat in his room alone for hours. When he called for Martha, she found him with his Bible in his hands. Maria's death caused an uproar of grief and confusion in the household. "The day passed I do not know how," Martha's daughter Ellen, then eight, recalled. By the time she was taken to see her aunt, someone—likely a woman, Martha or Sally or one of the other slaves—had covered Maria's body "with a white cloth, over which had been strewed a profusion of flowers." Maria Jefferson Eppes was buried in the family graveyard two days later.

Jack stayed two or three weeks after his wife's death before returning to Washington. He left his baby behind at Monticello. No sooner had Jack departed than his mother arrived, just missing her grieving son. As she had once before, at the end of her visit Elizabeth Eppes brought a motherless child back to Eppington. She had pressed Jefferson to allow her to care for the baby, promising to bring her back to Monticello when Jefferson and Jack would return for the summer recess. "It will be a great comfort," Jefferson wrote to Jack, "to have been brought up with those of her own age, as sisters and brothers of the same house." As he struggled to look forward to a future without his daughter, Jefferson assured Jack that Maria's death would "in no wise change my views at Pantops." He would be happy to help Jack build the house that he anticipated would one day belong to Francis.

But Jack had lost all heart for the project. The outgoing man of the frank and engaging manners was undone by his wife's early death. His great love for her had not been able to save her. He buried his grief and memories so deeply, they never resurfaced. No portrait hung at Monticello to remind him of Maria. None had ever been commissioned, perhaps at her command. She had always hated compliments about her beauty, her niece Ellen remembered, "saying that people only praised her for that because they could not praise her for better things." Only two when his mother died, Francis would frequently lament that he had no recollection of her face because no image of his mother existed. Nor did his father ever talk about her, even after he had found happiness with a second wife. Unlike Jefferson, who frequently prefaced a story with "Your grandmother would say," Jack Eppes could not talk about his wife after she was gone. All he could do was keep her letters. If little Francis wanted to know anything about his mother, his aunt Martha and his grandfather would have to supply the history.

In his own suffering, Jefferson sank under a wave of pessimism as he responded to a friend's expressions of sympathy. "When you and I look back on the country over which we have passed, what a field of slaughter does it exhibit! Where are all the friends who entered it with us, under all the inspiring energies of health and hope? As if pursued by the havoc of war, they are strewed by the way, some earlier, some later, and scarce a few stragglers remain to count the numbers fallen." Death beset him on all sides, and he was fearful. "Others may lose of their abundance, but I, of my want, have lost even the half of all I had. My evening prospects now hang on the slender thread of a single life." But what if he lost Martha, too? In this world, he knew, he could count on nothing. "Perhaps I may be destined to see even this last cord of parental affection broken," he acknowledged in near despair. "The hope which with I had looked forward to the moment, when, resigning public cares to younger hands, I was to retire to that domestic comfort from which the last great step is to be taken, is fearfully blighted."

With Maria's death, Jefferson's most cherished dream of living out the rest of his days with his family gathered around his fireside was gone.

CHAPTER

8

Harriet's Monticello

. . . .

1804

. . . .

JEFFERSON HAD NOW BURIED HIS wife and five of the six children born of his marriage. His admission of his searing pain
was a rare view into his interior landscape, revealed only to a much-
trusted friend. But as he looked up from his letter, surveying his bleak
future, his vision failed him, editing out completely the little son and
daughter who were growing up on Mulberry Row. Martha was not his
only surviving child. By 1804, Sally Hemings had borne him five children, two of whom still lived: Beverley, six, and Harriet, three. And
before he left Monticello to return to Washington that dark spring, he
and Hemings would conceive another child, Madison, as Jefferson
fought the specter of death that threatened to overwhelm him.

Although born into slavery, Sally Hemings's children lived very differently from the hundreds of other slaves Thomas Jefferson owned
over the course of his lifetime. First and foremost, they knew they were
destined for freedom. The perpetuation of slavery required that enslaved
children be trained in habits of submission to their masters, even as
their parents attempted to raise them as individuals within their own
community of family and friends. Harriet was spared the brunt of the
tensions most enslaved children endured as they were caught between

these cross-purposes. Jefferson did not embrace Harriet as his third daughter, but neither did he train her for a slave's life.

With next to no documentation of her childhood, we must cobble together a picture of Harriet's world from a variety of sources: Jefferson and the overseers he employed, accounts from former Monticello slaves, and the stories that Jefferson's grandchildren would later tell to preserve his legacy as a beneficent slave owner. These records need to be scrutinized carefully, particularly because the subject of Jefferson and slavery has been so very contentious. Nonetheless, they can be quite useful in helping us understand the larger world of slavery on Jefferson's plantations and the place of the Hemingses within it, and to imagine what it was like for Jefferson's enslaved daughter to grow up knowing that one day she too could live her life in the pursuit of happiness.

HARRIET HEMINGS WAS BORN into a family that had stood at the apex of the slave community at Monticello ever since Elizabeth Hemings's arrival in 1775. In Virginia's slave society, whites considered it a mark of favor to position slaves in the plantation house at tasks that required skill and artistry, from woodworking to cooking. With only two exceptions (an undercook and a carriage driver), the positions of service closest to Jefferson's family were filled by Elizabeth Hemings's extended family. Jefferson's grandson even believed that the Hemingses' privileged position incited what he called "bitter jealousy" among the other slaves. We cannot rely on the master class to give us a true understanding of the dynamics of the relationships among their slaves, but even historians today who have pored over the historical records at length conclude that the Hemings family members were a caste apart. They experienced a stability of family life uncommon to most slaves, at Monticello or anywhere else; they were employed in positions of trust (as butlers, valets, chambermaids, and nurses) and of skill (as cooks, carpenters, and artisans); and, as products of interracial relationships, they were fairer-skinned than most slaves. Harriet, who was seven-eighths white (and therefore, under Virginia law, legally white), was described by Jefferson's overseer Edmund Bacon as "nearly as white as anybody, and very beautiful."

But not until February 1810, as Jefferson was assembling his Roll of

The first notation of Jefferson's daughter Harriet Hemings in his Farm Book appears on this page, dated 1810. Jefferson grouped enslaved families together, noting the year in which each person was born. At twelve, Beverley appears in the list of tradesmen. On the next leaf (not shown), Jefferson organized his workforce by age. On that list, he recorded that Harriet and Beverley had "run" in 1822.

Negroes in Albemarle County, would he make a note of her in his Farm Book: "Harriet. 01. May," he wrote, recording her birth date. Perhaps he recalled the year because he associated it with the beginning of his first administration as president, but nine years later he had forgotten the precise date. This was not unusual among slaveholders. Former slave Frederick Douglass recalled of his childhood in 1820s Maryland that "by far the larger part of the slaves know as little of their ages as horses know of theirs, and it is the wish of most masters within my knowledge to keep their slaves thus ignorant." Jefferson had been home during the last month of Sally's pregnancy. But after leaving money to pay the local midwife, he had left Monticello, returning to Washington on

April 29 to throw himself into the hard work of his new presidency. If he ever asked the birth date of his daughter, he did not record it. In any event, by 1810, Jefferson also entered the names of Harriet's two younger brothers, Madison, born January 19, 1805, and Eston, born May 21, 1808, below hers in the column headed "House," under their mother's name. Almost twelve, Beverley, the eldest, was already a "Tradesman" and listed in a separate column.

Paging through the Farm Book, where these records appear, provides a bird's-eye view from which to watch Jefferson manage the operations of his plantations, this world into which his enslaved daughter was born. This is where we see him recording the propagation of his mares, cattle, and sheep; distributing to his slaves blankets, yardage for clothing, bread, fish, and pork; moving his slaves over his various holdings; making plans for an efficient wheat harvest; deciding how and when enslaved children were to be put to work; and measuring the wasted scraps of an iron nail rod in proportion to the weight of usable nails hammered out from it. This spare little book, not quite eight inches tall and six and a quarter wide, tells a truth that his philosophical pronouncements, his family's fierce vindications, and his persistent apologists down the years cannot discount: in cataloguing the human beings he owned with his "work horses, mules, breeding mares, colts, steers, cattle, ewes, lambs, sows, shoats, and pigs," Jefferson participated fully in a system that dehumanized the more than six hundred people whose lives intersected with his, those, he rationalized, "whom fortune has thrown on our hands."

Through the Farm Book, for instance, we can watch Jefferson distributing food resources to his labor force. There are several pages headed "Bread list," for example; Harriet appears for the first time on the one dated February 1810. When eighty-three hogs were slaughtered at Poplar Forest in December 1795, ten were slated "for negroes" there; sixty were sent on to Monticello. He rationed out fish and beef, although in portions that were stingy in comparison with other slave owners. In Jefferson's accounting, four children counted as one adult, although he counted as half a person the girls who worked in his textile factory as spinners. To the men sweating their days out in the nailery, he allocated the full measure of pork. Corn fed both slaves and livestock; on one page, Jefferson calculated how much he would need to feed "90 persons . . . 44 weeks @ 4½ Barrels a week" and then distributed the leftovers to the "breeding sows," shoats, one plantation horse, six mules, sixty-three sheep, and four oxen. Slaves of all ages received the weekly ration of a peck of cornmeal—picture a gallon jarful—but no allowance was made for the different nutrition needs of adults. Field hands (male and female), pregnant women, and nursing mothers all received the same weekly allowance of one pound of meat, some fish, and occasionally salt and milk.

Because this was all the food that Jefferson provided to his slaves, they had to supplement their diets with their own garden produce. We do not know where their gardens were, but we do know what they grew. On Sunday afternoons, they would sell their produce to the Monticello family: watermelons, cucumbers, potatoes, squash, cabbages, and eggs from the hens they raised. The family of Jefferson's chief gardener, Wormley Hughes, must have kept a good number of chickens; on one day alone, he sold nine dozen eggs. The skills that Jefferson's enslaved workers brought to the plantation house, they used as well to feed their own families. Following the seasons, they too planted, harvested, and put up foods for winter; they made butter and cheese and brewed beer. Gardening particularly was a universal skill, cultivated for survival but, at Monticello, also turned to profit of a Sunday afternoon at the door of the master's kitchen.

Slave clothing was likewise spare. Most of Jefferson's slaves wore clothing made of osnaburg: a coarse, itchy linen fabric that was the universal uniform of the southern laborer. Twice yearly, in spring and in December, Jefferson's slaves would receive yardage for their clothing allotments: linen for summer and woolens for winter. Every three years, Jefferson instructed his overseers to supply his slaves "a best striped blanket." As with their food, clothing allotments depended on age, so, for instance, Jefferson decided in December 1794 that the blanket and linen supplied to a mother for her newborn infant "serves till the next clothing time"—that is, six months, until the next summer or winter allotments were distributed. The skeins of thread required to turn yardage into clothing were also carefully measured out, three to make each shirt, for example, along with an extra three for repairs. He also apportioned out hats, shoes, and stockings to adults. To slaves such as "Dick's Hanah," he awarded a bed and a pot, "which I always promise them when they take husbands at home," that is, from among his own slaves rather than a neighbor's, in hopes that "others of the young people follow their example."

Besides documenting the material life of slaves, the Farm Book is also a study in agricultural methods. Jefferson thought his plantations neglected and dysfunctional on his return from France in 1790, but he could not begin his reform measures in earnest until he retired to Monticello in 1794 after his dispiriting experience as secretary of state. Disappointed that neither the American people nor their government turned out to be as responsive to natural law as he had anticipated, he applied "the principles of reason and honesty" to the management of his farms and his slaves instead. In true Enlightenment fashion, Jefferson applied geometry, mathematics, and the clock to develop ways to maximize the efficiency of his plantation's operations.

Like many Virginia planters in the late eighteenth century, Jefferson diversified from tobacco, with its ruinous impact on the soil and constantly fluctuating markets, to grains. By 1799, his plantations were on a rotating schedule, producing wheat, rye, oats, corn, and tobacco. Tobacco crops required little skill: just hoes and the repetitive human labor to plant and weed the hills, deworm the plants, cut the harvest, and dry and package the leaves. Wheat, however, introduced new technologies and methods: mills, threshers, and scythes, and a hierarchy of jobs, even in the harvesting fields, from mowers to carters and the cooks who would feed his workers their lunch.

Dissatisfied with the inefficiency of the 1795 harvest operations, Jefferson laid out his plan for improvements for the following year in his Farm Book. Too much time was lost when proper advance arrangements were not made. He would begin, for example, by making sure that spare scythes were at the ready when replacements were required. His trusted slave and overseer, George Granger, would roam the field in a cart with his tools and grindstone, sharpening scythes dulled from work. These changes would eliminate the idle intervals Jefferson had observed while cutters waited for their useless implements to be sharpened. Jefferson also wanted the treading floors to be laid out before the harvest, allowing the work of separating the grain from the stalks to begin without delay after the cutting of the wheat. With an attention to detail that most slaveholders delegated to their overseers, Jefferson organized his army of agricultural workers—sixty-six in all just at Monticello—into the work classifications to which he thought them best suited: the most skilled workers for cutting and cradling the grain, women and strong boys who would bind the cut wheat, younger boys to gather up whatever was left behind, three strong men to load the carts, seven men to stack, four carters to drive, eight women to keep the plows going, and two cooks to feed the whole crew. "In this way," Jefferson reckoned, "the whole machine would move in exact equilibrio."

Every worker was a necessary cog in the machine, including enslaved women. Jefferson forbade his white overseers from keeping a woman from the work of his harvest by appropriating her labor for their own purposes. His calculations depended on every pair of hands. Four men and a girl working the threshing machine twelve hours could produce forty bushels of clean grain when the machine was working smoothly, he computed. When the harvest was done, he thought ahead to clearing more land for spring planting. Grubbing, as it was called, was a laborious process, using a hoe to clear the land of weeds, briars, rocks, and roots. It had taken two slaves three and a half hours to clear just one-seventh of an acre in the graveyard where his beloved wife and children lay buried. Based on that observation, Jefferson estimated that a "laborer will grub from half an acre to an acre a week of common brush land in winter."

Over all this work, Jefferson kept a close eye. "On the north terrace of Monticello was the telescope," former slave Peter Fossett recalled, a perpetual reminder of the master's watchful gaze. From there, Jefferson could watch work developing on his other plantations; Pantops (which interestingly means "all-seeing") and Tufton were clearly in his sight lines. So too was his beloved "academical village," the university being built three miles away in Charlottesville in the early 1820s. A worker on the project recalled Jefferson watching "we alls at work through his spyglass."

The next tier of enslaved workers toiled closer to his home, on the mountain in Mulberry Row, a thousand-foot-long tree-lined lane that separated the mansion from the vegetable terrace. In 1796, Mulberry Row contained seventeen buildings that were the industrial hub of Jefferson's plantations. One of the most profitable (at least initially) of Jefferson's enterprises along Mulberry Row was the nailery. Set up in

1794, the nailery alone made enough money to support his slaves, Jefferson reported with satisfaction the following year. It was the perfect place to train young boys between ten and sixteen who had been left idle in the switch from tobacco to wheat. In practice, it also proved to be the staging ground that would decide their future: The industrious, productive boys who forged the most nails with the least waste would be promoted to the best jobs in their adulthood. Wormley Hughes became Jefferson's head gardener, for example, and Burwell Colbert his personal valet and butler. Inept boys were sent to work "in the ground," forever to be part of Jefferson's agricultural machine. Rebellious boys were whipped and exiled, sold south never to see their families again. Each boy had until his sixteenth birthday to try to influence his master's decision about the course his life would take.

It was exhausting work and brutally hot, especially in sweltering Virginia summers. Four fires burned in the nailery, each surrounded by workers, each of whom held the tip of his iron rod in the flames until a nail-length piece of iron could be broken off. Laying the hot iron on the anvil, the boys then swung their hammers to shape a nail, point at one end and head at the other. Jefferson set daily goals for each worker, depending on his age, size, and other duties on the plantation. In a typical summer workday—fourteen hours long—twenty thousand swings of George Granger's son Isaac's hammer yielded an exceptional output of a thousand nails a day. Jefferson measured everything: the weight of each uncut rod and the resulting nails, as well as the profit or waste each worker generated. The discipline of the work and the productivity of industry, he hoped, would build character in his workers. Once, when he transferred nailers to duty chopping down trees, he argued that it would be good for their character. "It will be useful to them morally and physically . . . to give them full employment," he believed. And, of course, the profit they made supported his bottom line. It was a neat way to convince himself that "providence has made our interests & our duties coincide perfectly."

Mulberry Row housed other industrial activities as well, such as the smithy and the joinery. Jefferson built two coal sheds in 1790 to house a convenient supply of fuel to keep the fires going in the blacksmith shop and his home. As always, Jefferson began by hiring white men to train his slaves. Yet there were exceptions. Joseph Fossett, the grandson

of Elizabeth Hemings, was so successful in the nailery, rising to foreman by 1800, that Jefferson chose him for further training as a blacksmith under a talented but drunkenly erratic white man. When Jefferson
finally fired him, Fossett officially became the head of the blacksmith
shop he had actually been running for years. Fossett's ability, as Edmund Bacon noticed, to "do anything it was necessary to do with steel
or iron" was well known in the neighborhood, and he served area farmers as well as his master, who allowed him to keep one-sixth of his earnings.

Perhaps one of the most gifted artisans on Mulberry Row was John
Hemings, Sally's younger brother, who worked in Jefferson's joinery
shop. He had spent his boyhood chopping down trees, and building
various structures on Jefferson's plantations. In 1793, Jefferson hired
David Watson (a British deserter during the Revolution and another
notorious drinker) to train Hemings to "make wheels, and all sorts of
work," but Hemings's real abilities were unleashed when Jefferson hired
Irish immigrant James Dinsmore in 1798 to craft the interior woodwork in his newly remodeled home. Hemings was his assistant until
Dinsmore's departure in 1809, when Hemings then led the work of the
joinery. Like Fossett, Hemings commanded overseer Bacon's respect
for his work. "He could make anything that was wanted in woodwork,"
Bacon observed admiringly. His expertise ranged from carving the
beautifully crafted arch that separated Jefferson's cabinet from his library to repairing plows to fashioning furniture from sketches drawn by
Jefferson. He was the principal interior woodworker when Jefferson
built his retirement getaway home of Poplar Forest. Jefferson paid him
an annual gratuity and even allowed his clothing purchases in town to
be put on his master's account. Beloved by Jefferson's family, who called
him "Daddy," Hemings was devoted to Jefferson as well.

Jefferson was conscious of his obligations as master of people he saw
as both inferior to and wholly dependent upon him, so he also strove to
alleviate their labor with humanitarian principles, encouraging rather
than terrorizing them. As a French visitor commented after touring
Jefferson's operation in 1796, "He animates them by rewards and distinctions." Isaac Granger Jefferson remembered that Jefferson gave the
boys in the nail factory "a pound of meat a week, a dozen herrings, a
quart of molasses and peck of meal. Give them that wukked the best a

suit of red or blue: encouraged them mightily." Jefferson liked the idea, borrowed from a neighbor and recorded in his Farm Book, of providing financial incentives for slaves who produced more than their weekly requirement. There were also numerous instances in which he interceded to stave off punishments he judged degrading, believing that his favorable opinion would serve as better incentive to good behavior and productivity.

The son of Great George and Ursula Granger, Isaac Granger Jefferson was born at Monticello in 1775. He was with Jefferson when the British invaded Richmond, accompanied him to Philadelphia to learn tinsmithing in the 1790s, and was the most skilled worker in the nailery. Gifted to the Eppeses on their marriage, Isaac was later purchased by Tom Randolph, for whom he worked as a blacksmith. Pictured here a free man at age seventy-one, Isaac Jefferson was still vigorously plying that trade in Petersburg, Virginia, when he told his story to an interviewer in 1847.

But the Farm Book does not tell us everything about what it was like to live in slavery under Jefferson's mastery. It does not sound the gong that visitors to Monticello can still hear today, marking the passage of the long hours during which his slaves were forced to produce. It does not reveal the way in which his nailery was inspired by the latest theories of penal reform, such as he had seen in Philadelphia in the 1790s, which were designed to make productive workers of prisoners. And while the force of his personality and his system of rewards and distinctions may have bound slaves in the house and on Mulberry Row to him, that was not so with field hands, who toiled far from the main house under the disciplining hand of an overseer.

A master of the art of persuasion, Jefferson hated the whip. He was pleased when Thomas Mann Randolph, supervising his plantations in his absence in 1792, reported that his overseer Clarkson "has a valuable art of governing the slaves which sets aside the necessity of punishment almost entirely." "My first wish is that the labourers may be well treated," Jefferson replied magnanimously, commending his overseer. Later he acknowledged his obligation to feed, clothe, and protect his slaves "from all ill usage" and to require of them "such reasonable labor only as is performed voluntarily by freeman." He would not run his plantations with ill-fed, nearly naked, abused, and overworked slaves. Such sentiments may explain why Edwin Morris Betts, who edited Jefferson's Farm Book for publication, concluded that "life for the slaves on Jefferson's plantations was probably a happy one" or why Dumas Malone's six-volume biography judged Jefferson's slaveholding as "kind to the point of indulgence."

But the fact is that if Jefferson himself did not use the whip, he employed overseers who did. He hired William Page to supervise his slaves at Shadwell. So brutal a reputation did Page have that when Jack Eppes employed him for a year, he was unable to find anyone who would lease slaves to him. Jefferson had made a point of asking Tom Randolph to make sure that overseer Gabriel Lilly governed the nailery without resorting to the whip, except "in extremities," but he let pass, unremarked, Tom's reply that none of the nailery workers "have incurred it but the small ones for truancy." Although Jefferson preferred restraint for his productive nailers, Lilly did not need to worry about being chastised by his employer, so long as he kept Jefferson's customers supplied.

More than a year after this exchange, another incident occurred in the nailery in which Jefferson did intervene—this time, however, to ensure the severity of the culprit's punishment. Wielding one of the heavy hammers of his trade, Cary, a seventeen-year-old nailer, broke the skull of Brown Colbert, a grandson of Elizabeth Hemings. Amazingly, Colbert survived the attack, but hearing of the altercation in Washington, Jefferson was furious. "It will be necessary for me to make an example of him in terrorem [terror] to others," he instructed Tom Randolph. Cary was to disappear from Monticello. Immediately. A slave trader from Georgia was Jefferson's first suggestion, but if none could be had, then "he could be sold in any other quarter so distant as never more to be heard of among us." The effect for those remaining behind at Monticello, Jefferson emphasized, "would be as if he were put out of the way by death." Cary would not threaten a Hemings or Jefferson's nail business again.

Interestingly, however, Jefferson did not fire Lilly when he beat James Hemings, the seventeen-year-old son of Critta Hemings, Sally's older sister. The young man had been ill, and James Oldham, a white carpenter working on Jefferson's remodeling project, had been taking care of the sick boy and feared for his life. Oldham later provided Jefferson with an account of Lilly's "barbarity." Refusing to believe that he was too ill to work in the nailery, Lilly rousted Hemings out of bed and whipped him so severely that Hemings "was really not able to raise his hand to his head." Once recovered, James Hemings fled. Briefly recaptured in Richmond six months later, he was unpersuaded by Jefferson's pleas to return. Nor did Jefferson try further to pursue him. It is telling that even after losing a valuable slave—and a Hemings, at that—Lilly felt confident enough of Jefferson's approval of his methods to ask that his salary be doubled. Balking at the figure, Jefferson refused, although with regret. "Certainly I could never get a man who serves my purposes better than he does," Jefferson sighed ruefully to Tom Randolph as he let Lilly go.

Jefferson's "first wish" may have been leniency for his slaves, but his second and overriding policy was that his slaves "may enable me to have that treatment continued by making as much as will admit it." In other words, if they were cooperative, they would be spared. If they were not, there would be consequences. They might face a whipping. Or they might be demoted from his benign supervision on the mountain to fieldwork under a William Page or Gabriel Lilly, whose job was to ensure profitability. Or their master could make it seem as if they had dropped off the face of the earth.

As he did on the use of punishments, Jefferson had a mixed record on arguably the most important aspect of his slaves' existence: family life. Of course, no state in the union legally recognized the marriages of slaves: "Property" obviously could not marry. Nor would masters allow their convenience to be constrained by their slaves' marital or parental bonds if sale or dispersal made good business sense. But unlike many southern slaveholders, Jefferson at least professed concern for the integrity of his slaves' marriages and family bonds. In fact, he encouraged his slaves to choose partners from among his own slave communities. "Certainly there is nothing I desire so much as that all the young people in the estate intermarry with one another and stay at home," he wrote to his overseer at Poplar Forest, adding, "They are worth a great deal more in that case than when they have husbands and wives abroad." When he decided to sell some slaves to help reduce the inherited Wayles debt, he had approached his brother Randolph, hoping that he might be able to identify a buyer in his neighborhood for "Dinah & her family," since Randolph owned Dinah's husband, thus enabling the couple to live near each other.

Other instances of Jefferson's willingness to accommodate slave relationships occurred closer to home. When Jefferson returned from France, he found that Mary Hemings, Sally's eldest sister, had borne two children to his Charlottesville neighbor, a white man named Thomas Bell. A merchant in town, Bell had hired Mary from Jefferson during his absence. Two years after Jefferson's return, Mary Hemings asked to be sold to Bell. Acquiescing, Jefferson instructed his agent to "dispose of Mary according to her desire to Colonel Bell, with such of her younger children as she chose." Of course, in this case, Jefferson was also taking into account the wishes of a white man he respected. Nonetheless, his sale of Mary Hemings was of a piece with similar decisions he made to buy and sell other married slaves to unite them, such as blacksmith Moses Hern. Hern repeatedly requested that Jefferson buy his wife and children, who were owned by Jefferson's nephew Randolph Lewis, six miles away. Not until Lewis was picking up stakes to move to Kentucky did Jefferson finally yield, although he was clearly put out. "Nobody feels more strongly than I do the desire to make all practicable sacrifices to keep man and wife together who have *imprudently*," he judged, "married out of their respective families." In another case, he went "exactly counter" to his aim to retain strong young men for his own plantations and agreed to sell Brown Colbert (who wanted to remain with his wife, whose owner was moving to Kentucky), because he was "always willing to indulge connections seriously formed by those people"—at least "where it can be done reasonably." He did try to exact a surcharge of an extra one hundred dollars for Colbert's smithing expertise in the bargain, however.

Whatever his strong desire to accommodate enslaved families, Jefferson did separate families if it suited him. When he recommended that Isabel Hern escort little Maria across the Atlantic, he disregarded the fact that on that risky voyage of an indeterminate duration, Isabel was not only pregnant but would have left behind a husband (his trusted wagoner, Davy) and four children. Joseph Fossett and Edith Hern were probably already married when Jefferson took the fifteen-year-old Edith (the child with whom Isabel had been pregnant when Jefferson suggested that she accompany Maria to France) to Washington to learn French cookery during his presidency. He airily downgraded the commitment she and Joseph had forged together, from marriage to "formerly connected," perhaps to allow himself to separate them for eight years with no pangs of conscience. After four years, however, when Jefferson returned home for a holiday without Edith, Joseph disappeared from Monticello. He reappeared in the yard of the President's House in Washington, where his wife was working. Puzzled that Fossett had run away although he had "never in his life received a blow from any one," Jefferson alerted a loyal Irish servant at the White House to pursue him. Jailed for the night, Fossett was sent back to Monticello the next day, where he waited until Jefferson's second term of office was over to be reunited with his wife.

Nor did Jefferson always honor the bond between mother and child. Although he agreed to sell Mary Hemings to Thomas Bell along with their two children, her older children by other fathers, twelve-year-old Joseph Fossett and nine-year-old Betsy Hemmings, were decidedly not part of the deal and remained in Jefferson's possession. (He had already given away two of her other children as gifts.) And when the Jefferson family celebrated Maria's wedding to Jack Eppes, three enslaved families were forced to bid heartbreaking goodbyes to four children, ages ten to fourteen, gifts from Jefferson to the newlyweds who then moved to Eppington, three days' journey away.

THIS WAS THE WORLD into which Jefferson's third surviving daughter, Harriet Hemings, was born on a spring day in 1801. To some extent, the extended Hemings family was spared the pain of separation, although Maria's wedding gift had included two of Elizabeth Hemings's granddaughters: Betsy, the daughter of Mary Hemings Bell, and Melinda Colbert, the daughter of Sally's older sister Betty Brown. Sally's children were never to be sold or gifted away from her, however, although in their adulthood two would leave the mountain forever, likely never to see her again. Still, the relative security of her immediate family was itself a significant mark of distinction in the slave community at Monticello, even among the extended Hemings clan.

These distinctions are not readily apparent in Jefferson's Farm Book, however, where we can see Sally and her children receiving their portions just like everyone else. As a toddler, Beverley received his first woolens in 1799, his yard and a half exceeding Jefferson's rule of distribution by half a yard. Having received her blanket in 1798, his mother got a bed and a pair of shoes in 1799. Similarly, the Farm Book records blanket distributions for her in 1808 and for her four children in 1809. She is probably the Sally who received a bed in 1809, perhaps marking her move from Mulberry Row up the slope to the completed south dependency of the main house. In December 1812, they received their yardage of linen proportionate to their ages, as Jefferson's rule specified: Sally received her full seven yards; four-year-old Eston received two and one-third. Beverley received a hat in 1811, and by December 1813, as a fifteen-year-old, he was listed separately from his mother and younger siblings for his shirting, cotton plains, and woolens. And it was in the Farm Book's bread list that Jefferson recorded the birth dates of Sally's children. So Jefferson left almost nothing in the general run of his plantation record to alert even the closest reader that Sally Hemings and her children were unlike any other Hemingses at Monticello.

Jefferson did make clear to his overseers, however, that his house slaves—comprising mostly Hemingses—were different from all the others. After losing Gabriel Lilly, in 1806 he hired Edmund Bacon, who would work for him at Monticello for the next sixteen years. Returning to Washington, Jefferson left a memorandum of instructions for his new overseer. He was particular about his most favored slaves; they each had their own individual supervisor who alone directed their skilled labor. Bacon was to have nothing to do with them, Jefferson emphasized, except to provide their provisions. Nor was Bacon ever to send John Hemings to assist in the harvest. Bacon was also relieved of responsibility for clothing the house slaves, who were considerably better dressed than the field hands. "Mrs. Randolph always chooses the clothing for the house servants; that is to say, for Peter Hemings, Burwell, Edwin, Critta, and Sally," Jefferson directed. They received Irish linen instead of the rough osnaburg, calamanco (a soft wool with a high gloss), flannel (to make warm undergarments), and knitted cotton stockings rather than the baggy woven stockings worn by field hands. Bacon was to supervise the distribution of "colored plains," a woven wool cloth softer on the skin, to Jefferson's house slaves, Betty Brown, Betty Hemings, Nance, and Ursula. These women, Bacon remembered, were "old family servants, and great favorites" who remained at Monticello during Jefferson's absence. Remarkably, to Bacon at least, he "was instructed to take no control of them." They may have been the only enslaved women in the state free of an overseer's control.

So this too was little Harriet's world. It explains why she was able to spend her childhood at her mother's side—a deceptively simple observation but one that packs a punch. Harriet was almost eight before Jefferson returned to live permanently at Monticello. In the meantime, in his absences, the Hemings women "had very little to do," according to Bacon, except airing the house in preparation for Jefferson's twice-yearly visits and the cider-making that consumed two weeks every March, following Jefferson's persnickety directions. (Thirty years later, Bacon could still recall Jefferson's unusual "instructions to have every apple cleaned perfectly clean when it was made.") Harriet's earliest memories, then, were of growing up among a loving, relatively stable network of aunts, uncles, and cousins, her mother and brothers, and until she was six, even her grandmother. Without the driving presence of a master and an overseer, and exempt from field labor, Sally Hemings had more time than most enslaved women to devote to her small children and relations at Monticello. Until age fourteen, Sally's children spent their days at her side in the great house, unlike most slave families whose parents labored at sites away from their children.

Harriet's childhood was also exceptional because she was raised by a woman whose experiences as a young girl set her apart from every other slave at Monticello: She had survived the perils of transatlantic travel and had lived in the glittering city of Paris. During Harriet's earliest years, her father and sisters Martha and Maria were only intermittently at Monticello, and her uncle James Hemings had died tragically just months after she was born. So the only person who remained on the mountain consistently throughout Harriet's childhood, who retained the memories and who frequently told stories of those years, was her mother. Bacon listened to them, too. "They crossed the ocean alone," he said. "I have often heard her tell about it."

Sally Hemings had a lot of stories to tell. She had learned early in her life what it meant to be enslaved. In 1783, at age ten, she had been sent with Maria to Eppington, and then again the following year. Her mother had remained behind at Monticello, a twenty-seven-hour hard cavalry ride, or three days' coach travel, away from Eppington. We do not know how Elizabeth Wayles Eppes treated her house slaves, but certainly her constant visitors kept them busy. The warm hospitality for which she was known would not have extended to slaves, not even to Sally, whom she had last seen at the deathbed of their half sister Martha Wayles Jefferson. Elizabeth Eppes was there when, according to a Hemings family tradition, Martha gave nine-year-old Sally a bell, a token of their tie as sisters and as mistress and slave. But when Sally arrived at Eppington, Eppes probably sent her to the second floor, to sleep in the open space that was the nursery for the youngest children. Perhaps she slept on a pallet at the foot of Maria's bed, at hand if Maria awoke, crying in the night. There she would have helped Elizabeth Eppes care for the children stricken with whooping cough that terrible October 1784, perhaps fearing for her own safety with every coughing fit in that crowded room. Certainly Sally Hemings matured at Eppington in ways that Francis and Elizabeth Eppes recognized when they decided that she was the best choice to accompany their precious niece to France. Only fourteen, Sally Hemings then crossed the Atlantic virtually alone: No one provided her with a male protector to shield her from the coarse leers or worse of roughened sailors. As Bacon noticed in her accounts of those days, she felt her vulnerability keenly. Indeed, Harriet Hemings was raised by a mother who, of necessity, had learned how to stand on her own two feet at a very young age.

Once in Paris, as historian Annette Gordon-Reed remarked, Sally Hemings "learned that another type of life was possible." Under the tutelage and guidance of her elder brother James, she had experienced the sights and sounds of the city, mixing with other people of color to whom James introduced her. She had learned to speak French, watched the beginnings of revolution, and realized enough about French law regarding slavery to know that if she chose, she could remain in France, a free woman. She also had been inoculated against smallpox by the most prominent practitioner in Europe, spending six weeks away from Jefferson's household as she recuperated. She had mixed in elite Parisian society as a lady's maid, maybe attending Jefferson's daughters occasionally at their school but certainly present at the balls Martha frequented in her last months in Paris. As we saw, the girls' schoolmates even included greetings to "Mademoiselle Sally" in their letters. Sally Hemings was a caste apart from other slaves, then, even before she entered into a relationship with Jefferson. Learning self-reliance at an early age, and living in a much wider world than was visible from Monticello, Sally Hemings was a mother of uncommon character and experience in the slave community. And in the new life she had negotiated for herself on her return from France, she occupied a new status: no longer a lady's maid to either Martha or Maria, off-limits to the governance of the overseer, and a mother of children destined for freedom.

The names of Sally Hemings's children are another indication of the special status this family occupied at Monticello. It was a common enough practice of slave owners to name their slaves, frequently bestowing names like Zeus, Apollo, and Hercules that contrasted cruelly with their subordinate status. But the names for Sally's children, drawn from Jefferson's family lines and circle of friends, were meaningful to him. Each had a story attached to it. Harriet's name came from a beloved Randolph, a younger sister of Martha's husband, Tom, who had sought relief from her young stepmother at the more congenial fireside of Monticello. Jefferson and Sally Hemings used the name twice; Harriet was named for an elder sister, who had died in 1797 at two. William Beverley was likely named after a relative from Jefferson's mother's Randolph line, who in 1746 had traveled with Peter Jefferson on his first expedition to survey the far western reaches of Lord Fairfax's lands in Virginia. At the suggestion of Jefferson's family friend Dolley Madison, James Madison was named for Jefferson's closest friend and political associate, Thomas Eston for a favorite Randolph uncle. There had been no other Harriets in Jefferson's records before Sally's daughters; her sons' names are especially distinctive standouts in the Farm Book lists of slaves. And when we consider the names of Martha Jefferson Randolph's sons (James Madison, Benjamin Franklin, Meriwether Lewis, and George Wythe), the pattern of all the boys' names (Hemings and Randolph), one historian noted, resembles "the act of a white man who has no white sons to name."

But as a very young child, Harriet would have been unaware of these nuances of status. She may have played with the Randolph girls on their occasional visits to Monticello. Two were particularly close to her in age: Virginia, born just three months after Harriet in August 1801, and Cornelia, born two years earlier. It was not at all unusual in the eighteenth and nineteenth centuries for very young children, free and enslaved, to spend their days playing together until they began to learn their respective conditions in life. Nor would a stranger looking at the three little girls have been able to distinguish among them: Both Cornelia and Virginia had their father's dark coloring, with olive skin and dark hair. The Randolphs had prided themselves on their descent from Pocahontas, after all. We do not know the color of Sally Hemings's hair; Isaac Granger Jefferson had said only that she had "long straight hair down her back." Harriet may have had the auburn hair and gray eyes of her Jefferson line, as did her brothers; all four of Sally Hemings's children, Ellen Randolph wrote in 1858, were "fair," as was Ellen herself. Either way, Harriet would have fit right into a Randolph family tableau. Certainly her skin, "nearly as white as anybody's," Edmund Bacon said, would not have marked her as anything other than the freeborn white girls her Randolph nieces were.

But, of course, Harriet Hemings was no Randolph and so could not enjoy their privileges. It is not likely that she was a recipient of Jefferson's largesse in her childhood. She would not have received the kinds of gifts Jefferson bestowed with such a generous hand on his grand-daughters: a saddle and bridle, an elegant watch, a guitar, or silk dresses. But neither was Jefferson stern or cold to her. He was, Madison thought, "undemonstrative" by temperament, but at the same time "uniformly kind to all about him." But, he added, "he was not in the habit of show-ing partiality or fatherly affection to us [Sally's] children." So it is not likely that he bestowed the gifts upon Sally Hemings's children that he did upon Martha's.

Nor did Jefferson follow the example of many planter-fathers in his own day who lived openly with their slave consorts, claimed the chil-dren of those unions, and provided for them. Bachelor fathers in New Orleans made a point of asserting paternity in baptismal records. Prominent white Floridians had large mulatto families, freed and edu-cated their children, and provided for them in their wills, bestowing on them homes, land, and even slaves. In Jefferson's own state, there were multiple examples of fathers who freed their children with enslaved mothers, educated them, and bequeathed their own acreage to their progeny at their deaths. Of the several who also freed the mothers of their children, one even requested that he be buried beside her.

Against these fellow Virginians, Jefferson's provisions for Sally and her children were parsimonious by comparison, and always beneath the radar. On their return from Paris, he installed her, with her sister Critta, in the stone structure he had built in the 1770s for his hired white builders. But when he anticipated hiring white artisans for the remod-eling project in 1793, he instructed Tom Randolph to move them out to the new houses he had built for them on Mulberry Row. Sally Hemings's house was built of wood, with a wood chimney and, by Jef-ferson's own description, "earth floors." There she raised their children until the south dependency was completed in 1808 and they were moved to a room there. Tucked under the terrace that afforded Jeffer-son and his family and guests a pleasant outdoor promenade from the house to the south pavilion, the south dependency contained the kitchen, cook's room, dairy, smokehouse, and washhouse—all functions necessary to the smooth functioning of Jefferson's household but, like the slave labor required to run them, hidden from the family's view.

Ever conscious of the threat of smallpox endangering Martha's and

Maria's families, he vaccinated his slaves in several rounds: seventy or eighty of them in 1801, and dozens more in 1802, 1816–1824, and 1826. At four years of age, Beverley was in that second round of inoculations, as was Harriet, who may have reached her first birthday by that late May morning. Although the vaccination method was considerably safer than the inoculations practiced in the 1790s, Sally Hemings may well have felt as Martha Randolph had when she sent Anne and Jeff, six and five, to Richmond in 1797 for the procedure: "The idea of exposing my children to such a disease . . . makes me perfectly miserable. I never look at them but my eyes fill with tears to think how soon we shall part and *perhaps* forever." Or, remembering her own successful inoculation in Paris, she may have sent them off in confidence that they, too, would emerge unscathed and forever protected from the dreaded pox. Either way she would not have had a choice in the matter.

Jefferson would have entrusted Harriet's education to her mother, however, as tended to be true as well in most white households in the nineteenth century. The goal of white female education was the same, whether girls were schooled at home or in the numerous female academies that began to dot the southern landscape after the 1820s: to train them for lives of domesticity as wives and mothers. The "curriculum" was as various as the situations of the students themselves, whether daughters of wealthy slaveholders, urban artisans, or rural farmers, but at its most basic would have included at least reading and writing literacy, "ciphering" (basic math), and needlework. At home, mothers would also ensure that their daughters knew how to make a pudding, truss and roast a chicken, raise a vegetable garden, and tend a poultry yard. There is no reason to think that Sally Hemings would have wanted anything less for the daughter she knew would live her adult life in freedom.

We do not know if Harriet learned to read and write, but given the culture of learning and teaching on both Mulberry Row and in the great house, it is eminently possible that she learned at least the rudimentary skills necessary to position herself to be the wife of a respectable man one day—perhaps even a white man. Literacy was a key badge of both respectability and whiteness; ex-slave Israel Jefferson considered it "a legitimate fruit of freedom." Sally's older brothers Bob and James Hemings were literate; an inventory of Monticello kitchen equipment from February 1796 in James's hand has survived to this day. So, too, have several letters written by Sally's younger brother John to Jefferson and to his favorite Randolph, Martha's youngest daughter, Septimia. And archaeologists working on Mulberry Row have excavated a piece of slate bearing the chalk markings of a writing lesson, so Harriet could have learned to read and write from members of the enslaved community.

Or, as Madison had, it is possible that Harriet may have picked up literacy from her Randolph nieces. Madison recalled "inducing" the Randolph children to teach him his alphabet and more besides. Joseph Fossett's son Peter similarly remembered that "Mr. Jefferson allowed his grandson to teach any of his slaves who desired to learn, and Lewis Randolph first taught me how to read." We know that Harriet's youngest brother, Eston, had also learned how to read and write. Perhaps Virginia and Cornelia taught Harriet her letters as they were learning them as well. Or maybe Harriet learned from Ellen, five years her senior, who was actively interested in slave education. When Burwell Colbert's wife, Critta (not to be confused with Sally's sister), died in 1819, Ellen asked if she could have one of his daughters. She had been "lamenting very seriously that I had not secured one of her elder children. Mama promised I should have any one of them not disposed of," and Ellen was thinking she would like "little Martha." Even though she was not sure exactly which of Burwell's children was Martha, she hoped no one else had claimed her and assured her mother that "I am more than ever anxious to have it in my power to befriend, and educate her as well as I can." (Ellen's mother kept the child.) So even if Sally Hemings could not have taught Harriet to read and write, there were many ways to enlist someone who could. Tellingly, Jefferson took no notice of this daughter's education as he had of Martha's and Maria's.

Sally Hemings would certainly have taught her daughter the needlework skills for which she herself was well known and that were an essential part of a well-bred woman's preparation for marriage and housekeeping. Jefferson, who had recommended stitchery to Martha as a productive way for women to pass the time, would have heartily approved. Under her mother's eye, Harriet began with simple straight stitches to join seams, progressing to a hemming stitch for handkerchiefs, skirts, and sheets, and finally advancing to decorative stitches to adorn dresses, pillows, chair covers, and bed hangings. Sally would have passed to Harriet all the skills she had learned in Paris and continued to hone at Monticello as she looked after Jefferson's clothing and chambers. From a mother experienced in caring for a range of fabrics and garments, Harriet would have learned how to clean and preserve the clothes she created with the higher-grade fabrics Martha Randolph provided. Jefferson sometimes supplied piece goods as well; twice at Christmas he sent special packages from Philadelphia for Sally, Critta, and Betsy Hemings.

A central feature of female preparation for marriage was training in cookery, whether the bride would section, salt, and cure the ham herself or direct her servants or slaves to do so. No nineteenth-century woman was spared kitchen duties, regardless of her rank. The women of Jefferson's family both directed and cooked: One of Isaac Granger Jefferson's early memories was Jefferson's wife, Martha, perched on a kitchen stool, reading a cake recipe to Ursula Granger; Maria's father had constantly nagged her about whether she had yet learned to make a pudding. Therefore it is inconceivable that Sally Hemings would have neglected to arrange a culinary education of some sort for Harriet.

Just a few short months after Harriet was born, her uncle James, the French-trained chef, left Monticello for the last time to seek his fortune in the free black community in Baltimore. His younger brother Peter took charge of Jefferson's kitchen. As president, Jefferson hired a Frenchman named Honoré Julien to supervise his Washington kitchen and there train slaves Edith Hern Fossett and her sister-in-law Fanny Gillette Hern in French cookery. Their skills drew praise, both in the President's House and back at Monticello, where they returned in March 1809 to cook for Jefferson in his retirement. "Served in half Virginian, half French style," Daniel Webster noted after his visit in 1824, Edy Fossett's meals delighted. Her "balls" of ice cream "inclosed in covers of warm pastry" were a particular highlight of dining at Jefferson's Washington table and may have appeared in Monticello as well.

Edy Fossett's days began early to ensure that breads and muffins were baked and on the table by eight or nine A.M. Then followed the rush of the day to get the main meal prepared for serving by four P.M. The pace of kitchen work was compounded by the numbers of visitors to Jefferson's table, sometimes as many as fifty at a time. According to

Shown newly restored in this photograph, the kitchen in Monticello's south wing is Jefferson's re-creation of a French gourmet cuisine of that era. Completed in 1809, the kitchen was ready to serve Jefferson in his retirement. Note the eight-burner stove on the left as well as the bread oven in the rear, attesting to the skills of the enslaved cooks who prepared the elegant dishes and sauces that graced Jefferson's table.

Jefferson's records, Harriet was never assigned duty in the kitchen. But at exceptionally busy times, she may have worked under the supervision of the undercooks and taken her turn at whipping cream, stirring sauces, kneading bread, preparing vegetables, or learning to bake the muffins that were Peter Hemings's specialty and Jefferson's particular favorite. Harriet could have learned a great deal in the well-equipped kitchen of the French-trained chefs that Edy and Fanny had become, when they brought their skills back to Monticello with their master's retirement from the presidency. She would have been able to produce more elegant fare than most American girls and know how to serve it.

From the colonial period, housewives had also been responsible for planting kitchen gardens, from which they would harvest herbs and vegetables, and for raising poultry. Harriet had plenty of opportunity to cultivate these skills as well. It is clear that Monticello's slaves were enormously productive in both. Not only did they raise enough to supplement the meager diet their master supplied them, but as mentioned they sold great quantities of food to the great house, including cucumbers, cabbages, watermelons, potatoes, strawberries, and eggs and chickens. Martha Randolph had appointed her eldest daughter, Anne, to make and record these transactions, paid for in cash, as part of her preparation for managing her own household when she married.

Of the slaves who sold eggs and poultry to the Monticello household, Wormley Hughes sold the most, on forty-five different occasions over three years. But his prodigious output relied on the work of his wife and children; the care, housing, and maintenance of the poultry were community affairs. Adults built the henhouses; children chased away predators. Twenty years older than Harriet, Wormley Hughes, the son of Betty Brown, was her cousin; his wife, Ursula, a grandchild of Great George Granger, worked in the kitchen. Blood ties and their favored status at Monticello bound them all together. It is easy to imagine Harriet, who lacked a fond father, tagging along after Wormley, gathering eggs, peppering him with questions, and with a child's fascination with chickens, following them—perhaps with wailing protests—from the henhouse to the butchering table. This was not just the work of slaves: Only months before Maria's death, Jefferson was happily planning the establishment of her henhouse at Pantops, starting with the "two pair of beautiful fowls" he had received from Algiers; and from Washington, he had told his granddaughter Anne he would send her a pair of bantams to raise. Harriet, however, would have learned about this key element of nineteenth-century housekeeping directly from Monticello's most successful poulterer.

Cousin Wormley was also at the center of other activity in the spring seasons of 1807 through 1809, in which Harriet, too, may have been much interested. Thinking ahead to his retirement, Jefferson sent his wagoner, Davy Hern, on several trips from Washington back to Monticello, beginning in the fall of 1806, with carts laden with trees, bulbs, thorns (for natural fencing), and seedlings to begin laying out the gardens that today are a central feature of Monticello's beauty. Jefferson put Anne, who shared his passion for gardening, in charge of nursing his Peruvian grasses through the winter, and she and Ellen were responsible for riding over from Edgehill to Monticello to keep an eye on his tulips. Ornamental gardens were considered a perfectly suitable interest for well-bred girls, as was botany.

In the letters that flew between Jefferson and his two eldest grand-daughters, Anne and Ellen, their mounting excitement with each passing season is palpable. Wormley prepared the beds for Jefferson's design in the spring of 1808, and he, Jefferson, and Anne finished the project the following spring when Jefferson returned home, finally to begin his retirement from public life. Reminiscing years later, Ellen still smiled at the memory. Wormley planted each seedling under Jefferson's "own eye" with a "crowd of happy young faces," she recalled, who inquired "anxiously the name of each separate deposit."

Throughout these spring plantings, however, Harriet Hemings remains obscured in the shadows. Would she, too, have been interested in all the varieties of bulbs and plants going into the ground? Enjoying comparative freedom as a little girl, except as her time was structured by her mother, would she have dug tulip holes, or passed the bulbs to Wormley for planting, or checked for spring shoots before Ellen and Anne arrived from Edgehill? And in the process, could Wormley Hughes have furnished her with something of the warmth and care that Jefferson did not?

Thinking about Harriet's life requires peering into these shadows, asking questions to which answers are not always discoverable. Did she trail Jefferson in the quiet of the morning, when, as was his habit, he checked his flower beds right after breakfast? Did she share in the Randolph girls' delight over the rich colors of the flowers as they bloomed? Family passions and aptitudes do seem to be inheritable. True, you don't have to carry Jefferson blood to be entranced by the beauty of fifty-five hundred tulips on the west lawn; visitors still marvel at their appearance every spring, massed in their oval beds and ringing the reflecting pond. But in their adulthood, it became clear that Madison and Eston Hemings inherited their father's love of building and music; it is not too much of a stretch, then, to wonder if their sister inherited Jefferson's passion for gardening. It would have been a perfectly appropriate interest for a girl to pursue. It could also have been a way to connect with her rather distant father, especially if an approving word or smile occasionally broke through his reserve as together they bent their fair heads to a fragrant flower.

At least until she turned fourteen, when he decided her childhood was over and sent her to work in his textile manufactory.

An Enlightened
Household

. . . .

1809

. . . .

As she made her way to work each day, Harriet Hemings walked the path that led down the slope from the south dependency. Connecting Mulberry Row to the main house, the path ended directly across from the cottage that was now Jefferson's textile manufactory. Did she ever pause there, looking up to measure the short distance that separated her workday from that of her half sister Martha's? From the bottom of the slope, she could see the graceful curve of the brick wall that was the exterior of Jefferson's library. Above the library one of Monticello's four great chimneys was visible, rising behind the ornamental spindle railing that trimmed the roofline of the house. She could see, too, the pediment that crowned the four massive pillars at the east entrance of the mansion, covering the portico. It was barely twenty-four paces to the top. But it might have been a world away.

In his study, which he called his cabinet, Jefferson had started his day before breakfast. Just before the sun's rising he, too, had risen, bathed his feet in cold water as was his habit (he believed it staved off sickness), dressed, and sat at his desk to attend to his voluminous correspondence. Taking breakfast with Martha and her children at eight, he returned to his desk for a morning of reading and writing. His cabinet is furnished today much as it was in his own day: A tall handsome clock chimed the passing of each hour, which Jefferson could track in any event as the light that flooded his work space moved from the south windows on his left to the west-facing windows in front of him. His desk held a polygraph copying machine to create a duplicate of each letter he wrote, a book stand that permitted him to work with five books at a time, a copious supply of ink, and his spectacles. Two candles were rigged to his chair to provide light for evening reading, and a long upholstered bench allowed him to elevate his feet while he read.

Bathed in natural light, Jefferson's cabinet is visible through his library. Inspired by the apartments he enjoyed in Paris, Jefferson redesigned his home upon his return. The light from the double glass doors of the greenhouse to the left (unseen) illuminates his books (right). The graceful arch seen here is one of the surviving specimens of John Hemings's skill that can be seen at Monticello today.

Adjoining his cabinet was his library, composed of two rooms, their walls lined with books, designed so that each room opened to the next. The easy flow facilitated by the floor plan—from bookshelves to desk and back again—mirrors the exchange and development of ideas in which Jefferson delighted. Angled to capture the best light the Virginia sun could afford and sheathed in windows, Jefferson's cabinet was itself both symbol and wellspring of one of the greatest minds of the American Enlightenment. In his bright study, Jefferson took pen in hand and resumed his day's work. At the bottom of the path, his daughter Harriet opened the door to his textile manufactory, took her place at the spinning jenny, and put her hand to the wheel.

In the South Square Room, immediately off the entrance hall, Martha Jefferson Randolph began her working day. Measuring fourteen feet ten inches by fifteen feet four inches, the room offered cramped quarters for the several functions it had to serve, its meager floor space reduced further by a fireplace that jutted out into the room. One of the windows faced east, admitting morning light as Martha assigned the house slaves their tasks for the day; the other faced the east portico, allowing her to see approaching visitors. A small desk was tucked into the tiny corner alcove created by the fireplace's footprint, enabling her to literally turn her back away from the commotion in the room to concentrate on her work. Her sewing table, probably crafted by John Hemings, and chair were drawn up to the window to take advantage of the light. Here Martha supervised the running of her father's household and received the guests who congregated in the entrance hall in hopes of seeing him. And here as well, in this overcrowded room far from the glittering life she had known in Paris, Martha Jefferson Randolph schooled her children.

However remote her girlhood years in Paris may have seemed, they had decidedly molded her vision of female education as she constructed a plan for her own daughters. Her ideas for them contrasted sharply with her father's for her. For all the attention historians have lavished on Jefferson's ideas about education, it was instead the years spent in the company of girls and women devoted to the intellectual life, and supervised by an abbess who herself epitomized female intelligence, capacity, and energy, that shaped his daughter's ideas of the content and meaning of female education. Here at Monticello, under her instruction, her daughters would mature in the study of Latin, literature, history, and the sciences that they had begun as children at Edgehill. Over the years, they would delight in the life of the mind, vie with each other for precious study time away from housekeeping chores at Jefferson's Bedford

From the desk on the left, Martha Jefferson Randolph supervised the daily operation of her father's household. The books in the alcove on the right supplied the lessons she dispensed daily to her ever-growing family. In the center of the room stands her sewing table, made for her in the joinery at Monticello. Through the door can be seen Jefferson's own library, where Martha sometimes sat with him while she sewed.

County hideaway of Poplar Forest, and be praised as the best-educated young women in America. But as Jefferson expended the final energies of his life building the university that remains his monument, it never occurred to him that his brilliant and vivacious granddaughters should ever take seats in its classrooms. And, in fact, the architectural innovations that Jefferson designed at Monticello reveal important clues about his opinions of the contrasting ways men and women should live their lives, and help us to understand why he never envisioned his granddaughters at his university.

INSPIRED BY ALL HE had seen in France, Jefferson embarked upon a twenty-year renovation project to remake Monticello after his return. In the finished house, public and private spaces were clearly demarcated. The public north wing contained dining and tea rooms, located near guest bedrooms. Taking advantage of the light and warmth of a southern exposure, Jefferson's private apartments occupied almost the entire south wing. He ensured his privacy by keeping all three doors to his apartments locked, to the dismay of many a guest who observed how much more pleasant their stay might have been had they enjoyed access to Mr. Jefferson's books.

Family life, however, was architecturally all but invisible at Monticello. This is particularly curious given Jefferson's hope that his daughters and their families would be frequent visitors, if not residents, there with him. Although Jack Eppes had turned down Jefferson's offers to lodge at Monticello while he built a home at Pantops, the Randolphs found it convenient to move their family from Edgehill to Jefferson's mansion. Using his father-in-law's house as their headquarters, Tom could more easily help the aging Jefferson manage all their plantation operations and Martha could run his household and receive his guests. By 1809, most of his renovations were complete and the house was infinitely more comfortable, a fact Martha must have appreciated since she was expecting her tenth child when Jefferson returned home from Washington for the last time. Her son Meriwether Lewis was born in 1810; Septimia (so named because she was the seventh daughter) followed in 1814 and, last, George Wythe in 1818.

Viewed from the east entrance, the house seemed smaller than its eleven thousand square feet and appeared to be just a single story, graced by floor-to-ceiling windows. In fact, the tops of the windows extended up to the second floor—but only waist-high. The five second-story bedrooms were thus lit from the floor, while Jefferson's cabinet and library enjoyed the fullest benefit of natural light that full-length, south-facing windows could provide. In each wing, an impossibly narrow staircase ascended steeply from basement to third floor; positioned discreetly away from the guest rooms, the stairs were not visible to visitors, who could remain oblivious to clues of family life inside the house as well. Lacking natural light, the steps required the use of a candle to light the way, an additional encumbrance to hands already full. Two-year-old Septimia was scarred in more ways than one when she took a spill down those stairs in the arms of her brother's wife, Jane. Ever after, when anyone spoke of the incident, Virginia told Jane, "Septimia pitied her self very much, without bestowing a single thought on the bruises which you got in trying to save her."

Historians studying the home as closely as they have its builder have

This view makes clear the hazards of negotiating the interior staircases, particularly for women. Built into stairwells that are six-feet square, the steps are just twenty-four inches wide, have dangerously high risers, and ascend in almost a spiral, with two turns on each floor. The only illumination comes from a small skylight in the roof. Jefferson's design certainly rejected the grand European staircases, which were used to assert rank, but it does more: It reveals his lack of concern with his family's convenience, even as he ensured his own.

been puzzled by what they view as an architectural flaw in an otherwise convenient house. But if we acknowledge that Monticello is a "very self-centered" kind of house, to quote one architectural historian, the puzzle is solved: Jefferson never routinely climbed those stairs, carrying small children, bedclothes, laundry, chamber pots, or candles. Downstairs, where he lived, domestic efficiency *did* reign. He had learned the delights of private apartments at the Hôtel de Langeac; such refinements were unknown in America. But although his renovations of Monticello had clearly been inspired by European architecture, he ignored the precedents of seventeenth-century Rome—a most masculine city where men outnumbered women by a ratio of three to two. Even there, apartments for women were still very much a part of their architectural planning. A wife might have parallel apartments in a mirror image of her husband's, either across the house or upstairs from his. Newly married husbands remodeled their homes if they lacked space for the bride's needs. Yet in spite of his expectations that Maria and Jack Eppes would live with him after their wedding, Jefferson did not reconfigure his designs for Monticello to accommodate them, much less Martha's sprawling family.

In their design and allocation of space, then, Jefferson's personal apartments are a celebration of Enlightenment reason and its application to daily life. But this "great advocate of light and air," as Jefferson called himself, provided little of either for his family members on a floor with a series of small, poorly lit, nondescript rooms, none of which were even visible from the exterior. In its arrangement of space, light, and function, the very architectural design of Monticello daily taught implicit lessons about the *in*significance of female intellectual life. In spite of this, Martha Jefferson Randolph launched an education program for her daughters that was years ahead of both northern and southern schools. In her cramped quarters and in spite of interminable interruptions—a visitor once commented that her children "seem never to leave her for an instant, but are always beside her or on her lap"—she inculcated a love of reading and study in her six daughters, training them in habits of thinking that distinguished them from most young Virginia girls.

So admirably did she accomplish this work, Jefferson turned to her when he received an inquiry in 1818 from a Virginia friend about the best plan for female education. Admitting that the topic "has never been a subject of systematic contemplation with me" (his own daughters' education only "occasionally requiring" his attention, as we know), Jefferson then sketched out in broad strokes his recommendations: carefully selected novels only (since most, he thought, were inclined to result in "a bloated imagination and sickly judgment"); for the same reason, only select poetry to promote "style and taste"; and French, dancing, drawing, and music. It was an utterly conventional program of study, essentially unchanged in thirty years. Of lessons in household budgeting, Jefferson knew "I need say nothing," since running a household was a given for American mothers.

The catalogue he appended to his letter, however, was compiled by Martha and one of her daughters (probably Ellen), not by him, and it shows a very different approach. Martha's own education and formation at Panthemont are reflected in this more substantial program for female scholars, even for those of humbler rank than her children: French literature (to be read in French), all the luminaries of English literature, ancient history, modern histories of Europe, America, and Virginia, mathematics, geography, natural history, and science. Perhaps no works on the list prove the continuing influence of her French edu-

A woman of great intelligence and a master of several languages, Ellen Wayles Randolph lamented the futility of female education and the invisibility of female achievement in her day. Her lively letters, full of wit and astute observations—sometimes cutting, sometimes hilarious—reveal how much was lost by excluding women from universities and the professions.

cation more than the writings of Madame de Genlis; she recommended no fewer than four of her books! Genlis, whose *Adele et Theodore* (1782) had been translated and read across Europe and in America, believed in the transformational impact of education and in the rational capacity of women. Like the male Enlightenment figures of her generation, Genlis was convinced that proper education would prepare her students to take their places as useful, responsible, and respected members of society. The tutor of Louis-Philippe, the future king of France, Genlis was a firm believer in home education as much for the benefit of mothers as for their children. For Genlis, one scholar noticed, the role of teacher "gave the mother a strong sense of identity and made her life happier, more meaningful, and more fulfilled." In short, Genlis's work furnished nothing less than the blueprint for Martha Jefferson Randolph's transition from Paris to her life in rural Virginia.

In some respects Martha's reading suggestions very much mirrored the Anglo-American culture to which she had returned: William Shakespeare's plays, John Milton's *Paradise Lost,* John Dryden's *Tragedies,* Alexander Pope's *Works,* and the British periodicals that had been models of style and wit since the colonial period, *The Spectator, The*

Tatler, and *The Guardian.* Girls needed only a basic understanding of math and science, so Martha supplied only a single text for each subject: Nicolas Pike's *Arithmetic* and the Reverend J. Joyce's three-volume *Scientific Dialogues,* which was aimed at a juvenile audience. Her recommended geography and history books were all by English authors as well. For natural history, however, she turned to the famed French naturalist Comte de Buffon's multivolume *Histoire Naturelle,* in spite of his claim that the New World produced smaller and fewer animals than the Old (an assertion that her father had refuted in his *Notes on the State of Virginia* in the 1780s).

But Martha's immersion in French culture thirty years earlier is apparent also. French plays, novels, and histories, as well as French adaptations of classical literature, composed a significant portion of what she considered a well-rounded girl's education. Martha assigned the works of Molière, Racine, and Corneille; the plays and novels of Madame de Genlis; *Gil Blas;* a French translation of the Spanish novel *Don Quixote;* and the moral tales of Jean-François Marmontel. Her students read modern French history: Voltaire's *Histoire Générale* and his *Louis XIV,* Claude Millot's *Histoire de France,* and the Duc de Sully's *Memoires.*

Her emphasis on classical learning is particularly interesting, since that area was usually reserved only for boys. Martha recommended Gibbon's *The Decline and Fall of the Roman Empire* and Millot's *Histoire Ancienne,* both multivolume works, to give her students a foundation in the overarching contours of ancient history. From there, she introduced them to a plethora of primary sources from the ancient period, allowing them opportunities for more in-depth exploration. Titus Livius, her old nemesis from Panthemont, she had apparently decided was best appreciated in English. So, too, were Cicero's *Offices* and Sallust, Tacitus, Suetonius, and Plutarch. For students unlikely to read the originals in Latin and Greek, she liked John Dryden's translation of *The Aeneid* and Alexander Pope's of *The Iliad* and *The Odyssey.* But she recommended that Seneca be read in a French translation by Abbé de La Grange.

Two other works in French were inspired by the classics but were a modern take upon them: Fénelon's *Les Aventures de Télémaque* and Jean-Jacques Barthélemy's *Voyages du Jeune Anacharsis.* Adapted from the *Odyssey,* Fénelon's tale describes his hero, Telemachus, whose search for his father becomes a journey of self-discovery as well. Sent to Greece from Macedonia for his education, Barthélemy's hero produces a travel account that was an engrossing way for a young student to learn the geography of the ancient world. Both works were enormously popular in France. From this reading, Martha knew, girls would learn about virtuous leaders devoted to the common good, about tyrants and seekers of liberty, and about the moral life. Her daughters loved it; from childhood, Ellen recalled, "my heart would swell and my eyes would fill over the characters and exploits of the heroes of Greece and Rome."

Martha took her daughters' curriculum even further, however: They also studied Latin. As a girl in Panthemont, Martha had complained frequently to her father about plowing her way through Titus Livius, but she had read him in an "ancient Italian," not Latin. Although Jefferson had frequently remarked that the greatest gift his father had given him was a classical education—more so than "all the other luxuries his cares and affections have placed within my reach," he believed—he had not considered bestowing such a gift on his daughters. So Martha had been trained in French and Italian instead. But *her* daughters would not be deprived of that conventionally male curricular component. How exactly she accomplished this remains a mystery. Perhaps she relied on Ellen's elder brother, Jeff, to teach her as he himself was learning; or Ellen may have sat in on his lessons with their father. The least likely, yet still possible, alternative was that she struggled to teach them herself. Abigail Adams complained to her husband about the difficulty of instructing Nabby and John Quincy in Latin without knowing it herself, so we know that other determined women tried it.

Like the Abbess of Panthemont, who persisted in importuning her superiors for what she needed for her school, Martha Randolph could do the same thing with her father when she wanted something, and one way or another she secured Latin for her daughters. Their training began early. Anne was translating Justin's ancient history at age eleven. As the girls got older, however, they had to divide their time between their studies and their housewifery training, which is why they loved the weeks-long visits they were permitted to their grandfather's retreat of Poplar Forest. Preferring their books over all else, including company, Martha's daughters also found respite at Poplar Forest from the crowds of visitors and curiosity seekers who climbed the mountain for a sight of the retired president, and from the work of hospitality that fell to women. Uninterrupted, Ellen happily "poured over volumes of history which I should in vain have attempted to read at Monticello" or devoted seven to eight hours a day to her Latin. Like her grandfather, she appreciated the gift of this ancient language. Having mastered it well enough to read Virgil, Ellen swore, "I will never again tolerate a translation." The difference between the original and Dryden's translation she likened to that "between a glass of rich, old, high flavored wine, and the same wine thrown into a quart of duck-water." But Jefferson could only take two of the girls at a time since there were only two bedrooms in the small house. Left behind at Monticello, Mary once vented her frustration about "the precious time I am wasting from my *precious* studies." She daydreamed about having nothing to do for weeks but her Latin, but in the perennial conflict women have always had in their pursuit of the intellectual life, she had no idea how that "would be compatible with my house keeping duties."

Martha's curriculum for her daughters clearly differed from her own childhood in significant ways, but it was very like that which Jefferson had recommended for young *men* over the years. Both emphasized classical history, Latin, and French. In 1785, for example, Jefferson sent his nephew Peter Carr a detailed letter of a plan of education that, in contrast to that for his daughters, he had considered long and carefully, each component building on the one before, which he would lay out successively over time. Read ancient history, Jefferson advised the fifteen-year-old, in the original Latin. Two years later, he sent Peter a list that included all the classics Martha would later recommend for girls. And when his grandsons were old enough, Jefferson would ensure that the study of Latin figured prominently in their education. In his retirement, Jefferson invited Francis Eppes to Monticello, where he could have a total immersion experience of French "with aunt and cousins who speak it perfectly."

Jefferson's program of education for his nephews and grandsons was, of course, much fuller than that for girls. Boys added a variety of sciences—botany, chemistry, astronomy, anatomy, and agriculture—since he believed they, and not girls, looked forward to a life's work that would "advance the arts and administer the health, subsistence, and comforts of human life." For the same reasons, boys required deeper study in mathematics, history, geography, and politics. As Jefferson observed to Martha's husband, science was excellent preparation for planters, but if the boys were not able to farm, then the other subjects would be useful if they had to, as he viewed it, "resort to professions." But to his mind, women—who would neither contribute to what eighteenth-century Americans called "outdoor affairs" nor populate the professions—had no need of such advanced study. Recall how his letters to his young daughters had pestered them for progress reports on their drawing and music!

In fact, less than a year after their return, he may have already regretted Martha's Parisian education, which had given her so much more than mere ornamentals. Offering to bring his nephew Jack Eppes to Philadelphia to further his studies, he warned Jack's mother to "load him on his departure with charges not to give his heart to any object he will find there. I know no such useless bauble in a house as a girl of mere city education." Nor apparently was he much involved in Martha's daughters' education, except to ask the occasional question on the books they had read. Martha's husband would not have been the impetus for their daughters' unusually high level of learning, either; Tom argued instead that "the *elegant* and agreeable occupations of *Poetry* and the fine arts, sure become the delicate sex more, than tedious & abstruse enquiries into the causes of phenomena." If Ellen was, as their family friend Eliza Trist once observed, "perhaps one of the best Educated Girls in America, a perfect Mistress of the French Italian and Spanish languages," it was certainly because of the aspirations of her cultivated mother, rather than of her father or grandfather.

Martha's program for her daughters was remarkable for her time, even compared with female education in the North, which just about everyone admitted exceeded anything that could be found in the South. The 1820s was a crucial decade in which northern female seminaries began to teach such subjects as Latin, natural philosophy, and botany. In the fifteen-foot-square room Jefferson allocated for Martha's use, her daughters were studying those subjects a full decade earlier. The practice of extracting from their texts, a fixture of both Martha's education and later antebellum female academies, was central to Martha's daughters' learning as well. Carefully copying segments from their voluminous reading, students compiled a treasure trove of knowledge and recalled the wise words that had most resonated with them.

This work of transcription was both academic and deeply personal. So when all of Ellen's treasured keepsakes were lost in transit from Monticello to her new home in Boston, her sister Mary mourned the losses not only of Ellen's writing desk (handmade for her by John Hemings) and family letters but also of "your own notes & extracts the accumulation of which has been the employment of years." These pursuits (and her meticulous material record of them) had taught Ellen to refer to herself as a "bluestocking," that is, an elite female thinker. But such women were not usually sought out as wives. Ellen wrote that in her experience, north or south, a woman who "is believed to have received a *useful education* is really more welcome than a *blue-stocking Unitarian democrat* could possibly be."

This was no small consideration for the Randolph daughters, whose father's increasing indebtedness made it impossible for him to provide them with dowries large enough to attract the husbands they would need for their own financial stability. Tom's obligations had continued to pile up as he obtained bank loans he could ill afford to repay to keep creditors at bay. His continued efforts, into the 1820s, to sell off the heavily mortgaged Varina property were fruitless; he would sell the occasional slave instead to buy time. Elected to the Virginia Assembly in 1819, he was voted by that body to the governor's chair for three consecutive one-year terms. That salary brought some relief, but more to the point was the winter social scene in the state capital, to which the governor's daughters repaired to meet marital prospects. Ellen was not impressed with what she found there. She worried that her "mind would sink to the level . . . of stupidity," she encountered in "the folly and frivolity of the beings with whom I associate." Gay party chatter was no match for what she called the "feast of reason" that she enjoyed at home.

Ellen's observations cut to the central problem of female education in her lifetime. What purpose should it serve: practical or intellectual? In the years immediately following the Revolution, several prominent people had tried to formulate answers to that question, with mixed results. At the Young Ladies' Academy of Philadelphia, founded in 1787, girls took lessons not in ornamentals like French, drawing, and music but in bookkeeping, to become useful and economical wives. From Massachusetts in the 1790s, writer Judith Sargent Murray had urged that girls be educated to self-sufficiency, even as she also tried to argue that educated women would not threaten men's role as family provider. Maine's Eliza Southgate emerged from the best girls' school in Boston "with a head full of something, tumbled in without order or connection," as she put it, but at a loss as to what to do with any of it. Educators, parents, and most students agreed, however, that girls' education should be put to the service of the family, not to their self-actualization and advancement.

This is key to understanding the limits of the various courses of study, even one as advanced as Ellen Randolph's. Classical education became increasingly important in the curriculum of nineteenth-century American girls' schools. But it served much different purposes for girls than for boys. "Ancient history was acceptable for women, but the classical languages (especially Greek) were not," historian Caroline Winterer explained. "Admiring the heroism of Cicero or Scipio was acceptable, but tying the heroism to prescriptions for modern statecraft was not; reading about ancient orators was acceptable, while declaiming aloud less so." As was true of French schoolgirls in the ancien régime who attempted a grasp of classical studies, American girls also had to do so while understanding the limits of what they could do with their learning. Their hearts might thrill to the stories of worthy heroes, but their own lives could never imitate them.

Martha Jefferson Randolph had attempted to widen considerably the boundaries of female learning with her gift of Latin, but her daughters—however brilliant their education—remained otherwise confined by their sex. These limitations were dictated in large part by the gender conventions of antebellum America, whether in Boston, as Ellen would find, or in Charlottesville, which funneled young women to the route of domesticity. But they were also shaped by writers on female education, including Madame de Genlis, whose works such as her *Letters on Education* Martha so admired and recommended. An ardent Catholic and supporter of the French crown, Genlis did not challenge the idea that women were best suited for motherhood in the home. In that, she agreed with Enlightenment philosopher Jean-

Jacques Rousseau, who had spelled out his ideas on female education in his novel *Emile*. Genlis parted company with Rousseau, however, with her argument that women's intellectual capabilities were the equal of men's. She insisted that women, too, were capable of rational thought and judgment. For Genlis, all reading—even the novels that critics feared would provoke wild flights of imagination and passion—was valuable in the project of self-improvement.

This process of transformation required self-discipline, as Genlis understood from her own preparations to teach her two daughters and the four children (including the future Louis-Philippe) of the Duc d'Orléans, cousin to the king. Rather than assuming all the prerogatives that accompanied rank in prerevolutionary France, Genlis believed that she and her students needed to work to earn their privileges. As their teacher, she had to cultivate her own mind and talents, and in turn her students had to earn their position in society by their responsible behavior. But this approach only functioned to explain what these privileged students already knew about their lives in a hierarchal society: why they deserved the position into which they had been born. So in spite of declaring the equality of the female intellect, Genlis did not teach Martha Jefferson Randolph to make an argument that demolished notions of so-called natural hierarchies, whether of gender, of class, or, at home in the United States, of race. But she did provide her with a model for finding meaning in her life, both in Paris and in Virginia. Women's capacity for rational thought, combined with the rigors of self-discipline in study, rendered them as capable as men of asserting rank in a meritocracy based on intellect and character.

This use of education to validate status was not quite the same thing as republican motherhood, a new idea developing in private letters and in the pages of newspapers and magazines in America about the role of women in the new nation. Emerging from a history as monarchical subjects and creating a new one as republican citizens, Americans in the early republic were redefining what citizenship meant. A long history stretching back to Ancient Greece (a history that Martha's daughters were reading) emphasized that governing was a task that belonged to men only. And increasingly, white American men of all ranks asserted their equality in a system that became defined by "one man, one vote." An egalitarian rhetoric both promoted and reflected these changes, as the franchise broadened, state by state, cutting down the property requirements that previously barred less affluent white men from the ballot box. Jefferson's own party took the lead in this direction, although not incidentally disenfranchising free black men in the process. Barred from the ballot box, some American women nonetheless claimed the language and philosophy of republicanism in their writing, teaching, and mothering of future citizens.

But egalitarianism was not what Genlis had in mind; rather, she aimed for the preservation of rank by the cultivation of the rational mind through rigorous self-discipline. In France, her students could look forward to court life and the salons; but where, in the new republic, would American women display their learning and rank? Federalist women, sharing the inclinations of George Washington and John Adams in 1790s Philadelphia, attempted to counter the growing democratizing tendencies of the Jeffersonian Republicans by organizing a genteel life around visits, promenades, and salons that served as visible markers of elite status in the new nation. Several women who had experienced salon life in Paris even attempted to re-create it in Philadelphia. Anne Willing Bingham's gatherings in her mansion at the corner of Third and Spruce were particularly notable. Inviting Philadelphia's most fashionable people and her husband's Federalist connections, she hoped to establish a political salon in which women could exert influence, as she had seen in France. Federalist women from both northern and southern states found the national capital of Philadelphia a perfect ground for the visible display of women of status as a part of political society.

But the salons survived neither the move to Washington City nor the transition of power from the Federalists to the Jeffersonian Republicans in the election of 1800. Connected to the Virginia dynasty of presidents, some women such as Dolley Madison and Jefferson's friend and admirer Margaret Bayard Smith remained political players in social settings until the presidency of Andrew Jackson in 1829. Years after Jefferson's death, for example, Martha tapped her connection with Smith to secure a clerkship for her son-in-law and a position in the fledgling Navy for her son. But privileged women attempting to exercise political muscle had become suspect in the young republic. By the 1840s, all white men enjoyed the vote, and with the evolution of the two-party system, the wheeling and dealing of politics now took place in party caucuses, behind doors firmly closed to women.

And indeed, Martha Jefferson Randolph never did visit Philadelphia when it was the nation's capital; and when she visited her father in Washington during his presidency, she performed the filial duties of a loving daughter rather than the presiding duties of a salon hostess. At home in Virginia, she followed Genlis's precepts, devoting herself to the service of her students in her exclusive mountaintop home school, teaching them to deserve the elite position into which they had been born. Martha's life followed the formula by which Genlis herself had lived, if not quite as strictly. In 1781, Genlis's daughter Caroline mused, "It is curious indeed that at her age, when she was still young, pretty, and so talented, that she would renounce society life and all its pleasures in order to devote herself to her children and to their education. . . . I don't know how Mama withstands the life she leads: ten lessons to give every day, after which she works at her desk until two or three o'clock in the morning."

Martha's self-discipline was also evident in the scheduled order of her days and in her habits of industry, which were remarked upon by all who observed her. Jefferson's overseer for twenty years commented that "Mrs. Randolph was just like her father . . . she was always busy. If she wasn't reading or writing, she was always doing something. . . . As her daughters grew up, she taught them to be industrious like herself." Not quite twenty-two, Virginia was so desperate to find a place at Monticello where she could study uninterrupted, she converted a wasp-infested attic space into her "fairy palace," furnishing it with a couple of cast-off chairs, a sofa (that had lost its cushions), and two small tables. Counseling her daughter Septimia, who was struggling with her schoolwork, Martha spoke from experience when she admitted that desultory application to lessons "will weary you and you will not retain much of what you read under such circumstances. But," she reassured her, good study habits "will in time be formed and the improvement to your own mind and character my dear Septimia will repay you most amply for the weariness of your initiation." Through self-disciplined application to study, Martha was convinced that "to cultivate the good, and smother the bad [was] in the power of every rational creature."

For her strenuous efforts on their behalf, Genlis was rewarded by the devotion of her children. Caroline declared that she "preferred a thousand times more a quarter hour of conversation with Mama to all the parties and pleasures of Paris." Her words could just as easily have come from any of Martha's children about her. "She is *our sun,*" Virginia once asserted with emphasis. Away from home and worrying about her mother's health, Ellen was cheered to hear from Martha that her brother Jeff was taking good care of her, which was just what Ellen expected, given his "devoted attachment to you; an attachment which all your children feel to a degree that makes it a ruling passion." Ellen agreed entirely with her grandfather when he reflected upon the "excellences" of her siblings and attributed it to the "education and the influence of example" that Martha had provided.

But no matter how advanced their curriculum, how brilliant their minds, how steadfast their study habits, or how devoted they were to the life of the mind and to each other, Martha and her daughters were still confronted with the powerful message of that house every day. Architectural historians have helped us understand that buildings are not neutral; they are designed to convey messages, whether it is the cathedral spire that points to heaven or the snug bungalow that enchants a first-time home buyer. Aristocratic homes, both in England and Virginia, showcased the power of their owners. In the fortress-style houses of medieval England, visitors easily identified the center of power and understood their relationship to him: Their host sat upon a dais, elevated over them. By Jefferson's day, that personal mode of signifying order and rank had changed, now built into the very design of the house. In the sprawling classical country houses (think Blenheim, near Oxford, or even the fictional Downton Abbey), the family occupied the central quarters; guests, servants, and services were located progressively farther away from the center. With the increasing compartmentalization and privacy evident in these houses, the hierarchy of the people who lived and worked in them was spelled out. As a result the house itself actually structured how the family head, family members (male and female), guests, and servants (or slaves, as in Virginia) related to one another, in ways that were seemingly impersonal and immutable but actually quite carefully calculated.

A visit to Monticello makes the point crystal clear: the central quarters, where the master lived, at the home's core; the comfortable guest quarters at a distance from the master's, although on the same floor; the small rooms up a narrow staircase where his daughter and her family lived; and the kitchens and stables below the terraces that extended outward from the core of the house. Jefferson did not have to be home for his family, visitors, or slaves to understand where power resided. It is disconcerting to realize that in a household so devoted to the life of the mind, nowhere was space dedicated to the reading and writing that was utterly central to the Randolph women's existence. Instead their letters to be read and answered were scattered all over the house; whenever they could, they stole minutes from supervisory perches in the cellar or kitchen to scratch out a quick note. Never would they have presumed to use their grandfather's well-equipped study, even though he vacated it for several hours every day for his afternoon rides.

It was Jefferson's intention, then, rather than oversight or error, to design his home in a way that imposed order on his mountain: women and children relegated to the invisible upper floors, slaves and their work hidden beneath the terraces. For the Randolph daughters, these spatial arrangements were significant in reducing their access to knowledge, because, as one architectural historian explained, "gendered spaces separate women from knowledge used by men to produce and reproduce power and privilege," so "by controlling access to knowledge and resources through the control of space, the dominant group's ability to retain and reinforce its position is enhanced." The locked doors of Jefferson's library effected exactly that.

The bonds of blood and affection did not permit Jefferson's daughter and granddaughters to escape that order, much less challenge it. Rather, they became subject to it. Perhaps remembering those first awkward months of married life in which she knew nothing of managing a household, Martha remedied her own educational deficiency by instituting a monthly system in which the keys of housekeeping rotated from daughter to daughter. The keys certainly served as a symbol of their authority, since household valuables were locked up to prevent theft by slaves. But the Randolphs did not relish that authority; instead the keys' physical and psychic weight was palpable in the girls' complaints: Virginia could finally find time to write to Ellen, because she had just given up the keys after "one of the most troublesome months of housekeeping that I ever had." Mary complained of all she could not do since she had "carried the keys." Cornelia, the most artistic of Martha's daughters, bemoaned her "books lying covered with unmolested dust, my drawing boxes locked and never opened, the letters of my correspondents filling my desk and reproaching me for my neglecting to answer them" while she held the keys. The world was not to benefit from their intellectual gifts; instead these learned women would learn the female chores of running a household.

The spatial boundaries of Monticello maintained the inequality between master and female family, but there were at least brief moments of escape. In a world organized into separate gendered spaces, the solution for the studious Randolph girls was, literally, to change places. This explains why Jefferson's granddaughter Ellen felt most truly herself when she was at Poplar Forest. A retreat Jefferson built for himself to avoid the throngs of uninvited visitors at Monticello, Poplar Forest became a favorite getaway for his granddaughters as well. Aside from Jefferson's bedroom, the compact design of the house provided one other bedroom, a large center hall that served as a dining room, and a reading salon (south-facing, of course, for light and warmth). It was not a house that encouraged visitors, and few came. Here the Randolph daughters were able to spend far fewer hours in the kinds of housekeeping and hostess duties that bore down on them at Monticello, and many more in their intellectual pursuits. This was a house built for reading, long conversations, and evening walks on the terrace, and they adored their grandfather for sharing it with them.

They particularly loved having Jefferson all to themselves. It was not something they could count on, even when he was living at home with them at Monticello. Their mother had once complained to him—still bitter nine months after the fact—that during one of Jefferson's visits home from Philadelphia, she had not enjoyed "the pleasure of passing one sociable moment" with him. But it took three days over rough country roads to cover the ninety-three miles to their Poplar Forest retreat, and Jefferson was all theirs from the moment they left his mountain. On the way, they always stayed at the same little inns. Virginia treasured memories of these trips when Jefferson would choose a roadside spot at which to pull over for lunch. "Our cold dinner was always put up by his own hands," she recalled; "he was the carver and

Designed in the octagon shape that Jefferson loved, the house at Poplar Forest had a square dining room in the center, encircled by bedrooms at the east and west sides of the house, two small rooms to the north, and a reading parlor to the south. Built for quiet study rather than entertaining, the house was a refuge as well for his granddaughters, who cherished their evening walks with him on the terrace that topped the service wing, extending out from the east side of the house's lower level.

helped us to our cold fowl and ham, and mixed the wine and water to drink with it."

Their destination was a country house, furnished simply with four small bookcases, three dining tables, and four tea tables. The girls' room did not even have a set of drawers for their clothes until Ellen managed to persuade Jefferson to have them made at the woodworking shop at Monticello and carted to Poplar Forest. The sparseness of the furnishings is even more apparent when we consider a list of taxable items (kitchen and bedrooms were exempt) which were *not* in the house. Jefferson owed no taxes for anything in category 30, which included portraits, pictures, prints, mirrors, fortepianos, harpsichords, organs, and harps; nor for category 31, which included bureaus, secretaries, and drawers; nor did he own the niceties that suggest entertaining, enumerated in category 32: urns for coffee or tea; candlestick lamp chandeliers, decanters, pitchers, bowls, and goblets. Ellen missed her music, though, worrying that she would "be falling off there" without a piano.

The four small bookcases that furnished the reading room were

filled with duodecimos, tiny books—perhaps seven by five inches—
formed by folding a sheet of printing press paper into twelve leaves. The
small size allowed portability as Jefferson and his granddaughters
packed for a month or two of solid reading. As Cornelia blissfully anticipated her turn to take the trip, the two months ahead seemed "as
long as two years." But when she surveyed "the long row of books I
brought," she confessed that "I began to think the time was scarcely
sufficient to do it in." Requests for forgotten books were always flying
between Monticello and Poplar Forest. Cornelia asked for a "little English dictionary . . . very small" for "Daddy" (slave John Hemings) in
one letter; in another, she asked for a "key" or index to a domestic encyclopedia kept at Poplar Forest.

When Jefferson sold his duodecimos to Congress in 1815, they were
valued at a dollar apiece (about fifteen dollars today), a far cry from his
elegant folios, which were at least seventeen by twenty inches in size.
His three-volume set in folio of Theodore de Bry's *Great and Small
Voyages* alone was worth £400 sterling (almost twenty-nine thousand
dollars today). Folios were intentionally weighty books, their size com-
mensurate with the importance of their subject. By contrast, women's
reading was typically printed in duodecimo: intellectually less weighty
but also cheaper, smaller, and easier to carry in one's pocket in case a
quiet moment presented itself during a busy day of housekeeping. But
at Poplar Forest, the physical aspects of their books did not separate
Jefferson's reading from his granddaughters', which may have encouraged them to feel that their study paralleled his.

With a heart brimming with nostalgic gratitude for the enchantment of these weeks at Poplar Forest, Ellen years later wrote a full description of a typical "cheerful and uneventful" day. Together they would
take a leisurely breakfast, then break for the morning's reading—
Jefferson to the sunny drawing room, the girls to their bedroom. Dinner was at three, which "like all his other meals, he took leisurely." As
he lingered over his wine ("he never took more than three glasses,"
Ellen observed), they delighted in his conversation. It was, she recalled,
"easy, flowing, and full of anecdote." Many times he would tell them
stories of his long-dead wife, "whose memory he cherished with deep
and tender affection. He often quoted to us her sayings and opinions
and would preface his own advice with 'Your grandmother would have

told you,' and 'Your grandmother always said.'" After dinner, they again separated for work, until they took their afternoon walk on the terrace. They spent the remainder of the day with him, drinking tea and reading, occasionally pausing to read aloud an interesting passage to the others.

As he did at home in Monticello, Jefferson occupied the sunniest room for reading at Poplar Forest, while his granddaughters retreated to their bedroom to study. The campeachy chair shown here (named after the Mexican province of Campeche, which supplied the wood) was Jefferson's favorite reading chair, providing comfort against his rheumatism. John Hemings made several based on the design. At least five of Jefferson's campeachy chairs are known to survive today.

Perhaps Jefferson's favorite, Ellen accompanied her grandfather to Poplar Forest almost every time. She treasured her days there; it was where she learned to think of herself as a bluestocking. Certainly it mattered mightily to Ellen that while they were there, Jefferson "interested himself in all we did, thought, or read" and that he in turn shared with her what he was reading. But the secluded location, only occasionally intruded upon by a few visitors, mattered as well. That Ellen associated this space with study is apparent in the reflections she wrote during a visit, three years after her first one. She roamed nostalgically from room to room, reveling in the memory of her studies in each, and later calculated that she had enjoyed four times the leisure to read at Poplar Forest than at Monticello. Jefferson attested to her study habits; at Poplar Forest, he told Martha, Ellen and Cornelia "are the severest students

I have ever met with. They never leave their room but to come to meals." The results of their disciplined study were obvious to all who met them. Visiting Monticello in 1820, for example, a Maryland engineer was clearly impressed by his evening's conversation with Martha and "her highly polished and highly instructed daughters," for whom "it seems to be a matter of equal facility with them to write or converse, in French, Spanish, Italian, or their mother tongue."

Quiet rural living did not always provide the society that kept such educated minds stimulated, however; Ellen once complained that "Bonaparte might die, or the pope turn turk, and we should be none the wiser for it." That may be why, at twenty-seven, Ellen was so attracted to a young New Englander who made the trip to Monticello to meet Jefferson in the spring of 1824. Joseph Coolidge, Jr., the son of a wealthy trading family in Boston, had graduated from Harvard seven years earlier and just completed his grand tour of Europe. The two young people took an instant liking to each other, and Coolidge so impressed Ellen's mother and grandfather that when he asked them the following spring if he could visit again, their reply informed him that they could not provide her with a dowry. Coolidge didn't care; he returned to Monticello, married Ellen in Jefferson's parlor in May 1825, and brought her home to Boston.

In spite of her trips to Richmond in search of suitors, Virginia also met her husband at home at Monticello. Like Coolidge, Nicholas P. Trist, the grandson of Jefferson's old friend Eliza House Trist, was drawn there by Jefferson's reputation. At eighteen, Trist spent a year reading law with Jefferson, during which time he and seventeen-year-old Virginia fell in love. Although Martha grew to love Nicholas like a son, she thought the pair too young to marry and asked them to wait. Nicholas left to study at West Point and to attend to property he owned in Louisiana. But ever steadfast in his love, he returned to Monticello to claim Virginia for his bride after six years in 1824.

The prospects for livelier intellectual society for the remaining Randolph daughters improved markedly when their grandfather began his project of building a university in Charlottesville, and they followed its progress with great interest. Jefferson had chosen Francis Walker Gilmer, a young local lawyer whose education he much admired, to go to Europe to recruit the finest minds to teach in his university. As they began to arrive in Virginia, it was with great anticipation that the new professors and their wives were welcomed to dine at Monticello, where Jefferson's granddaughters took the opportunity to look them over. They were "more and more pleased with Dr. Dunglison both as a man and a physician," Cornelia wrote to Ellen, who had just moved to Boston. Robley Dunglison, a Scotsman who had been hired to teach anatomy and medicine, increasingly endeared himself to Jefferson's family through the relief his ministrations offered to Jefferson's chronic complaints.

Mary thought Mrs. Bonnycastle, the new wife of the professor of natural philosophy, "no very great acquisition to our neighborhood . . . but apparently perfectly inoffensive." Generally Cornelia agreed, finding that "as we become better acquainted with all of the professors and their wives we like them better." The exception was Mrs. Blaettermann, the wife of the German professor hired to teach modern languages, "who from all accounts is a vulgar virago." Cornelia's pen reproduced the reputation the unfortunate Mrs. Blaettermann acquired in Charlottesville. "If she does not steal," she said cuttingly, "it is very probably because she has no occasion to do so." Judge Dade, who had been offered the law professorship, on the other hand, pleased the young Randolph women mightily. "He has that frankness about him that you would suppose was the effect of perfect honesty and integrity. . . . It is so rare to meet with a Virginian who is a man of education it is always an agreeable surprise to me," Cornelia said of the distinguished forty-two-year-old judge; "I am quite in love with him."

Jefferson intended his university to train the young men of the southern states for productive lives in civic service, agriculture, commerce, or manufactures. The champion of the separation of church and state, Jefferson intentionally rejected any religious affiliation that, until this point, had been the raison d'être of American colleges. Indeed, one of only three achievements he wanted included on his tombstone was his authorship of the Virginia Statute of Religious Freedom, passed in 1786. Instead his university would school students in habits of reason, discipline, and virtue in preparation for the leadership roles they would assume in their adulthood. Some of the young men would disappoint Jefferson severely; within six months of the university's opening, three students (of an enrollment of about one hundred) were expelled for two successive nights of alcohol-fueled rioting that included throwing bottles through windows, cursing the European professors, and striking with both sticks and stones the professors who tried to restrain them. Jefferson did not forgive these three, but he did excuse the fourteen masked students who created a disturbance on the Lawn that weekend as just indulging in youthful hijinks.

Although the younger Randolph boys (Lewis, Benjamin, and George) would eventually attend the university, there was never any question that their studious and well-behaved sisters would not be able to do so. But the girls' avid reports of professorial hirings were only one indication of their great interest in Jefferson's university. They visited his "academical village," as he called it, whenever they were in Charlottesville and, to the extent they could, visited the library and attended public lectures. On one occasion, after attending an oration given by a student member of the Patrick Henry Society, Mary climbed to the gallery of the Rotunda to listen to the echo, which produced "the effect of a whispering gallery." Several times, she reported to Ellen, she visited the university's library, where she could browse through its holdings and sit and read like any student during the library's opening hours. But, she sighed, "it is forbidden to carry a single volume beyond the precincts of the Institution." Unable to bring a book home with her, Mary could not continue her reading in whatever pockets of time she could carve out of her housekeeping duties.

But as in the rest of America, admission to the university's classrooms was denied her. Charlottesville's celebration of the visit of the Marquis de Lafayette poignantly illustrates women's marginalization. In 1824, Lafayette was making a triumphant tour of the Unites States, whose independence he had been so instrumental in winning. Charlottesville went out of its way to welcome him. A grand dinner, attended by five hundred men of the community, was given at the Rotunda, which Jefferson designed after the Roman Pantheon and which remains today the very heart of the University of Virginia. A great number of women attended as well to pay tribute to the aging French patriot; however, they occupied a space in one of the wings of the Rotunda, invisible to the main event.

The Randolph sisters attended the grand dinner, but they also enjoyed quieter moments with their illustrious guest at Monticello, where they had witnessed firsthand the emotional reunion of the two old revolutionaries. In the portico on a "golden November day," Martha and her daughters stood at Jefferson's side as Lafayette arrived "with all the military show of gay scarfs and prancing horses, whose glittering accouterments flashed in the sunshine." As Jefferson embraced his friend, "all was so still that [they] heard the words distinctly, 'My dear Jefferson,' 'My dear Lafayette.'" This privileged group then followed the men into the house for a private dinner, quite different from the crush of the dinner celebration at the university. "A party of 20 ladies & gentlemen sat down to dinner," a niece of Martha's later recounted. "*Mr. Jefferson* sat at one side with *Mr. Madison & Genl. Lafayette* on the other. *Mr. Geo. LaFayette* was at the head of the table between *Miss [Ellen] Randolph* & her mother. As usual there were fewer gentlemen than ladies, & one side of the table showed an almost unbroken line of beautiful young girls." Even in this more intimate event, as at the university, women were necessary for the festivities, but as ornaments rather than full participants. For Jefferson they rounded out a picture of female beauty and domesticity in his well-ordered world that he wanted to display to his visitor.

Despite being surrounded with these women, loving them mightily, and even encouraging their reading, Jefferson demonstrates to the modern observer the limits of his revolution. Women should not be trained to contribute to a growing nation, or to prepare for citizenship; rather, their education should produce agreeable, rational companions and conversationalists. His perfect confidence in Martha's ability to educate her daughters in the privacy of his home was justified by the admiration and praise of his visitors. But for all that Martha Jefferson Randolph was, for all her learning, all that she cultivated within herself and her daughters, she was relegated to the sidelines, her brilliance confined to her fifteen-foot-square sitting room—as her father had designed.

Departure

. . . .

1815

. . . .

*B*OUND TO JEFFERSON BY THE strongest ties of admiration and love, Martha loyally ensconced herself in her cramped schoolroom. Happy in the company of her family, she would not have had it any other way. Harriet Hemings, however, would have preferred to be doing something else as she made her way down the slope from her home in the south dependency of the great house to Mulberry Row, where the textile manufactory stood. Opening the door, she braced herself for another workday. At least the brick floor and stone walls offered her cool respite on hot Virginia mornings; in winter, the stone chimney radiated warmth while the solidly built walls kept the wind at bay. A single story high, the stone cottage had been built in the late 1770s for the white artisans Jefferson had hired when he first began building his great home. Measuring thirty-four by seventeen feet, its proportions were much larger than the smaller wood houses he later ordered built for his slaves. Two windows flanked the central door; the second floor and gambrel roof that today's visitors to Monticello see were added after Harriet's day.

Others lived here in the stone cottage after the artisans left: Harri-

Now known as the textile workshop, this building saw numerous uses and renovations after Jefferson first built it in 1776 to house the white laborers he employed to erect his home. It housed Sally Hemings on her return from France, as well as her sister Critta; it then reverted to housing for white builders working on Jefferson's extensive renovations; and, finally, it was converted in 1814 into the textile manufactory where Harriet worked as a teenager. The gambrel roof and the addition on the left are twentieth-century changes.

et's mother, when she first returned from France, and then later the talented carpenter James Dinsmore, who had found Harriet's uncle John such an apt pupil. But since then, the building had been reconfigured from dormitory to factory when Jefferson moved his textile operations onto the mountain in 1814. Now, instead of workers, the stone cottage housed three spinning jennies, a carding machine to disentangle and clean the raw fibers of debris, and a loom. But, Harriet reminded herself as she closed the door behind her and looked around at her co-workers, this would not be her life forever. Her elder sister might draw her daily fund of endurance from the great love she bore her father and from the privileges he bestowed on her family. But Harriet would choose a different road.

IT IS UNCLEAR WHEN Harriet began working in the textile factory. Not until 1815, when she was fourteen, did Jefferson document her as a worker in his Farm Book, but with his extended absences during his presidency, his entries had been sporadic since her birth. It is possible that she was working as early as ten, one of the unidentified "spinning girls" Jefferson noted in 1811. More likely, however, Jefferson's record for Harriet aligns with the pattern her younger brother Madison Hemings recalled of his childhood, in which he was not sent to work as a carpenter with his uncle John Hemings until he, too, was fourteen. This was unusually late for the enslaved children owned by Thomas Jefferson to begin working. Even children under ten could be useful, he thought, helping the elderly women who were no longer productive in the fields to mind the youngest children. This, of course, freed their mothers to work for him. Between ten and sixteen, "the boys make nails, the girls spin," Jefferson directed, and at sixteen, they "go into the ground or learn trades." In this way, Jefferson maximized the returns on the labor of his youngest slaves as he also screened for and built an efficient workforce. But until Harriet became a spinner, she would have spent her days in Jefferson's home with her mother, running errands as Madison did as a boy and perhaps working as a child minder for the Randolph babies; Martha birthed several more children by the time Harriet had turned ten. However she spent her childhood, one thing is certain: It deviated significantly from the norm Jefferson set down for the rest of his workforce.

Jefferson made different kinds of arrangements for his sons. Beverley, Sally's eldest child, was already working as a tradesman's apprentice at age eleven, probably alongside Sally's brother John in the joinery. When they were young boys, Beverley, Madison, and Eston accompanied John Hemings on his working trips to Poplar Forest as his "aids," as Jefferson called them. There, as Hemings crafted the interior work on Jefferson's vacation home, Sally's sons learned the trade of carpentry far from the demands of life on Mulberry Row, apprenticed to a much loved and talented uncle. And in the relative isolation of Poplar Forest, they may also have spent time with their father. Building had always been a passion for Jefferson—he called Monticello his "essay in architecture"—and in the leisure afforded by his retirement it became one of his chief preoccupations. Born a decade beyond the days when Jefferson assembled his agricultural "machine" at Monticello, Madison Hemings remembered that Jefferson "had but little taste or care for agricultural pursuits." (He was correct; Jefferson was turning more and more of those responsibilities over to his grandson Jeff.) Instead "it was his mechanics he seemed mostly to direct and in their operations he took great interest. Almost every day of his later years he might have been seen among them." This daily contact apparently never translated into intimacy between father and sons—we remember Madison's comment that Jefferson never showed partiality to them. But the craft of woodworking did give them common ground on which to meet around shared interests, skill, and a passion to create objects of beauty.

Carpentry training prepared Sally Hemings's sons to earn their livelihood as free men, but of course that would not suit a girl in the nineteenth century, so Jefferson had to make other provisions for his daughter. There are several possible reasons why he decided that the best place for Harriet was his textile factory as a spinner. In his own youth, his mother and sisters owned spinning wheels; his sister Martha (who had married his best friend, Dabney Carr) received a spinning wheel when she was sixteen. Perhaps Jefferson saw spinning more as a polite hobby and accomplishment than a productive skill vital to the household economy. If so, then he may have been equipping his daughter for the life of domesticity he expected her to have in her life in freedom.

His reasons were probably more practical, however, particularly considering how the world had changed in the generations from his mother's day to his daughters'. Although Americans made most of their everyday clothing in the early eighteenth century, they relied largely on imports from Britain for cottons and luxury fabrics. With the colonial resistance movements in the 1760s and 1770s, however, women showed their patriotism by stepping up their production of cloth, demonstrating their independence from the British markets. When he was inaugurated president, George Washington wore a homespun suit as a matter of American pride. But American-made textiles would not really take off until the invention of the cotton gin in 1793 freed factory owners from dependence on British resources. And until Jefferson set up his own textile operation in 1812, he himself bought, rather than made, most of the clothing for his slaves.

In the next decade, small manufactories sprouted up all over the country, partially as a response to the embargo of 1807 that Jefferson imposed as president, hoping it would persuade Britain to cease its impressment of American sailors—between six and seven thousand, by his count. The economic sanctions had no impact on Britain and were ultimately lifted, but they did finally spur greater cloth production both in cities and on farms. When war with England did come in 1812, during the presidency of his friend James Madison, Jefferson could report that his whole neighborhood was immersed in household manufactures of cloth and clothing. He himself proudly reduced his own reliance on imports of coarse clothing for his slaves to less than 20 percent of his total requirements. "The embargo has set every body to making homespun," Martha's eldest daughter Anne had reported to him from Edgehill in 1808. "Mama has made 157 yards since October, you will see all the children clothed in it." By the end of the war, Jefferson boasted that his broadcloth could rival England's best. There would be no need ever again to import such items when the peace came; of that, he was certain.

Jefferson knew the industrializing Northeast was well ahead in this manufacturing trend, even before the second war with England erupted in 1812. As he contemplated his country's preparedness for an embargo of British goods, Jefferson had looked to Philadelphia for examples of how to set up home manufactories. He particularly appreciated a model in which children could work at home under the watchful eye of their parents, who would also ensure their health and exercise. Although Jefferson was thinking of rural domestic arrangements rather than urban, this plan may have been Jefferson's vision of Harriet's future. His own daughter's household had modeled this picture of an industrious family during his embargo. He may have satisfied himself that he met his obligations to Harriet by training her for her future role as a housewife in a working-class household, busily spinning and teaching her children to do the same under the family roof.

This is why Jefferson assigned his enslaved daughter to the newer technology of the spinning jenny rather than to the old-fashioned spinning wheel. Yet the spinning jenny was not generally found in private homes, as the colonial spinning wheel had been. It was too big, for one thing. When Jefferson gave his instructions for a weaving factory to be built in Poplar Forest, he told his overseer to make sure that the door was at least four and a half feet wide to accommodate the machine. For another, the spinning jenny was one of the machines that inaugurated the industrial revolution. In the old days, when one spinner produced a single spool of thread at a time, it required three spinners to keep up with one weaver. The genius of James Hargreaves's invention had been to devise a way in which one worker could spin eight to as many as 120 spindles at one time. Output on such a massive scale could be accomplished best in factories, and only by those with sufficient capital to set them up.

By 1815, Jefferson had bought three Hargreaves-type spinning jennies and transferred textile production to Mulberry Row, steps away from his house. There Harriet Hemings spent her days spinning wool. Although spinning requires skill to ensure the quality of the finished product, she may not have taken any pride in her ability to spin. Rather, because the workers were producing textiles to clothe her father's enslaved workforce, it is more likely that Harriet would forever associate spinning with her enslavement.

With his access to labor, the resources to hire an expert to build the machinery and train his workers, and a large building whose footprint could accommodate the work, Jefferson began thinking about a factory of his own. In June 1812 he estimated that he needed "2000 yards of linen, cotton, & woolen yearly, to cloathe my family," by which he meant his enslaved force. "This machinery, costing 150. Dollars only, and worked by two women & two girls, will more than furnish" what he needed for his workforce of 130 slaves, he thought, and at reasonable start-up costs. Together with his son-in-law Tom Randolph, Jefferson set up a factory at Edgehill in the summer of 1812. By 1814, Jefferson had one forty-spindle and three twenty-four-spindle jennies installed at Monticello, for a total of 112 spindles. He had experimented with a couple of other models, each inventor eagerly assuring him of the efficiency of his own manufacture. In the end, however, Jefferson decided to go back to the "antient Jenny," which had been patented in 1770, because its straightforward design made it easy for his workers to replicate and repair themselves. By March 1814, he was able to dismiss the man he had hired to train his slaves in the manufacture, repair, and operation of the spinning jennies.

Best of all, even a child could learn to operate the jenny. In 1813, Jefferson had moved a fifteen-year-old slave named Maria from Poplar Forest for training. Her teacher was "a girl younger than herself," Jefferson reported to her overseer. It is a tantalizing reference; if, in fact, Harriet had been spinning since 1811, she could well have been Maria's teacher. Jefferson recorded her success: Under her instructor's tutelage, Maria was already "becoming a capital spinner" in just a few days. Closely measuring Maria's output, he saw that "she does her ounce. & a half a day per spindle on a 12. spindle machine," producing approximately seventy-five yards of wool per spindle. With the longer days of spring and summer, he hoped she would get to two ounces, "a reasonable task," he judged. Sally on the other hand, another slave from Poplar Forest and the same age as Maria, he thought "hopeless. She seems neither to have the inclination nor the understanding to learn." As Jefferson did with his nailers, he gave her a warning: "If there be no improvement she must cease to spin more cloth and go out to work with the overseer," a reference that, Sally knew, meant field work, away from Jefferson's more benign supervision.

Work in the textile factory was not altogether unpleasant for Harriet. Her co-workers were young (at least nine of the twelve were between ten and seventeen years of age, four of them boys), and the factory seemed to lack strict oversight. At thirty-six, Cretia Hern was the elder in the factory; although she had been a house slave, in 1815 she was spinning cotton—and keeping the teenage boys in line. Two of them were her sons; another was Israel Gillette Jefferson, who would later serve Jefferson as postilion, a sign of his favored status, working in close proximity to his master. The boys carded, disentangling and cleaning the raw cotton and wool fibers to ready them for spinning. Agnes Gillette, seventeen, and Nanny Granger and Isabel, both fifteen, spun the hemp, which combined with some cotton was used for the slave children's clothing; Dolly, nineteen, and Mary Hern, thirty-five, each wove four yards of cloth per day. Ten-year-old Eliza removed the full spools from the jennies and brought them to the weavers' looms.

The supervision of the factory's output apparently fell to Martha Jefferson Randolph; in her presence the "work used to be weighed out . . . and partly with her own hands." As early as 1815, Jefferson's factory achieved his needed two-thousand-yard-per-year production level and even had so much left over that Bacon "sold wagonloads of it to the merchants." But if Martha attempted to impose a rigid order upon the textile workers, she was unsuccessful. Fifty years after Jefferson's death, one of his former spinners chuckled that "we were so bad, so troublesome, I wonder how mistress [Randolph] had the patience to bear with us as she did." The work of spinners and weavers was not so engrossing as to preclude sharing stories, jokes, gossip, riotous laughter, and other behaviors that Randolph found "troublesome." Because the textile factory was one of the few spaces on the plantation that were primarily female, overseen by Martha Randolph's quick visits and Cretia Hern's responsible eye, the women's stories and other talk could have forged deep connections among them. That four teenage boys were among the factory crew would only have added to the boisterousness, especially when the constant whirring of the wheels and clacking of the machinery required that they shout to be heard. So Harriet did not spend her working days under a strict regime enforced by the lash. Instead she worked in the company of other young people in a somewhat relaxed but still very productive environment.

The work in the textile factory was less onerous and physically taxing than most slave labor on the plantation, of course, but Harriet's work was easier still. She alone worked with wool, which is much easier to handle than flax or hemp. It is the easiest of all fibers to spin, and wool's natural lanolin would have been softer on her hands than the stiffness of flax or hemp, which irritates the thumb as it is drawn through the hand and needs constant wetting to keep it supple. And since Jefferson gave wool for stockings to those slaves who could spin and knit it themselves, Harriet was in a position to put her skills to work for her family's interests. Edmund Bacon recalled that Harriet "never did any hard work." An overseer's perspective would not align with a slave's, of course, so it is unclear whether he meant that she did not have to produce as much as everyone else did, or that he thought spinning was considerably easier than field work.

Although there is no evidence that she absented herself from work for a whole week as Beverley once had, Bacon's comment suggests that Harriet did not take her work in the manufactory very seriously. But Jefferson did. Sally Hemings's daughter was never going to be like his granddaughters; not for her would there be training on the harpsichord or guitar, or in Latin. The intellectual activities and feminine accomplishments that were so critical to the Randolph girls' sense of themselves as elite white women would not be a part of Harriet Hemings's training for adulthood. Nor would spinning be part of the Randolphs' training. Even as an eleven-year-old, Ellen laughed off her grandfather's suggestion that she spin him a waistcoat. "I cannot now even spin candle wick," she told him spiritedly, with no apparent interest in learning how. But for Harriet Hemings, the child of a slave, industry meant spinning, not writing. In fact, Jefferson had long associated spinning with women of color rather than white women. Early in his presidency, he had envisioned Indian men settling down to "cultivate their lands; and their women to spin and weave for their families." Of course, the task was also well suited to the enslaved women, whom he could readily assign to his textile manufactory. By the time Harriet turned fourteen, Jefferson thought this work matched her rank in life, both on the mountain and wherever she would live out her life in freedom.

And certainly, a critical part of education in the South was to learn one's status in the world as free or enslaved and its requisite behavior. This was not immediately apparent to the very young. Remembering his childhood at Monticello, former slave Peter Fossett pointed out that "a peculiar fact about [Jefferson's] house servants was that we were all related to one another, and as a matter of fact we did not need to know that we were slaves. As a boy I was not only brought up differently, but dressed unlike the plantation boys. My grandmother was free, and I remember the first suit she gave me. It was of blue nankeen cloth, red morocco hat and red morocco shoes." Living in freedom after Thomas Bell's death, Mary Hemings Bell delighted in dressing her grandson in colorful clothes that set him apart from the dull beige osnaburg the other slaves wore; he did not even think of himself as one of the "plantation boys." But he discovered what it meant to be a slave after Jefferson's death. He bitterly recalled the day just after his eleventh birthday when he was "put upon an auction block and sold to strangers." He would not be reunited in freedom with his family again for almost twenty-five years.

Harriet was just about the same age, weeks from her eleventh birthday, when she learned something about the meaning of slavery: At Jefferson's orders, the Monticello slave community was forced to witness the full authority of their master with the whipping of Jame Hubbard. Since his move from Poplar Forest, Hubbard had become one of the most productive workers in the nailery. He had worked hard at other tasks as well, eager for the pay that Jefferson gave as an incentive for doing extra work. But brought back to Monticello in irons after a second escape attempt, Hubbard had exhausted Jefferson's patience. So on that April day in 1812, Hubbard's no-nonsense owner determined to make an example of him. "I had him severely flogged in the presence of his old companions," he told Reuben Perry, who had contracted to buy Hubbard, "and committed to jail."

Hubbard had made a mockery of Jefferson's previous leniencies toward him. Using his earnings, the twenty-one-year-old slave had furnished himself with such a fine set of clothes that in his first escape attempt in 1805 he had gotten almost as far as Washington before he was challenged. Later, back at Monticello, Hubbard was Bacon's chief suspect when several hundred pounds of nails went missing. Mystified by the behavior of this "favorite servant," Jefferson had relented at Hubbard's tears and refused to order a whipping for a theft that was worth close to fifty dollars. Now, however, furious that his benevolent authority had been so completely flouted a second time, Jefferson ordered Hubbard's whipping as an object lesson to the rest of his slaves, before he turned him over to his next owner. "All circumstances convince me he will never again serve any man as a slave," Jefferson warned Perry. "It will therefore unquestionably be best for you to sell him . . . out of the state." The slave owners of the Deep South were notorious for breaking the spirits of recalcitrant slaves and ensured that escape to the free states in the North was almost impossible.

If the laws of God and nature had consigned women to the sole task of motherhood, so too, Jefferson believed, the inherent inferiority of people of African descent fitted them to work under the direction of whites. It is unlikely that Harriet Hemings would have watched Hubbard's brutal punishment, but she certainly would have heard talk about it. If she had not quite understood the full meaning of slavery before, she surely learned that day. Admittedly, Jefferson preferred the smooth operation of a system in which his natural inferiors acknowledged the legitimacy of his government in return for the indulgences he dispensed. But if he could not secure their assent, he had the whip. And like every other slaveholder in the South, he was the law on his plantations. Public whippings were a ritual of terror aimed at the entire community; Hubbard's would have made a deep impression on a young girl as she realized what her father could command in a system that would not restrain him.

Harriet had other lessons in rank and status at Monticello that were considerably less dramatic but no less real. Most slaves learned early to exhibit the deferential behavior their masters required even if it was more show than genuine, the price they paid to keep their families together, to earn indulgences, or sometimes just to survive. These lessons were relentless and were particularly clear to Harriet every time the Randolphs and the Eppeses arrived for their extended visits when Jefferson was in residence. Although it is true that, as Annette Gordon-Reed wryly observed, "there can be great comfort in knowing that visitors are eventually going to go home," little Harriet would have noticed substantial changes in her family's daily routine during these visits. Her mother, and indeed all her relatives, would have had considerably less time for her and one another as the focus of their daily duties shifted to the comforts of Jefferson and his white family. The house had to be aired and cleaned, meals cooked and delivered on schedule, and fires and lamps lit. Once, after the Randolphs had moved to Monticello permanently and Jefferson had taken Burwell Colbert with him to

Poplar Forest, Ellen complained, "You know we never have the comfort of a clean house whilst Burwell is away."

Years later, married and living in Boston, Ellen compared free white servants and southern slaves, providing an unwitting picture of the expectations of the white Monticello family and the work of the Hemings house slaves. In Boston, Ellen explained, servant women made the beds, straightened the rooms, and swept the carpets *once* each day; their work schedule was not interrupted by a hapless mistress who could not keep a room tidy. Unlike elite southern girls, Ellen was learning, northern ones "take care to require from the servants no running about from place to place," adding that Boston girls left "no clothes tossed about, no drawer open, combs, pins, curls, ribbons, trinkets here and there on the dressing table, shoes in the middle of the floor, and so forth." Watching her mother's sisters spending their days picking up after the Randolph girls would have taught Harriet a great deal about the privileges of whiteness and the place of slaves.

These differences became clearer still when Martha Randolph and her children moved into Monticello permanently in 1809. Harriet had been too young—just a toddler, in fact—to notice when the storm first broke around the Monticello family, disrupting the quiet arrangements Jefferson had made in his life with Sally Hemings and his daughters' equally quiet accommodation of them. Aggrieved that he had not been rewarded for past services attacking President Jefferson's political enemies, a hack journalist named James Callender publicly exposed Jefferson's relationship with Sally Hemings in the pages of the Richmond *Recorder*. "It is well known that the man, *whom it delighteth the people to honor,* keeps, and for many years past has kept, as his concubine, one of his own slaves," Callender charged in September 1802. "Her name is SALLY. . . . By this wench Sally, our president has had several children," he added, one of whom (a son) bears "features [that] are said to bear a striking resemblance to those of the president himself." Several more articles ensued, adding details—most of which turned out to be accurate—that Callender culled from Jefferson's neighbors.

Jefferson met Callender's accusations with silence, neither admitting nor denying them. The story did not go away, however. Almost ten years later, a Vermont schoolteacher named Elijah P. Fletcher visited

Monticello. His visit was cordial: Jefferson offered him wine and showed him his library. But Fletcher discovered that the story about "Black Sal is no farce," as he put it in a letter to a relative. As news of the arrangement continued to circulate in Charlottesville, Jefferson was "little esteemed by his neighbors, Republicans as well as Federalists," perhaps, Fletcher reasoned, because he "keeps the same children slaves." Although the New Englander saw that in Virginia "such proceedings are so common that they cease here to be disgraceful," Martha Randolph suffered the humiliation of this exposure greatly for years afterward, and in the fallout of her pain Sally Hemings and her children surely did as well, in the thousands of subtle gestures of daily life.

Such practices were common in the slaveholding South, of course, and white men had pursued them with impunity since the seventeenth century. No one should be surprised they persisted in Albemarle County when, as one of Jefferson's neighbors observed, "Mr. Jefferson's notorious example is considered." But after the Revolution, new conventions of etiquette required the protection of southern white womanhood from the sordid details. The unwritten rule of the day was that as long as the man was discreet and did not insist that his white family accept the children of his slave liaisons as one of them, neither his wife nor the community at large had anything with which to reproach him. But Callender's articles broke this southern consensus of silence, and Martha's suffering was acute. She "took the Dusky Sally stories much to heart," her son said more than fifty years later. Although she did not have the status of a wife to lodge a complaint, Martha was pushed to the breaking point by a poem she read a few years afterward that alleged Jefferson "dreams of freedom in his bondmaid's arms." "The calm, gentle Martha's passion-gust was irresistible," wrote Henry Randall, an early Jefferson biographer, describing the way she stormed into her father's library. "Mr. Jefferson broke into a hearty, clear laugh," which Martha chose to read as a denial.

But the question never receded. How could it, when after her move back to Monticello she was confronted daily with her father's visage in at least two of Sally's three sons? It bothered Martha's son Jeff as well. He told Randall that "the resemblance was so close, that at some distance or in the dusk the slave [probably Eston], dressed in the same way, might be mistaken for Mr. Jefferson." There was even the time when "a gentleman dining with Mr. Jefferson, looked so startled as he raised his eyes from the latter to the servant behind him, that his discovery of the resemblance was perfectly obvious to all." As Martha had confided to Ellen in 1825, she had endured "the discomfort of slavery" all her life. According to Jeff, if she had had her way, Sally Hemings and her children would have been moved off the mountain years before. That did not happen, of course, yet she still strove to mold her father's memory. Near the end of her life, Martha asked her sons Jeff and George to check their grandfather's records, directing them to notice that Jefferson had not been at Monticello for a full fifteen months before the conception of one of Hemings's children. "Remember this fact," she bade them. In fact, Jefferson's records showed precisely the opposite.

Schooled, then, by their mother and grandfather in the habits and attitudes of white slaveholding Virginians, the Randolph girls would also have given Harriet daily lessons in what it meant to be a slave. The curtain of silence that Jefferson drew down around his life with Sally Hemings veils the character of daily contacts between Sally's children and Martha's; beyond Madison's few words about "inducing the white children to teach me the letters," we simply do not know. But the Randolphs' later actions reveal what they were taught, explicitly or otherwise, about slaves and people of color, and those attitudes would have been inscribed in every look, gesture, and comment directed toward Harriet.

That the young Randolphs were as discomfited as their mother by the "yellow children," as Ellen called them, is apparent in their various attempts to explain them away. In 1858, Ellen wrote a long letter to her husband, Joseph, explaining that "there is a general impression that the four children of Sally Hemmings were *all* the children of Col. Carr." Ellen agreed with this assessment of Samuel Carr, her mother's cousin; his licentious "deeds are as well known as his name," she thought. It was Jefferson's principle to "allow such of his slaves as were sufficiently white to pass for white men, to withdraw quietly from the plantation," she stated categorically; "it was called running away but they were never reclaimed." There was nothing notable, then, about the "four instances of this, three young men and one girl, who walked away and staid away. Their whereabouts was perfectly known but they were left to themselves—for they were white enough to pass for white." The notion that Jefferson could have fathered Sally's children, Ellen flatly denied. "There are such things, after all, as moral impossibilities," she declared. Jeff Randolph, on the other hand, identified Sam Carr's brother Peter as the father of Sally's children to try to explain away the family resemblances that were so obvious to visitors.

The white family stories about the "yellow children" of Monticello are shot through with holes, inconsistencies, and inaccuracies that have been thoughtfully analyzed at length elsewhere. But there are several points to consider here as we think about Harriet's interactions with the Randolphs at Monticello. One is the way in which Ellen talked about Sally Hemings and her children. Although she had known Sally all her life and knew she was light-skinned, Ellen nonetheless still referred to her as "dusky Sally," the denigrating name given to her in sensationalized print stories almost sixty years earlier. When Madison Hemings told his family story to an Ohio newspaper in 1873, he named every one of Martha's eleven surviving children; in her account, Ellen refused to name Beverley and Harriet when she described the escaped slaves Jefferson never hunted down. Similarly, in his conversation with his grandfather's biographer, Jeff failed to explicitly identify the son who so resembled Jefferson but rather referred to him only as a "slave." In her feigned ignorance of their names, Ellen would like us to read an insurmountable distance between her world and theirs, a chasm that she neither cared nor was forced to bridge. But she *did* know them— she grew up alongside them; and as long as the stories linking them to Jefferson continued to circulate, she could hardly be indifferent. In fact, the whole point of Ellen's letter to her husband—otherwise inexplicable after more than thirty years of marriage—was to establish her credentials as Jefferson's legitimate descendant and consign her cousins to nameless oblivion, erasing Beverley, Harriet, Madison, and Eston Hemings from contention.

But Ellen and her family were also grossly indifferent to the plight of all the other female slaves at Monticello, who she admitted were at the mercy of the "Irish workmen" and the "dissipated young men in the neighborhood," and subsequently bore the "yellow" children whom visitors to the plantation noticed. Ellen's letter makes plain how little she thought of the humanity of the slaves who spent their days picking up after her and her sisters, but then suffered, unprotected, the sexual assaults of her grandfather's hired help and Jeff's schoolmates. To Ellen, slaves were inferior beings, no matter what color their skin might be. So certain was she of the truth of that view that when she weighed the relative freedoms of American and English women, she was comfortable omitting enslaved women entirely from her calculations. "Putting domestic slavery out of the question," she wrote, easily dismissing the weight of this American institution, "it has never been my lot to see any thing like oppression of the many by the few." Jefferson had been able to proclaim that all men were created equal without any sense of contradiction precisely because he denied the full humanity of slaves. So too could his privileged granddaughter judge American women as the freest in the world, by excising from consideration the many who were more oppressed by race than she was by gender.

But, as one jarring incident shows, not even well-bred and educated women could escape their part in upholding this system of oppression. "You will laugh to hear what disciplinarians we have turned out to be," Cornelia wrote to her sister Virginia from their rented home in Washington several years after Jefferson's death. When a young slave girl named Sally admitted stealing a pair of satin shoes from Septimia and some stockings, Martha and Cornelia conferred about her punishment. Not a week earlier, they had sent Sally for a whipping in the city's public facility where slaveholders could pay others to administer punishment, but it was, Cornelia thought in hindsight, "by far too moderate correction." To send her back would be an admission that the white women could not control a slave girl. Instead Cornelia continued, "we . . . took her down into the basement, Melinda & myself held her & mama inflicted the flagellation pretty severely." As much as they abhorred administering physical punishment, they nonetheless could sacrifice their discomfort to ensure their authority over their slaves.

Nothing in this family's record, then—their stories to "protect" Jefferson, their account of a slave's whipping, or their efforts to distinguish themselves from the children of a slave woman—suggests that the Randolphs would have treated Harriet Hemings as anything other than the slave that the law said she was. If Jame Hubbard's whipping taught Harriet about slavery, growing up with the Randolph girls taught her about the power of whiteness. It did not matter who her father was. All the Randolphs had to do was to look past her and, in their willful blindness, deprive her even of her name to ensure she understood her place.

Like Jefferson, Sally Hemings never publicly commented on their relationship or her relations with the Randolphs. She made no statement in the wake of Callender's firestorm. She left no memoir after Jefferson's death. So we cannot know exactly how she felt about her Randolph relations. Perhaps a French ointment pot, found by archaeologists on Mulberry Row, may provide a clue. By the time Jefferson retired from public life in 1809, the south dependency of the house had been completed. It housed his state-of-the-art French kitchen and several dormitory rooms. In one of them lived Sally Hemings and her four children. Two centuries after her move to the south dependency, Monticello archaeologists unearthed the shards of a pharmacy ointment pot in Mulberry Row. Carefully reassembled, it revealed its Parisian origins: "in Rue de Richelieu vis a vis [facing] Le Café Foi, Paris." If Sally Hemings had kept it for twenty years, a mute testimony to the significance of her two years in Paris, why did she not bring it with her up the slope to her new quarters in the south dependency? Did the pot represent a time in her life when she envisioned a life at Monticello absent the governing hand of a mistress? With her new status, Sally Hemings could reasonably have looked forward to that eventuality. But that prospect crumbled with Martha Randolph's move to the mountain in 1809. Perhaps Sally tossed her French memento into the trash pit, not wishing to be reminded of a scenario that would never be realized.

Broken, buried, and now resurrected, the ointment pot is not unlike the history of Sally Hemings's life, and both stories remain a tantalizing mystery. In the end, what Sally felt about her niece Martha Randolph, or Martha about Sally, really did not matter to the dynamics of life at Monticello. Like Martha, Sally was bound by Jefferson's will and determination to avoid confrontation. In the face of Ellen's sneers about "yellow children," or Jeff's discomfort with the resemblance her four "fair" children bore to Jefferson, or Martha's obvious unhappiness with the arrangement, Sally Hemings would have taught her daughter the value of holding her tongue. Discretion was a small price to pay for peace and the freedom that would be hers when she turned twenty-one.

Neither a Randolph nor an acknowledged Jefferson, Harriet none-theless knew that there were still tangible benefits to being Sally Hemings's daughter. During the newspaper revelations of 1802, readers learned that Sally Hemings was "treated by the rest of his house as one much above the level of his other servants." And at first glance, Harriet's transfer from the great house to the textile factory was not as dra-matic as her mother's had been, at the same age, from Virginia to Paris; Harriet's journey was a matter of steps, not thousands of miles. But unlike her mother, Harriet was no one's maid; with her work in the textile factory, Jefferson had ensured that. She grew up "measurably happy," as her brother Madison had said about their childhood, always with the knowledge that she would be free. And if Jefferson's white la-borers or Jeff's friends sexually exploited Jefferson's female slaves, Har-riet Hemings was clearly off-limits; there is not a whiff of a suggestion in the historical record to suggest she bore any children at Monticello. It is ironic that, as a slave, Harriet Hemings needed the protection of the very man who had impregnated his own sixteen-year-old slave, her mother. But unlike most enslaved women in the South, who bore chil-dren by age nineteen, Harriet was apparently held safe from sexual as-sault at Monticello. And tellingly, she would be the only female slave Jefferson ever allowed to go free.

In all these ways, then, Harriet Hemings was an utter anomaly: named by Thomas Jefferson, fair in her coloring, and clearly favored in the protections afforded her and her expectation of freedom, yet never comparable to her Randolph cousins who were born free and, in the language of Virginia law, "legitimate." In the way that the Randolph sisters cultivated a sense of themselves as a kind of Jeffersonian aristoc-racy, could not their aunt Harriet have done so as well, given all of her advantages? And in the insidious workings of the slave system, which created and enforced a color hierarchy, might Harriet have harbored some sense of superiority over dark-skinned slaves? If Harriet Hemings saw herself as privileged, and even deprived because she was not ac-corded the same privileges she saw her sister and the Randolph girls receive, it may help to explain why she decided to leave. "The slave is always the stranger who resides in one place and belongs in another," historian Saidiya Hartman learned when she journeyed to Africa to study the captives of the slave trade. Born at Monticello, Harriet Hemings was "of the house" that Jefferson built, but she had no stake in it.

Leaving Charlottesville may not have been what her mother initially intended for Harriet, although it is impossible to know with any certainty what hopes Sally Hemings harbored for her daughter's future. Perhaps she fondly hoped for the kind of extended family experience she herself had known at Monticello, except transplanted in freedom among the Charlottesville community. Relying on Jefferson's promise, Sally Hemings could reasonably have hoped that her own family would do even better than her sister Mary, who lived in town in quasi freedom with Thomas Bell and their two children. Several of Mary Hemings Bell's older children had remained enslaved, however. Sally Hemings, on the other hand, could have anticipated that *all* her children would live as free people of means, in the beauty and familiarity of Albemarle County, within easy reach of relatives both free and enslaved.

It was not to be. In 1806, the Virginia legislature mandated that henceforth all manumitted slaves must leave the Commonwealth within twelve months or be reenslaved. Six years earlier, Richmond had been shaken by the sophisticated organization of rebellious slaves who planned to torch the city, seize its arsenal of weapons, and capture the governor and his officials. Saved from the coup by torrential rains that prevented the conspirators from launching their revolt, Virginia legislators methodically began tightening the manumission laws that had been considerably loosened during the Revolution. Evading the 1806 edict was possible only by a successful petition to the legislature, but that would require a public declaration of responsibility that Hemings knew Jefferson would never make. His determined silence in the face of Callender's attacks had made that plain. Unless he would allow her to leave the state, Sally Hemings knew that her family would not be exempt from the enforced separations that were the daily lot of slaves in the United States. The law must have hit her with brute force as she looked upon her little children—then eight, five, and one—and realized she might have to prepare them to leave her forever.

The point of the law was to remove the obvious evidence that contradicted white claims—Jefferson's included—that people of African descent were incapable of caring for themselves. It was a maxim on which the system of slavery rested. But the law also highlighted the problem created when white men had sex across the color line: the growth of a significant population of mixed-race people. In their newspaper ads, white Virginians used at least sixty-one different phrases to describe the varying skin tones of their runaway slaves. This remarkable list itself was proof that, as one historian noted, "the racial order was breaking down." But even the law did not stipulate a neat divide between black and white. In 1785 the state legislature changed the boundary between whiteness and mulatto from one-eighth African ancestry to one-quarter, but it failed to address the ambiguous racial category of people with less than one-quarter African blood. They remained raceless, the law exempting them from the legal category of color but still unwilling to categorically denote them white.

In practice, white Virginians tended to be a bit lax about these racial categories when it suited them. No one in Charlottesville, for example, contested Thomas Bell's will, which left his property to Mary. Although Bell had never formally freed her, there was clearly a community consensus about Mary's free status, although it depended on the locals' acceptance of his standing and hers in the town. When the 1830 census taker knocked on Sally Hemings's door, he judged her, Madison, and Eston "white," an indication of both their skin color and the community understanding of their free status after Jefferson's death. Three years later, however, another official judged them mulatto. These are precisely the sorts of situations—endlessly duplicated—that explain the legislature's refusal to follow their reasoning to its logical conclusion and say that if you do not meet the criteria for black, you must be white.

Nothing was as simple as black and white in Jefferson's Virginia. Fair as they all were, Sally Hemings's children appeared in a list Jefferson entitled "Negroes retained," on which he sorted out those slaves he leased to his neighbors from those who remained to work for him. Ultimately, of course, one's status depended not on the lightness of one's complexion or hair but on the condition of one's mother. Because Beverley, Harriet, Madison, and Eston were the children of an enslaved woman, their emancipation would therefore require their departure. The inevitable separation, however, would not have altered their mother's essential goals for them: that all marry free persons, that her sons be well positioned to support themselves and their families, and that her daughter become the wife of a respectable man. These were not substantially different dreams than any free white mother would have nurtured for her children, but they were prodigiously challenging for an enslaved one. To the extent that her duties would allow, Sally Hemings had worked to make the most of their time together before the inevitable partings and to ensure her children's readiness when that time came; the same force of will that in Paris elicited Jefferson's promise of freedom for their children would only have been strengthened under these new circumstances.

With all these considerations, Harriet had a decision to make as her twenty-first birthday approached. What would she do? Would she leave Albemarle County? Where would she go? Her options presented her with a different kind of dilemma than her brothers faced. There was the obvious gendered difference common to almost all nineteenth-century women: Her brothers had marketable skills and could be self-supporting; Harriet, on the other hand, may not have even known how to read or write. Indeed, a self-supporting woman in the nineteenth century was synonymous with poverty. As for almost all women of her time, her survival strategy would have to center not on work but on making a good marriage.

Harriet also had to consider the gender differences inherent in the slave system. To avoid a paper trail that would connect them to him, Jefferson facilitated Beverley's and Harriet's departures without furnishing them manumission papers; in fact, for anyone who might examine his papers after his death, he wrote in his Farm Book "run [18]22" next to their names. So at law they remained fugitive slaves until the United States abolished slavery with the Thirteenth Amendment in 1865. Although some states had already abolished slavery or put it on the path to extinction by gradual emancipation before then, the force of the federal government had always been marshaled in support of slavery, first with the Fugitive Slave Act of 1793, and then its stronger successor in 1850. Not only was it a federal offense to assist fugitive slaves, the 1850 act required the free states to return runaways to their masters, so that even in the North they were not safe.

For forty-three years, then, Harriet risked forcible return to Virginia and slavery if her identity was discovered and reported. And because

Virginia law perpetuated slavery through women rather than men, Harriet's very body would condemn her children to that status if she was discovered. Thus her only hope to break the bonds of slavery in her generation was to disappear into the anonymity of the North. With her departure, Harriet did not reject her mother or her brothers, but whites' evolving definition of slavery. Like her father, who had compared Britain's rule to enslavement, she knew exactly what slavery was and, as he had, claimed independence as her right in her own pursuit of happiness.

We do not know for sure where she was headed the day she left Monticello. Bacon remembered that "by Mr. Jefferson's direction I paid her stage fare to Philadelphia and gave her fifty dollars." In fact, Philadelphia would have been an ideal place to begin her new life. First of all, she could get there, since her father had paid the fare; it was far enough away from Charlottesville that the Hemings name (if indeed she kept it) might not betray her origins; and, with a population of nearly sixty-four thousand, it would be easier than in Washington City to disappear into anonymity. The city had attracted many manumitted slaves from Delaware, Maryland, and Virginia, as well as from the Pennsylvania hinterlands, between 1790 and 1820. Its reputation for abolition appeared to have been justified by the 1820 census that for the first time entered a zero under the city's category of Slave. Hemings would have stayed far away from the free black community, of course, but she may have been reassured that Philadelphia's approach to slavery appeared to be very different from her home state's.

Jefferson would not have sent her to Philadelphia without making careful arrangements for her initial placement and care. He had known the city well and still had close and trusted friends there from his days serving as delegate to the Continental Congress, and later as secretary of state and vice president. Remembering his fond friendship with Francis Hopkinson, who had since died, he may have considered approaching Hopkinson's son, Joseph, drawing upon those old ties and Hopkinson's abolitionist sympathies to obtain a situation for Harriet. He may have asked his good friend Dolley Madison whether she had any old connections from whom he might request a favor. Or he may have made discreet inquiries through another Philadelphia contact, James Ronaldson, who had recommended so enthusiastically the small manufactories there. Might he suggest an available position for a well-bred though financially distressed young woman in his neighborhood who could spin and weave? Whether Jefferson entrusted his secret to anyone in Philadelphia or kept it hidden, the city would only have been a possibility for Harriet Hemings if her father had made it so. And in paying her fare to that city, it is clear that for him, at least, it was Harriet's destination.

But just because Jefferson thought spinning and weaving was a good job for a woman does not mean that Harriet and her mother thought so. More likely, Harriet Hemings would always associate spinning with her enslavement. Perhaps it could serve as a fallback position, but Harriet probably had very different ideas about her life as a free woman. In fact, Madison specified that she had gone to Washington, at least at first. If Harriet alighted from the stage at Washington City (as is most probable) rather than continuing to Philadelphia, it was because the Hemingses had made other plans. A new and growing city, Washington offered a wide variety of employment possibilities for women— with the notable exception of textile manufacturing.

Even though Harriet had never been there herself (there is no evidence that she ever left Charlottesville and environs before her final leave-taking), Washington was familiar to a lot of people at Monticello. Of course, Jefferson had spent eight years there, and his daughter Martha had taken two winter sojourns with him during his presidency. But more important for Harriet was the daily contact she enjoyed with Edith Hern Fossett, who had lived at the White House, and her brother Davy Hern, the driver who knew every inch of the roads between the capital and Monticello. Although the Herns left Washington in 1808 before Jefferson did, they clearly maintained contact with friends they had made there. When their younger brother Thruston ran away in 1817, Jefferson looked for him in Washington, where, he was sure, Thruston was "lurking under the connivance of some of his sister's old friends." Betsy Hemmings, the enslaved daughter of Sally's older sister Mary Hemings Bell, also knew Washington, staying there with Jack Eppes (after Maria's death) while he was serving in Congress. Betsy was apparently able to make the journey there alone. In one instance, after Jefferson had retired from the presidency, his Washington servant Joseph Dougherty arranged that she be charged with transporting some of Jefferson's valuable books home from Washington as far as Fredericksburg. Besides having at least two children with Eppes (who continued the pattern of shadow families begun by his grandfather John Wayles), Betsy served as a nurse for Francis and would have accompanied them to Monticello to visit her own relations when Francis and his father visited there in the years after Maria's death. Paul Jennings, the enslaved valet of James Madison, accompanied his master on his twice-yearly retirement visits to Monticello, beginning in 1817, and would have been another, more updated source on Washington as the time for Harriet's decision drew near.

This dizzyingly interconnected network of slaves and ex-slaves makes clear that while masters commandeered slave labor to facilitate their careers in Washington, their workers used every opportunity to shape their own lives even while enslaved and to study possibilities for constructing new futures for themselves in freedom. Indeed, one historian persuasively identified Paul Jennings as the person who helped Thruston Hern escape; Bacon guessed that the young man "had gone with Mr. Madison's cart to Washington, and had passed himself off as Mr. Madison's servant." One human link forged to another, layer upon layer, story upon story: Thus Harriet would have learned a lot about the city long before she decided to go there.

But perhaps the most important consideration of all was that her brother Beverley Hemings was there. We know from their brother Madison that "Beverley went to Washington as a white man." Although he had turned twenty-one in April 1819, Beverley had remained in slavery for almost three additional years, according to Jefferson's Farm Book. Never a meticulous daily record, the Farm Book is imprecise about the departure of brother and sister. One of the last records for both is when the entire family appears for the 1819–1820 cloth and blanket distribution, although twenty-one-year-old Beverley is listed apart from his mother and younger siblings, as he had been for several years. The last time Jefferson records both names is in January 1821, in his list of house slaves. It appears the two of them had left by the Christmas 1821 distribution of cloth, blankets, and hats, or at least, their departure was so imminent they did not receive allowances meant for the following year; Sally Hemings's name is joined only by Madison's and Eston's. Jefferson even made a point of scratching the siblings' names off the blanket list; given their ages and having received their blankets for 1818–1819, they would not need the next scheduled allotment three years later in 1821–1822. Perhaps it was Beverley whom Mary Randolph saw playing the fiddle during that otherwise quiet Christmas week in 1821—his last at Monticello?—"as he stood with half closed eyes & head thrown back with one foot keeping time to his own scraping in the midst of a circle of attentive & admiring auditors." As did her elder sister Ellen when talking about Sally Hemings's children, Mary left the talented enslaved musician unnamed.

Hemings scholars believe that Beverley probably left Monticello near the end of 1821. There is no particular evidence in the Farm Book to show that Beverley left before Harriet did, although it makes eminent sense that he would go ahead to scout out living quarters and work prospects before his sister joined him. Washington offered countless work opportunities for the young man, who was well trained as a carpenter and as a cooper.

We know very little about Beverley Hemings, but if he was anything like Paul Jennings, who was just a year younger, he was a man who claimed the right to improve his circumstances and to succeed. Jennings had learned to read and write as he stood attendance on his young master during his lessons; he spoke French; he played the violin with flair; he was scrupulously polite to the Madisons' guests, cultivating a network of potential contacts and allies; he negotiated a loan from the eminent Daniel Webster to buy his freedom; and after a career working for the government, he died possessed of valuable city property that he bequeathed to his sons. Such achievements were possible for well-placed slaves who adroitly made the most of the limited opportunities they were allowed, without alienating their masters upon whom their advancement depended.

We do know that Beverley was successful enough to win the hand of a white woman from Maryland whose family, Madison noted, "was of good circumstances." We also suspect, thanks to the account of another Monticello slave, that Beverley was the man who launched a hot-air balloon in Petersburg on the Fourth of July 1834, an event that Madison attended. That he would have inherited something of his father's intelligence and interest in science and innovation is perhaps not surprising; that he possessed the time and money to pursue such an undertaking is more so. It certainly indicates a man who, like Jennings, refused to let his talents and drive be stymied by his society's system of racial hierarchy. Instead Washington became Beverley's launchpad.

Whatever her mother or father thought best for her, in the end it was Harriet's own decision that prevailed. To Washington she would go. As Madison explained, "She thought it to her interest, on going to Washington, to assume the role of a white woman." His phrasing is interesting. "*She* thought," he said. The decision does not sound like either a parental directive or a family consensus. "To *her* interest," he said. Harriet would have recognized the difference between her situation and that of her brothers. Maybe there were long conversations about the priority of keeping the family together once Beverley turned twenty-one; we have seen how close a family the Hemingses were. The idea of allowing the law to force a permanent fracture may have been more than her mother and younger brother could bear. But in Madison's view, the family interest did not prevail; Harriet's particular individual interest did. "To assume the *role* of a white woman," he said. Madison's careful wording hints at anguished conversations about identity. Perhaps she had to assure him strenuously that she would be no less a Hemings because she had to drop the family name to pass, that she would be no less her mother's daughter or his sister. Perhaps she had to explain to him that it was a role the law forced her to play so that her children would be born white and free, with all the privileges of citizenship the Constitution afforded such people. Ultimately, we can only guess whether Madison's words convey Harriet's sensibility about what she was about to do, or his anger and grief at losing her to the white world.

What we do know is that Harriet played her role as a white woman perfectly. "By her dress and conduct as such," Madison continued more than fifty years after her departure, "I am not aware that her identity as Harriet Hemings of Monticello has ever been discovered." Lacking formal freedom documents, there would be no documentation to gainsay her ruse by pointing to her birth in slavery or to her distant African ancestor, her unnamed great-grandmother. She possessed the advantages of her father's fair coloring to play upon whites' unthinking assumption of her free status, and of her mother's beauty to play upon gender conventions to charm and disarm. In most levels of society, beauty and manners were enough to attract a husband, particularly in a racist society that assumed genteel manners could only be white. Still, there would be significant details to attend to, to ensure a smooth and unquestioned transition from "black" to "white."

Clothing was the most obvious detail, as universal a signal of status in Harriet Hemings's time as in our own. In the South, slave garb was a particularly striking demarcation between enslaved and free. In 1735, South Carolina had even passed a series of laws to ensure that the distinction was observed, for example forbidding slaves to wear the cast-off clothing of their masters. Jame Hubbard had relied on his new suit to carry him to freedom, and if it hadn't been for a poorly written pass, it would have worked. Harriet had never worn the costume of an enslaved woman: the jacket and loose-fitting short gown that allowed both mobility of movement for field work and layering in the winter, or an osnaburg shift in summer. She did not suffer the tortures of wearing coarse flax garments that Booker T. Washington remembered felt like "a dozen or more chestnut burrs, or a hundred small pin-points, in contact with his flesh." It is not likely she wrapped her head in the turban headdress characteristic of African women and carried to America. She never "worked in the fields in rags, breasts exposed," as a French visitor saw in Louisiana; she would not have worn "pantelettes made an' tied to dere knees, to wear in de fields to keep dew off dere legs," as a Mississippi slave recalled of her work clothing. Although there are no notations in Jefferson's accounts that he spent extra money on Harriet's clothing, he had authorized Martha to clothe well the Hemings women who served in the house. Not for them the defeminized, shapeless, identical clothing of the field hand; the master who sent them fabrics of different colors and patterns from Philadelphia was clearly conscious of the ways women should present themselves, particularly in his home. There is no reason to think that his sensibilities would not have extended to his daughter.

Even so, Harriet's trousseau for her life in freedom would have to look more like the Randolphs' clothing than her mother's. But a well-chosen wardrobe was a challenge, it turns out, even for the privileged Ellen Randolph. Feeling completely out of her depth in rural Albemarle as she prepared for her wedding trip and move to Boston in 1825, Ellen enlisted the aid of the mother of her brother Jeff's wife, who lived in the rapidly expanding port city of Baltimore. "The clothes which served me through my Richmond & Washington [husband-hunting] campaigns are gone," she wrote to her brother's mother-in-law, Margaret Nicholas. Ellen placed her trousseau entirely in Margaret's hands. "I have lived so much at home & particularly of late, have dressed so little, that I am completely ignorant of what I shall myself want. Will you then make out a list of such articles?" she asked, as Margaret "shall determine to be necessary." Although Harriet would have reduced the quantities considerably, the return list gives us an idea of the kinds of articles she would have needed to dress like a white woman of her class: fifteen pairs of cotton hose, six dozen silk hose, three pairs of corsets, a dozen pairs of gloves, twelve pairs of shoes, two worked capes, a black silk dress supplemented by two other silks (presumably in different colors), a dress cloak, a beaver bonnet for winter travel and straw for summer, eighteen pocket handkerchiefs, gauze hands (to protect arms and hands from summer sun, such as Abigail Adams had provided for Maria), breakfast dresses, a variety of muslin and edging for everyday capes, lace and edging for dresses, a trunk to cart it all in, and a carpetbag for stylish conveyance of articles one would prefer to keep close at hand. Harriet probably would have dispensed with the recommended bridal bonnet.

The tab for Ellen's ensemble ran just short of three hundred dollars, or a male day laborer's pay for a year and a half—hardly anything Harriet Hemings could have afforded. This list of necessaries for women of Ellen's rank also contrasts starkly with the clothing allotted female slaves, who received only two seasonal outfits and coarse woven stockings. They were lucky if they received a pair of shoes and a hat; there were no corsets, gloves, bonnets, silk or breakfast dresses, cloaks, lace edgings, or handkerchiefs. Slave mistresses certainly had no interest in enhancing the attractiveness of their female slaves, and given their limited mobility, slaves needed neither trunks nor carpetbags.

White women's dress differed noticeably in style as well. Their custom-fitted dresses were instantly distinguishable from the identical, shapeless, and color-restricted clothing of female slaves. All white women wore stays or corsets to provide shaping; this practice continued even as the fitted bodices of the eighteenth century gave way to the high-waisted comfort of empire dresses of the next. Dresses were long enough to cover the ankles, although in the fashion of the early 1820s they featured low necklines. Whether of homespun or of silk, in their colors, trimmings, and embellishments white women's dresses were as varied as the women wearing them. True, the choice of textile was significant in denoting class: For both formal occasions and everyday, middling-class women wore not silk but worsted wool. But it was comfortable, durable, and unlike slave clothing, draped well about the body to make the most of the fashions of the period.

Worsted wool would have been an excellent middle ground for Harriet's clothing, and the sewing skills her mother taught her would have been critical for her to fashion a wardrobe that would enable her to pass as a white woman. It is not difficult to imagine the Hemings family pooling their resources to outfit Harriet for her departure: perhaps giving up some of their own fabric allowance; or persuading Martha Randolph to allocate them just a little bit more than last December; or John Hemings apportioning some of his clothing charge account in Charlottesville to add to Harriet's trousseau; or Wormley Hughes selling some eggs or chickens to the main house to raise cash to buy necessaries in town. And if John Hemings lovingly crafted a lap desk for Ellen Randolph before her departure, surely it is not a stretch to imagine the trunk he could have presented to his niece. If Jefferson did not send her away empty-handed, it is inconceivable that her relatives would have.

Madison's reference to "dress," then, is not a difficult word to decipher; but what could he have meant by "conduct"? Perhaps, thinking about his brother Eston, he meant an attitude of reserve, or speech and vocabulary, or carriage, or one's choice of associations. An article written about Eston almost fifty years after his death by a former neighbor vividly recalled "a remarkably fine looking" man, tall, "well proportioned, very erect and dignified; his nearly straight hair showed a tint of auburn, and his face, indistinct suggestion of freckles." But more impressive than his appearance was his bearing. "Quiet, unobtrusive, polite and decidedly intelligent, he was soon very well and favorably known to all classes of our citizens, for his personal appearance and gentlemanly manners attracted everybody's attention to him," one of his Ohio neighbors remembered. Sold to another family after Jefferson's death, even eleven-year-old Peter Fossett found the tables turned when, "being with and coming from such a family as Mr. Jefferson's, I knew more than they did about many things." Perhaps white conduct meant forgetting forever the kind of spirited dances she could have known in the slave quarters and learning instead the more fashionably restrained dances of the Randolph sisters during their soirées, for which Beverley used to play.

What would it mean for a woman to "act white"? We do not know if Harriet was tall like Eston (who was six foot one, like his father and perhaps Beverley) or shorter like Madison, who stood just under five foot eight. Either way, wearing stays or corsets would straighten her back, forcing the regal posture common to white women even when seated. In addition, respectability dictated that women refrain from gossip, loud voices, and expressions of anger. They were to cultivate grace in their demeanor and carriage. This emphasis on manners became more important just as Harriet was coming of age, as Americans tried to throw off the last vestiges of colonial habits of deference to social superiors and to develop manners that would reflect democratic sensibilities instead. Interestingly, conduct books addressed their advice to both men and women, as the presence of women outside of their own homes, in the streets, markets, shops, and theaters, became increasingly taken for granted in the nineteenth century.

Cleanliness in her person and clothing would also have been important. This was not a subject to which Jefferson had ever been indifferent. Almost forty years earlier, he had lectured eleven-year-old Martha about "the subject of dress, which I know you are a little apt to neglect." "Let your clothes be clean, whole, and properly put on," he began. She was not to wear clothes repeatedly until "the dirt is visible to the eye." She was to dress neatly, as if for company, from the moment she rose in the morning. "Nothing," he finished sternly, "is so disgusting to our sex as a want of cleanliness and delicacy in yours."

Sally Hemings would have taught this important lesson to her daughter. Once described as "an industrious and orderly creature in her behavior," Sally Hemings modeled exactly the virtues that Harriet would need to enter with confidence the world into which her mother must send her. At precisely this time, Americans were beginning to pay a great deal more attention to the question of health and hygiene (Jefferson had been somewhat ahead of that curve in the 1780s), charging

mothers with ensuring the freshness of the air in their homes, the sani-
tation of their households, and the good health and appearance of their
families. As cleanliness became a concern of middle-class households,
so too did related questions of body control around coughing, sneezing,
and spitting tobacco juices. As a result, attention to questions of posture, manners, cleanliness, neatness, and even the use of handkerchiefs
(recall Margaret Nicholas recommending that Ellen get eighteen!) had
further set respectable white Americans off from enslaved blacks. Far
from leveling societal barriers in the young democracy, then, manners
solidified them. But the Hemings family had always been a caste apart,
and Harriet was evidently successful in passing as a freeborn white
woman in Washington City. From Eston's "personal appearance and
gentlemanly manners" and Peter Fossett's critiques of whites who did
not live up to standards he had seen at Monticello, we begin to understand how.

When she left for her new life is unclear. The fact that Jefferson
noted 1822 for both siblings suggests that, at least in his mind, her
departure was coordinated with Beverley's—whether that meant that
Beverley would take care of Harriet when she arrived in Washington,
or that he would return to escort her, or that they left together. Maybe
they left during the Christmas season when slaves traditionally were
given the week off from their year's labors and allowed passes for visiting. When Bacon said that Harriet left "when she was nearly grown,"
perhaps he meant before her twenty-first birthday, in May 1822, had
actually arrived. The weather had been bleak that year as winter set in.
At Monticello, Martha Randolph found December a "month . . . of unusual discomfort here." Her husband was serving as governor and their
daughters had gone to be with him in Richmond for the social season.
Madison and Eston may have been gone as well; a week before Christmas, Jefferson told John Hemings down in Poplar Forest that "the boys
set off this morning" for the three-day trip from Monticello, and gave
instructions that "Eston must drive the cart." With the house thus
emptied, it might have been a good time to leave without fanfare.
Through one of the elegant windows of the house, bound to Monticello
by her love for their father, Martha may have watched her younger sister go.

The pain of Harriet's final leave-taking with her mother and brothers is past imagining. Madison was just turning seventeen and Eston was not yet fourteen when they said goodbye to her forever. They all knew she could never risk the exposure of her enslaved origins by visiting them. There is no indication of a fond farewell with Jefferson; he seems to have delegated responsibility for her departure to his overseer, who relayed to her a sum the equivalent of three months' wages for a laboring man. Jefferson intended it not as a dowry but to cover her expenses on the road; twenty years earlier, he had given James Hemings thirty dollars for lodging and food for the week's trip to Philadelphia, and to his two other daughters one hundred for their trip to Washington.

Jefferson would have ensured that she had an escort who would not raise the eyebrows of her fellow travelers. Perhaps a white man: maybe Joseph Dougherty, Jefferson's Irish employee who had served him so well in Washington during his presidency and continued to write and visit Monticello from Washington long afterward. Or perhaps Jefferson sent one of the slaves with her. Peter Fossett remembered that "Mrs. Randolph would not let any of the young ladies go anywhere with gentlemen with the exception of their brothers, unless a colored servant accompanied them." Maybe his gardener Wormley Hughes: Jefferson had once entrusted Francis Eppes to Hughes for the eighty-mile trip between Monticello and Eppington. Or his valet, Burwell Colbert, who could combine the errand with a visit with his sister Melinda, who lived in the city. Indeed, a Hemings relation would be particularly suitable: He would be protective of her and she would be comfortable traveling with him. Or—least likely but nonetheless a possibility—did Ellen accompany her? We know Ellen traveled to Washington for the winter social season in November 1821. That may have been too early for Harriet to leave, but one wonders, did Madison name his youngest daughter Ellen Wayles Hemings as a tribute to the Randolph who escorted his sister into freedom?

However unobtrusive her departure from Monticello may have been, it caused quite a stir in the town of Charlottesville. "There was a great deal of talk about it," Bacon said. "People said he freed her because she was his own daughter." From Court Square in the small town of about four hundred houses, they could easily see Jefferson's home perched atop his little mountain. Over whiskey or peach brandy in

Charlottesville's Swan Tavern or the Eagle Hotel, Jefferson's neighbors had freely discussed, among themselves and with snooping strangers, his relations with Sally Hemings and the children who looked so much like him. Now, jaws agape, they animatedly sought to explain why Jefferson would free Harriet Hemings. Everyone knew, as Jefferson himself acknowledged, that an enslaved "woman who brings a child every two years [is] more profitable than the best man of the farm." That would explain why Jefferson had never done such a thing before. Why else would the man let a perfectly healthy young female slave leave, tavern patrons demanded of one another, if she wasn't his daughter?

Frustratingly, we simply do not know the details of Harriet Hemings's departure. Nor can we know what she was feeling the day she left. She had heard so much about Washington, and now it was time to go. If Beverley was not at her side, he was waiting for her at the end of the line. True, she carried no manumission papers that would secure her the privileges of freedom, but neither would there be any clues for another James Callender to ferret out years later and bandy about in the newspapers.

Sally Hemings had trained her daughter well for this day. From her, Harriet had learned that in spite of the insidious laws that governed the lives of Virginia slaves, including her mother's, *she* could, with care, craft her own future. Now, dressed in her new traveling clothes, her baggage secured and fifty dollars in her reticule, she boarded the stage and left Charlottesville forever, ready to begin the performance of her life.

Passing

. . . .

1822

. . . .

*I*T WAS A THREE-DAY TRIP to Washington: three days of cramped, shoulder-to-shoulder, bone-bruising travel. The heavy steel springs on which the carriage was suspended did nothing to absorb the jarring thumps of the rough Virginia roads. It was a good road, and safe, Jefferson had told Martha when she prepared for her visit to the capital twenty years earlier. But the route became hilly as one approached Alexandria, requiring the driver to ask passengers to get out of the carriage at several points to lighten the load for the horses.

However uncomfortable Jefferson found stage travel, it presented additional challenges for women. Just four years after Harriet's departure, Cornelia Randolph journeyed to Boston to visit her sister Ellen. She found the crowded stagecoach "excessively disagreeable," complaining that "the being squeezed in among so many strange men frightened me & the thought of their falling upon me & crushing or suffocating me in case of an upset not infrequently occupied my mind." Her elder brother, Jeff, accompanied her, but even he could not shield Cornelia from suffering the affronts for which her pampered life at Monticello had not prepared her. At first she had found tavern keepers kind and hospitable, and she enjoyed the dutiful attendance of their slaves who served her at each stop, leading her to a room reserved for women where she could rest apart from the men. She detected the attention to white female sensibilities fading, however, as they approached Maryland, and by the time they reached Washington the difference was quite striking. Forced to stand in a crowded passageway along with male travelers, she found herself eye to eye with one of them in spite of her efforts to avoid contact. Brunswick, New Jersey, was even worse. There, to her great dismay, Cornelia found "perfect equality of ranks & sexes, that is, we all had to serve ourselves and I soon found that my being a woman was no sort of reason why the men should yield me a place at table or a chair when I was standing."

What Cornelia found daunting and excessively disagreeable as she traveled north from Virginia may have been utterly refreshing to Harriet Hemings. The press of bodies in the coach might have been distasteful, but the gradual disappearance of slaves would not have been. And what Cornelia Randolph had expected as her due as a southern woman, an experienced English traveler thought exhibited "the cool selfishness with which they accept the best of everything." In other words, it was only proper that others make sacrifices for her comfort. But once the stage had been emptied of anyone who knew her origins, Harriet, like Cornelia, may also have enjoyed the solicitous concern of gentlemanly travelers who gallantly helped her in or out of the coach, provided a sheltering umbrella when needed, or made sure she was comfortably seated at table.

As her stage headed north and each mile took Harriet farther away from her enslaved origins, a whole new world was opening up for her. How she navigated her way through that world is the question. People leave their historical tracks in many different ways: the great portraits, writings, and speeches; the less visible people of the past can sometimes be found in letters, baptismal records, or court complaints. Or they leave no traces at all—or at least not in the usual places historians are trained to look. So to begin the project of finding Harriet Hemings, we must first imagine a range of possible theories on which we can base our plan of investigation. From there we can begin to search for the surviving records from this period that might yield any useful information. Finally, we must settle in, with patience and curiosity, prepared to go down an infinite number of rabbit holes. To map the terrain, we shall take a look, through Harriet's eyes, at the city that would become her home.

REACHING THE CAPITAL, HARRIET's coach drew to a halt in front of the Indian Queen. The hotel occupied practically the entire block on the north side of Pennsylvania Avenue between Sixth and Seventh streets. Its proprietor, Jesse Brown, was a popular tavern keeper and much respected by his fellow townsmen. The dining hall took up most of the second floor and was said to be the largest in the city; indeed, some Washingtonians boasted, in the whole country. There Brown's fresh repasts, including vegetables grown in his own garden, drew a lively and lucrative trade. In the winter season, when Congress was in session, the Indian Queen was a social center where Brown hosted numerous dancing assemblies. His hotel could accommodate one hundred people at a time; for seven to ten dollars a week, patrons could rent a chamber, as the rooms were described, each furnished with a fireplace. From here, stages left almost hourly for Baltimore, every four hours for Georgetown, and daily for the West. Hacks (horse-drawn taxis) were easily called to get to the steamboats that served points south. Brown's hotel was both a Washington landmark and a bustling depot—in short, a destination for anyone arriving in the city. It was precisely the sort of place where Beverley would have arranged to meet his sister at the end of her trip before taking her to the lodgings he had arranged for them.

As she stepped out of the coach onto the packed dirt of Pennsylvania Avenue, Harriet could clearly see the Capitol building high above the city on the hill in one direction and the President's House in the other. Both had been burned by the British just eight years before but since restored; by 1819 both houses of Congress had resumed business in their usual quarters. The Capitol presented a different prospect for Harriet than it would have for later travelers. Not for another two years would the original rotunda and its first dome be completed, linking the north and south wings.

The placement of these two buildings in the landscape had been carefully designed by Pierre Charles L'Enfant, George Washington, and Harriet's father, as they imagined a capital city that would embody the very principles of the new republic: separation of powers, transpar-

Occupying a strategically located block on Pennsylvania Avenue, Jesse Brown's Indian Queen Hotel was an important transit depot in early Washington City. Its elegant entrance welcomed visitors; its impressive size could accommodate one hundred guests; and a good view of the city could be enjoyed on the rooftop walkway five floors above-ground. The Indian Queen is likely the spot where Harriet Hemings began her new life in Washington.

ency of government, and government's accountability to the governed. High upon the hill, in separate wings but linked together in a single building, the people's representatives would do their work in clear sight of the electorate. The executive branch was located a mile and a half away from the legislative, so that the traffic of people, ideas, and legislation between it and Capitol Hill would be clearly visible on the broad way of Pennsylvania Avenue. And the diagonal spokes of roads emanating from both branches symbolized government's accountability and accessibility to the American people, far beyond the boundaries of the District.

As the stage had made its way up Pennsylvania Avenue, Harriet caught her first glimpses of the city. She saw the great variety of grocery, apothecary, dry goods, and fancy goods stores that had sprung up to serve Washington's residents. A gentlemen's tailor shop was located conveniently across the street from Brown's hotel. Milliners and boardinghouses were a few blocks west. The avenue was lined with the Lombardy poplars Jefferson had planted in his first term as president, forming delineated walkways for pedestrians.

But the bustle and buildings of Pennsylvania Avenue were hardly typical of the entire city. Washington was a capital still very much in the making in 1822, its population a mix of affluent planters from the outlying areas and Alexandria and Georgetown merchants, joined by an array of government clerks, office holders, and white and black laborers. By the time Harriet and Beverley arrived in Washington, its population was only thirteen thousand, but growing. In the next decade it would increase almost 50 percent to nineteen thousand, with an influx of government workers to staff a growing bureaucracy, construction workers, newly manumitted freedmen and -women, and a variety of shops to serve the expanding population. Even so, vast empty distances would separate the city's most prominent buildings, and many of L'Enfant's streets lacked any houses at all.

Familiar only with the little town of Charlottesville, Harriet Hemings may not have been as put off by the cityscape as were so many better-traveled European visitors, who viewed it as an enormous design blunder. English visitors, particularly disinclined to admire anything about the capital of their former colonies, complained about the haphazard way in which houses were often situated a quarter of a mile apart. Paying calls required leaps across ditches and walks across grassy fields to get from one street to another. One 1822 visitor guessed that it would be many years before even half of the city, with its vast scale, would be completed.

But to a young person fresh from rural Albemarle County, Washington was new and exciting. In the spring of 1822—just the time of Harriet's departure—Jeff Randolph's mother-in-law feared that when Ellen came home to Monticello after spending the winter season in the capital, she "will find this place very *dull* and heavy," adding that a certain "Miss Spear has just got home . . . and speaks in raptures of the joys of Washington." And even though unfinished, the Capitol may have impressed Harriet as it had English author Frances Trollope, who remarked on her return to England that she had never "expected to see so imposing a structure on that side of the Atlantic."

Most significantly, Harriet would have arrived at the national capital with a clearer understanding of the city's meaning and what it represented than most visitors. She certainly knew the difference between free and unfree, and who got to enjoy the privileges of freedom that the capital city was meant to embody and celebrate, and who did not. What did she think when she first saw the presidential mansion in which her father had been living when she, his enslaved child, was born? As she first strolled alongside the trees he had planted? As she first climbed Capitol Hill and saw below her the city he helped design? For twenty-one years, she had been excluded from all that the new city seemed to promise; her mother would forever be so. How would the daughter of Sally Hemings and the former president now go about claiming the rights that her father had so eloquently declared universal but clearly had meant for whites only? They could belong to her now. She could use her fair skin to take advantage of the presumptions of other whites who would see her as no different from themselves. Newly freed, her enslaved origins buried, and clothed in her new dress and identity, Harriet surveyed the place where she would start her new life.

This very early view of the Capitol shows the building before it was burned by the British in the War of 1812. Saved from utter destruction by a timely rainstorm, the Capitol would be repaired after the war. The construction of the center building connecting the wings would have been under way when Harriet Hemings arrived in Washington; she would have watched the ascension of the copper dome over it in 1826. Note the rows of poplar trees planted during Jefferson's presidency.

Exactly how she did so is a mystery, but stories of passing from the antebellum era give us an idea of how Harriet accomplished her deception. One escaped slave, later described as being "well dressed, and of genteel deportment," boarded a steamboat in New Orleans in 1852. He boldly "sat at the first table, in the cabin, near the ladies," and made it as far as Memphis before he aroused any suspicion. With the "appearance of an unassuming gentleman," he had traveled almost eight hundred miles, easily mixing with white society before a steward's suspicions launched an onboard investigation. In another case, a Monsieur Dukay arrived in Memphis in 1838 with a manufactured history: In his affected French accent, Dukay told his new friends that he sought to escape the malarial climate of the South. Charming the ladies "who smiled delightedly in his presence" and talking "eloquently of finance" and of his two sugar plantations, he ensured that no party that summer was complete without him. Fleecing his newly made friends, Dukay quietly left town with a new horse, saddle, bridle, and even a diamond ring for a sister he had invented. In what was a much more common scenario, a young seamstress passed for white in the home of the mother of a young tradesman. He became enamored of her and married her in 1849, fully convinced that she was white. His subsequent discovery that she was a slave, and therefore black, voided the marriage, but her story shows how it would be possible to cross the color line, even without the flamboyant performance skills of Monsieur Dukay.

That Harriet Hemings was successful cannot be doubted—she obliterated her historical tracks so well, there has not yet been a single credible claim of descent from her. She may have started by trying out her freedom in small steps: following the servant who guided her to the ladies' chamber at the various tavern stops, as her cousin Cornelia had; or accepting the hand to steady her as she alighted in Washington; or making her first independent purchases there. When a fugitive slave named Harriet Jacobs arrived in Philadelphia after her escape from North Carolina in 1842, she decided to buy some veils and gloves. Like any tourist befuddled by an unfamiliar currency, when told the price she held out her largest denomination, a gold coin, and waited for the change that would tell her how much her purchases actually cost her. Harriet would not have been quite so inexperienced, given the shop trade in Charlottesville and her aunt Mary's common-law marriage to merchant Thomas Bell, but her first purchase in freedom would have been quite different with the clerk's respectful "May I help you, miss?" and her full command of her own money and choices.

Still, with years of preparation, all would not have been experimental firsts; there had been time to map out a strategy for her new life. Given Jefferson's notation in his Farm Book that both Beverley and Harriet had "run, [18]22," it stands to reason that their departures from Monticello or their arrivals in their new city (or both) were somehow connected. Jefferson's paternalism would not have allowed him to let a pretty young woman travel unprotected. An escort to Washington (or to Philadelphia) and a safe place to stay when she got there were critical to her safety and to his purposes: keeping his promise to Sally Hemings and relieving his daughter Martha of a source of mortification and tension. At the very least, it is reasonable to believe that Beverley was part of Harriet's life, even if just initially, in Washington. There is no evidence that Harriet or Beverley ever returned to Charlottesville or saw their mother again. As a white man, Beverley would have enjoyed infinitely greater mobility than his sister and might have visited his mother, but it is unlikely that Harriet ever did. So it makes sense that, having to hide their Monticello family connections, brother and sister would have concocted a new family history and agreed on a new last name, the better to conceal their origins and to preserve the one remaining family tie they could openly claim. Because names are central to one's identity, and Beverley would carry their choice for the rest of his life, the name might have had some meaning for him, particularly. At the very least it needed to be sufficiently innocuous to avoid drawing attention.

Their anonymity would not have been threatened by Washington's relatively smaller population, since new faces were the norm in a city of transients. And the Hemingses were more fortunate than most fugitive slaves in that their former owners had no interest in tracking them down and exposing them. In fact, it is likely that the Randolphs did not keep track of Harriet and Beverley at all once they left. In 1836, Jeff Randolph had to ask a relative in Washington for help in locating Beverley, presumably to inform him of the death of his mother fourteen years after his departure. ("I will make every inquiry," the reply read, "but from the length of time will render it very doubtful whether any trace can be found of him. I have no recollection whatever of him.") In any event, the friends of Jefferson and his family had no incentive to expose Harriet or Beverley, resurrecting a subject that had only caused Martha Randolph much pain. And if Harriet Hemings's path ever crossed those of Martha and her children (who resided for a time in

Washington after Jefferson's death), the family records are silent on the matter.

The ability to earn a livelihood was also key to a successful transition from slavery to freedom. In assigning Beverley to an apprenticeship under the highly skilled John Hemings, Jefferson had ensured that his son was prepared with the skills necessary to support himself. Opportunities for skilled carpenters were ubiquitous in Washington City, making it a perfect place for Beverley Hemings to build his new life. Dolley Madison had thought the new capital infinitely preferable to the former one, as she advised a future grandson-in-law of Jefferson's, where "people in straightened circumstances enjoy greater advantages of society than they do elsewhere."

Temporary living quarters were also available in the growing city until Beverley decided where to settle. Mrs. Stewart's boardinghouse was the first option a new arrival would notice, right across the street from the Indian Queen. "Gentlemen preferring comfort and retirement" might favor Mrs. C. P. Gardiner's "two single rooms at $8 [per week], fire and candles included," in the quieter neighborhood on Twelfth Street. Once he had accumulated some means, Beverley could also consider John Hughes's two-story brick house, "situated near the corner of E and 12th Streets."

Under the protective wing of her brother, Harriet, too, could establish herself. Few government employees who boarded in the city brought their families with them in these early years, so working women supplied the needs ordinarily tended to at home by wives and daughters. The directory to the city, published the very year that Beverley and Harriet arrived, shows that women ran boardinghouses, schools, grocery stores, and "fancy" stores; they were milliners, seamstresses, and in a couple of cases "tailoresses," who undoubtedly catered to a male clientele. In her search for employment, Harriet may have advertised her skills in the *Daily National Intelligencer,* the paper begun by Samuel Harrison Smith, the husband of Martha Randolph's friend Margaret Bayard Smith. Perhaps she placed the ad that ran that year, seeking "a situation" that would make use of her "thorough knowledge of the Dress maker business, and . . . management of domestic affairs." To preserve her anonymity, she omitted her name and instead directed interested parties to a local bookseller. Or she may have been the "young lady well skilled in both . . . millinery and mantua making," recently hired by Mrs. Seaver, whose business three blocks down from Brown's hotel pledged to "execute work in the most fashionable style." If she was literate, Harriet may have applied to teach in one of several small schools headed by women. The infant city was ripe for talented, hard-working people looking to make their way in the world, and Harriet's white skin would open more doors for her than for women of color.

But as was true for any nineteenth-century white woman, Harriet's best bet for a secure future rested on her ability to identify a good marital prospect and to cultivate his interest. She would not have had to read one of the many advice writers for young women to know, as one book warned, that this decision would shape "the destiny of [her] life and the whole of its happiness." Nor, as she pondered the qualities to look for in a potential husband, would she disagree with its counsel that "industriousness and regular habits . . . should weigh more in a decision of this nature than any *possession of present wealth,*" which, in the volatile and changing economies of the nineteenth century, could evaporate in an instant. The financial Panic of 1819 had plunged Jefferson deeply—and, as it turned out, irrevocably—into debt, as Harriet could have overheard from the anxious conversations that followed in his home.

For her part, we know Harriet Hemings possessed beauty, a critical attribute on the marriage market. Did she polish that presentation by cultivating the manners that were becoming the mark of middle-class respectability: expecting to be accorded the right of way on a crowded sidewalk, refraining from saying someone's name too loudly when met on the street, walking along with an acquaintance to talk rather than intruding on their time by stopping them on the street? Her sewing skills would likewise recommend her as a wife, enabling her to adorn a home with the pillows, bedclothes, curtains, and chair covers that distinguished a middling-class home and to clothe herself and her children well.

Any training she received in cooking would have been essential for her to perform one of the primary chores of housewifery throughout the day. She would know how to lay a good fire for warmth, knead and set the bread to rise, and prepare breakfast; and, after clearing breakfast, to turn her attention to pulling together a "standing dinner," such as that which Margaret Bayard Smith supervised daily in her Washington home, which was composed of soup, meat, and vegetables. A good housewife would tend a garden to provide vegetables and chickens for eggs. In Washington, Harriet would have had access to the Centre Market, an enormous farmers' market stretching two full blocks on Pennsylvania Avenue. Smith occupied an entire morning "running about" and "salting away beef" herself, even with all the help she was able to employ. Harriet may have known how to serve her dinners in the "half Virginia, half French style" that Daniel Webster had enjoyed at Jefferson's table, and to change plates with each course. (A cousin once told Ellen Randolph that "Monticello is the only place I can ask for a clean plate in America.") Even by age eleven, slave Peter Fossett had learned enough about elite manners from his observations of Jefferson's family to be disdainful of whites who lacked them. Harriet had had twenty years at close range to see how to present a table with the taste and abundance that guests like Webster so appreciated.

All of these attributes would have been particularly crucial for Harriet Hemings, since she did not have the family connections to secure a good alliance or to tempt a husband looking for a hefty dowry. With its growing population of government clerks and other minor officials, tradesmen, and builders, Washington drew many ambitious men on the make, who may not have cared as much about traditional family alliances as rural gentry did. A beautiful woman, neatly presented, who could transform a home with her needle and keep a good table would have been a most appealing candidate for a wife. As Jefferson's friend Benjamin Franklin had advised young men in his popular almanac so many years earlier, "He that hath not got a Wife, is not yet a Compleat man."

Whatever the details, with courage, intelligence, and grit, Harriet Hemings honored her mother's gift to her in her ability to pass as the freeborn white wife of a "white man of good standing in Washington City," whose name Madison knew but refused to reveal "for prudential reasons." "She raised a family of children," Madison continued (whether in Washington or elsewhere, he never specified), and as late as 1863 he was "not aware that her identity as Harriet Hemings of Monticello has ever been discovered." Her continued invisibility in the historical record is the best measure of the achievement of her mother's training and provides the most convincing evidence that Harriet successfully adopted the dress and conduct of a white woman. But how did her life play out? Is it possible today to ferret out the details that Madison Hemings rightly hid in 1873? The historian—*this* historian—yearns to know.

My search began with all the key sources about and by the Monticello slave community. Jefferson's Farm Book, taken together with his overseer's recollections and the various explanations of Jefferson's grandchildren to explain away the "yellow children," constituted one set of sources. Madison Hemings's family story, augmented by Isaac Granger Jefferson's and a close study of Jefferson's own actions as recorded by himself and others (for example, freeing all of Sally Hemings's children), constitutes another. A third set of sources is the remarkable Getting Word project on Monticello's website, designed to locate descendants of the Monticello slave community and chronicle their stories. Recorded there is the testimony of Edna Jacques, a descendant of Elizabeth Hemings through the line of Betsy Hemmings (the enslaved consort of Jack Eppes), who recalled her elderly "Auntie" Olive Rebecca Bolling (1847–1953), saying sometime in the 1940s that "Sally Hemings's and Thomas Jefferson's daughter's white family lives right here in Washington DC." Her curiosity piqued (she was a little girl at the time), young Edna "asked about that. And they said 'as a matter of fact, yes, they had a daughter and she passed for white and her family's prosperous and lives right here now.' Matter of fact." Pressing for details, the little girl was silenced. "Somebody said shhh. It's family business. That meant 'don't ask me any more' . . . That's family business." To this day, Edna Jacques cannot provide a name in answer to my inquiries. But the clue is still an important one: Harriet Hemings's family remained in the capital district at least until the 1940s, in a way that was, if not prominent, present in some way in the historical records.

The prospects are tantalizing. I take the plunge. I am quickly convinced that Harriet and Beverley constructed a new family history for themselves, since it becomes immediately clear that they dropped the telltale Hemings name; it does not appear in marriage or census records for the District of Columbia or its immediate environs. None of the Beverleys I locate in the census records are a match, so Beverley seems to have dropped that name also as too distinctive. Remembering that Madison named one of his sons William Beverley, I begin to look instead for a William or William B. In the District's marriage records, I look for a surname shared by both a Harriet and a William B. But Beverley married a "white woman in Maryland," Madison had said, while Harriet probably married in the District, so their names would not necessarily appear on the same registry. I look for a family into which Harriet might have married that has longevity in the District. Most of all, I look for children's names. As historian Annette Gordon-Reed noted, "The Hemingses had a positive mania for naming their children after one another." *If* Harriet had sons, and *if* her husband allowed her the privilege of naming any of them (a big "if," given nineteenth-century gender conventions), and *if* she used any of her brothers' distinctive names (which would stand out in a sea of names such as James, John, Joseph, or Thomas), I could make an argument that I had found the start of the path that would lead to Harriet Hemings.

From the outset, however, the simplicity of that plan is foiled by nineteenth-century record-keeping at both the federal and District levels. The national government did not mandate that the names of *all* persons in a household be entered in the federal census until 1850, rendering wife, children, other relatives, servants, slaves, and any other live-ins unidentified between 1790 and 1840. Nor did the city fathers order the registration of births in the District of Columbia until 1874. (Deaths were registered beginning in 1855.) What may have been a straightforward if somewhat tedious task of reading through the census records of 1830 and 1840 and the city's birth rolls instantly becomes more complicated. Instead children's names must be retrieved from baptismal records contained in scattered church records.

This strategy presents several immediate problems. Not all Washingtonians were Christians or churchgoers, so before I even begin, the net that may have gathered Harriet's children is pocked full of holes. Even of those who were, many were not baptized as infants; some Presbyterians, for example, required an adult confession of faith for baptism. Identifying the churches presents another challenge. The earliest city directories, in 1822 and 1827, listed the churches that existed in Washington within the most likely years of Harriet's marriage, but most have since changed their names or locations or been absorbed into other congregations. In other words, one must first construct a genealogy of the churches to know where to look for any existing records, and then hope the records have survived the various transformations and moves over almost two centuries. Even if the records can be located, they would not have been kept with any consistency. Instead they reflect the idiosyncratic preferences of the particular clergyman with respect to what information he considered important to record, over what period of time, and with what standardization of spelling and legibility of penmanship. Only two of the original churches remaining in the city today possess records dating to 1822: First Presbyterian Church and St. John's Episcopal Church. My searches in each church's baptismal records for children with the distinctive Hemings family first names turn up empty.

These few existing church records do not yield any likely brides named Harriet, either. But my hopes rise when I discover that, beginning in 1811, all marriages had to be registered with the District. Extracting the name of every Harriet married between 1822 and 1830 from *Marriage Licenses of Washington D.C. 1811 Through 1830,* I compile a list of fifty-eight. The marriage record lists the names of the bride and groom, their race (only if they were "black" or "mulatto"), and their wedding date—nothing more; no parents' names or witnesses, or date and place of birth. There is not a single Hemings listed in the entire book. But fifty-eight Harriets constitute a much more discrete sample to research than an entire city population of thirteen thousand. More important, I learn the names of their husbands, whose tracks as heads of household, workers, taxpayers, property owners, and devisors of property are much easier to follow than those of women, who tend to disappear from the historical records once they marry.

The most logical place to begin this work is the Daughters of the American Revolution library, which has collected voluminous genealogical records to help researchers determine whether their ancestors fought during the Revolutionary War. There one finds a database created from the work of the DAR's Genealogical Record Committee (GRC). This early-twentieth-century project preserved by transcription a mass of early church, town, county, and court records, including wills. They even transcribed gravestone inscriptions. Entering the name of each Harriet (duplicating the entries with various spellings, such as Harriot, Harriott, and Harriett) and each husband into the database, and searching in the District of Columbia, Maryland, and Virginia, I am able to eliminate several possibilities. For example, baptism records at Rock Creek Church reveal that, in spite of her suggestive last name, Harriet Free had been baptized there in 1800, Harriet Higdon at Christ Church in May 1807, Harriet Dyer in the Presbyterian church in Alexandria in 1809, Harriot Hughes in February 1801, and Harriet O. Graves at Rock Creek Church in 1809. With their births and parents firmly established in the Washington area records, these Harriets could not have been Hemingses. Baptized at the First Baptist Church in 1831, Harriet Sales was a woman of color and so could also be eliminated.

Marriage records taken from both church and District records in the GRC database are also useful. Although Harriet Narden was married in December 1823, a date well after Hemings had arrived in Washington, the GRC also showed that she had married previously in 1819, far too early to have been Hemings. Similarly, Harriet Wallice, who married William Ridgeway in June 1823, was almost certainly the widow of Richard D. Wallace, whom she had married in 1816. (The different spellings are not enough to raise a question; clerks frequently spelled phonetically.) Harriet Nicoll, who married in November 1824, had also been married previously, and was bringing so much property to her second marriage that she protected it with a marriage settlement (what today we would call a prenuptial contract).

Other records show how vital are the details of Madison's account in the search for his sister. For example, funerals recorded in the GRC database lead me to eliminate Harriet L. Cruttenden, who had married Dr. Hezekiah Magruder in 1830. She died in 1836, long before the period 1863–1864, when Madison Hemings last heard from his sister. When George Sweeny, onetime chief clerk of the post office, prepared his will in 1849, his wife, Harriet Burgess, was already dead. Elsewhere, an obituary in 1851 for her brother, Thomas Shields (age thirty-five), eliminates Harriet Ann Shields, who married Washington bookbinder James P. McKean in 1830. Even if Beverley had taken his father's name, Thomas Shields was eighteen years younger than Beverley; nor, in 1873, had Madison given any hint that Beverley was dead.

My list of Harriets narrows my search through the District's probate records to find a will that may have devised property to children bearing the distinctive names of Harriet's brothers. But only a handful of the couples married in the 1820s filed a will with the District of Columbia, a sobering reminder of the importance of both class and

mobility in nineteenth-century America. Not everyone possessed sufficient goods to leave a will, nor had the capital lost its reputation as a
city of transients, with its ebb and flow of hopeful job seekers with each
changing administration. Although none of the wills point in Harriet
Hemings's direction, they do eliminate two more Harriets from my list.
Harriet Castle's husband, John Cromwell, died in 1835 with no children, an unlikely candidate for someone who "raised a family of children." Probate records at the National Archives reveal that Harriet
Bohrer was the sister of physician Benjamin Bohrer.

A variety of other sources help me to eliminate more contenders.
Less than eight months after his marriage, Martin Steel posted a notice
in the *National Intelligencer:* "My wife, Harriet Steel, having eloped
from my bed & board without any just provocation, this is to forewarn
all persons from crediting her on my account, as I am determined to
pay no debts of her contracting." Harriet Tolliver Steel clearly did not
follow the conventions of respectable white womanhood, much less
"raise a family of children" that would indicate she could have been
Harriet Hemings.

Harriet Bell married William J. Cooper in 1826. Her last name
draws my interest because it echoes a family tradition that Sally
Hemings had received a bell from her dying half sister Martha Wayles
Jefferson. Bell's husband was an English-born printer, a rising and respectable occupation in the early republic. When he died in 1871, he
was mourned as a man who "filled with honor several positions of trust
under the former government of the city of Washington." This sounds
like the man Madison Hemings described as his sister's husband, and I
begin to hope that I might be on the right track. Cooper was visible in
the way that counted most for nineteenth-century male identity: He
was a skilled craftsman, a good provider, and civic-minded, as his official positions attested. In these ways, he seems to have been exactly the
kind of citizen upon whom Jefferson pinned his hopes for the survival
of the republic and an intriguing possibility for Harriet Hemings's husband. Although he named no children in his will, the 1850 census
showed he had six. With the exception of one-year-old Jane, however,
none bear names connected to the Monticello families, white or black.
Still, it is only when I visit Congressional Cemetery that I'm forced to
eliminate Harriet Bell. There, next to the stone marking the graves of

Harriet Bell Cooper and her husband, is one for Harriet's father, Charles Bell.

Another intriguing early possibility is Harriet Cottringer, who married Robert Young Brent in 1824. Brent's father had served as the city's mayor during Jefferson's and Madison's administrations. Certainly, then, Brent fit Madison's description of a "man in good standing in Washington City." But a letter written in 1823 by Charles Francis Adams, grandson of John Adams, casts doubt on the likelihood that Harriet Cottringer could have been Harriet Hemings. Remarking that it was high time that Cottringer got married, "for she has passed the grand climacteric and is now going down hill" (she was twenty-four at the time), the sixteen-year-old Adams reflected that although he did not doubt that she would make a good wife, he would prefer "something like pleasure for so disagreeable a step" as marriage. "Excellence is good," the young man concluded, "but it is not much without beauty." Since Jefferson's overseer, Edmund Bacon, had said that Hemings was quite beautiful, Cottringer was not likely to have been Hemings. Further research reveals that Harriet Cottringer was from a Philadelphia family; born there in 1799 and baptized in St. Mary's Catholic Church, she could not have been Hemings.

A more exciting possibility arises with the case of Harriet Walker, who married John Newton in May 1825. The last name is certainly suggestive: Martha's daughter Ellen had spoken of the "three young men and one girl, who walked away," and we know that in spite of Jefferson's notations, neither Harriet nor Beverley had "run." In addition, the District's marriage records list a William B. Walker who married just two months after Harriet Walker did. Could he possibly be Beverley? William B. Walker was a coach painter, not entirely unlikely for Beverley; Jefferson's valet, Burwell Colbert, was a talented coach painter as well. And the man who voluntarily endured almost three additional years of slavery to wait for his sister to turn twenty-one could well have waited a mere two months for her to marry before establishing his own household. But there are thirty-five other Walkers (excluding two identified as black) in the marriage register; if Harriet and William B. were related to any of them, they obviously were not Hemingses.

More sleuthing in both church and census records rewards me by establishing a clear connection between John and Harriet Newton and

William B. Walker. In October 1839, William's wife, Maria, stood as sponsor for the baptism of John and Harriet's infant daughter. The close relationship of Harriet Newton and her sister-in-law connects Harriet Walker and William B. Walker as brother and sister, raising my hopes further. But then the 1830 census finally eliminates Harriet Walker from contention: Although William B. Walker and his wife were white, John Newton was a free man of color, and Madison had been emphatic that his sister had married a white man.

Aside from checking baptismal records, I am only able to identify most of my fifty-eight Harriets through the historical imprints of their husbands. However, a sizable minority, twenty of the fifty-eight men, seem to have disappeared from the landscape after their marriages were recorded by the District's clerk. This is particularly puzzling given the advent of the Internet, which, coupled with a phenomenal rise of interest in family genealogy as a hobby, has made this kind of search possible in ways that it would not have been thirty years ago. Databases such as Ancestry.com and Family Search that make available both original records as well as individually uploaded family trees allow me to cast a net nationwide, rather than assuming that these husbands remained in the capital district. Even so, the trail stops cold for John Anchors, who married Harriet Ann Hess, Joseph Askins and Harriet Wilson, John Barry and Harriet Farland, and many more. Nor does my reading of Washington's 1850 and 1860 census records reveal their presence. Their invisibility reminds us of the haphazard nature of record-keeping and record survival. In any event, remembering Olive Rebecca Bolling's comment in the 1940s that Harriet Hemings's family was "prosperous and lives right here now," the invisibility of these men in the records makes me believe it less likely that any of the Harriets who married them was Harriet Hemings. Prosperous men own real estate, run businesses, and pay taxes—all of which would be discoverable in the records.

Two last Harriets of my original fifty-eight still offer intriguing possibilities, in cases that are at once suggestive and questionable. Harriet Simpson married Rezin Pumphrey in January 1824. Pumphrey was a laborer who, even as late as the 1860 census, when he identified himself as a farmer, still had not managed to amass any real estate at all; his personal property amounted to only one hundred dollars. He had lived in Virginia, where, if we can rely on the distinctiveness of his name, the

1820 census seems to have counted him twice, in both Brooke and Ohio counties (now West Virginia). This is not necessarily to be wondered at, when it took eighteen months to compile the census, for it shows the imperative for landless men to be on the move to find work. It also suggests that he was not skilled in a viable trade. His name appears in the Washington newspapers twice, both times in reports of violence. A meeting with a John Long broke out into a fight in which Long assaulted Pumphrey and left him for dead in 1853; and Pumphrey was injured during a shooting at the Navy Yard in 1858.

None of what we can glean about Rezin Pumphrey, then, comports with Madison's description of a "man in good standing." Not even the names of their ten children, which include John, Martha, Ann, and Mary—all names that could be found at Monticello during Harriet's childhood—persuade me to take another look. Rather, along with their other children's names (Sophia and Lloyd), they all echo the Pumphrey family line. There are also about two dozen other Simpsons in the District's marriage register, and Simpson is a common name in Prince George's and Montgomery counties in Maryland as well. It is likely that Harriet was related to one of those families; indeed, the wedding announcement of a Rezin S. Simpson in Baltimore in 1821 may indicate a tie of long standing between the two families long before Rezin and Harriet's marriage.

Nonetheless, one wonders. Could Olive Rebecca Bolling have been referring to the Pumphreys when she talked about the prosperity of Harriet's descendants? By the 1940s, a Pumphrey family had been in the funeral and undertaking business in the capital district for over one hundred years. In 1928, they purchased a home in Rockville, Maryland, where their undertaking business still operates; and the Bethesda location on Wisconsin Avenue continues to serve as the business's headquarters, as it has since 1934. In other words, this visible and thriving business, managed by a family with a distinctive name, could well explain why Bolling thought Hemings's descendants were prosperous. However, the line of Pumphrey undertakers was not Rezin's; rather, it descended from his brother William. The Pumphreys were a large and prolific family in the Washington-Baltimore corridor; Bolling could be forgiven if she confused one branch with another. It is possible, then, that Harriet Hemings married Rezin Pumphrey, and if Madison thought his sister had done well, it could be because she had exaggerated her success in her reports to her brother, either to cover her own discomfiture or to keep him from worrying about her.

But given what we have learned about the successful lives of Hemings family descendants from Monticello historian Lucia Stanton and the Getting Word project, it seems unlikely that Harriet Hemings was so imprudent as to choose a luckless laborer to raise her fortunes. Or perhaps, I admit to myself as I consult my list for other possibilities to explore, I just want a happier ending for Harriet Hemings than she would have known as the wife of Rezin Pumphrey. Maybe that's why I eagerly turn my efforts to a tantalizing new trail.

Harriet Garner (as she appears in the marriage register) or Gardner (as reported in the newspaper's wedding announcement) married Benjamin Williamson on July 13, 1822. If Garner was Harriet Hemings, she made her decision about her future livelihood quickly but well. Williamson was a Scottish immigrant who had arrived in the city about four years earlier. His very ethnicity may have appealed to Harriet: As a Scotsman, he had no experience of or investment in the institution of slavery, nor is there any indication for the rest of his life that he ever owned a slave. As a recent migrant, he did not have family or connections who would have scrutinized those of a prospective wife. (Interestingly, there are several examples of Scotsmen who marry women of color in this period.) He was a carpenter by trade and so could have moved in Beverley's orbit, explaining how he would have met Harriet so soon.

Benjamin was no ordinary carpenter, however. In today's parlance, he was a contractor and developer. "In the '30's," a Washington history recounted in 1908, "Benjamin Williamson erected a row of two-story and basement frames . . . and Williamson's row was as well-known as was the grocery of Michael Sardo, erected at the southeast corner of 10th and H streets." The savvy Scotsman knew, as Jack Eppes had advised Jefferson two decades earlier, that investing in building the capital city would yield "a handsome interest on money and would perhaps be better property than United States paper, being more permanent."

Just a quick sampling of deeds from the 1840s at the National Archives shows Williamson's deep immersion in buying, developing, and selling improved lots in Washington City. In that decade, he was busily "erecting some frame houses on the corner of 11th and K streets," creating a neighborhood in what had been a gravel bank. By 1860, he owned more than seventeen thousand dollars' worth of property in the city. When he died in 1864, his widow hired thirty carriages to carry the mourners from their home on Eleventh Street (near K) to his burial site in Congressional Cemetery. Benjamin certainly met Madison's description of a man of good standing, as did his sons John and Joseph, who followed his trade. The Williamson men literally helped build Washington, D.C., including buildings that still stand on the block formed by K and Eleventh streets NW. In 1898, Benjamin's son Joseph B. Williamson joined the Society of the Oldest Inhabitants with pride, and when Joseph helped build a new building for Fourth Presbyterian Church in 1898, the church reserved pews for the Williamson family.

Harriet and Benjamin "raised a family of children." Seven survived childhood; they buried at least three who did not. Sons John, Joseph, and Charles all bore the middle initial *B*. As expected, the eldest son carried his father's name, John Benjamin. But might Joseph or Charles have received Beverley's name? My exhaustive search in every public record imaginable—baptismal, marriage, census, deeds, even his death certificate in 1914—fails to turn up a document that spelled out Joseph's middle name. Not until I meet with a descendant who showed me his Bible, inscribed by his mother as a wedding gift, do I finally confirm that he too was named Benjamin. Charles migrated to Missouri, but neither his marriage nor death certificates in that state spell out his middle name.

Harriet Garner Williamson may not have named her sons, but she appears to have named her daughters. As was entirely conventional in this period, she named her first daughter after herself. Next followed Virginia in 1832 (after the place of her birth or Virginia Randolph, also born in 1801?), Sarah in 1836 (after her mother?), and Elizabeth in 1838 (after her grandmother?). Taken separately, of course, these names prove nothing; their use is quite unremarkable in this era. But considered in the aggregate, in precisely the sphere in which Harriet would have had leverage, they are intriguing.

Almost certainly propelled by Benjamin's Scottish sensibilities (his ethnicity is even proclaimed with pride on his tombstone in Congressional Cemetery), Harriet and Benjamin presented themselves for marriage to a Presbyterian minister, the Reverend James Laurie, also a Scottish immigrant. They may not have heard the story of Reverend Laurie's encounter with Jefferson almost two decades earlier, but Harriet would surely have relished it if she had. As church historian Elaine Morrison Foster relates, "Laurie was conducting a service in the Capitol on one occasion when Thomas Jefferson entered the gallery. Laurie used for his text the second chapter of 2 Peter, which speaks of false teachers who try to deceive with feigned words and speak evil of things they do not understand, and who shall perish in their own corruption. The Massachusetts congressman Abijah Bigelow, who reported the incident to his wife, declared that he had it from the parson's 'own mouth' that Jefferson never spoke to him again." In an era of fierce political partisanship, Federalists had accused Jefferson of being an atheist whose election would bring destruction to Christianity in America. Presbyterian preachers typically spoke extempore rather than from prepared notes, so Laurie would have had no trouble shifting gears when he noticed the president join his congregation that day.

But just as her husband worked his way up from off-the-boat-immigrant to American success story, Harriet Williamson also worked her way to respectability as befitted her sex. Like many women of her middling rank, she turned to religion. In May 1835, "having applied for admission to the church" and been "examined with reference to her Christian knowledge and experience," the records note, Harriet Williamson was received by the elders into Fourth Presbyterian Church. With the exception of a two-year interval beginning in 1845, she was a faithful member of that congregation for the rest of her life, and when she returned in April 1847 she brought Benjamin with her. Her devotion to her faith clearly overflowed the bounds of dutiful church attendance and spilled into her home. From 1848, when Harriet's son John and his wife, Mary, brought their firstborn, Harriet Elizabeth, to be baptized, until well into the 1870s, when Harriet Elizabeth, now married and a mother herself, brought her son to the baptismal font, the records of Fourth Presbyterian Church document the succeeding generations' commitment to Harriet's church. In 1897, Harriet's son Joseph was elected vice president of the church's board of trustees; the following year, he joined the committee to build a new church, replacing the one that his family had attended at 9th and G streets NW for decades. When Harriet's youngest daughter, Elizabeth, died in 1917, she had been a member for sixty-five years.

Literacy was another mark of middling-class status that Harriet Williamson eventually acquired. When Benjamin sold a lot on L Street in June 1847 that he and his wife had bought the previous September, both transactions required Harriet's written consent. This feature of the law of coverture (recall, *not* overturned by the Revolution) was designed to help wives retain their dower right to property, that is, the percentage a widow could claim for her support if her husband died without a will. But Harriet could not sign her name; instead the clerk supplied "Harriet Williamson, her mark" next to her X. By 1864, however, the year her husband died, Harriet had learned to write. Among the bills and receipts in Benjamin's probate records is a signed promissory note in her hand.

This question of literacy is an important one, as we consider how Harriet Hemings could have kept in touch with her younger brother. If Harriet Williamson was actually Harriet Hemings, Benjamin's death in 1864 could well have ended her communication with Madison. The timing certainly fits Madison's memory. Perhaps Benjamin knew of Harriet's background and had been her point of contact with her brother during the years of her illiteracy. But since she had learned to write by the time her husband died, why did she not stay in touch with her brother? It may be that she felt her secret was safer if her husband was the conduit of information. Unlike their wives, nineteenth-century men enjoyed unquestioned rights to privacy for their business and personal affairs. Benjamin could receive letters with unfamiliar writing, or from unexplained places—such as Ohio—in ways that Harriet most certainly could not. With his death, that link would have been broken, particularly if they had destroyed Madison's letters after they were read, leaving Harriet with no address for him and no way to find one. (Where Beverley was at this juncture is a mystery; if he had been providing news to Madison about their sister, by this point he obviously was not any longer.) Ultimately, of course, Harriet's priority was to protect her children's white identity; that could have entailed keeping from them any knowledge of their enslaved origins that may have been betrayed by an unexplained letter. Whether by accident of Benjamin's death or her own determination to protect her secret, Harriet could have sacrificed her connection with Madison.

Finally, when I weigh the case for Harriet Williamson's candidacy, the Williamson family's longevity in the Capital District is an important factor. Here, too, Harriet Garner's descendants are a fit. When Harriet's son Joseph B. Williamson died in 1914, his obituary recalled that he had been "prominent in the affairs of the city." His son Joseph Boteler Williamson lived until 1955. He too was a successful builder who supported members of his wife's large Italian family in addition to his own. Charles Williamson, son of Harriet's son John, was a wealthy attorney by the 1940s, whose wife appeared in *The Washington Post*'s society pages. These are but a few examples of a large extended family, many of whom remain in the District and surrounding areas today.

But if there is a case to be made that Harriet Garner Williamson could well have been Harriet Hemings, there is also evidence to suggest that she was not. On June 6, 1821, a year prior to *our* Harriet Garner's marriage, a William Jones published a warning to the public against a Harriet Garner's charges that he stole "two copper candle sticks, a copper hoop, and a rat trap." She had reported the theft to his superior, Captain Cassin, but Jones retorted that her claim was malicious, "as it is said that she is not given to speak the truth and a person who has no right to claim the character of a decent woman." It is highly unlikely that Harriet Hemings was in Washington that early; nor would she have risked calling attention to herself in that way. There were other Garners in the city, and a later marriage record, in 1847, places another Harriet Garner in the District, so it is possible that the Garner of the ad was not the woman who married Benjamin Williamson. But the ad certainly raises questions.

There are other inconsistencies, although considered in the context of someone trying to pass, they may actually help make the case for Harriet Garner. In her determination to hide her origins, Harriet Hemings would have manufactured information about her birth dates and parental origins, easily enough done when we remember the uneven state of record-keeping in the late eighteenth and early nineteenth centuries. Conveyed to her children, who would then report it in official documents like census records and death certificates, that information becomes both legitimate and permanent. So her birthday became November 5, 1805, rather than the May 1801 date Jefferson recorded. Census records variously attribute Harriet Garner's birthplace to Maryland or Washington, depending on who was giving the census taker the information; in contrast, her children were never confused about their father's Scottish origins. Harriet Garner Williamson's death certificate says that her parents were born in Prince George's County, Maryland, which, if true, clearly would eliminate her as Hemings, but I have not been able to find a marriage record for Joseph and Mary Garner there or in neighboring Montgomery County, nor baptismal records for a Harriet Garner to substantiate that claim. For a researcher trying to see through the smokescreen created by someone intentionally trying to cover her tracks, the public record can be a cleverly placed red herring.

The most compelling reason to dismiss Harriet Garner Williamson, however, may lie in Congressional Cemetery. In 1844, the cemetery interment books show, Benjamin Williamson paid $2.50 for "opening a grave in Range E East No 109 for Mrs. Garner." Walking out to the gravesite from the cemetery offices, I find the headstone. Parts of the inscription are difficult to read, but one can see that it marks the final resting place of Joseph Garner, who died in 1824, and Mary Garner, who died in 1844. Beneath their names, clearly etched in the stone are the words: "Erected by their affectionate daughter, Harriet Williamson." If Joseph and Mary Garner are the parents of Harriet Williamson, clearly Sally Hemings and Thomas Jefferson could not be.

Yet again, I wonder. If Mary Garner really was Harriet Williamson's mother, why did not Mary's name appear in any one of Harriet's *six* daughters' names? Harriet even named one of her children (who died in childhood) Amelia Victoria in honor of her English friend Amelia Stanley. Why would her mother not merit such a distinction? And why does Elizabeth (the name of the Hemings matriarch, we remember) recur so frequently? Daughters Virginia and Sarah both bore Elizabeth as their middle names, as did granddaughter Harriet, and Harriet's youngest was named Elizabeth.

Could Harriet Williamson née Hemings have erected the gravestone for another purpose? Slave graves and cemeteries were usually unmarked. Freed slave Elizabeth Keckley, Mary Todd Lincoln's dressmaker, grieved that she could never visit her enslaved mother's grave.

She had been buried in an anonymous burying ground, Keckley explained, where her grave was "so obscure that the spot could not be readily designated." Likewise, no one knows if Sally Hemings's grave had ever been marked, but by 1837 her sons had left Charlottesville for Ohio, leaving their mother's grave untended after their departure. Since then, Sally Hemings's gravesite has been completely lost to us. (Today historians guess that her remains lie under the paved parking lot of a Hampton Inn on Main Street.) In any event, Harriet could never go there again. Perhaps this is why Harriet Williamson erected and signed the gravestone for Mary Garner. If Mary Garner had taken Harriet in when she arrived in Washington, serving as a surrogate mother, perhaps Harriet tended her grave as a way to honor Garner's gift to her, when, like Keckley, she did not know where her own dead mother lay. In any event, the inscription certainly discourages any detective on the trail of Harriet Hemings, an effect that may well have been just what Harriet intended.

It is impossible to say, of course. But whoever she was and whatever her origins, Harriet Garner Williamson became the founding matriarch of a large family, whose many descendants went on to live successful lives and who named daughters and granddaughters after her. Just like the family of Elizabeth Hemings.

In such shadows, alternately seeming to lift and then darkening again, does the search for the identity of Harriet Hemings proceed. In so many important ways, Harriet Garner Williamson seems to be the most likely of the fifty-eight Harriets on my list to have been Harriet Hemings, but the historian can ignore neither the contradictions raised by the public record nor the evidence literally engraved in stone. Lacking any other viable options on my list, I concede defeat. Harriet Hemings will keep her secret.

But does it really matter if we never find her? If we are never sure? True, it is jarring to realize how easily we lost the president's daughter. But it is also instructive to see how effortlessly new identities could be created and accepted in the antebellum period; it certainly gives new meaning to the much proclaimed American ideal of the self-made man. Harriet's success also shows how necessary was the collusion of others—whether of Jefferson or the Randolphs and their friends, or of the free black community forming in Washington (many from Albemarle and

Orange counties, who would have known her), or of Harriet's husband and perhaps even her children. All had a stake in preserving the secret of her bold imposture as a white woman who had been born in freedom.

It is a tale almost as fantastic as the sixteenth-century story of a French imposter, Arnaud du Thil, who strolled into the village of Artigat one day, claiming to be the long-lost soldier Martin Guerre. Guerre had gone off to war eight years earlier, leaving behind his wife, children, four sisters, and an uncle. If he did not look exactly as they all remembered, they chalked that up to the effects of war and welcomed him home—his wife, Bertrande, particularly. For three years, the imposter ingratiated himself in the community, only to find himself in court when his business dealings ran afoul of Guerre's suspicious uncle. In a plot twist that defies belief, the real Martin Guerre turned up unexpectedly at the trial, just as the judge was trying to sort out the contradictions between the uncle's accusations and the insistence of Bertrande and Guerre's four sisters that du Thil was the real Martin Guerre.

Stories of assumed identities fascinate. Martin Guerre's story has been taken up by novelists, playwrights, and movie scriptwriters. Part of the attraction, historian Natalie Zemon Davis explained, is that they remind us "that astonishing things are possible." Davis's deep research into this episode penetrated a world rarely visible to historians: She showed how French peasantry thought, believed, felt, and related to one another in times of tumultuous change. Davis's careful exploration of the characters in the French tale revealed more about peasant life than historians had understood before, precisely because she was undeterred by the conventional wisdom that it was unknowable.

So, too, in the search for Harriet Hemings we stumble upon hidden stories not usually seen of the ordinary people who built Washington. They are not exactly secrets, since all this information is there to be mined from the records if we will just look. But they are stories that have been muscled aside by heroic narratives of great politicians and social elites. Collectively, the lives of ordinary men and women tell us a great deal about Harriet Hemings's Washington: the successes of many men in government jobs, trade, and business; the difficulties for unskilled laborers like Rezin Pumphrey even in a city that seemed to offer potential for work, because so much of that work was still being done by slaves; the ways in which the city grew in the forty years (at least) that Harriet Hemings lived there; the daily labor of women to sustain their families with their gardening, marketing, cooking, and sewing; the women who died in childbirth; and the heartbreak of women who rose from childbed only to bury their children who had hardly had a chance to live. In the process, we can begin to imagine Harriet Hemings's life, ordinary in its surface appearance but extraordinary in the secret it concealed.

But there is another history of Washington to consider as well, one that Harriet Hemings would have followed with both interest and horror, however detached her white skin rendered her from it: the worsening predicament of blacks, free and enslaved. Unlike many states, the District of Columbia did not at first impose restrictions on newly freed men and women that constrained their movements or work opportunities. As a result, the free black population expanded rapidly after the capital's founding. By 1850, free and enslaved blacks made up almost a quarter of the population, and their increasing numbers made many whites nervous. Even as early as the War of 1812, Martha Randolph's friend Margaret Bayard Smith feared that "our enemy at home"—the city's enslaved workforce—would join the British in their attack on Washington.

Initially, the District's regulations governing free black workers had resembled those of northern cities, as, for example, when the 1820 Washington city charter required that all free blacks post a bond to ensure they would not become a public charge, requiring government assistance. But just seven years later, the city fathers attempted to slow the number of free blacks entering the city by requiring residency permits, and they tried to control any attempts at resistance by placing limits on blacks' ability to assemble in groups. In 1828 blacks were even forbidden to be on the Capitol grounds unless they had been sent there on business.

Contrary to Margaret Smith's suspicions that blacks would destroy the city, however, the black population of Washington built it up, energetically erecting churches and schools. Mt. Zion Methodist Negro Church was constructed in 1814, and the first African Methodist Episcopal church was built in 1820. In the 1820s, blacks founded schools to educate their children for American citizenship, offsetting the efforts of southern whites who had established the American Colonization Society to repatriate its enslaved population in Africa. Schools met under trees or as Sunday schools. A few black children even attended white schools. With the general emancipation of the District's slaves on April 16, 1862, a generation that became known as the First Freed formalized these efforts, which, they were convinced, explained their great financial and social successes for the remainder of the century, especially compared with slaves who were not freed until after the end of the Civil War.

In spite of Washington's increased fear and regulation of its free black residents, antislavery sentiment began to build in the city in the antebellum period, although slowly. A black press began publishing a newspaper, *The National Era,* in 1847 to point out the evils of slavery, particularly in the nation's capital. Even the much loved Dolley Madison, revered for her courage in saving the Stuart portrait of George Washington from the British torching of the White House, came under attack in the abolitionist press because of her slaveholding. Leading the charge for abolition from Boston, William Lloyd Garrison excoriated her in his famous publication, *The Liberator,* for selling slaves in the nation's capital. "This thing is not done, let it be noted, in the darkness of the Alabama cotton-field, or of the Louisiana cane-brake," he thundered in March 1848, "but at the heart of the Federal City" and, he pointed out, "in the midst of genteel, fashionable life." Public rebukes continued the following month, after a failed attempt of seventy-seven slaves to escape from Washington on a ship, the *Pearl.* One of the fugitives was Dolley's slave Ellen Steward, whom Dolley promptly punished by selling her to a slave dealer, who in turn would sell her far away in the Deep South. Remembering the woman who had been such an intimate friend of the white family at Monticello but who had defaulted on her promise of a gift to her mother if Sally had named her son James Madison, Harriet would have read these attacks with grim satisfaction.

The abundant evidence of the capacity of Washington's free black community to be productive citizens of the republic might seem to indicate progress for blacks in the capital. But even though it would have served the nation's diplomatic purposes to outlaw slavery and the slave trade in the District (European diplomats were appalled at seeing slavery at every turn), Congress did neither. Just four years after Harriet's arrival, a free black from New York who was sightseeing in the city was arrested as a runaway and saved from a lifetime of enslavement only by the governor's intervention. Blacks who could not prove themselves free could be jailed and sold back into slavery if they could not pay the fine. Visitors observed with disgust processions of slave coffles driven through the streets of the District, men, women, and children bound together with ropes or irons. Like Charleston, a bastion of slave society in the South, the national capital had its own correctional facility in the city jail to which masters could send recalcitrant slaves to be whipped. So even if Washington residents could not actually import slaves into the District, the city served as a kind of depot for slaves en route to other destinations and perpetuated all the barbarities of the institution.

This illustration appeared in A Popular History of the United States, *published in New York a dozen years after the end of the Civil War. The unfinished Capitol building overlooks the procession of chained slaves as they transit Washington in 1815. The absence of the dome highlights the two chambers that housed the people's elected representatives, who, unlike foreign visitors, were oblivious to the contradiction between this iconic American symbol of freedom and the American practice of slavery. The image reminded* A Popular History's *readers of the awful cost of that willful blindness.*

Then, barely a dozen years after the Hemingses' arrival, Washington in 1835 erupted in its first race riot. The alleged attempted murder of a white woman, Anna Maria Thornton, widow of Capitol architect William Thornton, frightened whites, already jittery about the numbers of freed blacks who were settling in the District. Thornton had been awakened in the middle of the night by Arthur Bowen, her drunken nineteen-year-old slave, who appeared at her bedroom door, ax in hand. Although Bowen had fled without harming anyone in the house (including his mother, who was sleeping in the same room as Thornton), the story spread like wildfire. Three days later, a newspaper report accused him of having shouted threats at his owner that could only have been inspired by the antislavery materials he had been reading. Fearing that Bowen's attack was meant to launch a slave rebellion, whites unleashed a wave of rioting that targeted successful blacks in the city.

A particular object of the crowd's wrath was Beverly Snow, an enormously successful restaurateur, whose fresh daily menus, prepared on request for patrons seated at their own rather than a common table, were a striking departure from the usual tavern operations. But amid the swirling rumors of slave rebellion were whispers that Snow had been heard disparaging the wives and daughters of the city's white laborers. So when a mob was thwarted in their attempts to drag Arthur Bowen from his jail cell and lynch him, they turned instead to Snow's restaurant. Protected by his friends and employees, who stalled the crowd, Snow fled out the back door of his restaurant, barely escaping with his life. He would eventually head for Canada, where he operated a restaurant in peace for the rest of his life.

Blacks remaining behind in Washington, however, found that thenceforth their job options were overwhelmingly restricted to menial labor such as digging foundations or moving vast quantities of building materials in a city that was rising from the swamps. Very quickly, then, anywhere they turned in their adopted city, Beverley and Harriet could see the fate they escaped when they decided to pass as freeborn whites.

Harriet Hemings's story also teaches us about the power of community consensus and the costs of breaching that consensus. During the course of Harriet's life, the United States strengthened its commitment to the preservation and spread of slavery in several important ways: the Missouri Compromise of 1820, which prevented free states from outnumbering slave states; the gag rule of 1836, which forbade discussion of slavery and antislavery petitions on the congressional floor; the defeat of the Wilmot Proviso in 1846, which would have outlawed slavery in Texas territory; and the Compromise of 1850, which made it a federal crime for any citizen anywhere to assist fugitive slaves. In addition, most northerners and southerners agreed, almost without exception in the nineteenth century, on the idea of the natural inferiority of nonwhites. In such a nation, the exposure of Hemings's secret would have been catastrophic: Before the outbreak of the Civil War, it would have meant a return to slavery for her and, by law, all of her children. After the war, exposure would have meant exclusion from the white community and all its privileges. Her crime: the violation of racial boundaries by "posing as white" (her white skin notwithstanding) when she knew she carried African blood. She would not have suffered physical death, as did the sixteenth-century French imposter, but she would have died a social one.

Instead, by passing, Harriet Hemings won the privileges of white womanhood. Her fair skin entitled her to the presumptions of purity and piety, and because her parents had protected their daughter's marriageability, she conformed to standards of white female virtue. None of this was remotely possible for enslaved women, even Harriet's formidable mother. Nor would she have to settle for a common-law marriage, as had her aunt Mary Hemings. Instead she would enjoy the full legal sanction of the institution. She could bear and raise her children in freedom. She would never have to worry that her husband and children would be beaten or sold away from her. She could be mistress and the emotional center of her home, claiming the moral authority that was increasingly ceded to wives and mothers during this period. She could join a church, apply gentle pressure on her husband to join her there, and put her piety to work outside her home in benevolent societies that helped the poor, orphaned, and widowed. She, too, could read *Uncle Tom's Cabin* and, from the safe distance her color, sex, and rank allowed, look on the plight of slaves with horror and pity.

But these gains came at great cost. Harriet had to give up the Hemings name of which the family was so proud and endure a permanent separation from her mother and her younger brothers. She would have to live in a state of eternal vigilance so that she never betrayed her enslaved origins and fugitive status by a stray letter or utterance. Although no infant of questionable skin color ever gave her away, each pregnancy brought with it the terror of exposure. And if she ever saw the features of her mother or father or brothers in the faces of her children, it would have been a bittersweet knowledge she would have to keep to herself. To the extent that she was proud of her connection with the great statesman Thomas Jefferson, she would have to remain mute whenever she heard him discussed. She would face the unique kind of loneliness that such a secret would forever inscribe on all her relationships, particularly if she kept it from the family she created in Washington.

We will never hear her story in her own voice. As Saidiya Hartman observed, "Silence was the only reasonable position to be assumed by a descendant of slaves," especially by one who passes. We are fortunate that Madison Hemings refused to be defined by slavery or bound by silence. But in his account, the pain of a fractured family is palpable as he reflected on his family's experience of slavery and all that was lost to him when his brothers and sister crossed to the white side of the color line, leaving him behind. Not even the destruction of slavery restored his family to him. In 1873, the process of rebuilding the country with a new vision of citizenship that admitted black men as well as white met with severe and violent challenges in the Reconstruction South. With the withdrawal of federal troops from the former Confederate states in 1877, the northern states would also abandon the project. But even before our country once again surrendered to racism, Madison's language makes clear how important it was that Harriet's neighbors never suspected her of being "tainted with African blood" or that "the white folks" of Beverley's neighborhood never knew that his daughter "had any colored blood coursing in her veins."

For their life in Washington, Harriet and Beverley Hemings created a new story of their origins. As Linda Schlossberg, a scholar of American literature, has said, passing is "the creation and establishment of an alternative set of narratives." This would not necessarily have been a new experience for Harriet. If, as Schlossberg observed, it is true that every person's history "is a work in progress—a set of stories we tell ourselves in order to make sense or coherence out of a frequently confusing and complicated past"—Harriet had been working on that history long before she left Monticello. She had to construct for herself an alternative narrative to the Virginia laws that defined her and her family as property. She needed to dismantle the stories told by the infinitely more powerful Jefferson-Randolph family when they perpetually denied Jefferson's paternity, to get to the real truth about her parentage. She had to cut through the Randolphs' condescension toward the Hemingses to claim an appreciation of her own intelligence, strength, and capability. "Poor creature," Martha Jefferson Randolph had said of Sally Hemings's older brother Robert, who bought his freedom in 1795; and of John, her younger one, freed in Jefferson's will, she had clucked, "His liberty poor fellow was no blessing to him." One of the "yellow children" to whom Ellen Randolph Coolidge referred, Harriet would have detached herself from the elitist world of the Jefferson-Randolph family even while she still lived among them.

Ultimately, Harriet's decision to pass was about setting her world to rights, rejecting her classification as property. In asserting her humanity, she claimed for herself the rights to life, liberty, and the pursuit of happiness—at least to the extent to which white women could enjoy them in the nineteenth century. "Passing never feels natural," one journalist commented in light of America's racialized contemporary culture. "It is a second skin that never adheres." Maybe so. But for Harriet Hemings, it was the artificiality of legal codes and social custom that rendered her black and enslaved that did not feel natural. Passing, she could do.

Legacies

. . . .

1835

. . . .

*F*OR NINE DAYS RUNNING, MARTHA had been complaining of headache and nausea. Worried, Virginia decided to keep watch in her mother's room. Camping out on the sofa, she dozed a little, but woke up just after one A.M. Martha's sleep had been restless and she had woken suddenly, her pulse racing. Gently, Virginia tried to pacify the sick woman, murmuring her reassurances and urging her not to worry about anything. But convinced she was dying, Martha would not be soothed back to sleep. "There was no knowing what might happen the next day," Virginia recalled her mother insisting, and there was urgent business she had left undone. To put Martha's mind at rest, Virginia reluctantly agreed to help her with her last will and testament.

Virginia hastily assembled paper, pen, and ink and knelt on the floor by the lamp's light, prepared to serve as scribe for her mother's last words. She dated the will carefully: "April 18th [1835] at 2 o'clock in the morning Friday." Martha's first concern was her daughters. "To my five daughters, I wish to bequeath my property in the funds," she began. The "funds" were what was left of two issues of bank stock worth ten thousand dollars each, which South Carolina and Louisiana had granted to her in Jefferson's memory. Her eyes, Martha once said, "often filled with tears of gratitude and affection when I look round upon the comforts, and consider the life of ease and quiet" she owed to them. Her life had taught her much about women's vulnerability in this world, even under the protective mantle of her father's roof. His revolution had done little to improve the position of women, who remained excluded from the professions, the pulpit, and colleges, barred from voting and holding political office, and still rendered legally invisible by marriage. So Martha's impulse was to protect her daughters the best she could, bequeathing them the means that custom and law prevented them from earning and owning.

Even more vulnerable than white women in this society, however, were slaves. Weakened though Martha was by her persistent illness, debilitated as she was by her financial distress, the dying woman held the future of seven people in her hands. She disposed of two in short order, transferring ownership of them to her sons Ben and Lewis. But the remaining five were a different case altogether. They were Hemingses. And as Martha Jefferson Randolph agitatedly dictated her will through labored breaths that night, the long history of their two families weighed heavily on her. "The happiness of so many depended on the arrangements she wished to make," Virginia remembered her mother saying. Emily and Martha Ann Colbert, two of Elizabeth Hemings's great-granddaughters, could look forward to freedom in the near future, Martha decided. "To Betsy Hemmings, Sally [Hemings] & Wormley [Hughes] I wish my children to give their time," she directed, ensuring that the informal freedom the former slaves were already enjoying in Charlottesville would not be jeopardized by her death. Unlike many Virginia families who challenged such bequests, Martha knew she could rely wholly on her children's love, admiration, and respect to carry out her dying instructions, as her father had on hers.

To her son and sons-in-law, she left small mementos of the Monticello household, now broken up forever. She divided the family silver among them; she particularly wished Jeff to have the casseroles, and Ellen's husband, Joseph, the silver duck, which the family used as a chocolate pot. To Virginia's husband, Nicholas, she bequeathed the clock that had always been at the head of Jefferson's bed. To her youngest son, George, the darling of her elder years, "I have nothing but my love to leave," she finished.

"Written at Mama's request," Virginia documented at the bottom of the page. She rose from the floor and went to her mother's bedside. "It's done," Virginia assured her, hoping that Martha would now rest. "Should I not sign it?" Martha asked anxiously. Virginia shook her head, reminding her that the doctor had forbidden all exertions. Still, Martha remained distressed. The daughter of a lawyer, she was not sure that a will dictated on a slip of paper in the middle of the night would have any legal standing without witnesses. She asked Virginia to summon Ellen and Cornelia to her sickbed. Not until she had repeated all her wishes to them was she satisfied. Finally, having discharged the last of her obligations to her father and children, Martha fell back on the bed. Perhaps her blinding headache receded with the release of that burden. She was like her father in so many ways; he, too, had suffered debilitating headaches when grief and anxiety pressed in on him. Tranquil now, she rested.

Still, as Martha reviewed her meager legacy, she may have fretted that she had nothing but her love to devise to her cherished youngest child. How could her life be summed up by so little? She was the daughter of one of the most prominent founders of the nation. She had grown up in a house of such beauty that a European visitor had remarked that Jefferson was "the first American who has consulted the fine arts to know how he should shelter himself from the weather." She had lived in Paris, gone to school with princesses and daughters of diplomatic officials, and danced with French aristocrats. She had met some of the leading *salonnières* of the Enlightenment. Life had been so rich with promise then.

But her life in Virginia as a planter's wife had been difficult. Although she bore twelve children on whom she doted, Martha's marriage had become progressively troubled by her husband's brooding depressions. His violent explosions alienated their eldest son, Jeff, as well. Tom's volatile temper added to Martha's already incalculable affliction when their eldest daughter, Anne, only thirty-five, died in February 1826. "Her husband has gone on since his daughter's death more like a demon than ever," a relative reported; "he has given her positive orders not to let either of the younger children go down to Tufton [Jeff's home] that the very moment they cross that threshold he will take them from here—did you ever hear of such a brute?" Then just four months later, Jefferson's death dealt Martha yet another bitter blow. By January 1827, Monticello—the house, its contents, and its slaves—were all heaped on the auction block to repay the massive debt Jefferson left behind.

Jefferson had not meant to leave his daughter penniless, but neither had he confronted his deplorable financial situation until the waning months of his life. He had racked up considerable debt from decades of spending, and his creditors were becoming insistent. Further, after Tom's financial reverses, he had taken over the support of his daughter's large family and then found himself on the hook for a friend's note for twenty thousand dollars, which he had guaranteed with his own signature. With the slide in land values during the financial Panic of 1819, Jefferson's hopes to recoup his own fortunes had turned bleak.

In desperation, Jefferson proposed that Virginia hold a lottery; the prize would be his mills and a thousand acres. The proceeds, he hoped, would bail him out of the financial morass he could no longer ignore. The legislature authorized the lottery but attached a condition: Jefferson's beloved Monticello must be included in the prize. Jefferson blanched when his grandson broke the news, incapable of speech, but he acquiesced when assured that the winner would not take immediate possession of the house. Jefferson could remain in his home until his death, and his daughter would be guaranteed residence there for at least two years beyond that.

Reassured that he had provided for his daughter and her family, Jefferson died at peace. He "cheerfully committed his soul to his god," Jeff wrote a week later, and "his child to his country." He never knew that the lottery would fail and that the auction would not draw even half of what was needed. Indeed, buoyed by renewed hope, the very last letter he wrote arranged to pay custom duties to release a shipment of the expensive French wines he loved so much.

Martha fled the mountain (and her husband) after her father's death to stay with her daughter Ellen in Boston. She did not return until 1828, after an absence of almost two years. Virginia and her husband, Nicholas, served as caretakers in the meantime, adjusting their lifestyle to their reduced circumstances after the auction had left them with little furniture and few slaves. To economize, they learned to live in discrete sections of the big house, and Virginia drew up a plan to make do with a skeletal staff. Hearing of her cutbacks, Ellen warned from Boston that Virginia would need to leave behind the old ways of life. "You will be obliged dear Virginia, to adopt Yankee habits if you follow Yankee fashions," she said with wry humor. Just before Martha's return, Tom Randolph applied to Nicholas for permission to return to Monticello. In March 1828 he took up residence in the north pavilion, living apart from the family. Just three months later he died there at age fifty-nine, having reconciled at last with his wife and eldest son.

This portrait of Martha Jefferson Randolph, painted in Philadelphia a year before her death, illustrates the "delicate likeness" she bore to her father, as well as her lively intelligence and cheerful temper, famously unruffled despite the many storms of her life.

With Monticello's sale in 1831, Martha Jefferson Randolph was homeless. She spent the rest of her life shuttling among the homes of her children, from Boston to Washington to Virginia, constantly battling financial insolvency and the indifference of an ungrateful public who did not feel obliged to maintain Jefferson's family to demonstrate their appreciation of his legacy. "Supporting a large family in genteel society, upon very limited means" was a challenge, she said, even in a Washington rental. Outfitting her daughters for the winter social scene (a key venue for husband-hunting) was a constant drain, although she cut corners by remaking and trimming dresses and doing her daughters' hair, "at which I am quite a proficient," she crowed, as she had been since her first days in Paris. And winter days found the whole household—sometimes as many as nineteen, including the slaves—all crowded about the same fire, "without the possibility of enjoying elbow room or quiet or privacy even for an hour in the day," she complained. In spite of all her efforts, she had never been able to make the money stretch far enough.

Jeff owned that he bitterly regretted Jefferson's decision to pursue the lottery that left his family vulnerable to "the mortification of neglect from an ungrateful country," but his sisters uttered no such reproach of their grandfather. It seems surprising that Monticello—an uncomfortable house (Martha called it "a comfortless winter residence") in which they had been relegated to the household duties of their sex—should have been the object of Jefferson's granddaughters' yearnings in the years after his death. But with its vistas, gardens, woods, paths, and hideaways, the mountain had been for them shelter, comfort, and a world apart, even as it had been a magnet for visitors.

Martha herself had experienced those woods as solace and healer. When she gazed out from the terraces of her father's home, feeling that "'all the Kingdoms of the world, and the glory there of' lay spread before me," she reflected in her daughter Mary's commonplace notebook, "every feature of that landscape has it's own spell upon my heart, can bring back the living breathing presence, of those long mingled with the clods of the valley[;] can renew for a moment youth itself. Youth, with it's exquisite enjoyments, it's ardent friendships, and oh! dearer than all, it's first, purest, truest love!" Those woods had been consecrated by her father's grief after his wife's death; no wonder that every square foot seemed to bring back his "living breathing presence" for her.

Martha's daughters poured out their grief and memories in Mary's book as well. Ellen copied the poetry of Byron: "There is pleasure in the pathless woods. . . . There is society where none intrudes." Cornelia inscribed lines she attributed to Goethe: "Know'st thou the mountain? And its Lonely peak / Know'st thou it well? Tis there, 'tis there! / Oh father lies our way! Let us go there." Aching for Monticello after its sale, Mary copied a prayer for resignation, that in the "tranquility of nature" she might learn "the beautiful order of thy works / [to] Learn to conform the order of our lives!"

For Ellen and Virginia, the pain of their memories outweighed their pleasure; but for Cornelia, whose artist's eye noted the evening's "deep indigo & bold outline of the blue ridge . . . against the bright gold coloured or orange western sky," the landscape sometimes brought "unmixed delight." Still, as she prepared to vacate the mountain, she acknowledged that "I do not feel at home or happy anywhere but at Monticello. I miss the very emotion excited by that beautiful scenery. . . . I want those familiar haunts which . . . seem as if grandpapa was still there."

Married and living in Boston, far removed from these bittersweet scenes, Ellen found it strange that when she dreamed of Monticello, "I never find myself within the house; I am always wandering through the grounds or walking on the terrace." There, in her dreams, the "glorious prospect lays open before me. I seem to have 'leaped a gulf' of fifteen years, to have retraced my steps, and losing sight of all present ties, forgetting even my children, to be what I was at sixteen." Cornelia well understood that their pleasure in the beautiful Monticello views was because "every thing is so strongly associated with our dear grand father that he seems yet to be present." But their nostalgia for the mountain landscape tells us more: It also helps explain their view of themselves as accomplished intellectuals, a Jeffersonian aristocracy, in spite of the limits of the house and their sex. The glorious prospects from the mountain promised infinitely more than the crowded rooms on the second floor to which they had been shunted.

Ellen's dreams allowed her to return to her girlhood, when the world was her oyster because she was the charming, well-educated, and distinguished granddaughter of Thomas Jefferson. Her dreams of the future could still take flight, unencumbered by the weight of household keys or maternal responsibility. Older now, her subconscious had filtered out all memory of the gendered constraints that the house (and its architect) had imposed on her. Martha had taught her daughters that, like their grandfather, they too could enjoy the life of the mind, and she had encouraged them to seek out spaces—architectural and interior—to develop their minds and to break free of the chains by which gender conventions bound them. The sisters mourned the loss of the apparently boundless landscape at Monticello precisely because it had suggested possibilities for an internal terrain so vast in its potential, they could overlook and maybe even transcend the physical limits of their upper-floor rooms and attic hideaway. In their veneration of Jefferson after his death, his granddaughters attempted to claim that legacy of the mind he bequeathed to them.

They were to be disappointed at every turn. Ellen realized early that her mother's efforts had raised her daughters' expectations to an unattainable level. "I was brought up too tenderly—rendered unfit for an ordinary destiny," Ellen reflected ruefully at thirty-two. "My friends, in their love, seem to have thought that I could command fortune and direct the events of my life." But as it turned out, not even the daughter and granddaughters of the author of the Declaration of Independence would be permitted that freedom; in spite of their scholarly attainments, they remained, after all, women.

Ellen had begun to understand this, even before Jefferson's death. Once, ruminating on her childhood education, she regretted that she had not earlier read English philosopher John Locke's *Essay Concerning Human Understanding*. Locke had argued that people were not born with innate ideas; rather the mind was a tabula rasa, a blank slate, whose ideas were shaped over time by education and circumstances. "In former years," Ellen recalled, "I read because it amused me and because I wished to make myself a companion for those intelligent and well-informed persons in whose society I most delighted." Until she read Locke, however, "it never occurred to me that it was necessary to do anything but read. . . . *Understanding* what I read . . . I conceived to be nothing more than to have an image presented to my mind." Not until she was almost thirty did she become aware that "the proper and healthy employment of the mind is *to think*, and not to *dream*." She was tempted to start her education all over again, she said, beginning with a child's hornbook. "As it is," she despaired, however, "I am nothing but a woman, and could promise myself no competent reward for so much trouble."

Without any apparent destination for female education, then, Ellen even questioned the journey. Despite all the attention that Martha Jefferson Randolph devoted to her children's education, it was not meant—for her daughters, at least—to cultivate the Revolutionary ideal of an autonomous self, able, in Jefferson's words, to judge "what will endanger or secure his liberty." Rather, it was a discipline of behavior and practice, Ellen realized, to teach the "praise of *method and order.*" (One historian's description of the ideal woman of the early republic as "astute enough to be politically null" fits the Jefferson and Randolph daughters perfectly.) So despite its apparent similarities to an Enlightenment education, that which Martha gave to her daughters failed to reach its benchmark: a rigorous discipline of critical thought that resulted in the development of an independent, self-sufficient person.

But that was not what Martha had ever intended. She never meant to challenge a structure in which men were the acknowledged political actors. Rather, shaped with reference to the past, from which she learned how elite women influence men rather than make history, she trained cultivated and pleasing women. At Monticello, they willingly enacted the roles the Scottish Enlightenment had created for them: placing female education at the disposal of the head of the household and offering the rational society and ordered calm that restored men buffeted by the storms of political life. It was surely no coincidence that Martha named a daughter after Cornelia, the Roman matron who refused to remarry after her husband's death and who spent the rest of her life selflessly promoting her sons for the good of Rome.

Martha Jefferson Randolph's story, like those of Mesdames de Genlis and de Staël, highlights the doggedness of traditional gender conventions even in the age of the transatlantic revolutions that, it has been said, ushered in the modern world. As it turned out, both Genlis and Staël were shunted out of France, while women's tentative claims to participation in politics were similarly thrust aside in the United States. Even a postrevolutionary world was not prepared to receive such educated women.

But these women themselves did not always understand that the power of their intellect was sufficient ground for claiming the authority men enjoyed. It is striking that Madame de Staël, who was such a thorn in the side of the emperor Napoléon that he banished her and her salon from Paris, did not even own a desk until after the successful reception of her second novel, *Corinne.* "I really want a big table," she told her cousin longingly; "it seems to me that I now have the right to one." Martha's great convent revolt, which her father had stymied in Paris, would fizzle to the "regular siege" she mounted—at age forty-nine—to persuade her father to turn an alcove in her bedroom into a closet. Whether it housed her clothing or a tiny writing space, complete with table, chair, and writing implements, we shall never know. However she used it, she was pleased with her small victory. "You have no idea how much it has added to my comfort," she sighed with satisfaction.

In addition to her diligent cultivation of the life of the mind, Martha also leveraged her great devotion to her father to offset the stultifying life of a rural plantation wife. She taught her daughters to treasure the blood ties with Jefferson that, in their view, gave them more than any marriage could have. In their association and identification with their famous grandfather, the Randolph women were different, and they knew it. "Ellen would be greatly admired if she had not such a telltale countenance," a neighbor once said of her; "she shows too plainly that she feels her superiority." Cornelia could not contain her disdain of Richmond society; one letter dripped so "full of slanders," her aunt feared that if it got into the wrong hands they would have to "take horse and leave Richmond with all speed." Even Martha's daughter-in-law once puzzled, "I don't think they think like other people." Nor could Cornelia conceal her contempt for those "prophane" people "who respect no more the house of Thomas Jefferson than that of one of themselves & who would turn it into a boarding house." They were utterly incredulous that the public had no interest in maintaining Monticello as a shrine to the dead president or in purchasing the volumes of Jefferson's correspondence they had labored many a tedious hour to transcribe.

In spite of all their hopes, however, in the end their association with Jefferson could not protect them. Their lives make clear the benefits and perils for women of relying upon men—even wealthy, well-intentioned men of reputation—for one's life's meaning and livelihood. Martha had been left destitute, her education, brilliant mind and manners, and famous connection all insufficient defenses against the vagaries of life. Not until 1878 could her daughter Virginia bring herself to acknowledge that connections alone did not suffice to support women. "Girls should be brought up to be able to maintain themselves in these days," she asserted, almost ninety years after Massachusetts's Judith Sargent Murray had argued the same thing in the wake of the Revolution. Even in our own time, a strategy to rely on the male breadwinner with the higher salary may seem to make sense in the short term, but it leaves mothers and their children economically vulnerable in the long run. As Jefferson's daughter and granddaughters learned in the nineteenth century, today's highly educated women—lagging behind in wages and leadership positions—are also discovering that love, good intentions, and connections are not enough to soften patriarchy's very rough edges.

Of course, female education in the early republic was not calculated to produce self-sufficient women, any more than it had been in the colonial period. Such women would have presented too much of a challenge to a patriarchal system that insisted on the preservation of the male prerogative in all areas of life. And if Martha Jefferson Randolph had little interest in changing this system, Maria Jefferson Eppes had even less. She had been raised deep in rural Virginia by a gentry slaveholding family, so firmly rooted there that even in their great distress over sending her to Paris it apparently never occurred to them to pack up and take her there themselves. In a society so strictly demarcated by race and gender, white girls learned to use their racial superiority to offset their gender inferiority. They would be the least likely to dispute that order, then, since to do so would upset the fragility of the slave society on which white Virginians depended, and their privileged place in it.

In her aspirations for a husband, children, and a stable family life of her own, Maria Jefferson Eppes was typical of Virginia gentry women of the late eighteenth century. She had little interest in excelling in her studies or her music or her writing. Intellectual challenges, such as attempting to read *Don Quixote* in the original Spanish, did not delight her. Before he left for France in 1784, Jefferson had borrowed a copy, bought a Spanish dictionary, and occupied the long hours of the voyage teaching himself Spanish. He would insist that his daughter Martha follow suit, and as a young matron Martha required that Maria do the same. The year before she died at eighty, Virginia congratulated herself that she had finally read the novel in the original Spanish, in what had become something of a family tradition almost one hundred years after Jefferson accomplished the same feat. Maria, on the other hand, had looked for any excuse not to cart the book and her Spanish dictionary about as she accompanied her newlywed sister on her honeymoon visits.

Raised by her aunt according to the principles of genteel female education, Maria instead endeared herself to everyone with her beauty and modest self-deprecation, rather than with displays of learning. Like her father, who also hated large gatherings, she shone in smaller circles. "When alone with you," their friend Margaret Bayard Smith remarked, Maria had the most "communicative and winning manners." She had a gentle sense of humor, once chiding her brother-in-law for not having replied to the letter she had intended to write to him. In short, Maria followed her culture's prescriptions for proper female behavior, pleasing those around her and entering into a loving marriage. But her life was cut short by childbirth, a death common to countless women, from time out of mind, for whom motherhood was a woman's only acknowledged calling.

Her only surviving child knew little about her. Francis had no portrait of her, no art from her days at Mrs. Pine's school or the convent, no needlework from Mrs. Fullerton's. Her death when he was just two deprived him of any maternal letters to guide him as he grew. His father never spoke of her. In fact, Jack Eppes had taken comfort after Maria's death by following the example of his grandfather and father-in-law: he took an enslaved consort, Betsy Hemmings (who was a wedding gift from Jefferson in 1797), and fathered a shadow family with her. And five years after Maria's death, Eppes remarried; with his new wife, Martha Burke Jones, he had four more children. Except for Francis himself (his baby sister, Maria, died at two), then, no evidence of Maria Jefferson Eppes's life seemed to have survived.

So Francis's accidental discovery, years after her death, of his mother's neglected harpsichord and her rotting music books must have pierced his heart. Once, as they traveled from Monticello to Poplar Forest in early September 1820, his cousin Ellen and his grandfather had called in at Jack Eppes's plantation home. Jefferson wanted to see what had become of Maria's harpsichord, thinking he might take it to Poplar Forest. Rummaging about, Francis and Ellen found it in the cellar. It was in very bad shape, Ellen reported to her mother, "the soundboard split for 12 or 14 inches, the strings almost all gone, many of the keys swelled so that when pressed down they do not rise again, and the steel part of the different stops so much rusted that several of them refuse to obey the hand." When Francis reached for his mother's music books, they fell apart in his hands, "dropping to pieces," Ellen said. They had lain in the basement—about "six or seven years," the second Mrs. Eppes guessed vaguely—where she had consigned them to the damp and mold. Ellen was appalled.

Gently, she helped her stupefied cousin retrieve his mother's books. Together they gingerly went through each one. Turning them over, they saw Maria's handwriting everywhere. "We found the name of Maria Jefferson, & the initials of M. E. written in Aunt Maria's own hand in a great many different places," Ellen said. And not only her signature; they also discovered entire song manuscripts that she had copied. It had been sixteen years since Maria's death; Ellen was only eight at the time and had practically forgotten her. But in the cellar that day, carefully going through Maria's moldy music with her eighteen-year-old only child, surrounded by "so many mute memorials," Ellen felt the loss anew. "I don't know how Francis felt," she wrote in this fresh burst of grief, "but when I looked round that comfortable establishment, and saw all those blooming children I could not help feeling as if a stranger had usurped *her* rights, and as if none other should have been mistress or mother *there*."

Her life cut short at twenty-five, Maria's only legacy was those mute memorials. But would she even have chosen these as her legacy? We know how reluctantly she practiced, yet in the way that young girls in the early republic lovingly proclaimed their ownership of their favorite novels, Maria claimed her music by inscribing every book with her name. She had even written out some songs by hand, a discovery that must have stunned her son, who had never even owned a letter by which to remember her. Ellen ached for the lost life and lost potential. "Had *she* lived," Ellen grieved, "*I* should have been *at home* at this sweet place and in this charming family." Even more, she dreamed on, "in my mother's sister and her children, I should have found another mother & other brothers and sisters."

Lacking the technologies of birth control available to women today, of course, Maria Jefferson Eppes had no way to limit the hazards of childbirth that had killed her mother as well. Maria's seven-year marriage produced four pregnancies (three live births and a miscarriage), and not even her husband's great love could protect her from the genetic inheritance that rendered childbirth so dangerous for her. Neither she nor her sister seem to have entertained the thought of a small family, a pattern of family planning that one historian has noted began in the Revolutionary era. White family size declined precipitously and deliberately, from 7.4 children in 1800 to 3.56 by the end of the nineteenth century. Not all women were able to limit their pregnancies, but those who did were upper- and middle-class women who lived in the North and Middle Atlantic. This trend does not appear to have spread to the southern states, where both free and enslaved women served the organic function of reproduction without limits. So thoroughly ingrained was that idea for southern women, Ellen overlooked completely the toll that pregnancy and childbirth had extracted from Maria's fragile body as she imagined the additional cousins she might have had, had Maria lived.

There is no evidence that Maria Jefferson Eppes wanted to limit the number of her pregnancies in spite of the suffering they brought her; but she would not have had many contraceptive choices if she had. There is little evidence from this period about how northern couples succeeded in reducing family size, although an occasional letter makes clear that their efforts were intentional. But in an age when women waited for quickening (feeling movement) to confirm a pregnancy, they sought other options until then to clear what they understood to be a menstrual blockage. Eighteenth-century physicians still understood human health to be governed by the four humors: black bile, yellow bile, blood, and phlegm. Illnesses resulted when these bodily humors were out of balance; remedies such as purges and bleeding restored balance. The absence of menstrual blood (a "hot" humor), for example, meant that a cold humor was dominant, and so the hot humor had to be induced to restore balance. In such a medical universe, it was possible to confuse a pregnancy with rheumatism, consumption, pleurisy, or similar ailments that involved an obstruction of humors.

We are long past the day when physicians confuse pregnancy with a cold. Technologies exist to ensure the good health of both mother and child. However, the effect of twenty-first-century policies that increasingly restrict women's access to reproductive healthcare is to return women to the conditions endured by their nineteenth-century forebears. So the questions raised by the story of Maria Jefferson Eppes remain both timely and crucial.

Maria's hopes for a long and happy life with her little family were tragically cut down by her early death in childbed. Martha Jefferson Randolph had raised her daughters with great expectations that were deflated both by conventions of female domesticity and by their country's apparent indifference to Jefferson's legacy. Unlike most enslaved girls, Harriet Hemings, too, had harbored great expectations for her life, but while Maria and Martha had played by the rules of a patriarchal society, Hemings had broken one of the most inviolate of them when she rejected racial hierarchy. In expanding the boundaries of the life into which she had been born, she was spectacularly successful, arguably even more so than the privileged Jefferson and Randolph women had been.

But unlike the Randolphs, whose voluminous letters map out lives devoted to one another and to Jefferson's legacy, Harriet lived out her life in the oblivion of exile. We can't know how heavily Harriet's motherlessness, forced upon her fourteen years before Sally Hemings actually died, weighed on her. We don't know when her correspondence with her brother Madison began, or what she knew about her family's lives after Jefferson's death, or when or how she learned of the death of her mother. Was she at least able to maintain an open relationship with Beverley, so that she was not cut off from all her family members? "Slaves did not possess lineage," historian Saidiya Hartman pointed out. "The 'rope of captivity' tethered you to an owner rather than a father and made you offspring rather than an heir." Harriet may have been Jefferson's offspring, but as the daughter of Sally Hemings and the granddaughter of Elizabeth Hemings, she was an heir of the proud Hemings line, which would have meant as much if not more to her. But passing forced her to bury that lineage.

It was only because Madison refused to be defined by slavery and left a public testament to the Hemings pedigree that we know something of what happened to Harriet's family. Careful research has revealed even more. Back home in Charlottesville, Sally Hemings had left the mountain sometime after Jefferson's death. Madison and Eston bought a house on West Main Street, between Jefferson's university and the town, where the three lived together. Sally's sons married free women of color. While Eston settled with his bride in a two-story brick building on East Main Street that the couple received from the bride's parents, his mother remained with Madison in the house on West Main. Sally Hemings died in 1835, living long enough to see her first grandchild born in freedom.

Within two years of their mother's death, Eston and Madison headed west to the free state of Ohio, pressured to leave by Virginia's increasing restrictions on free blacks in the wake of a slave rebellion that had killed dozens of whites. Eston settled in Chillicothe, a town in the foothills of the Appalachian Mountains, in a topography that bears a striking resemblance to the little town he had left behind. There he bought a house and, with the talents he had inherited from his father, supported his wife and three children as a carpenter and musician. "A master of the violin," one of his neighbors remembered, Eston was "an accomplished 'caller' of dances [who] always officiated at the 'swell' entertainments of Chillicothe." Madison put down roots in nearby Waverly, among other free blacks who had also migrated from Virginia. He, too, worked as a carpenter, and raised ten children with his wife. By 1865, he owned a sixty-six-acre farm. His white neighbors admired him as a man "whose word," they said, "was bond."

But even in a free state neither man could escape the burdens imposed by a white supremacist society. In Madison's neighborhood, one resident remembered, whites "made almost constant war" on the successful free people of color who lived there. Madison held his ground, but by 1852, Eston quietly pulled up stakes. In an effort to avoid the fracture that had separated him from his elder brother and sister, he took his family to Madison, Wisconsin, before his teenagers reached marrying age. There he changed his name, relegating Hemings to an innocuous middle initial and claiming his father's name. Eston H. Jefferson then passed as a freeborn white man.

Eston's daughter, Anna, likewise passed and married a white man. His sons served in white regiments in the Union army as officers during the Civil War and later went on to lucrative careers. Beverley Jefferson owned a hotel and launched a successful omnibus company in Madison; his three sons graduated from the University of Wisconsin with degrees in medicine and law. Beverley's brother John Wayles Jefferson moved to Memphis, where he became a successful cotton broker after the war. He never married, perhaps because of his anxiety about the secret he hid. A chance meeting with a Chillicothe friend during the war revealed the depth of his fear of being discovered. "He begged me not to tell the fact that he had colored blood in his veins," his friend recalled. None of the white soldiers under his command suspected a thing.

The prosperity he enjoyed as a businessman is apparent in this photograph of William Beverley Frederick Jefferson (left) and his three sons. The younger son of Eston Hemings Jefferson, Beverley served in the first volunteer Wisconsin regiment raised during the Civil War. Thereafter, he returned to run the family business, a successful restaurant in Madison. Without the discriminatory restrictions that bound many of Madison Hemings's descendants, Eston's descendants flourished in careers as doctors, lawyers, and businessmen.

There are no portraits of Sally Hemings or any of her children; this is the first generation of whom we have images. John Wayles Jefferson, elder son of Eston Hemings Jefferson, served as a major and then colonel in the Union army during the Civil War. His men praised him for his bravery, gallantry, and coolness under fire, and idolized him for his kindness and courtesy off the battlefield, never guessing that the man who commanded them was the son of an ex-slave.

Although Madison remained on the black side of the color line all his life, his descendants did not all follow suit. Two of his sons, William Beverley Hemings and Thomas Eston Hemings, served in the Union army in white regiments. Thomas Eston died during the war, probably at the infamous Confederate prison of Andersonville. William Beverley died alone and unmarried in a veterans' hospital decades later. Other stories of grandsons who passed populate Monticello's Getting Word project. "They tended to cross over to the white community," one descendant said, and communication was just "sort of cut off." Some returned to their Ohio families, such as the relative who resurfaced as a mysterious uncle whose Italian accent matched his olive skin tone. His sister, who had remained a member of the black community, cared for him until his death.

By this time, of course, the Union victory in the Civil War had destroyed slavery, so arguably Madison's grandsons should not have had any need to leave their families behind to pass as white, since they were already free. When masters posted runaway slave ads before the Revolution, they often referred to fugitives who dressed and posed as free, regardless of their skin color. One slave owner thought his escaped slave might "go to Sea and Pass for a free Negro," for example. But by the 1820s, when Harriet left Monticello, this fluidity in categories of race and condition was calcifying, marking the turn one historian has traced from "passing as free" to "passing as white." We need to see how this happened if we are to understand why, long after the abolition of slavery, people continue to cross the color line.

Emboldened by the refusal of the Founding Fathers to eradicate slavery after their Revolution, southern state legislatures and courts busily redefined the meaning of skin color. As the practice of hiring white servants was dying out, especially in the South, unfree labor became increasingly associated with black skin. The landmark case *Hudgins* v. *Wright* (Virginia, 1806) made that link explicit, ruling that skin color determined a person's condition as free or enslaved. That same year, by forcing freed slaves to leave the state, Virginia legislators attempted to cement this racialized regime by expelling any evidence of self-sufficient free blacks, whose very presence contradicted the white rationale that slavery was good for blacks, since they were incapable of caring for themselves. The federal government would not disturb the

Revolutionary settlement, as the Missouri Compromise of 1820 made clear when it admitted Maine as a free state and Missouri as a slave one to maintain the tenuous balance between free and slave states.

In any event, Harriet could not follow the example of many fugitive slaves who dropped their pretense of being freeborn whites once they arrived in a free state and sought out communities of free blacks instead. Her journey to Washington had not ended in free territory; the capital district protected slavery until its Compensated Emancipation Act in 1862. Instead, in this increasingly racialized society, she used her white skin and its implicit claim of free birth to protect herself and her children from enslavement. And while it is true that the abolition of slavery in 1865 and Reconstruction's project to incorporate newly freed slaves into citizenship were important historical markers in the transition from "passing as free" to "passing as white"—abolition having eliminated the reason to pass as free—neither provided Harriet with any incentive to reveal her origins.

By the end of the Civil War, Harriet Hemings had successfully manufactured a white history and lineage for her children while becoming a new person herself. As one novelist reflected in a fictional rendering of Harriet's life, it was not only that she had reinvented herself but also that people saw her differently. Not a single one of her neighbors saw a former slave when they looked at her. The end of Reconstruction, with the withdrawal of federal troops from the South in 1877 (if Harriet Hemings lived long enough to see that day), would only have confirmed her choice to claim the privileges of whiteness, as northerners turned their attention to matters more important to them than the rights of freed black men and women. Of course, Harriet could not have foreseen the passage of laws by the 1890s known as Jim Crow that would sharply segregate Americans by racial categories. Still, little in her experience would have led her to expect anything other than this improvised legal system of segregation that southerners borrowed from its more experienced northern practitioners. "The dangers of blackness," a professor of ethnic studies observed, remained for all who shared African ancestry, dangers unrelieved by abolition.

That is why the practice of passing, which has its own troubled history, has continued from Harriet's time through to our own. After abolition, passing as white brought tensions into black communities that passing as free during the slave regime had not. Black activists had made good use of Reconstruction's political opportunities, filling legislative seats and judicial benches. It was an auspicious time, full of promise, however short-lived. Even when they were ejected from government by Jim Crow laws in the 1890s, black activists continued the fight on many fronts, such as educational and occupational, but also in restaurants and on rail- and streetcars. So to pass as white in this era was to desert not only one's family and community but the cause of black equality as well.

In their relentless efforts to forge what one historian called the "bright-line differences between blacks and whites," white Americans supplied light-skinned blacks with many reasons to cross. For example, Harriet's home state of Virginia passed one of the nation's first "one-drop rule" laws. In 1924 the Act to Preserve Racial Integrity for the first time defined a white person as one who has "no trace of other blood." (They exempted the white descendants of Pocahontas, however; too many of Virginia's first families, including Tom Randolph's, proudly laid claim to descent from her.) To ensure racial purity, the law also prohibited interracial marriage. That kept whites in line by banishing to blackness anyone who accepted a black person as a spouse. The law was a return to the strategy of their forebears, who had legislated the same thing in 1691. These efforts at marking the bright-line differences were further enforced at the federal level when the 1930 census dropped the mixed-race mulatto category, leaving Americans with only two choices: to identify themselves as either black or white.

This hostile climate explains why Clare Kendry, the main character in Nella Larsen's 1929 novel, *Passing,* believed more "coloured girls" should pass. "If one's the type," she declared in a fit of bravado, "all that's needed is a little nerve." But it was desperation to feed her family, rather than nerve, that propelled the grandmother of legal scholar Cheryl I. Harris to pass as white to obtain a job at a Chicago department store in the 1930s. Harris watched the pain flit across her grandmother's face when she told stories of those days, remembering the monumental effort of self-effacement they required. "She was transgressing boundaries, crossing borders, spinning on margins, traveling between dualities of Manichean space, rigidly bifurcated into light/dark, good/bad, white/Black," Harris now understands. Because she had migrated far from her

Mississippi roots, her grandmother had left behind the neighbors and friends who could have identified her. She could therefore "enter the white world, albeit on a false passport, not merely passing, but trespassing." Surely echoing the lesson Harriet Hemings had learned a century earlier as she hid her family story behind the impassive façade of her white face, Harris's grandmother knew that "accepting the risk of self-annihilation [of her black identity] was the only way to survive."

The inducement to pass as white in a one-drop-rule America has not disappeared. In spite of the mid-twentieth-century civil rights movement, whiteness has retained value as a material asset that has been consistently upheld by the courts. "Property is a legal construct by which selected private interests are protected and upheld," Harris explained. "In creating property 'rights' [such as the right to white identity], the law draws boundaries and enforces or reorders existing regimes of power."

Americans have made use of this idea in many ways. Property rights allow the right to *exclude,* as when white Americans limit blacks' access to certain jobs, home mortgages, and education. The courts protected their right to do so. To take another example, slander and libel are infringements for which the offended also have legal recourse. To call a white person "black," American jurisprudence repeatedly determined throughout the 1950s, was defamation.

White Americans understand this well, even if they know nothing about legal theories of whiteness as property. When a group of white students was asked in the early 1990s how much compensation they would require if, through no fault of their own, they had to live the next fifty years of their lives as blacks in America, "most seemed to feel that it would not be out of place to ask for $50 million, or $1 million for each coming black year."

The students' responses make perfect sense in a culture that unthinkingly makes the leap from what historian and sociologist W.E.B. Du Bois in 1911 called "the differences of color, hair, and bone," to ideologies based on nineteenth-century theories of race. Du Bois debunked the theories, fashionable in his time, that linked size and structure of the skull (Du Bois's "bone") to the varying mental capacities of different races. "Such things are on the whole, poorly correlated with genetic difference," he asserted. His beliefs have been borne out time and again, for example, by studies that have found no reason to isolate rare blood types to any particular racial category, proving that all human beings are of the same blood. Nonetheless, there are those who still argue a biological foundation for race. As the British sociologist Stuart Hall remarked, "The biological, physiological, or genetic definition [of race], having been shown out the front door, tends to sidle around the veranda and climb back in through the window."

But we can no more discern a person's genetic code from their skin color than could the nineteenth-century Virginia judges who used what was visible to the eye to declare the existence of what was not visible, that is, race defined by blood. Those who continue to believe that blood is synonymous with race have taken advances in genetic technology to further the two-century-old racial equation rather than to challenge it. "But once invoked," as the authors of *Racecraft: The Soul of Inequality in American Life* argue, "the metaphor launches a logical program of its own: If 'blood' is synonymous with 'race,' and 'DNA' is synonymous with 'blood,' then 'DNA' is synonymous with 'race.'" To be taken in by a logic that equates genetic with racial is to fall for the tricks of the long discredited nineteenth-century pseudo science of racialism.

Indeed, genetic indicators of ancestry are often invisible. For example, almost a third of white Americans possess up to 20 percent African genetic inheritance yet look white; while 5.5 percent of American blacks have *no* detectable African genetic ancestry. Marriage practices in the United States explain why: Whites tend to marry those that look like them. This helps us to understand how Eston Hemings's children Anna and Beverley could marry white spouses, even when the story of his parentage had followed him to Wisconsin. Eston's Chillicothe friends had heard the rumor that he was "a natural son of President Thomas Jefferson" and so knew his enslaved origins. It was a story, they said, "a good many people accepted . . . as truth, from the intrinsic evidence of his striking resemblance to Jefferson." When Beverley died half a century after his father, a Wisconsin admirer wrote to the Milwaukee *Tribune* that Beverley's "death deserves more than a passing notice, as he was a grandson of Thomas Jefferson." As "one of God's noblemen—gentle, kindly, courteous, charitable," Beverley Jefferson had clearly crossed the tribal line of acceptability by whites, even if he had not passed as white in the sense of deceiving anyone about his origins. Since the national consensus around the one-drop rule in the 1920s, however, that flexibility has disappeared. That explains why even now between thirty-five thousand and fifty thousand blacks still cross the color line each year.

As an authority on the history of passing observed, these numbers make glaringly clear how both "specious but utterly real" racial categories remain in America today. As a biological category, racial difference has been exposed as a sham, yet as political, economic, and social categories, racial difference and its consequences remain profoundly real. White Americans face fewer inconveniences and challenges at polling booths. Whites obtain home mortgages more easily and at cheaper interest rates, rendering the American dream of home ownership much more accessible to them than to blacks, who for decades have paid higher rates. That is why, as Cheryl I. Harris observed of her grandmother's experience in 1930s Chicago, passing has "a certain economic logic."

Passing is also about survival. Despite their numerical minority, blacks, both male and female, have been and are still incarcerated in epic proportions compared to whites. The long devaluation of black lives since the seventeenth century has created a white way of seeing, so deeply ingrained that most white Americans are unconscious of the way it shapes their thinking. The lesson we take away from all of this is that Americans are not color-blind. Quite the contrary: The meaning of color remains deeply significant. The care with which they have crafted laws to regulate categories of race makes clear that whites insist on the right to know who carries the drop of African blood that renders a person black. And whites enforce penalties when a passing person is exposed as such, as though blacks have trespassed onto the grounds of white privilege, from which, blacks are supposed to understand, they are barred.

This was exactly the problem with Harriet Hemings. In her birth into slavery and its long history of oppression, she was black, but the Virginian jurists of her day, who based their rulings on the skin color they saw, would have judged her white; she was neither free—because Jefferson gave her no manumission papers—until the Thirteenth Amendment abolished slavery in 1865, nor enslaved, since she lived as a free person. She does not fit any of the terms that seem to have such clarity of meaning in our American experience. This is why her story is so important, whether we find her or not. Her invisibility, then and now, is precisely the point. When we can so easily lose the daughter of a president and his slave, it forces us to acknowledge that our racial categories are utterly fallacious and that our racialized systems are built on a science that has been thoroughly discredited.

As far as the Randolphs were concerned, however, Harriet Hemings was a trespasser, properly barred from the privileges of their common descent from Jefferson of which they were so proud. Trespass remains a sore point between recognized Jefferson descendants, who claim the right of burial in the Monticello graveyard, and any Hemings descendants who seek access to the same. A rapprochement may have seemed faintly possible in 1999, when Hemings descendants were invited for the first time to a meeting of the Monticello Association, an organization of Jefferson descendants through the lines of Martha and Maria. But in 2002, the association roundly voted down a proposal to admit Hemings descendants to the graveyard. A dozen years later, when white Jefferson descendant Tess Taylor arranged to meet slave descendant Gayle Jessup White at Monticello, they walked to the graveyard together. "I unlocked the gate," Taylor recounted simply, apparently unconscious of the fullness of that moment, sitting atop two centuries of family history: the white person in possession of the key, while the other remains locked out.

BELIEVING THAT SHE WAS living her last night on earth, Martha Jefferson Randolph had labored to shape her own legacy with her newly dictated will. But how does one account for one's life as it is drawing to a close? Ellen would later recall her mother's "deep affections, her high principles, her generous & magnanimous temper, her widely diffused benevolence, her sound judgment and glowing imagination, [and] her highly cultivated understanding." But was that enough of a legacy? Even Ellen, who could "never think, speak, or write of my mother without forgetting, for the time, all other things" (meaning the loss of everything they had known with her at Monticello), feared that it would not be. "She has passed away and the world has not known her," she la-

mented, "she has left no memorial but in the recollection of her friends
& the hearts of her children. . . . A few short years and perhaps all record, all remembrance of her name, her qualities will be gone."

Legacies are rarely simple or straightforward. Mired in debt, Jefferson had little materially to leave his daughter, but in the words "all
men are created equal" he bequeathed a national legacy that continues
to inspire Americans in the pursuit of justice. Yet that legacy was tar-
nished by his record as a slaveholder who, after the Revolution, consistently refused to lend his name to slavery reform and who, despite his
stated belief in the natural inferiority of slaves, fathered children with
one of his own. Even the legacies of Jefferson's beloved Revolution were
problematic: a firmer commitment to slavery, even as abolitionist agita-
tion was rising; a wider franchise that added increasing numbers of
white men, even as free black men were being excluded; a consensus
that domesticity and motherhood were women's only callings, even as
it meant permanently barring them from the equality proclaimed in the
nation's founding documents.

The legacies of Jefferson's daughters were no less complex, but until
now they have gone almost completely unremarked. Over the course of
her life, Martha Jefferson Randolph had seen the legacies of her father's
Revolution come to pass, but she was more preoccupied with those of
her family. She would live another year beyond that fitful spring night,
but her determination to leave a written legacy that would hold up in a
court of law was intentional and crafted. Like her father, who with the
help of his daughter and granddaughters assiduously kept an archive of
more than eighteen thousand of his letters, Martha understood the
value of the written word. And if she did not have much to leave behind
to her daughters besides their illustrious connection, she had flung
open for them the doors to the joys of the intellectual life that they had
treasured, relishing their studies and taking pride in their learning. Maria's legacy was less intentional: the moldy music books, covered with
her signature, the imprint of her identity, but falling apart in her son's
hands. Like most mothers of her era, Maria had hoped to establish her
legacy in her children. But her only surviving child could not remember
her and, in 1828, would turn his back on Virginia forever when he
moved his family to Florida.

Legacies depend on continuity. But in her departure from Monticello, Harriet Hemings broke with her history and, with her move to Washington, deliberately erased it from view. Her story, enabled in her own day by the colluding silence of Jefferson, the Hemingses, and the Randolphs, is certainly part of the national legacy of slavery and race in America. But we cannot forget that there is also Harriet's personal legacy, which must be reconstructed by historians from traces that are even more ephemeral than Maria's music books but no less significant than either of her sisters'.

It is the historian's job to excavate these buried stories, to capture these historical legacies, to make visible an invisible past. In the same way that Martha determinedly shaped hers, and a grieving Ellen struggled to articulate the value of her remarkable mother's life, I have tried to recover both Maria's and Harriet's legacies from the dustbin of history. As we look back at them, these stories prompt us to ask: Why were the lives, gifts, and passions of so many women excised from the Revolution's historical legacy? Why, long after the Revolution, were people still forced to choose between their family connections and the color of their skin? And why do the discredited ideologies of gender and race continue to control and separate Americans so powerfully?

The locked cemetery at Monticello, like Jefferson's locked library, cabinet, and wine cellars, marks boundaries of privilege that cannot be breached except by invitation. When Jefferson founded a public university to train an educated electorate and a productive citizenry, it too was a place of privilege: Only white men could attend. His limited vision could not comprehend the ways in which women and people of color could also cultivate the very civic virtues to which he devoted his life. The tragedy of the American experience is how much has been lost following Jefferson's lead. America's hope, however, lies in the vision of those who reject those limits and strive to build the legacy embedded in his most famous words.

Acknowledgments

I ENTERED THE WORLD OF JEFFERSON scholarship with some trepidation. Over the past century, it has been contentious to the point of acrimony. However, I have found it to be populated by historians of enormous talent and generosity, whose work made my own possible and who gave of their time to read and discuss my research. Their contributions have made this book infinitely better than it would have been otherwise. I am deeply grateful to them all.

For their helpful comments when I presented early versions of these chapters at conferences, I thank Jon Kukla, Cynthia Kierner, Sheila Skemp, Jeffrey Young, and the audiences at the Paris conferences sponsored by the European Early American Studies Association. I thank the anonymous readers of "The French Education of Martha Jefferson Randolph," who encouraged me to do a deeper reading of Martha's convent schooling. I am grateful to Elaine Forman Crane and the late C. Dallett Hemphill for their assistance in shepherding that article to publication in *Early American Studies: An Interdisciplinary Journal*. I have been particularly fortunate to count Cynthia Kierner as a friend as well as a colleague. From the day I talked with her over lunch in Charlottesville to make sure we were not writing the same book, her generosity in helping me map my way through the Jefferson/Randolph papers, discussing my ideas, and inviting me to contribute to *Virginia Women: Their Lives and Times* has been unparalleled. I thank Frank Cogliano for his unstinting support of my project and his invitation to contribute an essay to *A Companion to Thomas Jefferson*. Even though she was supposed to be retired, Lucia Stanton read and commented on that essay and several chapters of this book. As readers of the end-notes will see, my work owes a great debt to hers and to that of Annette Gordon-Reed, both of whom inspired my search for Harriet Hemings.

I am blessed beyond all measure to teach in the Department of History at Villanova. In their dedication to their students and their award-winning scholarship, my colleagues daily inspire me to give my best. Their supportive generosity to my project has been exceptional. I thank Marc Gallicchio for twice paving the way to allow me to accept the fellowships that were necessary for the research and writing, and my colleagues who have read chapter drafts and fellowship applications and devoted several Friday afternoons to discuss them, including Craig Bailey, Marc Gallicchio, Judith Giesberg, Elizabeth Kolsky, Adele Lindenmeyr, Andrew Liu, Whitney Martinko, Timothy McCall, Lynne Hartnett, Paul Rosier, Paul Steege. I thank my former graduate students (now friends) Jacqueline Beatty and Emily Hatcher McCloskey for reading drafts of articles and book chapters, and Claire Bohall, Nicholas Mumenthaler, and Michael S. Fischer for their research assistance along the way. My longtime friend in Virginia studies, Tatiana Van Riemsdijk, generously provided her careful and appreciative reading of the manuscript. For their willingness to serve as my general readers and to rein my slippages in to academic-ese, I thank Anne Horne Bridgers, Wendy Hamilton Hoelscher, and Justin Foster.

I am especially indebted to the many archivists who pointed me in all manner of helpful directions. I thank the staff of the Albert and Shirley Small Special Collections Library at the University of Virginia, especially Regina D. Rush; the staffs of the District of Columbia Public Library, the Historical Society of Washington, D.C., the Moorland-Spingarn Research Center of Howard University, and the National Archives; Anna Berkes of the International Center for Jefferson Studies; Linda Eaton, head curator of textiles, Winterthur Museum; and Margaret M. O'Bryant, librarian of the Albemarle Charlottesville Historical Society. For permission to publish images from their collections, I thank the Fenimore Art Museum, the Historical Society of Pennsylvania, the Massachusetts Historical Society, the Muscarelle Museum of

Art, Thomas Jefferson's Poplar Forest, the Thomas Jefferson Foundation, and the Museum of Wisconsin Art.

For enormously helpful discussions of my questions, I thank Ann Lucas Birle, Lisa A. Francavilla, Richard Guy Wilson, Martha King, and Allyson Hobbs. As are all researchers on Jefferson-related topics, I am indebted to Andrew O'Shaughnessy for his warm support of my project and his direction of the ICJS, which provides the most congenial environments in which to research, write, and discuss our work with other scholars. At Monticello I was fortunate to make a friend of Elizabeth Chew, whose passion for the Randolph sisters inspired my own. With her help, I was able to spend days poring over their schoolbooks in one of their second-story bedrooms (now renovated and open to visitors, owing to Elizabeth's research). She generously met with two Villanova student groups I brought to Monticello and put me in touch with Greg Graham, the owner of Edgehill. I thank him for graciously allowing me to visit the Randolphs' home.

In Washington, my detective work searching for Harriet Hemings was aided and abetted by the staff of the Daughters of the American Revolution Library; Ali Rahmaan of the District of Columbia Archives; Dayle Dooley and John Kreinheder of Historic Congressional Cemetery; Daniel Stokes of New York Avenue Presbyterian Church; J. Theodore Anderson of National Presbyterian Church and Center; Hayden Bryan of St. John's Episcopal Church; and Ruth Williams of Fourth Presbyterian Church in Bethesda, Maryland. I thank Elisabeth Williamson for her gracious response to the inquiries of a stranger, opening her personal family archive to me and even providing a DNA sample.

I have been enormously privileged to meet or speak with descendants of the extended Hemings family. I thank J. Calvin Jefferson and Karen Hughes White for their help and suggestions as I began my search for Harriet Hemings; Beverly Gray and Edna Jacques for conversations about where Harriet might have gone; and Rosemary Ghoston for her kind efforts to help me with the DNA samples that could make connections the archival records cannot.

I am profoundly grateful for the generous institutional support this project has received from the beginning. Fellowships at the International Center for Jefferson Studies, the Colonial Williamsburg Foundation, and the Virginia Historical Society supported my initial research. A full year's research was supported by the American Association of University Women, supplemented by my own institution. A fellowship from the Virginia Foundation for the Humanities, together with a sabbatical from Villanova University, enabled a full semester devoted solely to writing. I am grateful for Villanova's commitment to support faculty research, particularly the award of two summer grants over the course of this project and a generous subvention grant. Work in archives located in Washington was supported through the generosity of the Albert Lepage Research Fund and the department's Summer Research Fund.

I thank my wonderful agent, Howard Morhaim, for his immediate interest in this book and his help in preparing the proposal, and for finding it a home at Ballantine Books. Susanna Porter's editorial pen has smoothed out the prose, as has her editorial team, and Emily Hartley has patiently ushered me through the many steps of the publication process.

I reserve my final thanks for my friends and family who know well that I could not have finished this book without their unstinting love and support. For more hours than I can count, Wendy Hamilton Hoelscher and Sallie Cross listened to my stories of Martha, Maria, and Harriet and encouraged me to press on to bring them to the world. Elizabeth Ince Wright opened her gracious home to me on many a Washington research trip. As always, my children—Elizabeth Foster, Sarah Foster, and Justin Foster and his wife, Dani—are my raison d'être. I thank them for their love and unending pride in me, which will always mean more to me than the most glowing accolade the world can give.

I dedicate this book to James P. Whittenburg, my former professor and mentor, to thank him for setting me on this scholarly path and for his continued friendship, guidance, and encouragement over the years. A dedication is but a token; it cannot come close to repaying a debt. But I hope it conveys something of my deep gratitude and respect.

As I have written this book, I have had the happy experience of discovering, as Jefferson did, that "grandchildren . . . furnish me great resources of happiness." I hope that, unlike Jefferson's daughters, Everett, Luke, and Madeleine will know the grace of living in a world that respects the dignity of every human being.

Bibliography

PRIMARY SOURCES—MANUSCRIPTS

ALBERT AND SHIRLEY SMALL SPECIAL COLLECTIONS LIBRARY,
UNIVERSITY OF VIRGINIA

Burke and Trist Family Papers. Accession 5385 aa-t.
Burke and Trist Family Papers. Accession 5385f.
Burke, Randolph, and Trist Family Papers. Accession 10487.
Carr-Cary Family Papers. Accession 1231.
Carr-Terrell Family Papers. Accession 4757-d.
Cocke Family Papers. Accession 640.
Coolidge, Ellen Wayles Randolph Papers. Accession 9090.
Eppes Family Papers. Accession 7109.
Eppes, Maria. Letter. Accession 38-757.
Eppes, Maria, Thomas Jefferson, the Randolph Family Correspondence. Accession 3470.
Jefferson, Thomas. Letter. Accession 6860.
Meikleham, Septimia Anne Cary Randolph Papers. Accession 4726-b.
Nicholas, Wilson Cary, and the Randolph Family of Edgehill Papers. Accession 5533.
Randolph Family of Edgehill Papers. Accession 1397.
Randolph, Thomas Jefferson. Papers on Thomas Jefferson. Accession 8937.
Smith, Jane Blair Cary. "Carysbrook Memoir." Accession 1378.
Wayles, John. "Will and Codicil of John Wayles, 1760, 1772–1773." *Tyler's Quarterly Historical and Genealogical Magazine* 6 (1925): 268–70.

DAUGHTERS OF THE AMERICAN REVOLUTION

Genealogical Record Committee (GRC)

CONGRESSIONAL CEMETERY

Congressional Cemetery Records, Washington, D.C.
Daily Interments, July 1839–July 1849.
Range and Interment Records "Blue Book." Begun in 1858.

HISTORICAL SOCIETY OF WASHINGTON

Membership Applications. "Oldest Inhabitants Society." MSS 422, Series V.

INTERNATIONAL CENTER FOR JEFFERSON STUDIES (ICJS)

Eppes, Mrs. Nicholas (Susan) Ware. "Maria Jefferson Eppes and her Little Son, Francis."
Howard Rice Collection.
ICJS vertical files.

MARYLAND HISTORICAL SOCIETY

Redwood Collection. MS 1530.

MASSACHUSETTS HISTORICAL SOCIETY

Adams Family Papers.
Coolidge Collection.

NATIONAL ARCHIVES OF THE UNITED STATES

Record Group 21: Records of the District Courts of the United States.
Record Group 351: Deed books.

SOUTHERN HISTORICAL COLLECTION,
UNIVERSITY OF NORTH CAROLINA

Nicholas Philip Trist Papers. Accession 2104.

VIRGINIA HISTORICAL SOCIETY

Page Family Papers.
Randolph, Mary Jefferson. Commonplace Book.

PRIMARY SOURCES—CHURCH RECORDS

First Presbyterian Church (Washington, D.C.). Session records, vol. 1, 1812–1840.
St. John's Episcopal Church (Lafayette Square, Washington, D.C.). Fourth Presbyterian Church Records, First Session Book, Marriage and Baptism Record Book,
1828–September 1878.

PRIMARY SOURCES—NEWSPAPERS

Daily National Intelligencer (Washington, D.C.)
Daily Scioto Gazette
The Evening Star (Washington, D.C.)
Federal Gazette (Philadelphia, Pa.)
The Pennsylvania Mercury and Universal Advertiser
The Pennsylvania Packet
The Recorder (Richmond, Va.)
The Washington Post

PRIMARY SOURCES—ELECTRONIC

Congressional Cemetery. congressionalcemetery.org.

Crackel, Theodore J., ed. *The Papers of George Washington Digital Edition.* Charlottesville: University of Virginia Press, Rotunda, 2008.

Hening, Walter Waller. *Hening's Statutes at Large: Being a Collection of All the Laws of Virginia from the First Session of the Legislature, in the Year 1619.* Transcribed by Freddie L. Spradlin. vagenweb.org/hening.

Thomas Jefferson Foundation. "Jefferson Quotes & Family Letters." tjrs.monticello .org.

Jefferson, Thomas. *Thomas Jefferson Papers, 1606 to 1827.* Manuscript Division, Library of Congress (LOC), Washington, D.C. loc.gov/collections/thomas-jefferson-papers.

Looney, J. Jefferson, and Barbara B. Oberg, eds. *The Papers of Thomas Jefferson Digital Edition.* Charlottesville: University of Virginia Press, Rotunda, 2008.

Martin, Sara, ed. *The Adams Papers Digital Edition.* Charlottesville: University of Virginia Press, Rotunda, 2008–2017.

Shulman, Holly C., ed. *The Papers of Dolley Madison Digital Edition.* Charlottesville: University of Virginia Press, Rotunda, 2008.

Smith, John C. *Jehovah-Jireh: A Discourse Commemorative of the Twenty-seventh Anniversary of the Organization of the Fourth Presbyterian Church, Washington, D.C.* Washington, D.C.: Thomas McGill, 1855. *Sabin Americana.*

PRIMARY SOURCES—PRINT

Abell, Mrs. L. G. *Woman in Her Various Relations: Containing Practical Rules for American Females.* New York: J. M. Fairchild, 1855.

Adams, Abigail. *Journal and Correspondence of Miss Adams, Daughter of John Adams, Second President of the United States, Written in France and England in 1785.* Edited by her daughter. New York: Wily and Putnam, 1841.

Anburey, Thomas. *Travels Through the Interior Parts of America.* 2 vols. 1789. Reprint, Boston: Houghton Mifflin Company, 1923.

Bear, James A., Jr., and Lucia C. Stanton, eds. *Jefferson's Memorandum Books: Accounts, with Legal Records and Miscellany, 1767–1826.* 2 vols. Princeton: Princeton University Press, 1997.

Betts, Edwin Morris, and James Adam Bear, Jr., eds. *The Family Letters of Thomas Jefferson.* Charlottesville: University Press of Virginia, 1965.

Betts, Edwin Morris, ed. *Thomas Jefferson's Farm Book.* Charlottesville: Thomas Jefferson Memorial Foundation, 1999.

———, ed. *Thomas Jefferson's Garden Book.* Charlottesville: Thomas Jefferson Memorial Foundation, 1999.

Biddle, Clement. "Selections from the Correspondence of Clement Biddle." *Pennsylvania Magazine of History and Biography* 43 (1919): 193–207.

Birle, Ann Lucas, and Lisa A. Francavilla, eds. *Thomas Jefferson's Granddaughter in Queen Victoria's England.* Boston and Charlottesville: Massachusetts Historical Society and Thomas Jefferson Foundation, 2012.

Boyd, Julian P., ed. *The Papers of Thomas Jefferson.* 42 vols. Princeton: Princeton University Press, 1950–.

Brady, Patricia, ed. *George Washington's Beautiful Nelly: The Letters of Eleanor Parke Custis Lewis to Elizabeth Bordley Gibson, 1794–1851.* Columbia: University of South Carolina Press, 1991.

Cappon, Lester J., ed. *The Adams-Jefferson Letters.* 1959. Reprint, Chapel Hill: University of North Carolina Press, 1987.

Carter, Edward II, and Angeline Polites, eds. *The Virginia Journals of Benjamin Henry Latrobe, 1795–98.* 2 vols. New Haven: Yale University Press, 1977.

Chastellux, François Jean Marquis de. *Travels in North America, in the Years 1780, 1781, and 1782.* 2 vols. Dublin: Colles, Moncrieffe, White, 1787.

Cott, Nancy F., Jeanne Boydston, Ann Braude, Lori D. Ginzberg, and Molly Ladd-Taylor, eds. *Root of Bitterness: Documents of the Social History of American Women.* 2nd ed. Boston: Northeastern University Press, 1996.

Custis, George Washington Parke. *Recollections and Private Memoirs of Washington by His Adopted Son with a Memoir of the Son by His Daughter.* New York: Derby & Jackson, 1860.

Delano, Judah. *Washington Directory: Showing the Name, Occupation, and Residence of Each Head of a Family and Person in Business.* Washington: William Duncan, 1822.

Douglass, Frederick. *Narrative of the Life of Frederick Douglass: An American Slave, Written by Himself.* 2nd ed. Edited by David Blight. Boston: Bedford Books of Saint Martin's, 2003.

Elliot, Jonathan. *Historical Sketches of the Ten Miles Square Forming the District of Columbia.* Washington, D.C.: J. Elliot, Jr., 1830.

Elliot, S. A. *The Washington Directory.* Washington, D.C.: S. A. Elliot, 1827.

Farish, Hunter Dickinson, ed. *Journal and Letters of Philip Vickers Fithian: A Plantation Tutor of the Old Dominion, 1773–1774.* 5th ed. Charlottesville: University Press of Virginia, 1993.

Ford, Paul Leicester, ed. *The Works of Thomas Jefferson.* 12 vols. New York: G.P. Putnam's Sons, 1904–1905.

Fossett, Peter. "Once the Slave of Thomas Jefferson." *Sunday World,* January 29, 1898.

Gilmer, Peachy. "Peachy R. Gilmer Memoir." In *Francis Walker Gilmer,* edited by Richard Beale Davis. Richmond: Dietz Press, 1939.

Hemings, Madison. "Memoirs of Madison Hemings." In *Thomas Jefferson and Sally Hemings: An American Controversy,* by Annette Gordon-Reed, 245–48. Charlottesville: University Press of Virginia, 1997.

Hunt, Gaillard, ed. *The First Forty Years of Washington Society in the Family Letters of Margaret Bayard Smith.* 1906. Reprint, New York: Frederick Ungar, 1965.

Hunter, Alfred, compiler. *The Washington and Georgetown Directory.* Revised by Wesley E. Pippenger. Washington, D.C.: Kirkwood & McGill, 1853.

Jacobs, Harriet A. *Incidents in the Life of a Slave Girl, Written by Herself.* Edited by Jean Fagan Yellin. Cambridge, Mass.: Harvard University Press, 1987.

Jefferson, Isaac Granger. *Memoirs of a Monticello Slave As Dictated to Charles Campbell in the 1840's by Isaac, One of Thomas Jefferson's Slaves.* Charlottesville: University Press of Virginia for the Tracy W. McGregor Library, 1951.

Jefferson, Israel. "Memoirs of Israel [Gillette] Jefferson." In *Thomas Jefferson and Sally Hemings: An American Controversy,* by Annette Gordon-Reed, 249–53. Charlottesville: University Press of Virginia, 1997.

Keckley, Elizabeth. *Behind the Scenes, or, Thirty Years a Slave and Four Years in the White House.* New York: Oxford University Press, 1988.

Kimball, Marie G. "Unpublished Correspondence of Mme. De Staël with Thomas Jefferson." *The North American Review* (1821–1940) 208, no. 752 (July 1918): 63–71.

La Rochefoucauld-Liancourt, François. *Travels Through North America, Canada.* London: R. Phillips, 1799.

Martineau, Harriet. *Society in America.* Vol. 3. London: Saunders and Otley, 1837.

———. *Retrospect of Western Travel*. Vol. 1, 1838. Reprint, New York: Greenwood Press, 1969.

Morris, Anne Cary, ed. *The Diary and Letters of Gouverneur Morris: Minister of the United States to France; Member of the Constitutional Convention, Etc.* Vol 1. New York: Charles Scribner's Sons, 1888.

"Mrs. Thomas Mann Randolph, Eldest Daughter of Thomas Jefferson, by a Granddaughter." *The American Monthly Magazine* 17 (1900): 21–30.

Murray, Judith Sargent. "On the Equality of the Sexes." *Massachusetts Magazine, or, Monthly Museum of Knowledge and Rational Entertainment*, March 1790.

Peterson, Merrill D., ed. *Visitors to Monticello*. Charlottesville: University Press of Virginia, 1989.

Pierson, Hamilton W., ed. *Jefferson at Monticello: The Private Life of Thomas Jefferson from Entirely New Materials*. 1862. Reprint, Stratford, N.H.: Ayer Company, 1971.

Randall, Henry S. *The Life of Thomas Jefferson*. 3 vols. New York: Derby & Jackson, 1858.

Randolph, Sarah Nicholas. *The Domestic Life of Thomas Jefferson. Compiled from Family Letters and Reminiscences, by His Great-Granddaughter*. Charlottesville: University Press of Virginia, 1978.

Randolph, Sarah Nicholas. "Mrs. Thomas Mann Randolph." In *Worthy Women of Our First Century*, edited by Agnes Irwin and Sarah Butler Wister. Philadelphia: Lippincott, 1877.

Teitelman, Robert, ed. *Birch's Views of Philadelphia: A Reduced Facsimile of the City of Philadelphia—As It Appeared in the Year 1800: With Photographs of the Sites in 1960 & 2000 and Commentaries*. Philadelphia: Free Library of Philadelphia, 2000.

Torrey, Jesse. *A Portraiture of Domestic Slavery, in the United States: With Reflections on the Practicability of Restoring the Moral Rights of the Slave, Without Impairing the Legal Privileges of the Possessor: And a Project of a Colonial Asylum for Free Persons of Colour: Including Memoirs of Facts on the Interior Traffic in Slaves, and on Kidnapping*. Philadelphia: John Bioren, 1817.

Trumbull, John. *The Autobiography of Colonel John Trumbull, Patriot Artist 1756–1843*. New Haven: Yale University Press, 1953.

Wright, F. Edward, compiler. *Marriage Licenses of Washington D.C. 1811 through 1830*. Silver Spring, Md.: Family Line Publications, 1988.

SECONDARY SOURCES

FAMILY AND GENEALOGICAL RECORDS

Brent, Chester Horton. *The Descendants of Hugh Brent, Immigrant to Isle of Wight County, Virginia, 1642*. Rutland, Vt.: Tuttle Publishing, 1936.

Clark, Edythe Maxey. *William Pumphrey of Prince George's County Maryland and His Descendants*. Decorah, Ia.: Anundsen Publishing, 1992.

Peden, Henry C., Jr., ed. *Marriages and Deaths from Baltimore Newspapers, 1817–1824*. Lewes, Del.: Colonial Roots, 2010.

Pumphrey, L. N. *The Pumphrey Pedigree*. Baltimore: Gateway Press, 2003.

Simpson, Dennis William, compiler. *Simpson and Allied Families*. Baltimore: Gateway Press, 1985.

Simpson, John Worth. *Simpson: A Family of the American Frontier*. Baltimore: Gateway Press, 1983.

Smith, Ralph D. *The Simpson Families of Southern Maryland, Western Maryland, and the District of Columbia to 1820*. Daytona Beach, Fl.: R. D. Smith, 1998.

BOOKS AND ARTICLES

Abbott, Carl. *Political Terrain: Washington, D.C., from Tidewater Town to Global Metropolis.* Chapel Hill: University of North Carolina Press, 1999.

Adams, William Howard. *The Paris Years of Thomas Jefferson.* New Haven: Yale University Press, 1997.

Allgor, Catherine. *Parlor Politics: In Which the Ladies of Washington Help Build a City and a Government.* Charlottesville: University Press of Virginia, 2000.

Baumgarten, Linda. *What Clothes Reveal: The Language of Clothing in Colonial and Federal America.* New Haven: Yale University Press, 2012.

Beiswanger, William L. *Monticello in Measured Drawings.* Charlottesville: Thomas Jefferson Memorial Foundation, 1998.

Belkin, Lisa. "The Opt-Out Revolution." *New York Times,* October 26, 2003.

Bloch, Jean. "Discourses of Female Education in the Writings of Eighteenth-Century French Women." In *Women, Gender, and the Enlightenment,* edited by Sarah Knott and Barbara Taylor, 243–58. 2005. Reprint, New York: Palgrave Macmillan, 2007.

Bloch, Ruth H. "The Gendered Meanings of Virtue in Revolutionary America." *Signs: Journal of Women in Culture and Society* 13 (Autumn 1987): 37–58.

Boydston, Jeanne. *Home and Work: Housework, Wages, and the Ideology of Labor in the Early Republic.* New York: Oxford University Press, 1990.

Branson, Susan. *Those Fiery Frenchified Dames: Women and Political Culture in Early National Philadelphia.* Philadelphia: University of Pennsylvania Press, 2001.

Brodie, Fawn M. *Thomas Jefferson: An Intimate History.* New York: Bantam Books, 1974.

Brown, Kathleen M. *Good Wives, Nasty Wenches, and Anxious Patriarchs: Gender, Race, and Power in Colonial Virginia.* Chapel Hill: Published for OIEAHC by University of North Carolina Press, 1996.

———. *Foul Bodies: Cleanliness in Early America.* New Haven: Yale University Press, 2009.

Burstein, Andrew. *The Inner Jefferson: Portrait of a Grieving Optimist.* Charlottesville: University Press of Virginia, 1996.

Carson, Cary, and Carl R. Lounsbury, eds. *The Chesapeake House: Architectural Investigation by Colonial Williamsburg.* Chapel Hill: University of North Carolina Press, 2013.

Chambers, S. Allen. *Poplar Forest and Thomas Jefferson.* Little Compton, R.I.: Fort Church Publishers, 1993.

Chase-Riboud, Barbara. *The President's Daughter.* New York: Crown Publishing Group, 1994.

Chew, Elizabeth V. "Inhabiting the Great Man's House: Women and Space at Monticello." In *Structures and Subjectivities: Attending to Early Modern Women,* edited by Adele F. Seeff and Joan Hartman, 223–52. Newark: University of Delaware Press, 2007.

Choudhury, Mita. *Convents and Nuns in Eighteenth-Century French Politics and Culture.* Ithaca: Cornell University Press, 2004.

Clark, Emily. *The Strange History of the American Quadroon: Free Women of Color in the Revolutionary Atlantic World.* Chapel Hill: University of North Carolina Press, 2013.

Clark-Lewis, Elizabeth. *First Freed: Washington, D.C., in the Emancipation Era.* Washington, D.C.: Howard University Press, 2002.

Coale, Ansley J., and Melvin Zelnik. *New Estimates of Fertility and Population in the United States.* Princeton: Princeton University Press, 1963.

Cogliano, Francis D. "Preservation and Education: Monticello and the Thomas Jefferson Foundation." In *A Companion to Thomas Jefferson,* edited by Francis D. Cogliano, 510–25. West Sussex, U.K.: Blackwell Publishing, 2012.

Cohen, Lizabeth. *A Consumers' Republic: The Politics of Mass Consumption in Postwar America*. New York: Alfred A. Knopf, 2003.

Cope, Virginia. "'I Verily Believed Myself to Be a Free Woman': Harriet Jacobs's Journey into Capitalism." *African American Review* 38 (Spring 2004): 5–20.

Cripe, Helen. *Thomas Jefferson and Music*. Charlottesville: University Press of Virginia, 1974.

Dalzell, Robert F., Jr. "Constructing Independence: Monticello, Mount Vernon, and the Men Who Built Them." *Eighteenth-Century Studies, Special Issue. Thomas Jefferson, 1743–1993: An Anniversary Collection* 26 (Summer 1993): 543–80.

Darnton, Robert. "The True History of Fake News," *New York Review of Books*, February 13, 2017.

Davidson, Cathy. *Revolution and the Word: The Rise of the Novel in America*. New York: Oxford University Press, 1986.

Davis, Natalie Zemon. *The Return of Martin Guerre*. Cambridge, Mass.: Harvard University Press, 1983.

———. *Women on the Margins: Three Seventeenth-Century Lives*. Cambridge, Mass.: Harvard University Press, 1995.

Diaconoff, Suellen. *Through the Reading Glass: Women, Books, and Sex in the French Enlightenment*. Albany: State University of New York Press, 2005.

Durey, Michael. *"With the Hammer of Truth": James Thomson Callender and America's Early National Heroes*. Charlottesville: University Press of Virginia, 1990.

Egerton, Douglas R. *Gabriel's Rebellion: The Virginia Slave Conspiracies of 1800 and 1802*. Chapel Hill: University of North Carolina Press, 1993.

Ellis, Joseph J. *American Sphinx: The Character of Thomas Jefferson*. New York: Alfred A. Knopf, 1996.

Fields, Karen E., and Barbara J. Fields. *Racecraft: The Soul of Inequality in American Life*. London: Verso, 2012.

Finkelman, Paul. *Slavery and the Founders: Race and Liberty in the Age of Jefferson*. Armonk, New York: M. E. Sharpe, 1996.

Foner, Eric. *A Short History of Reconstruction, 1863–1877*. New York: Harper and Row, 1990.

Fosseyeux, Marcel. "Une abbesse de Panthémont au XVIII siècle: Madame de Béthisy de Mézières, 1743–1789." *Revue du Dix-huitième Siècle* V (1918).

Foster, Elaine Morrison. "Founding a Church in a City on a Hill: Joseph Nourse, James Laurie, and the F Street Church." In *Capital Witness: A History of the New York Avenue Presbyterian Church in Washington, D.C.*, edited by Dewey D. Wallace, Jr., Wilson Golden, and Edith Holmes Snyder. Franklin, Tenn.: Plumbline Media, 2011.

Foster, Helen Bradley. *"New Raiments of Self": African American Clothing in the Antebellum South*. New York: Berg, 1997.

Fryer, Darcy R. "Mortality in the Colonial Period." In *Encyclopedia of American History: Colonization and Settlement, 1608 to 1760*, edited by Billy G. Smith and Gary B. Nash. Rev. ed., vol. 2. New York: Facts on File, 2009.

Gaines, William H., Jr. *Thomas Mann Randolph: Jefferson's Son-in-Law*. Baton Rouge: Louisiana State University Press, 1966.

Garrioch, David. *The Making of Revolutionary Paris*. Berkeley: University of California Press, 2002.

Gawalt, Gerald W. "Jefferson's Slaves: Crop Accounts at Monticello." *Journal of the Afro-American Historical and Genealogical Society* 13 (1994): 19–38.

Gillespie, E. D. *A Book of Remembrance*. Philadelphia: J. B. Lippincott, 1901.

Godineau, Dominique. "The Woman." In *Enlightenment Portraits*, edited by Michel

Vovelle and translated by Lydia G. Cochrane, 393–426. Chicago: University of Chicago Press, 1992.

Goodman, Dena. "Women and the Enlightenment." In *Becoming Visible: Women in European History,* edited by Renate Bridenthal, Susan Mosher Stuard, and Merry E. Wiesner, 233–62. 3rd ed. Boston: Houghton Mifflin, 1998.

———. *Becoming a Woman in the Age of Letters.* Ithaca: Cornell University Press, 2009.

Gordon-Reed, Annette. *Thomas Jefferson and Sally Hemings: An American Controversy.* Charlottesville: University Press of Virginia, 1997.

———. *The Hemingses of Monticello: An American Family.* New York: W. W. Norton, 2008.

Green, Constance McLaughlin. *Washington: Village and Capital, 1800–1878.* Princeton: Princeton University Press, 1962.

Gross, Robert A., and Mary Kelley, eds. *An Extensive Republic: Print, Culture, and Society in the New Nation, 1790–1840.* Vol. 2 of *A History of the Book in America,* edited by David D. Hall. Chapel Hill: University of North Carolina Press, 2010.

Hall, David D. "Books and Reading in Eighteenth-Century America." In *Of Consuming Interests: The Style of Life in the Eighteenth Century,* edited by Cary Carson, Ronald Hoffman, and Peter J. Albert, 354–72. Charlottesville: United States Capitol Historical Society by the University Press of Virginia, 1994.

Harris, Cheryl I. "Whiteness as Property." *Harvard Law Review* 106 (June 1993): 1707–91.

Hartman, Saidiya. *Lose Your Mother: A Journey Along the Atlantic Slave Route.* New York: Farrar, Strauss and Giroux, 2007.

Hayes, Kevin J. *The Road to Monticello: The Life and Mind of Thomas Jefferson.* New York: Oxford University Press, 2008.

Heilbrun, Carolyn. *Writing a Woman's Life.* New York: W. W. Norton, 1988.

Hemphill, C. Dallett. *Bowing to Necessities: A History of Manners in America, 1620–1860.* New York: Oxford University Press, 1999.

———. "Manners and Class in the Revolutionary Era: A Transatlantic Comparison." *William and Mary Quarterly* 63 (April 2006): 345–72.

Hobbs, Allyson. *A Chosen Exile: A History of Racial Passing in American Life.* Cambridge, Mass.: Harvard University Press, 2014.

Holt, Thomas. *Black over White: Negro Political Leadership in South Carolina During Reconstruction.* Urbana: University of Illinois, 1977.

Holton, Woody. *Abigail Adams.* New York: Free Press, 2009.

Honeywell, Roy J. *The Educational Work of Thomas Jefferson.* New York: Russell and Russell, 1964.

Howard, Hugh, and Roger Straus. *Thomas Jefferson, Architect: The Built Legacy of Our Third President.* New York: Rizzoli, 2003.

Hufton, Olwen. *The Prospect Before Her: A History of Women in Western Europe.* New York: Alfred A. Knopf, 1996.

Johnston, James Hugo. *Race Relations in Virginia & Miscegenation in the South 1776–1860.* Amherst: University of Massachusetts Press, 1970.

Justus, Judith. *Down from the Mountain: The Oral History of the Hemings Family. Are They the Black Descendants of Thomas Jefferson?* Fremont, Ohio: Lesher Printers, Inc., 1990.

Kaplan, Sara Clarke. "Our Founding (M)other: Erotic Love and Social Death in *Sally Hemings* and *The President's Daughter.*" *Callalo* 32 (Summer 2009): 773–91.

Kasson, John F. *Rudeness & Civility: Manners in Nineteenth-Century Urban America.* New York: Hill and Wang, 1990.

Kelley, Mary. *Learning to Stand & Speak: Women, Education, and Public Life in America's*

Republic. Chapel Hill: Published for OIEAHC by University of North Carolina Press, 2006.

———. "Female Academies and Seminaries and Print Culture." In *A History of the Book in America.* Vol. 2, *An Extensive Republic: Print, Culture, and Society in the New Nation, 1790–1840,* edited by Robert A. Gross and Mary Kelley. Chapel Hill: University of North Carolina Press, 2010.

Kerber, Linda K. *Women of the Republic: Intellect and Ideology in Revolutionary America.* Chapel Hill: Published for OIEAHC by University of North Carolina Press, 1980.

Kern, Susan. "The Material World of the Jeffersons at Shadwell." *William and Mary Quarterly* 62 (April 2005): 213–42.

———. *The Jeffersons at Shadwell.* New Haven: Yale University Press, 2010.

Kerrison, Catherine. *Claiming the Pen: Women and Intellectual Life in the Early American South.* Ithaca: Cornell University Press, 2006.

———. "Sally Hemings." In *A Companion to Thomas Jefferson,* edited by Francis Cogliano, 284–300. West Sussex, UK: Blackwell Publishing, 2012.

Kierner, Cynthia A. *Beyond the Household: Women's Place in the Early South, 1700–1835.* Ithaca: Cornell University Press, 1998.

———. "Martha Jefferson and the American Revolution in Virginia." In *Children and Youth in a New Nation,* edited by James Marten, 29–47. New York: New York University Press, 2009.

———. *Martha Jefferson Randolph, Daughter of Monticello: Her Life and Times.* Chapel Hill: University of North Carolina Press, 2012.

Kilbride, Daniel P. "Cultivation, Conservatism, and the Early National Gentry: The Manigault Family and Their Circle." *Journal of the Early Republic* 19 (1999): 221–56.

Kimball, Marie. "Jefferson in Paris." *North American Review* 248 (Autumn 1939): 73–86.

———. *Jefferson: The Scene of Europe 1784–1789.* New York: Coward-McCann, 1950.

Klepp, Susan E. *Revolutionary Conceptions: Women, Fertility, and Family Limitation in America, 1760–1820.* Chapel Hill: Published for OIEAHC by University of North Carolina Press, 2009.

Kolchin, Peter. *American Slavery 1619–1877.* Rev. ed. New York: Hill and Wang, 1993.

Kroeger, Brooke. *Passing: When People Can't Be Who They Are.* New York: PublicAffairs, 2003.

Kukla, Jon. *Mr. Jefferson's Women.* New York: Alfred A. Knopf, 2007.

Landers, Jane. *Black Society in Spanish Florida.* Urbana.: University of Chicago Press, 1999.

Landes, Joan B. *Women and the Public Sphere in the Age of the French Revolution.* Ithaca: Cornell University Press, 1988.

Lee, Vera. *The Reign of Women in Eighteenth-Century France.* Cambridge, Mass.: Schenkman Publishing Company, 1975.

Lesko, Kathleen M. *Black Georgetown Remembered: A History of Its Black Community from the Founding of "The Town of George" in 1751 to the Present Day.* Washington, D.C.: Georgetown University Press, 1991.

Lewis, Jan. *The Pursuit of Happiness: Family and Values in Jefferson's Virginia.* New York: Cambridge University Press, 1983.

Lewis, Jan, and Peter S. Onuf, eds. *Sally Hemings & Thomas Jefferson: History, Memory, and Civic Culture.* Charlottesville: University Press of Virginia, 1999.

Loesser, Arthur. *Men, Women and Pianos: A Social History.* New York: Simon & Schuster, 1954.

Malone, Dumas. "Polly Jefferson and Her Father." *Virginia Quarterly Review* 7 (January 1931): 81–95.

———. *Jefferson the Virginian.* 6 vols. Boston: Little, Brown and Company, 1948–1981.

McLaughlin, Jack. *Jefferson and Monticello: The Biography of a Builder.* New York: Henry Holt, 1988.

McMaster, John Bach. *A History of the People of the United States: From the Revolution to the Civil War.* New York: D. Appleton and Company, 1914.

McNamara, Jo Ann Kay. *Sisters in Arms: Catholic Nuns Through Two Millennia.* Cambridge, Mass.: Harvard University Press, 1996.

Mires, Charlene. *Independence Hall in American Memory.* Philadelphia: University of Pennsylvania Press, 2002.

Morgan, Edmund. *American Slavery, American Freedom: The Ordeal of Colonial Virginia.* New York: W. W. Norton, 1975.

Morley, Jefferson. *Snow-Storm in August: Washington City, Francis Scott Key, and the Forgotten Race Riot of 1835.* New York: Doubleday, 2012.

Nash, Gary B. *Forging Freedom: The Formation of Philadelphia's Black Community.* Cambridge, Mass.: Harvard University Press, 1988.

Nash, Gary B., and Jean R. Soderlund. *Freedom by Degrees: Emancipation in Pennsylvania and Its Aftermath.* New York: Oxford University Press, 1991.

Nash, Margaret A. "Rethinking Republican Motherhood: Benjamin Rush and the Young Ladies Academy of Philadelphia." *Journal of the Early Republic* 17 (Summer 1997): 171–91.

Neiman, Fraser D. "Coincidence or Causal Connection? The Relationship between Thomas Jefferson's Visits to Monticello and Sally Hemings's Conceptions." *William and Mary Quarterly* 57 (January 2000): 198–210.

O'Brien, Michael. *Rethinking the South: Essays in Intellectual History.* Baltimore and London: Johns Hopkins University Press, 1988.

Onuf, Peter S., ed. *Jeffersonian Legacies.* Charlottesville: University Press of Virginia, 1993.

———. "The Scholars' Jefferson." *William and Mary Quarterly* 50 (October 1993): 671–99.

Patterson, Orlando. *Slavery and Social Death: A Comparative Study.* Cambridge, Mass.: Harvard University Press, 1982.

Pybus, Cassandra. *Epic Journeys of Freedom: Runaway Slaves of the American Revolution and Their Global Quest for Liberty.* Boston: Beacon Press, 2006.

Rapley, Elizabeth. *A Social History of the Cloister: Daily Life in the Teaching Monasteries of the Old Regime.* Montreal: McGill-Queen's University Press, 2001.

Reps, John W. *Washington on View: The Nation's Capital Since 1790.* Chapel Hill: University of North Carolina Press, 1991.

Rice, Howard C. *Thomas Jefferson's Paris.* Princeton: Princeton University Press, 1976.

Rothman, Joshua D. *Notorious in the Neighborhood: Sex and Families Across the Color Line in Virginia, 1787–1861.* Chapel Hill: University of North Carolina Press, 2003.

Rousseau, François. *Histoire de L'Abbaye de Pentemont depuis sa translation à Paris jusqu'a la revolution,* Société de l'Histoire de Paris et de l'Ile-de-France 45 (1918): 171–227.

Rousselot, Paul. *Histoire de L'Abbaye de Pentemont.* 1883. Reprint, New York: Burt Franklin, 1971.

Russell, Kathy, Midge Wilson, and Ronald Hall. *The Color Complex: The Politics of Skin Color Among African Americans.* New York: Doubleday, 1992.

Ryan, Mary P. *Cradle of the Middle Class: The Family in Oneida County New York, 1790–1865.* Cambridge: Cambridge University Press, 1981.

Scharff, Virginia. *The Women Jefferson Loved.* New York: HarperCollins, 2010.

Schlossberg, Linda, and María Carla Sánchez, eds. *Passing: Identity and Interpretation in Sexuality, Race, and Religion.* New York: New York University Press, 2001.

Schwartz, Marie Jenkins. *Born in Bondage: Growing up Enslaved in the Antebellum South.* Cambridge, Mass.: Harvard University Press, 2000.

Scranton, Philip. *Proprietary Capitalism: The Textile Manufacture at Philadelphia, 1800–1885.* Cambridge: Cambridge University Press, 1983.

Shackelford, George Green. *Jefferson's Adoptive Son: The Life of William Short, 1759–1848.* Lexington: University Press of Kentucky, 1993.

———. *Thomas Jefferson's Travels in Europe, 1784–1789.* Baltimore: Johns Hopkins University Press, 1995.

Shulman, Holly Cowan. "History, Memory, and Dolley Madison." In *The Queen of America: Mary Cutts's Life of Dolley Madison,* edited by Catherine Allgor. Charlottesville: University of Virginia Press, 2012.

Sobel, Mechal. *The World They Made Together: Black and White Values in Eighteenth-Century Virginia.* Princeton: Princeton University Press, 1987.

Sonnet, Martine. *L'Éducation des filles au temps des Lumières.* Paris: Les Editions du Cerf, 1987.

Sorensen, Leni. "Taking Care of Themselves: Food Production at Monticello," *Repast* 21 (2) (2005): 4–5.

Spain, Daphne. *Gendered Spaces.* Chapel Hill: University of North Carolina Press, 1992.

Spencer, Samia I. "Women and Education." In *French Women and the Age of Enlightenment,* edited by Samia I. Spencer, 83–96. Bloomington: Indiana University Press, 1984.

Spruill, Julia Cherry. *Women's Life and Work in the Southern Colonies.* 1938. Reprint, New York: W. W. Norton, 1998.

Stabile, Susan M. *Memory's Daughters: The Material Culture of Remembrance in Eighteenth-Century America.* Ithaca: Cornell University Press, 2004.

Stanton, Lucia. *"Those Who Labor for My Happiness": Slavery at Thomas Jefferson's Monticello.* Charlottesville: University of Virginia Press, 2012.

Stewart, Robert G. *Robert Edge Pine: A British Portrait Painter in America, 1784–1788.* Washington, D.C.: Smithsonian Institution Press, 1979.

Stoner, Gregory Harkcom. "Politics and Personal Life in the Era of Revolution," M.A. thesis, Virginia Commonwealth University, 2006.

Stuart, Andrea. *The Rose of Martinique: A Life of Napoleon's Josephine.* New York: Grove Press, 2003.

Sweet, Frank W. *Legal History of the Color Line: The Notion of Invisible Blackness.* Palm Coast, Fl.: Backintyme, 2005.

Taylor, Elizabeth Dowling. *A Slave in the White House: Paul Jennings and the Madisons.* New York: Palgrave Macmillan, 2012.

Treckel, Paula A. "Breastfeeding and Maternal Sexuality in Colonial America." *Journal of Interdisciplinary History* 20 (Summer 1989): 25–51.

Trouille, Mary Seidman. *Sexual Politics in the Enlightenment: Women Writers Read Rousseau.* Albany: State University of New York Press, 1997.

Waddy, Patricia. *Seventeenth-Century Roman Palaces: Use and the Art of the Plan.* Cambridge, Mass.: MIT Press, 1990.

Warner, Judith. "The Opt-Out Generation Wants Back In." *New York Times,* August 7, 2013.

Weigert, Roger Armand. "Un centenaire. Le temple de Pentemont, 1846–1946." *Bulletin de la Société de l'Histoire du Protestantisme Français* 94 (January–March 1947): 13–32.

Weigley, Russell F., ed. *Philadelphia: A 300-Year History.* New York: W. W. Norton, 1982.

Weisman, Leslie Kanes. *Discrimination by Design: A Feminist Critique of the Man-Made Environment.* Urbana: University of Illinois Press, 1992.

Welter, Barbara. "Cult of True Womanhood, 1820–1860." *American Quarterly* 18 (2) (1966): 151–74.

Wenger, Mark R. "Thomas Jefferson, Tenant." *Winterthur Portfolio* 26 (Winter 1991): 249–65.

Westcott, Thompson. *The Historic Mansions and Buildings of Philadelphia, with Some Notice of Their Owners and Occupants.* Philadelphia: Porter & Coates, 1877.

White, Deborah Gray. *Ain't I a Woman? Female Slaves in the Plantation South.* New York: W. W. Norton, 1999.

Wiencek, Henry. *An Imperfect God: George Washington, His Slaves, and the Creation of America.* New York: Farrar, Straus and Giroux, 2003.

———. *Master of the Mountain: Thomas Jefferson and His Slaves.* New York: Farrar, Straus and Giroux, 2012.

Wilentz, Sean. *Chants Democratic: New York City and the Rise of the American Working Class, 1788–1850.* New York: Oxford University Press, 1984.

Winterer, Caroline. *Mirror of Antiquity: American Women and the Classical Tradition, 1750–1900.* Ithaca: Cornell University Press, 2007.

Wise, Jennings Cropper. *Col. John Wise of England and Virginia (1617–1695): His Ancestors and Descendants.* Richmond, Va.: Bell Brooks and Stationary Company, 1918.

Wolf, Eva Sheppard. *Race and Liberty in the New Nation: Emancipation in Virginia from the Revolution to Nat Turner's Rebellion.* Baton Rouge: Louisiana State University Press, 2006.

Woloch, Nancy. *Women and the American Experience.* 4th ed. New York: McGraw-Hill, 2006.

Wood, Peter H. *Black Majority: Negroes in Colonial South Carolina from 1670 Through the Stono Rebellion.* New York: Alfred A. Knopf, 1974.

Woods, Edgar. *History of Albemarle County Virginia.* Bridgewater, Va.: C. J. Carrier Company, 1900.

Woodward, C. Vann. *The Strange Career of Jim Crow.* 1955. Reprint, New York: Oxford University Press, 2001.

Woody, Thomas. *A History of Women's Education in the United States.* 1929. Reprint, New York: Octagon Books, 1980.

Wright, Esmond. *Franklin of Philadelphia.* Cambridge, Mass.: Harvard University Press, 1986.

Zagarri, Rosemarie. "Morals, Manners, and the Republican Mother." *American Quarterly* 4 (June 1992): 192–215.

———. *Revolutionary Backlash: Women and Politics in the Early American Republic.* Philadelphia: University of Pennsylvania Press, 2007.

Zujovic, Danica. "A Short History of Pentemont." n.d. Pamphlet printed by the Eglise Réformée, Pariosse de Pentemont, Paris. Howard C. Rice Collection, International Center for Jefferson Studies.

Notes

ABBREVIATIONS USED IN NOTES

AA	Abigail Adams
ACR	Ann Cary Randolph
EWE	Elizabeth Wayles Eppes
EWR	Ellen Wayles Randolph
EWRC	Ellen Wayles (Randolph) Coolidge
Family Letters	*The Family Letters of Thomas Jefferson,* Edwin Morris Betts and James Adam Bear, Jr., eds. (Thomas Jefferson Foundation: University Press of Virginia, 1965)
Farm Book	Edwin Morris Betts, ed., *Thomas Jefferson's Farm Book* (Charlottesville: Thomas Jefferson Memorial Foundation, 1999)
FB	*Farm Book*, facsimile
FLDA	Thomas Jefferson Foundation, Inc., tjrs.monticello.org, 2017, Family Letters, Digital Archive
ICJS	International Center for Jefferson Studies
JWE	John Wayles Eppes
MJE	Maria Jefferson Eppes
MJR	Martha Jefferson Randolph
NARA	National Archives and Records Administration
PGWDE	*Papers of George Washington, Digital Edition,* Theodore J. Crackel, ed. (Charlottesville: University of Virginia Press, Rotunda, 2008)
PTJDE	J. Jefferson Looney and Barbara B. Oberg, eds. *The Papers of Thomas Jefferson, Digital Edition* (Charlottesville: University of Virginia Press, Rotunda, 2008)
SHC	Southern Historical Collection, University of North Carolina
TJ	Thomas Jefferson
TJMB	James A. Bear, Jr., and Lucia C. Stanton, eds., *Jefferson's Memorandum Books: Accounts, with Legal Records and*

Miscellany, 1767–1826, 2 vols. (Princeton: Princeton University Press, 1997)

TJR   Thomas Jefferson Randolph
TMR   Thomas Mann Randolph
ViU   Albert and Shirley Small Special Collections, University of Virginia
VJRT   Virginia Jefferson Randolph Trist

INTRODUCTION

ix   **"news of this change"** Paul Leicester Ford, ed., *The Works of Thomas Jefferson*, vol. 1, *Autobiography* (New York: G.P. Putnam's Sons, 1904–1905), 135. Jefferson also reported this incident to John Jay, TJ to John Jay, 19 July 1789, *PTJDE.*

CHAPTER 1: FIRST MONTICELLO

3   **Although petite, Martha carried** Isaac Granger Jefferson, *Memoirs of a Monticello Slave As Dictated to Charles Campbell In the 1840's by Isaac, one of Thomas Jefferson's Slaves* (Charlottesville: University Press of Virginia, 1951), 19–20; Sarah Nicholas Randolph, *The Domestic Life of Thomas Jefferson* (Charlottesville: University Press of Virginia, 1978), 43.

3   **"intelligence, with benevolence"** Henry S. Randall, *The Life of Thomas Jefferson* (New York: Derby & Jackson, 1858), 1:33–34.

4   **Forced to abandon both their carriage** "Reminiscences of Th[omas]. J[efferson]. by M[artha] R[andolph]," Burke, Randolph, and Trist Family Papers, Acc. 10487, University of Virginia (ViU).

4   **"They arrived late"** Ibid.

4   **They broke out a bottle** Randall, *Jefferson*, 1:45.

4   **"unchequered happiness"** Thomas Jefferson, "Autobiography," 27 July 1821, *Thomas Jefferson Papers*, LOC.

5   **He and Carr made a pact** Randall, *Jefferson*, 1:82–83; Dumas Malone, *Jefferson the Virginian* (Boston: Little, Brown and Company, 1948) 1:161; Randolph, *Domestic Life*, 45.

5   **He named the new tract** Malone, *Jefferson*, 1:17, 19.

5   **By the time he died** Malone, *Jefferson*, 1:31.

5   **"first map of Virginia"** Jefferson, *Memoirs*, quoted in Randolph, *Domestic Life*, 19.

6   **He later returned to Virginia** Susan Kern, *The Jeffersons at Shadwell* (New Haven: Yale University Press, 2010), 44.

6   **"whose name associated itself"** Randolph, *Domestic Life*, 21.

6   **Jane Randolph was proud** Ibid., 18.

6   **From her, Thomas gained his appreciation** Kern, *Jeffersons at Shadwell*, 19–20, 29–40, 54–68, 80.

6   **"To the south"** Randolph, *Domestic Life*, 17–18.

6   **"the Atlantic might be seen"** François La Rochefoucauld-Liancourt, *Travels Through North America, Canada* (London: R. Phillips, 1799).

6   **Slaves, many of them hired** Malone, *Jefferson*, 1:143.

7   **The following year, the dining room** Notes compiled for Monticello Foundation. 2/27/84 "Monticello Building Chronology," copy at International Center for Jefferson Studies, Charlottesville, Virginia (ICJS).

7   **The completion of the dining room** TJ to James Ogilvie, 20 February 1771, *The*

Papers of Thomas Jefferson, Digital Edition, Barbara B. Oberg and J. Jefferson Looney, eds. (Charlottesville: University of Virginia Press, Rotunda, 2008), *PTJDE.*

7   **It is unlikely that these rooms** "Monticello Building Chronology," ICJS.

8   **"good breast of milk"** TJ to Thomas Mann Randolph (TMR), 19 October 1792,
PTJDE.

8   **Shortly thereafter, he bought Ursula's husband** Lucia Stanton, "Free Some Day:
The African American Families of Monticello," in *"Those Who Labor for My Happi-
ness": Slavery at Thomas Jefferson's Monticello* (Charlottesville: University of Virginia
Press, 2012), 118; *FB,* 8; Malone, *Jefferson,* 1:81.

8   **Well nourished, little Martha** Stanton, "Free Some Day," in Stanton, *"Those Who
Labor,"* 118; Annette Gordon-Reed, *The Hemingses of Monticello: An American
Family* (New York: W. W. Norton, 2008), 124.

9   **To meet their insatiable appetite** See Edmund Morgan, *American Slavery, Ameri-
can Freedom: The Ordeal of Colonial Virginia* (New York: W. W. Norton, 1975);
Kathleen M. Brown, *Good Wives, Nasty Wenches, and Anxious Patriarchs: Gender,
Race, and Power in Colonial Virginia* (Chapel Hill: Published for OIEAHC by
University of North Carolina Press, 1996).

9   **The representatives, called burgesses** William Waller Hening, *Statutes at Large:
Being a Collection of All the Laws in Virginia from the First Session of the Legislature
in 1619,* vols. 1 and 2. Transcribed for the Internet by Freddie L. Spradlin.

9   **"act on the casual killing of slaves"** Hening, *Statutes.*

10 **Of course, many of the lawbreakers** Brown, *Good Wives, Nasty Wenches, Anxious
Patriarchs,* chapters 4 and 6.

10 **With the exception of a handful** Virginia Scharff, *The Women Jefferson Loved* (New
York: HarperCollins, 2010), 104–5.

11 **Ursula was even worth** Scharff, *Women Jefferson Loved,* 96.

11 **Her nursing efforts notwithstanding** *TJMB,* 1:341.

11 **Instead the market crashed** Gordon-Reed, *Hemingses,* 57–76.

11 **To Martha he left eleven** Gordon-Reed, *Hemingses,* 72.

12 **"A Roll of the proper Slaves"** *FB,* 5–19.

13 **"substitute for a wife"** John Hartwell Cocke, Diaries, 23 April 1859, Cocke Family
Papers, Acc. 640, ViU.

13 **Elizabeth Hemings was light-skinned** Jefferson, *Memoirs of a Monticello Slave,* 10.

13 **In the relationship that would last** This story is recounted in Gordon-Reed,
Hemingses, chapter 2.

13 **White Virginia women** Scharff, *Women Jefferson Loved,* 264.

13 **In his will** John Wayle's will, 15 April 1760, in *Tyler's Quarterly Historical and Genealogical Magazine* 6 (1924–1925): 269.

13 **She may have been relieved** At her deathbed, Martha extracted a promise from
Jefferson that he would never remarry, telling him that she "could not die happy if
she thought her four children were ever to have a stepmother brought in over
them." Hamilton W. Pierson, *Jefferson at Monticello: The Private Life of Thomas Jefferson from Entirely New Materials* (1862; repr., Stratford, N.H.: Ayer Company,
1971), 107.

13 **Less than a year after** Fawn M. Brodie, *Thomas Jefferson: An Intimate History* (New
York: Bantam Books, 1974), 149–50.

14 **"I have never received"** TJ to Francis Eppes, 7 November 1775, *PTJDE.*

14 **"is perfectly recover'd"** Francis Eppes to TJ, 3 July 1776, *PTJDE.*

14 **The despairing parents never** Jack McLaughlin, *Jefferson and Monticello: The Biography of a Builder* (New York: Henry Holt, 1988), 196–97.

14 **Martha endured far worse** Darcy R. Fryer, "Mortality in the Colonial Period," in *Encyclopedia of American History: Colonization and Settlement, 1608 to 1760,* eds. Billy G. Smith and Gary B. Nash, rev. ed., vol. 2 (New York: Facts on File, 2009).

15 **But her final pregnancy** Scharff, *Women Jefferson Loved,* 145.

15 **Jefferson's account book records** Scharff, *Women Jefferson Loved,* 93–94; 108; 113; 116–17; 124–26; 144–45.

15 **But it is unclear who** Scharff, *Women Jefferson Loved,* 130–31.

15 **Another period of silence follows** *TJMB,* 1:513.

16 **"in ten minutes not a white man"** Jefferson, *Memoirs of a Monticello Slave,* 7.

16 **Reunited with his family** Scharff, *Women Jefferson Loved,* 138.

16 **"all my barns"** TJ to Dr. William Gordon, 16 July 1788, *PTJDE.* Jefferson exaggerated; only eighteen slaves fled to the British, hoping for freedom. Cassandra Pybus, *Epic Journeys of Freedom: Runaway Slaves of the American Revolution and Their Global Quest for Liberty* (Boston: Beacon Press, 2006), 48–49.

17 **Perhaps that omission indicates** Cynthia A. Kierner, *Martha Jefferson Randolph, Daughter of Monticello: Her Life and Times* (Chapel Hill: University of North Carolina Press, 2012), 23, 28.

17 **"mild and amiable wife"** Marquis de Chastellux, *Travels in North America, in the Years 1780, 1781, and 1782* (Dublin: Colles, Moncrieffe, White, 1787), 2:45.

17 **Indeed, extended visits among** Kierner, *Martha Jefferson Randolph,* 23.

17 **Certainly it did not harbor** It is also possible that Martha Jefferson suffered her 1776 miscarriage at Monticello, although I think it more likely that, since she was experiencing problems with that pregnancy, she would have relied on her sister's care at The Forest and gone to Elk Hill for her recuperation the next week. Francis Eppes to TJ, 3 July 1776, *PTJDE.*

18 **Scholars have missed this point** Kierner, *Martha Jefferson Randolph,* 26–27; Scharff, *Women Jefferson Loved,* 284, 315.

18 **In any event, in this period** Thomas Anburey, *Travels through the Interior Parts of America* vol. 2, (1789; repr., Boston: Houghton Mifflin Company, 1923), 184; Catherine Kerrison, *Claiming the Pen: Women and Intellectual Life in the Early American South* (Ithaca: Cornell University Press, 2006).

18 **"in all respects"** Jacob Rubseman, 1 December 1780, *PTJDE.*

18 **girls were taught** Kerrison, *Claiming the Pen,* 14–15.

18 **"considerable powers of conversation"** Quoted in Kierner, *Martha Jefferson Randolph,* 27.

19 **"worth and abilities"** TJ to James Madison, 26 November 1782, *PTJDE.*

19 **For his part, the Marquis** Randolph, *Domestic Life,* 59.

19 **"during my Mother's life"** MJR, "Reminiscences of Th. J.," Acc. 10487, ViU.

19 **"a plan of female education"** TJ to Nathaniel Burwell, Monticello, 14 March 1818, *Thomas Jefferson Papers,* LOC.

19 **In other words, Jefferson described** Jon Kukla, *Mr. Jefferson's Women* (New York: Alfred A. Knopf, 2007), 172–77.

19 **But it is also clear** James Bear, "Jefferson's Advice to His Children and Grandchildren on Their Reading" (pamphlet: Rector and Visitors of the University of Virginia Tracy W. McGregor Library, 1967), 1.

19 **Martha Jefferson Carr** Malone, *Jefferson,* 1:431.

20 **The arrival of Martha Jefferson Carr's** Cynthia Kierner emphasized Jefferson's influence in this period. Cynthia Kierner, "Martha Jefferson and the American Revolution in Virginia," in *Children and Youth in a New Nation,* ed. James Marten (New York: New York University Press, 2009), 30.

20   "**taken my final leave**" TJ to Edmund Randolph, 16 September 1781, *PTJDE*.

20   **Ten-year-old Sam Carr** TJ to Overton Carr, 16 March 1782. Overton Carr was the brother of the deceased Dabney Carr. *PTJDE*.

20   **Martha may well have sat** Hunter Dickinson Farish, ed., *Journal and Letters of Philip Vickers Fithian: A Plantation Tutor of the Old Dominion, 1773–1774*, 5th ed. (Charlottesville: University Press of Virginia, 1993).

21   "**For the last four months**" MJR, "Reminiscences of Th. J.," Acc. 10487, ViU.

21   "**Mrs. Jefferson had been too ill**" Sarah Nicholas Randolph, "Mrs. Thomas Mann Randolph," in *Worthy Women of Our First Century*, eds. Agnes Irwin and Sarah Butler Wister (Philadelphia: Lippincott,1877), 10.

21   "**A moment before the closing scene**" MJR, "Reminiscences of Th. J.," Acc. 10487, ViU.

21   "**He kept to his room**" Ibid.

Chapter 2: To Paris

23   **Determined to remain in Virginia** TJ to George Nicholas, 28 July 1781, *PTJDE;* TJ to Thomas McKean, 4 August 1781, *PTJDE;* TJ to Edmund Randolph, 16 September 1781, *PTJDE*.

23   "**All the reasons**" Editors' note, From Robert Livingston, Enclosing Jefferson's Appointment as Peace Commissioner, 13 November 1782, *PTJDE*.

24   **Just as faithfully** Randall, *Jefferson*, 1:384; Kierner, *Martha Jefferson Randolph*, 36–37; Jefferson, *Memoirs of a Monticello Slave*, 11; Gordon-Reed, *Hemingses*, 137.

24   **After visiting them there** *TJMB*, 1:523, 30 October 1782, "Pd. A guide to Eppington 6/8."

24   **Familiar with the Suttons' methods** Gordon-Reed, *Hemingses*, 215–21.

25   "**From the calculations**" TJ to James Madison, 26 November 1782, *PTJDE*.

25   "**My only object now**" TJ to Marquis de Chastellux, 26 November 1782, *PTJDE*.

25   **On December 2** *TJMB*, 1:524.

25   **It was not Robert's first trip** Gordon-Reed, *Hemingses*, 214.

25   **Jefferson and Martha then made** TJ to [Anne-César] Chevalier de LaLuzerne, 7 February 1783, *PTJDE;* TJ to John Jay, 11 April 1783, *PTJDE;* Malone, *Jefferson*, 1:399.

25   **Three weeks later** TJ to John Jay, 11 April 1783, *PTJDE*.

25   **Finally, in early April 1783** Robert R. Livingston to TJ, 4 April 1783, *PTJDE*.

26   **Formally released by Congress** TJ to Robert R. Livingston, 4 April 1783, *PTJDE*.

26   **Did Martha look wistfully** *TJMB*, 1:531.

27   **In the meantime, two popular novels** TJ to François de Barbé-Marbois, 5 December 1783, *PTJDE*.

27   **As one historian observed** Rhys Isaac, "The First Monticello," in *Jeffersonian Legacies*, ed. Peter S. Onuf (Charlottesville: University Press of Virginia, 1993), 102.

27   **He had written to John Jay** TJ to John Jay, 3 January 1783, *PTJDE*.

27   "**I will ask the favor**" TJ to James Madison, 31 August 1783, *PTJDE*.

27   **Dislocated yet again** Kierner, *Martha Jefferson Randolph*, 42.

27   **Eliza Trist agreed** James Madison to TJ, 30 September 1783, *PTJDE*.

27   **On November 19** *TJMB*, 1:539.

27   **In accordance with Jefferson's wishes** TJ to MJR, 28 November 1783, Betts and Bear, *Family Letters*, 19.

27   **Her father had hired** Kierner, *Martha Jefferson Randolph*, 43.

28 **"The conviction that you would"** TJ to MJR, 28 November 1783, Betts and Bear, *Family Letters*, 19.

28 **Letters flew from Baltimore** Kerrison, *Claiming the Pen*, 164–69.

28 **"the many happy hours"** Rebecca Frazier to Anna Hopkinson Coale, 24 November 1790. Redwood Collection, MS 1530, Maryland Historical Society.

29 **"Disregard those foolish predictions"** TJ to MJR, 11 December 1783, Betts and Bear, *Family Letters*, 21.

29 **"consider . . . as your mother."** TJ to MJR, 28 November 1783, Betts and Bear, *Family Letters*, 19; Kierner, *Martha Jefferson Randolph*, 41, 44.

29 **"danced out the old Year"** Francis Hopkinson to TJ, 4 January 1784, *PTJDE*.

29 **"I have the Pleasure"** Ibid.

31 **"whose trade it is"** Malone, *Jefferson*, 1:406–9, quoting Jefferson, "Autobiography."

31 **Certainly Francis Hopkinson's five children** TJ to MJR, 15 January 1784, Betts and Bear, *Family Letters*, 23.

31 **"They would be more valued"** TJ to Francis Hopkinson, 14 August 1786, *PTJDE*.

32 **John Jay was returning** Malone, *Jefferson*, 1:418–19; TJ to William Short, 30 April 1784, *PTJDE*.

32 **By the twenty-eighth of May** Robert Hemings, who had been with Jefferson as his valet, also traveled to Boston but was sent home by Jefferson. Gordon-Reed, *Hemingses*, 160.

32 **He lodged Martha** Kierner, *Martha Jefferson Randolph*, 48–49.

33 **"all of whom papa knew"** MJR to Eliza House Trist, [August 1785], *PTJDE*.

33 **"The vaunted scene of Europe"** TJ to Charles Bellini, 30 September 1785, *PTJDE*.

33 **And as he watched the ship** Gordon-Reed, *Hemingses*, 160.

34 **"threw every day"** *TJMB*, 1:557, quoting *The Memoirs of Baron Thiébault*, trans. Arthur John Butler (New York: Macmillan, 1896), 1:44.

34 **At last, they crossed** See Hubert Robert's painting, *The Opening of the Pont de Neuilly*, with Jefferson's comment in William Howard Adams, *The Paris Years of Thomas Jefferson* (New Haven: Yale University Press, 1997), 80. An engineering marvel, the bridge is dwarfed by the skyscrapers of La Defense today. Howard C. Rice, *Thomas Jefferson's Paris* (Princeton: Princeton University Press, 1976), 108.

34 **"a perfect garden"** MJR to Eliza House Trist, [August 1785], *PTJDE*.

35 **There is not a sliver** A crowded Paris street. Balthazar Anton Dunker, illustrator, *Tableau de Paris* (n.p., 1787), in David Garrioch, *The Making of Revolutionary Paris* (Berkeley: University of California Press, 2002), 1, 18–20, 224. My description of Paris draws from Garrioch's.

35 **Less obvious from pictures** Garrioch, *Making of Revolutionary Paris,* 18.

35 **There, neighborhoods such as** Louis-Sébastien Mercier, *Tableau de Paris*, quoted in ibid., 20.

36 **By the time the Jeffersons** Ibid., 219.

36 **Once owned by a younger brother** Ibid., 218.

37 **Close enough for a commute** Ibid., 218; TJ to Buchanan and Hay, 13 August 1785, *PTJDE*.

37 **"appear a monster"** TJ to Virginia Delegates in Congress, 12 July 1785, *PTJDE*.

37 **But the rue Saint Honoré** Rice, *Jefferson's Paris*, 21–23.

37 **They arrived at their lodgings** Adams, *Paris Years of Thomas Jefferson*, 46–47.

37 **The very day they arrived** *TJMB*, 1:557–58.

38 **"there is not a porter"** Abigail Adams to [Cotton Tufts], 8 September 1784, Adams Family Papers, Massachusetts Historical Society. Interestingly, Jefferson

submitted, although he considered the process "an affliction" and was tempted to cut off his hair altogether to avoid it. Ibid.

39 **"I soon got rid of him"** MJR to Eliza House Trist, [after 24 August 1785], *PTJDE.*

39 **the most expensive** "Fourchette des tariffs de pensions pratiqués par les interants payants de 1760 á 1789," Martine Sonnet, *L'Education des filles au temps des Lumières* (Paris: Les Editions du Cerf, 1987), 329.

39 **He had been so impressed** Chastellux, François Jean, Marquis de, *Voyages de M. de le Marquis de Chastellux dans l'Amérique Septentrionale dans les Annés 1780, 1781, & 1782* (Paris: Prault, Imprimeur du Roi, 1786). This book was translated into English the following year.

39 **Such a well-placed advocate** George Green Shackelford, *Thomas Jefferson's Travels in Europe, 1784–1789* (Baltimore: Johns Hopkins University Press, 1995), 172n18.

39 **Martha and Jefferson** The following description is based on author's visit to this site.

41 **Next they were led** Notes of Howard C. Rice of his visit to Panthemont, 11 April 1948, in "Notebook *A*-10: Paris: Left Bank: Faubourg St.-Germain," Howard C. Rice Collection, ICJS.

41 **"I leave you to judge"** MJR to Eliza House Trist, [after August 1785], *PTJDE.*

41 **"the most monstrous article"** MJR to Septimia Randolph, 2 December 1832, Papers of Septimia Anne Cary Randolph Meikleham, Acc. 4726-b, ViU.

42 **Devoted to reforming children's education** Denis Diderot, *La Religieuse* (1760), quoted in Dena Goodman, *Becoming a Woman in the Age of Letters* (Ithaca: Cornell University Press, 2009), 275. On Rousseau and his influence, see Mary Seidman Trouille, *Sexual Politics in the Enlightenment: Women Writers Read Rousseau* (Albany: State University of New York Press, 1997), 30–33; and François Rousseau, *Histoire de L'Abbaye de Pentemont depuis sa translation à Paris jusqu'a la revolution* (Paris, 1918), 37–39. Rousseau describes Panthemont as a worldly institution at which a devotion to feverish gossip rendered "arid" such subjects as grammar and arithmetic.

42 **Revered in European and American culture** Olwen Hufton, *The Prospect Before Her: A History of Women in Western Europe* (New York: Alfred A. Knopf, 1996), 112; Elizabeth Rapley, *A Social History of the Cloister: Daily Life in the Teaching Monasteries of the Old Regime* (Montreal: McGill-Queen's University Press, 2001); Jean Bloch, "Discourses of Female Education in the Writings of Eighteenth-Century French Women," in *Women, Gender and the Enlightenment,* eds. Sarah Knott and Barbara Taylor (2005; repr., New York: Palgrave Macmillan, 2007), 243–44.

43 **As historians have documented** Mita Choudhury, *Convents and Nuns in Eighteenth-Century French Politics and Culture* (Ithaca: Cornell University Press, 2004), 18–19, 134–38; Hufton, *Prospect Before Her,* 112.

43 **The Mother Superior** Choudhury, *Convents and Nuns,* 15–16; Rapley, *Social History of the Cloister,* 119–22.

43 **Martha Jefferson's Panthemont** Sonnet, *L'Éducation des filles,* 27.

43 **A thin soup** Ibid., 285.

44 **Combined with Martha's basic tuition** Gordon-Reed, *Hemingses,* 180. Currency conversions from the eighteenth century are inexact and do not convey their buying power in a particular time and place. I followed the method at hornworld .me/2010/08/19/how-much-did-haydn-earn.

44 **These differences mattered little** Sonnet, *L'Éducation des filles,* 285–87; Goodman, *Becoming a Woman,* 74.

44 **The dismal state** Sonnet's *L'Éducation des filles* is the most thorough study of convent schools in Paris and much relied upon by scholars of this period.

44   **By 1800, only 27 percent** Dominque Godineau, "The Woman," in *Enlightenment Portraits*, ed. Michel Vovelle and trans. Lydia G. Cochrane (Chicago: University of Chicago Press, 1992), 409.

44   **But there was a deeper** Sonnet, *L'Éducation des filles*, 285–87.

44   **Marie-Catherine de Béthisy de Mézières** Paul Rousselot, *Histoire de L'Abbaye de Pentemont* (1883; repr., New York: Burt Franklin, 1971), 17.

45   **Founded in 1217** Danica Zujovic, "A Short History of Pentemont" (n.d., pamphlet printed by the Eglise Réformée, Pariosse de Pentemont), 1, Howard C. Rice Collection, copy at ICJS.

45   **"I must admit"** 26 March 1781. Translated in ibid., 3. *"Je vous avoue que j'ai été fort surpris d'y lire que vous comptiez sur un secours, de la part de la Commission, de 60 000 livres, et que votre confiance, à ce sujet, était si assurée que vous alliez, en conséquence, prendre des arrangements avec vos créanciers."* Quoted in Rousselot, *Histoire de L'Abbaye de Pentemont*, 36.

45   **She successfully recruited** Roger Armand Weigert, "Un centenaire. Le temple de Pentemont, 1846–1946," *Bulletin de la Société de l'Histoire du Protestantisme Français* 94 (January–March 1947): 13–32, 15–20. Howard C. Rice Collection, ICJS.

46   **master over all** Dumas Malone, "Polly Jefferson and her Father," *Virginia Quarterly Review* 7 (January 1931): 81.

CHAPTER 3: SCHOOL LIFE

47   **"spoke very little French"** MJR to Eliza House Trist, [after August 1785], *PTJDE*. This is the only letter Martha Jefferson wrote describing her life in Paris.

47   **"I am very happy"** Ibid.

48   **"really great difficulty"** MJR to TJ, 27 May 1787, Betts and Bear, *Family Letters*, 42.

48   **The Abbess allowed her father** MJR, "Reminiscences of Th. J.," Acc. 10487, ViU.

48   **"four rooms exceedingly large"** MJR to Eliza House Trist, [after August 1785], *PTJDE*.

48   **Panthemont, on the other hand** Sonnet, *L'Éducation des filles*, 59.

48   **In fact, as she told** *Journal and Correspondence of Miss Adams, Daughter of John Adams, Second President of the United States, Written in France and England in 1785*, ed. by her daughter (New York: Wily and Putnam, 1841), 27.

49   **"great entertainment"** Judith Randolph to MJ, 12 February 1785, Trist Papers, Acc. 2104, Southern Historical Collection, University of North Carolina (SHC).

49   **When Julia arrived** JA[nnesley] to MJR, 20 April 1786, Papers of the Randolph Family of Edgehill, Acc. 1397, ViU; Ann Lucas Birle and Lisa A. Francavilla, eds., *Thomas Jefferson's Granddaughter in Queen Victoria's England* (Boston and Charlottesville: Massachusetts Historical Society and Thomas Jefferson Foundation, 2012), 151. Arthur Annesley was first Earl of Mountnorris and eighth Viscount Valentia.

49   **"I will first give you"** JA[nnesley] to MJR, 27 April 1786, Acc. 1397, ViU.

50   **Martha would preserve** Martha Jefferson's List of Schoolmates, n.d., Acc. 5385-I, ViU.

50   **They were the nieces** Birle and Francavilla, *Thomas Jefferson's Granddaughter*, 164. He would later be more notorious for his liaison with Georgiana, Duchess of Devonshire.

50   **They would write** Elizabeth Tufton to MJR, 21 March 1790, Acc. 1397, ViU.

50   **"I shall be indulged"** MJR to Bettie Hawkins, March 1789, Acc. 1397, ViU.

50   **"Give me a description"** B[ettie] Hawkins to MJR, n.d., Acc. 1397, ViU.

51   **"always wild, your petticoat dragging"** Marie de Botidoux to MJR, 31 October 1798, Acc. 5385-aa, ViU.

51   **"held back for twenty years"** Ibid., 1798; 12 March 1790; 1 May 1790; 4 October 1809.

51   **Included in the three thousand** Rice, *Thomas Jefferson's Paris*, 65; Sonnet, *L'Éducation des filles*, 47.

52   **"pretty well"** MJR to TJ, Paris, 27 May 1787; MJR to TJ, 8 March 1787, in Betts and Bear, *Family Letters*, 42, 32.

53   **"The only kind of needlework"** MJR to TJ, 9 April 1787, in ibid., 37–38.

53   **Jefferson had told her** TJ to MJR, 6 March 1786, in ibid., 30.

53   **Martha Jefferson's copy** Nöel Antoine Pluche, *Nature Display'd. Being Discourses on such Particulars of Natural History as Were Thought Proper to Excite the Curiosity, and Form the Minds of Youth. Containing What belongs to Man Considered in Society*, vols. 1, 3, 5, 6, 7 (London: 1750). Jefferson had books sent to him in Paris from England, so it is certainly possible that Martha read this while in Paris. Kevin J. Hayes, *The Road to Monticello: The Life and Mind of Thomas Jefferson* (New York: Oxford University Press, 2008), 284. It is also possible that she read the work in its original French (Jefferson owned a French edition) and later obtained the English translation for her own children. Either way, she read the work and thought it valuable enough to teach them.

53   **Her French grammar book** Charles François Lhomond, *Grammaire de Lhomond: Éléments de la grammaire françoise*, 1780. Other inscriptions reveal the book's subsequent history: M Randolph [Martha's signature when married] Monticello/Virginia Randolph/Monticello/Martha Jefferson Trist.

53   **She read Alain Lesage's** TJ to François de Barbé-Marbois, 5 December 1783, *PTJDE*.

53   **And she relished** Jean-Pierre Claris de Florian, *Oeuvres de Florian: Galatee, Roman Pastoral* (Paris: 1785). Inscribed, "À Mademoiselle Jefferson"; also: "M. Randolph/ Monticello; Cornelia J. Randolph/Monticello." La Fayette, Marie-Madeleine Pioche de La Vergne, Comtesse de, *Ouevres de La Fayette: Zayde, histoire Espagnole, precedee d'un traite sur l'origine des Romans*, vols. 1–3 (Amsterdam: 1786). Inscribed, "M. Randolph/Monticello."

53   **"Are you still reading"** B. Hawkins to MJR, [1788 or 1789], Acc. 1397, ViU.

53   **She was introduced** Madame de Genlis, *Théâtre à l'usage de jeunes personnes* [Theater for the use of young people]; Antoine Denis Bailly, *Dictionnaire poetique de Bailly* (Paris: 1782). Martha's copy is inscribed, "MJRandolph, Edgehill." *Le Rime di Francesco Petrarca* (London: 1784). Inscriptions show that both TJ and Martha read this work.

54   **To perfect the art** Goodman, *Becoming a Woman*, 53. "The art of making extracts" and reading Sévigné's letters were a staple of French girls' education. Rousselot, *Histoire de l'education des femmes en France*, vol. 2, 147.

54   **"I am going to say"** Marie de Botidoux to MJR, 2 January 1790, Acc. 5385-aa, ViU. See Goodman, *Becoming a Woman*, 149–50, for an extract of Madame de Sévigné's letter breathlessly conveying momentous news from court.

54   **Because Martha left us** Sonnet, *L'Éducation des filles*, 27.

54   **One of its students** Quoted in ibid., 212. This described the day of Hélène Massalska, age six to ten, rather than Martha Jefferson, but its overall contours are similar.

55   **"reading and writing"** This school's students were trained as well in "double-entry

bookkeeping, receipts and expense accounts; and weights and measures of different countries," suggesting a somewhat different clientele than Panthemont's nobility. "Etat et conditions de la pension pour les jeunes demoiselles, relativement à l'éducation complette qu'on continue de leur donner dans le couvent des religieuses Angloises, à liège" (1770). I am grateful to Sally Mason, Omohundro Institute of Early American History and Culture, for providing a copy of this document.

55 **At Liège** Goodman, *Becoming a Woman,* 67.

55 **These comparable elite schools** Recent scholarship supports this picture of elite education. See Rapley, *Social History of the Cloister,* 236–38; Samia I. Spencer, "Women and Education," in *French Women and the Age of Enlightenment,* ed. Samia Spencer (Bloomington: Indiana University Press, 1984), 84–85.

55 **Following the lead** Weigert, "Un centenaire. Le temple de Pentemont," 19–20. See also, Rousselot, *Histoire de Pentemont,* 37–38.

55 **"This good woman"** Quoted in Choudhury, *Convents and Nuns,* 135.

55 **Indeed, some have thought** Bloch, "Mme Roland de la Platière," in *Women, Gender, and the Enlightenment,* Knott and Taylor, eds., 746.

55 **"Titus Livius puts me"** MJR to TJ, 25 March 1787, 27 May 1787, and 8 March 1787, in Betts and Bear, *Family Letters,* 33, 42, 32.

55 **But her letters** MJR to Eliza House Trist, Paris, [after August 1785], *PTJDE.*

56 **"*Priests* can't marry"** J. Annesley to MJR, 20 April 1786, Acc. 1397, ViU.

56 **"I remember her"** Madame de Staël to TJ, 25 April 1807. Marie G. Kimball, "Unpublished Correspondence of Mme. De Staël with Thomas Jefferson," *The North American Review* 208, no. 752 (July 1918): 64.

56 **For both serious scholars** This is the main argument of Dena Goodman's *Becoming a Woman.*

56 **The solution** Ibid., 15.

56 **In fact, so standardized** Photographed in Goodman, *Becoming a Woman,* 107.

57 **"little nothings"** Ibid., 6, 269.

57 **"The need to write"** Ibid., 264.

57 **"Tell me who are friends"** Bettie Hawkins to MJR, n.d., Acc.1397, ViU.

57 **"Tell me all about her"** Bettie Hawkins Curzon to MJR, [1789], Acc. 1397, ViU.

58 **"I am grateful"** Gabrielle D'Harcourt to MJR, [1789], in "Jefferson Quotes & Family Letters," FLDA.

58 **"your lady ship stands much"** Bettie Hawkins to MJR, [1788], Acc. 1397. ViU. None of Martha's letters to her schoolmates have been located.

58 **"had as many steps"** MJR to Eliza House Trist, [after August 1785], *PTJDE.*

59 **"The abbess in charge"** Letter of Jean Armand Tronchin, 10 March 1788, translated in Marie Kimball, *Jefferson: The Scene of Europe 1784–1789* (New York: Coward-McCann, 1950), 13–14.

59 **"there are in it"** TJ to Mary Jefferson Bolling, 23 July 1787, *PTJDE.*

59 **The Jeffersons had not been** MJR to Eliza House Trist, [after August 1785], *PTJDE.* For a description of the ceremony, held on 14 October 1784, see *Journal and Correspondence of Miss Adams,* 23–27.

60 **"impossible to describe"** *Journal and Correspondence of Miss Adams,* 24–25.

60 **"fine, white woolen dresses"** Ibid., 26–27.

60 **At nineteen, Nabby Adams** Abigail Adams had confessed her "false prejudices" about the convent to Jefferson when she expressed her concern about his plan to lodge the lively Maria at Panthemont with her sister. AA to TJ, 10 September 1787. Lester J. Cappon, ed., *The Adams-Jefferson Letters* (1956; repr., Chapel Hill: University of North Carolina Press, 1987), 197.

60 **But Nabby had also** *Journal and Correspondence of Miss Adams,* 26. The memoir of Hélène Massalska, who attended the Abbaye-au-Bois in Paris, describes an identical ceremony there, quoted in Jo Ann Kay McNamara, *Sisters in Arms: Catholic Nuns Through Two Millennia* (Cambridge, Mass.: Harvard University Press, 1996), 537.

62 **The first church building** Hugh Howard and Roger Straus, *Thomas Jefferson, Architect: The Built Legacy of our Third President* (New York: Rizzoli, 2003), 183.

62 **"When do you make abjuration?"** Bettie Hawkins to MJR, n.d., Acc. 1397, ViU.

62 **"seduce[d] Miss Jefferson"** *Morning Post* (London), 16 May 1788. I am grateful to my assistant, Emily Hatcher McCloskey, for locating this notice.

62 **"the earliest intelligence of it"** These quotes come from three undated letters from Bettie Hawkins to Martha Jefferson, although archivists have appended the dates 1788 and 1789 in brackets. Acc. 1397, ViU. With the newspaper notice, it is clear the last dates to 17 May 1788.

62 **A revolt** Sarah Nicholas Randolph, a great-granddaughter of Jefferson, published this story, much told in Jefferson-Randolph family tradition. Randolph, *Domestic Life,* 146. No documentation from either Jefferson or his daughter survives to support it, however. In any event, it was eleven months from the newspaper report to Jefferson's withdrawal of his daughters from the school.

63 **"seems to have great tendencies"** Quoted in Julian P. Boyd, ed., *The Papers of Thomas Jefferson* (Princeton: Princeton University Press, 1950), 14:356.

63 **Marie de Botidoux** Marie de Botidoux to MJR, January 1790, Acc. 5385-aa, ViU.

63 **"At your age"** MJR to Septimia Randolph, 2 December 1832, Acc. 4726-b, ViU. Jefferson assembled a new book he called *The Life and Morals of Jesus of Nazareth* for his use.

64 **As Martha saw in Paris** Rousselot, *Histoire de Pentemont,* 37; Vera Lee, *The Reign of Women in Eighteenth-Century France* (Cambridge, Mass.: Schenkman Publishing Company, 1975), 82.

65 **The Abbess had persuaded** Marcel Fosseyeux, "Une abbesse de Panthémont au XVIII Siècle: Madame de Béthisy de Mézières, 1743–1789," *Revue du Dix-huitième Siècle* 5 (1918), 1–16.

65 **In spite of the abolition** Choudhury, *Convents and Nuns,* 176–83. Choudhury points out the irony of their position, however: "Women religious came to represent the crimes and excesses which some of them had opposed in the eighteenth century."

65 **But it is to say** Natalie Zemon Davis, *Women on the Margins: Three Seventeenth-Century Lives* (Cambridge, Mass.: Harvard University Press, 1995). See particularly Marie de l'Incarnation.

65 **As we have seen** Marquis de Chastellux to TJ, Paris, 24 August 1784, *PTJDE.*

66 **"entirely at your disposal"** Rice, *Thomas Jefferson's Paris,* 61–62. On the invitation to Versailles, Adrienne de La Fayette to TJ, 26 August 1786, *PTJDE.* On dining at their home, TJ to MJR, 14 June 1787, in Betts and Bear, *Family Letters,* 44. George Shackelford notes that "Patsy's sponsor [at Panthemont] was Comtesse de Brionne, the niece of the Abbess Béthisy de Mézières." Shackelford, *Thomas Jefferson's Travels,* 172n18.

66 **Just blocks away** Anne Cary Morris, ed., *The Diary and Letters of Gouverneur Morris: Minister of the United States to France; Member of the Constitutional Convention, Etc.* (New York: Charles Scribner's Sons, 1888), 1:35–36.

66 **Probably the most brilliant salons** The function and influence of the salons in French culture are an ongoing historiographic debate that is beyond the scope of

this book. My point here is to argue that on all sides, Martha Jefferson saw lively, educated, elite women engaged in conversations with men about all branches of learning. Joan B. Landes, *Women and the Public Sphere in the Age of the French Revolution* (Ithaca: Cornell University Press, 1988).

66   **In her fifties** Kimball, *Jefferson: The Scene of Europe*, 101; Hayes, *Road to Monticello*, 297.

66   **"quite the first salon"** Morris, *The Diary and Letters of Gouverneur Morris*, 188.

67   **Gouverneur Morris** See, for example, ibid., 8, 166.

67   **Young as she was** *Journal and Correspondence of Miss Adams*, 1 September 1784 and again on 9 May 1785, 17 and 74.

67   **Madame Houdetot** "Maria Jefferson Eppes and her Little Son, Francis," by Mrs. Nicholas (Susan) Ware Eppes, ICJS, 9; Madame Houdetot to TJ, 7 July 1789, *PTJDE*.

67   **The affectionate relationship** De Tessé loved British novels and often conducted readings of them in her salon evenings. George Green Shackelford, *Jefferson's Adoptive Son: The Life of William Short, 1759–1848* (University Press of Kentucky, 1993), 24–25.

67   **"You need not dress"** Caroline Tufton to MJR, Wednesday 1 July [1789], FLDA.

67   **"the Dutchess of Devonshire"** Ibid., [1789].

67   **"And beaucoup [a lot]"** Randolph, "Mrs. Thomas Mann Randolph," 20–21.

68   **Jefferson's lodgings** William Short to TJ, 14 March 1788, *PTJDE*.

68   **Kitty (Catherine) Church** TJ to MJR, Paris, 16 June 1788; TJ to MJ, 28 June 1787, in Betts and Bear, *Family Letters*, 44–45. Andrew Burstein, *The Inner Jefferson: Portrait of a Grieving Optimist* (Charlottesville: University Press of Virginia, 1995), 108.

68   **"Make it a rule"** TJ to MJ, 4 November 1786, in Betts and Bear, *Family Letters*, 31.

68   **Martha would have been** *Journal and Correspondence of Miss Adams*, 44, 50.

69   **Sundays featured concerts** Élisabeth Vigée Lebrun quoted in Marie Kimball, "Jefferson in Paris," *North American Review* 248 (Autumn 1939): 73–86. Nabby Adams recorded two January 1785 visits to the Palais Royal: one with her brother, after the theater, and another to meet Anne Bingham. *Journal and Correspondence of Miss Adams*, 39, 44.

69   **"one of the principal ornaments"** TJ to Dr. James Currie, 14 January 1785, *PTJDE*.

69   **She, Caroline and Elizabeth** Marie Ball to MJR, Wednesday [Tuesday?] morning 23 June [1789], FLDA.

69   **Nabby Adams had noticed** *Journal and Correspondence of Miss Adams*, 34.

69   **With its strategic mix** Frederic Masson, quoted in Weigert, *Un Centenaire: Le Temple de Pentemont*, 20. Following Masson, Andrea Stuart argues that Caribbean-born Rose de Beauharnais's sojourn in Panthemont was key to her integration to French society and to polishing the presentation that would one day attract the attentions of Napoléon Bonaparte. Andrea Stuart, *The Rose of Martinique: A Life of Napoleon's Josephine* (New York: Grove Press, 2003), 76–79.

69   **These older women boarders** Zujovic, "Short History of Pentemont," ICJS. This pamphlet includes floor plans for the three floors of the convent and school.

69   **This was a common practice** The separation of boarders from students was also usual. Rapley, *Social History of the Cloister*, 236.

69   **A former student** Jeanne-Louise-Henriette Campan, quoted in Fosseyeux, "Une abbesse de Panthemont," 5. See also Lee, *The Reign of Women*, 7; Sonnet, *L'Éducation des filles*, 27.

70   **"if every husband"** MJR to TJ, 9 April 1787, Betts and Bear, *Family Letters*, 37–38.

70 **She was very much** Rousselot, *Histoire de Pentemont,* 39; Samia I. Spencer, "Women and Education," 86; Goodman, *Becoming a Woman,* 78.

70 **Three princesses** *Journal and Correspondence of Miss Adams,* 27; Sonnet, *L'Éducation des filles,* 96; Maria (Polly) Jefferson joined her sister in the summer of 1787.

71 **"for fear of taking"** MJR to TJ, 25 March 1787, in Betts and Bear, *Family Letters,* 33.

71 **Some thought** MJR to TJ, 8 March 1787 and 3 May 1787, in Betts and Bear, *Family Letters,* 32, 39.

71 **"demon of democracy"** Botidoux to MJR, 4 November 1789; 4 December 1789, Acc. 1397, ViU.

71 **Pensionnaires were allowed** MJR to TJ, 9 April 1787, in Betts and Bear, *Family Letters,* 37.

71 **"Know exactly"** TJ to MJR, 16 June 1788, in Betts and Bear, *Family Letters,* 44–45.

71 **The daughter of the Duc** Rousselot, *Histoire de L'Abbaye de Pentemont,* 38.

72 **"I think we are kept"** J[ulia] Annesley to MJR, 20 April 1786, Acc. 1397, ViU.

72 **Nevertheless, within a year** MJR to Eliza House Trist, [after 25 August 1785], *PTJDE.*

72 *"Ah! Mais vraiment"* Randolph, "Mrs. Thomas Mann Randolph," 17–18.

CHAPTER 4: FAMILIES REUNITED

73 **"had we met with her"** TJ to Elizabeth Wayles Eppes (EWE), 28 July 1787, *PTJDE.*

73 **The warmth of the day** *TJMB,* 1:790.

73 **She was undoubtedly wearing** Abigail Adams (AA) to TJ, 10 July 1787, Cappon, *Letters,* 185.

74 **"As she had left"** AA to TJ, 6 July 1787, Cappon, *Letters,* 183.

74 **Or perhaps the Virginia** Gordon-Reed, *Hemingses,* 204–5.

74 **"lying messengers"** TJ to Maria Cosway, 12 October 1786, *PTJDE.*

75 **It was a tie** Burstein, *Inner Jefferson,* 79–85; Kukla, *Mr. Jefferson's Women,* 98–103.

75 **"What she thinks"** AA to TJ, 10 July 1787, Cappon, *Letters,* 185.

75 **"reconcile her little Sister"** AA to TJ, 26 June 1787, Cappon, *Letters,* 178.

75 **"When she arrives"** TJ to MJR, 7 April 1787, in Betts and Bear, *Family Letters,* 36.

76 **"render my happiness"** MJR to TJ, 9 April 1787, in ibid., 37.

76 **No portrait was ever** "Account of Mrs. Nicholas Ware Eppes," ICJS.

76 **"beautifull girl"** AA to Mary Smith Cranch, 16 July 1787. *The Adams Papers Digital Edition,* ed. Sara Martin (Charlottesville: University of Virginia Press, Rotunda, 2008–2017).

76 **"lovely Girl"** *Extract from Diary of Nathaniel Cutting at LeHavre and Cowes,* 12 October 1789, *PTJDE.*

76 **"beautiful"** Gaillard Hunt, ed., *The First Forty Years of Washington Society in the Family Letters of Margaret Bayard Smith* (1906; repr., New York: Frederick Ungar, 1965), 34.

76 **"She was low"** Jefferson, *Memoirs of a Monticello Slave,* 5; Peachy Gilmer, "Peachy R. Gilmer Memoir," in *Francis Walker Gilmer,* ed. Richard Beale Davis (Richmond: Dietz Press, 1939), 373.

76 **"large, loosely made"** Gilmer, "Memoir," 373.

76 **"a delicate likeness"** Hunt, *First Forty Years of Washington Society,* 232.

76 **"dignified and highly agreeable"** Randall, *Jefferson,* 2:223.

76 **"beaming with intelligence"** Hunt, *First Forty Years of Washington Society,* 232; Gilmer, "Memoir," 373.

77   **"delicacy and sensibility"** 27 January 1785. *Journal and Correspondence of Miss Adams*, 45.

77   **"frank, communicative"** [Unknown] "Mrs. Thomas Mann Randolph, Eldest Daughter of Thomas Jefferson" by a Granddaughter, *The American Monthly Magazine: Historic, Patriotic* 17 (July 1900 by DAR): 30.

77   **"break so painful"** MJR to TJ, 8 [March] 1787, in Betts and Bear, *Family Letters*, 32.

77   **"I have not been able"** TJ to MJR, 7 April 1787, in Betts and Bear, *Family Letters*, 36.

77   **"leading her"** TJ to EWE, 28 July 1787, *PTJDE*.

77   **Francis Eppes** *TJMB*, 1:522.

78   **"not wish its continuance"** TJ to EWE, [3? October 1782], *PTJDE*.

78   **"mightily like her sister"** Jefferson, *Memories of Monticello Slave*, 15.

78   **"Here all is good humor"** Edward C. Carter II and Angeline Polites, eds., *The Virginia Journals of Benjamin Henry Latrobe, 1795–98* (New Haven: Yale University Press, 1977), 2:259.

78   **"you would have found"** TJ to Eliza House Trist, 15 December 1786, *PTJDE*.

78   **Eppes's cordial empathy** TJ to Francis Eppes, 24 January 1786, *PTJDE*.

79   **It may be something** Scharff, *Women Jefferson Loved*, 151.

79   **Eppes coordinated** Martha Jefferson Carr to TJ, 2 January 1787, Boyd, *Papers*, vol. 15, Supplementary Documents, 632–33.

79   **"Dear little Polly"** Ibid.

80   **"often mentions you"** Francis Eppes to TJ, 22 December 1783, *PTJDE*.

80   **"dear Poll"** TJ to Francis Eppes, 10 November 1783, *PTJDE*.

80   **"I was mighty glad"** Mary Jefferson to TJ, 1 April 1784, in Betts and Bear, *Family Letters*, 25.

80   **Francis and Elizabeth Eppes** Genealogical records are incomplete for this family. Francis Eppes to TJ, 22 December 1783; Francis Eppes to TJ, 14 October 1784, *PTJDE*; pennock.ws/surnames/fam/fam13935.html, accessed 14 November 2012.

80   **"prittyly"** Martha Jefferson Carr to TJ, 6 May 1785, *PTJDE*.

80   **"Mrs Eppes is Extreemly anxious"** Martha Jefferson Carr to TJ, 22 May 1786, *PTJDE*.

80   **"French English erethmatick"** Francis Eppes to TJ, 31 August 1786, Boyd, *Papers*, 15:631.

81   **"Books are her delight"** AA to TJ, 6 July 1787, Cappon, *Letters*, 184.

81   **"No," she replied** TJ to Francis Hopkinson, 13 March 1789, *PTJDE*.

81   **An inventory taken** "Inventory of the property of Elizabeth Wayles Eppes," in Martha McCartney, "A Documentary History of Eppington, Chesterfield County, VA," 67–69. Typescript report, February 1994. ICJS.

81   **"quickest sensibility"** AA to TJ, 6 July 1787. Cappon, *Letters*, 183.

82   **"They as well as"** Francis Eppes to TJ, 16 September 1784, *PTJDE*.

82   **"It is almost impossible"** EWE to TJ, 13 October 1784, *PTJDE*.

82   **"the Complicated evils"** Dr. James Currie to TJ, 20 November 1784, *PTJDE*. Elizabeth Eppes's letter was not received until 6 May 1785. TJ learned of his daughter's death from this letter, which arrived on 26 January 1785, having been brought to France by Lafayette. Editors' notes, *PTJDE*. Martha Jefferson Carr to TJ, 15 April 1784. Boyd, *Papers*, 613. On treating pertussis, see: medicinenet.com/pertussis/page5.htm#what_is_the_treatment_for_whooping_cough, accessed 15 November 2012.

83   **"It is in vain"** TJ to Francis Eppes, 5 February 1785, *PTJDE*.

83   **"Mr Jefferson is a man"** *Journal and Correspondence of Miss Adams*, 68.

83 **"wish to have Polly"** TJ to Francis Eppes, Summary Journal of Letters, 13 January 1785, *PTJDE*.

83 **"I must have Polly"** Editors' note, *PTJDE*. TJ to Francis Eppes, 11 May 1785.

83 **"hang on my mind"** TJ to Francis Eppes, 30 August 1785, *PTJDE*. A great loss is the letter of the same date that Martha wrote to Elizabeth Eppes, accompanying her father's. Only Nabby Adams's observations remain to testify to Martha's grief.

84 **"some strange fatality"** Francis Eppes to TJ, 11 April 1786, *PTJDE*.

84 **"very much afraid"** Martha Jefferson Carr to TJ, 5 May 1786, *PTJDE*.

84 **"tho after much ado"** Martha Jefferson Carr to TJ, 22 May 1786, *PTJDE*.

84 **"Nothing but force"** Francis Eppes to TJ, 23 May 1786, *PTJDE*.

85 **Eppes would later blame** Francis Eppes to TJ, 31 August 1786, *PTJDE*.

85 **"not withstanding"** John Wayles Eppes to TJ, 22 May 1786, *PTJDE*.

85 **"She says she has"** Martha Jefferson Carr to TJ, 22 May 1786, *PTJDE*.

85 **"I long to see you"** Maria Jefferson to TJ, [22 May 1786], Betts and Bear, *Family Letters*, 31.

85 **"as many dolls"** TJ to Maria Jefferson, 20 September 1785, Betts and Bear, *Family Letters*, 29.

85 **But so intractable** Eliza House Trist to TJ, 24 July 1786, *PTJDE*.

85 **A regular visitor** James Currie to TJ, 9 July 1786, *PTJDE*.

85 **"I can not go"** Maria Jefferson to TJ, [31 March 1787], Betts and Bear, *Family Letters*, 36.

86 **"countermanding your orders"** EWE to TJ, [31 March 1787], *PTJDE*.

86 **"must at last"** Martha Jefferson Carr reporting EWE's words to TJ, 2 January 1787, *PTJDE*.

86 **stranded at home** EWE to TJ, 7 May 1787, *PTJDE*.

86 **The pangs of grief** TJ to Francis Eppes, 26 May 1787, *PTJDE*.

86 **Jefferson's sister** Mary Jefferson Bolling to TJ, 3 May 1787, *PTJDE*; Martha Jefferson Carr to TJ, 27 April 1787, *PTJDE*; EWE to TJ, 7 May 1787, *PTJDE*.

86 **"vexation and the affliction"** Andrew Ramsay to TJ, 6 July 1787, *PTJDE*.

86 **"as rough as"** AA to TJ, 6 July 1787, Cappon, *Letters*, 183.

86 **in accommodations** Mary Jefferson Bolling to TJ, 3 May 1787, *PTJDE*.

86 **"She was so much attached"** AA to TJ, 26 June 1787, Cappon, *Letters*, 178.

87 **Ever wary of** AA to TJ, 27 June 1787, Cappon, *Letters*, 179.

87 **the little girl confided** AA to TJ, 6 July 1787, Cappon, *Letters*, 183.

87 **"Oh, now I have"** AA to TJ, 20 May 1804, Cappon, *Letters*, 269.

87 **"Polly had learned"** Scharff, *Women Jefferson Loved*, 184.

87 **"did not succeed"** Dumas Malone, "Polly Jefferson and Her Father," *Virginia Quarterly Review* 7 (January 1931): 95.

88 **"could ride a horse"** Scharff, *Women Jefferson Loved*, 148, 278.

89 **"If I must go"** AA to TJ, 10 July 1787, Cappon, *Letters*, 185.

89 **"to go out"** TJ to Maria Jefferson, 20 September 1785, Betts and Bear, *Family Letters*, 30.

89 **"She fancies"** TJ to AA, 30 August 1787, Cappon, *Letters*, 193–94.

90 **Ten-year-old Sally Hemings** Gordon-Reed, *Hemingses*, 143.

91 **the girls were very fond** AA to TJ, 27 June 1787, Cappon, *Letters*, 179.

91 **Elizabeth could have** Scharff, *Women Jefferson Loved*, 176–80.

91 **to supply the comfort** Gordon-Reed, *Hemingses*, 201.

91 **"the old Nurse"** AA to TJ, 26 June 1787 and 27 June 1787, in Cappon, *Letters*, 178–79.

91   **"the girl she has"** AA to TJ, 6 July 1787, in Cappon, *Letters*, 183.

91   **Whatever the cause** Gordon-Reed, *Hemingses*, 194–95, 205–6.

91   **Captain Ramsay had** Andrew Ramsay to TJ, 6 July 1787, *PTJDE*.

91   **knew no such attentions** Gordon-Reed, *Hemingses*, 207.

92   **"accustomed to her"** AA to TJ, 26 June 1787, Cappon, *Letters*, 178.

92   **It required courage** Scharff, *Women Jefferson Loved*, 180–82.

92   **the new clothes** AA to TJ, enclosure to letter, 10 July 1787, Cappon, *Letters*, 186–87.

92   **For Sally's part** Gordon-Reed, *Hemingses*, 209.

92   **James had been training** Gordon-Reed, *Hemingses*, 163–66.

93   **When his sister arrived** Gordon-Reed, *Hemingses*, 226.

93   **a different way of life** Annette Gordon-Reed has discussed James Hemings in Paris at length; see *Hemingses*, chapters 7, 8, 11, and 12.

93   **he paid dearly** *TJMB*, 7 November 1787, 1:685; Gordon-Reed, *Hemingses*, 216, for today's equivalent.

93   **"may have been"** Gordon-Reed, *Hemingses*, 221, 223.

93   **received wages** *TJMB*, January, November, and December 1788, 1:690, 718, 722.

93   **"well above that"** Gordon-Reed, *Hemingses*, 235–38.

94   **Hemings-Jefferson controversy** For a more detailed account of this debate, see Catherine Kerrison, "Sally Hemings," in *A Companion to Thomas Jefferson*, ed. Francis Cogliano (West Sussex, UK: Blackwell Publishing, 2012), 284–300.

95   **Such a woman** Gordon-Reed, *Hemingses*, 269 and chapters 13 and 15.

95   **The calculations of this relationship** Gordon-Reed, *Hemingses*, chapters 16 and 17.

96   **"To induce her"** Madison Hemings, "Memoirs of Madison Hemings," in *Thomas Jefferson and Sally Hemings: An American Controversy*, Annette Gordon-Reed (Charlottesville: University Press of Virginia, 1997), 246; Gordon-Reed, *Hemingses*, chapter 14.

96   **"During that time"** Hemings, "Memoirs," 246.

96   **the word *concubine*** Gordon-Reed, *Hemingses*, 107.

96   **a longer history** britannica.com/technology/castle-architecture#ref257455, accessed 23 January 2016.

97   **"in consequence of his promise"** Hemings, "Memoirs," 246.

CHAPTER 5: TRANSITIONS

99   **"with a view"** Ford, *Autobiography*, 1:157.

99   **he had decided** MJR to Nicholas P. Trist, 25 June 1823, Acc. 3470, SHC.

99   **He had been thinking** TJ to EWE, 12 July 1788 and 15 December 1788, *PTJDE*.

99   **"Humphries, Short, and myself"** TJ to Francis Eppes, [30 August 1785], *PTJDE*.

100   **"too wise to wrinkle"** TJ to Anne Willing Bingham, 11 May 1788, *PTJDE*.

100   **"filled with political debates"** TJ to the Marquise de Bréhan, 9 May 1788, *PTJDE*.

100   **Eliza Trist had quietly** Eliza House Trist to TJ, 13 December 1783, Acc. 2104, SHC.

100   **Jefferson's reproach** TJ to MJR, 28 June [1787], Betts and Bear, *Family Letters*, 44.

100   **"chez vous"** Bettie Hawkins to MJ, [Fall 1788], Acc. 1397, ViU.

100   **"the cloak you have sent"** Bettie Hawkins Curzon to MJR, March 1789, Acc. 1397, ViU.

100   **Jefferson's accounts** *TJMB*, 1:730–34.

101   **"The story you told"** Bettie Hawkins to MJR, 1786 or 1787, Acc. 1397, ViU.

101 **"I hope I have not"** Elizabeth Tufton to MJR, 18 September [1789], Acc. 1397, ViU.

101 **Abbé Edgeworth de Firmont** Edgeworth was Irish-born; his given name was Henry Essex Edgeworth. He served as chaplain to the doomed Louis XVI and was noted for his courage in accompanying the king to the guillotine, at great risk to his own life. Dominic Aidan Bellenger, "Edgeworth, Henry Essex (1745–1807)," in *Oxford Dictionary of National Biography,* Oxford University Press, 2004, oxforddnb .com/view/article/8475, accessed 28 June 2015.

101 **"Do you know"** Julia Annesley to MJR, [1788], and 20 April 1786, Acc. 1397, ViU.

101 **"I wish out of mere spite"** Julia Annesley to MJR, 27 April 1786, Acc. 5533, ViU.

101 **"You cannot think"** Elizabeth Tufton to MJR, 13 August 1789, Acc. 1397, ViU. I have not been able to discover the identity of "Tom," but it was not Thomas Mann Randolph. There is no evidence that he was ever in Paris.

102 **"I thank you"** Bettie Hawkins to MJR, [1788], Acc. 1397, ViU.

102 **"spent the nights"** Marie de Botidoux to MJR, 21 June [1801], FLDA; Rice, *Thomas Jefferson's Paris,* 53.

102 **"without the least formality"** *Journal and Correspondence of Miss Adams,* 45.

102 **favorite of her mother's** AA to her niece, quoted in Randolph, *Domestic Life,* 77.

103 **"that he hopes"** Elizabeth Tufton to MJR, [1789], Acc. 1397, ViU.

103 **"the duke seemed"** Maria Ball to MJR, Wednesday [Tuesday?] morning 23 June [1789], FLDA.

103 **"fond remembrance"** John Frederick Sackville, Duke of Dorset, to MJR, n.d., FLDA.

103 **"sent to the American"** Elizabeth Tufton to MJR, 23 October 1789, Acc. 1397, ViU.

104 **"Mlle Jefferson"** Marie de Botidoux to MJR, 4 November 1789, Acc. 5385-aa, ViU.

104 **"I recollect"** Bettie Hawkins to MJR, [1788], Acc. 1397, ViU.

104 **"All I can tell you"** Bettie Hawkins to MJR, [April 1788], Acc. 1397, ViU. Bettie used a different spelling for her fiancé's last name. Genealogical information available at thepeerage.com/p16040.htm#i160396.

104 **"a Mr Maxwell"** Bettie Hawkins Curzon to MJR, 2 July 1789, Acc. 1397, ViU.

104 **"fatal vessel"** Julia Annesley to MJR, [1788], Acc. 1397, ViU.

105 **"is now Lady Julia"** Bettie Hawkins Curzon to MJR, [late 1789], Acc. 1397, ViU.

105 **"I am really *un peu dérangée*"** Bettie [Hawkins] to MJR, [17 May] 1788, Acc. 1397, ViU.

105 **"a Mr Dashwood"** Bettie [Hawkins] Curzon to MJR, 2 July 1789, Acc. 1397, ViU.

106 **"necessary in the world"** Bettie Hawkins to MJR, [n.d. 1788], Acc. 1397, ViU.

106 **closely resembled** See chapter 3, "School Life."

106 **"so mature an understanding"** AA to Elizabeth Cranch, 16 July 1787, *Adams Papers Digital Edition.*

106 **"Her reading, her writing"** TJ to EWE, 28 July 1787, *PTJDE.*

106 **"easily enough"** TJ to EWE, 12 July 1788, *PTJDE.*

106 **Martha's devoted friends** Martha Jefferson's List of Schoolmates, Acc. 5385- I, ViU. Although undated, the list in Martha's hand was composed between September 1786 and September 1787; Martha listed her age as fourteen.

106 **"to attach herself"** TJ to EWE, 28 July 1787, *PTJDE*; AA to TJ, 10 July 1787, Cappon, *Letters,* 185.

107 **strangers who vied** TJ to AA, 16 July 1787, Cappon, *Letters,* 188.

107   **"It does not signify"** Bettie Hawkins to MJR, n.d., from London, Acc. 1397, ViU.

107   **"answer her charming"** Bettie Hawkins to MJR, [1788], Acc. 1397, ViU.

107   **Tufton never wrote** See for example, Caroline Tufton to MJR, 2 May 1789, Acc. 1397, ViU.

107   **"a universal favorite"** TJ to EWE, 28 July 1787, *PTJDE.*

107   **Caroline Tufton must have** Caroline Tufton to MJR, 21 March 1791, Acc. 1397, ViU.

107   **"and describe to me"** Abigail Adams to Elizabeth Cranch, 16 July 1787, *Adams Papers Digital Edition.*

107   **"it is impossible"** TJ to EWE, 25 July 1787, *PTJDE.*

108   **"the theme"** TJ to EWE, 12 July 1788, *PTJDE.*

108   **"I know she will undertake"** TJ to EWE, 12 July 1788, *PTJDE.*

108   **"hard for her to learn"** Malone, "Polly Jefferson and Her Father," 86.

108   **"He seated his little daughter"** Eppes, "Maria Jefferson Eppes and her Little Son, Francis," 8, 10, ICJS.

109   **purchase in June 1786** *TJMB,* 9 June 1786, 1:629; Rice, *Jefferson's Paris,* 51–53.

109   **"very elegant one"** MJR, "Reminiscences of Th. J.," Acc. 10487, ViU.

109   **"oval salon overlooking"** This description is taken entirely from Kimball, *Jefferson: The Scene of Europe 1784–1789,* 110. The house no longer stands.

110   **Jefferson paid fifty livres** Rice, *Jefferson's Paris,* 52.

110   **a semipublic building** Gordon-Reed, *Hemingses,* 162.

111   **"an indisposition"** TJ to EWE, 15 December 1788, *PTJDE.*

111   **"My daughters"** TJ to John Trumbull, 12 January 1789, *PTJDE.*

111   **symptoms of the disease** umm.edu/ency/article/001363sym.htm, University of Maryland Medical Center, accessed 12 December 2012.

111   **Maria was on the mend** TJ to William Short, 22 January 1789, *PTJDE.*

111   **"At last, dear Jefferson"** Marie de Botidoux to MJR, [1789], Acc. 5385-aa, ViU.

111   **"introduced into society"** Randolph, "Mrs. Thomas Mann Randolph," 20–21.

111   **No longer needing** Randolph, *Domestic Life,* 146–47.

112   **"A Gentleman told me"** Maria Ball to MJR, 23 June 1789, FLDA.

112   **"of course require"** TJ to Overton Carr, 16 March 1782, *PTJDE.*

112   **Gordon-Reed has suggested** Gordon-Reed, *Hemingses,* 246.

112   **Sally Hemings's duties** Gordon-Reed, *Hemingses,* 236–48.

113   **her wages of twelve livres** Gordon-Reed, *Hemingses,* 236.

113   **expenditure constitutes evidence** Fawn Brodie argues that these expenditures demonstrated Jefferson's growing interest in Hemings in Brodie, *An Intimate History,* 301–2.

113   **not unusual in French families** Gordon-Reed, *Hemingses,* 230–31.

113   **the honorific "mademoiselle"** Gordon-Reed, *Hemingses,* 230.

113   **These conversations** Gordon-Reed, *Hemingses,* 381–82.

113   **"She refused to return"** Hemings, "Memoirs," 246.

114   **Martha and Maria shopped** Susan Ware Eppes Memoir; Madame d'Houdetot to TJ, 7 July 1789, *PTJDE.*

114   **"We are in such confusion"** Elizabeth Tufton to MJR, [August 1789], Acc. 1397, ViU.

114   **"I shall value it"** Caroline Tufton to MJR, [Friday, London, 1789], Acc. 1397, ViU.

114   **"adieus are painful"** TJ to Madame de Corny, 14 October 1789, *PTJDE.*

115   **"I do not recollect"** Nathaniel Cutting diary, 28 September–12 October, 1789, *PTJDE.*

115   **Jefferson party arrived** Ibid.; *TJMB,* 1:745–47.

115 **They sailed** TJ to Nathaniel Cutting, 15 September 1789, *PTJDE;* Malone, *Jefferson,* 2:235.

115 **twenty-nine days** TJ to William Short, 21 November 1789, *PTJDE.*

115 **"Maria, who is at my elbow"** TJ to Nathaniel Cutting, 21 November 1789, *PTJDE.*

115 **"as thick a mist"** MJR, "Reminiscences of Th. J.," Acc. 10487, ViU.

116 **"but for the politeness"** Ibid.

116 **sleep in a hammock** *TJMB,* 24 November 1789, 1:748.

116 **"the *idea* you had formed"** Elizabeth Tufton to MJR, 19 December 1789, Acc. 1397, ViU.

116 **"Pray tell me"** Bettie [Hawkins] Curzon to MJR, [late 1789], Acc. 1397, ViU.

117 **"some emotion of chagrin"** Nathaniel Cutting to MJR, 30 March 1790, *PTJDE.*

117 **"*Mais c'est bien"*** Randolph, "Mrs. Thomas Mann Randolph," 23.

117 **Maria's delight** TJ to EWE, 12 July 1788, *PTJDE.*

117 **proceeded slowly through Virginia** *TJMB,* 1:748.

117 **she met again** Thomas Mann Randolph may not have been at his father's home during the Jeffersons' visit; he had fought with his father and fled to a cousin's home for the shooting season. William H. Gaines, Jr., *Thomas Mann Randolph: Jefferson's Son-in-Law* (Baton Rouge: Louisiana State University Press, 1966), 24.

117 **"The negroes discovered"** MJR, "Reminiscences of Th. J.," Acc. 10487, ViU.

118 **positioned to defeat** Gordon-Reed, *Hemingses,* 342.

118 **Jefferson gave him money** *TJMB,* 10 December 1789, 1:749.

118 **"down a curtain"** Gordon-Reed, *Hemingses,* 371.

118 **protections for slavery** See, for example, Article 1, section 9, of the Constitution and Paul Finkelman, *Slavery and the Founders: Race and Liberty in the Age of Jefferson* (Armonk, New York: M.E. Sharpe, 1996), chapter 1.

118 **By 1810, free blacks** The actual numbers are: 23 percent in Maryland; 75.9 percent in Delaware; 32.1 percent in Washington, D.C. Peter Kolchin, *American Slavery 1619–1877,* rev. ed. (New York: Hill and Wang, 1993), 241.

120 **nature and role of women** Dena Goodman, "Women and the Enlightenment," in *Becoming Visible: Women in European History,* eds. Renate Bridenthal, Susan Mosher Stuard, and Merry E. Wiesner, 3rd ed. (Boston: Houghton Mifflin Company, 1998), 233–62.

120 **he concluded** Ibid., 238.

121 **the view of Scottish Enlightenment** Ibid., 238–39.

121 **only 27 percent** Ibid., 242.

121 **"If you love me"** TJ to MJR, 28 November 1783, in Betts and Bear, *Family Letters,* 20.

121 **a kind of semi-independence** Kierner, *Martha Jefferson Randolph,* 56.

122 **"Her young friends"** Randolph, "Mrs. Thomas Mann Randolph," 22; Adams, *Paris Years of Thomas Jefferson,* 289–90.

122 **"woman's country"** Morris, *Diary and Letters of Gouverneur Morris,* 1:179.

122 **"Society is spoilt"** TJ to Madame de Bréhan, 9 May 1788, *PTJDE.*

122 **French women of all ranks** Darline Gay Levy and Harriet B. Applewhite, "A Political Revolution for Women? The Case of Paris," in Bridenthal, Stuard, and Wiesner, eds., *Becoming Visible,* 268–72, 276.

123 **female suffrage** Rosemarie Zagarri, *Revolutionary Backlash: Women and Politics in the Early American Republic* (Philadelphia: University of Pennsylvania Press, 2007), 26, 29.

123 **"our high and mighty Lords"** Priscilla Mason, "Oration," 15 May 1793. Quoted in Linda K. Kerber, *Women of the Republic: Intellect and Ideology in Revolutionary*

America (Chapel Hill: Published for OIEAHC by University of North Carolina Press, 1980), 222.

124   **"both unjust and detrimental"** Ibid., 49.

124   **New Jersey legislators** Zagarri, *Revolutionary Backlash*, 30–36.

124   **"like a monkey"** Charles Brockden Brown, *Alcuin*, quoted in Kerber, *Women of the Republic*, 277; *Register* (Salem, Massachusetts), 4 October 1802, quoted in ibid., 279.

124   **"dove-like temper"** Parson Weems, quoted in ibid., 281.

124   **her father's assessment** TJ to John Jay, 29 July 1789, *PTJDE*.

125   **elements of female education** TJ to EWE, 28 July 1787, *PTJDE*.

Chapter 6: Becoming American Again

126   **Tom was well educated** Gaines, Jr., *Thomas Mann Randolph*, passim.

127   **sliding on ice** Virginia Jefferson Randolph Trist Memoir, Acc. 1397, ViU.

128   **"scrupulously suppressed my wishes"** TJ to Madame de Corny, 2 April 1790, *PTJDE*.

128   **"her sufferings"** Virginia Jefferson Randolph to Nicholas P. Trist, 4 February 1823, FLDA.

128   **"*the* important Crisis"** Elizabeth Smith Shaw Peabody to Abigail Adams Smith, 27 November 1786, *Adams Papers Digital Edition*.

128   **"and her only"** TMR to Septimia Randolph, 6 August 1827. Copy at ICJS.

128   **rebellious in the face** Gordon-Reed, *Hemingses*, 422.

128   **"you are both too young"** MJR to Nicholas P. Trist, 20 September 1818, Acc. 3470, Trist Family Papers from the SHC, ViU.

130   **from his friend James Madison** James Madison to TJ, 24 October 1787, *PTJDE*.

130   **Jefferson raised only two objections** TJ to James Madison, 20 December 1787, *PTJDE*.

131   **Print proliferated** David D. Hall, "Books and Reading in Eighteenth-Century America," in *Of Consuming Interests: The Style of Life in the Eighteenth Century*, eds. Cary Carson, Ronald Hoffman, and Peter J. Albert (Charlottesville: United States Capitol Historical Society by the University Press of Virginia, 1994), 357. By 1810, that numbered had climbed to 350.

131   **"most agreeably surprized"** Elizabeth Tufton to MJR, 21 March 1790, Acc. 1397, ViU.

131   **"being settled"** Caroline Tufton to MJR, 21 March 1790, Acc. 1397, ViU.

131   **"in the course"** Elizabeth Tufton to MJR, 24 September 1789, Acc. 1397, ViU.

131   **"for this month past"** Bettie Hawkins to MJR, [April 1788], Acc. 1397, ViU.

131   **Marie de Botidoux continued** Marie de Botidoux to MJR, 4 November 1789, 4 February 1790, 12 March 1790, 1 May 1790, Acc. 5385a, ViU.

132   **she had difficulty** MJR to Nicholas P. Trist, 1 September 1822, Acc. 3470, ViU.

132   **a trial so arduous** Birle and Francavilla, *Thomas Jefferson's Granddaughter*, 160.

132   **He rapidly concluded** TMR to TJ, 25 May 1790, *PTJDE*.

132   **Martha was impatient** TJ to MJR, 6 June 1790, Betts and Bear, *Family Letters*, 57. MJR's letter is missing; TJ's refers to her "resolution to go to housekeeping."

133   **"much averse"** MJR to TJ, 25 April 1790, Betts and Bear, *Family Letters*, 53.

133   **"took fire"** MJR to TJ, 20 February 1792, Betts and Bear, *Family Letters*, 94; Gaines, *Thomas Mann Randolph*, 34.

133   **her own premarital calculations** TJ to MJR, 17 July 1790, Betts and Bear, *Family Letters*, 60–61; Bettie Hawkins to MJR, [April 1788], Acc. 1397, ViU.

133   **"Take care my dear"** Bettie Curzon to MJR, April 1790, Acc. 1397, ViU.

133   **"To own the truth"** Elizabeth Tufton to MJR, 21 March 1790, Acc. 1397, ViU.

133   **"You are truly unbelievable"** Marie de Botidoux to MJR, 1 May 1790, Acc. 5385-aa, ViU.

134   **Marriage to Jefferson's daughter** Kierner, *Martha Jefferson Randolph*, 84.

134   **called Anne Cary** TJ to MJR, 24 March 1791, Betts and Bear, *Family Letters*, 76; see also Maria's repeated requests, 6 March and 26 March 1791, in ibid., 73, 77.

134   **financial difficulties** Gaines, *Thomas Mann Randolph*, 37.

135   **"labour, envy, and malice"** TJ to MJR, 15 January 1792, Betts and Bear, *Family Letters*, 93.

135   **"ease, domestic occupation"** TJ to François d'Ivernois, 6 February 1795, *PTJDE*.

135   **Ellen died** Kierner, *Martha Jefferson Randolph*, 100.

135   **"It was all"** Madame Brunette Salimbeni to MJR, 15 March 1800, FLDA.

136   **"Bruny has told me"** Marie de Botidoux to MJR, 31 October 1798, Acc. 5385a, ViU. Translated by Lucia Stanton, TJF. "Bruny" likely was Mme. Brunette Salimbeni.

136   **Martha's home was sited** Visit to site by author, courtesy of owner, Greg Graham. 7 May 2009.

136   **"I wish"** MJR to TJ, 3 May 1787, Betts and Bear, *Family Letters*, 39.

136   **"we shall see"** Elizabeth Tufton to MJR, September 1789, Acc. 1397, ViU.

137   **Tom was no more enamored** TMR to Nicholas P. Trist, 22 November 1818, Acc. 10487, ViU.

137   **"All men have"** TMR to Nicholas P. Trist, 5 June 1820, Acc. 3470, ViU.

137   **"aversion to increase"** TMR to TJ, 5 March 1791, *PTJDE*.

137   **owner of thirty-eight men** Kierner, *Martha Jefferson Randolph*, 87.

137   **"sorrows in all their bitterness"** MJR to EWRC, 2 August 1825, Acc. 9090, ViU.

137   **"I wonder"** Bettie Hawkins to MJR, [1788], Acc. 1397, ViU.

137   **"my little darling"** Bettie (Hawkins) Curzon to MJR, 2 July 1789, Acc. 1397, ViU.

137   **At Edgehill, Martha** MJR to TJ, 31 May 1804, Betts and Bear, *Family Letters*, 261.

138   **"hoped tis her last"** Dolley Madison to Anna Payne Cutts, 28 August 1808, *The Papers of Dolley Madison Digital Edition*, ed. Holly C. Shulman (Charlottesville: University of Virginia Press, Rotunda, 2008).

138   **"the education of my children"** MJR to TJ, 31 January 1801, Betts and Bear, *Family Letters*, 193.

138   **"but in such broken"** MJR to TJ, 16 January 1793, Betts and Bear, *Family Letters*, 109.

138   **Five-year-old Ellen** Ellen Wayles Randolph to TJ, November 1801, Betts and Bear, *Family Letters*, 212.

138   **"raise his eye"** VJRT, 26 May 1839. Quoted in Randolph, *Domestic Life*, 347.

138   **"After breakfast"** Hunt, *First Forty Years of Washington Society*, 70, 67–68.

139   **"Mrs. Randolph was"** Pierson, *Jefferson at Monticello*, 87.

139   **"Few such women"** Ibid., 86. Carolyn Heilbrun has noted that "above all other prohibitions, what has been forbidden to women is anger," both in daily life and in their writing. Carolyn Heilbrun, *Writing a Woman's Life* (New York: W. W. Norton, 1988), 13.

139   **"All Mrs. R's. children"** Hunt, *First Forty Years of Washington Society*, 70.

140   **"the habit will"** MJR to Septimia Randolph, 30 July 1832, Acc. 4726-b, ViU.

140   **they lacked horses** MJR to TJ, 25 April 1790, Betts and Bear, *Family Letters*, 52.

141   **"the dictionary is too large"** MJE to TJ, 25 April 1790, Betts and Bear, *Family Letters*, 53.

141   **"Your last letter"** TJ to MJE, 23 May 1790, Betts and Bear, *Family Letters,* 57.

141   **By the end of May** MJE to TJ, 23 May [1790], Betts and Bear, *Family Letters,* 56–57. Maria was reading William Robertson, *The History of America* (Dublin: 1777).

141   **"You must make"** TJ to MJE, 13 June 1790, Betts and Bear, *Family Letters,* 58.

141   **"improves visibly"** MJR to TJ, 16 January 1791, Betts and Bear, *Family Letters,* 68.

141   **"Books are her delight"** AA to TJ, 6 July 1787, in Cappon, *Letters,* 184.

142   **"The lovely girl"** Diary of Nathaniel Cutting, 10 October 1789, *PTJDE.*

142   **Cutting saw the presage** Ibid., 12 October 1789.

142   **His parting letter** TJ to MJE, 11 April 1790, Betts and Bear, *Family Letters,* 52.

142   **"I am really jealous"** TJ to EWE, 13 June 1790, *PTJDE.*

143   **"She is very pretty"** MJE to TJ, 13 February [1791], Betts and Bear, *Family Letters,* 72.

143   **They left Monticello** *TJMB,* 2:836.

143   **"I had no more idea"** George Washington to Alexander Hamilton, 14 October 1791, *PGWDE.*

143   **drove the twenty miles** George Washington to Alexander Hamilton, 17 October 1791, *PGWDE;* TJ to TMR, 25 October 1791, *PTJDE.*

143   **Martha Washington took charge** TJ to TMR, 25 October 1791, *PTJDE.*

143   **the tallest building** There are splendid images of Grays Ferry in 1787 and 1792 in S. Robert Teitelman, ed., *Birch's Views of Philadelphia: A Reduced Facsimile of the City of Philadelphia—As It Appeared in the Year 1800: With Photographs of the Sites in 1960 & 2000 and Commentaries* (Philadelphia: Free Library of Philadelphia, 2000). They are also available at publicpleasuregarden.blogspot.com/2013/05/1790-grays -gardens-in-philadelphia.html.

143   **They had taken the route** TJ took this route on his travels from Monticello to Philadelphia. *TJMB,* 2:836, 879.

144   **a laurel wreath fell** *Columbian Magazine,* May 1789; quoted in John Bach Mc-Master, *A History of the People of the United States: From the Revolution to the Civil War* (New York: D. Appleton and Company, 1914), 538. This is one of many stories about how Washington was crowned and by whom.

144   **"greene Country Towne"** Quoted in Mary Maples Dunn and Richard Dunn, "The Founding 1681–1701," in *Philadelphia: A 300-Year History,* ed. Russell F. Weigley (New York: W. W. Norton, 1982), 2, 5–10.

144   **With a population of forty-four thousand** Susan Branson, *Those Fiery Frenchified Dames: Women and Political Culture in Early National Philadelphia* (Philadelphia: University of Pennsylvania Press, 2001), 7.

145   **Homes that had been** Gary B. Nash, "Philadelphia," in Weigley, *Philadelphia,* 156.

145   **first public building** Ibid., 175–76.

145   **Birch recorded the building** Teitelman, *Birch's Views.* These images can most readily be seen at ushistory.org/birch/plates/plate01.htm.

145   **marked the outskirts** Map, Teitelman, *Birch's Views;* William Temple Franklin to TJ, 20 July 1790, *PTJDE.*

146   **"constitute what the french"** William Franklin to TJ, 20 July 1790, *PTJDE.*

146   **Jefferson's new home** Mark Wenger, "Thomas Jefferson, Tenant," *Winterthur Portfolio* v. 26 (4) (Winter, 1991): 249–65.

147   **"particularly attended to"** TJ to TMR, 25 October 1791, *PTJDE.*

147   **"been honored with"** The women were: Mrs. John Adams, Mrs. Edmund Randolph, Mrs. David Rittenhouse, Mrs. Jonathan D. Sergeant, Mrs. Nicholas Baker

Waters, and Mrs. [Benjamin] Davies. TJ to MJR, 13 November 1791, in Betts and Bear, *Family Letters*, 91.

147 **the house he had rented** Thompson Westcott, *The Historic Mansions and Buildings of Philadelphia, with Some Notice of Their Owners and Occupants* (Philadelphia: Porter & Coates, 1877), 317. Jefferson described his lodgings to James Mease, 16 September 1825, as "a new brick house, three stories high, of which I rented the second floor, consisting of a parlor and bedroom, ready furnished. In that parlor I wrote habitually, and in it I wrote this paper [the Declaration] particularly." Quoted in ibid., 308.

148 **to the home of artist** Charlene Mires, *Independence Hall in American Memory* (Philadelphia: University of Pennsylvania Press, 2002), 41.

148 **Adrien Petit** *TJMB*, 2:829n91. Petit arrived 19 July 1791.

148 **Because Pine had been** George William Fairfax to George Washington, 23 June 1785, *PGWDE*. The prominent English historian, Catherine Macaulay, thought Pine's portrait "bore the strongest resemblance to the original of any I had seen." Catherine Sawbridge Macaulay Graham to George Washington, 10 October 1786, *PGWDE*.

149 **first art museum** Mires, *Independence Hall*, 39; Robert G. Stewart, *Robert Edge Pine: A British Portrait Painter in America, 1784–1788* (Washington, D.C.: Smithsonian Institution Press, 1979), 25.

149 **advertised a new** *Pennsylvania Packet*, 28 March 1789.

149 **the number of scholars** The 1790 census showed ten women (including Mary Pine and her daughters) above the age of sixteen. Stewart, *Robert Edge Pine*, 35.

149 **Through his secretary** Tobias Lear to Clement Biddle, 6 November 1790, "Selections from the Correspondence of Clement Biddle," *Pennsylvania Magazine of History and Biography* 43 (1919): 197; E. D. Gillespie, *A Book of Remembrance* (Philadelphia: J.B. Lippincott, 1901), 26; Maria Jefferson to TMR, 29 January 1792, *Thomas Jefferson Papers*, LOC.

149 **"It is possible"** TJ to Thomas Leiper, 19 May 1791, *PTJDE*.

149 **"being the whole front"** Advertisement, "To be Sold," *Pennsylvania Packet*, 10 November 1790.

150 **He had hoped** TJ to Thomas Leiper, 16 December 1792, *PTJDE*.

150 **Another Philadelphia teacher** TJ to MJR, 11 May 1792, Betts and Bear, *Family Letters*, 99.

150 **"made young friends"** TJ to MJR, 13 November 1792, Betts and Bear, *Family Letters*, 91.

150 **"been to Mrs Pines"** MJE to TMR, 27 November [1791], *Thomas Jefferson Papers*, LOC. LOC dates this letter to 1792, but Maria's comment makes clear the error.

150 **A footnote here** Betts and Bear, *Family Letters*, 91, 99, 101; *TJMB*, 2:837, 884. Scharff's *Women Jefferson Loved* did not consider Maria Jefferson's education in Philadelphia.

151 **Mary Pine's school** Stewart, *Robert Edge Pine*, 35.

151 **"there is no rank"** Quoted in ibid., 36.

151 **"care and instruction"** *Pennsylvania Packet*, 28 March 1789.

152 **"Accustomed only to my"** Rembrandt Peale, "Reminiscences," *The Crayon 3* (1856), quoted in Stewart, *Robert Edge Pine*, 25.

152 **They often finished** Peale, "Reminiscences," 5, quoted in Stewart, *Robert Edge Pine*, 29.

152 **he thought "indifferent"** TJ to William Morgan, 4 February 1809, quoted in *TJMB*, 2:871.

152   **"Among genteel ranks"** Arthur Loesser, *Men, Women and Pianos: A Social History* (New York: Simon & Schuster, 1954), 268.

152   **hired John Christopher Moller** *TJMB*, 31 October 1792, 2:882.

153   **"The poor girl"** George Washington Parke Custis, *Recollections and Private Memoirs of Washington by His Adopted Son with a Memoir of the Son by His Daughter* (Derby & Jackson, 1860), 408.

153   **"They often practiced"** TJ to TMR, 20 February 1792, *PTJDE*.

153   **"I am in great want"** MJE to TMR, 25 December 1791, *Thomas Jefferson Papers*, LOC.

153   **the academy offered courses** Kerber, *Women of the Republic*, 210–14.

153   **As the historian Margaret Nash** Margaret Nash, "Rethinking Republican Motherhood: Benjamin Rush and The Young Ladies Academy of Philadelphia," *Journal of the Early Republic* 17 (Summer 1997): 186–88.

154   **Although Adams took an avid** This portrait emerges from Woody Holton, *Abigail Adams* (New York: Free Press, 2009).

154   **Adams would not compare** AA to John Adams, 21 February 1776; AA to John Adams, 17 June 1782; AA to Mary Smith Cranch, 21 May 1786, *Adams Papers Digital Edition*.

155   **particularly true in Philadelphia** Branson, *Those Fiery Frenchified Dames*, 38–49.

155   **"life of a cat"** Eleanor Parke Custis to Elizabeth Bordley, 23 November 1797, in Patricia Brady, ed., *George Washington's Beautiful Nelly: The Letters of Eleanor Parke Custis Lewis to Elizabeth Bordley Gibson, 1794–1851* (Columbia: University of South Carolina Press, 1991), 41.

155   **Nor did the return** TJ to TMR, 1 June 1792, *PTJDE*.

155   **Fullerton was American** *Pennsylvania Mercury and Universal Advertiser*, 13 July 1787, *Pennsylvania Packet*, 4 July 1788, *Federal Gazette*, 11 April 1792; TJ to TMR, 12 October 1792, *PTJDE*; *TJMB*, 20 November 1792, 2:884.

155   **"Mrs Fullerton"** MJE to TMR, 13 January 1793, *Thomas Jefferson Papers*, LOC.

155   **Sarah (Sally) Corbin Cropper** Jennings Cropper Wise, *Colonel John Wise of England and Virginia (1617–1695): His Ancestors and Descendants* (Richmond, Va.: Bell Brooks and Stationery Company, 1918), 90.

155   **Family lore** Ibid., 96.

156   **Jefferson's memorandum book** *TJMB*. See 2:825–29, for three examples between 20 June and 17 July 1791.

156   **"2. to 4. hours a day"** TJ to Francis Eppes, 15 May 1791; TJ to Francis Eppes, 8 April 1793, *PTJDE*.

156   **"out of love"** TJ to EWE, 15 May 1791, *PTJDE*.

156   **"but one at a time"** TJ to TMR, 30 March 1792, *PTJDE*.

156   **"scribbling and rubbing out"** TJ to TMR, 12 May 1793, *PTJDE*.

156   **One letter to her sister** TJ to MJR, 13 December 1792, Betts and Bear, *Family Letters*, 107. MJR kept a letter from Maria from Philadelphia, dated 3 June 1792, Acc. 2104, SHC.

157   **"the security of the thing"** TJ to MJR, 14 January 1793, and n. 2 in Betts and Bear, *Family Letters*, 108–9.

157   **"I have been very much entertained"** MJE to TMR, 13 January 1793, *Thomas Jefferson Papers*, LOC.

157   **An image painted** Residence of Thomas Jefferson, David J. Kennedy, 1793. The Historical Society of Pennsylvania.

157   **By the summer** TJ to MJR, 9 April 1793 and 7 July 1793, in Betts and Bear, *Family Letters*, 114, 121.

157   **"Under them I breakfast"** TJ to MJR, 7 July 1793, in Betts and Bear, *Family Letters*, 121–22.

157   **Maria enjoyed picnicking** TJ to MJR, 26 May 1793 and 21 July 1793 in Betts and Bear, *Family Letters*, 119, 122; *TJMB*, 1:765n80.

157   **"two young ladies"** TJ to David Rittenhouse, 6 September 1793, *PTJDE*.

158   **"long and severe"** TJ to TMR, 16 March 1792, *Thomas Jefferson Papers*, LOC.

158   **plagued with colds** TJ to MJR, 5 December 1791, in Betts and Bear, *Family Letters*, 91, and TJ to TMR, 16 March 1792, *PTJDE*.

158   **"having always retained"** MJR to Anne Cary Randolph Morris, 16 May 1827, quoted in Kierner, *Martha Jefferson Randolph*, 66.

158   **In early April** TJ to MJR, 8 April 1793, in Betts and Bear, *Family Letters*, 115.

158   **"Doctors always flatter"** TJ to Martha Jefferson Carr, 14 April 1793, *PTJDE*.

158   **"well . . . tho not"** TJ to MJR, 26 May 1793, in Betts and Bear, *Family Letters*, 119.

159   **counting the weeks** TJ to MJR, 18 August 1793, in Betts and Bear, *Family Letters*, 123.

159   **end of her formal education** Kierner, *Martha Jefferson Randolph*, 97.

159   **packed up a spinet** *TJMB*, 28 March 1792 and 19 May 1793, 2:866, 895.

160   **correcting the steward's entry** Helen Cripe, *Thomas Jefferson and Music* (Charlottesville: University Press of Virginia, 1974), 48.

CHAPTER 7: A VIRGINIA WIFE

161   **"Follow closely your music"** TJ to MJE, 17 November 1793, in Betts and Bear, *Family Letters*, 126.

161   **"Mr. Giles is at Monticello"** Martha Jefferson Carr to Lucy Carr Terrell, 25 August 1795, Carr-Terrell Family Papers, Acc. 4757-d, ViU.

162   **"affectionately, Th. J."** For example, TJ to William Branch Giles, 31 December 1795, *PTJDE*.

162   **Giles would acquire a reputation** "William Branch Giles," *Dictionary of American Biography* (New York: Charles Scribner's Sons, 1936); Joseph J. Ellis, *American Sphinx: The Character of Thomas Jefferson* (New York: Alfred A. Knopf, 1996), 154.

162   **launched a merciless attack** *The Autobiography of Colonel John Trumbull, Patriot Artist 1756–1843* (New Haven: Yale University Press, 1953), 174–75.

162   **"saw him talking"** Jefferson, *Memoirs of a Monticello Slave*, 39.

162   **"Mr. Giles joined us"** TJ to John Wayles Eppes (JWE), 3 September 1795, *PTJDE*.

162   **"Maria Jefferson has discarded"** Martha Jefferson Carr to Lucy Carr Terrell, 26 March 1796, Acc. 4757-d, ViU.

162   **A family story** Eppes, "Maria Jefferson Eppes and her Little Son, Francis," ICJS, 12.

163   **elite female education** Kerrison, *Claiming the Pen*, passim; Cathy Davidson, *Revolution and the Word: The Rise of the Novel in America* (New York: Oxford University Press, 1986), 110–50.

163   **"retired to my home"** TJ to Maria Cosway, 8 September 1795, *PTJDE*.

164   **"Could I hope"** JWE to TJ, 25 September 1796, *PTJDE*.

164   **"All obstacles to my happiness"** JWE to TJ, 19 December 1796, *PTJDE*.

165   **"to see Maria"** TJ to MJR, 8 June 1797, Betts and Bear, *Family Letters*, 146.

165   **"I learn, my dear Maria"** TJ to MJE, 14 June 1797, Betts and Bear, *Family Letters*, 148.

165   **"We shall all live"** TJ to MJE, 14 June 1797; and TJ to MJR, 8 June 1797, Betts and Bear, *Family Letters*, 148, 146.

165   **formal negotiations** TJ to Francis Eppes, 24 September 1797, *PTJDE* and editors'
       notes.
166   **"To say how much"** EWE to TJ, 10 October 1797, *PTJDE*.
166   **"Tell my Dear Martha"** TMR to TJ, 6 November 1797, *PTJDE*.
167   **Eppes was a handsome man** Jefferson, *Memoirs of a Monticello Slave,* 11.
167   **thick, curly dark hair** John Wayles Eppes portrait on page 166. Engraving created/
       published [1805]. Charles Balthazar Julien Fevret de Saint-Mémin, artist. LOC
       Prints and Photographs Division, Reproduction Number LC-USZ62-105849.
167   **"Mr Eppes was a gay, good-natured"** Ellen Wayles Randolph Coolidge (EWRC)
       Letter Book, 13 March 1856, 58–59, Acc. 9090, ViU; Randolph, *Domestic Life,*
       246.
167   **"the author of the Declaration"** Malone, "Polly Jefferson and Her Father," 95.
167   **"fretful child"** Scharff, *Women Jefferson Loved,* 303, 301.
167   **In the construction zone** TJ to TMR, 22 January 1797, and TJ to Henry Tazewell,
       28 November 1797, *PTJDE*.
168   **"Maria's foot improves"** JWE to TJ, n.d., received by TJ 18 November 1797,
       PTJDE.
168   **made the visiting rounds** MJE to TJ, 8 December 1797, Betts and Bear, *Family
       Letters,* 149–50.
168   **"their inclinations concur"** TJ to Francis Eppes, 24 September 1797, *PTJDE*. By
       the date of this letter, Congress had only been in session four months in 1797:
       January 1–March 3 and May 15–July 10. When next it met, 13 November 1797,
       however, Congress would sit until July 1798.
169   **"too generous"** EWE to TJ, 10 October 1797, *PTJDE*.
169   **"Aunt Eppes"** MJE to MJR, 1 April 1798, Acc. 2104, SHC.
169   **"my dear mother"** MJE to TJ, 21 June 1802, Betts and Bear, *Family Letters,* 229.
169   **"Mama"** MJE to TJ, 21 April 1802, Betts and Bear, *Family Letters,* 224.
169   **his daughter believed** EWRC Letter Book, 26 January 1856, 42–45, Acc. 9090,
       ViU.
169   **"would give you"** TJ to JWE, 9 October 1801, *PTJDE*.
170·   **"If I could conveniently"** JWE to TJ, 11 May 1802, *PTJDE*.
170   **"As she is equally"** JWE to TJ, 25 June 1802, *PTJDE*.
170   **"out of my power"** Ibid.
171   **wife's patient submission** TJ to MJE, 7 January 1798, Betts and Bear, *Family Let-
       ters,* 151. Jefferson's "sermon," as he called this letter, was his response to Maria's
       report of the unhappiness Mary Jefferson Bolling's abusive alcoholic husband
       caused their marriage. Perhaps if his sister did not complain about her husband's
       drinking, Jefferson suggested, his sister's marriage would be more bearable.
171   **"raptures and palpitations"** MJR to TJ, n.d., received 1 July 1798, Betts and Bear,
       Family Letters, 166.
171   **"The agonies of Mr. Randolph's"** MJR to TJ, 18 November 1801, Betts and Bear,
       Family Letters, 213.
172   **"The more I see of her"** MJE to TJ, 27 February [1797], *PTJDE*.
172   **"in the most tender love"** MJE to TJ, 2 February [1801], Betts and Bear, *Family
       Letters,* 194.
172   **Jefferson replied immediately** TJ to MJE, 15 February 1801, Betts and Bear, *Fam-
       ily Letters,* 196.
172   **"interwoven with her existence"** MJE to TJ, 26 June 1799, Betts and Bear, *Family
       Letters,* 178.
172   **Jefferson at the center** Scharff, *Women Jefferson Loved,* 275.

172   **"intellectually *very greatly*"** EWRC Letter Book, 14 January 1856, 41, Acc. 9090, ViU.

172   **"If I must go I will"** AA to TJ, 10 July 1787, Cappon, *Letters,* 185.

174   **"every sound we heard"** TJ to MJE, 13 July 1798, Betts and Bear, *Family Letters,* 166–67.

174   **"her miscarriage"** JWE to TJ, 14 July 1802, *PTJDE.*

174   **"too thinly clad"** JWE to TJ, 24 November 1798, *PTJDE.*

174   **"From Mont Blanco"** MJE to TJ, 26 June 1799, Betts and Bear, *Family Letters,* 178–79.

174   **"a sharer in a species"** JWE to TJ, 1 January 1800, *PTJDE.*

175   **In the eighteenth century** Paula A. Treckel, "Breastfeeding and Maternal Sexuality in Colonial America," *Journal of Interdisciplinary History,* 20 (Summer 1989): 27.

175   **sores broke through** JWE to TJ, 7 February 1800, *PTJDE.*

175   **Dr. Philip Turpin** Turpin (1749–1828), Jefferson's cousin, was a noted physician in Chesterfield County who had studied at the University of Edinburgh. Gregory Harkcom Stoner, "Politics and Personal Life in the Era of the Revolution," M.A. thesis, Virginia Commonwealth University (2006): 50–52, 68.

175   **But the doctor's remedies** TMR to TJ, 22 February 1800, *PTJDE.*

175   **before word reached Martha** MJR to TJ, 30 January 1800, Betts and Bear, *Family Letters,* 182.

176   **"revived a little"** JWE to TJ, 20 February 1800, *PTJDE.*

176   **"We found Maria"** TMR to TJ, 22 February 1800, *PTJDE.* William Bache was the son of Benjamin Franklin's daughter, Sarah Franklin Bache.

176   **"some female friend"** TJ to MJE, 26 December 1803, Betts and Bear, *Family Letters,* 250.

176   **"The continuance of her indisposition"** TJ to JWE, 8 March 1800, *PTJDE.* Even after the losses his daughters had endured by March 1802, Jefferson could still write of an acquaintance that she "expects to be in the straw every hour." TJ to JWE, 3 March 1802, *PTJDE.*

176   **"The sores on her breast"** JWE to TJ, 16 February 1800 and 16 March 1800, *PTJDE.*

177   **"she has not"** JWE to TJ, 22 April 1800, *PTJDE.*

177   **They had been forced** TMR to TJ, 18 January 1800, *PTJDE.*

177   **Jefferson traveled home** TJ to TMR, 14 May 1800, *PTJDE.*

178   **"The distance is so moderate"** TJ to MJE, 4 January 1801, Betts and Bear, *Family Letters,* 190–91. The election was finally settled in Jefferson's favor on 17 February 1801, on the thirty-sixth ballot.

178   **Maria assured him** MJE to TJ, 28 December 1800, Betts and Bear, *Family Letters,* 190.

179   **"Always in a crowd"** MJR to TJ, 31 January 1801, Betts and Bear, *Family Letters,* 193.

179   **"The carpenters are still"** MJE to TJ, 28 December 1800, Betts and Bear, *Family Letters,* 189–90.

179   **"regret entirely the disappointment"** TJ to JWE, 22 February 1801, *PTJDE.*

179   **Jack declined** JWE to TJ, 18 March 1801, *PTJDE.*

179   **"the servants we shall carry"** MJE to TJ, 18 April 1801, Betts and Bear, *Family Letters,* 202.

179   **In June she left** MJE to TJ, 18 June 1801, Betts and Bear, *Family Letters,* 204.

180   **Martha did not think** MJR to TJ, 25 July 1801, Betts and Bear, *Family Letters,* 209.

180   **Attended by a local midwife** *TJMB,* 2:1051.

180   **Nor did Maria** JWE to TJ, 3 October 1801, *PTJDE*.

180   **"We have considerable apprehensions"** Ibid.

180   **"He has now struggled"** MJE to TJ, 6 November 1801, Betts and Bear, *Family Letters*, 211.

180   **"My God what a moment"** MJR to TJ, 18 November 1801, Betts and Bear, *Family Letters*, 213.

180   **"in a very precarious"** Ibid.

180   **"Maria was entirely"** TJ to MJR, 17 January 1802, Betts and Bear, *Family Letters*, 216, reporting on the letter of 6 January 1802 that he had received from JWE.

181   **"The perils he has passed"** JWE to TJ, 11 March 1802, *PTJDE*.

181   **outbreak of measles** MJE to TJ, 21 June 1802, Betts and Bear, *Family Letters*, 230.

181   **"We are entirely free"** MJR to TJ, 10 July 1802, Betts and Bear, *Family Letters*, 233.

181   **"There are no young children"** TJ to MJE, 2 July 1802, Betts and Bear, *Family Letters*, 232.

181   **"Mr. Eppes thinks"** MJE to TJ, 17 July [1802], Betts and Bear, *Family Letters*, 235.

181   **"how large a portion"** JWE to TJ, 14 July 1802, *PTJDE*.

182   **"cease to be novelties"** Quoted in Malone, "Polly Jefferson and Her Father," 91.

182   **"with his hands extended"** MJE to JWE, 25 November 1802, FLDA.

182   **"very near losing"** JWE to TJ, 10 February 1803, *PTJDE*.

182   **"It is in the best health"** MJR to TJ, 14 January 1804, Betts and Bear, *Family Letters*, 252.

182   **longing for the "baby"** MJE to TJ, 1 April 1784, Betts and Bear, *Family Letters*, 25.

183   **"now venturing across"** MJE to JWE, 25 November 1802, FLDA.

183   **"resolved to answer"** TJ to Catherine Church, 27 March 1801, *PTJDE*.

184   **Jefferson hoped that Maria** TJ to MJE, 27 November 1803, Betts and Bear, *Family Letters*, 249.

184   **"this tedious interval"** MJE to TJ, 10 February 1804, Betts and Bear, *Family Letters*, 256.

184   **"temper, naturally mild"** EWRC to Henry S. Randall, 15 January 1856, in Randall, *Jefferson*, 3:102.

184   **Martha thought the long winter's** MJR to TJ, 14 January 1804, Betts and Bear, *Family Letters*, 252.

184   **"I confess I think"** MJE to JWE, 21 January 1804, FLDA.

185   **Jefferson wrote confidently** TJ to MJE, 29 January 1804, Betts and Bear, *Family Letters*, 255.

185   **"would revive me"** MJE to JWE, 6 February 1804, Maria Eppes, Letter, Acc. 38-757, ViU.

185   **Jefferson wrote his congratulations** TJ to MJE, 26 February 1804, Betts and Bear, *Family Letters*, 258.

185   **"to get down and brake"** JWE to TJ, 9 March 1804. Copy at ICJS.

186   **Martha too had been** EWRC to Henry S. Randall, 15 January 1856, in Randall, *Jefferson*, 3:101.

186   **"be of good cheer"** TJ to MJR, 8 March 1804, Betts and Bear, *Family Letters*, 259.

186   **"it cannot be discerned"** JWE to TJ, 12 March 1804, ViU. Copy at ICJS.

186   **"the house, its contents"** TJ to JWE, 15 March 1804, Thomas Jefferson Letter, Acc. 6860, ViU.

186   **"A rising of her breast"** JWE to TJ, 19 March 1804, ViU. Copy at ICJS.

186   **"a mere walking shadow"** JWE to TJ, 23 March 1804, ViU. Copy at ICJS. See also, EWRC to Henry S. Randall, 15 January 1856, in Randall, *Jefferson,* 3:101.

186   **"Maria is not worse"** JWE to TJ, 26 March 1804, ViU. Copy at ICJS.

186   **"I found my daughter"** TJ to James Madison, 9 April 1804 and 13 April 1804, quoted in Brodie, *An Intimate History,* 508.

187   **"We have no longer"** 16 April 1804, TMR to Caesar Rodney, Huntington Library, San Marino, California. Copy at ICJS.

187   **"died Apr. 17, 1804"** Betts and Bear, *Family Letters,* 259n1.

187   **"The day passed"** EWRC to Henry S. Randall, 15 January 1856, in Randall, *Jefferson,* 3:101.

187   **two or three weeks** A rough calculation, given by TJ to JWE, 4 June 1804 and TJ to MJR, 14 May 1804, Betts and Bear, *Family Letters,* 259–60.

187   **"It will be a great comfort"** TJ to JWE, 4 June 1804, Huntington Library, San Marino, California. Copy at ICJS.

188   **"saying that people"** EWRC to Henry S. Randall, 15 January 1856, in Randall, *Jefferson,* 3:102.

188   **"Your grandmother"** EWRC Letter Book, 13 February 1856 to Henry Randall, 51, Acc. 9090, ViU; Eppes "Maria Jefferson Eppes and her Little Son, Francis," ICJS.

188   **"When you and I look"** TJ to John Page, 25 June 1804, *Thomas Jefferson Papers,* LOC.

CHAPTER 8: HARRIET'S MONTICELLO

189   **enslaved children be trained** Marie Jenkins Schwartz, *Born in Bondage: Growing up Enslaved in the Antebellum South* (Cambridge, Mass.: Harvard University Press, 2000).

190   **"bitter jealousy"** Thomas Jefferson Randolph (TJR) on TJ, n.d., Acc. 8937.

190   **a caste apart** Lucia Stanton, "Free Some Day: The African-American Families of Monticello," in Lucia Stanton, *"Those Who Labor for My Happiness": Slavery at Thomas Jefferson's Monticello* (Charlottesville: University of Virginia Press, 2012), 171.

190   **stability of family life** Gordon-Reed, *Hemingses,* 27–28.

190   **"nearly as white"** Pierson, *Jefferson at Monticello,* 107.

191   **"by far the larger part"** David Blight, ed., *Narrative of the Life of Frederick Douglass: An American Slave, Written by Himself,* 2nd ed. (Bedford Books of Saint Martin's, 2003), 39.

191   **leaving money to pay** 25 April 1801, *TJMB,* 2:1039.

192   **Jefferson also entered** *FB,* 128.

192   **"work horses, mules"** *FB,* 132.

192   **"whom fortune has thrown"** TJ to Edward Coles, 25 August 1814, *PTJDE;* Stanton, "Jefferson's People," in *"Those Who Labor,"* 56.

192   **"Bread list"** *FB* 43, 50, 134.

192   **When eighty-three hogs were slaughtered** *FB,* 48.

192   **rationed out fish and beef** *FB* 51, 56; Stanton, "Jefferson's People," in *"Those Who Labor,"* 61.

192   **To the men** *FB* 135. Jefferson refers to the nailers as "boys"; but in 1809 Edmund Bacon said the youngest was twenty-two. Edmund Bacon to TJ, 19 January 1809. I thank Lucia Stanton for this reference. This may reflect a change in practice from the mid-1790s, however, when, for example, fourteen-year-old Joe Fossett was

working in the nailery and Jefferson himself wrote in his *FB* of using boys between ten and sixteen for that work.

193   **"90 persons . . . 44 weeks"** *FB* 163.

193   **no allowance was made** Leni Sorensen, "Taking Care of Themselves: Food Production at Monticello," in *Repast* 21 (Spring 2005): 5.

193   **sell their produce** 25 July 1808. Gerald W. Gawalt, "Jefferson's Slaves: Crop Accounts at Monticello," *Journal of the Afro-American Historical and Genealogical Society* 13 (1994): 29–30.

193   **skills that Jefferson's enslaved workers** Sorensen, "Taking Care of Themselves," 5.

193   **"a best striped blanket"** TJ's Memoranda to Edmund Bacon [1805–1806], in *Farm Book,* 25.

193   **"serves till the next"** *FB,* 41.

193   **The skeins of thread** Ibid.

193   **"which I always promise"** TJ to Jeremiah Goodman, 6 January 1815, in Edwin M. Betts, ed., *Jefferson's Garden Book* (Charlottesville: Thomas Jefferson Memorial Foundation, 1999), 540. See *FB,* 137, for TJ's list of awards to slave women in 1809 and 1810.

194   **"the principles of reason"** TJ to John Adams, 28 February 1796, *PTJDE.*

194   **In true Enlightenment fashion** Stanton, "Perfecting Slavery": Rational Plantation Management at Monticello," in *"Those Who Labor,"* 71.

194   **rotating schedule** *FB,* 58, 97.

194   **Jefferson laid out his plan** *FB,* 46; Cary Carson and Carl R. Lounsbury, eds., *The Chesapeake House: Architectural Investigation by Colonial Williamsburg* (Chapel Hill: University of North Carolina Press, 2013), 192–94.

195   **Jefferson forbade his white** *FB,* 76.

195   **Four men and a girl** *FB,* 67.

195   **"laborer will grub"** *FB,* 64.

195   **"On the north terrace"** Peter Fossett, "Once the Slave of Thomas Jefferson," in *Sunday World,* Cincinnati, 30 January 1898.

195   **"we alls at work"** Quoted in Stanton, "Perfecting Slavery," in *"Those Who Labor,"* 85.

196   **Jefferson reported** TJ to James Lyle, 10 July 1795, *Farm Book,* 430.

196   **In practice, it also proved** Stanton, "Those Who Labor for My Happiness," in *"Those Who Labor,"* 11; Henry Wiencek, *Master of the Mountain: Thomas Jefferson and His Slaves* (New York: Farrar, Straus and Giroux, 2012), 93.

196   **daily goals for each** See Stanton, "Perfecting Slavery," in *"Those Who Labor,"* 80, for a photograph of TJ's nailery accounts, 1796.

196   **yielded an exceptional output** Jefferson, *Memoirs of a Monticello Slave,* 37; Stanton, "Free Some Day," in *"Those Who Labor,"* 128.

196   **Jefferson measured everything** Stanton, "Perfecting Slavery," in *"Those Who Labor,"* 80–81, 128.

196   **The discipline of the work** TJ to TMR, 23 January 1801, *PTJDE.* Writing that "under my government, I would chuse they [his nailery workers] should retain the stimulus of character," TJ obviously believed that he instilled a desire in his workers to prove themselves to him by meeting his expectations. See also Stanton, "Perfecting Slavery," in *"Those Who Labor,"* passim.

196   **"It will be useful"** TJ to TMR, 29 March [1801], *PTJDE.*

196   **"providence has made"** TJ to Joel Yancey, 17 January 1819. In *Farm Book,* 43.

196   **Jefferson built two coal sheds** *FB,* 454.

196   **hiring white men** Stanton, "Perfecting Slavery," in *"Those Who Labor,"* 80.

197   **"do anything it was"** Pierson, *Jefferson at Monticello,* 109.

197   **"He could make anything"** Ibid.

197   **His expertise ranged** Stanton, "Free Some Day," in *"Those Who Labor,"* 192–93.

197   **Jefferson paid him** Gordon-Reed, *Hemingses,* 611.

197   **strove to alleviate** Stanton, "Perfecting Slavery," in *"Those Who Labor,"* 71–72.

197   **"He animates them"** Ibid., 79.

197   **"a pound of meat"** Jefferson, *Memoirs of a Monticello Slave,* 51–52.

198   **providing financial incentives** *FB,* 110, 113.

198   **interceded to stave off** Stanton, "Those Who Labor for My Happiness," in *"Those Who Labor,"* 15.

199   **nailery was inspired** Stanton, "Perfecting Slavery," in *"Those Who Labor,"* 77–79.

199   **"has a valuable art"** TMR to TJ, 27 March 1792, *PTJDE.*

199   **"My first wish"** TJ to TMR, 19 April 1792, *PTJDE.*

199   **"from all ill usage"** TJ to Edward Coles, 25 August 1814, *Farm Book,* 39.

199   **"life for the slaves"** *FB,* 7; **"kind to the point"** Malone, *Jefferson,* 1:163.

199   **when Jack Eppes employed him** Stanton, "Those Who Labor for My Happiness," in *"Those Who Labor,"* 15.

199   **"have incurred it"** TMR to TJ, 31 January 1801, *PTJDE.* This disturbing detail from Randolph's reply, a postscript to his wife's letter, was omitted from publication in *Farm Book,* 443. This was a major point made by Henry Wiencek in *Master of the Mountain,* 120–21.

199   **Lilly did not need** Ibid.; TJ to TMR, 23 January 1801, *PTJDE.*

200   **"It will be necessary"** On Cary's age, see *FB,* 55; TJ to TMR, 8 June 1803, *PTJDE,* and *Farm Book,* 19.

200   **"barbarity"** James Oldham to TJ, 26 November 1804, quoted in Stanton, "Free Some Day," in *"Those Who Labor,"* 178.

200   **"Certainly I could never"** TJ to TMR, 5 June 1805, quoted in Wiencek, *Master of the Mountain,* 123.

200   **"first wish"** TJ to TMR, 19 April 1792, *PTJDE.*

201   **"Certainly there is nothing"** TJ to Jeremiah Goodman, 6 January 1815, *PTJDE.*

201   **"Dinah & her family"** TJ to Randolph Jefferson, 25 September 1792, in *Farm Book,* 14.

201   **"dispose of Mary"** TJ to Nicholas Lewis, 12 April 1792, *PTJDE.*

202   **"Nobody feels more strongly"** TJ to Randolph Lewis, 23 April 1807, *Farm Book,* 26, italics mine; Stanton, "Free Some Day," in *"Those Who Labor,"* 137.

202   **"exactly counter"** TJ to John Jordan, 21 December 1805, *Farm Book,* 21.

202   **recommended that Isabel Hern** Stanton, "Free Some Day," in *"Those Who Labor,"* 135–36.

202   **"formerly connected"** Stanton, "Free Some Day," in *"Those Who Labor,"* 188–89.

202   **"never in his life"** TJ to Joseph Dougherty, 31 July 1806, *Farm Book,* 22–23.

202   **bond between mother** The nineteenth-century paradigm of white motherhood fixed mothers as the pious, pure, and moral center of the home. Barbara Welter, "Cult of True Womanhood, 1820–1860." *American Quarterly* 18 (1966): 151–74; Mary P. Ryan, *Cradle of the Middle Class: The Family in Oneida County New York, 1790–1865* (Cambridge: Cambridge University Press, 1981).

202   **twelve-year-old Joseph Fossett** Stanton, "Free Some Day," in *"Those Who Labor,"* 189. Joseph's father was probably William Fossett, a white workman at Monticello; Betsy's father may have been an enslaved man, since she carried the matriarch's Hemings name for the rest of her life, only altering the spelling.

203   **given away two** Stanton, "Monticello to Main Street," in *"Those Who Labor,"* 217.

203   **three enslaved families** Stanton, "Perfecting Slavery," in *"Those Who Labor,"* 77.

203   **Maria's wedding gift** Stanton, *"Those Who Labor,"* 321n29, citing TJ's comparison of marriage settlements [1797].
203   **Beverley received his first woolens** *FB*, 55.
203   **the Farm Book records blanket** *FB*, 137.
203   **In December 1812** *FB*, 139.
203   **Beverley received** *FB*, 143, 144.
204   **"Mrs. Randolph always chooses"** Memorandum, TJ to Edmund Bacon [1805–1806], *Farm Book*, 25; *FB*, 41; Stanton, "Free Some Day," in *"Those Who Labor,"* 171. See also, Pierson, *Jefferson at Monticello*, 48–49.
204   **"old family servants"** Pierson, *Jefferson at Monticello*, 66, 48, 107.
204   **"had very little to do"** Ibid., 107.
205   **Until age fourteen** Hemings, "Memoirs," 248.
205   **"They crossed the ocean"** Pierson, *Jefferson at Monticello*, 108.
205   **twenty-seven-hour** Author visit, summer 2005.
205   **Hemings family tradition** Gordon-Reed, *Hemingses*, 144.
206   **"learned that another"** Gordon-Reed, *Hemingses*, 193.
206   **experienced the sights and sounds** Gordon-Reed, *Hemingses*, 193, chapters 8–12.
206   **names for Sally's children** Gordon-Reed, *Controversy*, 197–201; Hemings, "Memoirs," 247.
207   **It was not at all unusual** For the eighteenth century, see Farish, ed., *Journal and Letters of Philip Vickers Fithian*, and Mechal Sobel, *The World They Made Together: Black and White Values in Eighteenth-Century Virginia* (Princeton: Princeton University Press, 1987); for the nineteenth century, see Blight, *Life of Frederick Douglass*.
207   **Both Cornelia and Virginia** Pierson, *Jefferson at Monticello*, 88.
207   **"long straight hair"** Jefferson, *Memoir of a Monticello Slave*, 10.
207   **"fair," as was Ellen** EWRC Letter Book, 24 October 1858, 101, Acc. 9090, ViU.
207   **"nearly as white"** Pierson, *Jefferson at Monticello*, 110.
208   **the kinds of gifts** Randall, *Jefferson*, 3:348–51.
208   **"undemonstrative" by temperament** Hemings, "Memoirs," 247.
208   **Bachelor fathers in New Orleans** Emily Clark, *The Strange History of the American Quadroon: Free Women of Color in the Atlantic Revolutionary World* (Chapel Hill: University of North Carolina Press, 2013), 101.
208   **Prominent white Floridians** Jane Landers, *Black Society in Spanish Florida* (Urbana: University of Illinois Press, 1999), 150–53.
208   **In Jefferson's own state** Joshua D. Rothman, *Notorious in the Neighborhood: Sex and Families Across the Color Line in Virginia, 1787–1861* (Chapel Hill: University of North Carolina Press, 2003), 42–43; Philip Morgan, "Interracial Sex in the Chesapeake," in *Sally Hemings & Thomas Jefferson: History, Memory, and Civic Culture*, eds. Jan Lewis and Peter S. Onuf (Charlottesville: University Press of Virginia, 1999), 64.
208   **in the stone structure** Monticello.org—stone house, Building E. See also TJ's map of his property, 1796, in *Farm Book*, 6; TJ to TMR, 19 May 1793, *PTJDE;* Stanton, "Free Some Day," in *"Those Who Labor,"* 175.
209   **vaccinated his slaves** TJ to Dr. Henry Rose, 23 October 1801, *PTJDE*, and *Farm Book*, 18–19.
209   **Beverley was in that** 26 May 1802. List of Inoculations, *PTJDE*. See also, Gordon-Reed, *Hemingses*, 694n15. The vaccinations began on May 10, but the first two were unsuccessful; they tried again on May 19, and Harriet and Beverley, among others,

were vaccinated on the twenty-sixth. Might the late vaccination date hint that Harriet's birthday was late in the month, since her procedure took place on the last day?

209   **"The idea of exposing"** MJR to TJ, 31 March 1797, Betts and Bear, *Family Letters,* 143.

209   **entrusted Harriet's education** Julia Cherry Spruill, *Women's Life and Work in the Southern Colonies* (1938; repr., New York: W. W. Norton, 1998); Cynthia A. Kierner, *Beyond the Household: Women's Place in the Early South, 1700–1835* (Ithaca: Cornell University Press, 1998); Kerrison, *Claiming the Pen.*

209   **"a legitimate fruit"** Israel [Gillette] Jefferson, "Memoirs of Israel Jefferson," reprinted in Gordon-Reed, *Controversy,* 251.

210   **archaeologists working on Mulberry** Stanton, "Free Some Day," in *"Those Who Labor,"* 165.

210   **"Mr. Jefferson allowed"** Fossett, "Once the Slave of Thomas Jefferson."

210   **Eston, had also learned** A letter from MJR to Thomas Jefferson Randolph referred to "Eston's letter," charging her for work he had done. MJR to TJR, 11 July 1830, Acc. 1397, ViU.

210   **"lamenting very seriously"** Ellen Randolph to Virginia Randolph, 31 August 1819, FLDA.

210   **Ellen's mother kept** Stanton, "Free Some Day," in *"Those Who Labor,"* 183.

211   **twice at Christmas** TJ to MJR, 4 December 1791 and 13 December 1792, Betts and Bear, *Family Letters,* 91, 107.

211   **The women of Jefferson's family** Jefferson, *Memoirs of a Monticello Slave,* 7; TJ to MJ, 11 April 1790, 13 June 1790, 25 July 1790, in Betts and Bear, *Family Letters,* 52, 58, 62.

211   **"Served in half Virginian"** Quoted in Stanton, "Free Some Day," in *"Those Who Labor,"* 187.

211   **get the main meal prepared** Ibid., 188.

211   **as many as fifty** Dr. Robley Dunglison to Randall, n.d., Randall, *Jefferson,* 3:515.

213   **Martha Randolph had appointed** Sorenson, "Taking Care of Themselves," *Repast,* 4.

213   **Wormley Hughes sold the most** Gawalt, "Jefferson's Slaves," 20, 29.

213   **Adults built** Sorensen, "Taking Care of Themselves," *Repast,* 5.

213   **"two pair of beautiful fowls"** TJ to MJE, 29 January 1804 and TJ to Anne Cary Randolph (ACR), 9 January 1804, Betts and Bear, *Family Letters,* 256, 251.

213   **Jefferson sent his wagoner** TJ to MJR, 21 November 1806, ACR to TJ, 12 December 1806, TJ to EWR, 8 February 1807, in Betts and Bear, *Family Letters,* 290, 292, 295.

213   **Ornamental gardens** Caroline Winterer, *Mirror of Antiquity: American Women and the Classical Tradition, 1750–1900* (Ithaca: Cornell University Press, 2007); Mary Kelley, *Learning to Stand & Speak: Women, Education, and Public Life in America's Republic* (Chapel Hill: Published for OIEAHC by University of North Carolina Press, 2006).

214   **Wormley prepared the beds** TJ to ACR, 16 February 1808, Betts and Bear, *Family Letters,* 328.

214   **Jefferson's "own eye"** EWRC to Henry Randall, n.d., Randall, *Jefferson,* 3:347.

214   **delight over the rich colors** Ibid.

CHAPTER 9: AN ENLIGHTENED HOUSEHOLD

219   **dismay of many a guest** Margaret Bayard Smith, "The Haven of Domestic Life,"
in *Visitors to Monticello,* ed. Merrill D. Peterson (Charlottesville: University Press of
Virginia, 1989), 48.

219   **move their family from Edgehill** Kierner, *Martha Jefferson Randolph,* 146–47.

219   **impossibly narrow staircase** The stairs are only twenty-five inches wide.

219   **"Septimia pitied her self"** Virginia Jefferson Randolph to Jane Hollins Nicholas
Randolph, 18 February 1816. FLDA.

220   **an architectural flaw** McLaughlin, *Jefferson and Monticello,* 5–7.

220   **a "very self-centered"** William L. Beiswanger, *Monticello in Measured Drawings*
(Charlottesville: Thomas Jefferson Memorial Foundation, 1998).

220   **precedents of seventeenth-century Rome** Patricia Waddy, *Seventeenth-Century
Roman Palaces: Use and the Art of the Plan* (Cambridge, Mass.: The MIT Press,
1990), 25, 28, 30.

220   **his expectations that Maria** TJ to Catherine Church, 11 January 1798, *PTJDE.*

221   **"great advocate of light and air"** TJ quoted by Colonel Isaac A. Coles to General
John Hartwell Cocke, 23 February 1816, Acc. 640, ViU.

221   **"seem never to leave her"** Bayard Smith, "Haven of Domestic Life," 48.

221   **"has never been a subject"** TJ to Nathaniel Burwell, 14 March 1818, *Thomas Jefferson Papers,* LOC.

222   **had been translated** Trouille, *Sexual Politics in the Enlightenment,* 238.

222   **transformational impact of education** Suellen Diaconoff, *Through the Reading
Glass: Women, Books, and Sex in the French Enlightenment* (Albany: State University
of New York Press, 2005), 99, 98.

222   **"gave the mother"** Spencer, *French Women and the Age of Enlightenment,* 92.

222   **Martha's reading suggestions** TJ to Burwell, 14 March 1818, *Thomas Jefferson Papers,* LOC.

223   **Martha assigned the works of Molière** Ibid.

223   **Her emphasis on classical learning** Primary sources included: Tully (Cicero)'s *Offices* (in English); LaGrange's translation of Seneca; Dryden's Virgil; Pope's *Iliad &
Odyssey;* Titus Livey (in English); Sallust [histories] [trans] by Thomas Gordon [in
English]; Plutarch's *Lives;* Tacitus by [Arthur] Murphy; Seutonious's [*Lives of the
Poets*], trans. by [Alexander] Thomson. TJ to Burwell, 14 March 1818, *Thomas Jefferson Papers,* LOC.

224   **"my heart would swell"** EWR to Nicholas P. Trist, Monticello, 22 December 1823,
FLDA.

224   **an "ancient Italian"** MJR to TJ, 25 March 1787, 27 May 1787, and 8 March 1787,
in Betts and Bear, *Family Letters,* 33, 42, 32. Interestingly, TJ had told TMR not to
bother learning Italian if he already mastered Spanish and French, even as he was
admonishing Martha not to give up on her ancient Italian Titus Livy. TJ to TMR,
6 July 1787, *PTJDE.*

224   **"all the other luxuries"** TJ to John Brazier, 24 August 1819, in Ford, *Works* 10:1423.
Ellen also recalled that he frequently said the same to her in their conversations at
Poplar Forest.

224   **Abigail Adams complained** Winterer, *Mirror of Antiquity,* 20.

224   **when she wanted something** MJR to Virginia Jefferson Randolph, Monticello,
10 January 1822, FLDA.

224   **Anne was translating** ACR to TJ, 26 February 1802. She was translating Marcus

Junianus Justinus, *De historiis Philippicis et totius Mundi originibus.* Betts and Bear, *Family Letters,* 217.

225 **"poured over volumes"** EWR to MJR, Poplar Forest, 18 July 1819, FLDA.

225 **"between a glass"** EWR to MJR, 11 August 1819, FLDA.

225 **"the precious time"** Mary J. Randolph to Virginia J. Randolph (Trist), 31 January 1822, FLDA.

225 **Jefferson sent his nephew** TJ to Peter Carr, 19 August 1785, *PTJDE.*

225 **Two years later** TJ to Peter Carr, 10 August 1787, *PTJDE.*

225 **And when his grandsons** MJR to TJ, 16 April 1802. "Jefferson is reading latin with his Papa but I am seriously uneasy at his not going to school." Betts and Bear, *Family Letters,* 222.

225 **"with aunt and cousins"** TJ to John Wayles Eppes, 1 June 1815. Copy at ICJS.

225 **"advance the arts"** TJ, "Report to the Commissioners," 4 August 1818, in Roy J. Honeywell, *The Educational Work of Thomas Jefferson* (NY: Russell and Russell, 1964), 250.

226 **"resort to professions"** TJ to Thomas Mann Randolph, Monticello, 30 July 1821, *Jefferson Papers,* LOC.

226 **"load him on his departure"** TJ to EWE, 31 October 1790, *PTJDE.*

226 **ask the occasional question** EWRC to Randall, 1856, in Randall, *Jefferson,* 3:342.

226 **"the *elegant* and agreeable"** TMR to ACR, 1788. Quoted in Jan Lewis, *The Pursuit of Happiness: Family and Values in Jefferson's Virginia* (New York: Cambridge University Press, 1983), 150.

226 **"perhaps one of the best"** Eliza House Trist to Catherine Bache, 22 August 1814, FLDA.

226 **Martha's program for her daughters** Martha Laurens Ramsay's sons read the New Testament in Greek, but she confined her daughter's language training to French. Winterer, *Mirror of Antiquity,* 70; Kerrison, *Claiming the Pen,* passim.

226 **The 1820s was a crucial** Kelley, *Learning to Stand & Speak,* 28. See also Mary Kelley, "Female Academies and Seminaries and Print Culture," in *A History of the Book in America,* vol. 2, *An Extensive Republic: Print, Culture, and Society in the New Nation 1790–1840,* eds. Robert A. Gross and Mary Kelley (Chapel Hill: University of North Carolina Press, 2010), 336–38. Thomas Woody's survey of seminaries shows Latin, Greek, and French appearing in female seminaries but in an even later period, 1830–1871. Thomas Woody, *A History of Women's Education in the United States* (1929; repr., New York: Octagon Books, 1980), Appendix.

227 **"your own notes"** Mary J. Randolph to EWRC, 10 November 1825, FLDA.

227 **These pursuits** Susan M. Stabile, *Memory's Daughters: The Material Culture of Remembrance in Eighteenth-Century America* (Ithaca: Cornell University Press, 2004), treats the significance of the ways in which women preserve the historical memory of their families in eighteenth-century Pennsylvania.

227 **"is believed to have received"** EWRC to MJR, 19 August 1828, FLDA.

227 **His continued efforts** Kierner, *Martha Jefferson Randolph,* 144, 162, 192.

227 **"mind would sink"** EWR to MJR, 28 January 1818, FLDA.

228 **writer Judith Sargent Murray** Judith Sargent Murray, "On the Equality of the Sexes," *Massachusetts Magazine, or, Monthly Museum of Knowledge and Rational Entertainment* (March 1790): 132–35.

228 **"with a head full of something"** Eliza Southgate to Moses Porter, May 1801, in *Root of Bitterness: Documents of the Social History of American Women,* eds. Nancy F.

Cott, Jeanne Boydston, Ann Braude, Lori D. Ginzberg, and Molly Ladd-Taylor, 2nd ed. (Boston: Northeastern University Press, 1996), 100.

228   **"Ancient history was acceptable"** Winterer, *Mirror of Antiquity,* 14–15.

229   **Genlis parted company with** Trouille, *Sexual Politics in the Enlightenment,* 243.

229   **For Genlis, all reading** Diaconoff, *Through the Reading Glass,* 99, 98.

229   **needed to work to earn** Trouille, *Sexual Politics in the Enlightenment,* 245.

229   **But this approach** Clarissa Campbell Orr, "Aristocratic Feminism, the Learned Governess, and the Republic of Letters," in Knott and Taylor, *Women, Gender, and the Enlightenment,* 319.

230   **some American women nonetheless** Kerber, *Women of the Republic* and Zagarri, *Revolutionary Backlash.*

230   **Anne Willing Bingham's gatherings** Branson, *Those Fiery Frenchified Dames,* 133–41.

230   **Federalist women** Daniel Kilbride, "Cultivation, Conservatism, and the Early National Gentry: the Manigault Family and their Circle," *Journal of the Early Republic* 19 (1999): 221–56. Alice Izard, a New Yorker married to South Carolina's Ralph Izard, and her daughter, Margaret Izard Manigault, were two examples of this.

230   **But the salons survived** Catherine Allgor, *Parlor Politics: In Which the Ladies of Washington Help Build a City and a Government* (Charlottesville: University Press of Virginia, 2000). Martha herself would make use of her connections to secure a place in the Navy for her son George Wythe, but that did not denote a sense of political participation.

231   **"It is curious indeed"** Quoted in Trouille, *Sexual Politics in the Enlightenment,* 245.

231   **"Mrs. Randolph was just like"** Pierson, *Jefferson at Monticello,* 87.

231   **"fairy palace"** VJR to Nicholas P. Trist, 5 June 1823, FLDA.

231   **"to cultivate the good"** MJR to Septimia Randolph, 30 July 1832, Acc. 4726b, ViU.

232   **"preferred a thousand times"** Quoted in Trouille, *Sexual Politics in the Enlightenment,* 245.

232   **"She is *our sun*"** VJRT to Nicholas P. Trist, 12 July 1832, Acc. 2104, SHC.

232   **"education and the influence"** EWR to MJR, 28 July 1819, FLDA.

232   **designed to convey messages** Robert F. Dalzell, Jr., "Constructing Independence: Monticello, Mount Vernon, and the Men Who Built Them," *Eighteenth-Century Studies: Special Issue: Thomas Jefferson, 1743–1993: An Anniversary Collection* 26 (Summer 1993): 554; Leslie Kanes Weisman, *Discrimination by Design: A Feminist Critique of the Man-Made Environment* (Urbana: University of Illinois Press, 1992), 86.

233   **scattered all over the house** Elizabeth V. Chew, "Inhabiting the Great Man's House: Women and Space at Monticello," in *Structures and Subjectivities: Attending to Early Modern Women,* eds. Adele F. Seeff and Joan Hartman (Newark: University of Delaware Press, 2007), 223–52.

233   **It was Jefferson's intention** Hugh Howard pointed out that Jefferson the architect "knew intuitively that nowhere in his life had he a better chance at achieving order than in architecture." Howard, *Thomas Jefferson, Architect,* 20.

233   **"gendered spaces separate"** Daphne Spain, *Gendered Spaces* (Chapel Hill: University of North Carolina Press, 1992), 3, 15–16.

233   **"one of the most troublesome"** VJRT to EWRC, 3 September 1825, FLDA.

234   **"carried the keys"** Mary Jefferson Randolph and VJRT to EWRC, 11 September 1825, FLDA.

234   **"books lying covered"** Cornelia Jefferson Randolph (CJR) to EWRC, 24 November 1825, FLDA.

234   **to change places** Spain, *Gendered Spaces,* 16.

234   **A retreat Jefferson built** S. Allen Chambers, *Poplar Forest and Thomas Jefferson* (Little Compton, R.I.: Fort Church Publishers, 1993).

234   **This was a house** TJ to MJR, 31 August 1817, in Betts and Bear, *Family Letters,* 419.

234   **"the pleasure of passing"** MJR to TJ, 31 January 1801, Betts and Bear, *Family Letters,* 193.

234   **"Our cold dinner"** VJRT to Nicholas P. Trist, quoted in Randall, *Jefferson,* 3:344.

235   **Ellen managed to persuade** EWR to MJR, 14 April 1818, FLDA.

235   **list of taxable items** 1815 Bedford County, Northern District: Personal Property Tax books, in Virginia State Library, Reel 37. I am grateful to Gail Pond for allowing me access to Poplar Forest research notes.

235   **"be falling"** EWR to MJR, 24 August 1819, FLDA.

236   **"as long as"** CJR to VJR, 18 July 1819, FLDA.

236   **"little English dictionary"** CJR to VJR, 25 October 1815, FLDA. The work was probably *Willich's Domestic Encyclopedia with Maese's Additions.* I am indebted to Gail Pond, Poplar Forest, for sharing her notes on the Poplar Forest library with me.

236   **When Jefferson sold** Hayes, *Road to Monticello,* 556.

236   **cheaper, smaller, and easier** Kerrison, *Claiming the Pen,* 61.

236   **"cheerful and uneventful"** EWRC to Henry Randall, in Randall, *Jefferson,* 3:343.

237   **"interested himself"** Ibid.

237   **She roamed nostalgically** EWR to MJR, 18 July 1819, FLDA.

237   **four times the leisure** EWR to MJR, 24 August 1819, FLDA.

237   **"are the severest students"** TJ to MJR, 31 August 1817, in Betts and Bear, *Family Letters,* 419.

238   **"her highly polished"** Isaac Briggs, "A Cordial Reunion in 1820," in Peterson, *Visitors to Monticello,* 92.

238   **"Bonaparte might die"** EWR to VJR, 9 January 1820, FLDA.

238   **Jefferson had chosen** Malone, *Jefferson,* 6:399.

239   **"more and more pleased"** CJR to EWRC, 3 August 1825, FLDA.

239   **"no very great acquisition"** Mary Jefferson Randolph to EWRC, 16 April 1826, FLDA.

239   **"as we become"** CJR to EWRC, 3 August 1825, FLDA.

239   **Jefferson intended** Jennings L. Wagoner, Jr., "'That Knowledge most useful to us': Thomas Jefferson's Concept of 'Utility' in the Education of Republican Citizens." Curry School of Education, UVA. (Prepared for the conference "TJ and the Education of a Citizen in the American Republic," Library of Congress, 13–15 May 1993, 36–37.) Copy at ICJS.

240   **he did excuse** Malone, *Jefferson,* 6:465.

240   **"the effect of"** Mary Jefferson Randolph to EWRC, 6 June 1826, FLDA.

240   **"it is forbidden"** Mary Jefferson Randolph to EWRC, 23 October 1825, FLDA.

240   **A grand dinner** Eliza House Trist to Sarah M. Thompson, 1 December 1824, Acc. 5385-ac, ViU.

241   **"golden November day"** Jane Blair Cary Smith, "Carysbrook Memoir," n.d., Acc. 1378, ViU.

CHAPTER 10: DEPARTURE

242   **the stone cottage** TJ Insurance plat, 1796, in *FB,* 6; McLaughlin, *Jefferson and Monticello,* 158–59, believed the house was built in 1770, but current estimates are 1776–1778. My thanks to Lucia Stanton for the correction.

243 **building had been reconfigured** TJ to John George Baxter, 16 July 1815, *Farm Book*, 490.

244 **"spinning girls"** *FB*, 135.

244 **Madison Hemings recalled** Hemings, "Memoirs," 248.

244 **"the boys make nails"** *FB*, 77.

244 **deviated significantly** Jefferson apparently did not keep regular records in his *FB* during these years, resuming in 1815, so it is possible that Harriet began work there before that year. However, I follow Madison Hemings's testimony that his siblings generally started work at age fourteen.

244 **Beverley, Sally's eldest child** *FB*, 128; "roll of Negroes. 1810. Feb. in Albemarle."

244 **When they were young boys** TJ to Yancey, 13 September 1816, *PTJDE;* TJ to Francis Eppes, April [6, 1825], in Betts, *Garden Book*, 616.

244 **Sally's sons learned** Gordon-Reed, *Controversy*, 52; *FB*, 77, 152. TJ's notations on page 152 are undated but lie in pages between those dated 1814 and 1816; Hemings, "Memoirs," 248.

244 **spent time with their father** Gordon-Reed, *Hemingses*, 617–18.

244 **"essay in architecture"** TJ to Benjamin Latrobe, 10 October 1809, *PTJDE*.

245 **"had but little taste"** Hemings, "Memoirs," 247.

245 **"it was his mechanics"** Susan Kern, "The Material World of the Jeffersons at Shadwell," *William and Mary Quarterly* 62 (2005): 24.

246 **between six and seven thousand** TJ to Philip Mazzei, 29 December 1813, *PTJDE*.

246 **proudly reduced his own reliance** TJ to William Thornton, 14 January 1812, in *Farm Book*, 469.

246 **"The embargo has set"** ACR to TJ, 18 March 1808, in Betts and Bear, *Family Letters*, 334.

246 **Jefferson boasted** TJ to Philip Mazzei, 29 December 1813, *PTJDE*.

246 **looked to Philadelphia** TJ to James Ronaldson, 13 October 1808, in *Farm Book*, 466; Philip Scranton, *Proprietary Capitalism: The Textile Manufacture at Philadelphia, 1800–1885* (Cambridge: Cambridge University Press, 1983), 75–134.

246 **His own daughter's household** TJ to Charles Willson Peale, 8 May 1816, in *Farm Book*, 492.

247 **Jefferson gave his instructions** TJ to Jeremiah Goodman, 5 March 1813, *Farm Book*, 483.

247 **"2000 yards of linen"** TJ to Thaddeus Kosciuszko, 28 June 1812, *Farm Book*, 478.

248 **Jefferson set up a factory** TJ to William Thornton, 9 June 1814, *Farm Book*, 486; ibid., 465; TJ to Philip Mazzei, 29 December 1813, in *PTJDE*.

248 **each inventor eagerly assuring** See *Farm Book*, 469–78.

248 **"antient Jenny"** TJ to William Thornton, 9 June 1814, *Farm Book*, 486.

248 **By March 1814** TJ to William Maclure, 16 October 1813, and TJ to "Whoever it concerns," *Farm Book*, 484–86.

248 **"a girl younger than herself"** TJ to Jeremiah Goodman, 5 March 1813, *Farm Book*, 483; on Maria and Sally, see *FB*, 129. I thank Lucia Stanton for the suggestion that Harriet may have been Maria's teacher. Maria's twelve-spindle machine was the Barrett, used to spin wool.

248 **Her co-workers were young** Jefferson, "Memoirs," 250.

249 **Agnes Gillette** *FB*, 128, 152; Stanton, "Free Some Day," in *"Those Who Labor,"* 159. See also TJ's estimates on production in *FB*, 116, and information on Monticello's website: monticello.org/site/plantation-and-slavery/mary-hern, accessed 15 July 2013.

249 **Ten-year-old Eliza** monticello.org/mulberry-row/work/spinning-and-weaving, accessed 15 July 2013.

249 **"work used to be"** Sarah Nicholas Randolph to [H.S. Randall], quoting EWRC, 30 [*sic*] February 1876, Acc. 1397, ViU.

249 **As early as 1815** TJ to James Maury, 16 June 1815, in *Farm Book*, 490; Pierson, *Jefferson at Monticello*, 69.

249 **"we were so bad"** Quoted in Stanton, "Free Some Day," in *"Those Who Labor,"* 160.

249 **that were primarily female** Helen Bradley Foster, *"New Raiments of Self": African American Clothing in the Antebellum South* (New York: Berg, 1997).

249 **added to the boisterousness** Stanton, "Free Some Day," in *"Those Who Labor,"* 160.

249 **relaxed but still very productive** Sarah Nicholas Randolph to [H.S. Randall], quoting EWRC, 30 [*sic*] February 1876, Acc. 1397, ViU.

249 **It is the easiest** Interview, Linda Eaton, Head Curator of Textiles, Winterthur Museum, 6 April 2009.

250 **"never did any hard work"** Pierson, *Jefferson at Monticello*, 48, 110.

250 **no evidence that she absented** Gordon-Reed, *Hemingses*, 601.

250 **"I cannot now even"** EWR to TJ, 26 February 1808, Betts and Bear, *Family Letters*, 330.

250 **"cultivate their lands"** TJ to Handsome Lake, 3 November 1802, *PTJDE*.

250 **"a peculiar fact"** Fossett, "Once the Slave of Thomas Jefferson."

251 **whipping of Jame Hubbard** TJ to Reuben Perry, 16 April 1812, *Farm Book*, 34.

251 **"I had him severely flogged"** Ibid., 35.

251 **"favorite servant"** Stanton, "Free Some Day," in *"Those Who Labor,"* 149–50.

251 **"All circumstances convince me"** TJ to Reuben Perry, 16 April 1812, in *Farm Book*, 35.

252 **"there can be great comfort"** Gordon-Reed, *Hemingses*, 603.

253 **"You know we never"** EWR to MJR, 27 September 1816, FLDA.

253 **"take care to require"** EWRC to VJRT, 15 October 1830, FLDA.

253 **"It is well known"** James Callender, *Recorder* (Richmond, Va.), 1 September 1802.

253 **articles ensued, adding details** Michael Durey, *"With the Hammer of Truth": James Thomson Callender and America's Early National Heroes* (Charlottesville: University Press of Virginia, 1990), chapter 7.

254 **"Black Sal is no farce"** 24 May 1811, Elijah P. Fletcher to Jesse Fletcher, Esquire of Ludlow, Vermont. Copy at ICJS.

254 **"Mr. Jefferson's notorious"** Journal of John Hartwell Cocke, 26 January 1853, Acc. 640.

254 **The unwritten rule** Rothman, *Notorious in the Neighborhood*, 13, 50–51.

254 **"took the Dusky Sally"** Henry Randall to James Parton, 1 June 1868, in Gordon-Reed, *Controversy*, 255.

254 **"dreams of freedom"** Randall, *Jefferson*, 3:118–19.

254 **chose to read** Jan Ellen Lewis, "The White Jeffersons," in Lewis and Onuf, *Sally Hemings & Thomas Jefferson*, 138, 146–47.

254 **"the resemblance was so close"** Randall to Parton, 1 June 1868, in Gordon-Reed, *Controversy*, 254.

255 **"the discomfort"** MJR to EWRC, 2 August 1825, FLDA.

255 **According to Jeff** Randall to Parton, 1 June 1868, in Gordon-Reed, *Controversy*, 256.

255 **"Remember this fact"** Randall to Parton, 1 June 1868, in Gordon-Reed, *Controversy*, 255.

255 **Jefferson's records showed** Fraser D. Neiman, "Coincidence or Causal Connection? The Relationship between Thomas Jefferson's visits to Monticello and Sally Hemings's Conceptions," *William and Mary Quarterly* 57 (January 2000): 198–210.

255 **"inducing the white children"** Hemings, "Memoirs," 247.

255 **"there is a general impression"** EWRC to Joseph Coolidge, 24 October 1858, EWRC Letter Book, 98–101, Acc. 9090, ViU.

256 **The white family stories** See Gordon-Reed, *Controversy;* Lewis, "White Jeffersons" and Rhys Isaac, "Monticello Stories Old and New," in Lewis and Onuf, *Sally Hemings & Thomas Jefferson,* 114–26.

256 **Jeff failed to explicitly** Lewis, "White Jeffersons," 150. It would not have been Madison, who at not quite five feet eight inches lacked Jefferson's height.

256 **In her feigned ignorance** Gordon-Reed, *Hemingses,* 619.

256 **"Irish workmen"** EWRC to Joseph Coolidge, 24 October 1858, EWRC Letter Book, 100, Acc. 9090, ViU.

257 **"Putting domestic slavery"** *Diary,* 30 January 1839, Birle and Francavilla, *Thomas Jefferson's Granddaughter,* 198.

257 **"by far too moderate"** CJR to VJRT, 11 August 1833, FLDA. Melinda Colbert Freeman, a former Monticello slave, was a freed person by this time, married and living in Washington. It is possible that she was related to Sally. Email communication, Lucia Stanton, 16 March 2014. Cornelia's account also included Martha's efforts to discipline an unruly grandson.

258 **But that prospect crumbled** Gordon-Reed, *Hemingses,* 604.

258 **Like Martha, Sally** Gordon-Reed, *Hemingses,* 559–60.

259 **"treated by the rest"** *Frederick Town Herald,* reprinted in *Recorder* (Richmond, Va.), 8 December 1802.

259 **But unlike her mother** Gordon-Reed, *Hemingses,* 598.

259 **unlike most enslaved women** Deborah Gray White, *Ain't I a Woman? Female Slaves in the Plantation South* (New York: W. W. Norton, 1999), 97.

259 **enforced a color hierarchy** See Kathy Russell, Midge Wilson, and Ronald Hall, *The Color Complex: The Politics of Skin Color Among African Americans* (New York: Doubleday, 1992), 9–23.

259 **"The slave is always"** Saidiya Hartman, *Lose Your Mother: A Journey Along the Atlantic Slave Route* (New York: Farrar, Straus and Giroux, 2007), 87, 88.

260 **Six years earlier** Douglas R. Egerton, *Gabriel's Rebellion: The Virginia Slave Conspiracies of 1800 and 1802* (Chapel Hill: University of North Carolina Press, 1993).

261 **sixty-one different phrases** Rothman, *Notorious in the Neighborhood,* 204.

261 **"the racial order"** Eva Sheppard Wolf, *Race and Liberty in the New Nation: Emancipation in Virginia from the Revolution to Nat Turner's Rebellion* (Baton Rouge: Louisiana State University Press, 2006), 86.

261 **They remained raceless** Rothman, *Notorious in the Neighborhood,* 204, 208–10.

261 **When the 1830 census taker** Stanton, *Those Who Labor,* 345n5.

261 **"Negroes retained"** FB, 160.

262 **"run [18]22"** FB, 130.

263 **"by Mr. Jefferson's direction"** Pierson, *Jefferson at Monticello,* 110.

263 **population of nearly sixty-four thousand** 1820 census. census.gov/history/www/fast_facts/012344.html, accessed 14 April 2009.

263 **The city had attracted** Gary B. Nash, *Forging Freedom: The Formation of Philadelphia's Black Community* (Cambridge, Mass.: Harvard University Press, 1988), 137.

263 **Philadelphia's approach to slavery** The disappearance of slavery by 1820 most emphatically did not mean the disappearance of bigotry and discrimination, as

black Philadelphians knew. White Philadelphians responded to the growing black population with laws and practices that increasingly restricted their rights, including barring black men from the franchise by 1836. See Gary B. Nash and Jean R. Soderlund, *Freedom by Degrees: Emancipation in Pennsylvania and Its Aftermath* (New York: Oxford University Press, 1991).

263 **sent her to Philadelphia** I thank Beverly Gray, historian of Monticello's Getting Word project, for the suggestion that Harriet Hemings may have begun her free life in Philadelphia. Phone interview, 3 April 2009.

264 **In fact, Madison specified** Hemings, "Memoirs," 246.

264 **"lurking under the connivance"** TJ to John Barnes, 14 June 1817, *PTJDE.*

264 **In one instance** Joseph Dougherty to TJ, 3 July 1809, *PTJDE.* Unlike her aunt Sally, Betsy Hemmings spelled her name with two *m*'s.

265 **Paul Jennings** Elizabeth Dowling Taylor, *A Slave in the White House: Paul Jennings and the Madisons* (New York: Palgrave Macmillan, 2012).

265 **Indeed, one historian** Taylor, *A Slave in the White House,* 76; Pierson, *Jefferson at Monticello,* 110–11.

265 **"Beverley went to Washington"** Hemings, "Memoirs," 246.

265 **One of the last records** FB, 164. "They [also] appear on the 1820–1821 cloth distribution list, a page that got separated from the FB over the years. . . . Both of their names have brackets around them, as do the names of three others, including Billy (William Hern, born 1801), who ran away in 1820." Communication from Lucia Stanton, 17 March 2014.

265 **The last time** FB, 171. The list is under his corn calculations, dated January 1821.

265 **Sally Hemings's name** FB, 172.

265 **Jefferson even made** FB, 165.

266 **"as he stood"** Mary J. Randolph to VJR, 27 December 1821, FLDA.

266 **Hemings scholars believe** Gordon-Reed, *American Controversy,* 33. Relying on an edited version of the *Farm Book,* Gordon-Reed follows an error made in *The Garden and Farm Books of Thomas Jefferson,* ed. Robert C. Baron (Golden, Colorado: Fulcrum, 1987), 479. Baron placed Harriet's name under Sally's in the year 1822. Jefferson's *Farm Book* omits both Beverley's and Harriet's names in 1822. However, the latest record of Harriet's presence at Monticello is early 1821 (between January and July), *FB,* 171.

266 **as a cooper** TJ to Edmund Bacon, 29 November 1820. Massachusetts Historical Society, quoted at monticello.org/site/plantation-and-slavery/coopering. See also, Edmund Bacon to TJ, 4 September 1819, Massachusetts Historical Society. "Davy & Beverly are with cooper they have not failed to deliver 108 barls every week since they began to make and they dress their timber as they go."

266 **anything like Paul Jennings** Taylor, *A Slave in the White House.*

266 **"was of good circumstances"** Hemings, "Memoirs," 246.

266 **We also suspect** Jefferson, *Memoirs of a Monticello Slave,* 10.

267 **"She thought it"** Hemings, "Memoirs," 246.

267 **"By her dress and conduct"** Ibid.

268 **In 1735, South Carolina** Foster, "New Raiments of Self," 134–35; Peter H. Wood, *Black Majority: Negroes in Colonial South Carolina from 1670 Through the Stono Rebellion* (Alfred A. Knopf, 1974), 145.

268 **costume of an enslaved woman** Linda Baumgarten, *What Clothes Reveal: The Language of Clothing in Colonial and Federal America* (New Haven: Yale University Press, 2012), 96, 120, 136; Foster, "New Raiments of Self," 162.

268 **"a dozen or more"** Quoted in Foster, "New Raiments of Self," 91.

268   **"worked in the fields"** Quoted in ibid., 171.

268   **clearly conscious of the ways** Gordon-Reed, *Hemingses*, 119, 122; Baumgarten, *What Clothes Reveal*, 135–36.

269   **"The clothes which served"** EWR to Margaret Nicholas, 26 March 1825, Acc. 1397, ViU.

269   **the return list** Sarah Elizabeth Nicholas to Jane Nicholas Randolph, Randolphs of Edgehill, 25 June [1822], Acc. 1397, ViU. Although archivists have guessed at 1822 as the date for this letter (Margaret [Peggy] Nicholas marshaled the advice of her daughters to reply to Ellen), this letter is most likely the reply to Ellen's dated letter of March 1825.

269   **The tab for Ellen's ensemble** Fifty dollars in 1822 was the equivalent of three months' pay. Gordon-Reed, *Controversy*, 30.

269   **White women's dress** A beautiful example of this is pictured in Baumgarten, *What Clothes Reveal*, 44.

270   **"a remarkably fine looking"** "A Sprig of Jefferson was Eston Hemings," *Daily Scioto Gazette*, Chillicothe, Ohio, 1902.

271   **"being with and coming"** Fossett, "Once the Slave of Thomas Jefferson."

271   **Beverley used to play** Lucia Stanton, "Free Some Day," in *"Those Who Labor,"* 116. Isaac Granger Jefferson remembered Jefferson's brother Randolph, who would "come out among the black people, play the fiddle and dance half the night." Jefferson, *Memoirs of a Monticello Slave*, 50. A white woman, however, could never be seen in such company without risking her reputation.

271   **We do not know** Albemarle County Minute Book, 1832–1843, 12, cited in Stanton, *Those Who Labor*, 338n261.

271   **In addition, respectability dictated** Dallett C. Hemphill, *Bowing to Necessities: A History of Manners in America, 1620–1860* (New York: Oxford University Press, 1999), 114–16, 144, 187.

271   **"the subject of dress"** TJ to MJ, 22 December 1783, Betts and Bear, *Family Letters*, 22.

271   **"an industrious and orderly"** *Frederick Town Herald*, reprinted in *Recorder* (Richmond, Va.), 8 December 1802.

271   **question of health and hygiene** Kathleen M. Brown, *Foul Bodies: Cleanliness in Early America* (New Haven: Yale University Press, 2009), especially chapter 9, "Redemption."

272   **questions of body control** John F. Kasson, *Rudeness & Civility: Manners in Nineteenth-Century Urban America* (New York: Hill and Wang, 1990), 124–25.

272   **Far from leveling** Hemphill, *Bowing to Necessities*, 130.

272   **"when she was nearly"** Pierson, *Jefferson at Monticello*, 110. This is also the thinking of Lucia Stanton, communication 17 March 2014.

272   **"month . . . of unusual"** MJR to Nicholas P. Trist, 8 January 1822, FDLA.

272   **Her husband was serving** Kierner, *Martha Jefferson Randolph*, 182–84.

272   **"the boys set off"** TJ to John Hemings, 18 December 1821, Coolidge Collection, Reel 11, Massachusetts Historical Society.

273   **seems to have delegated** Pierson, *Jefferson at Monticello*, 110.

273   **given James Hemings** *TJMB*, 2:1084; TJ to MJR, 3 June 1802, Betts and Bear, *Family Letters*, 227.

273   **"Mrs. Randolph would not"** Fossett, "Once the Slave of Thomas Jefferson."

273   **We know Ellen traveled** EWR to MJR, 19 November 1819, FDLA.

273   **"There was a great deal"** Pierson, *Jefferson at Monticello*, 110.

273   **in the small town** Edgar Woods, *History of Albemarle County Virginia* (Bridgewater, Va.: C. J. Carrier Company, 1900), 39.

274   **"woman who brings a child"** TJ to JWE, 30 June 1820, in *Farm Book,* 45–46.

CHAPTER 11: PASSING

275   **It was a good road** TJ to MJR, 3 June 1802, Betts and Bear, *Family Letters,* 227.

275   **"excessively disagreeable"** CJR to VJRT, 16 April 1826, Burke and Trist Family Papers, Acc. 5385ac, ViU.

276   **"the cool selfishness"** Harriet Martineau, *Society in America* (New York: Saunders and Otley, 1837), 3:90.

276   **the solicitous concern** CJR to VJRT, 16 April 1826, Acc. 5385ac, ViU.

277   **The hotel occupied** Judah Delano, *Washington Directory: Showing the Name, Occupation, and Residence of Each Head of a Family and Person in Business* (Washington: William Duncan, 1822), 20.

277   **Its proprietor, Jesse Brown** Jonathan Elliot, *Historical Sketches of the Ten Miles Square Forming the District of Columbia* (Washington, D.C.: J. Elliot, Jr., 1830).

277   **numerous dancing assemblies** *Daily National Intelligencer,* 12 December 1821.

277   **steamboats that served** Elliot, *Historical Sketches.*

277   **embody the very principles** Constance McLaughlin Green, *Washington: Village and Capital, 1800–1878* (Princeton: Princeton University Press, 1962), 13–14; Allgor, *Parlor Politics,* 58–59.

278   **She saw the great variety** Delano, *Washington Directory,* passim.

278   **The avenue was lined** TJ to Thomas Munroe, 21 March 1803, *PTJDE;* Capitol, Engraving by Alfred Jones, 1848, in Green, *Washington,* figure 15. Benjamin Latrobe preserved an 1812 view, showing a gracious tree-lined street coming down from the Capitol in ibid., figure 7. Although unsuited to Washington's climate, the poplars seem to have persisted until at least the 1840s.

279   **its population was only** This figure does not include Georgetown's 7,360 or Alexandria's 8,345 people. 1820 census.

279   **In the next decade** Carl Abbott, *Political Terrain: Washington, D.C., from Tidewater Town to Global Metropolis* (Chapel Hill: University of North Carolina Press, 1999), 28–38, 47–48.

279   **English visitors** Harriet Martineau, *Retrospect of Western Travel* (1838; repr., New York: Greenwood Press, 1969), 1:237, 266.

279   **One 1822 visitor** Anonymous English traveler, 1822, quoted in John W. Reps, *Washington on View: The Nation's Capital Since 1790* (Chapel Hill: University of North Carolina Press, 1991), 68.

279   **"will find this place"** Margaret (Peggy) Nicholas to Jane Nicholas Randolph, 24 April 1822, Acc. 1397, ViU.

279   **"expected to see"** Quoted in Reps, *Washington on View,* 76.

280   **"well dressed"** James Hugo Johnston, *Race Relations in Virginia & Miscegenation in the South 1776–1860* (Amherst: University of Massachusetts Press, 1970), 207–10.

281   **When a fugitive slave** Harriet A. Jacobs, *Incidents in the Life of a Slave Girl, Written by Herself,* ed. Jean Fagan Yellin (Cambridge, Mass.: Harvard University Press, 1987), 159. On this moment, see also Virginia Cope, "'I Verily Believed Myself to Be a Free Woman': Harriet Jacobs and Her Journey into Capitalism," *African American Review* 38 (Spring 2004): 5–20.

282   **"I will make"** Robert Carter Nicholas to TJR, 25 June 1836, Trist Family Papers, SHC, quoted in Judith Justus, *Down from the Mountain: The Oral History of the Hemings Family. Are They the Black Descendants of Thomas Jefferson?* (Fremont, Ohio: Lesher Printers, Inc., 1990), 130–31. TJR's letter has not been found.

283   **"people in straightened"** Dolley Madison to Nicholas P. Trist, quoted in Kierner, *Martha Jefferson Randolph,* 230.

283   **Mrs. Stewart's boardinghouse** *Daily National Intelligencer,* 8 January 1822.

283   **"Gentlemen preferring comfort"** *Daily National Intelligencer,* 1 January 1822.

283   **"situated near the corner"** *Daily National Intelligencer,* 23 January 1822.

283   **"a situation"** *Daily National Intelligencer,* 19 March 1822.

283   **"young lady well skilled"** *Daily National Intelligencer,* 31 January 1822.

284   **several small schools** Delano, *Washington Directory,* passim and 33.

284   **"the destiny of"** Mrs. L. G. Abell, *Woman in Her Various Relations, Containing Practical Rules for American Females* (New York: J. M. Fairchild, 1855), 202, 207. Italics in the original.

284   **The financial Panic** Jefferson had co-signed a note for twenty thousand dollars for his grandson's father-in-law, Wilson Cary Nicholas, that Nicholas was unable to pay. Land values also plunged, effectively negating Jefferson's plan to sell land to offset his debts. Dumas Malone recounts this story in *Jefferson,* 6:303–5, 308–14.

284   **cultivating the manners** Hemphill, *Bowing to Necessities,* 146, 151; see also Hemphill, "Manners and Class in the Revolutionary Era: A Transatlantic Comparison," *William and Mary Quarterly* 63 (April 2006): 345–72 .

285   **Centre Market** Described in Jefferson Morley, *Snow-Storm in August: Washington City, Francis Scott Key, and the Forgotten Race Riot of 1835* (New York: Doubleday, 2012), 17.

285   **"running about"** Hunt, *First Forty Years of Washington Society,* 48–49.

285   **"Monticello is the only place"** EWRC to Henry Randall, 22 February 1856, in EWRC Letter Book, 53, Acc. 9090, ViU.

285   **Even by age eleven** Fossett, "Once the Slave of Thomas Jefferson."

285   **guests like Webster** Daniel Webster, "A Yankee Congressman Pens a Portrait," in Peterson, *Visitors to Monticello,* 99.

285   **"He that hath not"** *Poor Richard's Almanac,* February 1744, quoted in Esmond Wright, *Franklin of Philadelphia* (Cambridge, Mass.: Harvard University Press, 1986), 43.

285   **"white man of good standing"** Hemings, "Memoirs," 246.

286   **Getting Word project** Edna Jacques, "Getting Word," Monticello.org.

286   **To this day** Author interview, 4 December 2012.

287   **"The Hemingses had a positive mania"** Gordon-Reed, *Hemingses,* 517.

287   **some Presbyterians** John C. Smith, *Jehovah-Jireh: A Discourse Commemorative of the Twenty-seventh Anniversary of the Organization of the Fourth Presbyterian Church, Washington, D.C.* (Washington, D.C.: Thomas McGill, 1855), 33. *Sabin Americana.*

288   **Only two of the original** Session Records, vol. 1, 1812–1840, First Presbyterian Church, Washington, D.C. I am grateful to Theodore Anderson for his assistance. Marriage and Baptism Record Book, St. John's Episcopal Church, Lafayette Square, Washington, D.C. I am grateful to Hayden Bryan, who provided access to this record.

288   **Extracting the name** F. Edward Wright, compiler, *Marriage Licenses of Washington, D.C. 1811 through 1830* (Silver Spring, Md.: Family Line Publications, 1988).

288   **For example, baptism records** Genealogical Record Committee (GRC), Daughters of the American Revolution. Free: GRC vol. 16, Rock Creek Church Records, baptismal records, 1803–1804; Higdon: Christ Church, Alexandria, records, May 1807; Dyer: Register of baptisms, marriages, and funerals, Presbyterian Church of Alexandria, 11; Hughes: GRC vol. 16, 58; Graves: GRC vol. 16, 71. Rock Creek records.

289   **Sales was a woman of color** GRC series 1, vol. 82, 27.

289   **Harriet Nicoll** For the marriage settlement, see bulk.resource.org/courts.gov/c/US/49/49.US.10.html.

289   **Other records show** Obituary, Thomas Shields, congressionalcemetery.org; on McKean, see Alfred Hunt, compiler, *The Washington and Georgetown Directory*, ed. Wesley E. Pippenger (1853; rev. ed., Lewes, Del.: Colonial Roots, 2004), 68.

289   **District's probate records** GRC: Record of Wills, vol. 4 (1799–1837), as recorded in the Office of Register of Wills, Municipal Court, Washington, D.C., 297–99; dated 10 August 1835; probated 29 September 1835.

290   **Harriet Bohrer** National Archives: Record Group 21, Entry 115: Old Series Case files, 1801–1878, Acc. 4581.

290   **"My wife, Harriet Steel"** *Daily National Intelligencer,* 4 January 1827.

290   **"filled with honor"** *Evening Star,* 9 December 1871. The "Oldest Inhabitants" was a Washington men's society.

290   **nineteenth-century male identity** On definition of masculinity and its connection with work in this period, see Jeanne Boydston, *Home and Work: Housework, Wages, and the Ideology of Labor in the Early Republic* (New York: Oxford University Press, 1990); and for laboring men, see Sean Wilentz, *Chants Democratic: New York City and the Rise of the American Working Class, 1788–1850* (New York: Oxford University Press, 1984).

290   **visit Congressional Cemetery** Congressional Cemetery, Range and Interment records, "Blue Book," begun in 1858, unpaginated, Range 72; gravestone, Charles Bell, "Died Aug 15, 1845, Aged 80 years."

291   **Brent's father** Chester Horton Brent, *The Descendants of Hugh Brent, Immigrant to Isle of Wight County, Virginia, 1642* (Rutland: Tuttle Publishing Company, 1936), 133–35.

291   **"for she has passed"** Charles Francis Adams, 26 December 1823, Adams Family Papers, Massachusetts Historical Society.

291   **baptized in St. Mary's** Records of the American Catholic Historical Society of Philadelphia, 18:73–75, at DAR.

291   **the case of Harriet Walker** Baptism: GRC vol. 038:40 at St. John's Roman Catholic Church, Forest Glen, Md.; Walker-Martin marriage: GRC marriage records, vol. 22:351.

292   **Family Search** Family Search is the website of the Church of Latter Day Saints.

292   **Pumphrey was a laborer** S. A. Elliot, *The Washington Directory* (Washington, D.C.: S. A. Elliot, 1827); 1860 census.

293   **appears in the Washington newspapers** *Daily National Intelligencer,* 14 January 1853; *Evening Star,* 24 February 1858.

293   **Not even the names** On Pumphrey family genealogy, see Edythe Maxey Clark, *William Pumphrey of Prince George's County Maryland and His Descendants* (Decorah, Ia.: Anundsen, 1992); L. N. Pumphrey, *The Pumphrey Pedigree* (Baltimore: Gateway Press, 2003).

293   **wedding announcement** Ralph D. Smith, *The Simpson Families of Southern Mary-*

land, Western Maryland, and the District of Columbia to 1820 (Daytona Beach, Fl.: R. D. Smith, 1998); Dennis William Simpson, compiler, *Simpson and Allied Families* (Baltimore: Gateway Press, 1985); John Worth Simpson, *Simpson: A Family of the American Frontier* (Baltimore: Gateway Press, 1983); Henry C. Peden, Jr., compiler, *Marriages and Deaths from Baltimore Newspapers, 1817–1824* (Lewes, Del.: Colonial Roots, 2010), 205, pumphreyfuneralhome.com, accessed 3 June 2015.

294 **Williamson was a Scottish immigrant** Obituary, congressionalcemetery.org.

294 **several examples of Scotsmen** See, for example, Allyson Hobbs, *A Chosen Exile: A History of Racial Passing in American Life* (Cambridge, Mass.: Harvard University Press, 2014), 84.

294 **"In the '30's,"** James Croggon, *Historical Sketch,* Second Part, "The Blocks between I and M, 10th and 11th Streets—Once an Enormous Gravel Bank," *Evening Star,* 16 February 1908.

294 **"a handsome interest"** John Wayles Eppes to TJ, 11 May 1802, *PTJDE.*

294 **Just a quick sampling** NARA Deed books, Record Group 351, Entry 112; see, for example, WB 89 (1841) 302/239; WB 98, 1842–1843; WB 130, 1846, 1847, Lot 2, Square 414.

295 **"erecting some frame houses"** Croggon, *Historical Sketch.*

295 **By 1860** 1860 Census, Washington, D.C.

295 **widow hired thirty carriages** NARA, Probate Records. Record Group 21, Entry 115: Old Series Case files, 1801–1878, Acc. 5011.

295 **Williamson joined the Society** Joseph B. Williamson application to the Association of the Oldest Inhabitants, 4 June 1898, MSS 422, Series V: Membership Applications, Container 2, Folder 53, Historical Society of Washington.

295 **even his death certificate** I am grateful to the archivist Ali Ramaan from the District of Columbia Archives for finding the death certificate, which had initially proved elusive.

295 **meet with a descendant** Interview with Elisabeth Williamson, 22 March 2014.

295 **Charles migrated to Missouri** 28 December 1863 Charles B. Williamson married Fanny B. Brady, Marion County, Missouri Marriage Records, 1805–2002; Ralls County Death Certificate, 4 August 1910.

295 **presented themselves for marriage** *Washington Gazette,* 16 July 1822.

296 **"Laurie was conducting a service"** Elaine Morrison Foster, "Founding a Church in a City on a Hill: Joseph Nourse, James Laurie, and the F Street Church," in *Capital Witness: A History of the New York Avenue Presbyterian Church in Washington, D.C.,* eds. Dewey D. Wallace, Jr., Wilson Golden, and Edith Holmes Snyder (Franklin, Tenn.: Plumbline Media, 2011), 40. It must also be noted, however, that on 15 January 1805, Jefferson contributed fifty dollars to the new church Laurie was building. Ibid.

296 **"having applied for admission"** Fourth Presbyterian Church Records, *First Session Book: 1828–Sept 1878,* May 1835, 44. I am grateful to Ruth Williams at Fourth Presbyterian Church for access to its archives. Baptism and marriage records from Laurie's F Street Church do not begin until the 1880s, and the 1824 session minutes do not list the Williamsons in their membership roll. Email communication with Daniel Stokes, New York Avenue Presbyterian Church historian, 9 July 2013.

296 **Joseph was elected** Board of Trustees: *Evening Star,* 10 April 1897, 23; new church: *Evening Star,* 11 March 1898.

297 **member for sixty-five years** Obituary, *Washington Post,* 9 January 1917.

297 **"Harriet Williamson, her mark"** Benjamin Williamson Deed to John T. Towers, NARA Deeds, Record Group 351, Entry 112, WB 136, 26 June 1847, 307/250.

297   **a signed promissory note** Note, 11 June 1864, NARA, Record Group 21, Entry 115: Old Series Case files, 1801–1878, Acc. 5011.

298   **"prominent in the affairs"** *Evening Star,* May 12, 1914.

298   **builder who supported** Interview with descendant, 22 March 2014. Joseph Boteler Williamson is often referred to as Joseph B. Williamson, Jr., although his middle name was different from his father's.

298   **Charles Williamson** Probate records, Charles J. Williamson, Acc. 61737, D.C. Superior Court Probate Division; "Anniversary Is Celebrated by Pendexters," *Washington Post,* 23 March 1946.

298   **"two copper candle sticks"** 6 June 1821, *Washington Gazette,* 3.

299   **So her birthday became** Harriet Williamson death certificate, 4 November 1883, District of Columbia Public Records Office; tombstone, Congressional Cemetery.

299   **not been able to find** Harriet Williamson death certificate. The only Joseph Garner who appears in the District is a black man who was advertised as a runaway slave in *National Intelligencer,* 8 December 1821.

299   **"opening a grave"** Daily Interments, July 1839–July 1849, vol. 2, unpaginated. Congressional Cemetery Archive.

300   **"so obscure that the spot"** Elizabeth Keckley, *Behind the Scenes, or, Thirty Years a Slave and Four Years in the White House* (New York: Oxford, 1988), 240–41.

301   **story of a French imposter** Natalie Zemon Davis, *The Return of Martin Guerre* (Cambridge, Mass.: Harvard University Press, 1983).

301   **"that astonishing things"** Ibid., 125.

301   **difficulties for unskilled laborers** Green, *Washington,* 96.

302   **worsening predicament of blacks** Abbott, *Political Terrain,* 49.

302   **"our enemy at home"** Quoted in Green, *Washington,* 58.

302   **But just seven years later** Abbott, *Political Terrain.*

302   **In 1828 blacks were even forbidden** Green, *Washington,* 99.

302   **energetically erecting churches** Ibid., 100.

302   **blacks founded schools** Ibid.

303   **First Freed** Elizabeth Clark-Lewis, *First Freed: Washington, D.C. in the Emancipation Era* (Washington, D.C.: Howard University Press, 2002), passim.

303   **"This thing is not done"** "Mrs. Madison's Slaves Again," *Liberator,* 31 March 1848, quoted in Holly Cowan Shulman, "History, Memory, and Dolley Madison," in *The Queen of America: Mary Cutts's Life of Dolley Madison,* ed. Catherine Allgor (Charlottesville: University of Virginia Press, 2012), 65.

303   **One of the fugitives** Shulman, "History, Memory, and Dolley Madison," 65–66.

304   **Blacks who could not prove** Green, *Washington,* 97.

304   **Visitors observed with disgust** Jesse Torrey, *A Portraiture of Domestic Slavery, in the United States* (Philadelphia: John Bioren, 1817), 33–34.

305   **object of the crowd's wrath** Morley, *Snow-Storm in August,* 21.

305   **Blacks remaining behind** Kathleen M. Lesko, *Black Georgetown Remembered: A History of Its Black Community from the Founding of "The Town of George" in 1751 to the Present Day* (Washington, D.C.: Georgetown University Press, 1991), 12; Abbott, *Political Terrain,* 49.

306   **died a social one** Orlando Patterson, *Slavery and Social Death: A Comparative Study* (Cambridge, Mass.: Harvard University Press, 1982).

307   **of questionable skin color** Frank W. Sweet, *Legal History of the Color Line: The Notion of Invisible Blackness* (Palm Coast, Fl.: Backintyme, 2005).

307   **"Silence was the only"** Hartman, *Lose Your Mother,* 71.

307 **"tainted with African blood"** Hemings, "Memoirs," 246.

307 **"the creation and establishment"** Linda Schlossberg and María Carla Sánchez, eds., *Passing: Identity and Interpretation in Sexuality, Race, and Religion* (New York: New York University Press, 2001), 4.

308 **"Poor creature"** MJR to TJ, 15 January 1795, in Betts and Bear, *Family Letters,* 131; MJR to Septimia Randolph Meikleham, 27 March 1833, Acc. 4726b, ViU.

308 **would have detached herself** Linda Schlossberg, "Rites of Passing," in Sánchez and Schlossberg, *Passing: Identity and Interpretation,* 4. The different stories the Randolph grandchildren invented to explain the "yellow" children at Monticello show that they, too, needed to make sense of their complicated past. EWRC to Joseph Coolidge, 24 October 1858, Acc. 9090, ViU; Thomas Jefferson Randolph on Thomas Jefferson, n.d., Acc. 8937, ViU.

308 **"Passing never feels natural"** Brooke Kroeger, *Passing: When People Can't Be Who They Are* (New York: PublicAffairs, 2003), 8.

Chapter 12: Legacies

309 **"There was no knowing"** VJRT to Nicholas P. Trist, 17–20 April 1835, Acc. 2104, SHC.

309 **"April 18th [1835]"** Will of Martha Jefferson Randolph, 18 April [1835], Acc. 1397, ViU.

309 **"often filled with tears"** MJR to TJR, 8 February 1833; and Joseph Coolidge to Thomas Jefferson Randolph, 23 July 1830, Papers of the Randolph Family of Edgehill and Wilson Cary Nicholas, Acc. 5533, ViU.

310 **She disposed of two** Martha Jefferson Randolph named and devised these slaves in her 1836 will.

310 **"The happiness of so many"** VJRT to Nicholas P. Trist, 17–20 April 1835, Acc. 2104, SHC.

310 **Emily and Martha Ann Colbert** Because MJR did not die after she dictated this will, these women remained enslaved. Indeed, Martha Ann Colbert would later be given to Lewis Randolph, who took her to Arkansas. Colbert does not appear in the records again, so presumably she died there.

310 **She divided the family silver** Joseph Coolidge to TJR, 18 December 1826, Edgehill Randolph Papers, ViU.

310 **To Virginia's husband** Jane Blair Cary Smith, "Carysbrook Memoir," n.d., 5, Acc. 1378, ViU.

311 **"It's done"** VJRT to NPT, 17–20 April 1835, Acc. 2104, SHC.

311 **"the first American"** Chastellux, *Travels in North America,* 2:42.

311 **"Her husband has gone on"** Jane Margaret Carr to Dabney Carr, 27 February 1826, Carr Cary Papers, Acc. 1231, ViU.

312 **Jefferson blanched** Hetty Carr to Dabney Carr, 13 March 1826, Acc. 1231, ViU; Malone, *Jefferson,* 6:479.

312 **"cheerfully committed his soul"** TJR to Dabney Carr, 11 July 1826, Acc. 1231, ViU.

312 **He never knew** Francis D. Cogliano, "Preservation and Education: Monticello and the Thomas Jefferson Foundation," in *A Companion to Thomas Jefferson,* ed. Francis D. Cogliano (West Sussex, UK: Blackwell Publishing, 2012), 510.

312 **the very last letter** TJ to George Stephenson, 25 June 1826 (transcription), Page Papers, Virginia Historical Society.

313 **"You will be obliged"** EWRC to VJRT, 10 January 1830, FLDA.

313 **took up residence** Thomas Mann Randolph to Nicholas P. Trist, 10–11 March 1828, FLDA.

313 **he died there** MJR to EWRC, [30] June 1828, and CJR to EWRC, 6–8 July 1828, FLDA.

313 **"Supporting a large family"** MJR to Ann Cary Randolph Morris, 6 September 1829. Copy at ICJS.

314 **"at which I am quite"** MJR to Thomas Jefferson Randolph, 16 March 1830, Acc. 1397, ViU.

314 **"without the possibility"** Mary Jefferson Randolph to EWRC, 25 September 1831, and MJR and VJRT to EWRC, [ca. March 1832], FLDA.

314 **"the mortification of neglect"** TJR to Jane Nicholas Randolph, 7 December 1826, Acc. 1397, ViU.

314 **"a comfortless winter residence"** "Monticello is a very expensive and comfortless *winter* residence." MJR to EWRC, 21 June 1831. FLDA.

314 **"'all the Kingdoms of the world"** Mary Jefferson Randolph Commonplace Book. Jefferson, Randolph, and Trist Papers, Acc. 5385-ac, ViU.

314 **"There is pleasure"** Ibid.

315 **"deep indigo & bold"** CRJ to EWRC, 11 September 1826, FLDA.

315 **"I do not feel at home"** CJR to EWRC, 28 August 1831, FLDA.

315 **"I never find myself"** EWRC to VJRT, 13 May 1828, FLDA.

315 **"every thing is so strongly"** CJR to EWRC, 6 July 1828, FLDA.

316 **"I was brought up"** EWRC, "Two Autobiographical Papers," 15 June 1828, FLDA.

316 **"In former years"** EWR to NPT, 30 March 1824, FLDA.

317 **"praise of *method*"** EWRC to VJRT, 3 May 1829, FLDA.

317 **"astute enough to be"** Allgor, *Parlor Politics,* 31.

317 **roles the Scottish Enlightenment** On the influence of the Scottish Enlightenment on gender roles see Rosemarie Zagarri, "Morals, Manners, and the Republican Mother," *American Quarterly* 4 (June 1992): 192–215, and Ruth H. Bloch, "The Gendered Meanings of Virtue in Revolutionary America," *Signs: Journal of Women in Culture and Society* 13 (Autumn 1987): 37–58. By 1820, the South may even have been more Scottish than English. Michael O'Brien, *Rethinking the South: Essays in Intellectual History* (Baltimore and London: Johns Hopkins University Press, 1988), 49.

317 **women's tentative claims** Zagarri, *Revolutionary Backlash.*

317 **"I really want a big table"** Quoted in Goodman, *Becoming a Woman in the Age of Letters,* 235.

318 **"regular siege"** MJR to Virginia Jefferson Randolph, 10 January 1822, FLDA.

318 **"Ellen would be greatly"** Dr. Horace Holley to his brother, 6 September 1824, quoted in Cripe, *Thomas Jefferson and Music,* 36.

318 **"full of slanders"** Harriet Randolph to Jane Hollins Randolph, 1 February 1822, Acc. 1397, ViU.

318 **"I don't think"** Jane Nicholas Randolph to Sarah Nicholas, [n.d. but after August 1831], Acc. 1397, ViU.

318 **"prophane" people** CJR to EWRC, 6 July 1828, FLDA.

318 **"Girls should be brought"** VJRT to Mary Jefferson Randolph, 5 November 1878, Burke and Trist Family Papers, Acc. 5385f, ViU.

319 **today's highly educated women** Judith Warner, "The Opt-Out Generation Wants Back In," *New York Times,* 7 August 2013, revisiting Lisa Belkin's "The Opt-Out Revolution," *New York Times,* 26 October 2003.

319 **Jefferson had borrowed** *TJMB,* 5 June 1784, 1:551.

319   **The year before she died** "Memories of Ellen Wayles Harrison, Daughter of Thomas Jefferson Randolph," transcribed by Martha Jefferson Trist Burke, 1888. Copy at ICJS.

320   **"When alone with you"** Bayard Smith, 26 December 1802, Hunt, *First Forty Years of Washington Society,* 34.

320   **once chiding her brother-in-law** MJE to JWE, 10 December 1803, Eppes Family Papers, Acc. 7109, ViU.

320   **fathered a shadow family** Edna Bolling Jacques, "The Hemmings Family in Buckingham County Virginia," buckinghamhemmings.com, accessed 15 May 2012. Jacques is Betsy Hemmings's great-great-granddaughter. Hemmings is buried in a well-marked grave next to Jack Eppes; Martha Burke Jones Eppes is buried at a different plantation.

320   **"the sound-board split"** EWR to MJR, 13 September 1820, FLDA.

321   **"We found the name"** Ibid.

321   **girls in the early republic** Davidson, *Revolution and the Word,* 75–79.

321   **"Had *she* lived"** EWR to MJR, 13 September 1820, FLDA.

322   **a pattern of family planning** Nancy Woloch, *Women and the American Experience,* 4th ed. (New York: McGraw-Hill, 2006), Appendix A-2; citing, *Statistical Abstract of the United States,* Bureau of the Census, U.S. Department of Commerce, 1983, 1992, 1998; Ansley J. Coale and Melvin Zelnik, *New Estimates of Fertility and Population in the United States* (Princeton: Princeton University Press, 1963).

322   **those who did** Susan E. Klepp, *Revolutionary Conceptions: Women, Fertility, and Family Limitation in America, 1760–1820* (Chapel Hill: Published for OIEAHC by University of North Carolina Press, 2009).

322   **There is little evidence** Ibid., 206–13.

322   **Eighteenth-century physicians** Ibid., 179–85.

323   **"Slaves did not possess"** Hartman, *Lose Your Mother,* 77.

323   **Back home in Charlottesville** Stanton, "Free Some Day," in *"Those Who Labor,"* 200–201; Lucia Stanton and Dianne Swann-Wright, "Bonds of Memory: Identity and the Hemings Family," in Stanton, *"Those Who Labor,"* 248–49.

324   **"A master of the violin"** "A Sprig of Jefferson Was Eston Hemings," *Daily Scioto Gazette,* Chillicothe, Ohio, 1 August 1902.

324   **"whose word"** Stanton, "Bonds of Memory," in *"Those Who Labor,"* 236–37.

324   **"made almost constant war"** Stanton, "Fulfilling the Declaration," in *"Those Who Labor,"* 284.

325   **"He begged me"** Stanton, "Bonds of Memory," in *"Those Who Labor,"* 239.

326   **"They tended to cross"** Ibid., 238.

326   **"go to Sea"** Quoted in Hobbs, *Chosen Exile,* 34.

326   **from "passing as free"** Ibid., 35.

326   **landmark case *Hudgins* v. *Wright*** Sweet, *Legal History of the Color Line,* 164–65.

326   **The federal government** Hobbs, *Chosen Exile,* 41–43.

327   **As one novelist** Barbara Chase-Riboud, *The President's Daughter* (New York: Crown Publishing Group, 1994), 243.

327   **that southerners borrowed** C. Vann Woodward, *The Strange Career of Jim Crow* (1955; repr., New York: Oxford University Press, 2001).

327   **"The dangers of blackness"** Sara Clarke Kaplan, "Our Founding (M)other: Erotic Love and Social Death in *Sally Hemings* and *The President's Daughter,*" *Callalo* 32 (Summer 2009): 783.

328   **Black activists had made** See for example, Thomas Holt, *Black over White: Negro Political Leadership in South Carolina During Reconstruction* (Urbana: University of

Illinois, 1977); Eric Foner, *A Short History of Reconstruction, 1863–1877* (New York: Harper and Row, 1990).

328   **"no trace of other blood"** Sweet, *Legal History of the Color Line,* 12.

328   **dropped the mixed-race** Hobbs, *Chosen Exile,* 23, 128–29. Not until the 2000 census were Americans allowed the option to "mark one or more." Karen E. Fields and Barbara J. Fields, *Racecraft: The Soul of Inequality in American Life* (London: Verso, 2012), 47.

328   **more "coloured girls"** Nella Larsen, *Passing* (1929; repr., Rutgers University Press, 1986), 157–58.

328   **"She was transgressing"** Cheryl A. Harris, "Whiteness as Property," *Harvard Law Review* 106 (June 1993): 1710.

329   **"In creating property 'rights'"** Ibid., 1730.

329   **Property rights allow** Ibid., 1714, 1736.

329   **To call a white person "black"** Ibid., 1730, citing J. H. Crabb, Annotation, *Libel and Slander: Statements Respecting Race, Color, or Nationality as Actionable,* 46 A.L.R. 2d 1287, 1289 (1956).

329   **"most seemed to feel"** Andrew Hacker, *Two Nations: Black and White, Separate, Hostile, Unequal* (New York: Charles Scribner's Sons, 1992), 32, cited in Harris, "Whiteness as Property," 1759.

329   **called "the differences of color, hair, and bone"** W.E.B. Du Bois, "The Conservation of Races," quoted in Stuart Hall, "Race: The Floating Signifier" (1997), 6, mediaed.org/transcripts/Stuart-Hall-Race-the-Floating-Signifier-Transcript.pdf, accessed 23 April 2015.

330   **no reason to isolate** Fields and Fields, *Racecraft,* 48–70. Physical anthropologists have also been at the forefront of rejecting bio-race as a useless concept, as a survey of 365 showed. Matt Cartmill, "The Status of the Race Concept in Physical Anthroplogy," *American Anthropologist* 100 (September 1998): 651–60. Cited in Sweet, *Legal History of the Color Line,* 67–68.

330   **"The biological, physiological"** Hall, "Race: The Floating Signifier," 7.

330   **"But once invoked"** Fields and Fields, *Racecraft,* 52–53.

330   **almost a third** Sweet, *Legal History of the Color Line,* 154, 28. Italics mine.

330   **Marriage practices** Ibid., 35. An endogamous group is one from which a person is considered a suitable marriage partner.

330   **"a natural son of President"** "A Sprig of Jefferson Was Eston Hemings," *Daily Scioto Gazette* (Chillicothe, Ohio), 1 August 1902.

330   **"death deserves more"** A. J. Munson, "Letter to the Editor," *Tribune* (Milwaukee), 12 November 1908.

331   **however, that flexibility** Sweet, *Legal History of the Color Line,* 155–57.

331   **between thirty-five thousand** Sweet, *Legal History of the Color Line,* 73.

331   **"specious but utterly real"** Hobbs, *Chosen Exile,* 8.

331   **White Americans face** Lizabeth Cohen, *A Consumers' Republic: The Politics of Mass Consumption in Postwar America* (New York: Alfred A. Knopf, 2003), especially Part III.

331   **"a certain economic logic"** Harris, "Whiteness as Property," 1713.

331   **incarcerated in epic proportions** David Crary, "Record Number of Americans in Prison," *New York Times,* 28 Feburary 2008. "While one in 30 men between the ages of 20 and 34 is behind bars," the Pew Center on the States reported in 2008, "for black males in that age group the figure is one in nine." For women, the differences were equally stark: "One of every 355 white women aged 35 to 39 is behind bars, compared with one of every 100 black women in that age group," the report revealed.

331   **she was black** "The term 'black,'" the sociologist Stuart Hall says, "is referring to this long history of political and historical oppression. . . . It's not referring to biology." Hall, "Race: The Floating Signifier," 4–5.

332   **A rapprochement may have** Leef Smith, "Jeffersons Split over Hemings Descendants," *Washington Post*, 17 May 1999.

332   **"I unlocked the gate"** Tess Taylor, "Cousins Across the Color Line," *New York Times*, 26 January 2014.

332   **"deep affections, her high principles"** EWRC Diary, 11 January 1839, Birle and Francavilla, eds., *Thomas Jefferson's Granddaughter*, 160.

333   **eighteen thousand of his letters** Peter S. Onuf, "The Scholars' Jefferson," *William and Mary Quarterly* 50 (October 1993): 692.

Image Credits

4   South pavilion and wing of Monticello. © Thomas Jefferson Foundation at Monticello.

30   Francis Hopkinson home. Author photo.

36   Rue de Grenelle. Public domain.

38   *Thomas Jefferson* by Mather Brown. Oil on canvas, 1786. National Portrait Gallery, Smithsonian Institution; bequest of Charles Francis Adams.

40   Panthemont, courtyard view. Author photo.

52   Marie de Botidoux portrait. © Thomas Jefferson Foundation at Monticello.

61   Panthemont chapel dome. Author photo.

64   *The Morning Post*, 1788. Public domain.

70   *Vue de Nouveau Palais Royal,* by F. M. Mayeur, c. 1788. Courtesy of the Thomas Jefferson Foundation at Monticello.

79   Eppington. Author photo.

88   *Abigail Adams.* Fenimore Art Museum, Cooperstown, New York. Bequest from the Estate of Frances J. Eggleston, Oswego, New York. NO150.1955. Photograph by Richard Walker.

103   *Portrait of William Short.* Oil on canvas, 1806. Muscarelle Museum of Art at the College of William and Mary in Virginia. Gift of Mary Churchill Short, Fanny Short Butler, and William Short. 1938.004.

110   Hôtel de Langeac. Library of Congress.

127   Thomas Mann Randolph, Jr. (copy, c. 1919). © Thomas Jefferson Foundation at Monticello. Loaned by University of Virginia, Alderman Library.

146   William Bingham home, Philadelphia. Public domain.

158   *The Residence of Thomas Jefferson,* David J. Kennedy watercolors collection [V61], Historical Society of Pennsylvania.

166   John "Jack" Wayles Eppes. Library of Congress.

173   View of Monticello from Edgehill. Author photo.

183   Francis Wayles Eppes, miniature portrait, c. 1805. © Thomas Jefferson Foundation at Monticello.

191   Farm Book 1774–1824, page 128. Coolidge Collection of Thomas Jefferson Manuscripts. Collection of the Massachusetts Historical Society.

198   Isaac Granger Jefferson. © Thomas Jefferson Foundation at Monticello. Tracy W. McGregor Library of American History, Special Collections, University of Virginia Library.

212   Kitchen at Monticello. © Thomas Jefferson Foundation at Monticello.

216   Jefferson's cabinet. © Thomas Jefferson Foundation at Monticello. Photo by Robert Lautman.

218   South Square Room. © Thomas Jefferson Foundation at Monticello.

220   Staircase at Monticello. © Thomas Jefferson Foundation at Monticello. Photo by Robert Lautman.

222   Ellen Wayles Randolph portrait by Francis Alexander, c. 1836. © Thomas Jefferson Foundation at Monticello. Gift of Ellen Eddy Thorndike.

235   Exterior view, Poplar Forest. Courtesy of Thomas Jefferson's Poplar Forest.

237   Parlor, Poplar Forest. Courtesy of Thomas Jefferson's Poplar Forest.

243   Textile workshop, Monticello. Courtesy of the Thomas Jefferson Foundation at Monticello. Photo by Catherine Kerrison.

247   Hargreaves spinning jenny. Public domain.

278   Indian Queen Hotel. Library of Congress.

280   Early view of the Capitol. Library of Congress.

304   Slave coffle. Library of Congress.

313   Martha Jefferson Randolph portrait by Thomas Sully, c. 1836. © Thomas Jefferson Foundation at Monticello. Gift of Burton H. R. Randall.

325   Top: William Beverley Frederick Jefferson and his sons. Courtesy of the Thomas Jefferson Foundation at Monticello; bottom: *John W. Jefferson* by Alexander Marquis. Oil on canvas, 1874, Museum of Wisconsin Art Collection.

Index

Page numbers of illustrations and their captions appear in *italics*.
Abbreviated references: Harriet = Harriet Hemings; Maria = Maria Jefferson
Eppes; Martha = Martha Jefferson Randolph; TJ = Thomas Jefferson

abolitionism, 10, 32, 33, 263, 303, 333
Adams, Abigail, 38–39, 48, 59, 73, *88*
   conservatism of, 154
   educating her children, 224
   Maria and, 73–76, 81, 86–87, 89,
      106, 107, 141, 147, 269
   reaction to Sally Hemings, 91, 92
   rights of women and, 154
Adams, Charles Francis, 291
Adams, John, 32, *38,* 48, 73, 136, 230
   TJ as vice president, 136, 165, 177
Adams, John Quincy, 224
Adams, Nabby, 48, 59–60, 67, 68, 69,
   77, 83, 102, 224
Adele et Theodore (Genlis), 222
Alien and Sedition Acts, 178
American Colonization Society, 303
American Philosophical Society, 29
American Revolution, xi, 7, 15–16, 20,
   23, 98, 116
   Daughters of Liberty, 123
   legacy of, 333
   slave status and, 136
   Treaty of Paris, 26, 27, 30–31, 119,
      129
   women's status and, 310
Ancestry.com, 292
Annapolis, Md., 26, 28, 30, 32
Annesley, Arthur, 49

Annesley, Julia, 49–50, 57, 61, 72, 101,
   104–5, 114
Arnold, Benedict, 15
Articles of Confederation, 129

Bache, Deborah, 149, 151
Bache, William, 176
Bacon, Edmund, 139, 204, 205, 249,
   251
   on escape of Thruston Hern, 265
   on Fossett's skill as blacksmith, 197
   on Harriet, 190, 207, 250, 272, 273,
      291
   on Martha, 139
Balbastre, Claude, 51, 152
Baltimore, Md., 25, 28, 269, 277, 293
   free black community in, 211
Barthélemy, Jean-Jacques, *Voyages du
   Jeune Anacharsis,* 223, 224
Bell, Mary Hemings, 15, 201, 202,
   203, 251, 261, 264, 281, 306
   enslaved children of, 202, 203, 251,
      260, 264
Bell, Thomas, 201–2, 251, 261, 281
Bermuda Hundred, 165, 170, 174,
   179, 181
Béthisy de Mézières, Marie-
   Catherine de, 44–45, 46, 48, 59,
   65, 70, 217, 224

Betts, Edwin Morris, 199
Bigelow, Abijah, 296
Bingham, Anne Willing, 68, *146*, 159, 230
Bingham, William, *146*
Birch, William, 145, *146*
Blanchard, Jean Pierre, 156–57
Bolling, Mary (TJ's niece), 141
Bolling, Mary (TJ's sister), 86, 117
Bolling, Olive Rebecca, 286, 292, 293
Boston, 32, 54, 303
    challenges of travel to, 275–76
    Ellen Randolph Coolidge in, 238, 239, 253, 268–69, 275
Botidoux, Marie de, 50–51, *52, 54,* 57, 63, 71, 100–104, 111, 113, 116–17, 123, 124, 131–34, 136
Bowen, Arthur, 305
Brionne, Comtesse de, 39
Brodeau, Ann, 150
Brodie, Fawn, 94
    Thomas Jefferson, 94
Brown, Betty, 204, 213
Brown, Jesse, 277, *278*
Bry, Theodore de, *Great and Small Voyages,* 236
Buffon, Comte de, 66
    Histoire Naturelle, 223
Burr, Aaron, 178

Callender, James, 253, 254, 258, 260
Cannet, Sophie, 56–57
Carr, Dabney (TJ's brother-in-law), 5, 20, 245
Carr, Dabney (TJ's nephew), 20
Carr, Martha Jefferson, 19–21, 32, 79, 84–86, 117, 161, 162, 164, 245
Carr, Peter, 20, 225, 255
Carr, Sam, 20, 255
Carroll, Catherine, 54–55
Carroll, Charles, 54
Carter, Robert, 20
Cary, Archibald, 24
Catholicism, 41, 58, 64, 65, 72, 105
    Martha and "convent revolt," 41, 58–59, 61–65, *64,* 100, 111, 317

Ceres (ship), 33
Cervantes, Miguel de, *Don Quixote,* 27, 53, 223, 319
Charleston, S.C., 304
Charlottesville, Va., 18, 26–27, 61, 116, 178, 201, 240, 273–74, 300
    gossip about Harriet, 273–74
    Hemings family in, 323
    University of Virginia, 195, 238–40
Chastellux, Marquis de, 17, 19, 25, 39, 41, 65
Church, Kitty, 68, 107, 183
Clermont (ship), xi, 115–16
Colbert, Brown, 200, 202
Colbert, Burwell, 196, 204, 210, 253, 291
Colbert, Emily, 310
Colbert, Martha Ann, 310
Colbert, Melinda, 203
College of Pennsylvania, 29
Confessions (Rousseau), 66
Constitutional Convention, 66, 130
Continental Army, 129, 154
Continental Congress, 7, 14, 119, 148, 155, 263
Coolidge, Ellen Wayles Randolph, 138, 167, 172, 173, 180, 184, 207, 210, *222,* 227, 232, 250, 279, 316
    accidental discovery of Maria's harpsichord and music, 320–21
    as bluestocking, 227, 237
    in Boston, 238, 239, 253, 268–69, 275
    "Dusky Sally" references by, 256
    education and, *222,* 224, 225, 226, 227, 237–38, 316–17
    on female intellectual life, 221, 228, 238, 315–17
    free white servants vs. slaves, 253
    legacy of her mother, 332–33
    love of books, 224, 225, 237
    marriage of, 238
    Monticello and, 213–14, 233, 253, 314–15
    mother's death, 310
    at Poplar Forest, 224–25, 234–38

slaves seen as inferior by, 256–57
status as TJ's granddaughter, 318
TJ and, 234–38
TJ's slave children, denial of his
    paternity, 255–56, 266, 308
trousseau for, 268–69, 270
Coolidge, Joseph, Jr., 238, 255, 256,
    310
Cooper, Harriet Bell, 290–91
Corinne (Staël), 317
Cornwallis, General Lord Charles, 16
Corny, Madame de, 68, 114
Cosway, Maria Hadfield, 74–75
Cosway, Richard, 74
Cottringer, Harriet, 291
Cropper, John, 155
Cropper, Sarah Corbin, 155, 157
Currie, James, 81–82, 85
Curzon, Bettie Hawkins, 104, 105,
    116, 128, 131
    as friend of Maria and Martha, 50,
        53, 57–58, 61, 63, 100–102, 104,
        107, 114, 116, 137
Curzon, Henry Francis Roper, 104
Custis, Nelly, 147, 149, 151, 153, 155
Cutting, Nathaniel, 76, 115, 117,
    141–42

Daily National Intelligencer, 283
Dashwood, Rachel, 101
Daughters of the American
    Revolution library, 288
Davis, Natalie Zemon, 301
Declaration of Independence, x, 26,
    29, 54, 119, 129, 148, 153, 316
"Declaration of the Rights of Woman
    and Female Citizen" (Gouges),
    122–23
Descartes, Réne, 120
Diable Boiteux (Lesage), 53
Diderot, Denis, 42, 66
Dinsmore, James, 196–97, 243
Don Quixote (Cervantes), 27, 53, 223,
    319
Dougherty, Joseph, 264, 273
Douglass, Frederick, 191

Du Bois, W. E. B., 329–30
Dugnani, Antonio, 63
Dunglison, Robley, 239

Edgehill plantation, 132, 134–38, *173,*
    177, 182, 184, 245, 248
Edgeworth de Firmont, Abbé, 101,
    104
Elk Hill estate, 7, 14, 16, 17, 26
Emile (Rousseau), 229
Enlightenment, 31, 42
    in France, 42–43, 44, 55, 230
    Martha and, 139–40, 316–17
    rational self-control and, 139, 230
    reform of female education and, 44
    Scottish circles, 120, 121, 126, 317
    TJ and, 194, 217, 316–17
    women and, 42, 120–22, 229,
        316–17
Eppes, Elizabeth, 14, 15, 17, 21, 73,
    78, 111, 167
    children of, 80, 81, 117
    death of Lucy Jefferson and, 81–82
    Maria and Lucy fostered by, 22, 24,
        26, 32, 75
    Maria's death and, 187
    Maria's education and, 80–81, 106,
        141
    Maria's infant cared for by, 187
    as Maria's second mother, 34,
        79–83, 88, 89, 107–9, 142, 169,
        174, 181
    Maria's wedding missed by, 165–66
    sends Sally Hemings to France,
        90–92
    slaves of, 205
    TJ and, 78–79, 125, 168–69
    TJ's sending for Maria and, 84–86
    whooping cough and, 81–82, 205
Eppes, Francis (Maria's son), 180–82,
    183, 187, 225, 265, 273, 333
    accidental discovery of Maria's
        harpsichord and music, 320–21
    death of Maria and, 188, 320, 333
Eppes, Francis (TJ's brother-in-law),
    14, 24, 77, 80, 82–86, 91–92, 165

Eppes, John "Jack" Wayles, 80, 85, 141,
    164, *166*, 167, 169, 219, 226, 294
  and Betsy Hemmings, 264, 320
  birth and death of daughters,
    174–75, 186, 320
  grieving Maria, 188
  law practice, 156, 164, 169
  Maria's final illness and, 185–87
  as Maria's suitor, 155–56, 161,
    162–65
  marriage of, 165–74, 183–85
  in Philadelphia, TJ and, 155–57
  political offices held by, *166*, 170,
    183–84, 264
  remarriage, 265
  residences (*see* Bermuda Hundred;
    Mont Blanco)
  shadow family, *166*, 265, 320
  slaves of, 199
  son, Francis, and, 180, 181, 182
  studies at university, 156
  wedding gifts and dowry of land
    and slaves, 165, 168, 203
Eppes, Lucy Elizabeth, 80, 81–82
Eppes, Maria (infant), 186, 320
Eppes, Maria Jefferson, x, 185
  Abigail Adams and, 73–74, 76, 81,
    86–87, 106, 141, 269
  appearance of, 73–74, 75, 76, 77,
    159
  astuteness about TJ, 89
  attachment and loyalty to TJ,
    167–68
  birth of, 14
  birth of children, 174–75, 180, 185
  compared to Martha, 87, 171–73
  conventional life of, 159, 319–22
  courtship by Jack Eppes, 161–65
  death of, 187
  death of sister Lucy and, 81–82
  desire for a family, 182
  disposition to please, 108
  Don Quixote and, 141, 319
  education, 80–81, 93, 106–7, 109,
    140–42, 148–53, 155, 159, 160,
    319

endearing personality of, 81, 86, 89,
    106–7, 159–60, 320
  fear of displeasing TJ, 108–9
  feelings toward TJ, 75, 79–80,
    171–73
  feminism and, 155
  friends of, 106, 107, 147, 150, 153,
    155, 157
  harpsichord or spinet played by,
    152, 159, 160, 320–21
  illness and, 110–12, 158–59,
    175–76, 181, 184–87
  injury at Monticello, 167–68, 174
  instability in life of, 87–88
  last letters to Jack, 185
  legacy of, 321, 333, 334
  letter-writing and, 80, 89, 92,
    107–9, 141, 147, 156, 157, 167,
    171, 172, 177, 182, 183, 185, 188,
    320
  love of books, 81, 141–42
  marriage, 166–74, 183, 184–85
  marriage residences, 169, 170, 174,
    179, 181 (*see also* Bermuda
    Hundred; Mont Blanco)
  measles outbreak and, 181–82
  mother's death, 88
  opposition to joining TJ in France,
    83–86, 167
  in Paris, xi, 73–77, 107, 108–12
  pattern of detachment, tears,
    resignation, and passionate
    attachment, 86, 87–88, 90, 142
  peripatetic childhood, 16, 17, 87–88
  in Philadelphia, 143, 147–55, 157,
    158
  pregnancies and miscarriages,
    174–76, 179, 184, 321–22
  raised by Elizabeth Eppes, and life
    shaped by, 24–26, 32–34, 79–83,
    79, 88, 89, 107–9, 142, 169,
    320
  relationship with Martha, 77,
    175–76
  relationship with Sally Hemings,
    90–91, 179

resolve and strength of character, 88–90, 172–73, 182
scholars' view of, 167, 172, 173
self-identity of, 89
smallpox inoculation, 24
son Francis and, 180–82, 320–21
suitors, 155, 156, 161–63
TJ as president and, 178, 183
TJ's expectations of, 87
TJ's wedding gift, 165, 168
training for marriage, 161
voyages of, 86–87, 115–16
wedding, 165–66
Eppes, Martha Bolling, 80, 82
Eppes, Martha Burke Jones, 265
Eppes, Mary and Matilda, 117
Eppington, 24, 25, 32, 77–79, 79, 81, 117, 125, 164, 168, 169, 182, 205
description, 77–78
inventory of, 81
Maria gives birth at, 174–76
Maria's education at, 80–81, 106
Essay Concerning Human Understanding (Locke), 316

Fairfax, George William, 148
Family Search, 292
Federalists, 178, 230, 296
Fénelon, *Les Aventures de Télémaque*, 223–24
Fine Creek plantation, 16
Fletcher, Elijah P., 253–54
Floyd, Kitty, 95
Fontaine, Jean de La, 53, 54
Forest, The, 3, 11, 12, 15, 24, 78
Fossett, Edith Hern, 211–12, 264
Fossett, Joseph, 196–97, 202, 210
Fossett, Peter, 195, 210, 250, 251, 270–71, 272, 273, 285
Foster, Elaine Morrison, 296
France, 23, 50
American Quasi War with, 177–78
aristocratic matchmaking, 104
Assembly of Notables, 71
cost of alliance with America, 98
Enlightenment in, 42–43, 44, 230

Estates General, 98–99
National Assembly, ix, 71, 98, 99, 123, 132
slavery in, 93, 95, 113, 136
suppression of female religious orders, 43
TJ as ambassador to, 93, 98
women's literacy in, 121
women's status and influence in, 65–67, 122, 123, 154, 317
See also Paris
Franklin, Benjamin, 23, 28, 31, 32, 37, 66, 149, 285
Franklin, William Temple, 145
free blacks, xi, 9–10, 119, 123, 211, 230, 314, 326, 327, 333
in Washington City, 263, 300–304
French Revolution, ix–x, 55, 71, 98, 120, 121–22, 154
Fugitive Slave Act, 262
Fullerton, Richard, 155
Fullerton, Valeria, 155, 159

Garrison, William Lloyd, 303
Genlis, Madame de, 53, 222, 223, 230, 231–32, 317
Adele et Theodore, 222
Letters on Education, 228–29
Female education and, 222, 229–31
George III, King of England, 131
Georgiana, Duchess of Devonshire, 67, 154
Gil Blas (Lesage), 27, 53, 223
Giles, William Branch, 161–62, 163
Gillette, Agnes, 249
Gilmer, Francis Walker, 238
Gordon-Reed, Annette, 90, 93–94, 118, 206, 287
Gouges, Olympe de, "Declaration of the Rights of Woman and Female Citizen," 122
Granger, Archy, 8
Granger, Great George, 8, 15, 194, 198, 213
Granger, Nancy, 249
Granger, Ursula, 8, 11, 15, 198, 211

Great and Small Voyages (Bry), 236
Great Britain, x, 22, 30–31, 119, 123,
    130, 245, 246, 263
  Act of Toleration, 41
  aristocratic homes in, 232
  Catholicism in, 105
  women's literacy in, 121
  See also American Revolution; War
    of 1812; *specific individuals*

Hamilton, Alexander, 68, 107, 130,
    135, 143, 144, 157, 162
Harcourt, Gabrielle D', 57, 58
Hargreaves, James, 247, *247*
Harris, Cheryl I., 328–29, 331
Hartman, Saidiya, 259–60, 307, 323
Helvétius, Madame, 66, 67
Hemings, Anna, 324
Hemings, Betsy, *see* Hemmings, Betsy
Hemings, Beverley. *See* Hemings,
    William Beverley
Hemings, Critta, 200, 204, 208, 211,
    243
Hemings, Elizabeth, 12–13, 15, 22,
    200, 203, 205, 286, 300, 310, 323
Hemings, Eston. *See* Hemings,
    Thomas Eston
Hemings, Harriet
  appearance of, 190, 207, 259, 284,
    331
  assumed identity ("passing"),
    267–72, 274, 280, 281, 285–86,
    300–301, 306–7, 308, 327, 329,
    331
  author's search for, 286–301
  Bolling on whereabouts, 286, 292,
    293
  childhood as measurably happy, 259
  date of birth, 191, 299
  duties at Monticello, 212, 250
  education and skills, 209–13, 246,
    247, 248, 283, 284–85
  employment possibilities, 283–84
  exceptional childhood of, 205
  farewell to family, 272–73
  flogging of slave and, 251, 252, 257

  freedom granted, 189–90, 258
  fugitive slave status of, 262–63
  gossip about paternity, 273–74
  home at Monticello, 189, 204–5,
    215, 242, 258
  importance of her story, 332
  lack of historical record on, 190,
    214, 276–77, 281, 285–86, 323
  leaves Monticello, 261, 263, 272–74
  legacy of, 334
  as legally white, 190
  lessons in rank and status, 252, 255,
    257–58
  listed in Farm Book, 191, *191*, 192,
    265–66
  loss of true identity, 306–7, 323
  manumission papers, lack of,
    262–63, 274, 331
  marriage to a "white man of good
    standing in Washington City,"
    284, 285, 288–93, 295
  name of, 206–7, 259
  new family history for, 282, 286,
    300–301, 307–8, 327
  new identity unknown, 267, 281,
    285
  only female slave freed by TJ, 259
  privileged position of, 249–50, 259
  "raised a family of children," 285,
    290, 295
  Randolph family and, 207, 255,
    256, 257
  Randolph family denies paternity
    of, 254–56, 308, 332
  rejection of racial hierarchy, 323
  smallpox inoculation, 209
  status of, 207–8, 244, 257
  TJ arranges her relocation, 263
  TJ's expectations of, 245, 246
  TJ's records as "run," *191*, 262,
    282
  twenty-first birthday, 272
  in Washington City, 264–65, 267,
    272, 277–80, *278*, 285, 291, 301
  work at textile manufactory, 214,
    242, 243, 244, 245, 248–50, 259

Hemings, James (Sally's brother), 22,
 33, 93, 26, 148, 205, 206, 273
 as chef, 92–93, 113, 211
 in France, 32, 33, 92, 93, 95, 110
 leaves Monticello, 211
 literacy of, 209–10
 return to Virginia (1789), 116, 118
 TJ frees, 119–20
Hemings, James (Sally's nephew), 200
Hemings, James Madison, 94, 95, 96,
 192, 207, 210, 245, 255, 261, 303
 appearance of, 261, 271
 childhood, 244, 259
 children of, 286, 324, 326
 color line and, 326
 importance of information, 323
 information on brother Beverley,
  265, 266, 287
 information on sister Harriet, 267,
  285, 289, 297, 298
 life in Charlottesville, Va., 323–24
 life in Waverly, Ohio, 324
 literacy of, 210
 marriage of, 323
 skills of, 244, 324
 tells his story, 256, 286, 287, 307
Hemings, John, 197, 204, 210, *216,*
 217, 227, 244, 270, 272, 308
 called "Daddy," 197, 236
 campeachy chairs made by, *237*
 Hemings boys with, 244, 245, 283
Hemings, Madison. *See* Hemings,
 James Madison
Hemings, Mary. *See* Bell, Mary
 Hemings
Hemings, Peter, 120, 204, 211, 212
Hemings, Robert, 25, 209, 308
Hemings, Sally, 15, 181
 accompanies Maria to Paris, 90–92
 appearance of, 91, 92, 261
 birth of, 13
 births of children, 189, 191–92, 203
 character and personality, 206, 262
 children's appearance, 207, 254–55,
  271, 330
 children's names, 206

children's paternity, 94–95, 96, 254,
 255, 256
closeness of family, 267
clothing for, 92, 112, 113, 204
deathbed of TJ's wife and gift of a
 bell, 90, 205, 290
death of, 282, 323
domestic duties, x, 93–94, 95, 112
educating her children, 209, 210–11
emancipation of children requiring
 their departure, 261
at Eppington, 22, 90, 91, 205
and freedom for her children, 96,
 118, 120, 189–90, 206, 259, 260
and goals for her children, 260,
 261–62
Gordon-Reed's study, 90, 94, 118
gossip about her children, 273–74
grandchildren of, 197
informal freedom of, 310
life after TJ's death, 323–24
lost grave of, 300
as Martha's maid, 112–13
midwife for, 191
Monticello residences, *4,* 114, 189,
 203, 208, *243*
as mother, 205–6, 209–11, 259–62
as paid employee, 93–94, 113
Paris and, x–xi, 91–92, 93, 95–96,
 110, 112, 113, 114, 206–7
pharmacy pot from Paris, 114, 258
pregnancies of, 96, 112, 118, 179
privileged position, 190, 203–6,
 259
Randolphs deny her children's
 paternity, 254–56, 258, 308, 332
smallpox inoculation, 93, 206
stories passed down from, 205
as "substitute for a wife," 94, 95, 96,
 112, 118
TJ's arrangements for his sons, 244,
 245
TJ's Christmas packages, 211
TJ and her children, 208
TJ's life with exposed, 253–54,
 258

Hemings, Sally (*cont'd*):
  TJ's negotiations with, 96, 97,
    113–14, 118, 120, 189–90, 206,
    262
  TJ's secretiveness about, 208
  TJ's treatment of and loyalty to, 118
  virtues modeled by, 271
Hemings, Thomas Eston, 94, 192,
    203, 207, 210, 244, 272
  children of, 324, *325,* 330
  in Chillicothe, Ohio, 324, 330
  description of, in Ohio, 270, 272
  emancipation requiring his
    departure from Virginia, 261
  life after TJ's death, 323
  in Madison, Wis., 324
  marriage of, 323–24
  name change and "passing," 324
  resemblance to TJ, 254, 271, 330
  skills of, 244, 324
  skin color of, 261
Hemings, Thomas Eston (son of
    James Madison Hemings), 326
Hemings, William Beverley, 189, 203,
    250
  author's search for, 289, 291–92,
    297
  date of leaving Monticello, 266,
    272
  death of his mother, 282
  emancipation requiring his
    departure from Virginia, 261
  fugitive slave status of, 262, 282
  Harriet and, 272, 274, 277
  hot air balloon launched by, 266
  listed in Farm Book, *191,* 192, 203,
    265–66, 282
  manumission papers, lack of, 262
  marriage of, 266, 287
  naming of, 207
  new family history, 282, 286, 307–8
  paternity of, 189, 256
  resemblance to TJ, 271
  skills of, 244, 266, 283, 294
  smallpox inoculation, 209
  as successful, 266–67

TJ's records as "run," *191,* 262, 282
  in Washington City, 265, 266, 274
Hemings, William Beverley (son of
    James Madison Hemings), 286,
    326
Hemmings, Betsy, *166,* 202, 203, 211,
    264–65, 310, 320
  shadow family of, 265, 286
Hern, Cretia, 248–49
Hern, Davy, 202, 213, 264
Hern, Edith, 202
Hern, Fanny Gillette, 211, 212
Hern, Isabel, 83–84, 85, 90, 202, 249
Hern, Mary, 249
Hern, Moses, 201–2
Hern, Thruston, 264, 265
Histoire Naturelle (Buffon), 223
History of the Roman People (Livius),
    51, 55, 140, 223, 224
Hopkinson, Francis, 27, 28, 29, *30,* 31,
    263
Hopkinson, Joseph, 263
Hopkinson, Mary, 27, 28–29, 31,
    147
Hopkinson, Thomas, 29
Houdetot, Comte and Comtesse d,'
    37, 66, 67
House, Mary, 25, 27
Hubbard, Jame, 251–52, 257, 268
Hughes, Ursula, 213
Hughes, Wormley, 193, 196, 213, 270,
    273, 310
Hume, David, 121

Ivry, Pierre Contant, 45

Jackson, Andrew, 230
Jacobs, Harriet, 281
Jacques, Edna, 286
James II, King of France, 44
Jay, John, 23, 27, 32, 130
Jefferson, Isaac Granger, 16, 17, 196,
    198
  family story of, 286
  on Harriet, 207
  memories of Maria, 76, 162, 167

memory of Jefferson's wife, 211
on slaves in nailery, 197–98
Jefferson, Israel, 209, 249
Jefferson, Jane Randolph (TJ's
daughter), 13–14, 18
Jefferson, Jane Randolph (TJ's
mother), 5–6, 18
Jefferson, John Wayles, 324–25, *325*
Jefferson, Lucy Elizabeth (first, and
deceased in infancy), 14
Jefferson, Lucy Elizabeth (second), 14,
16, 21, 24–26, 34, 75, 81–83
Jefferson, Martha Wayles, 3, 7, 11–18
acquiring of slaves Elizabeth
Hemings and Ursula Granger, 8,
11, 12, 13
births and deaths of children, 7, 8,
13–14, 16, 18, 21
character of, 88–89
as daughter Martha's teacher, 18
death of, 21
described by Chastellux, 17
father as slave trade broker, 11
marriage to TJ, 3
at Monticello, 4–5, 7, 15, 17
sister Elizabeth and, 15, 17, 21, 78
TJ grieving, x, 21–22, 78, 83
TJ's devotion to, 14, 21, 236
Jefferson, Peter, 5, 16, 207
Jefferson, Randolph, 201
Jefferson, Thomas
agricultural methods, 194–95, 213
American Revolution and, 15–16,
20, 25
appearance of, 3, *38*, 254, 271, 330
appointments to France, 23–26,
32, 83
attitude toward childbirth, 176
author's search for documentation
on Harriet and, 286
birth of, 5
births and deaths of daughters and
sons, 13–14, 18, 21
books and library of, 197, 215, 216,
216, 218, 219, 233, 236, 237, 254,
265, 334

building as passion for, 244–45
classical education of, 224
on cleanliness, 271
as congressman, 26, 28, 30, 31, 32
Constitution and, 130
death of, 312
death of daughter Lucy, 81–83
death of wife, Martha, 21
Declaration of Independence and,
x, 26, 119, 148, 316
descendants of, 332
design for nation's capital, 277–78
on education for boys, 20, 225–26
on education for girls, 19, 20,
51–53, 151, 153, 209, 217, 218,
221, 224, 226
encounter with Rev. Laurie, 296
Enlightenment ideas, 194, 217,
316–17
as executor for John Wayles, 11–12
Farm Book, 12, 191, *191,* 192–94,
198, 199, 203, 207, 265, 282, 286
favorite foods of, 212
first grandchild born, 134
French language and, 47, 48
French Revolution and, ix–x, 98–99
French women and, 95, 100, 122,
153
as governor of Virginia, 15, 20
grieving his wife, x, 21–22, 78, 83
Hamilton as enemy, 135, 157, 162
"Head and Heart" letter, 75
health issues of, 113, 239
Kentucky Resolutions, 178
Lafayette and, 67, 82, 241
legacy of, 333
letters archived, 333
lottery to sell estate, 312, 314
marriage to Martha Wayles, 3
Monticello, 3–7, *4,* 135, 139, 141,
143, 192–203
Monticello, typical day at, 215–16
Monticello renovations, 218–21,
220, 232–34
Notes on the State of Virginia, 66,
223

Jefferson, Thomas (*cont'd*):

Panic of 1819 and debt, 284, 312

in Paris (1784–89), ix–xi, 34–39, *38*, 65–69, 73–75, 94–95, 109–14

Paris, Hôtel de Langeac and, 51, 68, 73, 102, 109–11, *110*, 114, 220

Paris, relationship with Sally Hemings begins, 94, 95

Paris, negotiations with Sally Hemings to return to Monticello, 96, 97, 113–14, 118, 120, 262

Paris, preparation for and journey to, 32–34

Paris, reasons for leaving, 99

Paris, return from (1789), 117–18

Parisian affair, 74–75

paternal attentiveness lacking, 73–75, 77, 142, 163

paternity of Hemings's children, 94–95, 96, 189, 255–56

in Philadelphia, 145–59, *158*

Philadelphia friends of, 31

Poplar Forest estate, 16–17, 197, 201, 217–18, 234–38, *237*, 253

as president, 178, 191–92, 211, 231, 245

relationship with Elizabeth Eppes, 78–79, 84–86, 125, 168–69

relationship with Sally Hemings (*see* Hemings, Sally)

relationship with sons by Sally Hemings, 244, 245

religion and, 296

resignation from Washington's cabinet, 135

as slaveowner, 8, 11, 12, 24, 119, 137, 191–214, 251, 308 (*see also* Monticello; *specific individuals*)

slaves seen as inferior beings, 257

smallpox inoculation and, 24, 209

theology and, 28–29, 64

University of Virginia and, 195, 218, 238–40, 334

"valedictory" letters, 32

as vice president, 136, 164, 177

in Virginia House of Burgesses, 3

and Virginia Statute of Religious Freedom, 66, 239

as Washington's secretary of state, 125, 128, 140

women's place, views on, 27, 94, 100, 125, 141, 171, 209, 241

—DAUGHTER HARRIET HEMINGS AND

appearance of, skin color and resemblance to TJ, 190, 207

childhood of, 207–8

date of her birth noted, 191

date of her leaving Monticello, 272

departure delegated to overseer, 273

education of, 209, 210

freedom given to, 259, 262

gossip about paternity, 273–74

kindness to, 208

life of domesticity for, 245, 246

manumission papers, lack of, 262–63

privileged position given to, 259

provides fare and travel money to leave Monticello, 263, 273

record of, 191, *191*, 244

recorded as "run," *191*, 262, 282

sent to textile manufactory, 214, 244–50, 259

smallpox inoculation for, 209

—DAUGHTER MARIA AND

birth of, 14

conditional love and, 89

death of, grief and, 187, 188

desire to have at Monticello after her marriage, 168, 169–70, 179, 180, 220

education of, 106–7, 141, 142, 148–53, 155–56, 159, 161

Eppes as suitor and, 164–65

Giles as suitor and, 161–62, 163

her final illness and, 185–87

her illnesses and, 176, 177, 184

his expectations of, 87, 108, 141, 142

leaves her in Virginia, 22, 25

letter writing, 80, 85, 89, 108–9,
141, 142, 157, 167, 172, 183
in Paris with, xi, 73–77, 107–12
in Philadelphia with, 143, 147–57,
158
relationship with, 89, 147–48, 150,
155, 157, 163, 167–68, 171–72
return from France, escorting to
Virginia, 114
sends for, from Paris, 83–86, 90
—DAUGHTER MARTHA AND
admired by her friends, 51, 71
approval of husband for, 127–28
birth of, 8
boarding her in Philadelphia, 25,
26–31
Catholicism of and, 59, 61–64, 112
children of and, 138
education for, 19, 20, 27, 29, 45–59,
69–72, 109, 121, 159, 217, 221
expenditures for clothing, 38, 100,
112–13
marriageability of, 99, 100, 112
Monticello as home during
marriage, 134, 136, 138–39, 169,
215, 219, 220, 231, 252–53, 272
Monticello household supervised
by, 217, *218*, 233–34, 268, 270
in Paris with, x, 22, 34–77, 111–15
at Poplar Forest estate with, 234–35
relationship with, 18, 28, 41, 47, 59,
77, 121, 171, 172, 179, 224, 234,
272
return from France with, 114
Jefferson, William Beverley Frederick,
325, *325*, 330–31
Jennings, Paul, 265, 266
Joséphine (Rose de Beauharnais), 45
Julien, Honoré, 211

Keckley, Elizabeth, 299–300

La Fayette, Adrienne de, 66
Lafayette, Marquis de, x, 37, 65–66,
67, 82, 121–22, 240–41
Larsen, Nella, *Passing,* 328

Latrobe, Benjamin, 78, 81
Laurens, Henry, 23
Laurie, James, 296
Lavoisier, Marie Marguerite Émilie, 56
Lear, Tobias, 149
L'Enfant, Pierre Charles, 277–78, 279
Lesage, Alain, 54
Gil Blas and *Diable Boiteux,* 53,
223
Les Aventures de Télémaque (Fénelon),
223–24
Letters on Education (Genlis), 228–29
Lewis, Randolph, 201–2
Liberator, The, 303
Lilly, Gabriel, 199–200, 201, 204
Lincoln, Mary Todd, 299
Livius, Titus, *History of the Roman
People,* 51, 55, 140, 223, 224
Locke, John, 121
*Essay Concerning Human
Understanding,* 316
Loesser, Arthur, 152
Louis-Joseph de Bourbon, Prince, 93
Louis-Philippe, Prince, 222, 229
Louis XIV, King, 45, 48
Louis XVI, King, ix, 23, 36, 66, 98
Lowell, John, 32
Luynes, Cardinal of, 45

Madison, Dolley, 138, 207, 230, 263,
283, 303
Madison, James, 23–24, 25, 27, 95, 99,
130, 143, 144, 152, 178, 187
enslaved valet of, 265
Malone, Dumas, 87, 167, 173, 199
Marbois, François de Barbé-, 28
Marie Antoinette, Queen, 67
Maryland, 119
See also Baltimore, Md.
Mason, Priscilla, 153
Massalska, Hélène, 54–55, 106
Moller, John Christopher, 152
Monroe, Elizabeth, 149
Monroe, James, 149
Mont Blanco plantation, *166,* 170,
174, 177, 179

Monticello, 17, 46
  agricultural methods, 194–95, 245
  architectural design as gendered,
    219–21, *220*, 232–34
  architectural renovations, 164,
    218–21, *220*, *243*
  books from Martha's Paris days, 53
  breaking up of household, 310
  Carr children at, 19, 20
  cemetery of, 332, 334
  chefs and food at, 211–12, *212*
  Christmas week in 1821, 266
  construction of, 3–7, *4*
  death of TJ's wife, x, 20–21
  description (1809), 215–17, *216*,
    219–21, *220*
  Enlightenment ideas applied to,
    221
  Farm Book, 12, 191, *191*, 192–94,
    198, 199, 203, 207, 265, 282, 286
  female intellectual life and, 218,
    218, 220–22, 231–34, 314–16
  female slaves, vulnerability, 256–57
  food and clothing for slaves,
    192–94, 203, 204, 246, 268
  gardening and slave produce,
    212–13
  Getting Word project, 286, 294,
    326
  gong at, 199
  Hemings family, as privileged at,
    190, 203, 204, 243, 244, 268, 272
  Hemings family arrives at, 13
  hierarchy of slave labor at, 196, 249
  hierarchy of slave society at, 190
  historian Lucia Stanton at, 94, 294
  historical record on slave
    community of, 286
  house servants, 204, 250–51, 268
  kitchen at, *212*
  Lafayette visits, 240–41
  Madison visits, 265
  Maria and Martha give birth at
    (1801), 180
  Maria in residence, 140–41, 161
  Maria's injury at, 168

  Maria's death at, 186–87
  Maria's wedding at, 165–66
  Martha and Randolph family in
    residence, 134, 136, 138–39, 169,
    215, 219, 231, 233–34, 252–53
  Martha supervising, 217, *218*,
    233–34, 268, 270
  Mulberry Row, 114, 189, 195–96,
    199, 203, 208
  nailery, 195–200, *198*, 251
  newlywed TJ and wife arrive, 3–5
  operation of, 192–203, 208
  ornamental gardens, 213–14
  overseers, 139, 190, 197, 199–201,
    204 (*see also* Bacon, Edmund)
  return of TJ and daughters from
    Paris (1789), 117–18
  road to Washington City from,
    275
  room of Sally Hemings at, *4*, 203,
    208, 258
  runaway slaves, 200, 202, 251, 265
  sale of, 312, 313
  schoolroom at, 20
  Shadwell tract, 5, 6, 117, 199
  site for, 5–7
  slave children working at, 244
  slave deaths from quack medicine,
    175
  slave diet, 192–93, 197, 204,
    212–13
  slave families at, 201–3, 213, 250
  slave labor and, 6–7, 15, 194–98,
    198, 248–49
  slave literacy at, 209–10
  slave names at, 206–7
  slaves at, 94, 95, 192, 212 (*see also
    specific individuals*)
  slaves given as gifts, 165, 168, 202
  slaves inoculated, 25, 53, 83–85,
    209
  slaves sold, 196, 200–203, 251
  slave status and, 250
  slaves whipped and punished, 196,
    199–201, 251, 252
  slave training, 196–97, 211–12, 248

south dependency (wing) of, *4*, 203,
208, 215, 242, 258
south pavilion, 4, *4*, 7
spinning jenny at, 246–47, *247*
telescope at, 195
textile manufactory, 215, 242–49,
243, 247
TJ in residence at, 135, 141, 143,
163, 194, 204, 211, 258
TJ's day at, 215–16
TJ's desire for family at, 168,
169–70, 179, 180, 219, 220
TJ's "persnickety" directions, 204
TJ's relatives and, 32
view from, 6, 96, 314, 315
visitors to, 139, 197, 199, 211,
224–25, 241, 252, 285
winter of 1822, 272
world of, 204–5
"yellow children" of, 255–56, 258,
286, 308
Monticello Association, 332
Montpelier, 143
Morning Post, The (English
newspaper), 62, *64*, 104
Morris, Gouverneur, 66, 67, 122
Morris, Maria, 151
Morris, Robert Hunter, 151
Mount Vernon, 143, 144, 148
mulattoes, 10, 13, 261
census of 1930 and, 328
in Florida, 208
practice of passing, 272, 280–81,
306, 307, 308, 323, 326, 327–28
(*see also specific people*)
Murray, Judith Sargent, 124, 228, 318

Napoléon Bonaparte, 45, 317
Nash, Margaret, 153–54
Necker, Suzanne, 66
New Jersey, women's vote, 124
Newton, Harriet Walker, 291–92
New York City, 32, 130, 140, 144
New York State, 130
Nicholas, Margaret, 269, 272
Noailles, Adrienne de, 37

Norfolk, Va., x, 116, 117
Notes on the State of Virginia (TJ), 66,
223

Oldham, James, 200
*On the Current Circumstances Which
Can End the Revolution* (Staël),
122
On the Equality of the Sexes (Poulain),
120

Page, William, 199, 201
Paine, Thomas, *Common Sense*, 154
Panthemont (Abbaye Royale de
Panthemont), *36, 39–77, 40, 61*
Abbess Marie-Catherine, 44–45,
46, 48, 59, 65, 70, 217, 224
Abbess's table, 43–44, 69–70
art of letter-writing and, 54, 57
British aristocrats at, 70–71
Catholicism and, 58–61
cost of, 43–44
dames des chambres at, 69, 70
description of, 40–42
Maria's education at, 93, 106–7, 151
Martha acquires taste/polish, 100
Martha's desire to join convent,
61–65, 111
Martha's education at, 45–46,
47–59, 69–72, 159, 217, 221
Martha's friends at, 49–51, *52,*
57–58, 101, 105, 106, 111
Martha's role models at, 45
protocols by rank, 71–72, 151
subjects and curriculum, 51–57
TJ visits his daughter there, 59
TJ withdraws daughters from, 109,
111, 159
Pantops plantation, 165, 168, 169,
170, 187, 195, 213, 219
Paris, x
American peace talks in, 26, 27, 30
Bois de Boulogne, 109
bridge at Neuilly and, 34
Champ de Mars, 123
Champs-Élysées, 36, 37, *110*

Paris (*cont'd*):
  convent schools, 42–44, 54–55, 69, 106
  description of (1784, 1787), 34–35
  famous women of, 66–67
  Faubourg Saint-Germain, 35–36, 39
  Faubourg Saint-Honoré, 37
  female influence in, 72
  Grille de Chaillot, 110
  Hôtel de Langeac, 51, 68, 73, 102, 109–11, *110,* 114, 220
  Hôtel des Invalides, 45
  Hôtel d'Orléans, 37, 39
  La Fontaine des Quatre-Saisons, *36*
  Machine de Marly, 34
  Palais Royal, 68–69, *70,* 111–12
  Place Louis XV, ix, 37
  Right Bank, 36–37
  rue de Grenelle, 35–36, *36,* 39, 45
  salons in, 66, 122, 230
  TJ, daughters, and entourage in (1784–89), ix–xi, 34–39, *38, 65*–69, 73–75, 94–95, 109–14
  Tuileries Palace, 35, 37
  typhus in, 110–11, 112
  volatility of, 99
passing (as white), 272, 280–81, 306, 307, 308, 323, 326, 328–29, 331
  and fractured families, 261, 272, 324, 326
  See also specific people
Passing (Larsen), 328
Peale, Charles Willson, 148, 152
Peale, Rembrandt, 151–52
Penn, William, 144
Pennsylvania Abolition Society, 33
Perry, Reuben, 251
Petit, Adrien, 73, 74, 75, 87, 89, 110, 148
Petrarca, Francesco, 54
Philadelphia
  abolitionism in, 263
  Bartram's Garden, *158*
  Blanchard's hot air balloon, 156–57
  building in, 145
  as capital of U.S., 134, 144–45, 178, 231
  Congress in, 26
  description of (1791), 143–45
  Enlightenment figures in, 31
  first art museum, 149, 151–52
  free blacks in, 263
  French salons and, *146,* 159, 230
  Fullerton's school, 155
  Harriet given fare to, 263
  Hopkinson home, 29, *30*
  manumitted slaves in, 263
  Maria in, 148–55
  Martha in, 25, 26–31, 147
  Mrs. Pine's school, 148–52
  paintings of, by Birch, 145, *146*
  penal reform and, 199
  Pine house, 149, 151
  runaway slaves in, 281
  size of, 144, 263
  TJ drafts Declaration of Independence in, 148
  TJ in, as vice president, 165
  TJ's association with, 263
  TJ's home and office, 145–47, 149, 150
  TJ's life and social activities, 156–57
  Washington welcomed in, 143–44
  yellow fever epidemic, 158–59
  Young Ladies' Academy, 227–28
Phlipon, Manon (Madame Roland), 55, 56–57
Pine, Mary, 148–52, 155
Pine, Robert Edge, 148–49, 151, 152
Polignac, Madame de, 71
Polignac family, 67–68
Poplar Forest estate, 16–17, 197, 201, 217–18, 224–25, 234, 244, 253, 272
  accidental discovery of Maria's harpsichord and music, 320–21
  architectural design of, 234
  campeachy chair at, *237*
  description of, 234–36, *235*

female intellectual life and, 225–26, 235–39
Martha and family at, 234–38, *237*
TJ's granddaughters' visits to, 217–18, 224–25, 234–37, 320
weaving factory at, 247, 248
Poulain de La Barre, François, *On the Equality of the Sexes,* 120
Princeton, N.J., Congress in, 26
Pumphrey, Harriet Simpson, 292–94
Pumphrey, Rezin, 292–94, 301

Quakers, 10
Quasi War with France, 177–78

race
  blacks seen as inferior, 10, 252, 257, 260–61
  color hierarchy, 259
  construction of, in Virginia, 8–10
  hierarchy of slave society, 190
  laws against miscegenation, 10, 96
  mulattoes, 10, 13, 261
    census of 1930 and, 328
    in Florida, 208
    practice of passing, 272, 280–81, 306, 307, 308, 323, 326, 327–28
  U.S. commitment to hierarchies of, 305-6, 326-27
  See also passing (as white), slavery, whiteness
Racecraft, 330
Ramsay, Andrew, 86, 87, 91, 92
Randall, Henry, 254
Randolph, Anne Cary, 134, 138, 143, 209, 213–14, 224, 245, 311
Randolph, Benjamin Franklin, 207, 240
Randolph, Cornelia, 137, 180, 207, 210, 234, 236, 237–38, 239
  challenges of travel, 275–76
  loss of Monticello and, 315
  mother's death, 310
  naming of, 317
  privileged position of, 276

slavery and, 257
status as TJ's granddaughter, 318
Randolph, Edmund, 147
Randolph, Ellen Wayles (first, infant), 134, 135, 164
Randolph, George Wythe, 207, 219, 240, 255, 310
Randolph, Isham, 6
Randolph, James Madison, 207
Randolph, Jane, 219
Randolph, Jenny, 143
Randolph, Judith, 49, 117
Randolph, Martha Jefferson
  adored by her children, 232
  appearance of, 51, 67, 68, 76, 100, 101, *313*
  bedroom closet fought for by, 318
  birth and death of infant daughter, Ellen, 134, 135, 163–64
  birth of, *4, 8*
  births of children, 134, 137–38, 143, 184, 219
  Catholicism and, 41, 58–59, 61–65, *64,* 100, 111, 317
  charm of, 18, 67
  children's smallpox inoculation, 209
  conduct of a proper woman and, 100–101
  courtship of, 125–26
  dancing and balls loved by, 67–68
  death of, 332
  disappointments, 133
  discipline of her children, 139
  Edgehill as home, 133–38, *173,* 175, 177, 180–82, 184, 219, 248
  educating her children, 138–40, 217–18, 221–28, 232, 241, 315–16, 333
  educating Maria, 140–42, 319
  education of, father's direction, 19, 20, 27, 121
  education of, gender conventions, 121
  education of, in France, 19, *36,* 39–65, *40, 61,* 69–72, 75, 89, 100, 109, 159, 221–22

Randolph, Martha Jefferson (*cont'd*):
  education of, in Philadelphia,
    26–27, 29, *30,* 31, 147
  education of, taught by mother, 18
  financial distress of, 313–14, 318
  France, preparation and voyage,
    32–34
  France, shaping of character and
    future and, 33, 89, 121
  French language, 47–48, 53, 72, 99
  French life appealing to, 99–100
  French literature and, 53–54
  French Revolution and, x, 99,
    121–24
  Genlis's precepts followed by, 231
  handwriting of, 56
  household accounts, 213
  housekeeping instruction, 132
  as industrious, 139, 231
  influence of Hopkinson, 28–29
  last will and testament, 309–11, 332
  leaves Paris and voyage to Virginia
    (1789), 115–16
  legacy of, 332–33
  letter-writing and, 28, 31, 48, 49,
    50–51, 53, 54–55, 57–58, 62–63,
    100, 131, 133, 134, 165, 178–79
  letter-writing and female identity,
    29, 55–56, 58–59, 132
  Maria's engagement and, 164, 165
  Maria's illness and, 175–76
  marriage of, 125, 127–28, 131,
    133–40, 171, 310, 312
  marriage, ideas about, 105–6
  marriageability of, 99, 100, 101, 112
  Monticello, love of, 314
  Monticello as home during
    marriage, 134, 136, 138–39, 169,
    215, 219, 220, 231, 252–53
  as Monticello supervisor, 217, *218,*
    233–34, 249, 268, 270
  motherhood and, 136, 137
  mother and, 17, 18, 21
  names of her children, 207
  naming of, 8
  needlework and, 18, 53

  in Paris, x, 22, 34–77, 110–12
  Paris friendships, 49–51, *52,* 57–58,
    65–69, 72, 100–102, 105, 106,
    111, 113–15, 121, 131–36
  Paris goodbyes, 114–15
  Parisian influence, xi, 72, 73, 105–6,
    222–25
  Parisian temptations, 99
  Parisian wardrobe and style, 37–39,
    100, 112–13
  pastimes of, 127
  peripatetic childhood and favorite
    homes of, 16, 17–18, 26
  personality and temperament of, 49,
    51, 76, 127, 136, 140, *313*
  in Philadelphia (1782–84), 25,
    26–31, *30,* 147
  political positions unknown, 124
  readjustment to American life, 132
  rejection of titles and, 105
  relationship with Maria, 75–77,
    163–64
  relationship with Sally Hemings,
    254–55, 258, 310
  relationship with TJ, 18, 28, 41, 47,
    59, 77, 112, 224, 234
  relegated to the sidelines, 241
  return to Monticello (1789), 124
  romances of, 101–4, 112, 114
  self-identity of, 72, 100, 105–6, 140,
    217–18, 221, 224, 229, 317–18
  skill at riding, 18, 127
  slavery and, 100, 136–37, 257, 310
  smallpox inoculation, 24, 209
  status as TJ's daughter, 318
  TJ as emotional anchor for, 171,
    172, 179, 272
  TJ's death and, 312
  TJ's gifts, 112
  TJ's grief and, 21–22
  TJ's presidency and, 178–79, 183,
    231
  TJ's relationship with Sally
    Hemings and, 254–55, 282–83
  Varina plantation and, 132, 134, 135
  Virginia (1789) and, 116–17

in Washington City, 282–83
whooping cough of children, 180
Randolph, Mary Jefferson, 184, 225,
    233–34, 239, 240, 266, 314–15
Randolph, Meriwether Lewis, 207,
    210, 219, 240
Randolph, Septima Anne, 210, 219,
    231
Randolph, Thomas Jefferson "Jeff,"
    134, 209, 224, 232, 245, 275, 310,
    311, 314
  sons of Sally Hemings and, 254,
    255, 282
Randolph, Thomas Mann
  antislavery bill proposed by, *127*
  appearance of, 126, *127,* 207
  character of, 127, 167, 171, 310
  courtship of Martha, 126–27
  death of Maria and, 187
  debt of, 169, 227
  dislike of Jack Eppes, 167
  dowries for daughters, 227
  Edgehill and, 133–38, *173,* 175,
    177, 180–82, 184, 219, 248
  education of, 117, 126, 128
  education of his daughters and, 226
  as governor of Virginia, *127*
  illnesses of, 135, 163–64, 166, 171
  inheritance of Tuckahoe, 128, 133
  as justice of the peace, 134–35
  managing TJ's estates, 134, 136,
    199, 200, 219
  Maria and, 150, 153, 156, 157, 176
  marriage, 125, 127–28, 133–40, 171
  as militia captain, 135
  political office, 227
  rescue of Francis Eppes, 182
  return of Martha from Paris and,
    117
  slave Isaac Jefferson and, *198*
  as slaveowner, 137
  TJ's education for boys and, 226
  Varina plantation and, 132, 133,
    134, 135, 136, 170, 172, 227
  as Virginia governor, 272
  weaving factory and, 248

Randolph, Thomas Mann, Sr.,
    127–28, 133, 134
Randolph, Virginia. *See* Trist, Virginia
    Randolph
Rittenhouse, David, 29, 31, 157
Rittenhouse, Hannah, 147
Rittenhouse, Joseph, 29
Robert (ship), 86
Roland de La Platière, Jean-Marie, 55
Ronaldson, James, 263–64
Rousseau, Jean-Jacques, 42, 228–29
  Confessions, 66
  Emile, 229
Rush, Benjamin, 153, 154

Sackville, John Frederick, Duke of
    Dorset, 50, 70, 103–4, 113, 115,
    132
Saint-Lambert, Marquis de, 66
Salimbeni, Brunette "Bruny," 135–36
Scharff, Virginia, 88–89
Schlossberg, Linda, 307–8
Sergeant, Thomas, 155
Sévigné, Madame de, 54, 56, 57
Shays's Rebellion, 129
Short, William, 32, 102–4, *103,* 110,
    114, 134
Simitière, Pierre Eugène, 29–30, 31
Skelton, Bathurst, 7
Skelton, John, 7, 8
Skipwith, Anne, 32, 117
Skipwith, Henry, 32, 117
slave graves and cemeteries, 299–300
slave rebellions, 260, 305
slavery, 96
  abolished in American North, 119
  abolished in France, 93, 95, 113,
    136
  abolished in U.S., 327, 331
  antislavery bill by Randolph, *127*
  birthdates of slaves, 191
  children working, 244
  Christmas leave, 272
  color hierarchy, 259
  common slave names, 206
  Constitution and protection of, 119

slavery (*cont'd*):
  construction of, in Virginia, 9–10
  Dutch slave trade, 8–9
  English common law and, 10
  escaped slaves, passing as white,
    280–81, 326
  free white servants vs., 253
  Hartman on, 259–60, 323
  hierarchy of slave society, 190
  laws against miscegenation, 10, 96
  legacy of, 334
  lessons in rank and status, 250, 252,
    253, 255
  literacy and, 209–10
  at Monticello (*see* Monticello)
  payment to slaves, 197
  planter-slave relationships, 208, 254
  runaway slaves, 251–52, 281, 326
  selling of slaves, 196, 251
  shadow families and, 265, 320
  slave food and clothing, 192–94,
    268, 269
  slaves' lives as insignificant, 118
  slaves manumitted in Delmarva
    Peninsula, 119
  slaves of John Wayles, 11, 12
  slaves seen as inferior, 10, 252, 257,
    260–61
  status of, xi, 96
  sugar plantations and, 8
  tipping of slaves, 15, 25
  TJ and (*see* Hemings, Sally;
    Jefferson, Thomas; Monticello;
    specific individuals)
  TJ attempts to condemn in
    Declaration of Independence,
    119
  U.S. commitment to, 305–6,
    326–27
  Virginia laws and, 260–63, 326
  in Washington City, 303–5, *304*
  well-placed, opportunities for,
    266
  whipping and punishment, 196,
    251, 252, 257
  women doing field work, 195

smallpox inoculation, 24, 209
  of slaves, 25, 83–84, 85, 93, 209
  Sutton method, 24, 93
Smith, Margaret Bayard, 76–77, 138,
    230, 283, 284–85, 302, 320
Smith, Samuel Harrison, 283
Snow, Beverly, 305
Southgate, Eliza, 228
Staël, Madame de, 56, 66, 67, 122,
    154, 317
  Corinne, 317
  *On the Current Circumstances Which
    Can End the Revolution*, 122
Stanton, Lucia, 94, 294
Steward, Ellen, 303
Sutton, Robert, 24, 93

Tarleton, Banastre, 16
Taylor, Tess, 332
Tessé, Madame de, 66, 67, 122
Thil, Arnaud du, 301
Thomas Jefferson (Brodie), 94
Thomas Jefferson Memorial
    Foundation, 95
Thornton, Anna Maria, 305
Thornton, William, 305
Trist, Eliza, 25, 27, 29, 38, 39, 41, 49,
    53, 78, 85, 226, 238
Trist, Nicholas P., 238, 310, 312
Trist, Virginia Randolph, 137, 138, 180,
    207, 210, 219, 231, 232, 233, 309
  Don Quixote and, 319
  loss of Monticello and, 315
  marriage of, 238
  penury at Monticello and, 312–13
  women's financial independence
    and, 318
Trollope, Frances, 279
Tronchin, Jean Armand, 59
Trumbull, Jonathan, 110, 111, 162
Tuckahoe, 26, 117, 126, 128, 133
Tufton, Caroline, 50, 57, 67, 69, 107,
    114, 131
Tufton, Elizabeth, 50, 57, 67, 69, 101,
    103–4, 107, 114, 116, 131, 133,
    136

Tufton farm, 50, 195
Turpin, Philip, 175, 176

United States
  abolition of slavery, 119, 327, 331
  acts and laws upholding slavery in,
    305–6, 326–27
  American identity and, 130–31
  Anglo-American culture, 222–23
  Catholicism in, 41, 54, 59
  dictionary of English, 131
  dollar-based currency, 31
  economic depression, 129
  egalitarian rhetoric, 229–30
  federal census, 287
  female suffrage, 123
  first government, xi
  fragility of union, 129, 178
  gender conventions in, 228
  gender equality and, 130–31
  health and hygiene in, 271–72
  industrializing the North, 245
  Jim Crow laws, 327, 328
  literacy in, 131
  manners in, 271, 272
  Ohio admitted to the Union, 181
  Panic of 1819, 284, 312
  race and, 328–31 (*see also* passing;
    slavery; Virginia)
  republican citizens of, 229
  republican experiment of, 120
  Revolution of 1800 (TJ's election),
    178
  Shays's Rebellion, 129
  social class in, 271, 272
  textile manufacture in, 245–46
  theater in, 54
  voting in, 123, 124, 229–30
  whiteness as property, 329
  women shut out of politics, 230–31
  women's rights debated in, 123–24
University of Pennsylvania, 156
University of Virginia, 195, 218,
  238–40, 334
U. S. Congress, 129, 130, 264
  Alien and Sedition Acts, 178

Quasi War with France, 178
  spring session (1802), 181
  in Washington City, 277
U. S. Constitution, xi, 119, 129–30,
  177

Varina plantation, 132, 133, 134, 135,
  136, 170, 172, 227
Versailles, 34, 66
Vindication of the Rights of Woman, A
  (Wollstonecraft), 123, 154, 155
Virginia
  Act to Preserve Racial Integrity,
    328
  Albemarle County, 5
  American Revolution in, 15–16, 20
  antislavery bill by Randolph, *127*
  aristocratic homes in, 232
  Blue Ridge Mountains, 5
  bonded servants, black, 9
  female education in, 18
  free blacks in, 9
  government at Charlottesville, 16
  House of Delegates investigation of
    Jefferson, 23
  Hudgins v. *Wright* (1806), 326
  interracial marriage prohibited, 328
  Jamestown as capital of, 9
  law on hereditary slavery, 97, 263
  laws against miscegenation, 10
  manumitted slaves required to leave
    the Commonwealth, 260–61,
    326
  mulattoes in, 10, 261
  "one-drop rule," 328, 329, 331
  planter-slave relationships in, 208,
    254
  privileged blindness to slavery, 137
  racial hierarchy/white supremacy
    in, 10–11
  Randolph as governor, 272
  ratification of the Constitution, 130
  Richmond as capital of, 15, 272
  slave system in, 8–10
  theater in, 54
  TJ as governor, 15, 20

Virginia (*cont'd*):
   TJ's Statute of Religious Freedom,
      66, 239
   typical gentry woman in, 319
   view of slaves as inferior beings, 10
   women's rights in, 12
Voltaire, 42
Voyages du Jeune Anacharsis
      (Barthélemy), 223, 224

Walker, William B., 291–92
War of 1812, 245, 302
Washington, Booker T., 268
Washington, George, xi, 24, 125, 128,
      143, 149, 177, 230, 245, 277–78
   cabinet of, 147
   Pine portrait, 148
   Stuart portrait, 303
   TJ as secretary of state, 125, 128,
      140
   TJ's resignation from cabinet, 135
Washington, Martha, 143, 147, 153,
      159
Washington City (Washington, D.C.)
   Beverley Hemings in, 265, 266,
      283, 294
   black churches and schools, 302–3
   black press in, 303
   boardinghouses in, 283
   as capital of U.S., 144, 178, 230
   Capitol building, 277, *280*
   Capitol Hill, 278
   census, 287, 292
   churches of, 287–88
   Compensated Emancipation Act,
      327
   Congress in session and, 277
   description, 277–79, *278, 280*
   design for, 277–78
   emancipation in and First Freed,
      303, 327
   employment for women in, 283–84
   food sources in, 285
   Harriet in, 264–65, 267, 272, 277,
      278, 279–80, 285, 291, 301
   Hern family in, 264

   housewifery in, 284–85
   Indian Queen Hotel, 277, *278,* 283
   Monticello people in, 264
   opportunities for carpenters in, 283
   population of, 279
   President's House, 277
   race riots, 305
   Randolph family in, 282–83
   size of, 263
   slaves and free blacks in, 302–5, *304*
   stage travel to, 275
   temporary living quarters in, 283
   Williamson as developer in, 294–95
Watson, David, 196–97
Wayles, John, 11–12, 265
Wayles, Martha Eppes, 8, 12–13
Webster, Daniel, 211, 266, 285
Webster, Noah, 131
West Point, U.S. Military Academy at,
      181, 238
White, Gayle Jessup, 332
whiteness, 11, 209, 253, 257, 260–61,
      271, 306–7, 327–31
William III and Mary II (of
      England), 44
Williamson, Benjamin, 294–99
Williamson, Charles, 298
Williamson, Elizabeth, 297
Williamson, Harriet Garner, 294–300
Williamson, John, 295, 296
Williamson, Joseph B., 295, 296–97,
      298
Williamson, Joseph Boteler, 298
Wilson, James, 148
Winterer, Caroline, 228
Wollstonecraft, Mary, 120–21, 154–55
   *A Vindication of the Rights of
      Woman,* 123, 154, 155
women, 122
   age differences with spouse and, 95
   art of letter-writing and, 54, 56
   as authors, 131
   bluestocking, 227, 237
   books for, printed in duodecimo, 236
   botany, gardening and, 213

Catholic communities offering
  opportunity and power, 64–65, 72
childbed fever and, 175
cleanliness and, 271–72
clothing for elite women, 269–70
clothing for female slaves, 269
danger of seduction, 163
demeanor of elite women, 271
education, traditional, 27–28
education in colonial America, 18,
  20, 26–27, 31
education as gendered, 227–31,
  315–19
education in North versus South,
  226
education in post-Revolutionary
  America, 151, 153, 154
elite female identity, 56, 57, 58
Enlightenment and, 42, 44, 120–21,
  229, 317
enslaved, 306
equality of, 130–31, 333
Federalists, 230
female suffrage, 123, 124
femme savante, 44
financial independence of, 318–19
French, 66–67, 69, 72, 122, 154
French, education of, 42–44, 51–57,
  69, 106
friendships and, 57–58
gender conventions, 154, 228
housewifery, 141, 224, 284–85
law of coverture, 12, 171, 297
literacy and, 121, 297
manners and status, 271

marriage and, 104, 128, 171, 284
Martha and education of, 217–18,
  221–28
nervous brides, 128
novels by and for, 163
patriarchal system and, 153, 163,
  319, 323
politics, shut out of, 230–31
post-Revolution, 310
pregnancy, childbirth, and family
  size, 321–22
reproductive healthcare, 322
revolutions and role of, 120,
  122–23, 131
rights debated, 123–24, 131,
  154–55
Rousseau's ideas on education, 229
single women and contracts, 12
social education for girls, 81
stage travel, challenges of, 275–76
TJ's association of spinning with
  women of color, 250
TJ's idea of "natural equality," 27
TJ's ideas of education for, 19, 20,
  51–53, 151, 153, 209, 217, 218,
  221, 224, 226
TJ's view of duties and place of,
  27, 94, 100, 125, 141, 171, 209,
  241
university admission denied to, 240
Virginia gentry and, 319
writing instruction, 18

Young Ladies' Academy of
  Philadelphia, 153

CATHERINE KERRISON is a professor of history at Villanova University, where she teaches courses in colonial and Revolutionary America and women's and gender history. She holds a Ph.D. in American history from the College of William and Mary. Her first book, *Claiming the Pen: Women and Intellectual Life in the Early American South,* won the Outstanding Book Award from the History of Education Society. Kerrison lives in Berwyn, Pennsylvania.

Twitter: @CKerrisonPhD